ONTARIO SERIES

V

THE TOWN OF YORK

1793-1815

LIEUTENANT GOVERNOR JOHN GRAVES SIMCOE, BY JEAN LAURENT MOSNIER. [Toronto Public Library.]

THE TOWN OF YORK 1793-1815

A Collection of Documents of Early Toronto

Edited with an introduction by

Edith G. Firth

THE CHAMPLAIN SOCIETY
FOR THE GOVERNMENT OF ONTARIO
UNIVERSITY OF TORONTO PRESS
1962

SCHOLARLY REPRINT SERIES
Reprinted in paperback 2017
ISBN 978-0-8020-7031-9 (cloth)
ISBN 978-1-4875-9855-6 (paper)
LC 62-4422

FOREWORD

THE log houses and fortified embankments of Old Fort York, now a popular tourist attraction, are about all that remains in the immediate Toronto area of the physical assets of the late eighteenth century. In this fifth book of the Champlain Society's "Ontario Series," the editor and author has compiled a fascinating documentary history to show how primitive York began to assume the characteristics of modern Toronto.

Miss Edith Firth, head of the Canadian history and manuscripts section of the Toronto Public Library, has searched deeply into the old records for her book *The Town of York*, framing it within the period of Simcoe's arrival in 1793 and the time the news of peace reached York in the spring of 1815. In this factual book, which I am confident will be of interest to both layman and student alike, an attempt is made to show why York was chosen for settlement in the first place, the kind of community that was developing, and the effect of the War of 1812 on its social, religious, and business structure. The problems of defence, commercial development, local government, administration of justice, communications, politics, religion, and education are illustrated through contemporary documents.

York was a hot-house community, forced ahead of its natural growth by its importance and social position as a capital. Nevertheless, it lagged behind Kingston at this time, because of Kingston's commercial prosperity and pre-eminence as the military and naval centre of the province. The War of 1812 made an integral community out of such diverse elements as senior civil servants, who tried to live the leisurely life of their counterparts in England; the merchant class, who were mainly Scottish immigrants; and the tradesmen and labourers, who were mainly discharged soldiers from the British Army and arrivals from the United States. By 1815, many of the characteristics of present-day Toronto were beginning to show through the rough exterior of the pioneer town.

Our purpose in this Ontario historical series is not to interpret history, but rather to record it—to provide a solid foundation of source material for an interpretive historian and, at the same time, to sketch a detailed picture of the frontier age for the general reader.

Ontario has a rich, colourful heritage which is in danger of being lost to future generations unless preserved in readable book form. It is our hope that many of Ontario's historical records, existing only in manuscript form in private homes and offices, will be brought to light in the future works of this series.

Ours is a co-operative undertaking shared by the Ontario government and the Champlain Society, which has been directing the production of historical studies for more than 50 years. The Society chooses and guides the editors of the various works and the government defrays the cost of preparation and publication.

Since the first book of this series, *The Valley of the Trent*, was published in 1957, our aim has been to publish one volume each year. We now have on our bookshelves volumes on *Royal Fort Frontenac*, *Kingston Before the War of 1812*, and *The Windsor Border Region*. Under preparation are volumes about the early histories of the Muskoka-Haliburton region and the Valley of the Grand River.

Only by knowing our past may we advance with wisdom and knowledge into the future, and I take this opportunity of thanking Miss Firth for her contribution in helping add another page in the history book of Ontario.

JOHN P. ROBARTS
Prime Minister of Ontario

London and Toronto
Nov. 27, 1961

PREFACE

ON AUGUST 26, 1793, an Indian chief before a council of his people held at the site of Toronto said, "We earnestly hope that the great man now here will rekindle the fire that the chimney may be strong, that it may never be extinguished." The earlier fire which had been lit by the French in the first quarter of the eighteenth century had indeed gone out, but the great man, Lieutenant Governor Simcoe, succeeded, as the chief had hoped, in building a strong chimney. The fire has never been extinguished.

Modern Toronto really began in that summer of 1793 when Simcoe and the Queen's Rangers started to plan and build a town on the shores of Toronto Bay. The earlier Indian and French settlements had no influence on the development of the present city, nor did the abortive plans of Lord Dorchester affect its later history. This volume, therefore, begins with Simcoe's arrival at Toronto, and records the development of the town of York from that time to the end of the War of 1812. The final date was chosen because York entered a new stage in its growth after the war, when the heavy post-Napoleonic immigration brought major changes and greater complexities to every aspect of life in the community. Although the period covered in this book is thus a comparatively short one, it includes Toronto's formative years.

A number of the documents in this collection have already been printed in the published correspondence of Simcoe and Russell, in the reports of the Public Archives of Canada and the Department of Public Records and Archives of the Province of Ontario, and in other historical works. This re-publication has been unavoidable if a complete picture of the development of York was to be presented. Except where indicated, the transcriptions in this volume are from the original manuscript sources, and may vary slightly from earlier printed versions. An effort has been made, however, to include as much unpublished material as possible. The Introduction and Documents are divided into topical groups lettered from "A" to "H." The final section, "I," includes documents concerning military, economic, cultural, and social activities and conditions during the War of 1812. Within each group the documents are arranged in chronological order.

The editor is extremely grateful to Dr. W. Kaye Lamb and the staff of the Public Archives of Canada for their unfailing patience and practical help. This same assistance was cordially given by Dr. George W. Spragge and the staff of the Department of Public Records and Archives of Ontario, and by the staffs of the Archives of the United Church of Canada, Toronto; the Department of Lands and Forests of Ontario; the Douglas Library, Queen's University; the Royal Canadian Military Institute, Toronto; the Synod of Ontario Archives, Kingston; the Burton Historical Collection at the Detroit Public Library; the Historical Society of Pennsylvania, Philadelphia; the New York Historical Society, New York; and the William L. Clements Library, University of Michigan.

To the Toronto Public Library the editor owes a special debt. A leave of absence was kindly granted by the Board for work on this volume. Much is owing to the sympathy and understanding of the Chief Librarian, Mr. H. C. Campbell, and to the tolerance of fellow staff members with the enthusiasms and depressions that inevitably accompanied the work. To former members of the staff who were responsible for gathering together the Library's collection of Canadiana, every student of the area and period must be grateful.

The publication of a collection of documents is impossible without the co-operation of institutions such as these. They have all graciously given permission for the inclusion of their manuscripts in this volume. The Provost of Trinity College, Toronto, the York Pioneer and Historical Society, Mrs. Stephen Heward, and Mr. Christopher Robinson have also generously allowed publication of manuscripts and pictures in their possession. Unpublished Crown Copyright material in the Public Record Office, London, has been reproduced by permission of the Controller of Her Majesty's Stationery Office.

Valuable advice and information were received from Professor J. M. S. Careless, Professor E. R. Arthur, and Father E. J. Lajeunesse, of the University of Toronto, Professor S. F. Wise of Queen's University, Mr. C. W. Humphries of Mount Allison University, Mr. Verschoyle Blake and the late Mr. R. M. Lewis of the Conservation Branch of the Department of Planning and Development of Ontario, Mrs. Ross Glassford, and Mr. W. R. Wadsworth. Professor G. M. Craig of the University of Toronto read the manuscript and suggested many important corrections and improvements. Mr. Wallace Bonner was responsible for much of the photography, and Mrs. Milada Dufek patiently typed and retyped most of the material.

The editor wishes to thank the Prime Minister and Government of the Province of Ontario, and the Champlain Society, for making this publication possible. The general editor of the Ontario Series, Professor P. C. T. White, has been of great assistance, as have the editorial staff of the University of Toronto Press.

Although conscious of the imperfections of this collection, the editor is happy that these documents are now readily available to students of Toronto's history.

EDITH G. FIRTH

CONTENTS

B. DEFENCE

F. Political Ferment

PLATES

THE TOWN OF YORK, 1793–1815

INTRODUCTION

A. THE ESTABLISHMENT OF THE CAPITAL

THE SITE OF TORONTO has been of strategic importance from the beginning of Ontario's recorded history. It lay at the entrance to one of the oldest routes to the northwest, a route known and used by Huron, Iroquois, and Chippewa Indians.[1] From the Humber River, a portage of 28 miles led to the Holland River flowing northward into Lake Simcoe, which was connected, in turn, by rivers and portages with Georgian Bay. This route was used by Brulé, by LaSalle, by Du Lhut. The Senecas had a village, Teiaigon, near the mouth of the Humber; so did the Missisaugas. And here, about 1720, was built a little French trading post, which lasted for about ten years.

The English, meanwhile, established a trading post at Oswego, challenging the French Fort Frontenac at Kingston and French supremacy on Lake Ontario. The French retaliated by rebuilding Fort Niagara. In the spring of 1750 Fort Toronto or Rouillé was built across the lake from Niagara, to cut off Indians coming down from the Upper Lakes to trade at Oswego. This small fort was located on the Humber; in 1750–1 a more ambitious fort was built on the waterfront at the foot of the present Dufferin Street. It was not one of the major bastions of French domination—its usual complement was about ten men—but it did a respectable trade, and probably justified its existence in the cut-throat French-English rivalry for power. Always a subsidiary of Fort Niagara, it was destroyed by the French when Niagara was captured by the British under Sir William Johnson in 1759. The ruins were a landmark for many years afterwards.

The first 25 years of British control of Toronto were quiet ones. There were occasional independent fur traders at Toronto, some licensed by the Governor at Quebec, some not. There were the usual complaints of debauchery and drunkenness. After the American Revolution, the traders based in Montreal began to show some interest in the old Humber River route to the northwest, and on September 23, 1787, at the Carrying Place on the Bay of Quinte, Deputy Surveyor General John Collins, acting for the Crown, bought from three Missisauga chiefs a tract of land including about one-third of York County for about £1700 in cash and goods.

[1]See Robinson, *Toronto during the French Régime, passim.*

There were some doubts about the exact boundaries of the Toronto Purchase, which were settled by a second agreement in 1805.

The Governor in Chief, Lord Dorchester, was by this time fully aware of the potential importance of Toronto, and in 1788 a surveyor, Alexander Aitkin, was sent to Toronto to lay out a town-site. His plan[2] placed the town roughly between Spadina Avenue and Toronto Street, extending north nearly to Gerrard Street. The town was to be surrounded by a belt of commons about half a mile wide with government reserves beyond. The other plans of the pre-Simcoe period followed the same pattern, but enlarged the site to a mile and a quarter square, increased the government reserves, and moved the town further north and west. The garrison was placed by Aitkin on the site of Stanley Barracks.

Dorchester was not only planning a town on the site of Toronto before Simcoe's arrival; he and his Council were considering applications for land there. The most persistent applicant was one Philippe François de Rastel de Rocheblave, a French army officer who had transferred to Spanish service on the Mississippi in 1765, and to the British in Illinois about 1773. During the American Revolution he lost his possessions and was taken prisoner. He first asked for land at Toronto in 1785, as well as for the exclusive privilege of carrying goods from Toronto to Lake Simcoe. By 1788 others were also requesting land "near Monsieur De Rocheblave's tract," and on July 14, 1789, these applications were favourably received. On June 10, 1791, Deputy Surveyor General Collins wrote surveyor Augustus Jones at Niagara that Dorchester ordered 1000 acres laid out at Toronto for Rocheblave, and 700 acres each at the same place for two officers of the Provincial Marine, René-Hypolite LaForce and Jean Baptiste Bouchette.[3] The fate of this order is interesting. One year later, after Simcoe's arrival in Canada, Jones replied that he had just received these instructions, but that the District Land Board under whose orders he worked considered its powers dissolved by Simcoe's proclamation concerning the granting of land in Upper Canada. The Board recommended postponement until further instructions were received, presumably from Simcoe.[4] It is difficult to avoid the conclusion that the Land Board, composed of prominent Niagara citizens, intentionally disobeyed Dorchester. Whether this was an early instance of Niagara's desire

[2]Ontario, Department of Public Records and Archives (P.A.O.), Simcoe Papers, Aitkin's plan of Toronto, 1788.

[3]P.A.O., Crown Land Papers, District of Nassau Land Board, Letter Book 2, p. 40.

[4]*Ibid.*, p. 65.

to block the development of Toronto, as Mr. Verschoyle Blake suggests,[5] or whether it was done for other motives, is not now clear. In any case, Dorchester's plans for Toronto were overthrown, and Simcoe was able to plan and build his town unhampered by any previous commitment.

Simcoe arrived in Quebec on November 11, 1791, and spent the winter there. On July 1, 1792, he went to Kingston where the first meeting of the Executive Council was held. He arrived at Niagara[6] on July 26, 1792; here the Legislature met throughout his active administration. While still in the Lower Province, Simcoe had spent much time poring over maps and consulting those who knew Upper Canada. Less than a month after his arrival in Canada he wrote to Dundas that "if possible, I could wish to begin a settlement at Toronto."[7] On April 28, 1792, still in Quebec, he proposed three new settlements—Toronto, an unnamed capital of the province on the Thames River, and Long Point. Of Toronto, he wrote, "Toronto appears to be the natural arsenal of Lake Ontario and to afford an easy access over land to Lake Huron."[8]

It was not, however, until the spring of 1793, that Simcoe actually visited Toronto (A 1). He was impressed by the site, and wrote enthusiastically to General Clarke, acting Governor in Chief in Dorchester's absence (A 2). The most important advantage of Toronto was no longer the route to the northwest, but its excellent harbour and its defensibility. Simcoe proposed building fortifications on the western tip of the Peninsula (now Toronto Island) and on the mainland across from it, a naval arsenal and dockyard at the bottom of the harbour, a town (mentioned almost casually), and a sawmill on the Humber River. Clarke did not feel justified in incurring any expense for the establishment because of the imminence of Dorchester's return, but agreed that Simcoe could have anything in the King's Stores that might be useful (A 3).

In July, 1793, Simcoe and his family, a number of officials, and the Queen's Rangers arrived in Toronto (A 5); from that time there has been continuous settlement. The Governor and his family established themselves in a tent, while the Rangers began felling trees and hutting themselves on the site of Fort York. On August

[5]Ontario, Department of Planning and Development, *Don Valley Conservation Report*, General, pp. 20–2.

[6]Now called Niagara-on-the-Lake; formerly called Niagara, Newark, and West Niagara.

[7]Simcoe, *Correspondence*, ed. by Cruikshank, I, 88–91, Simcoe to Dundas, Dec. 7, 1791.

[8]*Ibid.*, I, 144, Simcoe to Dundas, April 28, 1792.

26, a group of Indians from the north came to the Humber for a council, and earnestly hoped "that the great man now here, will rekindle the fire that the chimney may be strong, that it may never be extinguished" (A 7). The following day, with all the meagre ceremony at his command, Simcoe christened his town site York, (A 6, H 1). This was after the Duke of York, later Commander in Chief of the army, in keeping with Simcoe's policy of substituting English for Indian place names. Apparently the new name did not have the unanimous approval of York's early citizens. In 1804 Angus McDonell, the member for York, requested leave to bring before the House of Assembly a bill to restore the name Toronto, because it was "more familiar and agreeable to the inhabitants."[9] He did not, however, proceed further in the matter. The Ridout family also preferred the old name, Toronto, and used it firmly in correspondence (I 7). York remained the name of the town, however, until its incorporation as the city of Toronto in 1834.

Simcoe chose York not as the capital of the province, but as its naval arsenal. For this purpose he thought that Kingston was too close to the American border for safety, and Niagara was even more exposed. In the event of war the maintenance of marine supremacy on Lake Ontario was obviously vital. Dockyards were therefore of the utmost importance; these he proposed to build at York, despite the fact that they were already being established at Kingston. Fortifications were also necessary to protect the shipbuilding and harbour, and it was to this end that Simcoe devoted most of his energy at York.

Besides means of defence, however, the new province needed a capital. Niagara, across the river from Fort Niagara, was unsuitable since Fort Niagara sooner or later would have to be given up to the Americans in fulfilment of the Treaty of Paris. Simcoe objected to Kingston as capital on the same grounds as he had refused to countenance the establishment of the dockyards there. It was therefore necessary, as William Jarvis sourly put it, to go "city hunting,"[10] and to found a new town in the wilderness for the capital. Before he left England, Simcoe thought that he had located the ideal place—London, on the River Thames. He visited this site before he visited Toronto and was convinced of its suitability. During the summer of 1793 he was still thinking of London as his capital and York as his naval post.

[9]"Journals of the Legislative Assembly of Upper Canada," 1804, *Sixth Report of the Bureau of Archives, 1909*, pp. 421, 432.

[10]"Letters from W. Jarvis . . . and Mrs. Jarvis to the Rev. Samuel Peters," Women's Canadian Historical Society of Toronto, *Transactions*, No. 23 (1922–3), 22, Jarvis to Peters, Sept., 1792.

Two things were essential for the founding of London and York —fortifications and additional troops; Simcoe was denied both by Dorchester (A 15). Without them, it was impossible to establish two new posts; by spreading available troops a little more thinly, the development of one was possible. The Home Secretary Henry Dundas approved Simcoe's choices of capital and arsenal, but wrote that "as the defence of the Colony is the first object, if that defence should be Maritime, it follows that the Settlement of York is the most important for the present, not as the future Capital, but as the Chief place of strength & security for the Naval force of the Province" (A 25). Simcoe, too, had concluded, reluctantly, that the founding of York should have priority. He did not, however, give up the idea of eventually establishing his capital on the River Thames. He realized that "it appears fated that the Arsenal of Lake Ontario must become the Capital of Upper Canada,"[11] but for him this was always a temporary expedient.

Dorchester's attitude was important in the development of York. Personal antagonism between Simcoe and Dorchester had begun during the American Revolution, and sprang to new and lusty life when Simcoe received his appointment over the head of Dorchester's preference, Sir John Johnson. Dorchester conceived the lieutenant governorship of Upper Canada as a post completely subordinate to his own; Simcoe regarded it as an independent command. He grudgingly consulted Dorchester, but only in the last extremity obeyed him. As Commander in Chief of the Forces, however, Dorchester was able to block the founding of London and hamper the founding of York by refusing more troops and money from the military chest for fortifications. Although he had earlier proposed settlement on the site, in his view York should not be fortified or be a station for troops, because it was "too far out of the way."[12] With the limited money and forces available for the defence of Upper Canada he thought that military installations should be concentrated where there were existing settlements, and recommended either Point Frederick or Gananoque as the arsenal of the province, with Kingston as the capital. There was thus a fundamental difference of opinion between the two men, as well as mutual dislike. Because of this, anything Simcoe did at York was in the face of Dorchester's freely expressed disapproval.

Simcoe's repudiation of Kingston as arsenal or capital was probably influenced by Dorchester's advocacy of it. Admittedly Kingston was closer to the United States than York, but the War of

[11]P.A.O., Russell Papers, Simcoe to Russell, Dec. 9, 1793.

[12]Simcoe, *Correspondence*, I, 203, Dorchester to Simcoe, April 14, 1794.

1812 showed that it was defensible. It lay, however, in the heart of Loyalist settlement, and had close ties both with the Johnson family, and with Montreal and Quebec commercial interests. As a new governor heading a new government, Simcoe preferred a new capital away from already entrenched positions and influences sympathetic to Dorchester. More important than this, however, was his hope that from York settlement would advance into the hinterlands of southwestern and northern Ontario.

During the summer of 1793, new plans for the town of York were drawn up by Alexander Aitkin.[13] They were much less ambitious than the earlier ones prepared for Dorchester. The town was to be further east and much smaller, consisting of only ten blocks bounded by the present George, Duke, Parliament, and Front Streets. The areas from Parliament Street to the Don and from Peter Street to the Humber were reserved for government and military purposes. North of Queen Street Simcoe planned a range of 100-acre lots which were to be granted as "douceurs" to the officials as compensation for having to move to York (A 25). The town commons disappeared completely. The greatly improved possibilities in this plan for the rewarding of favourites give some validity to the ill-natured rumour that Simcoe chose York over Kingston as capital because "York had the advantage of being able to afford lots for all his friends around it" (H 24). The reduction of the size of the town plot was probably wise; as Simcoe wrote, it would "prevent the scattering of the Inhabitants in such situations as their fancy or interest might induce them, which would ever prevent that compactness in a Town which it seems proper to establish" (A 25). The weakness of Simcoe's plan was that it did not provide adequate room for expansion. Despite Simcoe's enthusiasm for York, Dorchester had had a better grasp of its future possibilities.

The front town lots were reserved for the higher officials, who were supposed to build houses of a similar architecture (A 9, A 12). This plan for uniformity proved unworkable, probably because of the strong individuality of the householders involved, or the scorn so freely expressed by such critics as Richard Cartwright (A 17). In 1796, the Executive Council agreed that the front houses be built 12 feet back from the street "to allow a space for Pallisadoes, or other Ornaments," but these refinements were to be "at the Pleasure of the Occupant" (A 25). At the same time, it increased the size of these front lots and allowed the officials three

[13]Public Record Office (P.R.O.), "Plan of York Harbour surveyed by order of Lieut. Govr. Simcoe by A. Aitkin"; copy in Toronto Public Library (T.P.L.).

years in which to build, so that their houses might be "an Ornament to the Town."

The scramble for town lots began before the Executive Council on September 2, 1793 (A 10, A 11). Efforts were made to insure that only *bona fide* residents receive lots, and that speculators be kept out. Throughout the period there were periodic examinations to enforce the regulations requiring the clearing of lots, and although a considerable leniency was allowed (A 53), most of the lots had at least some work done on them fairly rapidly. There were, of course, a certain amount of trading about and some irregularities and venialities, but in general Simcoe's ten blocks were developed satisfactorily. The 100-acre lots went to members of Simcoe's official and personal entourage. Those families which had the foresight to hold them until the town was bursting its Queen Street limit subdivided and sold for very high prices. In the meantime, most of the owners cleared farms on them, and in some cases, like Peter Russell's Petersfield or Chief Justice Elmsley's Cloverhill, these farms were comparatively profitable.

Although the officials knew in the autumn of 1793 that York was to be the temporary capital (A 16), it was not until February, 1796, that they were ordered to move their offices to York, "the present Seat of this Government" (A 23). As at Niagara they were expected to provide their own office space, for which they received a government allowance (A 54). At the same time, Simcoe authorized the building of two wings of an eventual residence for the lieutenant governor, which would in the meantime serve for meetings of the legislature, sessions of the courts, and church services (A 22). These two brick buildings standing at the foot of Parliament Street were built by the Queen's Rangers following the plans of William Graham, and were not completely finished until 1798 (A 38, A 42, A 44). Even while giving directions for their building, Simcoe was considering their possible disposal when the capital would be transferred to the River Thames.

The moving of the capital from Niagara to York was not popular with the officials. They had with some difficulty established themselves at Niagara and had no desire to be again uprooted. When Simcoe left Upper Canada in the summer of 1796, none of the senior civilian officials had moved to York; they were still at Niagara, grumbling *sotto voce* about the hardness of their lot, or, like Russell, making lame excuses for their procrastination (A 26). Between 1796 and 1798 however, they recognized the inevitable, and one by one moved across the lake, with varying degrees of grace. The one who protested most loudly was, rather surprisingly, Chief Justice Elmsley who was a newcomer with no stake in Niagara (A 46, C 2). He too eventually moved to York, after a spirited exchange with President Russell.

Nor was the establishment of the capital at York popular with the powerful merchants of Niagara and Kingston who realized that the new town was a threat to their interests. People in Niagara had known that its days as capital were numbered, but had hoped that Kingston would be chosen, for there were always close commercial ties between the two towns, and both shared Loyalist background and interests. With the selection of York, the government moved out of the Loyalist sphere of influence. Simcoe's hopes of the northwest fur trade using the Humber River route also caused alarm among the Niagara merchants, who made a great deal of money from the trade passing through their area on its way to Detroit. As York's pretensions grew, critical comments on them from both Kingston and Niagara became common. Those by Cartwright (A 17) and the Rev. John Stuart (D 17) were typical of Kingston opinion. An example of Niagara's attitude was a satiric attack on a formal address of welcome to General Hunter from the citizens of York, published in the Niagara newspaper. "I found the word *capital*, rendered in plain English, York, and so I conclude that whenever I in future meet with 'we the inhabitants of the capital', it is to be translated into the vernacular tongue 'we the inhabitants of York, assembled at M'Dougal's over a capital glass of grog. . . .' "[14] Sniping at York was a favourite pastime of the rest of the province.

When Simcoe left Upper Canada in 1796, most of the original town lots and 100-acre lots had been granted. Some work had been done on most of them, but there were as yet few civilians living in York. Yonge Street had been opened, and farms were being cleared along it and in William Berczy's settlement in Markham Township. The two wings of the government house had been begun. The government officers were still at Niagara, and Simcoe himself was still insisting that York was only to be a temporary capital. The Executive Council had recommended that land in the town be reserved for a church, a jail, a court house, and a market (A 25), but this had not yet been done. A storehouse had been erected on the Peninsula, and a primitive wooden garrison had been built a mile and a half to the west of the town, separated from it by bush.

It was under Simcoe's successor, Administrator Peter Russell, that York was really established, both as the capital and as a town.

[14] *Canada Constellation*, Niagara, Sept. 27, 1799.

By the end of his administration there was no longer any talk of removing the capital to London or anywhere else. The capture of York by the Americans in 1813 revived the controversy, which continued sporadically into the 1820's, but in the years from Russell to Brock York was accepted as the permanent capital of the province. Amid difficulties of transportation and accommodation Russell met his first parliament at York in June, 1797.

In 1797, Russell extended the town westward, first to York Street, and then at Elmsley's insistence (A 40) to Peter Street.[15] The northern boundary was now Queen Street. Between this western New Town and Simcoe's town, he reserved land for a church, a school, a court house, a jail, a hospital, and a market (A44). To erect these buildings, however, military help was necessary, and it was not available (A 31). Only the jail was built in Russell's time (C 6). This extension of York was not opened as rapidly as the older section; Selkirk in 1803 commented on its lack of progress (H 24), and Williams' map of 1813[16] shows clearly that it was not nearly filled by that time. If Simcoe had underestimated the growth of York, Russell was too optimistic.

Russell made a strenuous effort to prevent land speculation in York. To receive a town lot during his régime it was necessary to prove that actual residence was intended. He was "determined to prevent as far as I can a Monopoly of the Lots," and in November, 1797, requested that no assignment for a town lot be issued without his sanction, so that he could "have an opportunity of Examining the Parties, and by cross questions discover the probability of their becoming settlers here" (A 43). From the record of grants during his administration, there seems to be no reason to question Russell's desire to encourage settlement. It was impossible to prevent all "improper Transactions," but Russell and his Council were able to limit their number.

In supervising the settlement of York, Russell faced many of the same problems as Simcoe. He was seriously hampered by the scarcity and consequent expense of labour. Even basic surveys were held up by this problem (A 34), which was aggravated by the reduction of the garrison. Provisioning was becoming easier; Russell never had to use government rations for civilians as Simcoe was forced to do several times (A 21). Simcoe had allowed govern-

[15]Plans of Russell's New Town with names of grantees are in T.P.L., D. W. Smith Papers.

[16]Public Archives of Canada (P.A.C.), Map Division, "Sketch of the Ground in advance and including York Upper Canada by Geo. Williams . . . Novr. 1813."

ment supplies to be borrowed for private use (A 28) and Russell continued this policy (A 48). Although his relations with Dorchester's successor, General Prescott, were better than those of Simcoe with Dorchester, Russell was still embarrassed by lack of sympathy in Quebec with the development of York (A 36). As settlement progressed during his régime, he was faced with the new problem of confusion arising from careless surveys (A 35).

Russell's successor, General Peter Hunter, had as Commander in Chief wider responsibilities than the earlier administrators and was frequently absent from York. He built a Government House as his official residence west of the garrison on the present site of Fort York; when he was succeeded by a civilian governor, this House was with difficulty wrested from military control.[17] He found Simcoe's Government Buildings inadequate for the purpose, and recommended that the British government contribute to the expense of replacing them with proper legislative and administrative buildings (A 54), but his request went unheeded. Apart from this problem, however, York was now able to progress without government assistance. Simcoe and Russell between them had built firm foundations for future growth.

It is one of the ironies of Toronto's history that Simcoe had intended to found a naval arsenal, but had in spite of himself established a capital. The resurrection of his original idea just before the War of 1812 led to capture and occupation, and to the revival of pressure to establish the capital at Dorchester's choice, Kingston.

[17]P.R.O., C.O. 42, v. 342, p. 53, microfilm copy in P.A.O., Gore to Wyndham, Sept. 6, 1806.

B. DEFENCE

SIMCOE BELIEVED that war with the United States was both inevitable and imminent. Defence therefore was always the primary object during his administration. York was chosen for the military and naval arsenal of the province; the establishment of a town and its choice as capital were subordinate to its military importance.

Simcoe's original plans for the fortification of York were outlined in a letter to General Clarke on May 31, 1793 (A 2). There was little danger of a land assault, but in Simcoe's eyes every possibility of an attack from the Lake upon the harbour. He therefore proposed building a combined storehouse and blockhouse on the western tip of the Peninsula with armament sufficient to stop any enemy vessel from entering the Western Gap. On the mainland side of the Gap he planned barracks for 250 men to the west of Garrison Creek, a small stream which meandered southeast from the present Trinity Park. At the mouth of the Creek he proposed placing his own tents with two huts for his own use; a row of huts was to be built north along the Creek, ending in a guardhouse. Another row of huts angled from the guardhouse to the shore, thus enclosing a triangular parade ground, and leaving the lake side of it open for a battery.[1]

In July, 1793, Simcoe brought the Queen's Rangers to York to begin the clearing and building (A 4), and began commandeering supplies from Kingston and Niagara. From Kingston, six 18-pounder and ten 12-pounder carronades were sent to York. From Carleton Island came six 18-pounder and six 12-pounder guns, all unserviceable. These offerings were accompanied by carronade carriages, shot, one non-commissioned officer and eight gunners of the Royal Artillery, three tents, a camp kettle, and a month's provisions.[2] Also from Kingston Simcoe requisitioned a complete set of punch-boring irons, and in October, thirty snowshoes for the Rangers. From Niagara came a brass 12-pounder belonging to the gunboat, 50,000 rounds of ball cartridges, powder, wadhooks and sponges, and ladles for the guns; provisions for the Rangers (A 8);

[1]A rough sketch by Simcoe of his proposals is owned by the Queen's York Rangers. It was published in University of Toronto, School of Architecture, Engineering Research School, *Bulletin 146, Old Forts in Upper Canada.*

[2]P.A.O., Simcoe Papers, "Memorandum of Guns & Carronades to be put on board his Majesty's Schooner Mississague," Aug. 6, 1793.

boards, nails, glass, and putty for the buildings.[3] The Rangers under Major Shank built 30 huts on the west side of Garrison Creek. These were roughly built of round logs and were expected to last only seven years. All the work done was impermanent; the first powder magazine "fell in" in 1795[4] and had to be replaced, and repair of the huts was constantly necessary. Palisades were built joining the huts together. The mouth of the Creek was widened for bateaux and a small wharf or landing place built for them. In September, 1793, Lieutenant Pilkington, R.E., submitted his estimate for the combined store and blockhouse on the Island, the first storey of which was to be made of masonry, but in November Simcoe decided that the Rangers were sufficiently adept at building with logs to make stone barracks unnecessary (B 3). This decision was probably influenced by Dorchester's flat refusal to countenance Simcoe's plans for York's defence; on October 7, 1793, Dorchester had written to Simcoe that "I cannot approve of any Fortifications being erected there at present" (A 15). Hampered by this command, Simcoe was forced to be content with his huts on the mainland and storehouses on the Island. A frame for a blockhouse was prepared, but not raised (A 30, B 8). In 1796 Dorchester withdrew two regiments from Upper Canada, so that it was necessary to remove most of the Rangers from York to man other posts. It was at this stage that Simcoe returned to England.

With the small garrison of 147 men left at York,[5] Russell found that little could be done; he constantly faced the problem of shortage of military labour in surveying, transporting provisions, and building. In 1797, however, the second battalion of the Royal Canadian Volunteers was ordered to relieve the Rangers at Niagara, Amherstburg, and St. Joseph, and Simcoe's regiment was once more concentrated at York. The problem of accommodation for the increased garrison arose, and although York was not an established military post, General Prescott, who had succeeded Dorchester as Governor in Chief, sanctioned the building of additional huts (B 5). Influenced by another war scare, Russell went beyond this authority and erected the first blockhouse on the mainland, on the east side of Garrison Creek, using the blockhouse frame built during the Simcoe régime (B 8). Early in 1799, Russell also built a blockhouse

[3]*Ibid.*, Littlehales to Capt. Porter, Sept. 20 and Oct. 25, 1793; to Major Smith, Aug. 9, Sept 9, and Nov. 25, 1793; to McGill, Oct 3, 1793; to Pilkington, Nov. 4, 1793.

[4]*Ibid.*, Littlehales to McGill, Oct. 13, 1795.

[5]Simcoe, *Correspondence*, IV, 344, "State of the Troops in the Province of Upper Canada," Aug. 1, 1796.

at the east end of the town itself, so that in case of attack there would be soldiers in the town and a place of safety for civilians to congregate (A 49). The town blockhouse was not particularly successful; it was too close to the Don marshes, and soldiers stationed there were constantly afflicted with fever and ague (B 15).

By 1800, the fortifications of York consisted of a number of log huts on both sides of Garrison Creek, a blockhouse on the east side of the Creek, a large provision storehouse, a powder magazine, and a two-storey storehouse for Indian presents. On Gibraltar Point on the Peninsula there were two combined store and blockhouses and a guardhouse; in York itself there was another blockhouse (A 52). This was the position when General Hunter arrived in the Province and made York a military post. During his régime only one extensive building was added—his own official residence, built on the west side of Garrison Creek, on the site of the present Fort York. More huts were built on the east side as they were needed. In 1802 a report on the public works and buildings at the military post included only twenty huts used for various purposes, two storehouses, and one blockhouse (B 14). "The Old Hutts on the west side of the Creek," presumably those built by Simcoe, were ordered torn down. In that year, the Royal Canadian Volunteers who were then in garrison at York were disbanded, as were the Queen's Rangers. They were replaced by a detachment of the 41st Regiment in September, 1802, who were, in turn, relieved the following May by two companies of the 49th Regiment under Lieutenant Colonel Isaac Brock.

The best record of the garrison at this time can be found in three sketches. The first,[6] dated May 31, 1803, by Lt. Sempronius Stretton of the 49th Regiment, shows the large, square, one-storey residence of General Hunter and a few huts on the west side of Garrison Creek, a small dock at the mouth of the Creek, and the palisaded garrison on the east side, consisting of a number of humble huts and a blockhouse. The second sketch,[7] also by Stretton, dated May 13, 1804, is a more finished painting, but has apparently gained in artistry at the expense of accuracy. Garrison Creek and the palisades are omitted altogether, and the buildings are compressed together and arranged more tidily than in either of the other sketches. The third drawing,[8] "View of the Garrison at Toronto or York Upper

[6]P.A.C., Picture Division, Lieut. Stretton's Sketch Book, 1803–6.

[7]*Ibid.*, York Barracks, Lake Ontario, May 13, 1804, by Lieut. Stretton.

[8]University of Michigan, William L. Clements Library, "View of the Garrison at Toronto or York Upper Canada . . . March 11, 1805."

Canada . . . March 11, 1805," is probably also by Stretton, and closely resembles the first sketch.

From this time until 1811, very little was done at York. There were of course repairs and such operations as whitewashing, but in general the little garrison remained unchanged. Late in 1805 the 49th Regiment was relieved by the 41st, but the following year the headquarters of the latter regiment were removed to Fort George, leaving only a small garrison at York.

In 1811 the situation changed, partly owing to the obvious possibility of war and the replacement of Gore by Brock as administrator. The most important reason, however, was the same as the one which originally influenced Simcoe in his selection of York as a military post—the weakness of Kingston as the naval centre of the province. All Simcoe's arguments against Kingston were revived—its proximity to the American border, particularly when the St. Lawrence was covered with ice, the weakness of its fortifications, and the consequences that would befall the communications with Lower Canada should Kingston be captured (B 24). Supremacy on the Lakes was to be vital in any war with the United States; the naval dockyards at Kingston would be of major importance. Because of the exposed situation of Kingston, it was proposed by both Brock and Prevost that the naval establishment be moved to York. Unhappily, Prevost at least did not realize that time was running out; he suggested in the spring of 1812 "that the removal of the Establishment should gradually take place, by laying out a Naval Yard upon a small scale, and by erecting Storehouses at York . . . as the buildings allotted for them at Kingston fall into decay" (B 25). At the same time he admitted that "no Works of any description have hitherto been constructed for its protection" at York (B 22). It was agreed that the best spot for such fortifications would be on the site of Hunter's Government House on the west side of Garrison Creek, and work was started here immediately. The building of the *Prince Regent*, a small schooner of 80 tons carrying 10 guns, was begun farther down the harbour early in 1812 (B 21), the first government vessel built at York since the *Toronto* thirteen years earlier. In April, 1812, Brock wrote from York that a temporary magazine for powder had been erected, and a ditch excavated for the proposed fortification on the site of the Government House.[9] The grandiose plans for a fortress, however, were not carried out. At the time of the capture of York a year later, the garrison was described as "a Block House, serving as Barracks without a Gun,

[9]P.A.C., C Series, v. 676, p. 103, Brock to Prevost, Apr. 22, 1812.

but on the Bank near to it were two Six Pounders behind a sod work.—At the Corner of the Government House was a Battery of two 12 Pounders. About 400 yards from the Govt House was a small half Moon work, thrown up without a Gun, & about the same Distance further on an 18 Pounder Battery which commanded the Anchorage & Landing."[10]

Simcoe, Prevost, and Brock all had the idea of a strong fort erected on the site of the present Fort York on the west side of Garrison Creek. This fort did not become a reality until the make-shift garrison to the east fell an easy prey to the Americans in 1813.

The defence of the province in this early period was in the hands of the British regular forces. There was, however, a large militia force, more or less untrained and unorganized, but impressive on paper. The first Militia Act in Upper Canada, passed in 1793, provided for the appointment of Lieutenants of each County by the Governor. The Lieutenant was responsible for the appointment of the officers and the organization of the militia, which consisted of every male inhabitant between the ages of 16 and 50[11] within his county. York County had three Lieutenants in the period before the war[12]—Æneas Shaw, D. W. Smith, and John McGill. Although Shaw was requested to get his militia into readiness during the war scare of 1797 (B 7), the York militia was first organized by D. W. Smith in 1798 (B 11, B 12) and included men from an area stretching from Whitby on the east to the Head of the Lake on the west. The men were to be drilled at least twice a year, but these occasions were not sufficient for any sort of training and seem to have been regarded even by the officers as almost social affairs. Ely Playter, a militia officer, recorded such an attitude to training days in his diary (H 23).

When relations with the United States again deteriorated in 1807, orders were received that one-quarter of the militia, chosen by volunteering or by ballot, was to prepare for actual service at an hour's notice (B 18), but the crisis passed and the militia returned to its almost casual footing. In 1811 when war once more seemed very near, a volunteer cavalry company was raised in Markham Township (B 20), and on May 4, 1812, following the passage of Brock's Militia Act, flank companies intended for active service

[10]P.A.C., Powell Papers, p. 1212, description of York and its fortifications in Powell's handwriting.

[11]In 1794 the age limit was raised to 60.

[12]The office of County Lieutenant became defunct during the War of 1812.

were chosen from the militia, and began to receive the first competent training ever given militia corps in Upper Canada (B 26, B 27). There were now three regiments of York militia. The First Regiment was drawn from the northern part of the county, the Second from the Western Riding which included Burlington and the Head of the Lake area, and the Third Regiment included men of the Town of York and its immediate environs. On June 26, 1812, the flank companies of the Third Regiment, 120 strong under the command of Major William Allan, marched into the garrison. Thus began the contribution of York's citizen army in the War of 1812.

C. LAW AND ORDER

THE ESTABLISHMENT OF AN EFFECTIVE SYSTEM of justice and local government in a new community takes a little time. Upper Canada did not experience the period of lawlessness beloved in the legend of the American West, but did suffer from occasionally faltering legal machinery and from a mixed population. Settlements like York which were the result of artificial creation rather than of natural growth needed a system to insure internal peace and order before they had time to shake down into a communal entity. York almost certainly did not deserve La Rochefoucauld-Liancourt's blanket condemnation of it, "les habitants n'y sont pas, dit-on, de la meilleure espèce,"[1] which reflects Niagara's attitude to the town which more or less superseded it. With York's labouring class, however, drawn so heavily from discharged soldiers at a time when the British army was recruited from the lowest classes, it did have its share of the dissolute and amoral. As the seat of government, it attracted drifters with no stake in the community and little pride in its development. The number of unsolved petty crimes recorded in the *Upper Canada Gazette* reflects both on the powers of detection of the authorities and on the probity of at least a segment of the population. It was fortunate that intelligence and criminal intent were so rarely found together; most of the crimes committed in this early period were bumbling and amateur, like the enterprising theft of Elisha Beman's property in 1798 (C 7).

The due process of law requires a number of things which the new community lacked—buildings both for the sittings of the courts and the detention of prisoners, a fairly large stable population to provide jurors, and men with various kinds of specialized training, from lawyers to hangmen. These deficiencies were stressed by Chief Justice Elmsley in his last ditch stand against the removal of the capital to York (C 2, C 3, C 5). (The Court of King's Bench and the sittings for the Home District were automatically held at the seat of government.) His opinion was overridden by the other members of the Council, however, and his dark prognostications of legal stagnation and disaster were not fulfilled. The courts met in the Government Buildings with relative convenience, although in May, 1805, one of the magistrates reported that the Court of Requests

[1]La Rochefoucauld-Liancourt, *Voyage dans les états-unis d'Amérique fait en 1795, 1796 et 1797*, II, 112.

was held "in the open field! which is equally uncomfortable, inconvenient & indecorous."[2] A primitive jail was built in 1798, "to restrain the Enormities of this increasing Town" (C 6). The jury problem took a little longer to solve—early court records show that there were frequent difficulties in getting enough jurors who were not exempt because of too recent jury service (C 11)—but increasing population brought a natural remedy. Lawyers tended naturally to gravitate towards the capital; other court and jail officials were appointed from the crowd clamouring for small government preferments. A hangman was fortunately not often needed; his job was badly bungled at York's first hanging in 1800 (H 16).

One legal problem in early York was the protection of the rights of the Indian. Contemporaries emphasized the need of protection for the European from the Indian, but it was the Indian who was in greater danger. York lay on the frontier between the two civilizations and was exposed to the friction created by the first attempts of the two races to live together amicably. Mrs. Simcoe might sentimentalize about an Indian chief holding her son at the christening of York, or about Jacob the Mohawk dancing Scots reels (H 1), but the average citizen's attitude to the Indians was a compound of fear and contempt. In York, as in Kingston, this erupted in the murder of a chief by a white man. Wabacanine, one of the three Missisauga chiefs from whom the Toronto Purchase was made, was murdered by a drunken soldier, Charles McEwan, in an unsavoury brawl on the waterfront in 1796 (C 1). President Russell was extremely conscious of the possibility of an Indian war at this time, and government machinery was immediately set in motion to placate the Indians.[3] The trial of the soldier, however, was something of a farce; no Indians were present, although invited, to prove Wabacanine's death, and McEwan was therefore released to continue to serve in the Rangers until honourably discharged with the disbandment of his regiment in 1802.

Local government was closely allied with law enforcement. In Upper Canada its establishment was complicated by Simcoe's distrust of any form of local elective assembly, engendered by the revolutionary results of the New England town meeting. Throughout the period, real power on the local level lay in the hands of the magistrates appointed by the governor, meeting by district in the General Quarter Sessions of the Peace. In 1796 the first magistrates

[2]T.P.L., McGill Papers, Alexander Wood to James Green, May 18, 1805.

[3]Russell, *Correspondence*, ed. by Cruikshank, I. 49–50, 117, Russell to Simcoe, Sept. 28 and Dec. 31, 1796.

in the York area were sworn in—John Small, William Willcocks, John Lawrence, Æneas Shaw, and possibly John McGill (A 30). This list was augmented as the population grew. Some of the magistrates attended the Sessions more regularly than others; the Home District Sessions became dominated by the Scottish merchant group—men like William Allan, Alexander Wood, and Duncan Cameron. In addition William Jarvis, William Willcocks, Donald McLean, and after 1811 Thomas Ridout, attended fairly regularly. It was an eminently respectable and conservative body, coping with an impossible task.

The expenses of the District were much greater than its income. The property taxes levied in York, Vaughan, and Markham in 1798 amounted to only £25.16.3[4] Currency and there was no guarantee that this would be collectible. The following year levied taxes rose to £81.5.6, and thereafter continued to rise slowly. Out of such sums as these, the magistrates were expected to pay the salaries of the members of Parliament of the two York ridings, the Sheriff, the High Constable, the clerk of the peace, the court keeper, the jailer, and the coroner, as well as the contingent expenses of these offices. They were responsible for the upkeep of the pound and of the jail (C 21), which like all York log buildings seemed to require constant attention. They paid a bounty on wolves, and occasionally were forced to spend part of their tiny income to provide for the poverty-stricken or insane (C 13), although they had some doubts about the legality of such expenditures (C 11). It is not surprising that they were constantly in debt, or that salaries were often badly in arrears.

As an administrative body, the General Sessions of the Peace issued regulations concerning the safety, convenience, respectability, and sanitation of the town. Like all frontier towns surrounded by forest and built almost entirely of wood, York was particularly exposed to the hazards of fire. Mrs. Simcoe records the burning of Scadding's cottage on January 31, 1794 (H 1); there were frequent fires throughout the period, but none spread to more than two or three buildings. When forest fires raged around York, as in the spring of 1806 (C 16), there was the danger of complete obliteration. In 1800 the magistrates ordered that every householder must have two fire-buckets and two ladders, one fixed on the roof for easy access to the chimney (C 10), and there were frequent inspections to enforce this ruling. In 1802 Lieutenant Governor Hunter

[4]Assessment roll of Home District, quoted in Robertson, *Landmarks of Toronto*, II, 990.

presented York with a fire engine (C 14), and a shed was built by public subscription to house it. There was no organized fire brigade in York at this time; everyone available was expected to assist when fire broke out.

The police force was appointed by the General Quarter Sessions. The High Constable, who until 1814 was paid only £10 a year, was the senior officer. His responsibilities included inflicting the summary punishments ordered by the courts; it is possible to feel sorry for the High Constable who "made a very rediculous appearance at the impilloring" of a woman convicted of keeping "a disorderly house, for the reception of loose, vicious and lewd persons," on April 28, 1804 (H 23). The High Constable was assisted by a number of unpaid constables appointed annually by the magistrates. These appointments were not popular, but refusal to serve was punished by the comparatively stiff fine of £2 (C 11).

The magistrates were also responsible for the repair and improvement of the streets and for the performance of statute labour on them. Most of the streets were rudimentary trails, on which the stumps may have been removed, but little more done. In York there was the additional problem of the many ravines and rivulets running through the town-site, over which bridges had to be built. Most of these bridges were crudely constructed; the editor of the *Upper Canada Gazette*, John Cameron, questioned this short-term policy in 1808 (C 18). Every householder had to work on the streets for an assigned number of days depending on his assessment, or pay for equivalent labour. The pathmasters were responsible for organizing this work, but the enforcement of their rulings lay with the General Quarter Sessions of the Peace (C 20). Only absolutely necessary work could be done by statute labour; other projects like the improvement of Yonge Street (E 11) or the building of a bridge to the Peninsula (C 17) were undertaken by special public subscription.

The magistrates were also responsible for such things as the regulation of the ferries across the Humber and Credit Rivers, the enforcement of standardized weights and measures, and the operation of the public market.

To insure respectability, the magistrates spent much time enforcing the liquor laws. They licensed all tavern keepers annually (C 12); in most years they refused as many licences as they issued. Illegal sale of liquor was summarily punished, and disorderliness even on licensed premises was discouraged. In 1802 the town wardens were directed to represent to the tavern keepers "the indecency and impropriety of allowing people to drink intoxicating liquors and be guilty of disorderly behavior . . . on the Sabbath days" (C 13). Respectability also lay behind the order of 1812 forbidding bathing in front of the town between sunrise and sunset.[5] As a magistrates' court the General Quarter Sessions dealt severely with disorderly houses, minor cases of assault, and general disturbances of the peace.

Drainage and sanitation were very primitive in early York. Occasional orders were made by the magistrates to safeguard the health of the town, for example that concerning butchers' garbage and offal in 1802 (C 13); but it was not until the first cholera epidemic thirty years later that strenuous efforts were made to enforce any adequate hygienic standards.

Besides the General Quarter Sessions, there was another more democratic institution for local government—the annual town meeting, attended by the inhabitants of the Town and Townships of York, Etobicoke, and Scarborough. The principal task of these meetings was the election of the town officers, including the town clerk, assessors, collectors, pathmasters, and town warden (C 4). In York two town wardens were elected until 1804; from that date only one was elected and the other appointed by the Anglican minister. The only regulations ever passed at these meetings concerned the running at large and the branding of cattle, and the height of fences.[6] Municipal government was thus in the hands of the magistrates. In the Home District they seemed to have been hard-working and conscientious. There is some evidence that there was occasional bias in the issuing of tavern licences and in the choice of streets on which statute labour was to be performed, but in general the Court of General Quarter Sessions of the Peace, working under financial difficulties, gave good government to York.

[5]P.A.O., Minutes of the General Quarter Sessions of the Peace, Home District, July 14, 1812.

[6]T.P.L., Minutes of Town Meetings and Lists of Inhabitants of York, 1797–1822.

D. COMMERCIAL DEVELOPMENT

TORONTO'S GEOGRAPHICAL ASSETS, which were to be so important in the future development of the metropolis, were not as readily realized as those of Kingston or of the towns on the Niagara River. Kingston was the gateway to the upper part of the province; all imports and exports to and from Lower Canada and Europe passed through Kingston, and were transferred there to lake or river boats.[1] The merchants on the Niagara, many of whom had connections with Kingston business interests, were also located on the main westward commercial route. Here again goods and produce were transshipped for the next stage of their journey. In addition, both Kingston and the Niagara towns had a well-populated hinterland behind them, settled by Loyalists in the 1780's. Before the War of 1812, York's advantages—a safe harbour and the pious hope that the northwest fur trade would use the Yonge Street route—were not sufficient to enable the infant capital to compete commercially with its more prosperous rivals.

In the beginning, the problem was one of basic survival. While Simcoe was ceremoniously christening his new town-site in 1793, his secretary was writing desperately to Niagara for food (A 8). In March, 1796, Simcoe was forced to issue a quantity of government provisions to the inhabitants to prevent starvation,[2] a gesture acidly condemned by Dorchester.[3] But while the townspeople in York were living on scanty rations, land was being cleared—to the north, especially by Berczy's settlers in Markham Township, to the east in Hope Township, and to the west near Burlington. Cartwright's expectation of selling flour in York (D 2) was fulfilled for only a short period. By 1801, the Yonge Street farmers were producing surplus flour, although "it is not in their power to carry it past" York (D 18). The development of agriculture around York was much faster than the people of Kingston would believe (D 17). Even in York there were doubts about the ability of the neighbourhood to feed the Town; in 1798 Peter Russell had written, "I fear the Increase of this Town bears no proportion to the Population round it—the Head will consequently I fear grow too big for the Body—& Scarcity

[1]Kingston's commercial development was entirely different from York's; see Preston, *Kingston before the War of 1812*.

[2]Simcoe, *Correspondence*, IV, 206, Simcoe to Dorchester, March 2. 1796.

[3]*Ibid.*, IV, 242, Dorchester to Simcoe, April 11, 1796.

& dearness of Provision are of course the inevitable Consequence— These keep up the prices of all kinds of labor and Materials."[4] The quantity and therefore the price of flour on the York market fluctuated a great deal, depending on the condition of the roads and crops. In 1802 the York merchant Alexander Wood wrote, "Flour is again very plenty. You know a small parcel gluts the Market of this place, so that it is Feast & Famine alternately, and these succeed each other frequently."[5] The following year, however, flour was scarce because of the drought, and "an uncommon influx of settlers."[6] This pattern continued throughout the period, while flour became the main export of the York area.

The only other export of any significance in the period was potash, a by-product of the clearing of land. Kendrick had a potashery on Yonge Street in 1799 (D 6), and William Allan one in York opposite the jail in 1800.[7] Pork was occasionally exported, although the problem of preservation and the reluctance of the farmers to use foreign salt complicated the business.[8] In the very early period, York salmon was regarded as a delicacy in Niagara and Kingston; in 1800 William Jarvis ordered a salmon seine because of the profits of the trade.[9] There was still some traffic in furs, although they were no longer an important part of the area's economy. Quetton St. George received a fair number of furs, mainly through his establishments at the Narrows at Lake Couchiching and at Amherstburg, and sold them in the United States (D 50). Duncan Cameron was also active in the fur trade. One merchant at least, Jacob Herchmer, hoped to build up a trade in ginseng for export to the Far East,[10] but was apparently unsuccessful. Throughout the period there were more general hopes that hemp could be grown commercially in the area (D 19, D 26), but nothing came of this aspiration. Other products like hams, beef, peas, beer, and whiskey were sold only locally.

These products, as well as garden produce, were usually sold

[4]T.P.L., Peter Russell Papers, Russell to Simcoe, Oct. 15, 1798.

[5]T.P.L. Alexander Wood Letter Books, Wood to Robert Hamilton, March 29, 1802.

[6]*Ibid.*, Wood to Ogilvy, Mylne & Co., Oct. 4, 1803.

[7]*Upper Canada Gazette*, York, Allan's advertisement, Nov. 22, 1800.

[8]Alexander Wood Letter Books, Wood to Irvine, McNaught & Co., July 2, 1802.

[9]He wrote that four men could land ten barrels of salmon in two hours at the mouth of the rivers during the salmon season, selling them when salted at $20 a barrel. (P.A.C., Upper Canada Sundries, Jarvis to recipient not stated, Jan. 18, 1800.)

[10]*Upper Canada Gazette*, York, Herchmer's advertisement, Aug. 29, 1801.

through the York merchants. A bill to establish a public market at York for direct sale between farmer and consumer was introduced in the House of Assembly by Ephraim Jones, member for Grenville, on June 13, 1798, and was passed with amendments by the House. The Legislative Council, however, amended it to "curtail the influence of the Market and the interference of the Magistrates to the mere limits of the Town Plot, whereas the original intention of the Bill extended to a circle of five miles"; the House of Assembly refused to accept these amendments, and the bill was lost.[11] A market was later established by the proclamation of Lieutenant Governor Hunter in 1803 (D 28), after he had consulted the Executive Council on the subject (D 24). An act to authorize the General Quarter Sessions of the Peace for the Home District "to establish and regulate a market" was however not passed until 1814.

Before the War of 1812, the few industries in the York area, besides grist mills and potasheries, probably produced goods for only local consumption. These included sawmills, tanneries, breweries (D 45), distilleries, and at least one pottery.[12] The most important mills in the immediate vicinity of York were the King's Mill built by the government in 1793 on the Humber near Bloor Street, Cooper's grist and sawmill built in 1806 on the Humber near Dundas Street, Skinner's grist and sawmill on the Don built in 1794, and Terry's sawmill further up the Don built in 1800.

Skilled tradesmen followed the government officials to York. Blacksmiths, carpenters, and masons were the earliest arrivals. A plan to reserve town lots for the most essential trades (A 51) was not proceeded with, probably because it was found to be unnecessary. In the advertisements in the *Upper Canada Gazette* we see the tradesmen arriving—the tailor (D 5), the hairdresser (D 7), the watchmaker (D 8), the baker (D 10), the chairmaker (D 22), the hatter (D 31), the druggist (D 32). It was a period when versatility was important; Eliphalet Hale, who won the contract for the improvement of Yonge Street in 1800,[13] began his career in York in 1799 as a bricklayer,[14] but advertised in 1806 as a shoemaker.[15] The prime example of over-all talents was William Cooper, who was variously a tavern keeper (D 13), a school teacher (G 1, G 4, G 5), a preacher (H 18), a butcher, a wharfinger, a miller, and an

[11]"Journals of the Legislative Assembly of Upper Canada," 1798. *Sixth Report of the Bureau of Archives, 1909*, pp. 61–3, 72–7.

[12]Alexander Wood Letter Books to James Dunlop, July 2, 1802.

[13]*Upper Canada Gazette*, York, Dec. 13, 1800.

[14]*Ibid.*, March. 30, 1799.

[15]*Ibid.*, March 15, 1806.

auctioneer. In most cases such diversity inspires doubts of competence. Some trades were not represented; for example in 1805 Alexander Wood complained of the absence of a silversmith,[16] and there were several times when there was a good opening for a baker.[17] Trades were taught by an apprenticeship system, in which children and adolescents were almost enslaved. Runaway apprentice advertisements were a common feature of the *Upper Canada Gazette* (D 53).

The men who were to become the real arbiters of York's commercial destiny, however, were not the farmers, millers, or tradesmen, but the shopkeepers. The first shopkeeper in York was probably Jean Baptiste Rousseau, a fur trader living at the mouth of the Humber from the time of the French régime. He automatically became a general merchant as well as a fur trader when English settlement began, and was a steady if small customer of Richard Cartwright of Kingston (D 1). In 1794 he entered a partnership with Thomas Barry; the accounts between the partners, drawn up when Rousseau withdrew to live in Ancaster in 1795, show the type of business the firm carried on (D 3). Its customers were mainly Queen's Rangers and a few farmers on Yonge Street and at the Head of the Lake; its goods were necessities. The more extensive account books of another early York merchant, Abner Miles, had greater emphasis on food and liquor—Miles was also keeping a tavern—but again show the simplicity of early life in York.[18]

Storekeeping in York received fresh impetus just before the turn of the century with the arrival of three very able men. Two of them were young Scotsmen from Aberdeenshire, William Allan and Alexander Wood; the third, Laurent Quetton St. George, came to Canada as a member of the Count de Puisaye's French royalist group in 1798. Allan and Wood entered a partnership which lasted until 1801, when each set up his own business. Probably, St. George's commercial beginnings in Upper Canada were fairly humble, but in a comparatively short time he was able to maintain a store not only in York, but in Niagara, Kingston, and Amherstburg. These three merchants divided the carriage trade among them through most of the period, and all three became wealthy.

There were, of course, many other storekeepers on a smaller scale in York, who seemed by their advertisements in the *Upper*

[16]Alexander Wood Letter Books, Wood to Leslie, McNaught & Co., Oct. 21, 1805.

[17]*Upper Canada Gazette*, York, Herchmer and Heron's advertisement, Aug. 30, 1800.

[18]T.P.L., Abner Miles' Account Books.

Canada Gazette to spend much of their time playing musical chairs with each other in the little shops on King and Market Streets. Competition was keen. The established merchants felt a particular resentment against American "birds of passage" who were able to undercut their prices (D 29), and against newcomers in the field (D 47).

It was the practice in York "to keep every kind of goods in one store" (D 20). Even stores with some degree of specialization, like the apothecary's shop, also carried a general line of merchandise (D 32). The big merchants sold to country storekeepers, but in general there was no organized wholesale business (D 54). Goods were often sent to York on consignment, but such attempts to sell articles chosen by those unfamiliar with local conditions were usually not very successful (D 27, D 54). Auction sales in taverns were held frequently, especially in the earliest period (D 9), but were not profitable as a means of unloading slow-selling stock (D 54). The York merchant's only chance of getting rid of his white elephants was to send them to the big auction sales at Montreal, but this again was accompanied by financial loss.

A surprising variety of imported goods was available in York. St. George, by far the most prolific advertiser in the period, regularly published long lists of articles for sale (D 25), as well as shorter more specialized advertisements (D 38). The other merchants also carried extensive assortments. There were, however, frequent scarcities; for example, the exceptionally cold winter of 1804–5 caused a shortage of blankets and heavy cloth.[19] A rather odd importation of the time was tombstones, because " we have neither materials nor artists here to execute in any thing more durable than Wood."[20]

One of the greatest problems of the merchant was the complete absence of banks combined with the extreme scarcity of specie (D 14, D 54). Goods were usually paid for by the farmers with produce (D 37), by tradesmen with produce or services, and by officials and army officers with promissory notes or bills on England (D 26). The situation was further complicated by the use of four systems of currency—the American dollar, pounds sterling equated at 4*s*. 6*d*. to the dollar, Halifax or Provincial Currency equated at 5*s*. to the dollar, and New York or York Currency equated at 8*s*. to the dollar. Merchants and ordinary citizens happily translated from one to the other with great facility. Counterfeit coins were

[19]Alexander Wood Letter Books, Wood to Ogilvy, Mylne & Co., Jan. 3, 1805.
[20]*Ibid*., Wood to John Radcliffe, Feb. 19, 1805.

another recurring difficulty to the merchant; in 1801 York's position on the fringe of two commercial empires was clearly demonstrated by the circulation of American coins counterfeited in England (D 15).

The system of barter and of credit which was developing had several important effects. The farmer was forced to give his produce to the storekeeper for the necessities he required, so that the storekeeper automatically became a middleman in marketing the area's one export product. The farmer usually became indebted to him through extravagance, bad harvests, or just bad luck. The rather pathetic dignity of Timothy Nightingale's letters to St. George (D 41, D 42) can be duplicated many times in the records of the early merchants. The end of the vicious circle of increasing indebtedness was often the merchant's gaining possession of the farm. Even if this extreme was not reached, the merchant had considerable control over the disposal of the farmers' crops; for example in 1810 a farmer had to deliver his potash furtively to Allan because he usually dealt with St. George (D 48).

Among the higher officials and army officers, the system of credit, combined with the fierce social competition, led to extravagance and debt. Solicitor General Gray left debts amounting to £1200 when he died,[21] and this was not an isolated case. In the capital, the time of payment of government salaries, which depended on the auditing of the public accounts and the governor's signature, was important to the merchant; then at least some debts would be paid (D 49). The problem of collecting debts in a shifting population led to co-operation between merchants of different towns. If a debtor remained in Upper Canada, a York merchant creditor could collect through other merchants wherever the debtor went.

All this is applicable to most of the successful merchants in York, or indeed in Upper Canada. There was, however, one area in which practices among the York merchants differed—the purchase of imported goods. The early merchants like Rousseau and Barry bought in Kingston or Montreal, sold at high prices, and made small profits. By 1800 when competition was increasing, the more ambitious merchants wanted to make more money, and turned their attention to direct importation from Great Britain or New York. They usually bought almost exclusively from one source or the other, supplementing their imports with goods bought in Montreal, and rums and brandy from the West Indies.

Alexander Wood was an example of an importer from Britain.

[21] *Ibid.*, Wood to Mrs. John Elmsley, Jan. 27, 1806.

Until the Embargo Act, he regularly bought only tea and tobacco from the United States, and even these were ordered through Niagara merchants. From Montreal he bought special orders for his customers, and items omitted for some reason from his annual shipment from Great Britain, or with greater demand than he had expected. These he tried to keep to a minimum, because of the additional cost of goods in Montreal (D 23). The bulk of his goods he bought abroad, ordering them once a year. The orders were made out in the early part of October, in time to be sent on the last ship sailing from Quebec. The goods were sent out with the spring fleet, and usually arrived in York in July or August of the following year. At the time the order was made, Wood had very little idea of British prices; these he discovered from the invoice which usually arrived after the goods themselves. If as usual he were paying in part with flour or potash, he would not know what price he would be allowed in Great Britain for them. With so much uncertainty, a great deal depended on the intelligence and common sense of the British exporter to adapt the order to changing conditions (D 20). He was handicapped, however, by his ignorance of Canadian circumstances. Upon arrival in Quebec, the goods were loaded on a boat for Montreal, where they were unpacked and checked for damage. Packed in smaller boxes they were transported to Lachine by waggon, and then shipped up the river to Kingston in small boats manned by French Canadians. The final stage of their passage to York was on the larger lake boats. Goods often arrived in a damaged condition, usually because of the rough treatment received in Canada. Poor marking of boxes (D 19) and careless packing (D 44) caused much inconvenience and loss. There was the additional hazard of seizure by French privateers (D 49).

Buying in New York was much simpler. Goods could be chosen by personal inspection on buying trips from merchants who were more familiar with the needs of pioneer communities. Transportation was not as time-consuming, although still somewhat cumbersome. Goods were shipped up the Hudson River to Albany, and transported by land to Schenectady. From there they could either follow the Mohawk route to Oswego and cross the lake by boat to York, or the land route from Schenectady to Lewiston, be ferried across the Niagara River to Niagara or Queenston, and again cross the lake by boat. St. George did most of his buying in New York until the American Embargo Act led to the impounding of his goods at Lewiston, and their rescue through the dramatic lawlessness of his clerks (D 43). The disadvantage of New York buying, however, was that the prices were often higher than in Great Britain, since many of the goods were of British manufacture and were naturally more expensive when not bought at source.

Importation from either direction was a costly and frustrating business. Delays were common on both routes, and there was keen competition among the merchants to be the first to get their yearly goods. In 1801 Alexander Wood wrote, that it was "an advantage to have the goods early at hand as the stores are very much culled by the month of May, of course who ever has his new supplies first is sure to meet a ready market."[22] This situation remained constant throughout the period; in 1810 St. George's clerks were nervously twittering about the delayed arrival of his goods from New York (D 46, D 47, D 48, D 49).

By 1812, however, a more or less satisfactory system had been established for supplying the York area with its wants and for selling its surplus produce. The leading merchants had warehouses for the storage of farm products, and a number of farmers were sufficiently in debt to them to guarantee that these warehouses would be constantly used. The established merchants were making money, although their biggest profits were still ahead in the war years. Then commissariat buying and inflated prices made their fortunes, and a real moneyed class emerged for the first time in York.

[22]*Ibid.*, Wood to Ogilvy, Mylne & Co., Oct. 1, 1802.

E. COMMUNICATIONS

THE ABSENCE OF ADEQUATE COMMUNICATIONS with the outside world was a problem for all who lived in York. In its earliest days York was completely cut off except in the summer when it could be visited by the few boats on Lake Ontario plying between Kingston, Niagara, and the American ports. During the Simcoe régime only one road from York was built—Yonge Street, leading north into the wilderness. In the winter months this isolation contributed greatly to the difficulties of provisioning and the privation of the inhabitants. York was founded not by the gradual expansion of existing areas of settlement, but because of its special geographical advantages. For this reason it could not depend (as normally growing communities could) on the natural development of roads built by statute labour linking adjacent settlements.

When the capital was actually established at York in 1797, these difficulties became acute. Until 1803, meetings of the Legislature were held in the summer at great inconvenience to farming members of Parliament, because it was too difficult to come to York in the winter. Even water communication was complicated by the reduction of the marine establishment on the Lakes and by the difficulty Russell had in commandeering the King's vessels. There was still not enough business in York to justify frequent visits by the few boats on the Lake. In the summer of 1799, Joseph Kendrick, captain of the *Peggy*, a schooner of "little more than twenty Tons" owned by two York merchants, was in a strong enough position to try a little gentlemanly blackmail to get port charges reduced (E 7). The launching of the government yacht, the *Toronto*, a month later (E 8), to be directly under the orders of the governor or administrator, made the problem somewhat less pressing; but it was not really solved until York grew sufficiently in population and commerce to make regular and frequent visits by commercial vessels profitable.

In 1797 there were no roads connecting York with the older communities in the province. Thriving settlements were established along the St. Lawrence to Kingston, on the Bay of Quinte and in Prince Edward County, in the Niagara Peninsula, and on the Detroit River, all separated from York by vast areas of unsettled bush. In 1799 the government made a contract with Asa Danforth to build a road eastward (E 5); Russell wrote that "we have Contracted with a man to cut bridge and causeway a Road from this to the Trent in the Bay of Quinte for about £2500 Hfx, which will be the making of this Town, and indeed the greatest thing ever done for this Province. I expect the Gratitude of the People will erect a Statue to my memory for it."[1] A road was also begun by the Queen's Rangers westward to the Head of the Lake. There was much agitation in York for the improvement of Yonge Street, which like all the early roads became an impassable bog in the spring and autumn. On April 2, 1807, Alexander Wood wrote that "from the Settlements about this place the roads are so very bad that all intercourse with Loads of any Kind is over till the month of June" (D 35). Yonge Street was of particular importance to York because so many essential provisions came from the farms to the north. To its citizens, however, who subscribed heavily to improve it, there was another strong incentive—the possibility of attracting the northwest fur trade.

In the years before the War, Yonge Street was more than a road; it was a symbol of the possible commercial ascendancy of York. From the very beginning of the period, Simcoe had seen the future of his town in the northwest trade using the Yonge Street route (A 19). In the early years of the century this remained a wistful dream. The *Upper Canada Gazette* in 1799 reported a rumour that the North West Company had contributed £12,000 towards the building of Yonge Street,[2] but this was unfortunately not true. Before 1810 a few consignments for the fur trade passed through York; Joel Beman of Newmarket was in town with "a load of Goods from North West—a large Canoe and a Number of Men" on August 22, 1809 (H 23). The usual route, however, was through Lake Erie and the Detroit River. The powerful merchants of the Niagara and Detroit areas had no intention of losing this lucrative business, and with their close connections with Montreal commercial circles kept a tenacious hold on the fur trade.

The threat of war changed the situation completely. The entire route from Montreal to Fort William lay along the border, in several places exposed to the guns of the American garrisons. For the first time, the North West Company took seriously the plaintive suggestions of Lieutenant Governor Gore and the citizens of York, and considered the possibility of using the Yonge Street route. In 1810 Archibald Norman McLeod travelled by it to the general meeting of the Company at Fort William to explore its possibilities (E 19). Apparently his report was favourable; a memorial was pre-

[1]T.P.L., Peter Russell Papers, Russell to John Gray, April 14, 1799.
[2]*Upper Canada Gazette*, York, March 9, 1799.

sented to the Governor by the Company pointing out the great benefits which would be gained by York and the other settlements through which the trade would pass, and asking in return for 2000 acres at both Penetanguishene and Kempenfelt Bay, and 200 acres at Holland Landing (E 20). While this request was referred to the British government and the whole question considered, war was declared, once more radically changing the situation. The North West Company was no longer in a bargaining position; it was now absolutely necessary to use an inland route. It was only with the war that Simcoe's dream of the northwest fur trade passing through York was fulfilled. Six years after the war the North West Company merged with the Hudson's Bay Company, and the northern route to the west was adopted. Thus the wealth and prominence that were to come to Toronto from the north and west were not to be based on the fur trade.[3]

Water and land communications were essential to supply York with settlers, food, clothing, shelter, and such luxuries as were available. They were also necessary for the dissemination of news and ideas. In the early years most letters were carried by private travellers. Regular postal service to York was slow in being established because of the unwillingness of the British General Post Office to lose money on routes that did not pay. It was only when Lieutenant Governor Hunter promised to cover any difference between expense and revenue that a courier service was begun between Montreal and York (E 10), and even then there were only four couriers each winter, and none in the summer (H 24). The service between York and Niagara was sporadic, especially in the winter (E 9). It was by this route that mail from the United States and much European mail reached the capital. Despite the weak Niagara-York link, the American route was faster than the Canadian for mails from Europe, because American postal service into the interior from New York was better than the more cumbersome British system from Halifax to Montreal and Kingston (E 15, E 16). The American route had several disadvantages. Alexander Wood complained that "the good people in the states generally open british letters" (D 29). This complaint of course was not confined to Americans; it was quite possible for Lieutenant Governor Gore, during the Thorpe excitement in 1806–7, to copy all relevant (and some irrelevant) correspondence among the opposition forces, pre-

[3]The North West Company's use of Yonge Street is discussed in Percy Robinson's "Yonge Street and the North West Company," *Canadian Historical Review*, XXIV, 253–65.

sumably with the active assistance of the York postmaster, William Allan. A more important effect was that news from Europe reached York filtered through American sources, and unofficial reports and rumours, like the one spread on October 3, 1803, that France had taken England (H 23), usually preceded accurate official accounts. Wild rumours like this were of only fleeting interest; more important was the isolation of York from direct British influence and the steady infiltration of the American viewpoint, spread even by the government paper, the *Upper Canada Gazette*, published in York from 1798. York lay at the crossroads of the two great routes into the interior, the British St. Lawrence and the American Hudson-Mohawk system. From the beginning both influences were important in its development.

F. POLITICAL FERMENT

POLITICS IN THE PERIOD before the War of 1812 were dependent more on personality and shifting cliques than on policy or party. Alignments were formed simply on the basis of being for or against the governor and council, and were often based on personal friendships and animosities, or on the possibilities of patronage. The leaders of the opposition included hot-headed Irishmen, like Joseph Willcocks and Robert Thorpe, who regarded opposition as an article of faith and combined a flaming demagoguery with a beautiful absence of logic. It included those who for some reason were left out in the distribution of loaves and fishes. The eclipse of Peter Russell's influence under Hunter, for example, carried his kinsmen, the Willcockses, and with them the Baldwins, beyond the golden circle of government patronage and into opposition.

Organized political parties were regarded with suspicion. Again and again candidates assured their electorate that they represented no party (F 31). Each candidate appealed as an individual, with his own platform and his own grievances. There were, of course, popular causes—the arbitrary nature of the "Act for the better securing this province against all seditious attempts or designs to disturb the tranquility thereof" passed in 1804, the rights and definition of the alien, the control the House of Assembly over expenditure, the repeal of Habeas Corpus in 1812. Beyond these basic issues, the candidate could produce his own issues; for example, Thomas Ridout in his campaign in 1812 against a radical who called for no repeal of the Habeas Corpus Act, championed "Education for the million" (G 20). Garbled appeals to the British "Constitution" were also popular, like Robert Henderson's manful demonstration of confused political thinking in 1808 (F 31).

Elections in York were still comparatively cheap; more than one candidate assured his constituents that he would abstain from canvassing because it was beneath the dignity of one who sought to represent the people (F 6, F 32). Still, there is evidence that the usual free meals and drinks were available. Gough spent $200 on his unsuccessful campaign in 1805 (F 21); Ridout's victory in 1812 cost between four and five hundred dollars (F 33), and unfriendly estimates of Thorpe's expenditure in the by-election of 1807 were considerably higher. Election days were gala ones in the lives of the ordinary citizen. Farmers came into York from miles around to cast their vote and enjoy the excitement. The enterprising showman exhibiting a monkey in a tavern at a shilling a head during the election of 1804 probably made a handsome profit (H 23). Even the schoolboys at the Home District Grammar School entered into the spirit of the occasion (G 20).

Because York was the capital, it contained a solid core of government supporters. The top officials did not necessarily belong to this group—the most effective government opponent in the period was one of the judges, Robert Thorpe. A Surveyor General, C. B. Wyatt, and an Attorney General, William Firth, were also prominent critics of the official policy or more precisely of the governor, as to a lesser extent was William Jarvis, Secretary of the Province. The real government support in York came from the great numbers of petty office-holders—the clerks, ushers, court criers, doorkeepers, and so forth—and from those who wished these preferments. The leading merchants, also, were always solidly behind the governor because their interests lay in maintaining stability.

On the other side were many of the farmers in the northern part of the riding. Most of them were indebted to the York merchants, and had also the pioneer distrust of the successful townsman. Dissatisfaction with the dilatory government land-granting machinery was widespread. Many of these settlers came from the United States in the early years of the century, and had lived under the Republic. There was a large block of Quakers, Mennonites, and other plain folk who were politically neutral but tended to support the opposition candidate, since the rallying cry of militant loyalty used by the government men did not appeal to them. This same area was later to provide William Lyon Mackenzie with much of his local support.

In the first two Parliaments of Upper Canada, York was included in the 1st Riding of Lincoln. With the redistribution of seats in 1800, a new riding was created consisting of the counties of Durham, Simcoe, and the East Riding of York, and in the general election of that year the first election was held in the capital.

Before the War of 1812, there were seven elections held in York—general elections in 1800, 1804, 1808, and 1812, and by-elections in 1801, 1805, and 1807. Information about all these elections is unfortunately somewhat fragmentary; the editors of the *Upper Canada Gazette* were severely reprimanded in 1800 for publishing a comparatively mild letter questioning the possible independence of a representative with "eminence of station" (F 2, F 3), and the *Gazette* was obviously never used as a forum for free discussion of political issues in this period. Of the two leading candidates in the first election, one, Judge Allcock of the Court of King's Bench, was never mentioned by name in the *Gazette* before the election, and the other, Samuel Heron, for reasons now obscure, advertised that he was not a candidate (F 5).

The first election was held in the colonnade between the two wings of the Government Buildings on July 24 and 25, 1800. Candidates for whom votes were cast were Henry Allcock, Samuel Heron, John Small, and William Jarvis, with the first two outdistancing their opponents. On the second day there was a disturbance at the hustings, involving "a drunken fellow," some soldiers, and the turbulent Willcocks-Weekes faction who were supporting Allcock; the Riot Act was read, and the polls were closed with Allcock two votes ahead (F 7). Samuel Heron and others petitioned against his election on the grounds that "very unwarrantable steps had been taken by the friends of Mr. Allcock to procure him to be returned" (F 11). The House of Assembly declared the election void in June, 1801, Allcock's only defence being to challenge the authority of the House to arbitrate in the matter. For this forbearance he was spoken to severely by Weekes, who seems to have been extremely active in the whole affair (H 15).

The by-election that followed was something of an anti-climax. There were two candidates only, John Small, who was now supported by Joseph Willcocks, and Angus McDonell, who had supported Heron in 1800, and had been dismissed from his government job through the agency of Allcock. McDonell won easily, and pursued an independent course in the House of Assembly.

In the general election of June, 1804, McDonell had the advantage of being the sitting member, and appealed to his constituents with a popular platform of reciprocal taxation and representation, and the shifting of the burdens of taxation from the "Industrious Farmers and Mechanics" to the "more opulent classes" (F 13). His opponents were William Weekes who appealed to those "who may be inclined to think with freedom, and to act with independency,"[1] and D. W. Smith, who had returned to England in 1802. Both these candidates were operating under a disadvantage. After the election Weekes claimed that his election address was not published in the *Gazette* because of government influence, a charge denied by the printer.[2] D. W. Smith's campaign was seriously hampered by his absence; his friends placed more and more plaintive promises of his imminent arrival in the *Gazette*,[3] but the handicap was too great.

[1] *Upper Canada Gazette*, York, March 17, 1804.
[2] *Ibid.*, March 2, 1805.
[3] *Ibid.*, April 7 and 14, 1804.

McDonell was again returned but sat for one session only before he was drowned in the loss of the *Speedy* in October, 1804.

In the by-election early in 1805, Weekes was finally returned, defeating the King's Printer, John Cameron (H 23). Weekes made a strong appeal against the Seditious Attempts Act passed during the previous session and against the spending of provincial funds without the sanction of the House of Assembly (F 15). He became one of the leaders of the opposition in the first unruly Parliament of Gore's régime, and a thorn in the flesh to the Governor. His days of influence, however, were numbered; in October, 1806, he was killed in a duel by William Dickson.

By this time the anti-government forces had received a new leader in the unlikely guise of one of His Majesty's Judges, Robert Thorpe. Thorpe had come to Upper Canada late in 1805 with the impressive support of Lord Castlereagh, but was disappointed in not receiving the Chief Justiceship when Allcock was moved to the Lower Province. He swiftly antagonized the ruling clique in York (H 27) and declared war on the "scotch Pedlars. . . . this Shopkeeper Aristocracy has stunted the prosperity of the Province & goaded the people until they have turned from the greatest loyalty to the utmost disaffection."[4] In his charges to juries he went far beyond the usual remarks on such occasions, and was openly and frankly critical of the governor and all his works.

Six days after Weekes' death, he began busily organizing his campaign to capture Weekes' seat (F 16) and to build up a strong organization among the malcontents of the area. That this was possible would seem to indicate either that he was personally more impressive than the eccentric ebullience of his writings would suggest, or, more likely, that there were many who were discontented or dissatisfied with Gore's autocratic government. Thorpe's strongest support understandably came from Yonge Street and the farming sections of the riding. William Bond declared that "not a Gentleman of respect except Mr. Wyatt and a Mr. Jackson . . . had voted for him."[5] This, however, was not quite true; Thorpe had the support of William Willcocks, William Jarvis, and Dr. Baldwin, among others.

The government candidate was the Yonge Street storekeeper, T. B. Gough, who had no chance against the supercharged emotionalism of Thorpe and his followers. He polled only 159 votes against Thorpe's 268 (F 26). The election caused considerable excitement, not only in York but throughout the province. John

[4]P.R.O., C.O. 42, v. 342, p. 209, microfilm copy in P.A.O., Thorpe to Sir George Shee, Dec. 1. 1806.

[5]*Ibid.*, v. 349, p. 235, William Bond to the Solicitor General, Nov. 3, 1809.

Strachan wrote from Cornwall, "The fame of your election extends to this remote part of the Province, it seems to have equalled Westminster. If this turbulent Judge proceed in the manner he has been doing, the peace and harmony of the Province will be destroyed. . . . You see we enter a little into your Politics, in truth the discontents which this man may very easily raise will render the situation of every respectable man in the Province much less agreeable."[6]

An attempt was made to unseat Thorpe on the grounds that a judge was ineligible for election to the House of Assembly, but this failed (F 26). He was suspended by Gore in 1807, and eventually went on to another colony to spread discord there, leaving a backwash of bad feeling, a number of debts, and a leaderless party. Of his lieutenants, Weekes was dead, Wyatt was also suspended, Jackson was quiescent. As for Joseph Willcocks who had moved to Niagara, Thorpe himself said, "that he was a mighty good young man, whose hobby was his horse and his hounds, that he was a good sportsman . . . but that he did not possess a sufficiency of brains to bait a mouse trap."[7] With Thorpe's departure organized opposition to Gore collapsed in York.

The election of 1808 was a quiet one, and Gough was returned for York. In the House of Assembly he supported government policies, against a noisy opposition including Joseph Willcocks who had been returned for Lincoln, Haldimand, and the West Riding of York.

The main issue in the election of June, 1812, was Brock's request for the repeal of the Habeas Corpus Act because of the imminence of war. This had been refused by the previous House of Assembly. Joseph Shepard was the no-repeal candidate in York, having won a toss-up with an opposition rival, Thomas Hamilton (H 23). This method of choosing a candidate was resented by Hamilton's supporters, and the government candidate, Thomas Ridout, was successful.

In this period York was not only the capital, and the home of most of the members of the Executive and Legislative Councils, but also the home of many of the leaders of the opposition. It was thus the centre of political activity before the War of 1812. How important was this activity? The conservative side was hardening into a cohesive group, but still lacked an effective leader, other than the governor himself. Patronage and self-interest were strong motives. The roots of the Family Compact can be clearly seen,

[6]T.P.L., Alexander Wood Papers, Strachan to Wood, Jan. 29, 1807.
[7]Broadside in *Upper Canada Gazette* microfilm at end of Sept., 1807.

particularly during the Thorpe crisis. The opposition movement was more individual and flexible. It was dominated by some of the oddest and most flamboyant personalities in Canadian politics. Even through the dozen years before the War it did not have a continuous existence, but ebbed and flowed around people rather than policies. Its basis was more often personal disgruntlement than principles. It is probably unfair to judge it by John Mills Jackson's "Damn the Governor and the Government . . . push about the bottle" (F 18) but it did seem to be singularly lacking in constructive ideas, and cannot be regarded as the antecedent of the later Reform movement.

G. RELIGION AND EDUCATION

Before the war of 1812, the Anglican Church had a monopoly on regular religious services in York. One reason for this was that it almost certainly had the largest number of adherents in the community at this time. Up Yonge Street were Methodist, Baptist, Quaker, and Lutheran strongholds, but York itself was predominantly Anglican. Then too, the Anglican Church was regarded as the established church; its clergymen were paid by the government, and assigned parishes by the Governor. Church and state were firmly intertwined; their separation was not even conceived of by the Governor or his Councils. The dissenters themselves were not yet demanding equality, but only the extension of certain privileges, like the right of their clergy to perform marriages. Another reason for the predominance of the Anglican Church in York was the basic difference of approach between the Anglican and dissenting communions concerning the best method of serving the new province. The Anglican practice was to assign its clergy to parishes with instructions to travel out from them, but with their first responsibility to their home church. York as capital naturally received a resident minister. The dissenting ministers in the province were sent out by American churches or missionary organizations with instructions to cover as wide an area as possible; to them York was merely one town of many to be visited at infrequent intervals in their long and gruelling travels through the bush. For the great number of settlements without an Anglican minister, the dissenting policy was undoubtedly better, but for the few places like York with a resident minister, the Anglican system was more effective.

The first religious services held in York were probably conducted outdoors for the Queen's Rangers, like the one on August 11, 1793, mentioned by Mrs. Simcoe (H 1). In November, 1796, the first resident minister, Rev. Thomas Raddish, arrived in York with his friend, Chief Justice Elmsley. Russell described Raddish as "just the sort of Clergyman most likely to impress on the Inhabitants of this new Country a proper Sense of their religious Duties, being a gentleman of an easy familiar manner, yet properly measured and respectable in his Conduct and of an Attracting Eloquence which constantly fills his Church and Arrests the attention of his Hearers."[1] Unfortunately this paragon remained in Canada for only one

[1]T.P.L., Peter Russell Papers, Russell to Bishop Mountain, July 31, 1797.

winter. In that time he acquired at least 4700 acres of land,[2] including a Park Lot in his own name which had been intended as a glebe. Raddish promptly sold it to Elmsley, thus alienating it from its original purpose.

Although six acres bounded by King, Church, Newgate (Adelaide) and New (Jarvis) Streets had been reserved for a church, no building was yet erected, so that Mr. Raddish's services were held in the Government Buildings. After his departure that ubiquitous jack-of-all-trades, William Cooper, read prayers and preached from a book of sermons on Sunday mornings at the Government Buildings, and at the jail to the prisoners in the evening. The evening services were apparently also attended by the townspeople (H 18).

Raddish resigned in 1799 (G 3), and in 1800 Rev. George Okill Stuart was nominated minister at York. He received £100 from the government and £50 from the Society for the Propagation of the Gospel in Foreign Parts, after assurances from Bishop Mountain that the additional sum was absolutely necessary (G 8). In his first report to the Society, Stuart reported good congregations including nominal dissenters, but few communicants (G 9). This situation, which also existed in the church at Kingston, continued throughout Stuart's ministry in York; in 1811 there were only 20 communicants.[3]

The most pressing need of the congregation was a church building. In 1802 there was some talk of building a church (G 9); fund-raising was organized at a meeting on January 8, 1803 (G 11). At first it was hoped that a stone church could be built, but this was found to be impracticable (G 15). By 1804 £400 had been subscribed (G 13). Expenses, however, exceeded available funds, and the church was not open for services until March, 1807. Pews were sold by auction on March 4, subject to a ground rent of $8 a year for a double pew, and $4 for a single one, payable quarterly.[4] Pew rents amounted to £35 Halifax Currency, which was used to complete the building (G 22). Although Lieutenant Governor Gore promised a pulpit, it was apparently built at general expense by Joshua Leach.[5] Stuart apologized to the S.P.G. for the cost—£25 Halifax Currency—but "the elegance of the design made it un-

[2]T.P.L., Alexander Wood Letter Books, Wood to Raddish, May 14, 1807.

[3]S.P.G. Journals, XXX, p. 212, microfilm copy in P.A.C., Stuart to the S.P.G., Oct. 8, 1812.

[4]*Upper Canada Gazette*, York, Feb. 28, 1807.

[5]Accounts of St. James' Church, quoted in Robertson, *Landmarks of Toronto*, II, 1025.

avoidable" (G 24). Most of the pews were rented by the higher officials and merchants; it was not until 1809 that a gallery was erected for poorer inhabitants, strangers, and soldiers (G 26). In 1810 part of the church grounds was enclosed, and the worst stumps around the door were removed.[6]

In 1811 Rev. John Stuart of Kingston died. Rev. John Strachan in Cornwall wanted the Kingston charge, but with a great show of nobility waived his claim in favour of Dr. Stuart's son, Rev. G. O. Stuart (G 33). Then began the complicated negotiations to bring Strachan to the vacant charge at York. The relations between Strachan and Bishop Mountain were already strained; for this and other reasons Strachan at first refused to go to York when asked by Mountain. When asked again by Brock, however, with the face-saving addition of the Chaplaincy of the Garrison, he accepted (G 35), and in July, 1812, arrived in the capital to take charge, in his capable way, not only of the Anglican Church and the Home District School, but also of the town itself.

Although there were no organized dissenting congregations in York before the War, there were occasional visits by dissenting ministers. The Methodist, Rev. Nathan Bangs, preached in York in 1801, and found its inhabitants "thoughtless and wicked" (G 7). He is probably the minister who preached the same sermon on September 10, 1802, as he had preached the year before, but with better delivery (H 23). Throughout the period other Methodist circuit riders like Coate, Case, and Perry visited York. Presbyterian ministers like McDowall, and Baptist ministers like Blood, Roots, and Kendrick occasionally held services, like the Methodists in private homes and taverns. Many dissenters not of their denomination attended; Ely Playter, for example, besides attending the Anglican services went to services conducted by Methodist, Presbyterian, and Quaker missionaries (H 23). All these missionaries were supported by American churches; early dissenters in York owed much to the New York and Genesee Conferences of the Methodist Episcopal Church, the Albany Presbytery of the Dutch Reformed Church, the Massachusetts Baptist Missionary Society, and the Shaftsbury (Vermont) Baptist Association. Because of the infrequency of their visits, however, the influence of these early missionaries was somewhat transitory. The coming of the War brought with it an almost complete withdrawal of American missionaries from Canada. It was not until after the War that dissent became a major factor in the religious life of York.

The Roman Catholics at this time were few in number in York—

[6]Scadding, *Toronto of Old*, p. 120.

the great days of Irish immigration were yet to come. Land was granted to them for a church in 1806, and there was some attempt at organization in 1807 (G 21), but without a priest and with little hope of getting one, not much could be accomplished.

Relations between the different denominations and faiths were relatively good. G. O. Stuart did not share the violent hatred of dissenters felt by Strachan, or by his own father at Kingston, possibly because the other denominations were still so weak in York. Unlike Strachan also, he did not appear to arouse antagonism among the dissenters. The Orange movement had not yet established itself. On November 20, 1800, Elmsley in York wrote to Lieutenant Governor Hunter describing in alarmist terms a subversive secret organization in Montreal called the Orange Society.[7] According to Elmsley, it recruited members with an ostensible purpose of opposing Roman Catholicism, but its real purpose, only revealed to members in the higher degrees of the order, was to overthrow the government in conjunction with the United Irishmen. Obviously Elmsley—and York—were unfamiliar with the movement. Ely Playter, who can be relied upon to be present in any excitement at York, makes no reference to the Glorious Twelfth until 1822, although he does refer to "Drunken Irishmen" on St. Patrick's Day in 1802 (H 23). In this period when there was only one church in York, most of the citizens attended its services regardless of their denomination or faith. For example, two of the most prominent Roman Catholics in York, Sheriff Alexander McDonell and Laurent Quetton St. George, were pewholders in the Anglican Church. The age of violent religious antagonisms had not yet come.

Turning from religion to education, we find that the creation of an adequate educational system in York was also beset with problems. In any new settlement the second generation is usually not as well educated as the original immigrants who came from older settlements with established schools and teachers. This was particularly true in York with its comparatively large group of upper officials and civil servants.

The first schools in York were small private ones. The best known and possibly the earliest of these was William Cooper's which existed from 1798 to 1801. This school was attended by young Macaulays, Ridouts, Chewetts, Playters, and Denisons, by the children of almost all the tavern keepers in York (G 5), and by the son of Peter Russell's slave (G 4). Cooper, who was licensed to teach in 1799, apparently restricted his instruction to reading, writing, arithmetic, and grammar.

[7] T.P.L., Elmsley Letter Book, Elmsley to Hunter, Nov. 20, 1800.

Primary education like this was the greatest need of the community. In 1805 a group of parents united to hire a teacher for their children at a salary of $15 a month, plus board and lodging, liquors excepted (G 14). For this the teacher, Alexander William Carson, was expected to teach a maximum of 25 children for five and a half days a week from eight to five during the summer and from nine to four in the winter. The subjects taught were again "the art of spelling—reading—writing and arithmetic." These basic skills were also taught in small dame schools in York. "Old Mrs. Dudley" who lost some of her work on June 2, 1806, when a child on fire sat on it (H 28) probably conducted such a school. There were also short-lived schools kept in taverns (G 27, G 34), and at least two attempts to establish night schools for apprentices (G 29).

More advanced educational facilities were harder to establish. Rev. G. O. Stuart took a few scholars from his first arrival in York in 1800 (G 8) to augment his meagre income, and in 1802 Dr. Baldwin advertised that he would teach a classical school (G 10). The usual solution to the problem of secondary education among the official class, however, was to send their sons down to Dr. Strachan's school in Cornwall. Their daughters were sent to friends in New York, Montreal, or Quebec to be finished.

After the passage of Upper Canada's first education act in 1807, a government school was established in York, and Rev. G. O. Stuart was appointed teacher (G 19). The fees were $16 a year. Most of the students came from homes of the official class, the merchants, or the prosperous tradesmen. Both girls and boys were admitted, ranging in age from Eliza Jarvis, age 6, to her elder sister Maria, age 19. Stuart was apparently not as good a teacher as Strachan. Admitting the tendency in school reminiscences to dwell on the rough-housing rather than on the learning, the reader is still impressed by the absence of both discipline and scholarship in Judge Jarvis' memories of his school days (G 20), which compare unfavourably with similar accounts of student life under Dr. Strachan.

With Strachan's arrival in the summer of 1812, the cause of both religion and education in York received a tremendous impetus. As a clergyman, a teacher, and a citizen, Strachan was outstanding. The first fumbling steps to create an Anglican Church and a grammar school were now over; under Strachan they expanded and prospered far beyond the expectations of those who helped to found them.

H. LIFE IN YORK

FOR THE FIRST TWO OR THREE YEARS, the settlement at York was really a military camp. Except for the surveyors almost all the men were soldiers. Most of them left their families at Niagara while some sort of habitation was chopped out of the bush. The indefatigable Mrs. Simcoe was there, however, and left the only detailed description of life in the earliest days of York (H 1). "Amid the beat of Drums & crash of falling Trees" she travelled about the area observing nature and sentimentalizing about the natural life in a fashion incongruously reminiscent of Jean Jacques Rousseau, noble savage and all. Her way of life, of course, cannot be considered typical; her position protected her from the worst privations.

Even for the senior officers, however, the early years in York were full of hardship. During the first summer they lived in tents, moving into log huts in the winter. The Simcoe tent was divided into two; in one part the Simcoes slept and entertained, while the other was used as a nursery for their children (A 9). During a storm in November, 1793, Captain Shaw's tent blew over in the night, leaving his large family exposed to the wind and rain (A 18). The huts were difficult to heat; in 1794 Mrs. Simcoe recorded that even wearing three fur tippets she "could hardly hold my Cards this Eveng" (H 1). There was no glass in the windows, and both rain and mosquitoes entered freely. Provisions were scarce, especially after the close of navigation in the fall. As late as 1797, York's detractors commented on the meagreness of the food supply (H 5). There were of course compensations. Camping in the woods has certain pleasures, and Mrs. Simcoe and her friends enjoyed riding, boating, fishing, skating, and picnics, especially in the winter. Mrs. Simcoe played whist, and dances were held on special occasions; ten ladies attended the New Year's Ball in 1796. Despite the hardships, Mrs. Simcoe obviously enjoyed her temporary return to nature. How the humble Queen's Ranger felt about it, painfully making a clearing and building huts without benefit of philosophy is not recorded.

When Simcoe returned to England, there were a few small houses built on his town-site, but extensive civilian settlement did not begin until 1796. The only official who had built at York was Simcoe himself. He erected a frame house in imitation of a Greek temple high above the Don, and christened it Castle Frank. This house, of course, was far outside the town, and was intended as a place of retreat rather than as a permanent residence. By 1796, however, when it was obvious that the transfer of the capital to York was inevitable, the officials began to make plans for their accommodation in the town itself. Some of them bought existing log houses, like John Small, who paid $50 for his (H 3) to discover later that it stood on the government reserve. Peter Russell also bought a house, only to have it destroyed by a fire caused by careless workmen employed in adding to it. Others like D. W. Smith (H 4) and William Jarvis (H 6) built new houses.

Whether building or renovating, the would-be citizen of York faced an almost insurmountable problem—the shortage of labourers and the consequent high wages they demanded. The few contractors like Samuel Marther, William Berczy, and the Kendrick brothers were in constant demand. In 1799 artificers received at least £150 a year.[1] Materials for building were also in very short supply. Even in 1803, to build a modest house cost about £1000 New York Currency (H 24). At that time, there were 75 houses in York.[2] The early houses were built of wood and were fairly simple. D. W. Smith described his house, Maryville, to a prospective buyer in England as a "cottage," and depreciated its workmanship and materials,[3] yet this house was one of the handsomest of its day in York. As time went on, more ambitious houses were of course erected, but the great majority were still unpretentious. In 1809 there were 14 round-log houses, 11 one-storey and 27 two-storey squared timber houses, and 55 one-storey frame houses in the town.[4] Increased population did not bring a solution to the difficulties of building; in 1810 when Dr. Baldwin was supervising the building of York's first brick residence for his friend St. George, he complained "that fretting has become our lot as well as all others who undertake house building" (H 36).

The population throughout the period was constantly changing. Most of the ordinary citizens in York were also owners of farms in the vicinity; for a few years they lived in town, and then moved to the country. Of the 72 heads of families listed in 1797 (C 4),

[1]Russell, *Correspondence*, ed. by Cruikshank, III, 107, Extract from Minutes of Executive Council, Feb. 5, 1799.

[2]"Abstract of the Home District for the Year commencing 7th March, 1803," quoted in Robertson, *Landmarks of Toronto*, II, 994.

[3]T.P.L., D. W. Smith Papers, Smith to C. B. Wyatt, April 11, 1805.

[4]"Abstract of the Home District," quoted in Robertson, *Landmarks of Toronto*, II, 995.

POPULATION OF YORK, 1797–1814*

		1797	1799	1800	1801	1802	1804	1805	1806	1807	1808	1809	1811	1812	1813	1814
Town of York	Men	144	266	261	136	120	140	154	137	139	159	195	169	234	158	189
	Women	97	155	142	66	74	97	130	113	114	137	162	149	164	149	172
	Children				134	126	195	189	152	161	192	220	366	305	318	330
	TOTAL	241	421	403	336	320	432	473	402	414	488	577	684	703	625	691
Townships of York, Scarborough, and Etobicoke	Men	116	137	175	190	124	163	201	190	195	177		207	210	161	178
	Women	80	111	149	155	86	129	156	159	173	148		147	155	135	156
	Children					219	289	324	389	402	337		286	391	380	402
	TOTAL	196	248	324	345	429	581	681	738	770	662		640	756	676	736
TOTAL		437	669	727	681	749	1013	1154	1140	1184	1150		1324	1459	1301	1427

*SOURCE: T.P.L., Minutes of Town Meetings and Lists of Inhabitants. This source is not completely reliable; its accuracy obviously varied with the ability and conscientiousness of the town clerk. From 1808 onwards Scarborough was not included, and after 1811 Etobicoke was also omitted.

at least 31 were settled in York's hinterland ten years later, at least six died, and at least four had left the area. The subsequent history of 16 is unknown. Only 15 were still in the town of York in 1807—four government officials, one half-pay officer, two merchants, three tavern keepers, one blacksmith, and four connected with the building trades. This exodus to the country caused the population of the town to drop during 1800, 1801, and 1802; in 1806 new arrivals were not numerous enough to compensate for those who moved to their farms. As the population increased there was more continuity, but on each annual list there were names that appeared and disappeared into the townships a year or two later. After 1800 there were more people in the townships than in York itself. As to be expected in a new pioneer community, there was a preponderance of men over women. The ratio of children to adults was high because of the relative absence of old people and because of the many large families.

In all, 552 heads of families were listed as living in the town of York at some time between 1797 and 1814. The vast majority had English names, with a few of Scottish and a very few of Irish origin. Many of these of course came to York from the United States. There was a large group of families of German extraction, most of whom came from New York or Pennsylvania. Less than a quarter of the names on the original list of 1797 appear in the United Empire Loyalist lists; this percentage decreased as the population grew. About 25 French-Canadian families lived in York at one time or another before the War of 1812.

In 1799 there were 15 Negroes in York, and another 10 in Peter Long's household east of the Don. By 1802 there were 18 in the town, including six children. Six were in service to William Jarvis, and six worked for Peter Russell. The Russell *ménage* consisted of a woman slave, her free husband, and their four children. The most prominent Negro of the period was Robert Franklin, who came to York with Russell as a senior servant, and eventually settled on a farm in York Township, after being refused land on Yonge Street. There was apparently co-operation among the Negroes; in 1799 they united to contract for the building of a road from Davenport Road to Castle Frank Road.[5]

Simcoe had hoped to establish an aristocratic society in the new province. The senior government officials who were to form the capital's upper class came from the towns of Great Britain and New

[5]Ontario, Department of Planning and Development, *Don Valley Conservation Report.*

England and brought with them the rigid provincial social pattern of the eighteenth century. This was complicated by the precariousness of their position in Upper Canada, since they owed their situation not to their ability but to the interest of an influential friend or protector in England, and therefore were in constant danger of eclipse from his downfall or death. Aware of their position in the lower strata of the vast patronage system by which Britain was governed, they were extremely jealous of each other, and constantly jockeyed for preferment. Each had a number of lesser folk attached to his coat-tails, hoping in turn for advancement through his influence. Even the smallest government job involved the interest of one of the great ones in York. In 1806 Mrs. Willcocks appealed to Peter Russell on behalf of her son for a minor position which *might* become vacant; Russell however had already requested it for another protégé, only to discover that President Grant had awarded it to his own son-in-law (H 28). To advance in government circles this sort of patronage was essential. The trick was to select as patron someone who would remain powerful, and then to ingratiate oneself sufficiently with him to insure his favour.

One person who blatantly pursued this policy was Joseph Willcocks. Shortly after his arrival in York he succeeded in establishing himself with Peter Russell whose strong family feeling attracted him to this personable distant cousin (H 16). Russell's power was however waning; Willcocks began to play off Chief Justice Allcock against Russell. This, combined with a piece of typical folly in his relationship with Russell's sister, lost him Russell's patronage but gained him Allcock's (H 15). Allcock did rather more for him than Russell; through his influence Willcocks became Sheriff of the Home District. Unfortunately Allcock was transferred to Lower Canada, and Willcocks was left without powerful backing. His next choice of protector was Judge Thorpe, but Thorpe's turbulent course of action soon lost all sympathy in government circles both for himself and for his protégé. Willcocks speedily became an outcast with the ruling class, lost the shrievalty, and was forced into a more or less impotent opposition. His career was an example of the impolicy of backing the wrong horse, or possibly of switching horses in midstream.

Naturally, this constant jostling for position among both the senior officials and those who depended on them for favours had a strong influence on the society taking shape in York. Rank and precedence became very important (H 29), and a keen competitive spirit manifested itself in every aspect of life. Cliques had developed while the government was still at Niagara, and divisions became deeper in York. Social slights were magnified beyond all significance; gossip was virulent. It was all so trivial, yet because of these people's position in the province it became important. Gossip led to the Small-White duel in 1800 (H 14). Its immediate result was the death of the Attorney General and the shredding of a number of reputations. Because of his part in the events leading up to the duel, D. W. Smith's appointment to the Legislative Council was postponed indefinitely.[6] Mrs. Small, whose virtue was questioned at the inquest, became a social pariah. The Gores, when they arrived in the summer of 1806, found that society in York was much divided, mainly by the personal obnoxiousness (H 27) and political activities of Judge Thorpe. In an attempt to do away with "the disgraceful contentions,"[7] they subscribed to the public assemblies and tried to enforce unanimous attendance. Unfortunately, by including Mrs. Small, they merely introduced a new storm centre in the teacup (H 31). Eight years after the event, the diehard moralists of York were willing to divide and disrupt society rather than to accept Mrs. Small in their ranks.

There were not many people belonging to this upper class, yet there was a complicated and shifting hierarchy within it depending on position, background, and closeness to the governor. It included the members of the Executive Council, the judges, a few of the senior officials, some of the lawyers, and the senior officers at the garrison. On a lower level but still within the group were those connected to it by relationship or patronage. Social position in general depended upon government position and influence, although personal popularity or lack of it played some part. The governor was of course the acknowledged leader of society; a change in governors resulted in changes of relative status right down the line, as each new governor chose his intimate advisers. Peter Russell, from being the most prominent man in the province, was swept aside in later administrations, until his sister was pathetically pleased by the smallest attention from the governor's wife (H 28).

Variations of background were also important. The accepted background was either middle-class provincial England, or professional army. The Loyalists with their American origin were not accepted on terms of complete equality, although American sympathies were rather surprisingly not entirely fatal. William Jarvis' brother-in-law and protégé, William B. Peters, crowned his activi-

[6]T.P.L., Elmsley Letter Book, Elmsley to Hunter, Dec. 24, 1800.

[7]T.P.L., Powell Papers, Mrs. W. D. Powell to George Murray, Dec. 13, 1806.

"YORK (OLIM TORONTO) THE INTENDED CAPITAL OF UPPER CANADA, AS IT APPEARED IN THE AUTUMN OF 1803," BY SURGEON EDWARD WALSH, 49TH REGT., SHOWING LEFT TO RIGHT, THE HOUSES OF DUNCAN CAMERON, DR. W. W. BALDWIN, WILLIAM ALLAN, PETER RUSSELL, THE GOVERNMENT BUILDINGS, AND THE TOWN BLOCKHOUSE. [William L. Clements Library, University of Michigan.]

ELMSLEY HOUSE. [T. A. Reed Collection, Toronto Public Library.]

CASTLE FRANK, BY MRS. SIMCOE. [Simcoe Sketches, Department of Public Records and Archives, Ontario.]

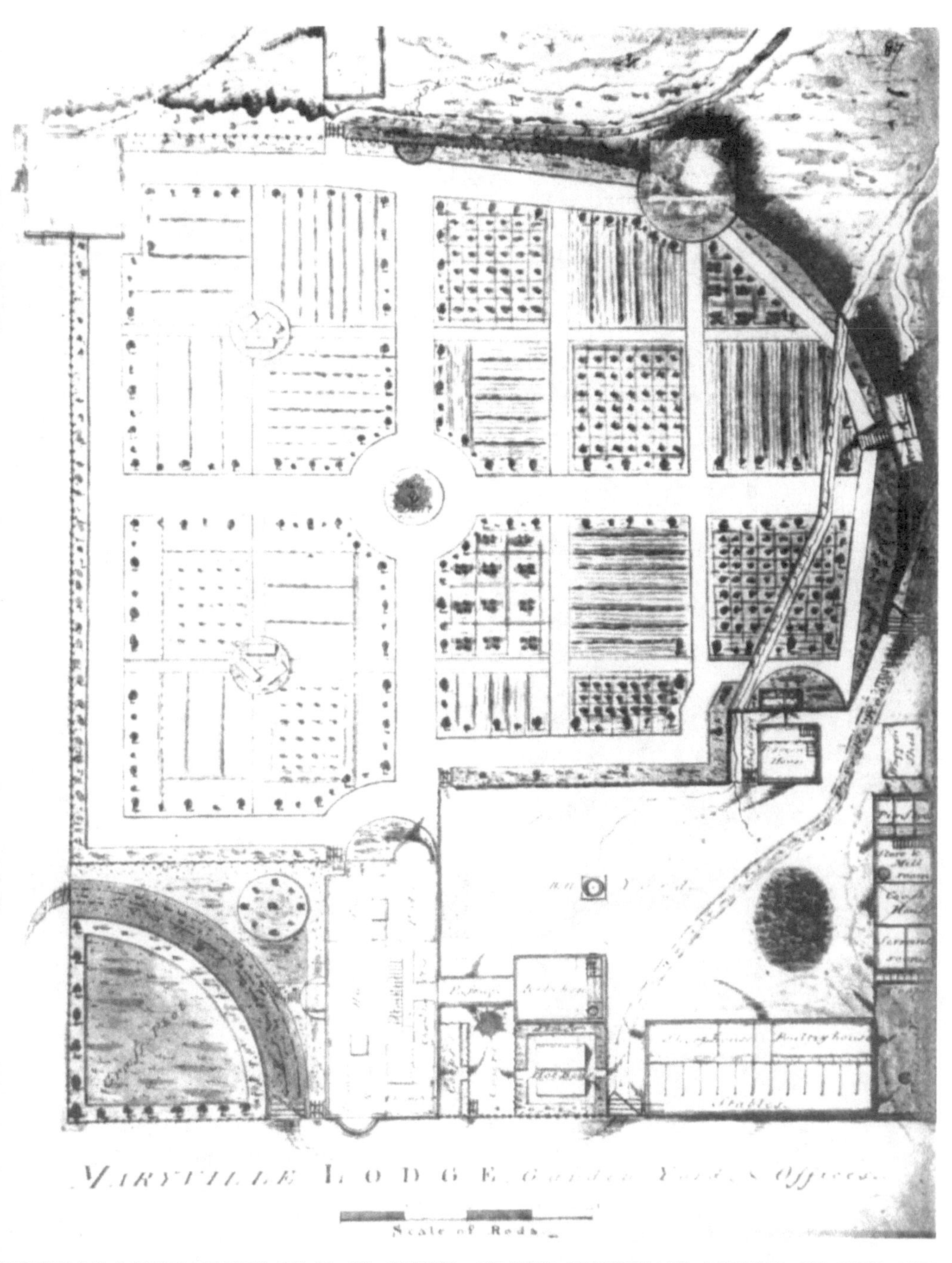

MARYVILLE LODGE, HOME OF D. W. SMITH, AT THE NORTHEAST CORNER OF KING AND ONTARIO STREETS. [D. W. Smith Papers, Toronto Public Library.]

FRONT STREET FROM PETER TO JOHN STREETS, ABOUT 1810, SHOWING LEFT TO RIGHT, THE HOUSES OF GEORGE CROOKSHANK, JOHN BEIKIE, A COMMISSARY STORE-HOUSE ON THE SHORE, AND THE HALF-WAY HOUSE. [Courtesy of Mrs. Stephen Heward.]

"VIEW OF THE GARRISON AT TORONTO OR YORK UPPER CANADA . . . MARCH 11TH 1805," PROBABLY BY LIEUT. SEMPRONIUS STRETTON. [William L. Clements Library, University of Michigan.]

"TAKING OF YORK, AND DEATH OF GENERAL PIKE." [From H. M. Brackenridge, *History of the Late War between the United States and Great Britain*, Philadelphia, 1839.]

FREDERICK AUGUSTUS, DUKE OF YORK, FROM A PRINT PUBLISHED BY RICHARD EVANS IN 1815.

PETER RUSSELL. [John Ross Robertson Collection, Toronto Public Library.]

THOMAS RIDOUT. [John Ross Robertson Collection, T.P.L.]

ALEXANDER MCDONELL. [John Ross Robertson Collection, T.P.L.]

ANGUS MCDONELL. [John Ross Robertson Collection, T.P.L.]

MRS. WILLIAM DUMMER POWELL. [John Ross Robertson Collection, T.P.L.]

MRS. JOHN SMALL. [John Ross Robertson Collection, T.P.L.]

REV. GEORGE OKILL STUART. [T. A. Reed Collection, T.P.L.]

REV. JOHN STRACHAN. [Trinity College, University of Toronto.]

WILLIAM ALLAN. [John Ross Robertson Collection, T.P.L.]

LAURENT QUETTON DE ST. GEORGE. [John Ross Robertson Scrapbooks, T.P.L.]

ALEXANDER WOOD. [Courtesy of Mrs. Stephen Heward.]

WILLIAM WILLCOCKS. [John Ross Robertson Scrapbooks, T.P.L.]

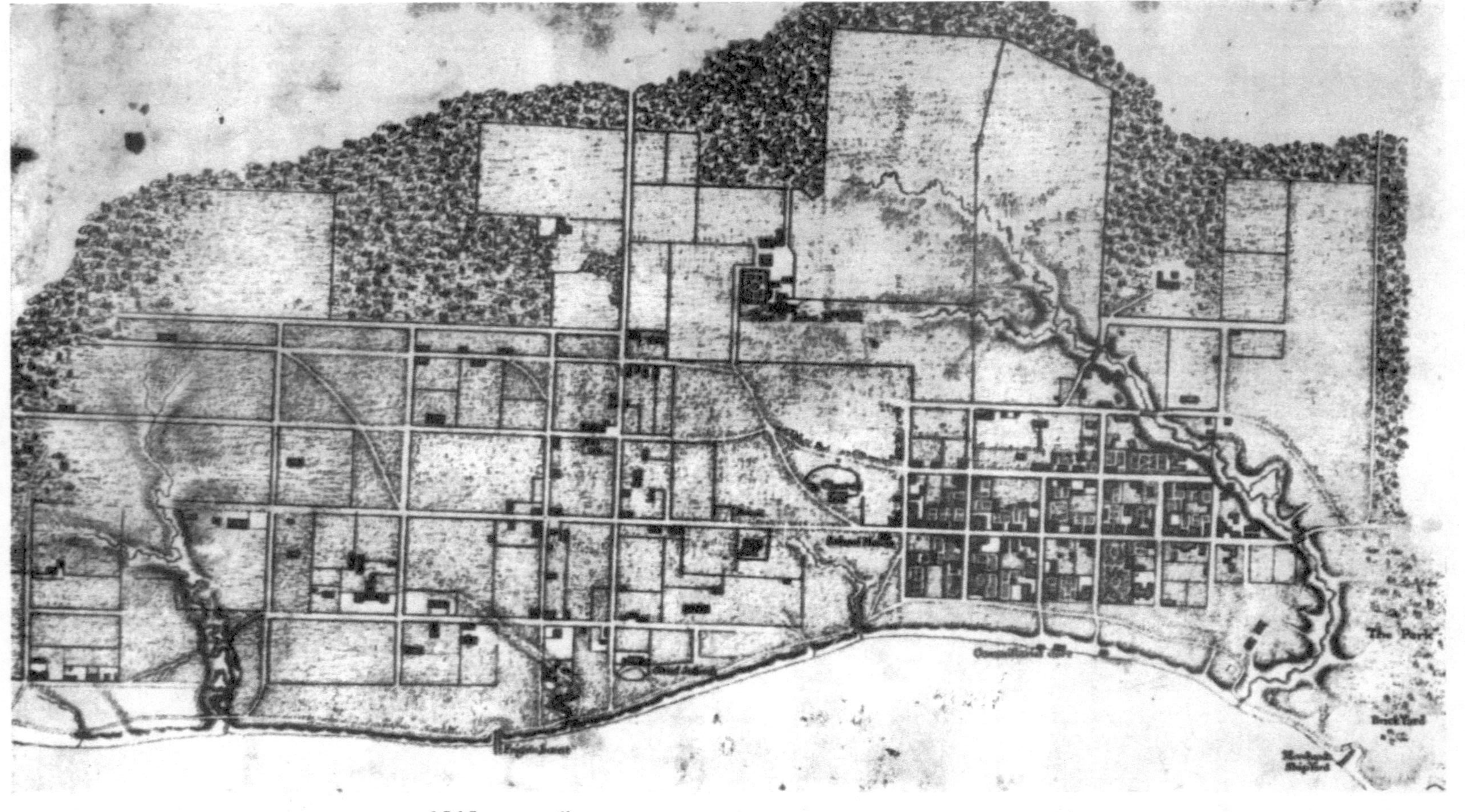

TOWN OF YORK, NOVEMBER 1813, FROM "SKETCH OF THE GROUND IN ADVANCE AND INCLUDING YORK UPPER CANADA BY GEORGE WILLIAMS . . . ." [Map Division, Public Archives of Canada.]

ties in York by welcoming the American invaders in 1813.[8] That Jarvis never reached the upper levels of prestige and power was due to his own regrettable temperament and inefficiency rather than to his relative's Americanism. The Scottish group, like the McGills, Crookshanks, and Beikies were not completely integrated into society, and tended to associate with the Scottish merchants rather than with the other officials. Their influence with Lieutenant Governor Hunter was resented. The accepted church was of course the Church of England. There were differences in moral standards corresponding to similar differences in English society of the time, which was after all portrayed by both Thomas Rowlandson and Jane Austen. Minor divergencies in behaviour became important in the stifling insularity of York; for example Dr. Baldwin was revolted by the table manners of the Powells.[9]

The upper class in York was not yet a closed circle; newcomers with the proper influence, position, and background were still accepted. It was difficult, however, to gain admittance by promotion from below. When St. George requested permission to pay his addresses to Anne Powell in 1807, her mother attributed his "presumption" to his "national and individual vanity" and "quietly but decisively rejected the proposal."[10] Occasionally real ability and forcefulness advanced someone beyond his position; by the end of the War, aided by his doughty behaviour during it, John Strachan had reached heights far above those of his predecessor Stuart.

None of these families was wealthy, and all were living beyond their means. Within the limited resources of a frontier society, great attempts were made to impress one's neighbours. Pretensions like the Ridout's fifty-pound carpet were acquired and were derided (H 28). The Jarvis family was most lavish in its ostentation; William Jarvis left debts amounting to over £1830 at his death.[11] All these families had large holdings of wild lands which were to make their descendants' fortunes, but the country was not yet sufficiently settled to make them of much monetary value before the War. In 1803 John McGill paid his carpenters in land in a settled part of Scarborough at the rate of six shillings New York Currency per acre.[12] It was not until the heavy postwar immigration that land

[8]P.A.C., Upper Canada Sundries, v. 16, no. 68, Information laid against inhabitants of Home District for sedition, etc.

[9]P.A.O., Baldwin Papers, W. W. Baldwin to William Firth, June 12, 1812.

[10]Powell Papers, Mrs. W. D. Powell to George Murray, Sept. 4, 1807.

[11]T.P.L., William Jarvis Papers, B55, p. 150–1, Memorandum [of debts].

[12]T.P.L., Alexander Wood Letter Books, Wood to Alexander McQueen, Oct. 28, 1803.

became a negotiable asset. With their salaries, private means, and credit, however, the gentry of York were able to afford many amenities. The list of things for sale from the Firth house in 1811 included "superb mahogany four post bedsteads," a silver dinner service, a "capital Eight Day Clock," a piano "inlaid with Sattinwood," "several hundred Volumes of Books," and a "beautiful Globe in Case" (H 39). This was fairly typical of an upper class home in York just before the War.

Like most immigrants and exiles, these families attempted to transplant to their new surroundings the way of life of their former homes. Habits and customs were rigidly retained after they had been given up elsewhere. For example, powdered hair remained in fashion in York long after it was outmoded in England. There was often incongruity in this remembrance of things past. Fox-hunting on the ice on the bay bore little resemblance to its English counterpart (H 19). D. W. Smith planned formal grounds around his home; Elizabeth Russell was proud of her garden, but at the same time turned her dogs loose on "pigs that were rooting up the grass before the house" (H 28). The Small-White duel might come up to accepted Regency standards, but the Baldwin-Macdonell duel of 1812 did not.[13] One of the greatest handicaps in the transplanting process was the scarcity of good servants. In a country where land was readily available and opportunities in other fields inviting, satisfactory domestic help was almost non-existent, and the gentry united with the wealthier merchants in bemoaning its absence (H 11, D 46). If standards were low, however, servants were at least plentiful. In 1808, 66 servants were employed by 39 masters in York. More than half of these worked in gentlemen's homes; the rest were employed in their businesses by merchants, tavern keepers, and tradesmen.[14]

The duties of the governing class were not onerous, and there was much leisure time. Regular subscription balls, in which the wealthier merchants and officers from the garrison joined, were organized as early as 1798.[15] The governor or administrator entertained officially at the Government Buildings on the King's and Queen's Birthdays (H 8, H 32). Frequent parties were held up the Don at Castle Frank.[16] There was incessant visiting, and a great deal of heavy drinking (H 10, H 28). After the first few years of scarcity, food

[13]Baldwin Papers, W. W. Baldwin to Firth, April 22, 1812.

[14]T.P.L., Minutes of Town Meetings and Lists of Inhabitants, 1797–1822.

[15]*Upper Canada Gazette*, York, Dec. 8, 1798.

[16]P.A.O., Ely Playter Diaries have a number of references to such parties.

was plentiful although the diet seems somewhat monotonous (H 15). Shooting wild pigeons provided a pleasant pastime in season, as did carioling, boating, sleighing, and horse-racing on the Peninsula. In 1810 a subscription library was organized, which did not survive the War (I 40). Reading novels or plays aloud was a favourite evening occupation (H 15, H 18). St. George and the other merchants sold a few of the standard authors, and in 1810 there was a bookstore in York (G 31). Books were scarce, however. McDonell wrote of going to Allan and Wood's shop to borrow "the Encyclopaedia" (H 10); to Wood's annoyance two volumes of this encyclopaedia inadvertently went with the retreating British army to Kingston after the American occupation of York.[17] A puppet show was performed on October 3, 1800 (H 15), and legitimate theatre from New York arrived at least as early as 1809 (H 33). Even with these signs of civilization, however, the stubborn adaptation of the life of older communities to pioneer conditions was difficult.

Although Simcoe described the site of Toronto as particularly healthy (B 2), it was found that fevers and ague resulted from the miasma arising from the Don marshes (H 21). The only qualified civilian doctors in York before the War were Dr. W. W. Baldwin, who also practised law, and possibly Dr. James Glennon. Two men called doctors, Thomas Stoyell and Amasa Stebbins, kept taverns; a third, Dr. E. Aspinwall, was a storekeeper before he entered the American service during the occupation of York.[18] Medical treatment was often given by laymen, like the setting of Mrs. John Playter's jaw in 1804 (H 23). Spectacles were traded about, and bought in a casual way from New York (H 25).

If there were variations in social status among the upper class, the merchants included representatives of every level of society, from men like Allan and Wood who were almost accepted by the gentry, to humble shopkeepers like James Pitney who whiled away the tedium of business life with stealing his neighbours' cabbages.[19] The leading merchants had small government appointments, but were not yet a power in provincial affairs like the merchants of Kingston or the Niagara towns. They were, however, influential in local matters through the Court of General Quarter Sessions of the Peace. Mostly Scottish in origin, the successful merchants were a

[17]Alexander Wood Letter Books, Wood to Joseph Forsyth, June 5, 1813.

[18]T.P.L., Papers relating to the Capitulation of York, signed by Chewett, Allan, Duncan Cameron, Samuel Smith, Strachan, Wood, and W. W. Baldwin, May 8, 1813.

[19]P.A.O., Miscellaneous, 1799, Papers concerning thefts by Pitney.

stabilizing force in the community, and formed a link between their lesser brethren and the gentry. There was as yet no clearly defined middle class.

The majority of the permanent citizens of York belonged to the petty bureaucracy or to the trades and labouring classes. Little is known of their lives; they appear in written records only as statistics or as senders of semi-literate bills. Ely Playter's diary (H 23) comes closest to presenting a picture of their ordinary life, but he was after all the son of a substantial farmer, and never had to face the basic problem of survival. Many of these men were discharged soldiers, with a leaven of American immigrants. Life for them was hard, and pleasures few. Its social centre was the tavern. As with the rest of the community, drinking was heavy. Besides liquor, however, the tavern provided a meeting place for town and country friends, an arena for wrestling, a stage for entertainments, and a block for auctions and raffles. A billiard table was available in at least one tavern. Many of these people were illiterate, or at least read and wrote with difficulty. Semi-lawless pleasures like the shivaree (H 23) or the patriotic breaking of William Willcocks' windows (H 10) were popular among the younger men.

A mile and a half beyond the town lay the garrison. The officers took an active part in York's social life; parties and assemblies always included the military. There is little evidence, however, that the ordinary soldier had much to do with the ordinary citizen. The garrison as a whole rendered much assistance to the townspeople. When fire threatened (C 16) or when there was difficulty landing goods (D 21) soldiers came to the rescue of civilians. Army doctors treated civilian patients (H 28). The commissariat, as well as individual officers and men, furnished an important market for the merchants' goods.

The relations of town and country were always close. Besides more distant holdings of wild lands, the upper classes had farms on their 100-acre lots in the first concession of York Township, and spent much time and money in developing them (H 15). Some of them, like McGill and Shaw, actually lived on their farms. The merchants were connected to the farming community by the profitable flour and potash business. The tradesmen served the farmers as well as the townspeople. Most of the farmers had for a time lived in York, and many drifted from town to country and back again. Thus the social and business community extended well beyond the limits of the town.

Before the War, then, York was a small but growing town with a population consisting mainly of artisans, labourers and transient farmers. There were a few merchants who were becoming comparatively wealthy, but who had not yet won political or social power. Because it was the capital, there was a high percentage of civil servants on all levels. A small group of senior government officials formed the upper class. The insecurity of their positions and their isolation from direct outside influence made them an inbred group, placing tremendous emphasis on trivialities. Divided by their intense rivalry and by differences of outlook and background, they were united in their opinion of their own importance, and brought on York the envy and opprobrium of the rest of the province.

I. YORK AND THE WAR OF 1812

THE WAR OF 1812 was one of the major influences in Toronto's history. It created new heroes, new villains, and a new class of society. For the first time, life in the ingrown backwoods community was directly and strenuously affected by outside influences. To most of the citizens of York it was a frightening experience. Those who lived through it, however, acquired status in the postwar community, rather like the United Empire Loyalists in older Upper Canadian settlements. The War of 1812 became to York, as to Upper Canada generally, a kind of St. Crispin's day. Legends sprang up around it of feats accomplished, of perils braved, of hardships overcome. At the time, however, its dominant characteristics in York were anxious apprehension and financial enrichment. Except for the week of occupation, the actual conflict was in the distance; in York itself another conflict raged between fierce loyalty and passive indifference.

The news that war was declared was received in York on June 27, 1812. It created bustle and confusion, but not panic (I 1). The possibility of disaster was not considered likely. The British regulars were immediately withdrawn from York, but their place at the garrison was taken by the militia, in whom the townspeople placed great confidence. Extravagant praise of the militia (I 2) was common; it was not realized that training was as important as patriotism, and that as the war progressed the first fine enthusiasm could be dimmed. The success of the 1812 campaign at Michilimackinac, Detroit, and Queenston Heights did nothing to dispel the general feeling of optimism. The flank companies of the York Militia were present at Detroit and Queenston Heights, and the citizens of York felt that they had had some part in these victories.

Meanwhile the battalion companies manned the local garrison. The usual pattern was that "the Militia after remaining a week or two in garrison here are marched off and replaced by raw Militia from the Country so that the garrison is continually changing" (I 4). Some men like Isaac Wilson remained for a longer time on duty; he reported that the food and beds were good, but complained of night sentry duty. In fact, "I thought I could stay there over summer very well but most of the men were very discontented and had come to a determination to go home as soon as they got their pay" (I 13). The garrison itself was much as Hunter had left it seven years before. Batteries had been built in front of the garrison and the Government House, and the Half-Moon Battery and Western Battery spread the defences further west. A magazine had been constructed near the Government House. Despite the urging of Brock, nothing further had been done to make the garrison capable of withstanding an attack.

The plans for the establishment of a dockyard were nevertheless carried out, thus making an attack extremely probable. In the winter of 1813 the keel of the *Sir Isaac Brock*, intended to be one of the largest vessels on the Lakes, was laid at York. It was to be finished by the opening of navigation in the spring of 1813. The work was under the superintendence of Thomas James Plunknett. Apparently to know him was to doubt his ability; he inspired misgivings in every officer who encountered him. After an inauspicious beginning (I 8) the work went forward, but the ship was not ready as soon as hoped, and it was destroyed by the British during the capture of York. No further attempts at shipbuilding in York were made. The building of the *Brock* had two effects on York—first it attracted the American attack of April, 1813, and second, it employed a great many York citizens. Between December, 1812, and February, 1813, there were 75 men on the payroll of the dockyard, most of them local residents.[1]

There was a general cessation of hostilities on the Niagara sector during the first winter of the War. The upper class in York spent it in patriotic activities. The ladies of York, inspired by Strachan, embroidered a banner for the 3rd Regiment, York Militia, which was presented with due ceremony in March, 1813.[2] In November, 1812, Strachan also organized a fund-raising campaign for comforts for York militiamen serving on the Niagara Frontier (I 6), and over £200 Halifax was contributed to this "Flannel Fund." It was felt, however, that "something more might be done of a permanent nature."

At a meeting of the principal inhabitants of York and its vicinity held on December 15, 1812, the Loyal and Patriotic Society of Upper Canada was organized, to afford aid and relief to militiamen and their families suffering because of the war, and to grant medals for "extraordinary instances of personal courage or fidelity."[3] Although the titular head of the Society was Chief Justice Scott, its most active director was once again John Strachan. Almost

[1]Royal Canadian Military Institute, Account Books of the Garrison of York.
[2]*Kingston Gazette*, April 20, 1813.
[3]Loyal and Patriotic Society of Upper Canada, *Report, passim.*

£21,500 Halifax Currency was contributed to this Society before March, 1815, of which the greater part came from Lower Canada, the Maritime Provinces, England, and the West Indies. The York subscriptions amounted to £1808.6.8 Halifax, but this included £200 from Sheaffe, £500 from Drummond, and several other smaller contributions from non-residents. Still, the citizens of York contributed handsomely to the fund, which was administered from York. The militia at the garrison gave one day's pay and the army officers also contributed.

One immediate result of the War was a shortage of food. On August 29, 1812, Wood wrote that "Every article in the grocery line is very scarce here."[4] Salt was in short supply, as was flour because "the harvest was very wet & the Farmers away from their homes so that much of the wheat had sprung before it was got into the Barn."[5] At the same time the tremendously increased purchases of the commissariat further reduced the quantity on the open market. The shortage became increasingly acute throughout the War; in December, 1814, neither flour nor pork was available in the York area (I 53).

To the merchants of York, commissariat buying brought handsome profits, and there was brisk speculation in flour, pork, and rum. Between November, 1812, and February, 1814, the commissariat paid over £50,458 to them, the lion's share going to St. George and Allan, with large sums also to Wood and Drean.[6] Not only did the leading merchants benefit financially from the war; smaller merchants and tradesmen like Joseph Cawthra and Jesse Ketchum also shared in the largesse. The lists of people to whom payments were made by the military included almost every citizen of York. This resulted in an artificial and temporary prosperity. The more lasting effect was the creation of a prosperous middle class. As with most wars, it was a time of full employment. In November, 1813, Wood wrote that "every hand every article of materials are in requisition & employed by Government."[7] Even the Government itself had difficulty finding workmen (I 44).

Another customary accompaniment of war, inflation, was also evident in York, as in all Upper Canada. Prices of provisions and manufactures skyrocketted because of scarcity (I 56). In the spring of 1814, the magistrates fixed prices for provisions (I 47), and revised these prices upwards from time to time. As always, high

[4]T.P.L., Alexander Wood Letter Books, Wood to James Leslie, Aug. 29, 1812.
[5]*Ibid.*, Wood to James Leslie, Nov. 11, 1812.
[6]Royal Canadian Military Institute, Account Books of the Garrison of York.
[7]Alexander Wood Letter Books, Wood to G. O. Stuart, Nov. 13, 1813.

prices were particularly hard upon those on a fixed income, as were so many of the government officers and employees in York. Judge Powell wrote that "we struggled through the war with less discomfort than might be expected considering our residence to have been twice in possession of the Enemy—our principal distress arose from the incredible Expense of living enhanced by the demands for the Army & consequent depreciation of our Salaries as the Mean of Income."[8]

Specie also became scarce. The commissariat issued army bills, but these did not completely solve the problem, particularly of handling small sums. On August 28, 1813, the merchants of Kingston joined to found the Kingston Association,[9] an organization for issuing small bills in return for the deposit of specie or army bills. No member of the Association would then accept a private individual's bills. This attempt at primitive banking failed because it did not win the support of all the major merchants in Kingston. On September 22, 1813, a similar organization was founded at York (I 39), with the significant difference that bills to the value of only £300 Currency would be issued; the Kingston Association proposed issuing £1000. The York Association was able to gain support of all the leading York merchants, but apparently also failed. Beyond the announcement of its organization and aims, nothing further can be found about it.

One of the greatest problems of the merchant through the War was transportation. The line of communication between York and Lower Canada was exposed to enemy attack throughout much of its length, and the merchants early realized the danger (I 5). All supplies for Upper Canada now came by this route. The Americans did not succeed in breaking this line, but were able to harass effectively commercial shipping on Lake Ontario. At the close of navigation in 1812, Alexander Wood lost his goods with the sinking of the *Simcoe* off Kingston (I 9), and for the rest of the War the merchants of York could not depend on water transportation for their goods. During the winter goods were brought in sleighs from Kingston (I 54, I 56); in January, 1815, this cost $6.50 per hundredweight, which was regarded as exorbitant.[10] It was extremely difficult to hire sleighs, because they were seized on sight for military or government use. This impressing of sleighs was enforced by the General Quarter Sessions of the Peace (I 45). During

[8]P.R.O., C.O. 42, v. 358, p. 56, microfilm copy in P.A.O., W. D. Powell to Mrs. Warren, Oct. 12, 1815.

[9]*Kingston Gazette*, Aug. 31, 1813.

[10]Alexander Wood Letter Books, Wood to William Mitchell, Jan. 13, 1815.

that last winter of the War, a more desperate expedient was resorted to, that of bringing goods up in small boats following the shoreline (I 52), but this was not entirely satisfactory, and many of the boats were wrecked.

In the spring of 1813, the whole fabric of York society was rudely torn to pieces. As soon as the ice was off the Lake, a squadron of 13 sail carrying 1700 men set out from Sackett's Harbour (I 21), and on April 26, 1813, were sighted off the Scarborough Bluffs. By chance there were 300 British regulars in York, most of them passing through on their way to the Niagara Frontier. In addition there were about an equal number of York militia and a group of Indians under Major Givins. Although such an attack was expected (I 11), Sir Roger Sheaffe could do little with the primitive fortifications and comparatively small force at his disposal, until at least he knew where the landing was to be made. On the morning of April 27, the American flotilla sailed past York, intending to land its men at the ruins of the old French fort, but easterly winds carried it beyond this point, and the landing was made on the site of the present Sunnyside Station. Sheaffe despatched troops to resist it. There was some confusion; the militia who were part of this detachment did not arrive in time, and the Grenadier company of the 8th Regiment was supported only by the Indians. Covered by murderous fire from their ships, the Americans succeeded in making a beachhead, and the company of the 8th was cut to pieces. This initial disaster had an unfortunate effect on both the militia and Indians; such untrained and inexperienced troops were easily dismayed by catastrophe, and little attempt was made to rally them. The Americans moved eastward toward the garrison, while their ships also moved in to shell the fort. An attempt was made at the Western Battery to halt their progress, but in the general confusion a portable magazine exploded, rendering the battery useless. The next battery was abandoned, and the American troops were advancing towards the Government House west of the garrison, when the magazine exploded, killing not only a number of Americans, including their commander in the field, General Pike, but also some of the British troops. Sheaffe withdrew the British regulars to the town, held a hurried council of war, and decided upon a retreat to Kingston, leaving the militia and townspeople to make what terms they could. Orders were given for the destruction of the naval stores and the *Sir Isaac Brock*. The losses of the British regulars were 62 killed and 76 wounded (I 25); the Americans lost 55 killed and

257 wounded.[11] Most of the British losses were at the landing, while the Americans lost most heavily in the explosion of the magazine.

The general impression of the episode—it cannot be called a battle—was of confusion and inefficiency. Militia officers like Allan and Chewett, and citizens like Strachan and Wood, were extremely critical of Sheaffe's handling of the affair. The main complaint was that he had no plan of attack and had given no orders (I 14). He had also failed to take advantage of the havoc created by the explosion of the magazine. Most of the militia were not engaged in action at all, but spent their time getting under cover waiting for orders (I 1) or trying to find a good vantage point from which to see the excitement (I 13). An attempt to form the militia in the ravine by the garrison failed because "the Men . . . refused to stand" when they saw the regulars in retreat (I 1). The Americans with their vast superiority in numbers would almost certainly have succeeded in their object no matter what Sheaffe had done, although they too were having difficulty with their high command (I 21). The usual modern criticism of Sheaffe is that he was wrong in wasting troops in opposing the Americans at all, that he should have retreated with his precious regulars before the action began.[12] Because of the outcry from York, however, he was removed from command and returned to England.

With his withdrawal from York, the complicated negotiations for capitulation were begun (I 14). Strachan took a leading role in them, and emerged as the acknowledged defender of the rights of the people of York. The terms of capitulation finally settled were "liberal & Satisfactory."[13] Public stores were to be given up, private property guaranteed to the citizens, and the militia paroled (I 15). This last removed the York militia from active combat for the rest of the War.

The American army remained in York from April 27 to May 1, and were storm-stayed in their ships in York harbour until May 8. It is difficult to get a clear picture of this occupation. On one hand there is Isaac Wilson's testimony: "It struck my mind very forcibly the evening after the battle was over to see men who two hours before were doing their utmost to kill one another now conversing together with the greatest familiarity. In the evening all seemed as

[11] *Niles Register*, June 12, 1813.

[12] E.g., Wood, *Select British Documents of the Canadian War of 1812*, I, 56.

[13] P.A.C., Powell Papers, p. 1204, Powell's account of the capture and occupation of York.

settled and quiet in York as if nothing had happened" (I 13). The usual description of these days, however, was one of lawlessness and plunder (I 17). On April 30, a General Order of the American army was issued supporting the civil authority of the magistrates and promising punishment for American soldiers guilty of "improper and irregular conduct."[14] The magistrates immediately swore in the principal householders as constables.[15] Some looting of private property was done by American soldiers (I 20, I 40), and the more dissolute elements of the local population also took advantage of the unsettled conditions. Powell wrote that "during the Interval from the retreat of the Troops to this ratification [of the terms of capitulation] the Inhabitants were exposed to every species of Insult & Plunder chiefly by our own people."[16] C. W. Humphries, however, from an examination of the war losses claims from York, has concluded that most of the looting was done by Americans, and that it was in any event not as extensive as contemporaries believed.[17] He believes that Canadian looting was considered prevalent because goods were given to the citizens by the Americans (I 13, I 24). The Parliament Buildings and most of the garrison were burned; public stores, public money (I 28), Sheaffe's baggage (I 22), some books from the subscription library (I 40), probably some private property, the mace, and the royal standard were carried off. The *Gloucester* which was in drydock undergoing repairs was towed away. On May 3, a meeting of the magistrates was held to enforce order (I 16), and the first occupation of York was over.

The capture of York had two major effects on its inhabitants. The first was great fear of subsequent attacks. From this time to the end of the war there were constant alarms and anxiety for the safety of the town and province (I 31, I 50). The citizens of York for the first time realized that capture was possible, and that British victory was not a foregone conclusion. The capture of Fort George a month later, followed by British reverses on the Niagara and Western frontiers, did nothing to increase confidence. With this fear went a distrust of the ability of the British commanders (I 49). Faith in the invincible British army was shaken; the armchair

[14]T.P.L., Papers relating to the Capitulation of York, General Order signed by N. Pinkney, April 30, 1813.

[15]Powell Papers, p. 1205, Powell's account of the capture and occupation of York.

[16]*Ibid.*

[17]Humphries, "The Capture of York," *Ontario History*, LI (1), March, 1960, 1–21.

generals of York saw much to criticize in the high command of both the army and the Provincial Marine.

The other result of the occupation was that the whole question of disaffection and treason in York was brought into the open. It had been present, of course, before the catastrophe, but there was little idea of the depth or prevalence of anti-British feeling. The definition of disaffection varied. To patriots like Mrs. Powell, gallantly invoking the spirit of Wellington (I 29), those who did not share their burning zeal were obviously pro-American. This probably explains her husband's report to Prevost that "in the Event of any serious disaster to his Majesty's Arms little reliance is to be had on the power of the well disposed to repress and keep down the Turbulence of the disaffected who are very numerous" (I 32). As the war progressed, there was certainly a dwindling of enthusiasm for sacrifice. Many of the inhabitants of York and its vicinity had lately come from the United States, and were uninterested in politics or governments. Of these some had returned to the United States at the outbreak of war. To many that remained, the War was an intolerable nuisance. Even some of the English immigrants like Isaac Wilson were perilously close to indifference about its outcome (I 13). Plundering and lawlessness had little to do with disaffection, but were merely the result of the dissolute element of the community taking advantage of unusual conditions.

On September 29, 1813, information was laid against 32 residents of the Home District for seditious activities.[18] Of the charges, the magistrates said that "some are mixed with prejudice, & some with malice, others are clear and pointed." Only two of these were residents of York, William B. Peters and John Young, both of whom were simply accused of uttering disloyal sentiments. Although the Acting Attorney General was instructed to proceed against five citizens of York for traitorously affording information to the enemy (I 33), no case was made against them.

The second occupation of York, however, on July 31 and August 1, 1813, clearly showed that the Americans were getting information from Canadians. Most of the inhabitants had retreated into the woods; the militia was still on parole (I 34). The Americans seized a quantity of flour, and then went up the Don in search of government stores hidden there after midnight the night before by George and Ely Playter (I 1). This had obviously been reported to them, and feeling ran high against the possible informants (I 36).

[18]P.A.C., Upper Canada Sundries, v. 16, no. 68, Information laid against inhabitants of Home District for sedition, etc.

The spectrum from vehement patriotism through indifference to active treason was present at York. It is difficult to assess the degree to which each was represented, but the citizens of York and its vicinity were probably less disaffected than Powell described, and less patriotic than the legends of the War would have us believe.

Another result of the capture of York was the rebuilding of the garrison on the site of Fort York. By July, 1814, seven buildings had been erected within the roughly triangular stockade, including two blockhouses.[19] Another blockhouse was built further up Garrison Creek (I 46). This was an example of locking the stable door; these buildings were never menaced, although shots were exchanged with an American ship in August, 1814 (I 50). During the campaigns of 1813 and 1814, York became the base hospital for the Niagara Frontier. As well as the small military hospital, the church (I 51), Elmsley House, and private billets (I 30) were used for the wounded. During the summer months of 1813 and 1814 the sick and wounded in the general hospital averaged from 370 to 420.[20]

York at the end of the War was very different from the town of 1812. Some men like John Strachan and William Allan had acquired more stature, others like Joseph Cawthra and Jesse Ketchum more money. A middle class developed of well-to-do merchants and tradesmen. Some men like John Young and William Peters lost their place in the community, and a number of American citizens had left it at the outbreak of hostilities. York's position as capital was threatened by the fact that it had been captured; for the next few years it was to fight a valiant and successful battle to prevent the capital being moved to Kingston. The ruling class had remained staunchly British, and were more firmly entrenched in power and more conservative than ever. The opponents of the government were discredited, and reform was not to rally until the post-Napoleonic immigration brought more British radicals to Upper Canada.

News of peace reached York on February 15, 1815. American trade and immigration recommenced; prices dropped instantly as the commissariat stopped buying. Normal times returned with the spring, as "the wild duck revisit our waters since peace was made" (I 58).

[19]P.A.C., Map Division. "Plan of the town and harbour of York, George Williams . . . 27 July, 1814."

[20]Strachan, *The John Strachan Letter Book*, p. 114, Certificate of W. Lee, March 14, 1816.

THE TOWN OF YORK, 1793–1815

DOCUMENTS

A. ESTABLISHMENT OF THE CAPITAL

A 1 LIEUTENANT GOVERNOR SIMCOE[1] VISITS TORONTO
[*Niagara*, Upper Canada Gazette, *May 9, 1793*]

On Thursday last his Excellency the Lieut. Governor accompanied by several Military Gentlemen set out in Boats for Toronto, round the head of the Lake Ontario, by Burlington Bay; and in the Evening his Majesty's Vessels the Caldwell,[2] and Buffaloe,[3] sailed for the same Place.

A 2 SIMCOE TO ALURED CLARKE[4]
[*Ontario, Department of Public Records and Archives (P.A.O.), Simcoe Papers*]

Navy Hall 31st May 1793

. . . As it cannot fail to strike your Excellency both in a civil and a military light, that the Safety of this Province should not depend upon so feeble a Barrier as (comparatively) the contemptible Fortress of Niagara, it is with great pleasure that I offer to you some Observations upon the Military Strength and Naval Conveniency of Toronto (Now York) which I propose immediately to occupy—I lately examined this Harbour accompanied by such Officers naval and military as I thought most competant to give me Assistance therein; and upon minute Investigation I found it to be without Comparison the most, proper situation for an Arsenal in every extent of that word that can be met with in this Province. The Spit of Sand which forms its entrance is capable of being so fortified with a few heavy Guns as to prevent any Vessel from entering the Harbour, or from remaining within it. From the diversity of the Sand Banks any small point of ground is sufficiently strong to be selected for the present purposes, and which as Circumstances shall require, may

[1]John Graves Simcoe (1752–1806) entered the British army in 1771. He served in America through the American Revolution, and from 1777 to 1781 he commanded the Queen's Rangers. In 1791 after the passage of the Constitutional Act, he was appointed the first Lieutenant Governor of Upper Canada, arriving in Canada the following year. After a brief stay at Quebec and Kingston, he established himself at Niagara, and met his first legislature there. He returned to England in 1796. In 1797 he spent some months as Commander in Chief of San Domingo. He resigned his Canadian appointment in 1798.

[2]The *Caldwell* was a 48-ton sloop, William Baker, master, manned by seven men, and carrying two guns. (Toronto Public Library (T.P.L.), Wolford Simcoe Papers, Book, 10.)

[3]The *Buffalo* was a gunboat of 20 tons, Charles Heslop, master, manned by five men. It was built at Kingston in 1792.

[4]Major General Alured Clarke (1745–1832) served through the American Revolutionary War. He was Lieutenant Governor of Quebec from 1791 to 1796. During the absence of Lord Dorchester in England, he acted as Administrator from 1791 to 1793, when he left Canada.

be occupied to the widest extent. At the Bottom of the Harbour there is a Situation admirably adapted for a Naval Arsenal and Dock Yard, and there flows into the Harbour a River [the Don] the Banks of which are covered with excellent Timber. Upon this River I purpose to construct as soon as possible a Saw Mill, principally for the benefit of the Settlement but which I have no doubt will at the cheapest rate supply every material that may be wanted for His Majesty's Service in the various Posts on Lake Ontario. I have fixed upon the Scite for a place for a Town on the main Shore—and another where I propose to build Barracks for the Kings Troops. These Barracks I have the Idea of constructing so as to hold 250 Men and Officers with health and conveniency. The ground not being as yet surveyed, I cannot transmit to your Excellency a Plan—but my general Idea is to build them of Stone, and in the form of an oblong of three sides, of a single story in height and closing the Angles to the Land with a kind of breastwork of Sod to leave an opening towards the Harbour for a Battery on barbette—I have heard of two eighteen pounders that were sunk in the Lake after the late Peace. They are described as being good Guns and easy to be weighed. If I obtain them, I should propose to place them and some heavy Carronades on the point of the Harbour opposite to the intended Barracks, where I should wish to build a Store House that might occasionally serve as a Block house to secure such Batteries as it may be necessary for the Troops to erect. I must observe to your Excellency that at this point there is an excellent Harbour for Batteaux It must be obvious for many reasons that the North Side of the Lake will be the most eligible communication between Kingston and Niagara. I have not as yet been able to cross from Toronto to Lake Huron. This I propose to do in the Autumn. But I have good information that a Road is very easy to be made to communicate with those Waters which fall into Lake Huron. . . . In forming a Naval Establishment it is apparent to me that the protection of the Shipping and the Union of the Artificers necessary for their building and Equipment, are the most important Considerations. In regard to the Harbour at Kingston it cannot be so fortified as to protect Shipping to this defect all other considerations are subordinate—nor do I see a reason that can justify the laying out any public money at that place. It can only at present be considered as a Harbour during the season of Transport, nor in this point is it so advantageously Situated as Gannanouqui [Gananoque]—York which is the best Harbour on the Lakes may be readily made very strong at a slight expence, and in the progress of the Country impragnable Shipping suited for every purpose of the Lakes may be built there at the cheapest Rates by Government for whom sufficient Reserves will be made to furnish materials for a long period. This Port is directly opposite and in sight of Niagara and Vessels from it may be at Sea in the spring generally speaking a fortnight sooner then from any other port on Lake Ontario. . . .

I feel it my duty to state to Your Excellency, & I hope you will communicate these Ideas to his Majestys Ministers, that I consider it my civil Duty immediately to occupy the Harbour of York without delay, with such troops as are not confined to the several Garrisons, & that I consider it to be indispensible for the protection of the province that the Harbour should be fortified, & I request of Your Excellency for this especial purpose some heavy Guns & ten Inch Howitzers, each of which should be provided with Carriages that may be used both for garrison Service & for the being placed in Gun Boats. The Wood & stone boats necessarily to be employed in the construction of the Garrison I purpose to build in such a manner as occasionally to supply this species of Armament. . . .

A 3 CLARKE TO SIMCOE
[*P.A.O., Simcoe Papers*]

Quebec 24th June 1793

. . . In hourly expectation of Lord Dorchesters arrival, and considering the restrictions under which I am placed with regard to Military Works and Fortifications, I do not feel myself authorized to incur expence on account of the Works proposed to be established in Upper Canada. As however you consider it your Civil duty immediately to occupy the Harbour of Toronto (now York) and fortify the same in such manner as you think is indispensible for the protection of the Province, I shall with pleasure afford Your Excellency every aid that the State of the King's Store here will admit of, and shall direct that you be furnished with the heavy Guns requested, as soon as I am favored with the number you may think necessary, together with the particular Calibre thereof, and agreeable to your desire shall by the earliest opportunity communicate your Ideas & intentions to His Majesty's Ministers.

With regard to the Howitzers there must be some difficulty as we have not many of that Species of Ordnance, and not one of the Size you mention; but I will enquire from Lieut. Colonel Walker[5] how far Carronades may be made to answer the purpose, if you should like to have them; and on being acquainted with your wishes will give the necessary directions thereupon. . . .

A 4 SIMCOE TO CLARKE
[*P.A.O., Simcoe Papers*]

Navy Hall
July 24th 1793

. . . I shall immediately proceed to Toronto (or York) whither I hope the whole of the Queens Rangers[6] will be encamped in a few days, when

[5]Lieutenant Colonel Ellis Walker entered the Royal Artillery in 1755, and served through the American Revolution. He became a general in 1812.

[6]The Queen's Rangers were first organized as a loyalist regiment at the beginning of the American Revolution, under the command of Robert Rogers, and then of Simcoe. It became part of the British regular army and was disbanded in New Brunswick in October, 1783. The regiment was reorganized by Simcoe in 1791,

I shall do myself the honor of making a more specific report on the subject of Fortifying that Harbour—Its extent, & the difficulty that any Enemy must have of bringing *heavy* cannon or Howitzers into the Province necessarily point out the advantages that must result from a few Guns of the largest Calibre—The Carronades meant for the Shipping, I have always purposed, to make use of & my intention has been to select some of the best Guns from Carleton Island,[7] that at the least expence, we may make the most formidable appearance, & in some measure fortify the most important post within the Territorial Line—Should the United States meditate attack, in the first instance, at least, it would be wise in them by manifesto "to declare that they restricted their operations simply to the recovery of the Posts[8] unjustly withheld from them, & which the continuation of the Indian War rendered indispensably necessary for their Interests." Upon this mode of reasoning I deduce an additional Argument for the immediate Occupation of a place of Arms, & am happy that York embraces so many different & permanent advantages for the welfare & protection of his Majesty's Government in a military as well as a civil View. . . .

A 5 The Queen's Rangers Arrive in York
[*Niagara*, Upper Canada Gazette, *August 1, 1793*]

A few days ago, the first division of his Majesty's corps of Queens Rangers left Queenstown for Toronto (now York), and proceeded in Batteaux round the head of Lake Ontario, by Burlington Bay; and shortly afterward another division of the same regiment sailed in the King's vessels, the Onondago and Caldwell for the same place.

On monday evening his Excellency the Lieut. Governor left Navy Hall, and embarked on board his Majesty's Schooner the Mississaga,[9] which sailed immediately for York, with the remainder of the Queens Rangers.

---

and went with him to Upper Canada. It was employed in the construction of roads, barracks, and such as well as in garrison duties, particularly at York. Upon its disbandment in October, 1802, many of its officers and men settled in or near York.

[7]Carleton Island, at the junction of Lake Ontario and the St. Lawrence River, was the site of Fort Haldimand and served as the British post of trans-shipment from 1778 to 1783.

[8]The Treaty of Paris, September 3, 1783, provided that the boundary between British North America and the United States would run through the middle of the Great Lakes and down the St. Lawrence to the forty-fifth degree of northern latitude. It was agreed that the British would evacuate their posts south of this line "with all convenient speed." The posts of Michilimackinac, Detroit, Fort Niagara, Oswegatchie (Ogdensburg), and Oswego, however, were not handed over to the Americans until 1796, as a result of Jay's Treaty in 1794.

[9]The *Onondaga* and the *Mississaga* were top-sail schooners of 120 tons, carrying six guns, and manned by 14 men. They were built in 1789–90, probably near Gananoque. The *Onondaga* was commanded by David Beaton, the *Mississaga* by Jean Baptiste Bouchette.

A 6 General Order Naming York
[*P.A.O., Simcoe Papers*]

York. August 26th. 1793.

G.O.

His Excellency the Lt. Governor having received official information of the success of his Majesty's arms under His Royal Highness the Duke of York,[10] by which Holland has been saved from the invasion of the French Armies; and it appearing that the combined Forces have been lately successful in dislodging their Enemies from an intrenched Camp supposed to be impregnable, from which the most important consequences may be expected; and in which arduous Attempt his Royal Highness the Duke of York and his Majesty's Troops supported the national Glory; It is his Excellency's Orders that on the raising of the Union Flag at Twelve O'Clock to morrow, a Royal Salute of Twenty one Guns is to be fired to be answered by the shipping in the harbour, in respect to his Royal Highness, and in commemoration of the of the naming of this Harbour, from his English Title, *York*.

Edward Baker Littlehales[11]
Major of Brigade

A 7 Rough Draft of Proceedings of a Council Held at St. John Rousseaux,[12] August 26, 1793
[*P.A.O., Simcoe Papers*]

Present
The Honble. the Chief Justice[13]
The Attorney General[14]
Major of Brigade Littlehales & several other gentlemen
22 Indians principally Chiefs & a Lake Huron Chief of consequence

The Lake Huron Chief spoke, addressing himself to Major Littlehales—

[10]Frederick, Duke of York (1763–1827), was the second son of George III and was Commander in Chief of the Army (1798–1809, 1811–27). In February, 1793, he commanded an expedition against the French in Holland, where he was successful in a series of skirmishes. The victory which prompted the ceremony of naming York was the siege of Famars, in May, 1793. Simcoe referred to the site as Toronto (now York) before the ceremony; see e.g. A 2.

[11]Edward Baker Littlehales (d. 1825) was Simcoe's military secretary in Upper Canada. In 1802 he was made a baronet and in 1817 he became by sign manual Sir Edward Baker, Bart.

[12]Jean Baptiste (St. John) Rousseau (1758–1812) was one of the earliest settlers at Toronto. He was a fur trader and lived near the mouth of the Humber River. His house was built in 1774. (T.P.L., Alexander Wood Letter Books, Alexander Wood to R. and S. Hatt, May 15, 1801.) In 1794 he entered a partnership with Thomas Barry dealing in furs and general merchandise, but moved to Ancaster in 1795.

[13]William Osgoode (1754–1824) was appointed first Chief Justice of Upper Canada in 1792. He was also Speaker of the Legislative Council. In 1794 he became Chief Justice of Lower Canada, but retired in 1801.

[14]John White (d. 1800) was called to the Bar at the Inner Temple in 1785. He

We are sorry our father the great man is sick, we wish to take him by the hand, have heard much of him, & that he is a good man—We hope he will take care of us—We have much to say & are sorry that we cannot understand each other—

Father—My heart is open, we will do what you wish, my children are desirous of obeying you—We now wish to speak regarding the lands we purchased from the Magedash Indians on Lake la Claie [Simcoe], they agreed to give us a mile on each side & a carrying place, which we paid for, but which they never complied with; Now my good father, we hope that you will assist us

Father—Some time ago a great man came to this place, & kindled a fire, he soon went away to our great surprise & never returned, we earnestly hope that the great man now here, will rekindle the fire that the chimney may be strong, that it may never be extinguished.

My good Father,—Our young men are very much in want of spear to kill their fish with, they are under the necessity of making use of wood, which by no means answers the purpose, & indeed they cannot procure subsistence, we therefore hope you will order us a blacksmith.—

Father—We trust you will prevent our being injured by any white people, we understand that you are sent here by the King our father to protect & take care of us, as our friend (speaking of Mr. St. John) is exceedingly ill, we will open our minds more fully next spring & speak at large; at the same time we hope that all our father's chiefs present have paid attention to our words, & we implore the great Spirit to protect them

Father—As we are in want of some little provisions, we hope you will give us some to carry us to our homes, and we also wish to have a walking stick to remember that we are supported by our father the great man near us; we also sollicit a small quantity of tobacco;

Delivered strings of white wampum

To which Major of Brigade Littlehales made the following reply

Children & Brothers

I shall faithfully communicate the words you have just uttered to the great man at this place the King your father's representative—

Children & brothers. the great man well laments that no person here but St. John who is exceedingly indisposed can interpret your language this is the principal & the only reason that he was prevented from taking all of you by the hand yesterday & from listening to your words, notwithstanding which he will be happy to see a few of the Chiefs tomorrow.

The King your fathers representative will take care of your interests, will guard & protect you, & prevent you being injured by any white person.

---

was appointed Attorney General for Upper Canada in 1791, and was elected a member of Legislative Assembly for Leeds and Frontenac in 1792. On January 3, 1800, he died from a wound received in a duel with John Small, Clerk of the Executive Council.

Children & Brothers

A Vessel is hourly expected with provisions, when I make no doubt the great man here will supply you with sufficient to carry you to your respective homes

E B. Littlehales

A 8 LITTLEHALES TO MAJOR SMITH,[15] COMMANDING AT NIAGARA
[*P.A.O., Simcoe Papers*]

York, Augt 28 1793

In obedience to his Excellency Colonel Simcoe's orders I have directed the Messessague to proceed with the utmost expedition to Niagara, & I am to represent to you that in consequence of no Vessel having arrived here, Provisions are *much* wanted for his Majesty's Corps of Queen's Rangers &ca. You will be so good therefore without the least delay, to order the Commissary to issue & put on board three months Provisions of all species for the above Regiment & you will desire the Capt of this Vessel to return as soon as possible after having received the quantity of Rations required. In case of any other of his Majesty's Ships having sailed from Niagara for this place, this order is to be nevertheless carried directly into execution.

Lieut. Pilkington[16] is desired to send by this opportunity his Excellency's Canvass house at Navy Hall with all its' apparatus, provided it does not detain the Messessague one moment; otherwise it is not to be sent.

A 9 PETER RUSSELL[17] TO ELIZABETH RUSSELL,[18] NIAGARA
[*P.A.O., Russell Papers*]

York Septr 1st 1793

Little Bouchette[19] arrived early this Morning—By him I received your Letter & am happy to hear that you are well. We had a rough but

[15]John Smith (d. 1795), of the 5th Regiment of Foot, was commanding officer at Detroit, 1790–2, and at Fort Niagara, 1792–5. He was the father of David William Smith.

[16]Robert Pilkington (1765–1834) entered the Royal Artillery in 1787. He transferred to the Engineers in 1789 and came to Canada the following year. From 1793 to 1796 he was on Simcoe's staff. In 1803 he returned to England, where he eventually became Inspector General of Fortifications.

[17]Peter Russell (1733–1808) came to America in 1776 as assistant secretary to Sir Henry Clinton, Commander in Chief of the British forces. After the Revolution he returned to England, and in 1792 was appointed Receiver General of Upper Canada and a member of the Executive and Legislative Councils. From 1796 until 1799 he was President of the Executive Council and Administrator of the province and was responsible for much of the practical planning of York.

[18]Elizabeth Russell (1754–1822) was the half-sister of Peter Russell, with whom she lived from 1786. She was a first cousin once removed of Mrs. William Warren Baldwin and left the considerable Russell property to her and her sister at her death.

[19]Joseph Bouchette (1774–1841) entered the office of his uncle Samuel Holland,

pleasant passage of four Hours, having saild from your River at Six & arrived here at ten—The Governor & Mrs. Simcoe[20] received me very graciously—but you can have no conception of the Misery in which they live—The Canvas house being their only residence—in one room of which they lie & see company—& in the other are the Nurse & Children squalling &c—an open Bower covers us at Dinner—& a tent with a small Table & three Chairs serves us for a Council Room—We had a Council of half an Hour yesterday—and another to day after Church of three Hours—But many more will be required before we can get thro' the Multiplicity of important Business that awaits our Decision. I attended his Excellency yesterday up the [mss torn] Town (about two miles from our Camp) Nothing can be pleasanter than this Beautiful Bason—bounded on one side by a number of low sandy Peninsulas,[21] & on the other by a bluff Bank of 60 feet, from which extends back a thick wood of large forest Trees. The Town occupies a flat, about 50 yards from the Water—the Situation I believe healthy, as the ground is perfectly dry—& consists for the present of four ranges of Squares—each containing five Squares—& each Square two rows of Houses, four in each row—The Ranges of Squares are bounded by broad Streets & the front houses are to be 46 feet in length & to be built after a uniform Model[22] with Columns facing the Water—When this plan is to be carried into Execution the Lord only knows—for no attempt has been yet made by any intended Inhabitant, except Mr. Robinson[23] who is making

---

Surveyor General of Quebec, about 1790. In November, 1792, he made the first survey of Toronto harbour. He was appointed Surveyor General of Lower Canada in 1804.

[20]Mrs. Elizabeth Posthuma (Gwillim) Simcoe (1766–1850) was born after her father's death, and her mother died shortly after. She was a considerable heiress when she married Simcoe in 1782, aged 16. She brought her two youngest children, Sophia (1789–1864) and Francis (1791–1812), with her to Canada. A third child, Katharine, was born at Niagara in January, 1793, and died at York in April, 1794.

[21]In 1830 a breach was made in the Peninsula at the head of Ashbridge's Bay, which opened and closed with storms and high water. Small vessels occasionally used this route. It was not until the bad storms of 1858 that a navigable channel for all shipping was formed at the eastern end of the harbour.

[22]On September 1, 1793, William Chewett was ordered by Simcoe to prepare elevations for two-storey houses of 46 and 36 feet in length, and a one-storey house 26 feet long. Chewett waited on the Governor in Council with four elevations on September 5, and was desired by the Chief Justice to make an elevation of a house 46 feet long with a colonnade. (Ontario, Department of Lands and Forests, Surveyors' Diaries, Notebook no. 121, William Chewett's Diary of Survey from June 3, 1793.)

[23]Probably Christopher Robinson (1763–98) who was with Governor Simcoe in the spring and summer of 1793. He was born in Virginia, joined the Queen's Rangers in 1781, and was demobilized in New Brunswick. In 1792 he come to Upper Canada, settling at Kingston and practising law. In 1793 he was appointed Deputy Surveyor General of the Woods and Reserves of Upper Canada. He moved to York in 1798 and died a few months later. He was the father of John Beverley Robinson. In 1795 Peter Russell bought Robinson's house and lot in York, then occupied by Berczy.

p[repar]ations for erecting a small back House—His E. makes much difficulty about granting either the Town or Farm Lots . . . H.E. has fallen so much in love with the land—that he intends to reserve from population the whole front from the Town to the Fort—a space of nearly three Miles—so that if we ever have a Town on this Principle, it must be fed from the Bay of Quinti instead of its fertile Neighbourhood. The Air on the opposite side is clear & healthy, & a hard Sand of several Miles to ride or drive a Carriage on. . . .

A 10 MINUTES OF EXECUTIVE COUNCIL

[*Public Archives of Canada (P.A.C.), Upper Canada Land Book C, pp. 324–9*]

At the Council Chamber, York (late Toronto) Upper Canada Monday September 2nd 1793

Present

His Excellency John Graves Simcoe, Esquire, Lieutenant General &ca &ca &ca

The Honorable William Osgoode, Chief Justice
The Honorable Peter Russell

The Deputy Surveyors[24] attended, and produced Maps and Surveys of the Town and Township of York, which were ordered to be laid on the Table.

Resolved that the two Center Squares, Front Lots of the proposed City of York, shall be at present reserved together with eight Lots of Two hundred Acres each, immediately behind the aforesaid Town Lots.

The following Petitions[25] for Lands in the Township of York, &c, were read Vizt

. . .

Messrs. Cozens[26] (Brothers) Praying for several Lots in the Township of York, and a Town Lot.

[24]Alexander Aitkin (d. 1799), Deputy Surveyor for Mecklenburg and the Midland District, surveyed York in the summer of 1793. His plan of the town consisted of 10 blocks bounded by George Street, Duke Street, Berkeley (now Parliament) Street, and Palace (now Front) Street. Aitkin was buried at Kingston on January 1, 1800.

[25]Only petitions for town lots have been printed. The following petitioned and received grants in the Township of York: John Scadding, John Cox, Frederick Brown, F. Willoughby Willard, George and Benjamin Mosley, John Matthews, Paul Wilcott, Jonathan Wilcott, John Ashbridge, Jonathan Ashbridge, Parker Mills, James McDonald, Andrew and James Hunter, John Coon, John and Thomas Hewitt, John Stoner, Joseph Dainty, St. J. B. Rousseau, Abraham Larroway, and Joseph Burk.

[26]There were a number of Cozens in early York. The father was Captain Daniel Cozens (d. 1801) who came from near Philadelphia and was a captain in the New Jersey Volunteers through the American Revolution. His sons included Samuel D. Cozens (d. 1808), who resigned a position in the Provincial Secretary's office in 1801; Joshua Y. Cozens, who was active in land speculation on the Grand

Ordered that they do receive No. 6, first Concession; No. 16—Second ditto; No. 24 and 25 fourth ditto; and a back Town Lot.

. . .

John Phillips[27] Praying for his Lands as a Loyalist amounting to 100 acres.

Ordered that he may receive the above quantity of Land in a back Concession and a Town Lot—Half No. 1, third Concession granted to him.

David Ramsay[28]Praying for a Town Lot and two hundred Acres.

Ordered that he may receive a Town Lot and 200 Acres near the Lake, or some River in the Township.—No. 2, first Concession, granted to him.

Mr. Christopher Robinson—praying for a Town Lot and 200 Acres.

Ordered that he receive a Town Lot in the back corner of One of the Front Squares, and No. 13 second Concession.

Magnus Swanson[29]—Praying for a Town Lot and 200 Acres.

Ordered that he may receive a Town Lot and 200 acres in a back Concession,—No. 13 third Concession, granted to him.

Mr. George Leith[30] praying for a Front Town Lot.

Ordered that he may receive the same.

. . .

John Henry Kahmann[31] for Two Town Lots.

Ordered that he do receive one.

Capt. J. B. Bouchette[32] (Naval Department) praying for a Front Lot for himself, and a back Town Lot for his Son, with the Land formerly

---

River, Benjamin Cozens, who carried on a tailoring business in partnership with one Richards in 1800 and was High Constable of York and Clerk of the Market; Daniel Cozens Junior; Jacob Cozens (b. 1766?); and Shivers Cozens (b. 1777?), who returned to New Jersey. The petitioners here are probably Samuel, Joshua, Daniel, and Benjamin, since they joined in other petitions in 1796 and 1799. (Petitions for Land Grants, 1796–9, Ontario Historical Society, *Papers and Records*, XXVI, 1934, pp. 141–3.)

[27]John Phillips served in Sir John Johnson's Regiment during the American Revolution.

[28]David Ramsay served in the Royal Navy at the reduction of Quebec and Louisbourg, and during the remainder of the war on private armed vessels. He served on Lake Ontario in 1764–5.

[29]In 1797 Lot no. 13, third concession, was declared vacant because of non-fulfilment of settlement duties.

[30]George Leith was a prominent Detroit merchant and one of the original settlers at Malden.

[31]John Henry Kahman (d. 1810) was listed in the supplementary list of loyalists as said to have been a sergeant in Colonel Creutzberg's Chasseurs. He was government blacksmith at York. On August 12, 1800, his property at the south-east corner of Duke and Princess Streets was to be sold in a sheriff's sale, at the suit of Samuel Heron. At his death on December 7, 1810, he was blacksmith to the Indian Department at York.

[32]Jean Baptiste Bouchette (1736–1804) served in the Canadian militia during the Seven Years War. He served in the Provincial Marine from 1777 and was commander of naval forces on Lake Ontario from 1794, with headquarters at Point Frederick. He was the father of Joseph Bouchette.

granted to him at Toronto, by the Honorable the Executive Council of this Province.

Ordered that he may receive Two Town Lots (One in Front) and 100 Acres in No. 24, first Concession, exclusive of the Land heretofore granted him by the Council,—and No. 29, second Concession 200 Acres, in part of the Land granted to him.

. . .

Samuel Heron[33]—praying for a Town Lot and Two hundred Acres.

Ordered that he may receive a back Town Lot.

William Smith[34]—praying for a Town Lot and 200 Acres.

Ordered that he may receive a back Town Lot, and No. 11 in the Third Concession.

. . .

Patrick Burn[35] praying for a Town Lot.

Ordered that he receive a back Town Lot.

Joseph King praying for permission to Build a Ferry Boat, and for a Lot of Land near the Water—

Ordered that there exists no objection to his building a large Boat of any description, for any legal purposes, and that he may receive a back Town Lot.

Peter Benville[36] praying for a Town Lot, and two hundred Acres;—and —Edward Gahan[37] for 200 Acres.

Granted for 100 Acres each to be in No. 4 first Concession the First—and No. 4 Second Concession.

. . .

William Demont[38] praying for a Town Lot and 200 Acres in part of His Majesty's Bounty as a Loyalist.

Granted the Land to be allotted to him in One of the back Concessions Viz: No. 2 third Concession.

[33]Samuel Heron (1770–1817) was born at Kirkcudbright, Scotland, emigrating to New York City, then to Niagara, and finally to York. In 1794 he married Sarah Ashbridge. He became a merchant in 1796, with a shop on King Street and a house on Duke Street, importing his goods from Montreal. In 1800 he was an unsuccessful candidate for Parliament. He subsequently settled on a farm near Hogg's Hollow, where he erected a sawmill, gristmill, potashery, and distillery.

[34]William Smith (d. 1819) was born in Nottinghamshire, England, and went to Cape Breton Island in 1774. He came to Niagara in 1792, spent the summer of 1793 in York, and moved his family to Lot 15 on the Don River in the spring of 1794. He was a builder and was responsible for many of the early buildings in York.

[35]Patrick Burn (Burns) settled in York Township, Lot no. 4, east side of the Don River, first concession, and raised a large family.

[36]Peter Benville (b. 1768?) was born in Quebec. In 1790 he entered the Marine Department on Lake Ontario.

[37]Edward Gahan (b. 1756?) was born in Waterford, Ireland. He entered the Marine Department on Lake Ontario in 1790 and was a boatswain.

[38]Captain William Demont (d. 1810) was apparently not a reputable citizen. Mr. Justice Thorpe was severely criticized for his intimacy with him. In 1799 Demont posted several advertisements in York, for which he apologized in the *Upper Canada Gazette* of May 11, 1799. He was the Worshipful Master of Rawdon Lodge, the first Masonic body in York.

Bemsley Peters[39] praying for a back Town Lot and 200 Acres in part of His Majesty's Bounty as a Loyalist.

Granted the Land in a back Concession Viz. No. 3 third Concession.

. . .

Mr. Joseph Forsyth[40] praying for a Front Town Lot.

Granted.

Mr. Jonathan Sills[41] praying for a Front Town Lot.

Granted.

Mr. William Willcocks[42] praying for a Front Town Lot.

Granted, and No. 15 first Concession, 100 Acres, and Half No. 24 second Concession, with his Son—

Mr. Charles Willcocks[43] praying for a Front Town Lot.

Granted, and No. 13 first Concession, 100 Acres, and Half No. 24, Second Concession with his Father (they having an Order of Council for the same).

Ordered that Mr. Aitkin Deputy Surveyor be directed to point out the Lots Granted to the several Petitioners herein mentioned, and to acquaint them, that, it is expected the same be immediately located.

Adjourned

(signed) E: B: Littlehales

A 11 Minutes of Executive Council

[*P.A.C., Upper Canada Land Book C, pp. 322–4*]

At the Council Chamber, York (late Toronto) Wednesday September 4th, 1793

Present

His Excellency John Graves Simcoe, Esquire, Lieutenant Governor &c &c

The Honorable William Osgoode, Chief Justice,
The Honorable Peter Russell

39Bemsley (Bensley) Peters (d. 1798) with other associated Loyalists first petitioned for lands at Toronto on October 13, 1792. He was buried at Kingston, October 4, 1798.

40Joseph Forsyth (1764–1813) was a prominent Kingston merchant.

41Probably a member of the Loyalist family of that name, in Fredericksburg.

42William Willcocks (1736–1813) was a first cousin of Peter Russell. Coming to Upper Canada from Cork, Ireland, in 1792, he petitioned for a township for himself and associates and was provisionally granted Whitby Township for settlement. In 1793 he returned to Ireland for settlers, was elected Mayor of Cork, 1793–4, and returned to Upper Canada in 1795. He was unable to fulfil his obligations in Whitby which was taken from him in 1797. He became an early merchant in York and was the first postmaster. Latterly, he was particularly interested in his property at Millbrook, Markham Township. His daughter, Phoebe, married Dr. William Warren Baldwin in 1803.

43Charles Willcocks (1762–1826) was the only son of William Willcocks. He came to Upper Canada with his sisters in 1797 and is mainly known for his difficulties with his distant kinsman Joseph Willcocks.

The following Petitions for Land in the Town and Township of York were Read and Granted

The Honorable William Osgoode, Chief Justice—
A Front Town Lot and No. 5 first Concession (100 Acres) and No. 26 in the Third Concession (200 Acres)

Peter Russell, Esquire, Receiver General—
A Front Town Lot and No. 14 first Concession (100 Acres) and No. 23 in the Second and Third Concession (400 Acres)

John White, Esquire, Attorney General—
A Front Town Lot and No. 4 first Concession (100 Acres)

John Small,[44] Esquire, Clerk of the Council—
A Front Town Lot and No. 3 first Concession (100 Acres)

William Jarvis,[45] Esquire, Secretary and Register—
A Front Town Lot and No. 2 first Concession (100 Acres)

Edward Baker Littlehales, Esquire—
A Front Town Lot and No. 1 first Concession (100 Acres)

David William Smith,[46] Esquire, Acting Surveyor General—
A Front Town Lot and No. 6 first Concession (100 Acres)

John McGill,[47] Esquire, His Majesty's Commissary, &c.—&c—
A Front Town Lot and No. 7 first Concession (100 Acres)

Mr. Justice Powell[48]—
A Front Town Lot and No. 11 first Concession (100 Acres)

The other Judge (not yet appointed)—
A Front Town Lot and No. 12 first Concession (100 Acres)

Solicitor General (not yet appointed)—
A Front Town Lot and No. 26 first Concession (100 Acres)

Incumbent—
A Front Town Lot and No. 9 first Concession (100 Acres)

[44]John Small (1746–1831) was born in Gloucestershire and came to Canada in 1792. He was Clerk of the Executive Council from 1793 until his death.

[45]William Jarvis (1756–1817) was born in Connecticut. He entered the Queen's Rangers in 1782 and came to Upper Canada with Simcoe as Provincial Secretary, a post he held until his death.

[46]David William Smith (Smyth) (1764–1837) was the son of Lieutenant Colonel John Smith. He joined the 5th Regiment of Foot in 1779 and in 1792 became Deputy Quartermaster General at Niagara. In September, 1792, he was appointed Acting Surveyor General of Upper Canada, and in 1800 Surveyor General. In 1792, 1796, and 1800 he was elected a member of the House of Assembly of which he was chosen Speaker in 1797 and again in 1801. In 1798 he was appointed Lieutenant of the County of York. He returned to England in 1802 and was created a baronet in 1821.

[47]John McGill (1752–1834) emigrated from Scotland to Virginia in 1773. He fought with the Queen's Rangers in the American Revolution and afterwards settled in New Brunswick. He came to Upper Canada in 1792 as Commissary of Stores and Provisions. In 1801 he became Inspector General, and in 1814 Receiver General.

[48]William Dummer Powell (1755–1834) was born in Boston and came to Canada in 1779. He practised law in Montreal, was appointed Judge of the Court of Common Pleas at Detroit in 1789, and a puisne Judge in the Court of King's Bench in 1794. In 1816 he became Chief Justice.

Major Smith—
A Front Town Lot and No. 27 first Concession (100 Acres)
Captain Shank[49]—
A Front Town Lot and No. 21 first Concession (100 Acres) No. 26 Second Concession and No. 27 Third Concession (400 Acres)
Captain Samuel Smith (Queen's Rangers)[50]—
A Town Lot and No. 22 first Concession (100 Acres); No. 27 Second Concession and No. 28 Third Concession (400 Acres)
Capt. Æneas Shaw[51]—
A Town Lot and No. 20 first Concssion (100 Acres) No. 28 Second Concession, and No. 29 Third Concession (400 Acres)
Captain Spencer (Queen's Rangers)[52]—
A Town Lot and No. 23 first Concession (100 Acres) No. 30 Second Concession (200 Acres)
David Burns,[53] Esquire, Clerk of the Crown—
A Town Lot and No. 25 first Concession (100 Acres)
James McCauley,[54] Esquire, His Majesty's Surgeon of Upper Canada—
A Town Lot and No. 10 first Concession (100 Acres)
Mr. Robert Richardson[55]—
A Town Lot and No. 31 Second Concession (200 Acres)

[49]David Shank (d. 1831) was a Scotsman who settled as a merchant in Virginia. From 1777 he served in the Queen's Rangers through the Revolution, returning to England in 1783. With the reorganized Rangers he came to Canada in 1792 and was the senior officer in the corps next to Simcoe. He returned to England in 1799. In 1803 he obtained permission to raise a regiment in Lower Canada, called the Canadian Fencibles.

[50]Samuel Smith (1756–1826) was born on Long Island, New York, and served in the Queen's Rangers during the Revolution. In 1783 he settled in New Brunswick and came to Upper Canada with the reorganization of the Rangers. He was Administrator of the government from June, 1817, to August, 1818, and again for four months in 1820.

[51]Æneas Shaw (d. 1815) was born in Scotland and served in the Queen's Rangers during the Revolution. In 1792 he came up from New Brunswick with Samuel Smith, Adjutant McGill, two other officers, and seven recruits on snowshoes to Quebec to join Simcoe. He was a member of the Legislative and Executive Councils, and in 1811 was gazetted a major general. During the War of 1812 he was Adjutant General of the Militia.

[52]George Spencer was a lieutenant serving in the 73rd Regiment when he was nominated for a commission in the reorganized Rangers by Simcoe. He was a master of the Spanish language.

[53]David Burns (d. 1806) served in the Revolution as surgeon of the 71st Regiment. Recommended to Simcoe by Sir A. Campbell, he was appointed surgeon to the Independent Companies of the Rangers and Clerk of the Crown and Common Pleas. Of intemperate habits, he died in York in 1806.

[54]James Macaulay (1759–1822) was born in Scotland, served as surgeon in the 33rd Regiment, and resigned the surgeoncy of the Botany Bay Corps to come to Upper Canada with Simcoe. He became Deputy Inspector General of Hospitals. When the Medical Board of Upper Canada was formed in 1819, he was the first President, a position he held until his death.

[55]Robert Richardson (d. 1832) was born in Scotland and came to Upper Canada as surgeon's mate in the Queen's Rangers, with which regiment he served at Queenston, York, and St. Joseph's Island, as surgeon's mate and assistant

Ensign & Adjutant McGill[56]—
A Town Lot and No. 25 Second Concession (200 Acres)
Mr. Donald McDonell—
A Front Town Lot
Sarah Cranford—
A Town Lot
George Playter,[57] Esquire—
A Front Town Lot, and No. 8 first Concession (100 Acres) No. 20 Second Concession (200 Acres) and No. 3 Second Concession (200 Acres)

. . .

Thomas Ridout[58]—
A Town Lot and No. 31, Third Concession, in part of the land he is entitled to, by Order of Council.

. . .

Adjourned

(Signed) E: B: Littlehales

A 12 RUSSELL TO JOHN GRAY,[59] MONTREAL
[*P.A.O., Russell Papers*]

Niagara, September 16, 1793

. . . I have now the pleasure to tell you that I am charmed with the Situation of the proposed City of York in the Bay of Toronto, & the fertility of the Country round it—Both which for Beauty, safety, & Convenience, exceeds every thing the most partial & prejudical wishes can form—The Bay is about 2½ Miles deep & 1¼ broad at the Mouth, formed by the Mainland on the North and a number of Sandy Peninsulas

---

surgeon. After the Rangers were disbanded, he became surgeon of the garrison at Amherstburg and Judge of the Court of Common Pleas, Western District. He was surgeon of the Provincial Marine on Lake Erie, 1812–13, when he was taken prisoner. His wife was the second daughter of John Askin, merchant and fur trader of Detroit and Amherstburg.

[56]Adjutant John McGill entered the British army about 1768, became a warrant officer about 1780, and served in the 40th and 16th Regiments. He became Ensign and Adjutant in the Queen's Rangers at its reorganization. He is often confused with Commissary John McGill. He is probably the John McGill who was later a captain in the Canadian Fencible Infantry under Lieutenant Colonel David Shank.

[57]George Playter (1736–1822) was born at Wapping on the Thames, Surrey, and emigrated to New Jersey, where he married Elizabeth Welding, a Quaker, in 1765. He was a Loyalist and lived in Kingston briefly before coming to York, where he lived on west side of the Don River above Castle Frank. He had a large family and many descendants.

[58]Thomas Ridout (1754–1829) was born in Sherborne, England, and emigrated to Maryland in 1774. He was captured by Indians in 1787 and brought to Canada. He was employed in the Commissariat and Surveyor General's Office, and in 1810 was appointed Surveyor General. He represented Simcoe, Durham, and the east riding of York in the House of Assembly from 1812 to 1816.

[59]John Gray (d. 1829) was a prominent Montreal merchant, who became first president of the Bank of Montreal, 1817–20.

on the South, which by a gradual Sweep join the Main land in the East—The Channel at the Entrance into this Bay is about a Quarter of a Mile over having nearly four fathoms on the Bar & deepining to six & upwards as you advance It lies nearer to the Main than the opposite point—on which there is a very secure Situation for Batteries & an inclosed work to Cover them—This with a corresponding Battery on the opposite Bank (25 feet high) will not only effectually protect the Entrance from any hostile naval attempt; but perfectly scour every part of the Bay should Boats with Troops happen to pass into it. Amongst these sandy Peninsulas are also excellent Coves for the reception of small Craft—& Wharfs may be run out from them into deep water where vessels may lie in the Winter free from all Injury by the Ice—Here is likewise an excellent Situation for building of Vessels, the Wood for which may be supplied in the greatest abundance from the neighbouring Shores—The Town is to be on the north side of the Bottom of this Bay—on a gentle Slope to the Water but elevated from it about ten feet—The Houses of the front Row are to be built on a uniform plan with a Colonade in front, & will have a Commanding View of every part of this beautifull Bason—Boats may now run up dry to the Center of the Town—but Wharfs may without much Expence be run out to eight feet Water for the landing of Stores Merchandize &c—Close to the Town on the East runs the River Don—abounding with Trout, Bass, Salmon & many other excellent fish & having a descent sufficient for working all sorts of Mills—About Six Miles to the West of this lies the River Humber—navigable for two Miles to the Falls—This River is about 100 yards across— & confined between abrupt & Steep Banks from two to three hundred feet high—formed of Sand Hills covered with tall Pines, Hemlock & Cedar, the ridges of which are so narrow in many places as scarcely to admit a foot path—And these Hills, which assume a variety of whimsical Shapes, cover nearly two Miles of the Country to the East of this River—The land then grows gradually better —& increases in goodness of Soil & Timber until you come to the Town from which it slopes away to fine Meadows—which are however at too great a distance to affect the health of the place, which I have no doubt will be found very salubrious . . .

A 13 MRS. WILLIAM JARVIS[60] TO THE REV. SAMUEL PETERS,[61] LONDON

[*P.A.C., William Jarvis Papers*]

Newark Septr 25 1793—

. . . The Governor & Family are gone to Toronto (now York) where it is said they Winter—and a Part of the Regiment—they have or had not four days since a Hut to Shelter them from the Weather—in Tents—

[60]Hannah Owen Peters married William Jarvis in 1785.

[61]Rev. Samuel Peters (1735–1826) was born in Connecticut, graduated from Yale, and in 1759 was ordained a priest in the Protestant Episcopal Church. He served at Hebron, Conn., until 1774 when his Loyalist sympathies forced him

no means of Warming themselves, but in Bowers made of the Limbs of Trees—thus fare the Regiment—the Governor has two Canvas Houses there . . . Every Body are sick at York—but no matter—the Lady likes the Place—therefore every one else must—Money is a God *many* worship . . .

A 14 Russell to Sir Henry Clinton[62]

[*University of Michigan, William L. Clements Library, Clinton Papers*]

Niagara September 29th. 1793

. . . You will unquestionably be surprised to hear that very little further progress has been as yet made in the Settlement of this Province. To what Cause this is owing I cannot presume to say for it must be acknowledged that the Governor by no means spares himself. He accompanied his Regiment to Toronto about two months since, with a view of expediting the Establishment of a Town on that Side of the Lake, and I was not a little disappointed, when I went there three weeks ago to attend a Council, to observe that not a House had been begun nor even a Hut built for covering the Troops in the Winter—yet there he is determined to remain with Mrs. Simcoe & the Children without other Accommodation than his two Canvas Houses & a Hut or two that may be probably added to them—and I am very sorry to say that he appears greatly broken & low spirited, tho he does not seem at all sensible of it himself. The Situation of Toronto (now York) is delightfull & promises to be healthy. The Town is to occupy the Bottom of a fine Bay three Miles deep & one Mile & a quarter across at the Entrance. The Channel, which inclines somewhat to the North Shore, is about 300 yards Wide & three fathoms Deep on the Bar, & is entirely under the Command of the Batteries on either Side—that to the South is formed by a Number of Sandy Peninsulas—on any one of which may be thrown up an impregnable Fortress to Secure the Post & cover a Naval Arsenal & Dock for which they are peculiarly suited; and the Continent to the North furnishes several commanding Eminences for Batteries. The Chief Advantages that recommend an Establishment at this place are, its being a Naval Station perfectly hors dInsult from any Attempt of the American States, should a War ever break out between us—and its Neighbourhood to the Forks of the la Tranche [Thames River] and the Waters that fall into Lake la Clé, (now Simcoe) from whence there is a direct free navigable Communication with Lake Huron & consequently with the Upper Lakes & Detroit—Whereas the States must make the Circuit of Lake Erie & work thro that Strait against

to withdraw to England. He was recommended by Simcoe for the bishopric of Upper Canada, without success. In 1805 he returned to the United States. He was the father of Mrs. William Jarvis and William Birdseye Peters.

[62] Sir Henry Clinton (1738?–95) was a British general who served in the American Revolution and was Commander in Chief in America 1778–81. Peter Russell served as his assistant secretary in America.

the Current of several Rapids to meet us there. The Negotiation for Peace between the States & the Indians is broken off—the former having refused to admit the Ohio to be the Boundary of their respective Territories, and the latter insisting on their Acquiescence previous to their meeting the American Commissioners in Council. Joseph Brandt[63] at the Head of the Six Nations dissented from the Western Indians on this Point & withdrew in consequence from their Councils—He now declares them to be neutral, & imputes the failure of the Treaty to the Intrigues of the English, in opposition to the asseverations of Colo. McKee[64] (our agent) who avers that he did every thing in his Power to accommodate matters & induce a parity of Sentiment among the Indian Nations. But should a renewal of the War be the Consequence I fear it will be impossible for the Six Nations to preserve their Neutrality—as it is highly probable they will be attacked for their defection by the Western Indians, and in that Case, as this part of the Province is exactly in the War Path, we have no small reason to apprehend its being laid waste & depopulated. Now Toronto is wholly out of the way of these Evils, is perfectly defensible against all Enemies in front, and has its rear well covered by a large Body of friendly Chippewas who are settled behind it; it has moreover a free Communication within land with lower Canada, by which we may easily fall back if hard pressed. All which plead strongly for an immediate Establishment there—I fear however that no Efforts of ours will be able to accomplish so desirable an Event unless Great Britain should incline to assist us very considerably in Artificers &c &c, which might perhaps be thought to cost more Money than this distant inland Province may be worth. . . .

A 15 DORCHESTER[65] TO SIMCOE
[*P.A.O., Simcoe Papers*]

Quebec 7th October, 1793

. . . I am also to desire you will inform me of the progress of Population and Agriculture on the North side of those Lakes, and how near they approach Toronto; the settling and cultivating the Country round

[63]Joseph Brant (1742–1807), principal chief of the Six Nations Indians, fought on the British side in the Revolution and after the war led the Mohawks to a new settlement on the Grand River.

[64]Alexander McKee (d. 1799), born in Pennsylvania, was deputy agent for Indian affairs at Fort Pitt before the Revolution. Of Loyalist sympathies, he escaped to Detroit in 1778 and became Deputy Superintendent General of Indian affairs.

[65]Sir Guy Carleton, first Baron Dorchester (1724–1808), first came to Canada as Wolfe's Quartermaster General. He was appointed Lieutenant Governor of Quebec in 1766 and was Governor from 1768 to 1778. In 1782 he became Commander in Chief of the British forces in North America, and from 1786 to 1796 was Governor in Chief of British North America. He disagreed with Simcoe over a number of questions, including the choice of capital; Dorchester preferred Kingston and was opposed to the development of York.

that Post, must facilitate and bring forward every advantage its situation can afford, and well deserves encouragement: prior thereto every attempt must be attended with difficulty; in laying out the Town I shall advise the System of wide Streets and Squares with Open Angles; but more especially that the Ground which Captain Mann[66] recommends for Public Works and Batteries be reserved; all which are marked on Mr. Collins's[67] Plan, a Copy of which I understand you have taken with you. I think it necessary to make these Reservations, tho' I cannot approve of any Fortifications being erected there at present. . . .

A 16 RUSSELL TO ALEXANDER DAVISON[68]
[*P.A.O., Russell Papers*]

Niagara 11th October, 1793

. . . Colonel Simcoe & family remain still with his Regiment at Toronto (now called York) and I much fear he is determined to Spend the Winter there—The Chief Justice & I are here, as there is no accommodations whatsoever at York for our Reception—We were both there about five weeks since to attend an Executive Council—and I was greatly pleased with the beauty & Defensibility of the Situation—as well as the apparent fertility of the Soil—But it is impossible to say how soon the Town & Country round it may be sufficiently inhabited to warrant the removal of the public offices thither—and I flatter myself His Excellency will not think of doing it before—for the high price of every necessary even here almost ruins us—they must be consequently double there for years to come . . .

A 17 RICHARD CARTWRIGHT[69] TO ISAAC TODD[70]
[*Queen's University, Douglas Library, Cartwright Letter Books*]

Kingston October 14th 1793

. . . The Governor is at present at Toronto where he has laid out

[66]Gother Mann (1747–1830) entered the army in 1763. In 1785–91 and 1794–1804 he was in command of the Royal Engineers in Canada. He made a plan of York in 1788, based on Aitkin's plan of the same year. The fort was placed near the site of Stanley Barracks, and the town plot lay roughly between Spadina and Toronto Streets, extending north to about Gerrard Street. The Collins plan of 1788 moved the town farther west and north. Simcoe apparently did not have access to all of these plans, and wrote in some mystification to Dorchester about them. (*Infra*, A 19.)

[67]John Collins (d. 1795) came to Canada in 1759 and was appointed Deputy Surveyor General in 1764. In 1787 he represented the Crown in the Toronto purchase from the Mississaugas at the Carrying Place on the Bay of Quinte, and in 1788 he surveyed the Toronto area and drew a plan of the proposed town.

[68]Alexander Davison (1750–1829) was a wealthy government contractor and friend of Lord Nelson.

[69]Richard Cartwright (1759–1815) was born in Albany and came to Upper Canada as a Loyalist. He lived at Kingston and was one of the foremost merchants of his day.

[70]Isaac Todd (1743?–1819) was a Montreal merchant and partner of James

a Town Plot which he has called York, and where I am told he intends to pass the Winter in his Canvas House, for there is yet no other built, nor Preparations for any, his Regiment is also to hut themselves there; This Situation for the Capital unites many Advantages, as it will contribute to the more speedy Settling of the vacant Lands on both Sides of it, and be a means of sooner uniting the Settlements above the Bay of Kenty, & below the Head of Lake Ontario; and also as it lays at the Entrance of a Communication into Lake Huron by Lake La Claye [Simcoe] which may bye and bye be found practicable and useful. But notwithstanding this he does not scruple to say that he has his Eye fixed on the River Tranch [Thames]; and tho' he may for a while put up with the Town of York, and the River Humber, he seems determined to be satisfied with nothing less than another Thames & a second London.—You will smile perhaps when I tell you that even at York, a Town Lot is to be granted in the Front Street only on Condition that you shall build a House of not less than 47 Feet Front, two Stories High & after a certain Order of Architecture; in the second Street they may be somewhat less in Front, but the two Stories & mode of Architecture is indispensible; and it is only in the back Streets and Allies that the Tinkers and Taylors will be allowed to consult their own Taste and Circumstances in the Structure of their Habitations upon Lots of 1/10 of an Acre. Seriously our good Governor is a little wild in his projects. . . .

A 18 Mrs. Jarvis to the Rev. Samuel Peters
[*P.A.C. William Jarvis Papers*]

Newark November, 13th 1793

. . . I mentioned that the Governor & Family with the Regiment were to spend the Winter at Toronto (now York) in my last—the Gun-Boat has arrived from there this Day and they are still in Camp—A Storm a few nights since blew over the Marqué of the Honorable Captn Lieutent Shaw, which left his Lady & seven Children exposed to the Rude eliments of Wind & Rain.—Major Littlehales with all his Papers & others shared the same fate—Mrs. Simcoe is in no want of a *fashionable Pad* . . . Captn McGill Commissary has received orders to join the Governor and remain the Winter—he has a Wife & sister and an Infant Daughter of five Weeks, who he is obliged to leave at Navy Hall—till he returns or they can follow . . . We are now situated thus—the Govr at York—the Chief Justice, the Attny Gl. the Receiver Gl., the Secretary, at Lincoln & Newark—the Acting Surveyor General at Niagara Fort—thus our Government is to spend the Winter at respectable distances. . .

McGill. He was one of the original partners in the North West Company, but withdrew in 1784 to trade in the Mississippi and Lake Michigan areas.

A 19 SIMCOE TO DORCHESTER
[*P.A.O., Simcoe Papers*]

York Decemr. 2nd 1793

. . . In respect to the progress of population & Agriculture on the North Side of the Lakes, and how near they approach to Toronto, on which Your Lordship desires to be informed, I beg to observe that in the course of this Year many Grants have been made by the Council of this Province in strict adherence to His Majesty's Instructions; but that in general few Emigrations have taken place, nor from the distance which the Persons who have applied for Grants have to convey their families could reasonably be presumed to take place, untill the ensuing Summer—

The Settlement of this Place whether it becomes the Capital of the Province or not will be attended with no difficulty, nor dependant on a continued and thin chain of Settlements between it and the Bay of Quinté. The soil between this and Lake aux Claies (now Simcoe) is perfectly calculated for farming, and before the summer the Road of Communication will probably be thickly settled—Thirty families are now on the Eve of being located in its Vicinity, and there is but little doubt but that by this Communication the North West Company will supply themselves with many of their heavy Articles instead of by the circuitous Rout of Lake Erie—The Inhabitants will soon raise abundance of Provisions, in the mean time they can procure them at a cheaper rate from the Bay of Quinté than they are to be met with at Niagara—The Rivers and Bays abound with Salmon, and the descent from the Higth of Land which separates the Lakes, being gradual, there are but few Swamps, and the Climate appears to be remarkably fine.—

The Town of York has been directed to be laid out on the personal Inspection of the Council, as appeared to them in the most proper manner and situation, and the whole Shore from the River Humber (St. Johns Creek) has been reserved for the Crown, including every spot that may be proper for Batteries, not only with that View, but that such Persons whose occupations and Employments ought to render them the Inhabitants of a Town, might of necessity be confined to the most eligible situation—And by their Condensation facilitate the growth of the Commerce and of the Power of the Province—

But I must observe that no reserves for Military purposes have been marked on any Plan I ever received from Mr. Collins—Mr. Aitkin the Deputy Surveyor will have the honor of conveying to Your Lordship a Survey of this place, and he is well qualified to give you any information which you may require.—

I am truly sorry that Your Lordship does not approve of any Fortifications being at present erected at this most defensible and important Spot. . . .

A 20 SIMCOE TO COMMITTEE OF THE PRIVY COUNCIL FOR TRADE AND PLANTATIONS
[*P.A.O., Simcoe Papers*]

Upper Canada
Kingston Decr. 20
1794

. . . Having stated to Mr. Secretary Dundas[71] the great importance which I attached to York (late Toronto) & received his directions to give due encouragement to that Settlement, It is with great pleasure that I am to observe that *Seventy families* at least are Settling in its vicinity, & principally on the Communication between York & Holland River, which falls into Lake Simcoe (La Clie, Shenyong or Oenteronk). . . .

A 21 LITTLEHALES TO MAJOR DODGSON,[72] COMMANDING AT KINGSTON
[*P.A.O., Simcoe Papers*]

Navy Hall, July 19th, 1795.

Major Smith of the Queen's Rangers has His Excellency Lt Governor Simcoe's permission to obtain from Kingston a certain quantity of Flour, not exceeding twenty Barrels, for the use of the Soldiers wives and Children of his Company, which is to be forwarded to York in any of His Majesty's Vessels bound to that post and Major Smith is directed to inform his Correspondent at Kingston thereof—

A 22 SIMCOE TO THE DUKE OF PORTLAND[73]
[*P.A.O., Simcoe Papers*]

York, Upper Canada,
Feby 27th 1796.

. . . I have given information to the Civil officers of Government that *York*, for the present, is to become the Seat of Government, & in consequence, I am preparing to erect such Buildings as may be necessary for the future meeting of the Legislature; the plan I have adopted is, to consider a future Government House, as a Center, & to construct the *Wings* as temporary Offices for the legislature, purposing that so soon as the Province has sufficient Funds to erect its own Public Buildings, that They may be removed elsewhere.

[71]Henry Dundas (1742–1811) was Home Secretary from 1791 until the summer of 1794. Colonial affairs were administered by the Home Office from 1782 to 1801.

[72]Major Richard Dodgson of the 60th Regiment commanded at Kingston from 1795 to 1798.

[73]William Henry Cavendish Bentinck, third Duke of Portland (1738–1809), succeeded Dundas as Home Secretary in 1794, which post he held until 1801.

But should the seat of Government be ultimately established on the River Thames as in my opinion every public Consideration & the Kings Service requires, the *Wings* now erecting together with the Lands appropriated for the Government House, may be hereafter sold,[74] so as materially to lessen if not to liquidate the Sums expended in their Construction. . . .

A 23 CIRCULAR LETTER FROM LITTLEHALES TO RUSSELL, JARVIS, D. W. SMITH, AND D. BURNS
[*P.A.O., Simcoe Papers*]

York, 28 Febr. 1796

I have the honour to signify to you His Excellency, the Lieut. Governor's directions, that immediately upon the conclusion of the ensuing meeting of the Provincial Parliament, you will be pleased to remove your office to York, the present Seat of this Government.

A 24 SIMCOE TO RUSSELL
[*P.A.O., Simcoe Papers*]

York
March 19th [1796]

. . . I must beg of you to turn your thoughts to proper regulations to be made & finally adopted relative to York. Its magistracy or police, & its uniformity in building. Mr Shaw seems to be of opinion that the front Blocks should admit of a further extension, & only be divided into two Houses, instead of three; I can have no objection to this or any other Arrangement that may promote the comfort of the Inhabitants or the Beauty of the town—do with Mr Smith & Mr White turn these matters in your thoughts; it may be the subject of conversation on your part; or of your Pen perhaps if not otherwise employed.

A 25 MINUTES OF EXECUTIVE COUNCIL AND YORK REPORT
[*P.A.C., Upper Canada State Book A, pp. 332–75*]

Council held at the Garrison at York April 6 1796—
Present—
His Excellency The Lieut. Governor
The Honble. Peter Russell
The Honble. Æneas Shaw—

His Excellency The Lieut. Governor requests the attention of the Honble. the Executive Council to ye carrying into execution such

[74]In a letter written the same day to Bishop Mountain of Quebec, Simcoe suggests that the building for the House of Assembly could be made a church "should as I hope for the Kings interest the seat of Government be only temporary at this place." (Quebec Diocesan Archives, Series C, vol. I, p. 75; printed in *Simcoe Correspondence*, ed. Cruikshank, V, 264.)

Measures as may seem proper to be taken to promote the Speedy Establishment and welfare of the Town of York, its Vicinity and Dependencies.—It seems necessary to premise that the Lieutenant Governor having represented the Importance of the Harbour of York, or Toronto, to Mr. Secretary Dundas, that Gentleman was pleased to agree with him in opinion.

The Lieutenant Governor having also communicated to Mr. Secretary Dundas the general "Plan of the Townships to be granted in future, together with the Exceptions proposed to be made at York, received Mr. Dundas's observations thereon, which will be laid before the Council for their Information.

This Statement will clearly appear to the Honourable the Council by the following Extracts from the Lieutenant Governor's Letters to Mr. Dundas, & his reply thereto—

Extracts of a Dispatch from Lieut Governor Simcoe, To the Right Honble Henry Dundas, one of His Majestys Principal Secretaries of State, &c &c &c. dated York the 16 September 1793,—

I do myself the honour of transmitting to You, the general Plan for the arrangements of future Townships in this Province, which the Executive Council have directed to be carried into execution as it seems to them to be properly calculated to enforce the provisions for the reserves of the Church & Crown, agreeably to the late Act of Parliament.

. . . The great importance that it appears to the Council to promote the Erection of Towns has also occasioned them to deviate from the general plan to assist the Settlement at Toronto or York. It was thought expedient to reserve the whole of the broken fronts for Garrison purposes, as well as to prevent the scattering of the Inhabitants in such situations as their fancy or interest might induce them, which would ever prevent that compactness in a Town, which it seems proper to establish, two or three of the front Concessions therefore are granted in this Township, and the reserves will be made in the back lands which in reality are far more valuable for agricultural purposes, but reserves to great extent are made near this Harbour of Timber, which must in time become valuable as it is proposed to furnish from hence all the Materials that may be wanted, for the service of the Crown, in the Fortresses on the Lakes, and which at present are purchased from the Merchants at a very exhorbitant price.

Extract of a Dispatch from Lieutenant Governor Simcoe, to Mr. Secretary Dundas dated York 20th. September 1793—[75]

. . .

Extract of a Dispatch from Mr. Secretary Dundas to Lieut. Governor Simcoe dated Whitehall 16th March 1794

The Plan for future Townships transmitted in Your Letter of the same Number and date with that which I have been answering seems in placing the reserves for the Crown and the Church to have properly attended to the Spirit and Principle of the late Canada Act.

[75]Simcoe quotes the two opening paragraphs of B 1.

Although there may be a good reason for making those reserves in the back Lands in the particular Townships of York, yet in that Township also there should be a reservation in the front Concessions for the Glebe & Residence to the clergyman, who shall be appointed the Rector, under the Provisions of the Act.

The next question is where to establish the Chief Naval Station of the Province and herein I am of opinion with You that York is the most proper place for it.

I also agree with you that the place upon the River Thames which You have marked as the Scite for London, is well situated & judiciously chosen for the future Capital, but as the defence of the Colony is the first object, if that defence should be Maritime, it follows that the Settlement of York is the most important for the present, not as the future Capital, but as the Chief place of strength & security for the Naval force of the Province

The Communication which by Your vigor & assiduity you have been enabled to trace between York & Lake Huron, is of great importance & must prove beneficial to the Province in the several points of view in which you have considered it.

In order to facilitate this communication You will of course give every encouragement for settling those parts of the Route, which are most convenient as the stages for the Traders & as Depots for all articles of Merchandize in their passage from York to Lake Huron.

Extract of a Dispatch from Lieutenant Governor Simcoe to Mr. Secretary Dundas, dated June 20th 1794

In the distribution of the front Lots of the Town of York as it seemed to be probable that for a time this Station would be the residence of the Government of the Country they were so laid out as to give one hundred acres to each of the Officers of Government as an inducement to build an House in the town & a remuneration for its expence but these grants I did not chuse to make final until I understood Your pleasure on the Subject—A Glebe and a residence for the Clergyman were amongst such appropriations, but with the intention that such lands should be reversionary with the Benefice.

In the course of a few days a final Ratification of the allotments will take place, when Your Instructions Sir, will be attended with all that Respect that is due to them.

I shall give every encouragement to the settling of the Communication between York and Lake Huron—

The Lieutenant Governor further informs the Honorable Council that Young Street the Road from York, to Gwilliambury from whence the Holland River becomes navigable into Lake Simcoe, the waters of which fall themselves into Lake Huron, has been opened this Year by the Soldiers—

The Honble. Executive Council are therefore requested to form themselves into a Committee in order to take this Statement into their Consideration.

The Council are perfectly aware of the Public Reasons which have hitherto prevented the final Settlement of the Seat of Government & which now operate to make it necessary to occupy York for that temporary purpose; His Excellency the Lieutenant Governor is confirmed daily in his Opinion that the Interest of His Majesty, and that of the Public require that the Seat of Government should so soon as possible be fixed internally on the Spot selected for that purpose on the River Thames, but as He He is under the immediate necessity, at present, of contracting those Views which he trusts hereafter will be properly expanded, He desires the Opinion of the Committee on such Arrangements as may be Necessary to give effectual support to the growth and welfare of the Town of York &c. &c. &c.—in consequence He directs the Honorable Council in Committee—

First To examine and report to His Excellency in Council upon all former proceedings of the Council relative to the settling the Lands of the Crown in the Town and Township of York, and in their Vicinity, and to state such parts thereof as shall seem just and expedient to be finally ratified and confirmed; For this purpose to call upon the Acting Surveyor General forthwith to lay before the Committee the several Plans in his Office of the Town & Township of York with a return of each & every Assignment, He has been directed to make therein, & any documents in his possession relative thereto.—

Secondly To summon every person to whom a Certificate or Order of Council has been given, or assignment has been made as a Settler on Young Street, to appear of himself or his lawful Agent before the Committee & to recommend the grant of Lands to those who may seem duly entitled to the same.

Thirdly To call upon the Settlers in the Township of York & to confirm such Grants therein as may be proper.

Fourthly To report what period in the opinion of the Committee ought to be allotted to each Officer of the Government for the construction of a House, in the front Lots of the Town of York, agreeably to a Plan that shall be recommended by the Committee to His Excellency provided such Officers receive one hundred Acres of Land respectively in the first Concession of the Township of York, and adjacent to the Town, in aid of the expence necessary to the Erection of such an House conformably to the original principal.

Fifthly To Assign such Portion of Land as may hereafter reimburse Government for the expences incurred in the opening of Young Street.

Lastly To adjust such regulations as may be expedient and not burthensome to give an architectural Uniformity to the Town, an object of very great importance in the Establishment of a new Province and to propose whatsoever may have a tendency to promote the welfare and speedy settlement thereof.

Queens Rangers It is necessary to state to the Committee of the Honorable the Executive Council the propriety of the reserves which in the opinion of the Lieutenant Governor, should take place, between the Humber and Smith's River or the Tobicoke for the express purpose of settling such soldiers as shall be discharged from the Queens Rangers or 1st American Regiment, agreeably to the system which has been recommended by Major General Simcoe and approved of by His Majesty's Ministers.

. . .

York, 5th April, 1796

To His Excellency Major General Simcoe Lieutenant Governor & Commander in Chief of Upper Canada, &c &c &c

Report[76] of a Committee of Council held at York, Apl. 6 1796, and continued by adjournments to the 28th of May 1796—

Sir,

The Committee of Council having taken into their Consideration the Instructions of Yesterdays date which Your Excellency has been pleased to order to be laid before them entirely concur with Your Excellencys Opinion that the Lots immediately butting on each side the Roads of Communication, particularly Young Street and Dundas Street, ought not to be granted to any but Bona fide settlers—

. . .

With respect to the Exceptions and Dispositions of the Reserves in the Vicinage of York it appears to the Committee to be unnecessary for them to enter into a Discussion thereof, as Your Excellencys Plan and Recommendation have been already approved by one of His Majestys Principal Secretaries of State with only one Additional Reserve for the Accomodation of the future Rector, and this they observe Your Excellency has amply attended to by Appropriating four hundred Acres for that Purpose, in the Concessions immediately behind the Town—

The Committee beg leave to lay before Your Excellency a Schedule of the Persons to whom farm lots have been ordered and to Recommend for Confirmation by Deed those to whom they find Assignments have issued, and those who tho' not under assignment they find either settled in the Vicinage of York or making some advance towards an Improvement in their Respective Lots—

. . .

The Committee having taken into Consideration the fourth Article of Your Excellencys Instructions respecting the City of York beg

[76]This report also included a list of all land grants in the town and township of York, with recommendations for confirmation or rejection.

leave to Recommend that the front Row of each Block in the front Range of Blocks shall be divided into two Tenements instead of three, comprising a Square of 132 feet, And that when the Town may be extended that the future front Blocks may be laid off on the same Principle—

But this Rule is not meant to preclude Your Excellency, from granting to the higher Officers of Government upon their Specifick Petitions to the Extent of half a Block—

The Committee begs leave likewise to recommend to yr Excellency that every Applicant for a Town Lot shall be obliged by his Licence of Occupation to lay down his House on a line which shall be marked for him by the Surveyor, which Line in the front of the First Range shall be retired twelve feet from the Edge of the Street, in order to allow a space for Pallisadoes, or other Ornaments in front of the Buildings at the Pleasure of the Occupant, and that the front of all other back buildings shall be on an exact line with the sides of the Streets—

It is also recommended that the Occupants of the Front Range of Houses shall be obliged by their Tenure to give them a front of at least forty six feet, which may be extended, but not diminished; And as it [is] hoped that the Occupants of the front Row of Houses will make a Point of raising such Buildings as shall be an Ornament to the Town and worthy of so beautiful a Situation, it is recommended to allow three Years for the Completion of their Plan before Officers of Government shall be considered as having forfeited their claim to the Douceur of 100 Acres in the first Concession as proposed by Your Excellency.

. . .

In Answer to the fifth Article of Your Excellencys Instructions, the Committee beg leave to recommend that the four Lots originally appropriated and under assignmt. for Mr. Berczy[77] on Condition that he laid out Yonge Street in the same Manner as Dundas Street, and Compleated the same in one Year from the 15th of September, 1794, may be sold for whatever sum they may bring and the Money applied for the Expences incurred in opening Yonge Street—or that they may be

[77]William von Moll Berczy (1748–1813) was born in Saxony and educated at the Universities of Leyden and Jena. In 1791 he became an agent of the Pulteney Associates in supplying German settlers in the Genesee country, but left this settlement in 1793, amid mutual recriminations. In 1794 he came with about 60 German families to Upper Canada, where he was granted Markham Township for settlement, and a personal grant on condition that he open Yonge Street past his settlement. Between 1794 and 1798 he settled 77 men with their families, mostly from Hamburg, in Markham, thus forming a settlement of great importance in the early provisioning of York. Although he ruined himself financially in this endeavour, he was not able to fulfil all the conditions, and his lands were taken from him in 1797, while Simcoe's more lavish promises to him were ignored. He left Upper Canada in 1799, going to Montreal, where he earned his living as a painter. Compensation was finally made to his son in 1818. When in York, Berczy acted as a contractor for building houses.

otherwise disposed of to reimburse Government, and as Mr. Berczy has justly forfeited his Claim to those Lots from a failure in the Conditions, but has been at some Expence in endeavoring to carry them into Execution, until he was obliged to stop by the Sickness of the Laborers he had employed on that Service—It is recommended by the Committee to Your Excellency to grant Mr. Berczy such a Portion of Land elsewhere in remuneration as Yr. Excellency may judge proper.

The Sixth & last Article of the Instructions has been already attended to in the previous Recommendations of the Committee, And it only remains for them to suggest the propriety of appropriating certain Blocks in Suitable Situations for a Church, a Gaol, a Court House, and a Market Place which is humbly submitted to Your Excellencys Wisdom—

. . .

28 May 1796. Signed Peter Russell
Chairman of a Committee of Council

York 15th. July. 1796
Signed J G Simcoe

A 26 Russell to Simcoe
[*P.A.O., Russell Papers*]

June 25 1796

I have the Honor to acknowledge to your Excelly. the Receipt of a Letter from your Secretary of yesterdays date, informing me that it was your Excellencys Command, "that I remove my Office to York, the Seat of this Government, without delay, as directed in his Circular letter of the 28 of February—and that your Excellency will not Sanction the Charge of any Allowance for an Office or its Contingencies at any other place"

It has excited in me no small Pain to observe that this is the third Mandate I have received by your Excellencys Orders, on this Subject; because it seems to imply a suspected unwillingness on my Part to execute your Excellencys Commands—Educated in the School of Obedience I have been accustomed to comply implicitly with the Orders of my Superiors—But the many obligations I feel myself under to your Excellency with the personal affection I have long had for you will always render this Obedience a pleasure; and I shall be consequently mortified in proportion whenever any insurmountable obstacle may happen to retard it . . . The instant I knew it was your Excellys. wish to settle at York & draw the Officers of Governmt. about you, I gave one Hundred Guineas for a small house there, tho' I could but ill afford it, and have been ever since endeavoring to find out some artificers who will undertake to add to it & prepare it for my Reception on reasonable Terms—but without Success—the prices demanded being such as not to be submitted to—When I received the subsequent Order from your Secretary of the 28th of febry.—I immediately expressed my Obedience to the Mandate, & assigned such reasons for my not immediately complying with it as I flatter myself were Satisfactory—I had in May last the Honor of another Order to the same purpose, in my answer to which I took the liberty of stating with all the Respect I owe to your Excellencys Station, that I could not, consistent with the Duty I owed to myself & my Securities, remove the Receiver Generals Office to York before I had prepared a place of safety there for the reception of the Money & Vouchers with which I was entrusted—that I was taking Measures to that end with all the Expedition I could, & that as soon as matters were properly arranged my Office should be removed to York agreeable to your Excellencys Commands. Your Excellency cannot be unacquainted with the great pressure of public Business with which I have had to struggle ever since last April—a Severe fit of Sickness having supervened—both together have necessarily prevented me from attending to this less important Duty—I cannot therefore avoid being exceedingly hurt at this fourth pressing order, when one ought to have been sufficient.—

No man can be more sensible than I am of the Utility & even Necessity of a Stationary & Compact Government—For if the Governor of a Province lives in one place—& the Counsellors under whose advice he is to act, are dispersed at a distance from him—almost all official Business must be at a Stand—and the Welfare of the Province consequently suffer—It would therefore have been a most fortunate Circumstance if Your Excellency could have at an early period determined upon the Seat of Government—and after having drawn farmers round it to feed the Inhabitants, & have built Courts of Justice & Offices for the Departments—& given time for the Counsellors & Officers of Government to raise habitations for themselves & families, caused the whole to remove thither together, as some hundred Pounds would have been saved to the Officers of Government, which will be now probably lost, and every man under your Excellencys Command would have been happy & satisfied—I am persuaded that this has been impossible—& the Officers of Government have consequently only to lament the peculiar Circumstances which have unavoidably so long procrastinated their Establishment. . . .

I hope your Excellency can have no doubt about my Settling at York if the Administration of the Government should devolve upon me during your Excellencys absence—especially as I have ever unequivocally declared it as my opinion that Niagara would be a most improper Situation for it, from the Moment the Americans should possess the opposite Bank of that River—Your Excellency has an undoubted Right to declare the Seat of Government—and I know of no Power I should have to alter it afterwards—But had I the power I should most certainly not have the inclination to make the smallest Change in your Excellencys arrangements—On the Contrary, should I be honored with the Administration, Your Excellency may be assured that I shall spare no pains to forward more implicitly all the Plans your Excellency may do me the honor to leave with me—and the establishing the Seat of Government at this place & accelerating its prosperity will consequently command my earliest attention—

Your Excellency will I hope do me the Justice to believe that I am unhappy in having occasion to write this Letter, as I have ever regarded your friendship as one of my most valuable acquisitions, and shall be miserable should any thing ever happen to interrupt it. . . .

A 27 SIMCOE TO JOHN McGILL
[*Toronto Public Library (T.P.L.), Wolford Simcoe Papers, Book 8*]

York, 15th, July, 1796

In consequence of the insufficiency of enclosed pasture for the King's horses and oxen to graze in at York, added to the frequent damages to which Government may be subjected to, by the horses running at large, you are hereby directed to dispose of the whole or such part of the horses (belonging to the Public) under your superintendancy, as you may conceive proper, and to purchase such an additional number of working oxen as may be adequate to the public services ordered at this place, and for so doing this shall be your warrant and authority.

A 28 SIMCOE TO McGILL
[*T.P.L., John McGill Papers*]

York July 16th 1796

believing that Major Shaw of his Majestys Executive Council, a Captain of the Queens Rangers during the late War, a UE, comes under the description of Persons to whom a reasonable allowance of materials may be lent from the public Store under gov directions to enable them to build a House in the Vicinity of this Place, you are hereby authorized & directed to issue such materials to him to be bona fidé employed in the erection of a dwelling House, & on the express Conditions that such materials, shall be replaced whenever called for reasonable notice being given to Major Shaw of the requisition—It seems necessary that he should sign a receipt to be duly kept in your office.

A 29 ALEXANDER BURNS[78] TO D. W. SMITH
[*T.P.L., Peter Russell Papers*]

Niagara 29th July 1796

. . . It being of importance to the Town of York that the land round it should be quickly settled,—His Honor is of Opinion that no individual

[78]Alexander Burns was Paymaster of the Queen's Rangers. He acted as Peter Russell's secretary during his administration.

should possess more than two Lots at most—It was the Governors own proposal at a very early period, that only one farm Lot should be granted to one person in the Township of York, His Excellency has however thought proper to deviate from this Rule in some instances —His Honor sincerely wishes he had not, and it will be His Honors endeavour to adhere to it in future. . . .

A 30 RUSSELL TO ÆNEAS SHAW
[*T.P.L., Peter Russell Papers*]

Niagara 27th August 1796

I am favored with your letter of the 19th. and am very happy that you have agreed to accept the Lieutenantcy of the County of York—A Commission for which I have directed Mr. Jarvis to prepare without loss of time—also a Dedimus to you & Mr. Small to swear in the Magistrates in your quarter, a list of whom will be sent you—If you have not been sworn in yourself—I think you should now be so, and act with the others—Mr. Small, Mr. Willcocks Mr. Lawrence[79] and yourself will form a respectable Bench for every purpose wanting at York—Is not McGill in the Commission also—if so he should give his mite in assistance

Capt. Shank calls for 30 men from York to assist in the Transport Service which he is incapable of managing without them—I have therefore been forced to consent—tho' the works at York must be retarded, and I am certain desertion will follow in consequence. The diminution of our Force renders it highly proper we should make the best provision we can for our security—I am therefore persuaded the Council will see the propriety of converting the Block house materials on the Peninsula to a Jail—and stockading the area round it in such a way as to supply a place of Refuge to the Inhabitants of the Town, & vicinage to defend themselves in should the Indians incline to be troublesome—The expence according to the estimate given me will amount to about £600 but I think the measure indispensible, and it must be submitted to

Mr. Chewitt[80] writes to the Surveyor General that he cannot protract the Town for want of assistance—You will therefore oblige me by requesting Major Smith to spare him three or four men for the purpose—I do not suppose it will take two days labor at farthest, the men will be paid by the surveyor the usual prices—I want him to lay off three or four Blocks more and select situations for the Jail, a Church, and a Court house—To each of which I think a Block at least ought to be

[79]John Brown Lawrence (d. 1798) was a New Jersey lawyer, who was imprisoned during the Revolution with Simcoe. He came to Upper Canada after Simcoe's appointment and was granted land and a mill site on the east bank of the Humber River.

[80]William Chewett (1753-1849) was born in London, England, and came to Canada in 1771. In 1791 he was appointed Deputy Surveyor General of Upper Canada and in 1799 became joint Acting Surveyor General with Thomas Ridout.

appropriated—The Scite for the Jail should be chosen high & dry, for the sake of health & defence—That for a Court house in the front Row of Blocks it being a handsome object from the Bay—and that for a Church on a heighth as nearly centrical as can be obtained—A Block should likewise be allotted in the middle of the Town for a Market place

If you could spare the time to walk with Mr. Chewitt, and chuse these different Scites you will be much thanked by every Member of the Council and more particularly by

Dear Sir &ca
(signed) Peter Russell

A 31 RUSSELL TO ROBERT PRESCOTT[81]
[*T.P.L., Peter Russell Papers*]

Upper Canada
Niagara 29th August 1796

. . . General Simcoe (as I had the honor of mentioning to your Excellency in a former Letter) has directed the seat of this Government to be removed to York—At present York is in a manner isolated, being cut off by the want of Roads from an easy land Communication with the rest of the Province—It has no Jail, no Houses for the meeting of the Legislature, none for the Courts of Justice, nor even Offices for the Departments. Our Dependence rested wholly upon the Queen's Rangers for assistance to raise these necessary Buildings make Bridges, cut Roads of Communication &ca. The Detachments taken from thence by Lord Dorchester's Orders reduced this assistance to 100 Men, and Major Shank finding himself incapable of Transporting the Indian Stores now calls for thirty more. I cannot presume to retard so important a service by refusing my consent—but everything at York must be at a stand in consequence—I therefore took the liberty of suggesting to Major Shank the propriety of drawing these thirty men from Kingston, where there are two Companies of the Canadian Volunteers, and no very material Duties to be injured by that temporary Reduction—But he does not judge himself at liberty to draw a man from Kingston. . . .

A 32 RUSSELL TO WILLIAM OSGOODE
[*T.P.L., Peter Russell Papers*]

Niagara 7th September 1796

. . . The withdrawing of the two Regiments from this Province and the great Desertions from the Queen's Rangers have reduced our Mili-

[81]Robert Prescott (1725–1816) entered the army in 1755. He came to Canada as Lieutenant Governor of Lower Canada and Administrator of the government of Canada in 1796. In 1797 he was appointed Governor in Chief. He returned to England in 1799, but retained his appointment until 1807.

tary assistance so low, that all public & private works are at a stand—and I consequently much doubt the possibility of putting York in any tolerable state of forwardness for receiving the Officers of Government and Provincial Parliament even by June next. As to the Courts of Justice I have no hopes—As the population there is too trifling to furnish Juries from that part of the District, and it would be a great hardship to compell the attendance of the Inhabitants of this quarter. I therefore long much for the arrival of the Chief Justice[82] that I may avail myself of his advice on these and other important points, which under my present circumstances I do not judge it altogether prudent to act on from myself. . . .

A 33 Samuel Smith to Russell
[*T.P.L., Peter Russell Papers*]

York Septr. 11th, 1796.—

As Indians are frequently here, and sometimes from a great distance, and asking for Powder, Ball and other Articles usually given to them. I have thought it proper to have such Articles as are here examined; and find by Mr. Givens's[83] report, that there are none of the following, and which he says are necessary Vizt. Gun Powder, Shot, Tobacco, Rum, fine blue Cloth and Hats (for Chiefs) Butchers Knives and Ribbon.—

A 34 D. W. Smith to Russell and Russell to Smith
[*P.A.C., Upper Canada State Papers, v. 78, p. 189*]

S.G.O., 6 Novr. 1796

Mr. Chewitt reports to me that he cannot get hands at the price allowed by the Department, so as to enable him to affix the Meridional Line at York—as no Labourer will work there under a Dollar, & some a Dollar & a half per day.

[Russell's answer is on the same page.]

In answer to your letter of yesterday respecting Mr. Chewitts requisition for a higher allowance to his laborers in consequence of a dollar

[82]William Osgoode was appointed Chief Justice of Lower Canada in February, 1794. His successor in Upper Canada, John Elmsley, was not appointed until November, 1796, and first took his seat as Chief Justice on January 16, 1797. In view of his disagreement with Russell on the moving of the courts, Russell's comment here is somewhat ironic.

[83]James Givins (1759?–1846) spent some years in the western fur trade. In 1791 he became a lieutenant in the Queen's Rangers. He was appointed Agent at York for Indian affairs in 1798, and became senior officer in the Indian Department in Upper Canada in 1827. During the War of 1812 he was provincial A.D.C. to General Brock with the rank of major in the Militia and was present at the capture of Detroit. During the capture of York in 1813 he commanded a company of Indians. Because of his connection with the Indians, his house was one of the few badly looted during the subsequent occupation.

& half a day being demanded at York—I can only say that I shall never warrant such enormous wages. If Mr. Chewitt cannot procure means (with the Assistance of the Troops when they can be spared) to execute the Surveying Duties alotted to him at York, he must be employed in some other place or in some other way—and the Meridional suspended until laborers can be procured on cheaper terms.

A 35 RUSSELL TO D. W. SMITH
[*T.P.L., Peter Russell Papers*]

Springfield 8 November 1796

I have read Mr. Chewitt's Report with your Answer, and looked over the plan of York, which you sent to me Yesterday evening.—

It is much to be Lamented that Mr. Aitkins and Mr. Jones[84] have not been more Accurate in laying off the Blocks.—But as the Evil is Committed, all we have to do is to remedy it in the best way we can.

I accede to your Opinion—That if the mere moving of Fences will bring all Square, it may be effected. But from Mr. Chewitts Report it appears that not only fences,—But Houses are to be removed—The latter would be a certain Injury and Expence to the possessor, without perhaps his having merited them by any fault of his own.—I should therefore propose to let the encroachments in front of the first Range stand as it is.—But Rear Line of the Second Range of Blocks must be retired to its proper Position, as far as the removal of the fences can do it.—The House and Kitchen which Mr. Chewitt mentions must of course stand; tho' their projection into the Street may have an Ugly appearance. However being in a back street, and next the open Country, the inconvenience may be dispensed with. The Advertisements Mr. Chewitt proposes I think Expedient; and request you will frame something to that purpose; and Let it be printed in Hand bills and posted up at York.—And notice given that no person in future shall presume to lay down a house, until the Surveyor examines the Spot, and declares it to be agreeable to the Regulations of Council.—But as well as I can remember something to the purpose has been already Communicated in Council. . . .

A 36 RUSSELL TO SIMCOE
[*T. P. L., Peter Russell Papers*]

Upper Canada, Niagara 24 November 1796

. . . Major Smith of your Excellencys Regiment having represented to me that it would be Conducive to the Kings Service if a small Assortment of Indian presents was lodged at York to be at his disposal for

[84]Augustus Jones (1763?–1836) was a Loyalist from Dutchess County, New York. On January 15, 1788, he was appointed a deputy surveyor. He made several surveys of the town and township of York, including one in 1791 called "Plan of the front line of Dublin."

satisfying the wants of such Lake Indians as may occasionally visit the Post of York,—I sent a Copy of his Letter to the Commander in Chief, to whom I submitted the propriety of His Excellencys Authorising the Storekeeper here to Comply with Major Smiths Requisition—But it has been refused in the following answer from the Military Secretary

"The General cannot Comply with Major Smiths wishes to Establish a Depot of Indian Goods at York.—The Storehouse at Niagara is the only place for that District from whence Indian presents can be Issued—Requisitions for which according to the Regulations must pass thro' the Officers of that Department with the Concurrence of the Officer at Navy Hall."

I was also equally unsuccessfull in Obtaining an order for the repair of the Huts at York—As by the following paragraph of the same Letter "The repairing the Huts at York and the Alterations in the Stockading stated in Major Smiths Letter of the 9th Ulto—His Excellency declines providing for from the Army Extraordinaries.—The Measure of Establishing them having been adopted in the first instance by Lieut. Governor Simcoe, without the Sanction of the Commander in Chief."—But as I understand from Captain McGill that he had your Excellencys orders to execute these Works for the Winter Accomodation of the Detachment at York I shall warrant money for defraying the Expence; and I hope to have your Excellencys Support with the Lords of the Treasury if I shall appear to their Lordships to have deviated into a line of Expence, which may not properly belong to the Civil Department of the Government

The Impossibility of making provision for the Officers, or raising Coverings at York to Shelter the Officers of Government, from the Scarcity of Artificers and Laborers and the Consequent high wages demanded by the few, who are there, has hitherto rendered it impracticable for me to Administer the Government there agreeable to your Excellencys wishes—And indeed the reduction of the Marine Establishment and Accidents that have happened to some of the Vessels would have caused a Stagnation to all functions of Government had I gone there, from the Consequent difficulty of Communicating from thence with the rest of the Province.—I have sent over Carpenters from hence to add to the House I have there; and tho' I have submitted to the most enormous Impositions in order to hasten the work, little or no progress has been yet made and I have now lost Sixteen or Twenty Pounds by the Mohawks[85] running on a ledge of Rocks in going out of this Harbour, which rendered it necessary to throw over some Articles and take out the rest to lighten her sufficiently to be got off—She had afterwards taken in her loading again in order to proceed with it to York.—but a Storm of Snow coming on accompanied with most severe frost which has continued these four days, has determined Major Shank to relinquish the sending her to York this Season, to which I have readily acceded from the apparent danger of the Attempt.—Everything in the

[85]A government schooner of 80 tons, launched on May 14, 1795, at Kingston.

building way must Consequently be at a stand at York, and I am much distressed for the Civil and Military Officers at York, whose stores must probably remain here this Winter.—Whether Commodore Bouchette or the Commandant at Kingston is to blame for keeping the Kings vessels there so long I cannot say—for at least five weeks elapsed between the two last arrivals at this place, and I do not recollect that I have been able to send one of them to York these Seven or Eight weeks past—So that I foresee many Difficulties and delays in my Correspondence with the rest of the Province after I reside there, unless I can Contrive to have a small Dispatch Boat capable of receiving passengers and being Navigated by three hands including the Master—This however must depend upon the Concurrence of the Council and the approbation of the Lords of the Treasury. . . .

A 37 Russell to Prescott
[*T.P.L., Peter Russell Papers*]

Upper Canada
West Niagara 28 Feby 1797

. . . In answer to your Excellencys desire of being informed what number of men I may think Sufficient to be sent to York, I have the Honor to Suggest that Carriage Roads from York to the Bay of Quinte & the Head of Lake Ontario will be absolutely requisite to enable the Person who administers this Government to execute the difft. Functions of his Station from thence. A Jail, a Court House and a Church must be built there; and a Dwelling House for the Governor and Buildings to receive the two Houses of Legislature had been ordered by Lieut. Governor Simcoe before his Departure, and are now erecting under the directions of Mr. Commissary McGill. These will of course require the Occasional aid of Troops, which in my humble opinion are indispensible also for giving Energy, Respectability and Protection to the Civil Governt.—Major Shank reports to me that the Huts built under the Lt. Governors orders at York may with some small alterations very well accomodate 200 Men; and I do not think a less number would answer the Services I have above stated. But if the Support of the Civil Magistrate and the Protection of the Town from Indian insults are the only objects of Consideration, I should imagine that one hundred men would be fully adequate. This is however submitted with all deference to your Excellency's superior Judgement. . . .

A 38 Russell to McGill
[*T. P. L., Peter Russell Papers*]

West Niagara 15 March 1797

Since my last I have had an Opportunity of speaking with Mr. Pilkington, and very much approve of the Alterations he proposes for the

Government House.—By these the two Wings will be 40 by 24 feet and joined to the Body of the House by something like a Colonade—But it will be necessary to advance the House as well as them Several Paces, and they will of course occupy a larger space in front than Mr. Grahams plan

Mr. Pilkington being apprehensive of some Mistake by conveying his Ideas to Mr. Graham[86] in writing, wishes that he may take some favorable Opportunity of coming to Newark, that he may explain his Plan fully to him—In the mean time your three Carpenters may be employed in planing the flooring & trying up the stuff for Windows and Doors & without exactly ascertaining the Dimensions, which may possibly differ in some cases from Mr. Grahams.—It is not my intention to Attempt more at present than the two Wings, as before they are finished I may expect to receive final Instructions from home, which will determine me respecting the propriety of entering into so large an Expence as the mansion will assuredly prove.—But these two wings by being joined by a temporary covered way to the two Buildings in their rear,—may be of great use for the present,—as Houses for the meeting of the Legislature, holding Councils[,] giving entertainments in, and back appartments for occasional lodgings

I have agreed with Mr. Berczy about the two Wings of my future residence at York, and he has I believe begun upon them. . . .

A 39 RUSSELL TO D. W. SMITH
[T.P.L., Peter Russell Papers]

Springfield 20 July 1797

. . . I can have no objection to the Honble Mr. McGill having No. 1 in front—to the West of the Reserves in York, for what was formerly No. 1 in the Rear is now become the front.—The small part of the old front now remaining had better be laid open, unless it is given separately to Mrs. McGill, for no person can have more than one acre—Mr. Jones cannot be given a front Lot.—

. . .

It is very much my wish that the Rear Lots in the old part of the Town of York are filled up before a single rear Lot shall be given away in the new Part.[87]—It is also my wish that no front Lots in the new

[86]William Graham served in the Duke of Cumberland's Regiment of Foot during the American Revolution as a captain lieutenant. He settled on Yonge Street in Whitchurch Township, became a captain of the Yonge Street Company of the York Militia in 1798, a magistrate in 1800, and the Colonel of the 1st Regiment of York Militia during the War of 1812. He was appointed Master Carpenter to superintend the building of the public buildings at York on July 25, 1794. (T.P.L., McGill Papers.)

[87]In June, 1797, York was enlarged from its former western boundary, New

Part are promised before the higher Officers of Government have made their choice begining with the Chief Justice.—Being under a promise to Mrs. Berczy in consequence of her having very handsomely accomodated me with a Quarter of the Block my house is on.—I request that either No. 3 or No. 5 in front of the new part may be appropriated to her—

The Street called Lot Street I have desired Mr. Chewitt to mark off one Chain & half, the half Chain to be taken from the rear Lots of the Town—I have no objection to oblige the Attorney General, if you can do it without spoiling the uniformity and arrangement of the Town, but I request you may consider what this may lead to, as other Gentlemen in similar situations will expect the like Indulgences. —You will be pleased to dispose of Mr. Ridout, John Holloway[88] and Mr. A. McDonell[89] as you think proper—Holmes,[90], Ridout, Piney,[91] Tully[92] and Willcocks to have the lots asked for.—

Bond,[93] Holloway and Conn[94] those asked for south of Dutchess

---

(Jarvis) Street, to York Street. A second addition extended it to Peter Street. The northern limit was now Lot (Queen) Street.

[88]John Hollaway, a farmer on Yonge Street, was granted Lot no. 2, south side of Duchess Street, through the agency of Thomas Ridout of the Surveyor General's Office, on the understanding that Hollaway would sell the property to Ridout for $25.00. After he had the land, Hollaway refused to sell to Ridout. The lot was finally assigned to Mrs. Ridout, and Hollaway received Lot 3, north side of Duchess Street. (T.P.L., D. W. Smith Papers.)

[89]Probably Angus McDonell (d. 1804), eldest son of Allan McDonell of Collachie and brother of Sheriff Alexander McDonell. In 1792 he was appointed first Clerk of the Legislative Assembly, but lost his position because of a controversy with the Comte de Puisaye in 1801. He was a member of the Assembly for Durham, Simcoe, and the east riding of York from 1801 until 1804, when he was drowned in the loss of the *Speedy*. He was a barrister, and Treasurer of the Law Society from 1801 to 1804. According to a biographical note in the *York Gazette*, July 4, 1807, he was an easy-going, pleasant companion, interested in chemical experimentation and the writing of bad poetry.

[90]Holmes was granted a lot on the northwest corner of Duke and Ontario Streets.

[91]Peter Piney or Pining was one of Berczy's German settlers in Markham. His lot was on the northeast corner of Duke and Caroline (Sherbourne) Streets.

[92]Malachi Tully received a lot on the northwest corner of Duke and Caroline (Sherbourne) Streets.

[93]William Bond first petitioned for land in June, 1794, wishing "to become an inhabitant of this Province." He was granted a lot on Yonge Street, on which Bond's Lake is situated. He was probably the first nursery gardener in York, with an extensive stock of fruit trees. In 1806 he went to England at the request of the principal members of the Agricultural and Commercial Society of Upper Canada to lay his plans for promoting agriculture before the Board of Trade, Arts and Science, arriving back in York in 1809. He had at first supported Judge Thorpe, but had become disillusioned. (P.R.O., C.O. 42, v. 349, pp. 233–5; microfilm copy in P.A.O.)

[94]John Conn was an ex-soldier, living on Yonge Street. His lot was at the southeast corner of George and Duchess Streets.

Street, Kirgan[95] Northside. W. Kendrick,[96] Turney,[97] Perrigo[98] & Pilney[99] W. side George Street.—

Hunt[100] must not be permitted to be in the new Town, he keeps a Tipling House, and must go to the Rear of the old Town.—

Doctor McAuly may have No. 2 in front and Mrs. McAuly the same number in the rear of it, in the new part.—Mr. Scoffield[101] No. 1 southside King Street, Adjnt. McGill and Hugh McLean[102] Nos. 2 and 3 Northside.—Chewitt No 8 Northside Market Street.—C. Robinson No. 4, southside same Street—The others must wait, as the rear of that part will not be filled up yet, or go into the Rear of the old Part. . . .

A 40 RUSSELL TO JOHN ELMSLEY[103]
[*T.P.L., Peter Russell Papers*]

West Niagara 10 Augt. 1797

I have the Honor to receive your letter of this date, and am extremely sorry that the directions I have judged proper to give to the Surveyor

[95]Thomas Kirgan received a lot on the northeast corner of George and Duchess Streets.

[96]There were four Kendrick brothers, with adjoining lots on the west side of Yonge Street north of Lawrence Avenue. Duke William Kendrick (b. 1766?) died on January 1, 1813, while on active duty as lieutenant of the 3rd Regiment of York Militia. John Kendrick (b. 1764?) was High Constable from 1800 to 1803. Joseph Kendrick was master of several vessels on the Lake and served during the War of 1812 on the *Prince Regent.* Hiram Kendrick's name is the one entered on the lot on the west side of George Street. The Kendricks worked as house-builders, but were mainly interested and employed on the lakes as sailors.

[97]Michael Tennery was granted the lot between Kendrick and Perrigo on George Street. On April 12, 1798, Samuel Marther claimed the property of Tennery, now dead, under an oral will but his claim was not allowed, and Tennery's appropriations were thrown open.

[98]The lot at the west end of Duchess Street on the west side of George Street was bought in Sergeant James Perrigo's name by William Jarvis, so that Duchess Street could be extended to New (Jarvis) Street. Lot (Queen) Street north of Duchess was in this section a bog, and Jarvis wished to make a detour around it via Duchess and New Streets. (T.P.L., D. W. Smith Papers.)

[99]James Pitney first petitioned for land in July, 1795. He received a grant on the east side of Yonge Street, on which Willcocks Lake is situated. In 1799 he confessed to a series of petty thefts of vegetables from gardens in York. At that time he had a small shop. (P.A.O., Miscellaneous MSS, 1799.)

[100]Joseph Hunt was a discharged sergeant. He kept a tavern on the north side of King Street for a number of years and died during the War of 1812.

[101]Thomas Schofield (1738?–1805) was an Englishman who became a prominent merchant in York. He formed a partnership with Thomas Mosley, which was dissolved in 1804 so that Schofield could return to England. He died on January 26, 1805, and had the biggest funeral yet seen in York.

[102]Hugh McLean was a reduced sergeant from the 40th Regiment, with a lot on Yonge Street. He was appointed Usher to the Court of King's Bench.

[103]John Elmsley (1762–1805) was appointed Chief Justice of Upper Canada in 1796. During the first years of Lieutenant Governor Hunter's administration, he was probably the most influential man in Upper Canada. In 1802 he became Chief Justice of Lower Canada.

General respecting York should meet with your Disapprobation, or Cause any Disappointment to you or the other Officers of Government, this being the first I have heard of it.—

After having your opinion, Sir, and those of the other Officers of Government, I endeavored so to benefit from each, that by improving and adding to what Genl. Simcoe had done, I might give to the Town of York every Beauty and Convenience which its situation is capable of;—But without limits there can be no perfection,—When you proposed to me therefore to extend the Town to the Garrison Reserve, I strongly objected to it, for the reasons which still operate with me. In such an extent it would be impossible to prevail upon the Inhabitants to build near each other, and years might elapse in Consequence before the place would assume even the appearance of a Town.—The present Plan of York, which indeed exceeds in Extent my original Design that I might Comply with your wishes to add to the number of front Lots occupies a full mile in length and more than half that in breadth.—a space much larger than we have any probability of filling with Inhabitants for many years. The Expence therefore of making Streets and public Sewers and keeping them in repair will fall heavy upon those who shall have Houses even in this confined space; but should the Town be extended as you desire, and the Houses not increased in proportion, the Expense to the thinly scattered Inhabitants would be doubled and Trebled, or the Town might remain for ever an Ugly, Miry, unhealthy Swamp.—However as the Reserve extends to the Garrison, the Town may be hereafter enlarged as the Population may call for it, the doing it sooner shall never receive my concurrence.—It is my wish in the meantime that this reserved Land (after Deducting an Area of five hundred Yards square for Military purposes) may be divided into Ten Acre Lots, and let the Inhabitants of the Town not having 100 Acre Lots for Parks (resumable at pleasure) at an Annual Rent of one Dollar each to make them some Amends for their being deprived of Park Lots, by the land in the rear of the Town being all engrossed by the Officers of Government

You will pardon me, Sir, if I profess myself ignorant what persons you allude to, who being entitled to front Lots remain unaccomodated —For I can safely declare that every person of that Description, who has done me the Honor of signifying his desires has been placed agreeable to his own wishes, and there still remains vacant one front Lot in the new part of the Town, and I believe several in General Simcoes part;—With respect to Mr Justice Powell, had he been anxious for a front Lot, he would have asked for one before his Departure.—but on the contrary he told me he would never build at York;—and I am determined to do all in my power to prevent any person whatever from having a Lot in York, who does not mean to build there.—The other Puisne Judge whenever he may be appointed and chuse to reside at York, may if he pleases have one of the front Lots on either side the intended Court House, which is as Eligible a situation as any in York.—

A 41 RUSSELL TO D. W. SMITH
[*T.P.L., Peter Russell Papers*]

Springfield 17 September 1797

As both the Lots No. 7 on the South and Northside Market Street are appropriated to Mr. Reddish[104] and Commodore Bouchette.—Mr. Jones request cannot be complied with.—The Lot No. 6 Northside is vacant which he may have.—But as Mr. Jones most probably does not mean to become a Resident at York by taking a Lot there, he only keeps out some one that does.—for I shall do all in my power to prevent the Lots at York to be taken up as objects of Speculation, and I hope to have your assistance in it. . . .

A 42 MCGILL TO RUSSELL
[*T.P.L., Peter Russell Papers*]

York 5th November 1797.

I was honored with your letter of this date at three oClock, and beg leave to congratulate Miss Russell and yourself on your safe arrival at York, which but for a lame Leg, and bad weather that has intervened, I should have done Personally at an earlier period—I am truly sorry to hear of your being so uncomfortably situated—But hope when the weather clears up, and necessary arrangement of your Baggage made, that you will find yourself more at ease—The fence of the Governors Park was put in a sufficient State of repair to keep in the Kings Oxen during the summer season, how, or in what situation it remains at the present time I know not—

I am sorry, that I have no power or authority over the Carpenters employed at work on the Government House, to order them upon any other service, unless they will agree to do it from choice, those engagements with me, being for that express service—If I am able to sit on Horse back, I will ride down and see what can be done towards your immediate accommodation—But I must beg at the same time to state, that it is highly expedient and necessary that the wing of the Government House should be enclosed and secured against damage by Frost, without the least possible delay, in order to preserve the Brickwork from utter destruction, after the great expence which has been already

[104]Thomas Raddish was the first clergyman in York, arriving in 1796. As the Bishop of Quebec observed, "after a little speculation in land he returned to England, and we have heard no more of him." (Bishop Thorpe Papers, Mountain to Moore, April 15, 1799, quoted in Millman, *Jacob Mountain, First Lord Bishop of Quebec*, p. 94.) Raddish was only in Upper Canada for about six months.

incurred & exertions made to have the House erected and enclosed before the winter sett in, and after having pressed and sollicited Major Shank for Masons and Labourers to bring the Building to a finish—I should humbly conceive myself not justificable to the Public, did I not persevere and by every means in my power endeavor to secure the Building in such a manner as to preserve the Brickwork from tumbling down By the injury which if left in its present State, it would assuredly receive during the Winter—

I have every reason to apprehend that your Honor has been misinformed with respect to the appropriation of the Government Hutt oposite to Capt. Smiths, this Hut was Built by order of Governor Simcoe solely for the purpose of accommodating the Military Artificers & such Civil Carpenters employed at work on the Public Buildings as chose to inhabit it—As such—and for the purpose of holding Tools & Stores at various times—it has been constantly used—and never to my knowledge (as suggested) been inhabited by any favorite whatsoever. If the Public Service for which your honor wants this Hutt is of such a nature as to supersede the services for which it was originally Built—of course the Hutt must be evacuated by discharging the Artificers from the Public employ. . . .

A 43 Russell to D. W. Smith
[*T.P.L., Peter Russell Papers*]

York 17 November 1797

I am every moment receiving Information of improper Transactions. This morning I wrote to you to stop a Description issuing to Josiah Bull on a Warrant of Survey for a Farm Lot, because he immedly. sold it to William Marsh and is gone off to the States.—I am now to desire that you will not assign a Town Lot to Cornelius Van de Walter, who has got an order of Council for one, because he has sold it to one Heywood—Nothing but the utmost vigilance in the Council, in you, and in me can put a stop to these Impositions on the Kings Bounty.—But with respect to the Town of York, I am determined to prevent as far as I can a Monopoly of the Lots in it.—I must therefore request that no assignment for a Town Lot issue from your Office without having first received my Sanction—that I may have an opportunity of Examining the Parties, and by cross questions discover the probability of their becoming settlers here—I shall likewise move the Council that the warrants of Survey for Town Lots may be Conditional, and no Description to issue upon them until they adduce to your Office sufficient proofs of their having Commenced a respectable Building thereon, —or Satisfy you in some other way that they actually mean to become Settlers in the Town, unless the Parties applying are known to be respectable and incapable of Deception—

A 44 RUSSELL TO SIMCOE
[*T.P.L., Peter Russell Papers*]

Upper Canada, York
December 9th, 1797

I have the pleasure to inform your Excelly. that I arrived here on the 3d. Ultimo with my family and all my effects, which were with great difficulty & some damage got on Shore, as a Violent Storm of Wind, Rain, & Snow came on immediately after, & has continued almost ever since with very little intermission accompanied by a most intense frost. So that our Harbor is now completely blocked up for the Winter, and I am not without apprehensions that the Inhabitants of this Settlement may suffer for want of flour, as their expected supplies of that Article have been cut off by this early visit of hard weather. Boards & scantling are likewise very scarce here and not to be procured now from the Mills. I am in consequence wholly uninclosed and without covering for my Horses, Oxen, or Poultry, and what is still worse my friend Mr. McGill has very unlike a friend neglected to lay in Hay for me altho' he was early requested to do so; And I cannot procure a Sufficiency for their Support at any price. The Attorney General and Mr. Smith have by very great exertions got themselves Housed the latter pretty comfortably. But Mr. Jarvis having not made the smallest effort for the removal of his Office remains still at Niagara and most probably means to do so until your Excellency's arrival. The Two wings to the Government House are raised with Brick & completely covered in. The South One, being in the greatest forwardness I have directed to be fited up for a temporary Court House for the Kings Bench in the ensuing Term, and I hope they may both be in a condition to receive the Two Houses of Parliament in June next, I have not yet given directions for proceeding with the remainder of your Excellency's plan for the Government House, being alarmed at the magnitude of the expence which Captain Graham estimates at (£10,000) I shall however order a large Kiln of Bricks to be prepared in the Spring and burnt, (as they will readily sell for what they cost if Government does not want them) and Boards & Scantling may be cut and seasoned upon the same principle—But I sincerely hope to have the pleasure of seeing Your Excellency here before we shall have occasion to proceed further with the building.—

I have extended this Town Westward towards the Garrison, & to the North as far as the Base of Hundred Acre lots, reserving between the part that was laid out by Your Excellency and this Addition, a large Space for public buildings (vizt. a Church, Court House, Jail, Market, Hospital, School House &c) most of the Lots have been already taken up, & about forty Houses erected & several more are beginning.

The Huts at the Garrison requiring considerable repair to render them Habitable in Winter, I have caused The Blockhouse (which

Your Excellency originally intended to place on the Peninsula) to be raised on the Knoll on this Side the Garrison Creek & fited as a Barrack for 70 Men. On the Top of it is put a light House, which renders it a convenient & conspicuous object to guide Vessels into the Harbor. Upon the Whole I flatter myself Your Excellency will not be displeased with what I have done at this place. . . .

A 45 Minutes of the Executive Council
[*P.A.C., Upper Canada State Book B, p. 93*]

Council Chamber at York 20th. Decr. 1797

Present
His Honor Peter Russell Esquire President
Honl. John McGill
Honl. David William Smith, Speaker of the Lower House

. . . The President laid before the Board a plan and estimate of a temporary lock up House which he requested they would take into their consideration.

Which, having done it was Resolved in consequence that it is absolutely requisite that some place of confinement shall be immediately provided in the Town of York to enable the Civil Magistrates to preserve the peace of the Town, and keep the people in order—But as a proper County Gaol may very soon be wanted, the further consideration of this subject is deferred until the arrival of the Chief Justice, that the Board may be assisted by his opinion thereon.

It having been reported to this Board that several persons, to whom Town Lots have been ordered in the Town of York, have instead of building and residing thereon as they have engaged to do, sold their location to others—that a stop may therefore be put to such proceedings which are very reprehensible for many reasons it is Resolved that the selling a Town Lot before a Deed or Patent issues to the Holder, unless permission has been previously obtained from the Council, be deemed a forfeiture of the location, and the order of Council in such persons favor be immediately rescinded—The Clerk of the Council to make this order of Council as public as possible

Adjourned

A 46 Elmsley to D. W. Smith
[*T.P.L., D. W. Smith Papers*]

Niagara Feb. 18th, 1798

. . . The President has written to me to inform me that the Duke of Portland has told him that York was chosen to be the Seat of Government on mature deliberation: he does not say the *permanent* seat; but I understand Mr Russell has everywhere announced it as such.

How peculiarly hard is the lot of the Civil Officers of Upper Canada, and how carefully they seem selected to be the sport of fortune!—But I am breaking the resolution I have made of uttering no more complaints, for I see it is all in vain, be they ever so well founded. . . .

With respect to your Idea of a Square, my Notion is, that you have an official right to lay out the Town as you please. When you do us the honour to consult us, I consider it as a compliment, & a mark of good will, which we shd not deserve, if we did not give you our Candid opinion: With all sincerity therefore, I approve highly of your Square; & wish there were more. Can you not before it is too late, lay off a handsome block of 8 or even 12 Acres for a College? I dropt the hint to Russell some time since, but he does not seem to relish it. . . .

A 47 MINUTES OF THE EXECUTIVE COUNCIL [*P.A.C., Upper Canada State Book B, p. 308*]

Council Chamber at York, 5th January 1799.

Present

His Honor Peter Russell Esquire President &ca. &ca. &ca.
Honl. John Elmsley Chief Justice
Honl. John McGill
Honl. David William Smith Speaker of the Lower House.

The President having informed the Board, that he has appointed Mr. Thomas Barry[105] Coroner for this part of the Home District, being the only Inhabitant he could find who was capable & willing to execute that office. But Mr. Barry refusing to accept of the Commission if he is required to pay the Fees of it, because he does not think the Emoluments of the office likely to reimburse him—The President moved, that the Secretary may be Instructed to deliver to Mr. Barry the Coroners Commission without demanding Fees from him which are to be charged against Government as other Fees on the Great Seal to Public Instruments.

Ordered accordingly. . . .

A 48 ELMSLEY TO MCGILL [*T.P.L., John McGill Papers*]

The Chief Justice requests the sanction of His Honour's permission to make use of the King's Oxen for two or three days, on condition of returning an equal number of Day's work with his own on The King's Works, whenever required: The impossibility of hiring Oxen that are capable of working, & the necessity of plowing his Garden immediately, are the reasons of this request.

[105]Thomas Barry (d. 1799) was one of the earliest York merchants. In 1794–5 he was in partnership with Jean Baptiste Rousseau. He bought and sold through Richard Cartwright in Kingston.

Permitted when the Indulgence
does not impede the public Service
Peter Russell

[Endorsed by McGill: "May 14th, 1799 The Presidents Sanction for sending the Government Oxen to assist the Chief Justice in plowing his Garden Rec'd in Council"]

A 49 RUSSELL TO PETER HUNTER[106]

[*Public Record Office (P.R.O.), C.O. 42, v. 324, pp. 230–3; microfilm copy in P.A.O.*]

York 20th August 1799.

. . . The only public Works on which I was engaged upon your Excellencys arrival, besides the above Road[107] and another from this Town to the beginning of the Yonge Street Settlements, are the Goal, a small armed Vessel[108] for the Use of the Civil Government, and a defensible Guard House intended by the Council & myself to cover such Troops as might be judged necessary for the Protection of the Town in Case of an Indian Rupture. My letter No. 51 Stated to the Duke of Portland the Reasons which influenced us to order a Goal to be forthwith erected in this Town for the Confinement of Criminals & Debtors; and my letter No. 64 represents to His Grace the Advantages & even Necessity of a land Communication between the Capital & the lower Parts of the Province, and reports the Contract we had entered into with one Darnford[109] for opening a Road to the Bay of Quinti for that purpose.

The Jail being just finished & the last Instalment ordered to be paid, the only Works remaining to be completed are the armed Vessel & the Guard House, and the two roads mentioned before. . . .

A 50 SAMUEL SMITH TO HUNTER

[*P.A.C., Upper Canada State Book B, p. 451*]

York 24th Septr. 1799

As there has been no person come forward to furnish Logs, Shingles &ca. (agreeably to an advertisement from the Commissioners) for the erecting of some additional Huts to accommodate the Queen's Rangers with Quarters, making it necessary I should request that the men of the Corps now employed in cutting Roads be called to assist in getting the

[106]Peter Hunter (1746–1805) was born in Perthshire, Scotland, and was appointed Commander in Chief of the forces in Canada and Lieutenant Governor of Upper Canada in 1799. His military appointment necessitated lengthy absences from York.

[107]Danforth Road to the Bay of Quinte.

[108]The *Toronto*, yacht.

[109]Asa Danforth (see E 5).

above materials, least a part of the Regiment should not be under cover before the Winter sets in. I shall therefore be happy to receive Your Excellency's directions on this head.

A 51 Lots in York Reserved for Particular Trades
[*P.A.C., Upper Canada State Papers, v. 99, p. 78*]

No	
19, 18, 17, 4	fronting on Lot Street
12, 9	fronting on Hospital Street
6, 5	fronting on Russell Square
10	fronting on Newgate Street

The whole Lots to be divided into half-lots, & to be reserved for persons who shall actually build & carry on the following trades thereon —:viz

Tinsmith
Blacksmith
Sadler
Wheelwright
Cooper
Shoemaker
Baker

Decr. 24. 99. In Council but not to be entered

A 52 General Statement of Public Property in This Province Commencing with the Year 1792 and Ending in 1799
[*P.A.C., Upper Canada Sundries*]

Saw Mill on the Humber.	Built in 1793, it being then contemplated to make York the Seat of Government, A Saw Mill was erected on the River Humber for the purpose of obtaining the necessary supply of Boards and other Lumber, required for Public Service, as could not be procured in a Wilderness Country distant from any Settlement more than fifty miles; This Mill has cut the greater part of the Boards used for the Public Service at York, and is lett for the Current Year at One fourth of the Lumber she may cut.
Garrison at York	Round Log Hutts were erected in 1793 and 1794 as Quarters for the Corps of Queen's Rangers.

Garrison at York	A Round Log Hutt was built for the Commissary of Stores and Provisions on the Army Staff in 1794.
York, Two Row Gun Boats with Oars, Rudders and Masts	Were built in 1794 for the purpose of transporting Troops with facility to whatsoever place they might be required, they were to have been manned chiefly by Militia, and to have carried a Six Pounder in the Bow; these two Boats are placed under a shed of Boards near to the Guard and Store Houses that have been erected on Gibraltar Point.
Large Scow	This Scow was built at the same time with the two Gun Boats, for the purpose of Landing Provisions and Public Stores, and for the transport of such materials as might be required for the Public Buildings to be erected at York.—This Scow is serviceable.
Oxen	Three Yoke were directed to be purchased in 1794 for the Public Services intended to be carried on at York. These Oxen as they became unserviceable were ordered to be sold and the amount Credited in the Commissary of Stores Public Account; other serviceable Oxen were purchased to replace those sold, as the Public Service might require. One Ox died in 1799, Two Yoke of serviceable Oxen now remain.
Dundas Street	Opened from York to the Grand River
Yonge Street	Opened from York to Lake Simcoe.
Gibralter Point; Two Block House, Store Houses,	These two Houses are built of Square Logs and are weather-boarded, and have Loopholes in the second Story, they were erected for the purpose of containing the Government Stores shipped at London in 1792, per the Scipio & ca,[110] and are now employed for that service.
and a Guard House.	This Guard House was built for the accommodation of the Guard necessarily required for the Protection of the Stores. It is upwards of 30 feet long divided into two apartments on the first floor with a Fire place in each; the materials are framed and Weather-Boards, fitted in with Brick, with a Gallery the whole length of the House.

[110]A large quantity of supplies for settlers was shipped from London on the *Scipio, Henniker,* and *Augustus* in 1792 and 1794. It included such things as axes, kettles, glass, building hardware, saws, scythes, paint, tools, iron, steel, and lead. Very little was distributed, causing some bitterness, and the rest was finally captured by the Americans in 1813.

Large Provision Store House at the Garrison of York for the Troops.

Canal, Locks and Wharf at the Garrison of York.—These were originally intended to lessen the expence incurred in landing Provisions and Stores as well as for the greater security of Boats and Batteaux.

Bridge and a Road	The Bridge was erected at the Garrison of York, and a Road opened from the Town of York to the Humber, for the better communicating with the Garrison.
Town of York, a Log Hutt.	Was erected for the Artificers and Men employed to work upon the Public Buildings. This Hutt was given with the concurrence of the Executive Government in exchange for a much larger One laying to the North East of the Brick buildings. This Hutt was used last Winter for the King's Oxen.
Government Park.	Inclosed for the benefit of the King's Oxen when employed.
Ground Cleared.	Where the Two Brick Buildings are erected in the Town of York.
Garrison of York.	A Powder Magazine of square Hemlock Logs, was built in 1795.
Batteaux.	Three Batteaux were sent to the Garrison of York in 1793, they have long been unserviceable; a new One was built in 1797 at York, which is since lost.
Stoccades	The intervals between the Hutts were ordered to be stoccaded, and Gates put up with Locks and Bars; likewise a large space afterwards stoccaded in front of the Hutts on the Parade.
Town of York.	A Log Hutt was erected in the Town of York, in order that a Blacksmith might reside therein: It has hitherto been given Rent free as an encouragement to have a Person at hand to do such work as the Public Service might at any time require.
Ox Sledges.	Several have been made which are no longer serviceable.
Ox Carts	Four. These Carts were made and used for the purpose of hawling Stones and other materials for Public Service at York; Two of them have long since gone to pieces, and the two remaining Ones stand in need of considerable repairs.
Two Brick Buildings at York, with Two other framed	The Brick Buildings were originally intended as Wings to a House for the Lieut. Governor, and the Houses in the rear of them to be advanced

Buildings in the rear	in front for Guard Houses and some other services. They now serve for the sittings of Parliament, Courts of Justice, and occasionally as Churches.
Wheel Barrows.	Ten were ordered to be made at York for Public Service. Chiefly expended.
Plow.	One made which is unserviceable.
Harrow.	Two made.—One of them stolen in 1799; and the other unserviceable.
Boat for Transport of Stone.	This Boat after tryal was found not to answer the service for which she had been built. She was therefore sold for Stones equal to her original Cost.
Garrison of York.	A large Block House Barrack occupied for the King's Troops.
A Light Row Boat	Built for the use of the Garrison of York.
York Garrison.	A Store House of two stories for the Indian Presents
Jail at York.	With the Jail yard stoccaded and Gates.
Toronto Yacht	This vessel was built for the service of the Civil Government of Upper Canada, and to be subject entirely to the orders of the Governor, Lieut. Governor or Person administering the Government.—1799.
A Block or defencible Guard House in the Town of York	This House was built as a Guard House for the Militia of York, should the Indian War with which we were threatened in the Winter of 1798 have required their being embodied.
Land cleared and inclosed near the Garrison of York.	For the more easy mode of procuring the quantity of Hay required for the King's Oxen, a Field of from Seven to Eight Acres was cleared, inclosed, and laid down with Grass Seeds

(Signed) Peter Russell

York 2d July 1800. lately Administering the Government of Upper Canada

Bricks.	Twenty-three thousand were delivered for the Public Services carrying on at the Garrison in 1800. Exclusive of which, upwards of Twenty thousand had at various times been supplied for the Building new Bakerys, and for the repair of Barrack Chimnies and Ovens.
Lime.	Thirty-seven Barrels supplied for the Public Services carrying on at the Garrison of York in

1799.—Besides which constant supplies of this Article had been from time to time furnished for the building of Ovens, as well as for the repair of Barracks and Ovens.—A small remains of this article is still in the Lime Shed

(Signed) John McGill

York 11th July 1800 Commissary of Stores & ca. Upper Canada.

A 53 Elmsley to Hunter

[*T.P.L., John Elmsley Letter Book*]

York March 6th. 1801

. . . The order for clearing the Lots in this Town has on the whole been well observed & the utility of the Measure will doubtless be sensibly felt next summer. In order to enforce a proper Obedience to it, we directed a return to be made to us, at the end of the first period of three Months, of the names of those who had made default in cutting & burning the underwood: & we gave Notice in the Gazette that their Lots would be forfeited unless saved by an Application for further time. Some have obtained that indulgence for the mere trouble of asking for it. The Second period is now elapsed, & it is our intention to direct a Similar return to be made & to allow one Month, as on the former occasion, for Applications for further time—This it is our intention to give on the same easy terms as before, & if at the end of the period proposed, the Order is not obeyed to its full extent, we still mean, provided something has been done, to accept of almost any excuse for the Omission. But with respect to those who shall be found, at the End of the Month, to have taken no notice whatever of the Order, to have offered no Apology for their neglect, & particularly those who have left the Town or its neighbourhood, we propose to recommend to Yr. Excy that both for the sake of Example, & that other more worthy applicants may be accommodated the appropriations in their favour be rescinded.

A 54 Hunter to Hobart[111]

[*P.R.O., C.O. 42, v. 334, p. 21; microfilm copy in P.A.O.*]

York, Upper Canada
10th April 1804.

I have the honor to transmit to your Lordship an Address to His Majesty by the two Houses of Legislature of this Province.

Your Lordship will perceive, that the Object which the prayer of this Address has in View, is an Aid from the United Empire, to enable the Province to erect at the Seat of Government proper Buildings for

[111]Robert, Baron Hobart (1760–1816), was Secretary for War and the Colonies, 1801–4.

the preservation of the public Records, the Assembling of the Legislative Council and House of Assembly, and for the Courts of Justice, and the transacting the other public Business.

Among the Acts of the Legislature of the last Session, which will be transmitted to your Lordship by the first safe Vessel that sails from Quebec, there is one (No. 4)[112] by which an annual Sum of £400, is charged on the Provincial Revenue for the Erection of these Buildings.

It seems almost unnecessary to point out, the total Inadequacy of such a Fund to the purpose for which this annual Sum has been granted, independent of which, it will occur to your Lordship, that the very slow Progress which would be made with so small a yearly Sum, would altogether defeat the necessary Object to be provided for, early Security to the public Records, and the means, within a reasonable space of time, of the Province being provided with Buildings adapted to the carrying on public business at the Seat of Government, with some degree of Convenience.

With reference to the Necessity which exists for the Erection of such Buildings, I submit to your Lordships Consideration, that there is not at present a single Building here, for any one public Office.

The Offices of the Executive Council, of the Secretary, the Register, the Auditor, the Clerk of the Crown and of the Courts of Probate and Surrogate all within the private houses of the Individuals who fill those respective Situations, and the Executive Council is obliged to meet in a very small room in the Clerks house, exposed to the hazard of having their discussions overheard. These houses are all built with Wood, and of course afford very slender Security to the public Records, and the hourly danger which awaits them is so manifest, that any Comment of mine would be troubling your Lordship unnecessarily, and for this very indifferent Accommodation, the public pays annually by way of Rent to the different proprietors of these Houses about the Sum of £350:—

As to the Building at present appropriated to the meeting of the two houses of Legislature, and for the Court of Appeal, the Court of King's Bench, the District Court and the Quarter Sessions, it only consists of two Rooms, erected about 8 or 9 years ago, as a small part of what was at that time intended for a Government house.

This Building is also obliged to be made use of for many other public Purposes, among the Rest as a Church, it being the only place which the Inhabitants of the Town could meet in for public Worship.

Neither is it calculated for any of these Uses, and it has been with the greatest difficulty and attended with every possible Inconvenience that the public Business has been hitherto carried on, and I assure your Lordship, that nothing but the Regret I felt at the Idea of troubling the

[112]This Act was repealed in 1813 and the fund accumulated under it "liberally granted in aid of the war." (P.R.O., C.O. 42, v. 335, p. 43, Drummond to Bathurst, March 31, 1814; microfilm copy in P.A.O.)

Kings Ministers with Applications for Aids of Money, at times when the United Empire was surrounded on all sides with such heavy Expenditures, as it has been for many years past that I have till now omitted, to Solicit your Lordship favorable attention to the situation of the Province in this respect . . .

With respect to the £400 per Annum which has been granted, although so unequal to the Object, it is certainly as much as the Revenues of the Province under all Circumstances enabled them to appropriate to these purposes, and as it is a perpetual Act, it will remain a Charge on the Province, subject to the Disposition of His Majesty, until any Aid which may be granted by the United Empire shall be repaid.

I beg leave further to state to your Lordship that I conceive the present Address to His Majesty has been brought forward by the two houses here in consequence of the very liberal aid which has been afforded by the parent Country to the Province of Lower Canada, to enable them to erect their Courts of Justice in Quebec and Montreal, and a Church at Quebec. The king's subjects here having frequent Intercourse with the Lower Province, and finding that a very considerable Sum had been granted by way of aid on Loan to that Province, alledge, that as they have by this Act, charged the Revenue of the Province, with as large a Sum as their Resources would enable them to appropriate to these purposes, they thought they might with humble Confidence rely on His Majesty's gracious Bounty to them, more especially as from the infant State of this Province, it must necessarily stand in greater Need of Protection and Assistance, than the Lower Province so much older and of greater Ability within itself.

No Estimate has yet been made of the Expence, which would attend the Erection of these Buildings, but probably with all the Oeconomy, that could be used, a very considerable Sum would, upon a moderate plan, be requisite to complete them. I shall procure from Major General Mann Commanding Royal Engineer in the Canadas, an Estimate[113] of the probable Expence, which shall, as soon as possible be forwarded to your Lordship. As to a Church, the Inhabitants of the Town of York, have subscribed very liberally and are about to build one this Summer. . . .

A 55 Heriot's[114] Description of York in 1807
[*Heriot*, Travels through the Canadas, *pp. 138–40*]

. . . York, or Toronto, the seat of government in Upper Canada, is placed in forty-three degrees and thirty-five minutes of north latitude,

[113]General Mann's estimate, dated "Quebec 16th July 1804" for a building 270 to 300 feet long and from 36 to 40 feet wide, was £15,120 Sterling. (P.R.O., C.O. 42, v. 336, p. 51; microfilm copy in P.A.O.)

[114]George Heriot (1766–1844) was Deputy Postmaster General of British North America, 1800–16.

near the bottom of a harbour of the same name. A long and narrow peninsula, distinguished by the appellation of Gibraltar Point, forms, and embraces this harbour, securing it from the storms of the lake, and rendering it the safest of any, around the coasts of that sea of fresh waters. Stores and block-houses are constructed near the extremity of this point. A spot called the garrison, stands on a bank of the main land, opposite to the point, and consists only of a wooden block-house, and some small cottages of the same materials, little superior to temporary huts. The house in which the Lieutenant-governor resides, is likewise formed of wood, in the figure of a half square, of one story in height, with galleries in the center. It is sufficiently commodious for the present state of the province, and is erected upon a bank of the lake, near the mouth of Toronto bay. The town, according to the plan, is projected to extend to a mile and a half in length, from the bottom of the harbour, along its banks. Many houses are already completed, some of which display a considerable degree of taste. The advancement of this place to its present condition, has been effected within the lapse of six or seven years, and persons who have formerly travelled in this part of the country, are impressed with sentiments of wonder, on beholding a town which may be termed handsome, reared as if by enchantment, in the midst of a wilderness. Two buildings of brick at the extremity of the town, which were designed as wings to a center, are occupied as chambers for the upper and lower house of assembly. The scene from this part of the basin, is agreeable and diversified; a block-house, situated upon a wooded bank, forms the nearest object; part of the town, points of land cloathed with spreading oak-trees, gradually receding from the eye, one behind another, until terminated by the buildings of the garrison and the spot on which the governor's residence is placed,[115] compose the objects on the right. The left side of the view comprehends the long peninsula which incloses this sheet of water, beautiful on account of its placidity, and rotundity of form; the distant lake, which appears bounded only by the sky, terminates the whole.

A rivulet, called the Don, runs in the vicinity of the town, and there are likewise other springs by which this settlement is watered. Yonge-street, or the military way leading to Lake Simcoe, and from thence to Glocester-bay on Lake Huron, commences in the rear of the town. This communication, which, in time, will be productive of great utility to the commerce of the country, is opened as far as Lake Simcoe, and as it is considerably shorter than the circuitous route, by the Straits of Niagara, Lake Erie, and Detroit, must become the great channel of intercourse from this part of the province, to the north-west county. . . .

[115]The lieutenant governor's house was built by Lieutenant Governor Hunter on the lake west of Garrison Creek, on part of the present site of Fort York.

B. DEFENCE

B 1 SIMCOE TO DUNDAS
[*P.R.O., C.O. 42, v. 317, pp. 283–95*]

York, Upper Canada
September 20th. 1793.

. . . The Winter Station and refitting Port of the Shipping on Lake Ontario is at Kingston; this Port which is at the mouth of the River St. Laurence, from its extent and situation is absolutely indefensible, and by being constantly frozen up during the Winter, is certainly liable at that Season to be destroyed, as it is at no great distance from the United States—

I propose therefore, that the Winter Station of the Fleet, and the refitting Port, and such naval Buildings as may be wanting, be at York, —this Post is at a great distance from the foreign shore, is capable of being easily defended; and the Grants of Land having been made by the present Government, sufficient Care has been taken, that great reservations of timber should be made for naval purposes—The floating Ice (and a Bridge which it makes from the Island near Kingston to the Continent) prevents the shipping in that Harbour, as well as in that of Niagara, from sailing for several days in the Spring, when it is practicable to be at sea from *York*—a Circumstance of no little moment when the growing Importance of this Colony is in Contemplation. . . .

. . . Upon the first news of the rupture with France,[1] I determined to withdraw the Queens Rangers from the unhealthy Vicinity of Niagara where they were encamped, and to occupy York—I submitted to the Commander in Chief my Intentions[2] and desired his Sanction to authorize me to construct a *Block House* to defend the Entrance of the Harbour, detailing to him Its properties and the security it would afford to the civil Government of the Province, at the same time stating in the Capacity of Civil Governor, that was I not obedient to his authority, I should certainly occupy and in some degree secure that Post, for the residence of the Civil Officers of Government, and that the only protection of the Country should not depend on such a miserable fortress as Niagara, situated within the Line of the United States.

As Major General Clarke was in expectation of the arrival of Lord Dorchester, He was not inclined to issue any Orders relative to the points which I had stated to him,[3] but permitted me to avail myself of such assistance as I had pointed out might be procured from some

[1]France declared war on Great Britain on February 1, 1793.
[2]Simcoe to Clarke, A 2.
[3]Clarke to Simcoe, A 3.

old Cannon that had been condemned (but which yet might be of specific Service) and some Carronades to give the appearance of fortifying the Harbour—

The lateness of the Season has prevented me from building *Storehouses* to lodge the Cargo of the Scipio and other public stores consequent to the Erection of the Government.—these I proposed to construct in such a manner as to serve for the defence of the Harbour . . .

The Occupation of the Harbour of *York* I totally take upon myself in that Capacity;[4] and I should forthwith proceed on the Storehouses which I propose to erect, as is most necessary for the publick Service, but at the same time being convinced that as permanent Storehouses may be so built as to contribute essentially to the strength of this important Post, and the whole Colony; and the incorporating such a military purpose, into the arrangement of what is necessary to preserve the public Stores, bringing it under the cognizance of the Board of Ordnance, I feel myself much embarrassed.

Under this difficulty, I have desired, the Engineer, Lieut. Pilkington, who is now here, in his way to accompany me to Lake Huron, to furnish me with the aggregate of his Estimate of the Expence which the proposed Storehouses and Block House will cost, and which I beg to submit for your Consideration.[5]—Having thus, Sir, entered into the System which I consider as absolutely necessary for the *defence* and *security* of the Province entrusted to my Charge, and in the most particular manner which His Majesty's Instructions direct, and which public Exigency seems at this period most peculiarly to require; I am with all respect most anxiously to solicit your speedy determination thereon—

The Stores which I have been furnished with for the Erection of public Buildings, Government Houses, &c., &c. are now dispersed in such places as have with difficulty been obtained from other purposes at Kingston and Niagara. . . .

B 2 SIMCOE TO DUKE OF RICHMOND[6]
[*P.A.O., Simcoe Papers*]

York (late Toronto)
Upper Canada
September 23d 1793

. . . I most respectfully beg leave to submit to Your Grace such a detail of the Principles of the Species of fortification which I wish to

[4]As civil governor.

[5]Pilkington submitted an estimate of £785 Sterling for workmanship only, to build a blockhouse 58 feet square, the lower part a powder magazine and store rooms built of masonry, and the upper part log barracks. (Pilkington to Simcoe, Sept. 6, 1793, printed in *Simcoe Correspondence*, ed. Cruikshank, II, 47–8.)

[6]Charles Lennox, third Duke of Richmond (1735–1806), was Master General of the Ordnance, 1782–95.

erect at York (or Toronto) & of the particular nature of the Ground as it is in my power to procure—The General Plan[7] will shew Your Grace the Position of the Harbour & Isthmus, which I propose to fortify; & the plan of the particular Point the exact nature of the Ground. Upon very mature consideration I have adopted as a general Principle, that in the establishment of this Province in its infant state, & taking into consideration the number of troops which are allotted for its defence, the force & the nature of the surrounding Nations, that Block Houses of Stone to be placed in Islands, on points of Land are the least Expensive & most proper species of fortification. Such Block Houses & in the Order I should wish them to be Constructed at *York*, the Island near the Harbour at *Long Point*, the Islands at *Bois Blanc* & Maisonville in the Streight of Detroit, & on Messisague Point, commanding the Niagara River, & some Point that may serve to command the Harbour & town of Kingston—

My first & Principal object is that of erecting a Block House to command York Harbour, an Explanation of which allowing for those deviations that the Situation of ground may occasion, may serve to elucidate the Ideas on which the whole may be formed—

To collect the numerous Stores for the civil purposes of the Government which are now dispersed into various places, as the Necessity of the case has compelled, I propose that the *store houses*[8] for these temporary purposes should be built so as to become the Cavalier or lower story of a Block House, which might serve for the Arsenals of the Country.

This Story as applicable to a permanent purpose, I proposed to make *Bombproof* & as the position admits, with such doors & apertures for Air, as in case of siege, might be a healthy Barrack for the Garrison to retire to.

Upon the roof of this Story, as on a Cavalier, I proposed to erect a Barbette Battery of the Heaviest Artillery, intermixed with lighter Pieces, which not only might effectually command the outworks & adjacent Batteries but also the Entrance of the Harbour, & all possibility of any Vessels which might enter therein from remaining there in safety—& I beg to observe to Your Grace, that this is a material object as there is no place within the Bay between Niagara & this place, where a Vessel that draws three feet of water can enter or anchor in safety—

The Upper Story I wished to form as a Blockhouse of Wood, Musket-proof, but slight; & which might serve generally as a Barrack for the Garrison, but which might be removed with the greatest facility, & if occasioned required it, embarked & put together in any given point at the shortest notice.

The enclosed Letter[9] which I do myself the Honor of submitting

[7]Probably Aitkin's "Plan of York Harbour" which was also sent with B 1.

[8]On Gibraltar (Hanlan's) Point.

[9]See note 5. Pilkington wrote that stone, lime, and timber could be easily procured.

to Your Grace from Lt Pilkington contains the aggregate of his Estimate—the particulars He left at Niagara, as his Presence here, was unexpected, my wishing him to accompany me across the Communication to Lake Huron.

Added to the materials which Lt. Pilkington speaks of as easily to be procured; I trust that I shall be able to establish a Brick Yard at a very cheap rate on a point I wish to level near to the proposed situation of the Barracks. In the Plan, Your Grace will observe the point[10] marked out for Barracks. It is an exceedingly healthy spot, capable of being easily fortified & in that case of essentially contributing to the protection of the Harbour. At present, if it be possible I mean to Hut the Queens Rangers, so that their Log Buildings may serve as a good security against any attacks of the Indians, should such be meditated, of which at their discontent & dissensions, & the Efforts of the United States to turn them against this Colony have spread an incredible Alarm amongst the Inhabitants.

A Saw Mill[11] is building for Government at a most convenient spot within three miles of the post & from which I propose to supply all such materials as may be wanted at any post on Lake Ontario at the Cheapest rate.

I have collected hither some condemned Eighteen pounders, which I purpose to have placed *Enpotrado* on a sandy point marked on the Plan—I have also procured five Eighteen Pound Carronades, & ten of twelve Pounders mounted upon slides—to these I have added an excellent Brass medium twelve pounder intended for a Gun Boat, all which may be placed in the Block House till it is supplied with Guns proper for its situation & advantages.

These Guns, I hope may be of the largest Calibre, & that Your Grace will also order me to be furnished with some Howitzers of ten Inches—I conceive that this Peninsula at some future period will be strongly fortified as the Harbour must become the Naval Arsenal of Lake Ontario. I beg to remark to Your Grace, that the Sandy Peninsula is so healthy, as that the native Indians have requested permission to encamp upon it with their families at the sickly Season—

B 3 SIMCOE TO RICHMOND
[*P.A.O. Simcoe Papers*]

York Novr. 22d 1793.

I do myself the honor of transmitting to Your Grace the Duplicate of my Letter of the 23d of September.

I take this opportunity of observing to Your Grace that the Season having been so favorable, the Troops are hutting themselves in this Post with great Expedition: from the Selection of the Materials, the Experience & Energy of the Officers & Soldiers, I have reason to believe

[10]Site of Fort York.

[11]The King's mill on the Humber River, near Bloor Street.

that they will build comfortable Barracks of *Log Work*, which will last, It is to be presumed, for Seven Years; this Circumstance precludes the necessity of my transmitting Estimates for *Stone Barracks* as in my dispatch I had intimated to your Grace. . . .

B 4 SAMUEL SMITH TO DAVID SHANK
[*T.P.L., Peter Russell Papers*]

York September 9 1796

I obtained an Order from Major General Simcoe, previous to his leaving this, to bring the Stockade into a smaller Compass, in Consequence of the few men likely to remain here. The manner I wish to have the Stockades put will lessen the Expence greatly by the Magazine being moved about twenty Yards, and as I forgot to mention this Circumstance to the M. General and obtain his order for so doing, I shall be glad to have your Instructions respecting the moving of it.—

As the Barracks appear to want something done to them to make the men Comfortable for the Winter, I have thought it proper to request Capt. Graham to inspect them and let me know what repairs are necessary to be made. —He informs me that the two Hutts formerly the old store require new Shingling, the Gavel ends newboarded, a hearth laid, and new plastering between the Logs, the Hut next to it a new hearth & plastering between the Logs and the one next to Mr. Cowells,[12] a new Chimney back, new door Posts, and the floor repaired; and the Hut that I am in requires some repairs also.—

From the great distance the Officers and men at this Post have now to bring their Winters fire wood, and thinking that the present Allowance of a Dollar per Cord not adequate to the destruction of the Mens' necessaries and Cloathing, I shall be glad to be informed if a greater allowance, Cannot be made or a Contract entered into by the Barrack Master or some other person with some of the Inhabitants of York for a Supply of even one half or a third of the Quantity wanted.—I am informed there are several People here would engage to supply a considerable Quantity, and I believe on Moderate terms.—Straw likewise will be wanted for the use of the men, and I believe may be had in the Neighborhood.

B 5 PRESCOTT TO RUSSELL
[*P.A.O., Peter Russell Papers*]

Quebec 21st June 1797

. . . I am sorry I cannot accede to your Request of making York a Military Post unless expressly directed so to do by One of His Majestys Secretaries of State—At your desire I changed my Plan of employing the Queens Rangers this year, and they were ordered to York; As the

[12]Lieutenant Robert Cowell served in the 99th Regiment and Queen's Rangers.

Troops must have quarters wherever they may be stationed, and the remaining Huts are reported from your personal Inspection of them to be insufficient for the numbers of the Regiment, you will please to desire an Estimate to be sent down thro the Engineer at Fort George of the expence for erecting so many Huts in addition to those already occupied as may conveniently lodge the Regiment, on which I will give what directions may be necessary. . . .

B 6 RUSSELL TO PRESCOTT
[*T.P.L., Peter Russell Papers*]

York 30 June 1797

. . . I must Submit to your Excellencys reasons for not taking York under your immediate Protection as an Established Post, to be supported from the Sums alloted for the Army Extraordinaries.—I shall in consequence move the Council for their Concurrence to my erecting a Block House for the accomodation of part of the Queens Rangers, and to be an occasional Shelter to the Inhabitants should any sudden Irruption of the Indians break in upon them, and I shall be obliged to your Excellency, if you permit the Engineer Lieut. Pilkington to give directions for laying out the Ground here to the best advantage for answering that end, and to draw out an Estimate of the probable Expence.

B 7 RUSSELL TO ÆNEAS SHAW[13]
[*T.P.L., D. W. Smith Papers*]

(Copy) West Niagara 18 July 1797

You will be pleased to send me a return of the State and effective strength of the Militia under your Command, and cause 100 men to be selected by Lot or their own voluntary Act with an adequate proportion of Commissioned and non Commissioned Officers to be in readiness to turn out for immediate Service in the field when called upon—[14]

I do not mean by this that these men and Officers shall be now taken from their present avocations, but that they shall hold themselves in readiness to be embodied on the shortest notice, which for the sake of the Country I do not propose to do until a very evident necessity may oblige them to take that measure—

The Officer commanding at Fort York will have directions to deliver to your order one hundred stand of small arms with five thousand Ball Cartridges, with a proportionable quantity of Flints—and I am to request that you will cause the Ammunition to be properly secured; and the Arms to be kept in constant good order until they may be wanted—

[13]Shaw was Lieutenant of the County of York until 1798, when he was succeeded by D. W. Smith.

[14]During the summer of 1797 and the following winter there was a danger of an Indian war. Russell was perhaps overly conscious of this possibility.

B 8 Russell to Prescott
[*T.P.L., Peter Russell Papers*]

Upper Canada 19 Augt 1797

. . . Before my receipt of your Excellencys Letter of the 21st. I had requested the favor of Lieut. Pilkington of the Royal Engineers to go over to York; and, after viewing the ground occupied by the Queens Rangers, to recommend such a Disposition of it as may supply that regiment with comfortable Winter Quarters at the least possible Expence to the public;—I gave him leave at the same time to make use of the frame of a Block House which had been prepared there under General Simcoes Orders, but never raised.—Upon Mr. Pilkington's return the day before yesterday he shewed me the Plan he had formed with the assistance of the Block House for providing a Barrack for seventy men, which with a little repair to the Huts within the Stockade of last Winter will amply accomodate the whole regiment.—Mr. Pilkington sends to Col. Mann by this Oppy. the plan of his proposed Work with an Estimate of the probable Expence. And tho' that Officer thinks that the Paragraph from your Excellencys Letter, which I communicated to him does not altogether warrant this sort of Arrangement; I have yet taken the liberty to request him to proceed immediately upon it, as it may give a more Military appearance to the Place, enable the Officers to keep their men under better Discipline, and provide at a trifling Expence a Beacon and light House for Vessels entering the Harbour.—Advantages which I trust may induce your Excellencys Aprobation; especially as Mr. Pilkington informs me that the Expence in Addition to the Block House will not be much; and were we to wait at this Season of the year for your Excellencys Answer, the winter might probably catch us before the men could be placed under cover.—However if this Arrangement should not accord with your Excellency's Intentions, I humbly request that no Censure may fall upon the Engineer, whom I have very much pressed for the reasons I have stated to proceed in the Execution of his Plan, without waiting the return of your Excellency's Pleasure. . . .

B 9 Russell to Prescott
[*P.A.C., C1206, pp. 189-91; printed in* Russell Correspondence, *ed. Cruikshank, II, 70-1*]

Upper Canada York 21st Jany. 1798.

I am extremely concerned to find by your Excellency's letter No. 20 that you are displeased with my having directed a Blockhouse to be erected for the accomodation of the Queen's Rangers, after my receiving your letters to me, numbered 7 & 12. I have therefore the honor to State to your Excellency in explanation, that having been requested by a Committee of the Executive Council to take immediate measures for putting this place in a State of Defence, and having the Materials of a Blockhouse by me, which had been already provided and paid for by the Lt. Govr., I judged that I could not carry the wishes of the Council more Œconomically into Execution, than by endeavoring to combine the object of them with that of the Covering which it was indispensibly necessary to provide for the Regiment stationed here. I was therefore induced to submit to your Excy. the arrangements which I had the honor of proposing in my Letter of the 19th of August last. And being apprehensive that my waiting for your Excy's answer might draw us too near to the approach of Winter for carrying these objects into Execution, I ventured to request the Engineer to proceed upon so much of his Estimate as might at least cover the erection of the Blockhouse in question, and the repairing as many Huts as might be wanted in addition for the Winter accomodation of the Troops at York. This I did on a presumption that the Expence of erecting a Blockhouse to hold Seventy men, would not greatly exceed what the building huts for the lodging an equal number might amount to; for I was assured that most of the old huts (which had outstood the time they were built for) were now so crazy they could not admit of repair. I considered moreover that forty huts at £20 each (which is probably rating them at less upon an average than they can be built for according to the present prices) would not fall much short of the Estimated Expence of all the Arrangements I had recommended; And I consequently flattered myself with the hopes of their meeting with your Excy's approbation, or I should not have presumed to cause a deviation from the Course which your Excy had pointed out.

Lieut. Pilkington having made a requisition for £375 to enable him to execute this service, I advanced that Sum to him in Novr. last by my Warrant on the Receiver Genl.—I shall now direct a Survey to be taken of the State of the Hutts, & that an Estimate of the probable expence of repairing or rebuilding (as may be found necessary) so many as would have been wanted for the accomodation of the Rangers, had the Blockhouse not been erected, may be forthwith prepared for your Excy's information.

B 10 Russell to Prescott

[*P.A.C., C1206, pp. 237–8; printed in* Russell Correspondence, *ed. Cruikshank, II, 162–3*]

York 28th May 1798.

A Paragraph in your Excy's letter No. 21, dated the 11th Sept. (which I received on the 20th Jany. last) having given me reason to suppose that your Excy is inclined to pay "what it might have cost to repair the old and construct addtl huts for the accomodation of the Queen's Rangers at York" I took the liberty of requesting Major Shank to order a survey on the Huts originally built for, and which the Regt. under his Command must have occupied had my arrangements for its accomodation not taken place; and of sending his report thereof to Lt. Pilkington with my desire that he would state to me the probable expence it might have taken to re-establish them.

I have now therefore the honor of transmitting to your Excy the report of said survey, and Capt. Pilkington's Estimate thereon amounting to £563.6.3¾ and to mention that the disbursements in the Engr. dept. and the purchase of materials for building the Blockhouse and repairing the huts I had directed (which were paid to him by my Warrant of the 3d Inst.) amounting to £408.13.4½ are nearly £150 less than the reestablishing the Huts for Lodging that Regiment would have probably taken. But I must at the same time observe that some Hutts may be still required for quartering its full complement of men and officers.

The Isolated situation of York, surrounded either by water or an unsettled Country makes me anxious to open Roads with as little delay as possible for communicating with the head of the Lake on one side and the Bay of Quinté on the other; that we may facilitate the supplies of Provisions from those Quarters, and thereby lessen the enormous Prices of them, to which the Civil Officers and every other Person whose business calls him to the Seat of Government, are at present exposed. I am therefore in hopes that your Excy may pardon my requesting to have the Detachments from the Queen's Rangers doing duty at Fort Erie & the Chippawa ordered (if the service can possibly admit it) to join the rest of the Corps at this place; that the Regt. may be employed on that and the other services in aid of the settlement of this Province for which it was originally raised.

B 11 Russell to D. W. Smith
[*T.P.L., D. W. Smith Papers*]

York 19th December 1798

I have carefully looked over the list of officers, their Distribution, and the Alarm Posts for the York Militia, which you sent me and judging the whole as judicious as the present State of Circumstances can admit, I return them to you with my Signature.

You have certainly acted with proper Delicacy in respect to Mr. Jarvis—tho no prior Commission from a Lieut. Governor (which I have no doubt Mr. Jarvis has, notwithstanding my never having heard of it before) can contravene an Act of the Legislature, which having given to the Lieutenant the Nomination of his Deputy leaves you of course at liberty to name to that office whomever you may judge proper —For if it was otherwise the Lieutenant might be often counteracted in his best Designs by his Deputy, who not being of his own chusing might not be equally confided in as if he was. The legislature ought however to have permitted the Governor to appoint Deputies to those counties, whose Inhabitants from their Number or Quality were not yet ripe for the Dignity of Lieutenants.

I have taken the liberty of lending to the Count de Puisaye[15] twelve stand of arms out of the hundred appropriated to your Militia which he is to return in the Spring. But should you in the mean time have occasion for more than eighty Stand, the Commander will have directions to supply you with the Deficiency out of the Spare Arms in Store. . . .

B 12 Officers of the York Militia, 1798
[*T.P.L., D. W. Smith Papers*]

Wm. Jarvis Esqr. Professing to have the Lt. Govrs. Commission as Depy. Lieut & Colonel of the York Militia	East Riding	Deputy Lieutenants
Richard Beasley[16] Esqr. JP. Member of Parliament	West Riding	Deputy Lieutenants
The Honble D W Smith Lieut of the County	Colonel	Field Officers
John Small Esqr. JP. Clerk of the Honble. EC & formerly Captain in the British Militia	Lieut Coll.	Field Officers

1. Mr. Wm. Graham formerly a Captain in the Kings Service, & now on half pay
2. Mr. Fred Baron dehaen,[17] formerly a Captain in the German troops, employed by his Majesty
3. Richard Beasley Esqr, Member of Parliament, now Capn. in the Lincoln Militia
4. John Wilson[18] Esq, Justice of the Peace, formerly Capn. of Militia, in Nova Scotia.
5. Mr. Wm. Chewitt, of the Sur Gens. Dept. formerly, Capn. of Militia in the Eastern District
6. Mr. Wm. Berczy, said to be already commissioned
7. Mr. George Playter, a U E Loyalist & Pensioner
8. Mr. Thos. Ridout, Lieutt. from the Lincoln Militia.
9. Mr. Alexr. Burns,[19] Secretary to His Honor the President.
10. Mr. Benj. Mallory,[20] son in Law to the late Mr. Dayton.

} To be Captains

---

[15]Joseph Geneviève, Comte de Puisaye (1755–1827), was the leader of a party of French royalists, who were settled in parts of Markham and Vaughan Townships in 1798. He himself chose to live near Niagara and returned to England in 1802. The settlement was a failure.

[16]Richard Beasley (1761?–1841) was one of the first settlers at the Head of the Lake and a prominent merchant.

[17]Frederick, Baron de Hoen (1764?–1816?), farmed on Lot no. 1, Yonge Street, at the northwest corner of Yonge and Eglinton Streets. He had financial difficulties and died unmarried about 1816.

[18]John Wilson (b. 1740?) was lessee of the King's Mill on the Humber.

[19]On January 11, 1799, Benjamin Wilson, formerly Captain of Militia under Governor Tryon, and one of the first settlers in Whitby, was appointed Captain, vice Burns, resigned.

[20]Benajah Mallory had large tracts of land in Burford Township, which had been assigned to his father-in-law, Abraham Dayton, for settlement in 1792. From

1 Mr. Jno. Denniston,[21] formerly an Officer in the British Militia. 2 Mr. Wm. Allan,[22] Lieutt from the Lincoln Militia. 3. George Chisholm[23] Esqr. Justice of the Peace. 4 Mr. Alexr. Wood,[24] Merchant 5 Mr. Jacob Herkimer[25] Do. brother in law to the Honble. R.H.. 6 Mr. Edward Wright,[26] formerly Qr. Mr. Queens Rang. 7 Mr. Archd. Cameron[27] Merchant, formerly Sergt. Q. Rangers 8 Mr. Thomas Barry, Merchant 9 Mr. Saml. Herron Merchant 10. Mr. Archd. Thompson,[28] formerly a Militia Officer 11. Mr. Wheeler Douglass,[29] Merchant Miller 12. A German, said to be commissioned	To be Lieutenants

1805 to 1812 he was a member of Parliament, but in 1813 he went over to the Americans and was second in command of Joseph Willcocks' Canadian Volunteers.

[21]John Denison (1755–1824) was born in Hedon, Yorkshire, and came to Upper Canada in 1792. He settled at Kingston, where he rented a brewery from Joseph Forsyth. In 1796 he moved to York and managed the Russell farm, Petersfield. His wife was a friend of Elizabeth Russell. He later moved to his own farm at Weston. He was the founder of the prominent Canadian military family.

[22]William Allan (1770–1853) was born near Huntly, Aberdeenshire. He came to Montreal in 1787 and worked as a junior clerk with Forsyth, Richardson & Co. Sometime prior to the spring of 1796 he came to York where he opened a general store and built a wharf. From 1797 to 1801 he was in partnership with Alexander Wood. He was appointed Collector of Customs, Inspector of Stills and Taverns, Postmaster of York, and Treasurer of the Home District. As Major, and in 1813 as Colonel of the 3rd Regiment, York Militia, he was active during the War of 1812. He was later president of the Bank of Upper Canada, and of the City of Toronto and Lake Huron Rail Road Company, governor of the British America Fire and Life Assurance Company, commissioner of the Canada Company, and member of the Legislative and Executive Councils. In July, 1822, he sold his business to J. W. Gamble & Co.

[23]George Chisholm (1745–1842) immigrated from near Inverness to New York State in 1773. He served in Burgoyne's army and settled near Shelburne, N.S., after the Revolutionary War but came to Upper Canada six years later. He settled in East Flamborough Township and was one of the earliest settlers on Burlington Bay.

[24]Alexander Wood (1772?–1844) was born near Aberdeen, and came to Canada about 1793. He became a partner with Joseph Forsyth and Alexander [?] Aitkin in the Kingston Brewing Company, but in 1797 came to York and opened a store in partnership with William Allan. After this partnership was dissolved in 1801, Wood became an independent and very successful merchant. After the War of 1812 he gradually retired. He was active as a magistrate from 1800, and was prominent in many of the York philanthropic societies. He was a friend of John Strachan. In 1810–12, 1817–21, and for the last two years of his life, he lived in Scotland, where he died.

[25]Jacob Herchmer (Herkimer) was a son of Johan Jost Herkimer, a Loyalist, and a nephew of General Nicholas Herkimer of the Revolutionary Army. He was a fur trader and merchant in York and at Rice Lake and was drowned in the loss of the *Speedy* in 1804. His sister Mary married as her second husband Robert Hamilton as his second wife.

[26]Edward Wright immigrated to America before the Revolution. He returned to England after it, and came to Canada as Quartermaster of the Queen's Rangers

1. Mr. James Ruggles,[30] Merchant, Nephew of B G Ruggles 2. Mr. Gamble,[31] from Ireland, Merchant 3. Mr. Jno. Tenbrook,[32] Son of Major Tenbrook 4. Mr. Saml. D. Cozens,[33] Son of Capt. Cozens, & asst. in Secys Office 5. Mr. Nat Ruggles,[30] Merct. Nephew of B G Ruggles 6. A German, said to be commissioned 7 vacant 8 Ditto	To be Ensigns
Mr. Alexr. McNabb[34] to be Adjt. with the Rank of Lieutt. Mr. Abner Miles,[35] to be Quarter Master	Staff

D W Smith
Lieut of the County of York

Approved
Peter Russell President &c &c &c

Cavalry. His son, Edward Graves Simcoe Wright, who kept the Greenland Fisheries Tavern for many years, is among the claimants for the title of first European child born in York.

[27]Archibald Cameron (d. 1806) had lands in Etobicoke and a shop in York.

[28]Archibald Thomson was a brother of David and Andrew Thomson, pioneer settlers in Scarborough Township.

[29]Wheeler Douglas (1750–1829) came from New York State in 1798 and built a mill on Whitemans Creek in Burford Township.

[30]James Ruggles (d. 1804) and his younger brother Nathaniel were nephews of Brigadier General Timothy Ruggles, who served in the army under Lord Amherst and was one of the most prominent Massachusetts Loyalists. They belonged to the sixth generation of their family in Massachusetts, and kept a shop on Yonge Street. James Ruggles was drowned in the loss of the *Speedy*. Nathaniel Ruggles declined serving in the militia.

[31]This could be Richard Gamble, or Nathaniel Gamble (d. 1833), or his son Nathaniel Gamble (1764–1836). Richard Gamble was granted Lot 17, south side of Hospital (Richmond) Street in 1798, but appears only once in the List of Inhabitants, in 1799. He also had a lot on the east side of Yonge Street, between Eglinton and Lawrence Avenues. The Nathaniel Gambles had Yonge Street lots too, and for a time kept a tavern. Nathaniel, Junior, served in the 1st Regiment of York militia during the War 1812. The Gamble nominated in 1798 refused to serve.

[32]John Ten Broeck was the son of Peter Ten Broeck, a Loyalist, who came from Albany County, New York, where the family had settled in the seventeenth century. Peter Ten Broeck served in the York Provincial Regiment during the Revolution and was one of the first settlers in the Niagara district.

[33]Cozens declined serving, and was replaced by Quartermaster Abner Miles.

[34]Alexander Macnab (d. 1815) was born in Virginia, the son of a surgeon who served in Major McAlpin's Corps of Loyalists. In 1797 he was appointed confidential clerk to the Executive Council. He became an ensign in the Queen's Rangers in 1800 and entered a British regiment after the Rangers' disbandment. As A.D.C. to Lt. General Sir Thomas Picton, he was killed at Waterloo.

[35]Abner Miles (1752?–1806) was one of the earliest store and tavern keepers in York. In 1792 with Samuel Heron he owned the merchant paquet, *York*. About 1802 he moved to his Yonge Street property in Vaughan Township at Richmond Hill and kept a tavern and general store there.

The following being only collateral anticipations, in case of His Honors approval, & not thought improper to be now communicated—

Officers as posted to Companies, til further Orders—

Company	No.	Officers	Alarm Post
Town Companys	No. 1	Captain Chewitt Lieuts. Allan, Wood	Alarm Post, The cross Street at Miles's Tavern
	No. 2	Captain Burns Lieuts. Denniston, Herkimer	
The Don Company		Captain Ridout Lieut. Herron Ens: Cozens	Alarm Post Scaddings Bridge
The Humber Company		Captain Wilson Lieut Barry Ens Ruggles Junr.	Alarm Post Humber Mill
The Yonge Street Company		Capn. Graham Lieut. Wright Ens: Ruggles Senr.	Heights above a ravine in a central situation
Markham Companys	No. 1	Capn. Dehaen Lieut. Cameron Ens: Gamble	Markham Mills
	No. 2	Capn. Berczy Lieut. A German, incog. Ens. Do. Do.	
Company of the Eastern Circle, incg Whitby, Pickering & Scarboro		Capn. Playter Lieut Thompson Ensign, vacant	Alarm post Centre front lot Whitby
Company of the Burlington Circle, (West Riding)		Capn. /Beasley Lieut. Chisholm Ens: Tenbrook	Alarm post, the Promontory above Mr Beasleys
Company of the Western Circle (West Riding)		Capn. Mallory Lieut Douglass Ens: vacant	Horners Mill

NB—The 8 first Companys are in the Eastern Riding—The 2 last mentioned in the West Riding—As the Town Companys, & those of the East riding increase; the west riding companies will be seperated from them; towards forming a small battalion of themselves—It is hoped also, that Whitby Pickering & Scarborough, will in the course of time, produce a second battalion for the East riding—

B 13 ÆNEAS SHAW TO JAMES GREEN[36]
[*P.A.C., C547, p. 26*]

York 19th. November 1801.

. . . The Kitchens at the Block House[37] in Town have been long finished, but I am sorry to say that I have not yet been able to obey The General's directions, to send a Party to occupy them, owing to the number of men necessarily employed in cutting Fuel, and a pretty full Hospital, but in a few days I shall be able to send some men there although not quite the number directed.

I hope I do not alarm you by mentioning our full Hospital, although there has been a good deal of Fever and Ague amongst the Inhabitants, we have had very little at the Garrison; our Hospital was filled with a variety of cases not arising from Climate, and all, one excepted, unimportant. The man of the 41st serving at the Generals is the only Fever and Ague case we have, and that appears to be pretty obstinate, having continued six weeks and does not yet give way to medicine, but the change the weather is now taking will probably restore him. . . .

B 14 R. H. BRUYÈRES[38] TO GOTHER MANN
[*P.A.C., C383, p. 6*]

12th Sept., 1802

[Copy certified by Gother Mann, 3rd Jan., 1803]

REPORT OF THE STATE OF THE PUBLIC WORKS AND BUILDINGS AT THE SEVERAL MILITARY POSTS IN UPPER CANADA

York

The several Hutts erected for temporary Quarters for Officers and Men, also the Block houses and Storehouses are in good repair for the number of men at present required to occupy them and Stores to be lodged. There are

		N. of men
7	officers' Hutts for 1 Capt. or 2 Subs ea	
2	do. for an Hospital	
1	do. Bakehouse	
1	do. Canteen	
8	do. Soldiers Quarters 16 men ea	128
1	Block house two floors	48
1	Block house town of York	48
	Total	224

[36]James Green, of the 26th Foot was military secretary to Lord Dorchester, General Hunter, and the other commanders of the forces in Canada, from 1795 to 1807.

[37]The blockhouse in York was built by Russell during the Indian scare of 1798. It stood east of the Government Buildings.

[38]Ralph Henry Bruyères (1765–1814) of the Royal Engineers served in Canada

1 Hutt for Guardhouse with an Officer's Room and Black hole adjoining
Magazine
Carriage and Engine Shed } Wood Buildings
Provision Storehouse } Wood Buildings
Indian and Commissarys Store } Wood Buildings
The Old Hutts on the West side of the Creek are condemned, and ordered to be pulled down.

B 15 Sir Isaac Brock[39] to Green
[*P.A.C., C922, p. 91*]

York July 29th, 1803

I have been dining with my Lord Bishop[40] at Justice Powell's. His Lordship had no idea of sailing till the morning, the favorable appearance of the evening has induced him to change his plan, and as he embarks immediately I must scribble a few words to say that the Grenadiers quartered in the Block House in town are falling ill of the Ague and Fever in great numbers. Within these three days ten have been removed to the garrison in consequence of being seized with these dreadful disorders. I have every reason to apprehend that the mischief is not likely to stop here. If I find that many more are affected with the same complaints I shall think it indispensably necessary to remove the whole to the garrison, altho' I am perfectly aware they will find but sorry accommodations. The garrison continues in perfect health which shews plainly that the character given of the situation of the Block House is too well founded. I shall write you more fully on the subject by the next conveyance. I have otherwise nothing particular to relate for General Hunter's information. The House, Garden and *Farm* get on in the usual quiet and improving style. I can assure you that I feel considerable uneasiness at this appearance of sickness. The General may rely on my exertions to stop if possible its progress.

---

from about 1800. In 1806 he was appointed Lieutenant Colonel commanding the Engineers in North America.

[39]Sir Isaac Brock (1769–1812) entered the army in 1785 and came to Canada as Lieutenant Colonel of the 49th Regiment in 1802. When a detachment of the 49th replaced the 41st Regiment at York in the spring of 1803, Brock was stationed briefly in York. He became a major general in 1811, and Administrator of Upper Canada just before the outbreak of the War. He was responsible for the capture of Detroit, but was killed at the Battle of Queenston Heights.

[40]Jacob Mountain (1749–1825) was the first Anglican bishop of Quebec, consecrated in 1793. In 1803 he made a pastoral visit to York, which was part of the diocese of Quebec until 1839.

B 16 Sir Roger Sheaffe[41] to Green
[P.A.C., C923, pp. 56–8]

York 9th. August 1805.

I have to acquaint you, for the information of Lt. General Hunter, that the two Deserters Privates Collins and Faulkner of the 49th Regt., who were in confinement here, effected their escape early in the morning of the 1st Instant, they were locked up in the blackhole and handcuffed, and were ascertained to be in it between the hours of twelve and one; on going in after Reveillé beating the Serjeant discovered that they had gone off by raising a plank of the floor, and digging a passage under the logs at the rear of the building; one pair of handcuffs and its lock were found on the floor, and also a nail, with its point turned, with which the lock had been picked; the Man, on whom those handcuffs had been, left his Jacket behind, but as neither the Jacket nor the handcuffs of the other were found, and his lock was the better one of the two, it is probable the nail was tried in vain to open it.—Parties have been employed in every direction, the woods have been searched, and descriptions have been dispersed—but hitherto, without success:—I do not, however, relinquish the hope of their being retaken, especially as it does not appear, that any boat or canoe belonging to York or its vicinity is missing. Though the circumstances attending the escape of those Men would lead to a belief that one or more of the Guard connived at it; yet on investigation I cannot find that proof of connivance can be fastened on any Individual belonging to it. . . .

B 17 William Derenzy[42] to Green
[P.A.C., C547, pp. 1–3]

York 18th January 1807.—

. . . I have also the honor to acknowledge the Receipt of a Letter from you, of the 3d. of November last,[43] respecting the repairs of the several

[41]Sir Roger Hale Sheaffe (1763–1851) was born in Boston and entered the British army in 1778. He served in Canada in 1787–97, 1802–11, and 1812–13. In 1804–5 he was commanding officer at York, as Lieutenant Colonel of the 49th Regiment. After Brock's death, he became Administrator of Upper Canada. He was in command at York during its capture by the Americans in April, 1813, and partly because of this defeat was recalled to England in June, 1813.

[42]Captain William Derenzy of the 41st Regiment was in command at York, after the Regiment's headquarters were moved to Fort George. The 41st replaced the 49th at York at the end of 1805.

[43]Green wrote to Derenzy that Brock had said that windows should be open when guns were fired and had asked what had happened to the trap doors to the lofts. Brock also thought that the damage to the berths must have been caused by neglect, which Derenzy was to prevent in future (P.A.C., C1214, pp. 40–1, Green to Derenzy, Nov. 3, 1806.)

Barrack rooms at York; Ordered by Colonel Brock, Commander in Chief of the Forces in both Canadas.

With respect to Colonel Brock's Observation on the Barrack Windows not being Opened during the time, the Guns were fired; that no destruction of Window Glass could have happened: I beg leave to observe, that the lower Sashes were all up, the Glasses that were broken, were in the upper Sashes which could not be moved.—respecting the Trap Doors for the Cellars, they are all present, but in such a bad state, as makes them dangerous, any man by chance steping on them is in danger falling through and being hurted thereby.—There are no Lofts in any of the Barrack rooms Occupied by the men, consequently there can be no Trap Doors wanted;—The Trap Doors mentioned were for the Cellars in the Barrack rooms.—As to the Boards of the Births, they are all present, but in such a bad State from long use, that the men Sleeping in the Top Births often fall thro'w on those sleeping in the lower Ones, likewise I have to observe; that it is the Opinion of Thomas Haynes Carpenter, that there are many of the Births not worth repairing. . . .

B 18 JOHN MCGILL TO WILLIAM JARVIS[44]
[*T.P.L., S. P. Jarvis Papers*]

York 29th November 1807

I herewith inclose for your information and guidance the Copy of a Letter which I have received from His Excellency the Lieutenant Governor dated the 26th. of the present month, ordering the Militia for the County of York to be immediately assembled, when one fourth of the whole number are either by Volunteers, or by Ballot to be selected and form a Detachment for actual Service, and after being Inspected are to be dismissed with orders to assemble at an Hours notice.

My attention for the purpose of carrying his Excellencys orders into effect, being turned to the Militia up Yonge Street and the adjacent Settlements

I am to request, that your attention for the same purpose, may be turned to the Militia settled in Etobicoke, York, Scarboro and Pickering to the South West of Duffins Creek, by ordering them to assemble at the Town of York on Saturday the fifth day of December next—and that the Militia to the North East of Duffins Creek, in Pickering and Whitby, be ordered to assemble at Mr Stevens House in Whitby on Wednesday the ninth day of December next, at Eleven oClock in the forenoon, at which times, and places, a draft of one Fourth of the whole, either by Volunteers, or by Ballot, is to take place, which

[44]McGill writes as Lieutenant of the County of York, to his Deputy Lieutenant, Jarvis. Relations with the United States had become very strained, and there was a strong possibility of war.

detachment of Militia after being Inspected, you will dismiss, at the same time ordering them when called upon to assemble immediately—the residents in Etobicoke, York, Scarboro & part of Pickering at the Government Buildings in York, and you are to order Officers in proportion to the number of men, who will be ready to take Command of them—

The Detachment belonging to Whitby and Pickering, you will order to be assembled in the first instance (when called upon for actual Service) at such place as you may appoint—they are however immediately afterwards to be marched under the Command of an Officer to Join the other detachments at York—

Should any of the Militia from the age of Sixteen to fifty be absent from this meeting, who are not exempt by Law, you are to take immediate measures for their being fined and the fine levied;[45] and in case of Quakers, Menonists and Tunkers having refused to pay their Composition money as directed by law—you are to cause execution to issue against such as have produced Certificates under the age of fifty.

B 19 Brock to Noah Freer[46]
[P.A.C., C550, p. 131]

York U.C.
November 10th 1811

Until very lately two Oxen were maintained at the public charge for the purpose of assisting in clearing the vast quantity of heavy timber which grows close to this Garrison—making roads—besides being usefully employed on other necessary service—

It appears very evident from the trifling progress made by the Military in this essential work for some years past, that the oxen were either kept idle, or employed for other purposes, which, I believe, occasioned their being sold—

Being anxious to continue the improvements begun by the late Lt General Hunter, I have to request His Excellency The Commander of the Forces to have the goodness to sanction the renewal of an establishment of such evident utility—

B 20 Freer to Brock
[P.A.C., Upper Canada Sundries]

Military Secretary's Office
Quebec 23d. January 1812.

I am directed to acquaint you that Orders have been given to the

[45]Any male inhabitant between the ages of 16 and 50 who was absent from training was fined 10 shillings. Quakers, Menonists, and Tunkers paid 20 shillings a year in peace, and £5 a year in war, for exemption from service.

[46]Noah Freer, of the Nova Scotia Fencibles, was appointed A.D.C. and military

Ordnance Storekeeper here for the issue of Fifty Swords and Fifty Waist-belts for the use of the Volunteer Cavalry[47] who have offered to enrol themselves at York, and that they have been transported to Montreal to be sent to Upper Canada by the most expeditious manner; And I am to request that you will direct One hundred Horse-Pistols may be furnished for the same purpose, from the Ordnance Store at Kingston.

B 21 ANDREW GRAY[48] TO SIR GEORGE PREVOST[49]
[*P.A.C., C728, pp. 77–8*]

York 29th Jany, 1812

. . . There is every inducement to build the new Schooner at York, as exclusive of the arguments already adduced in favor of establishing the Naval Yard at this place, there are the following considerations, which are of great importance at this moment—first, They have as much to do at Kingston as they can get through with at present, in fitting out the Moira[50] and mounting the Carronades &c. It will therefore extend our resources in Ship Building, if we could at the same time carry on the work at both places. This would also have the effect of paving the way for the removal of the Marine Depot from Kingston to this place, a change greatly to be desired. The Toronta[51] having been broken up here, furnishes an immediate supply of Iron Work, and a variety of other articles that may be worked up in the New Vessel, and in addition to what may be supplied by this means, there is a considerable assortment of Naval Stores appropriated to what is termed the Civil Service of the Province. This Store Genl. Brock will use as the service may require. I have gone round the Harbour with the General, and have examined, as far as the season of the year would admit of it, the different places for building a Vessel, and find there will be no difficulty on that head. The Genl. proposes putting the Superintendance of the

---

secretary to Sir George Prevost in 1811 and remained with him during his Canadian career.

[47]This troop, commanded by John Button of Markham, was attached to the 1st Regiment of York militia and served throughout the War of 1812.

[48]Andrew Gray (d. 1813) entered the army in 1808. He was appointed an Assistant Quartermaster General in 1812, and for the first 10 months of the year he was an Acting Deputy Quartermaster General. He was killed during the attack on Sackett's Harbour in 1813.

[49]Sir George Prevost (1767–1816) entered the army in 1784. In 1811 he became Governor and Commander in Chief of the Canadas. He was held personally responsible for the withdrawal after the attack on Sackett's Harbour in 1813, and the defeat at Plattsburg in 1814, but died a week before the date of his court martial.

[50]The *Earl of Moira*, built in 1805, was undergoing a complete overhaul at Kingston.

[51]The yacht *Toronto*, built by John Dennis in 1799, was wrecked on Toronto Island shortly before.

Work into the hands of the person who commanded the Toronto, who seems to be every way qualified for the task of Building, and commanding the New Schooner[52]. . . .

B 22 Prevost to Liverpool[53]
[P.A.C., C1218, pp. 170–1]

Mily Secretarys Office
Quebec 3rd March 1812

I have the honor to state for your Lordships information that York, the seat of Government in Upper Canada is a position well adapted for a Citadel and a deposit of Military Stores, for the land and Lake service, in that Province, and that I conceive it a matter of importance it should be occupied, but that in its present state it is entirely open to attack, and no Works of any description have hitherto been constructed for its protection.—

I beg leave to enclose herewith for your Lordships consideration the Copy of a Report which has been submitted by the Commanding Royal Engineer, upon a recommendation of Major General Brock, for fortifying the Kings reserve at York, whereon the Government House stands, and I have to acquaint your Lordship that I have in consequence directed the Ground proposed, and the Country in its Vicinity to be accurately surveyed and reported upon by an Officer of Engineer's, as soon as the season will permit; and as I intend to inspect that Post in the course of the Summer, I shall have the honor to communicate to Your Lordship upon this subject more distinctly. . . .

B 23 Bruyères' "Report Relative to the Present State of York Upper Canada"[54]
[P.A.C., C388, p. 165]

The position of this Post owing to the nature of the Ground is so unfavorable for defence that it would require the construction of a strong Work near the spot whereon the Government House is situated effectually to protect the entrance of the Harbor. It is at present defended by two small Batteries one on this point.— the other contiguous to the Block House within the enclosure of the Garrison.—These Batteries are

[52]The schooner *Prince Regent,* carrying 12 guns, was launched at York in June, 1812. She was built under the superintendence of Lieutenant Fish, formerly commander of the *Toronto.* In 1813 her name was changed to *General Beresford* and in 1814 to *Netley.*

[53]Robert Banks Jenkinson, second Earl of Liverpool (1770–1828), was Secretary for War and the Colonies, 1809–12.

[54]This report is undated by Bruyères, but has been endorsed in pencil "July, 1814." This date is obviously much too late: Bruyères died on May 15, 1814; there was no vessel built at York after April, 1813; and the defences described are those prior to the American occupation. It is probably the report sent by Prevost to Liverpool on March 3, 1812.

supplied with Furnaces for Heating Shot, and directions have been given to have them enclosed. Also to have Field Carriages prepared for the 12 Pdrs in order to move them to those points that may be found most advantageous on the approach of an Enemy.—

I do not consider that a Field Work capable of any efficient resistance could be constructed near the spot where the dock yard is at present established, in sufficient time to derive any essential benefit towards the protection of the Ship that is now Building, but every means that can be adopted towards placing the Guns that are on the spot in the most favorable situations to defend the approach towards the Ship will no doubt be resorted to by Lt. Col: Hughes[55] who has recd. Instructions to attend to this Service; and to use every possible exertion towards the protection of the Post.—

B 24 Gray's "Report upon the Expediency of Removing the Marine Establishment from Kingston to York, and upon Erecting a Fortress, or Place of Arms, at the Latter Station, and Making it the Principal Depot for Military Stores, &c"

[*P.A.C., C728, pp. 94–9; printed in Wood,* Select British Documents of the Canadian War of 1812, *I, 258–62*]

The very exposed situation of Kingston renders it an extremely unfit Station for our Naval Establishment upon Lake Ontario. During the whole of the Winter, while our Ships of War are dismantled, and locked up with the Ice, they might easily be destroyed, and the Military Stores carried off; as the River freezes over every winter opposite Kingston, and thereby deprives us of the defence afforded by our Marine, and exposes us to the Attacks of a Tumult[ua]ry force, which might be sufficient to accomplish this object, should Hostilities be determined upon. The impolicy of keeping the greater part of our means of defence for the Upper Province, at a frontier Post so defenceless and exposed as Kingston, must be obvious. Here we have not only our Marine Establishment (which entails the necessity of keeping the Ordnance, Ammunition and Stores of various sorts for the equipment of the Vessels); but there is likewise the Dock yard, and the Depot of Arms for the Service of the Militia &c. and all within a days march of a Neighbour who would not let so favorable an opportunity of striking a Blow escape him, should War be the result. A loss of this nature, at the commencement of the War would be irretrivable and at once decide the fate of the Province, as the communications with the lower Province would in all probability be cut off, so that we would have no opportunity of replacing the Military Stores, if we even possessed the Means. And the destruction of the shipping, would leave the whole of our Frontier bordering on Lake Ontario totally defenceless. At present the garrison of Kingston does not exceed 100 Men, of the Veteran Battalion, and many

[55]Lieutenant Colonel Philip Hughes, Royal Engineers.

of those are totally unfit for active service. And the nature of the ground is so peculiarly circumstanced, that the garrison and Dock Yards are seperated from each other by the Strait which forms the Harbour of Kingston. The High ground from which alone the Dock Yard can be defended, is also seperated from it by another inlet, called Navy Bay. Thus, the garrison occupies one situation, the Dock Yard another, and the ground commanding it remains unoccupied!

It would appear that York combines most of the advantages to be kept in view in the selection of a Naval Station. It has a safe and commodious Harbour, and is capable of affording shelter to any Number of Vessels, where they may lay at all times in perfect safety. It has also the advantage of being easily Fortified, as the entrance is narrow, and almost close to the Government House, near which it is proposed to establish a Military Work which will have the compleat command of the Passage. There is also reason to believe that Ship Timber, and all the facilities for Building Vessels are to be procured at York, equal if not superior to those had at Kingston; But this point cannot be decided till we see how we succeed with the New Schooner recently ordered to be built at York. The seat of Government being established at York, may also be considered as one of the inducements for removing the Naval Station to this place, where the Genl. Officer Commanding would have this important branch of our Military Establishment under his own eye, which would enable him the better to direct the operations of this branch of the Service.

But the most important consideration is the safety afforded against any Coup de Main of the Enemy. York will in all probability be held as long as we have a foot of territory in Upper Canada, as from its remote situation, and being so far retired from the frontier, it is secured from any sudden assault; nothing therefore can affect it but operations having for their object the subjugation of the Province, and which object this Post is admirably calculated to defeat, if it were fortified in a proper manner, and well garrisoned. If the enemy had even over-run the greater part of the Province, while we retain York and our Naval means entire, we might still find sufficient employment for them, and procure supplies for the Garrison.

One thing seems evident, and that is, that the Navy cannot winter anywhere in safety, without an adequat Military force to protect it, or unless it is placed under the Guns of a Fortress. While our Military Establishment in these Provinces remains on its present footing, there is but little chance of our being enabled to repulse everywhere the attacks of our enemies, throughout a frontier of a thousand miles in extent. I should therefore humbly conceive that it would be highly essential to the safety of Upper Canada, to establish a Military Work somewhere on each Lake, for the protection of the Marine during the Winter.

The narrow neck of Land formed between the Lake and the Ravine at the Govt. House, has been selected by Major Genl. Brock for a

Military Post. The ground seemed perfectly well adapted for the nature of Work the Genl. had in contemplation, namely, a small irregular Fort for the sole object of enclosing the new Barracks proposed to be built, and affording accommodation to the Garrison and public Stores. This although an important object, is still far short of the Work contemplated in this Report, as affording protection to the Navy, and as capable of being maintained against a superior force. Nothing I conceive short of a *strong regular Fort* will fully answer the end proposed. It does not appear absolutely necessary that this Work should be of a very great extent, I should rather prefer a small Pentagon, or Square, with one of the sides of the Polygon upon the Lake (or Harbour). The neck of Land at the Govt. House is too much contracted, and irregular in its shape, for such a Work; it might therefore be more adviseable to establish the Work between the Garrison and Town. This ground approaches nearer to the spot where the shipping would have to winter, and from the ground being a Plain (excepting the Ravine between the Govt. House and the Garrison) without any part having a sensible command over the immediate margin of the Lake, the figure of the Work may therefore be regular.

If the Fort were constructed in a strong permanent manner, and the Scarp and Counterscarp revetted with Brick or Stone, there would be but little expence incurred in keeping it in repair. And if at any time more cover, and extent of ground were required, to give protection to our Troops, or to the Inhabitants, in the event of the Enemy over-running the Country, it would be easy to surround the Fort with a Chain of Works (open to the Fort with the exception of a Pallisaded Line at the Gorge) that might enclose a considerable tract of country, and retard the approaches of the enemy. This extension of our Position, would of course be governed by our strength, and means of Defence. All the Out-Works might be temporary, and the construction of them left till they were likely to be wanted.

Quarter Master Generals Office
Quebec 9th March 1812.

B 25 Freer to Brock
[*P.A.C., Upper Canada Sundries*]

Military Secretary's Office
Quebec 27th. April 1812.

I have received the Commands of The Commander of the Forces to acquaint you with His Excellency's having some time since, submitted to the consideration of His Majesty's Government the propriety of strengthening the Post of York, by a regular Fortification, as the seat of Government in Upper Canada, and that, at your recommendation, He had directed the King's Reserve, whereon the Government House stands, to be accurately surveyed and laid out for that purpose.

I am at the same time instructed to inform you that a representation has been transmitted to Lord Liverpool, stating that, from the exposed situation of Kingston, His Excellency is induced to consider it an extremely unfit station for our Naval Establishment on Lake Ontario, and that the impolicy of exposing the greater part of our means of defence for the Upper Province, at a defenceless frontier Post like Kingston, being obvious, His Excellency esteems it prudent and proper that the Naval Establishment, Stores, &c, should be removed by degrees to York, a situation in every respect more eligible for the security of the Navy Yard and Shipping, and where it's safe and commodious Harbour, is capable of affording Shelter at all times to any number of Vessels;—

In suggesting the propriety of this change, it is not proposed, that it should instantly be carried into effect, but that the removal of the Establishment should gradually take place, by laying out a Naval Yard upon a small Scale, and by erecting Storehouses at York to receive the Marine Stores, as the buildings allotted for them at Kingston fall into decay, unless in the mean while, Hostilities with the United States should make a more expeditious removal indispensably necessary. . . .

B 26 Forming Flank Companies, York Militia
[*T.P.L., Copy of Orderly Book, 3rd Regt., York Militia*]

Regimental Orders, 2nd May, 1812.

His Honor the President, having been pleased by a Letter from Mr. Secretary Brock, of the 27th April last, to inform me, that Lieut. Johnson[56] of the Canadian Fencibles has been appointed to perform the duties of Adjutant under my Command, in Training the Flank Companies of the 3rd Regiment of York Militia, and the Volunteers having been ordered for Parade on the 4th. instant, at 8 o'clock in Morning, that a fair, and judicious selection of Men suitable to each of the said Companies might be made,—It is hereby to be understood that when the said selection shall have been made and the Men paraded under their respective Companies (Captain Cameron's[57] the Grenadiers, and Captain Heward's[58] the light Infantry) then the Lieut. Colonel will give his approbation of the Men attached to each. . . .

B 27 Training Flank Companies, York Militia
[*York*, York Gazette, *June 6, 1812*]

Thursday last being the Anniversary of His Majesty's Birth Day, the same was observed here with the usual demonstrations of joy—a Royal

[56]John Johnstone became a lieutenant in the Canadian Fencible Infantry in 1810.

[57]Duncan Cameron (1765?–1838) was born in Scotland and is listed in the List of Inhabitants from 1801. He was a merchant. His company of York militia was present at the Battle of Queenston Heights. From 1817 until his death he was Provincial Secretary.

[58]Stephen Heward (1777?–1828)was born in England and came to York via

Salute was fired from the Garrison. The Third Regiment of York Militia, also paraded very strong, and fired three Vollies. —It was highly gratifying to observe the expertness and correctness with which the two Flank Companies (composed of smart, active young Men, selected from the Volunteers of the Regiment) performed their Manoeuvres proving the great advantages of the new mode of Disciplining the Militia, adopted by his Honor GENERAL BROCK, and though drilled but a few times, shews how soon young Men animated by a zeal for the honor and defence of their Country, and prompted by an eagerness to learn, can be sufficiently trained fit for effective service.

B 28 GEORGE RIDOUT[59] TO T. G. RIDOUT,[60] QUEBEC
[*P.A.O., Ridout Papers*]

York 25th. June 1812.

. . . Hoping however that you are now in Quebec we anticipate the pleasure we will enjoy in seeing you next winter if your business will permit—that is to say if we are not disturbed by the Americans which at present appears not unlikely, since we understand that the Question for war has passed the congress by a majority of 16. Preparations are making here to receive them—the flank companies are paraded every week—a fort is building here preparations made at Niagara—with some new vessels on the lakes—but all this will avail but little without we are supported by a regular force of at least 10,000 men which number I am afraid it is impossible the English can spare—without that number to support them I don't think the Militia will be willing to serve —I have the Honor to be an Ensign in a Battalion Company viz the town one—*Col. Chewett* has given me to understand that in a short time I am to be promoted to a Lieutenancy in the Grenadier Compy. which is a Flank Compy. composed of picked men nearly of a size, & who are tolerably well disciplined. D. Cameron is the Captn. There was an express sent to Genl. Brock informing him that a Body consisting of 4,800 Indians are ready at a moments warning to offer their services to the British. The Americans have 1200 Kentucky men now at Detroit —a body of 600 at Niagara—and indeed both lakes on the South side are lined with them. I know not whether Father has told you that John[61]

United States and New Brunswick. He held a number of small government offices. From 1819 until his death, he was Auditor General of Land Patents. During the War of 1812, he was Captain of one of the flank companies of the 3rd Regiment of York Militia and took part in the capture of York. He married Mary, daughter of Christopher Robinson.

[59]George Ridout (1791–1871) was the second son of Thomas Ridout. He became a lawyer and practised in Toronto and Clinton.

[60]Thomas Gibbs Ridout (1792–1861) was the third son of Thomas Ridout. During the War he was Deputy Assistant Commissary General for Upper Canada. For many years he was cashier of the Bank of Upper Canada.

[61]John Ridout (1799–1817) was the fourth son of Thomas Ridout. He was killed in a duel by S. P. Jarvis.

is a Midshipman on Board the Royal George[62] on this lake with a pay altogether equal to about 150. dollars for the first year—with an increase of pay every succeeding year—John is quite contented & indeed delighted with it—he dresses in uniform and is quite snugly rigged off. He entered on Board the 24th. of May—draws provisions &ca among other things nearly a Barrel of Rum a year which he will sell as York is to be head Quarters for the Navy. John will remain with us next Winter, when he will avail himself of the opportunity to go to Mr Strachan's[63] school, who is hourly expected here as the wind is fair. Mr Stuart[64] goes to Kingston, little John Radenhurst[65] is now here, with a large Detachment of the Newfoundland Regt. which detachmt. is distributed on Board the several vessels on the lakes as Marines. it is likely that John Rad—will be on Board the same ship with John which will be pleasant for them both. . . .

[P.S.]

27. June

Since I wrote an Express has come here announcing to us that *War is declared*—every one is on motion Genl. Brock went off to Niagara last night dispatches to the Indians who are all in readiness—I do not know what we will do with our large family, the Militia is ordered out—I must now go. Adieu G.R.

62The *Royal George* was built at Kingston in 1809 and was renamed the *Niagara* in 1814.

63John Strachan (1778–1867) was born at Aberdeen and educated at the Universities of Aberdeen and St. Andrews. He came to Upper Canada in 1799 and taught at Kingston. In 1803 he was ordained priest in the Church of England and was appointed to Cornwall, where he also taught school. Many York families sent their boys to Cornwall to be educated. In 1812 he was moved to York, where he was a leader of anti-American feeling during the War. He became one of the most powerful men in Upper Canada. In 1839 he was consecrated first Bishop of Toronto.

64George Okill Stuart (1776–1862) was born at Fort Hunter, N.Y., where his father, Rev. John Stuart, was missionary to the Mohawks. He was educated at King's College, Windsor, Union College, Schenectady, and Harvard University. He was Rector at York from 1801 until 1811, when he went to Kingston to take his father's place as Rector of St. George's Church, a position he held until his death.

65John Radenhurst (1795?–1853) served in the Royal Newfoundland Regiment and the 8th Regiment. He was employed for many years in the Surveyor General's Office, until dismissed by Sir George Arthur in 1840. He married Mary, daughter of Thomas Ridout.

C. LAW AND ORDER

C 1 State of Case against Charles McEwan for Murder, 1796[1]
[*P.A.O., Miscellaneous MSS, 1796*]

State of Case—

The King vs. Charles McCuen	For murder—committed on the Body of Waipykanine an Indian Chief—

The Prisoner Charles McCuen a Soldier in the Queens Rangers, was, on the twentieth day of August last, at the Town of York, near the Dwelling House of a Mr Berry,[2] and in company with the said Waipykanine and other Indians, about the hour of Eight in the Evening, of the said day—during which time the Prisoner was heard to declare that the said Indians had got a Dollar and some rum of his, and insisted upon having it from them, upon being advised by Patrick Mealey[3] a Sergeant of the Queens Rangers, then present, not to proceed in his intentions, he still persisted, and demanded the dollar of the Indians, at the same time knocked the said Waipykanine down with something like a Stone—which blow has since occasioned the death of the said Waipykanine.—

Witnesses—

Call—Patrick Mealey—To prove that the Prisoner McCuen was about the middle of the Month of August in the Evening of the day in Company with two Indians and a Squa at York insisting upon having a Dollar and some rum from them that he saw an Indian fall to the Ground—and the said McCuen pick up a dollar which fell from the said Indian—

John Austin[4] To prove that the Prisoner knocked down Waipykanine —and that he knows the Prisoner from Patrick Mealey's calling him by the name of Charley—Patrick Mealey being then present; proves the situation of Waipykanine after he was knocked down.—

Archibald Steward[5]—To prove he saw the Prisoner with some Indians

[1]A slightly different account of this incident is given by Peter Russell (Russell to Simcoe, Sept. 28, 1796; printed in *Russell Correspondence*, ed. Cruikshank, I, 49–50). Charles McEwan had served for seven years in the 7th Regiment before enlisting in the Queen's Rangers in 1792. On December 13, 1796, at the Court of Oyer and Terminer and General Gaol Delivery, the Grand Jury found no bill, it not having been proved that Wabacanine was dead.

[2]Thomas Barry. The Indians were gathered about a campfire on the shore in front of York.

[3]Patrick Mealey was a sergeant in the Queen's Rangers. After the Regiment was disbanded, he kept a general store and tavern in York for many years.

[4]John Austin was a carpenter who lived with Thomas Barry.

[5]Archibald Stewart and Peter Haines lived at the Head of the Lake, whence they had come by boat.

at York on the 20th. August in the Evening confirms what Mealey proves—proves also the situation of the Indian having Examined him with Austin immediately after he received the blow—also proves that he left York the following day—and on his way Home stopped at the River Credit—and saw the Indian—and was told it was the same that was supposed to have been killed at York two nights before—

Peter Haines[5]—Proves that the Prisoner was at York with some Indians and struck an Indian man with something like a Stone—confirms what the other witnesses say—Assisted the Indian into a Cannoe. Stopped at the River Credit two days afterwards, & saw the same Indian he had helped into the Cannoe at York, who appeared to be very sick

C 2 John Elmsley to Russell

[*P.R.O., C. O. 42, v. 321, pp. 79–80; microfilm copy in P.A.O.*]

Newark February 2d. 1797

It is not without some degree of pain that I feel myself called upon by the duty of my station in this Province to request your Honors attention to a matter of the utmost importance to the Administration of Justice in it.

Your Honour knows that by Stat: 34 Geo: 3. C. 2., the Court of Kings Bench and the Sittings for the Home District are, until the Seat of Government is fixed, to be held at the place where the Legislature was last assembled.—On my arrival here in November last, I was informed that no place had yet been definitely fixed upon as the future Capital of the Province, but that in the mean time the Courts of Justice and the different offices of Government were to be removed from this place to the Town of York, and that His Excellency General Simcoe had left Instructions with your Honor to Convene the Legislature there.—What the object of this measure, so far as the Courts of Justice are concerned is, I have never heard: but be it what it may, it is my duty to request your Honor, that the execution of it may be suspended, at least until His Majesty's pleasure is known on the subject.—

The Town of York is as your Honor knows near forty miles beyond the most remote of the Settlements at the head of the Lake, and the road to it lies thro' a tract of Country in the possession of the Missasagues.[6] Besides this there is at York neither Gaol nor Court House, no accomodation whatever for Grand or Petty Jury, none for the Suitors, the Witnesses, or the Bar, and I believe but very indifferent for the Judges. So that the greater part of those whom business or Duty may call to York must remain, during their stay there, either in the open Air or Crowded together in Huts or Tents, in a manner equally offensive to their feelings and injurious to their health.—When to these circum-

[6]The tract of land between York and Burlington was bought from the Mississauga Indians in August, 1805.

stances your Honor adds that some of the Petty Jury (to say nothing of the Grand Jurors) may be called from the distance of Sixty or even Eighty Miles, and cannot be supposed to be absent from their own Homes for less than ten days, you will immediately perceive that there is no fine which it would be prudent or indeed, in the present Circumstances of the Province just to impose, as the Penalty of absence, which a man, who might otherwise want no inclination to discharge a public Duty, will set in the Scale against the fatigue, the Expence, the loss of time, and the personal inconvenience of attendance. So strongly am I persuaded that this will be the case, if the Sittings are removed to York, that I do not expect to be able to form a Jury there; and unless I have been much misinformed any interruption in the Course of Justice as at present by Law established will, from Causes which I need not bring to your Honors recollection, be of the most pernicious tendency, there being now several Causes in Court which ought to have been tried last Summer, but which if the Courts are removed to York will probably remain untried for another year, and for anything I can foresee for several years to come.

To point out to the Executive Government of the Province, the Effects which the measure in question may by possibility have on the Administration of Justice, I conceive to be the more immediate duty of the Station I have the Honor to fill in it. I am therefore most respectfully but most earnestly to request, that unless Your Honor has His Majesty's express Commands on the subject, or unless there are considerations of greater weight in favor of the Measure than those I have suggested against it, Your Honor will be pleased to Call the next meeting of the Legislature at this place, which will of course keep the Courts here also. Should either of those reasons make it impossible for Your Honor to alter your present intention, I shall feel it a necessary, tho' painful duty to request that I may be permitted to bring in a Bill as early as possible in the session for the purpose of continuing the Courts at this place, until a situation as easy of access and as convenient is provided for them elsewhere.—

C 3 Russell to Portland

[*P.R.O., C.O. 42, v. 321, pp. 75–6; microfilm copy in P.A.O.*]

Upper Canada,
West Niagara 26th February 1797

. . . The Chief Justice being apprehensive that the present Paucity of Inhabitants at York and in its Vicinage may render it impracticable for the Sheriff to collect Jurors for the Courts of Justice should they soon be obliged to follow the Legislature thither as the Law directs; has made me a formal Requisition by letter[7] (which I have the Honor

[7] C 2.

to inclose for your Graces Consideration) to suspend my removal of the Seat of Government to York until His Majesty's Pleasure may be known on the Subject, and to call the next Meeting of the Legislature at this place. But tho' I readily accord with the Chief Justice respecting the present probable difficulty of obtaining Jurors to the Courts of Justice at York without calling upon the Inhabitants on this Side the Water, yet looking upon the hardship of the distance to be reciprocal since the Inhabitants of that side would be equally obliged to attend Juries here when summoned, I cannot, my Lord Duke, consider the Emergency stated to be so very urgent as to warrant, without more evident Necessity or further Authority, an Alteration of Arrangements which have received His Majesty's Sanction.

Many of the Officers of Government as well as myself have expended very considerable Sums during their long Residence in this place in throwing Habitations over their Heads. A removal from hence must consequently be attended with great Inconvenience and Loss to most of us. Regardless however of all interested Considerations, I feel it to be my Duty, my Lord Duke, to acknowledge to your Grace that York is in my humble Opinion the most eligible Situation on this Lake for the Seat of Government; being a Port of commodious Access from all Parts of it, out of the reach of immediate Insult, and capable of Defence from every hostile attempt by Land or Water, being also sufficiently centrical for a land Communication with each extreme of the Province, and appearing to be at least equally Salubrious with any other Scite that has been named for the Capital of this Province. I do confess indeed, my Lord, that we may at first have some difficulties to encounter from the want of Roads, Farms to feeds us, and Vessels to bring our Supplies. I beg leave however with the most respectfull deference to suggest to Your Grace that the first may be removed by the assistance of the Troops and a judicious application of Funds to be raised by the Sale of Lands,—the rapid Population to be ever expected near a Capital will of course very soon supply the second,—and a small Vessel of about forty Tons, navigable by about three Hands, (whose expence of Outfit and Maintenance cannot be very great) would be amply sufficient for the last. Should York, therefore, be finally selected for the Seat of Government, I am advised by the Executive Council to submit to your Grace the Expediency of causing a Vessel of the above Burden to be immediately built there, & put entirely under the Orders of the Civil Governor for the purpose of communicating by Water with every inhabited part of the Province when wanted, and occasionally conveying Passengers, and the Stores of the Civil Officers; these being Services which since the reduction of the Marine Establishment cannot be well attended to by the Kings Vessels on the Lake, as being only two in Number, they are too closely employed in transporting Provisions & Indian Stores to admit of their visiting York so often as they may be required. . . .

C 4 Election of Town and Parish Officers, and List of Inhabitants[8]

[*T.P.L., Minutes of Town Meetings and Lists of Inhabitants*]

Agreeable to an Act of the Legislature passed in favour of the Township of York and the Townships adjoining—the inhabitants ware assembled on the 17th. Day July 1797—and Elected the following Persons for Town & Parish officers Viz—

Thomas Barry Town Clark
George Playter & Thos. Barry } Assessors
Saml. Heron Collector
Overseers of the High Ways Viz.
John Dennis[9] for the Humber
Wm. Berczy for the German Settlement
Nicholas Miller[10] for Yonge
John Ashbridge[11] for the Bay
Isaiah Skinner[12] for the Don
Abner Miles for the Town

Thos. Barry & Saml. Heron } Town Wardens
Duke Wm. Kendrick, John Coon[13] } Constables for the Town
Isaac Devins[14] Constable for the Humber
John Stern[15] Do. for German Settlement
Joseph Johnson[16] Do. for Yonge Street—

[8]An Act to provide for the Nomination and Appointment of Parish and Town Officers within this Province, 33 Geo. III, c. 2 (1793), established annual township meetings, at which a town clerk, two assessors, one collector, two to six overseers of highways, poundkeepers, and two town wardens (if no church) were to be elected. Before a township was eligible to hold a meeting, it must contain at least thirty inhabitant householders. The meeting was to be held on the first Monday in March. By 37 Geo. III, c. 2 (1797), special consideration was given to York, to allow a meeting as soon as convenient, without waiting until March.

[9]John Dennis was a Loyalist who lived for nine years in New Brunswick, worked at the dockyards at Kingston, and came to York in 1796. He was granted land on the Humber River near Weston. He was a shipbuilder and built the government yacht, *Toronto.*

[10]Nicholas Miller was an early German-speaking settler on Yonge Street, south of Langstaff, in Markham Township. He was a millwright from the Genesee and built the King's Mill on the Humber.

[11]John Ashbridge (1761–1843) came from Philadelphia in 1793, with his mother, three sisters, and brother. Their lands were on the lower reaches of the Don River, on Ashbridge's Bay.

[12]Isaiah Skinner was the son of Timothy Skinner, a Loyalist from New Jersey, who came to Niagara in 1784 and built a mill there. By 1796 Isaiah and his brother Aaron built a grist mill on the east bank of the Don River a mile above Castle Frank.

[13]John Coon had been a sergeant in Butler's Rangers. He had a farm about six miles up the Don River, with a house built in 1793. For a time he kept the government house of entertainment on the Credit River.

[14]Abraham, Isaac, and Levi Devins owned a tract of land on the Humber. They came from Pennsylvania, and helped build the King's Mill on the Humber.

[15]John Stamm (Stem) was one of Berczy's settlers in Markham.

[16]Joseph Johnson was a member of a family with holdings on Yonge Street between Finch and Steeles Avenues.

[17]John McDougall was a Highland Scotsman who served in the British Commissariat as a conductor of wagons in the American Revolution. After the war he moved to Shelburne, N.S., where he kept a store. He later came to Upper

List of the inhabitants of the Township of York and it's Vicinity In the Year 1797—

	Males	Females
The Honl. Peter Russell	3	1
The Honl. David Wm. Smith	3	4
John Small Esqr	4	1
Thos. Ridout Esqr.	3	6
John White Esqr	4	2
Wm. Chewitt Esqr	3	2
Doctr James Macauley	4	1
Wm. Willcocks	1	
David Burns Esqr	1	
Alexr. Burns Esqr	1	
Wm. Berzy	4	2
Capt Wm. Graham	4	2
Samuel Heron	3	2
Abner Miles	3	5
Thos. Barry	3	4
Wm. Allen	2	
Jacob Herchmer	1	
Archd Cameron	1	1
Archd Thomson	6	5
John McDougall[17]	3	5
David Thomson[18]	6	2
Andrew Thomson[19]	4	2
Parker Mills[20]	2	5
Samuel Marther[21]	2	1
Patrick Mealey	1	2
Edward Wright	5	3
Joseph Hunt	2	3
Wm. Smith	4	5
John Henry Kahman	1	3
John Coon	2	7
John Kindrick	1	5
Duke Wm. Kindrick	4	3
Joseph Kindrick	2	3
Wm. Cooper[22]	3	1
John Conn	1	
Peter Pining	2	
Job Loder[23]	2	
John McBride Sergt[24]	1	1
Wm. Dumont	2	
James Ruggles	2	
Bernard Carey[25]	3	2
Dayton Hendricks[26]	2	1
John McBride[24]	2	3
Gideon Badger[27]	2	2
Total	115	97

Canada, and kept a tavern in York for many years. About 1803 he moved to his lot on Yonge Street north of Eglinton Avenue, and kept a tavern there. He was the grandfather of the Hon. William McDougall.

18David Thomson (d. 1834) was a stone mason, born in Dumfriesshire, Scotland. When taking the oath of allegiance on July 2, 1801, he gave his age as 37. He immigrated to Canada in 1795, came to York in 1796, and was the first settler in Scarborough. He helped build the Government Buildings, as well as several houses in York.

19Andrew Thomson (1751?–1841?) was a brother of David Thomson and was also a stone mason.

20Parker Mills (1762?–1837) had a farm on the Don River. He married Mary Ashbridge.

21Samuel Marther was an early builder and contractor. He later kept an inn on the northeast corner of King and New (Jarvis) Streets, which he sold in 1801 to Benjamin Gilbert.

22William Cooper (1761?–1840), born in Bath, England, came to York in 1793, and, in a petition in 1823, claimed to have built the first house in York. He kept a tavern, the Toronto Coffee House, taught school, read the prayers on Sundays, was an auctioneer, and in 1806 built a grist and sawmill on the Humber River. He also owned a wharf at York, at the foot of Church Street.

23Job Loder does not appear in the List of Inhabitants after 1799.

24It is not clear whether this John McBride, a sergeant in the Queen's Rangers, or the other John McBride, U.E., became doorkeeper to the Executive and Legislative Councils, and died in 1801. His widow, Hannah, kept a tavern after his death. The other John McBride lived on Yonge Street.

25Bernard Carey was a Loyalist, recommended by the Duke of Portland.

26Dayton Hendricks does not appear in any later List of Inhabitants.

27Probably a member of the Bätger family, who were Berczy settlers in Markham Township.

Single Men in York

Jonathan Scott[28]	1	Malcolm Wright[38]	1
Shivers Cozens	1	James Nash[39]	1
Augustus White[29]	1	Fridk. Bush[40]	1
Joshua Leach[30]	1	Thos. Ward[41]	1
John McDonell Carptr	2	Michael Margh[42]	1
John Withers[31]	1	Daniel Tiers[43]	1
Ira Bissell[32]	1	Alexr. Bell[44]	1
Ephraim Payson[33]	1	James Pitnea	1
Andrew Johnson[34]	1	James Perrigo	1
James Elliott[35]	1	Thos. Tivy[45]	1
Daniel Cozens Junr	1	Henry Hutchins[46]	1
Saml. D Cozens	1	John Hollowell[47]	1
Jacob Cozens	1	Saml. Nash[48]	1
Robert Tate[36]	1		
John Endicott[37]	1		29

. . .

Thos. Barry, Town Clark

[28]Jonathan Scott had a farm on Yonge Street, at the southwest corner of Steeles Avenue.

[29]Augustus White does not appear in any later List of Inhabitants.

[30]Joshua Leach was a carpenter who lived at the northwest corner of Yonge and Hospital (Richmond) Streets where he later kept a tavern.

[31]John Withers last appears in the List of Inhabitants in 1799.

[32]Ira Bissell last appears in the List of Inhabitants in 1799.

[33]Ephraim Holland Payson was a military claimant.

[34]Andrew Johnson moved to Scarborough about 1800.

[35]James Elliott was an early Scarborough resident, possibly arriving with David Thomson.

[36]Robert Tate (Tait) last appears in the List of Inhabitants in 1799.

[37]John Endicott was a corporal in the Queen's Rangers. About 1804 he moved to Etobicoke Township. He served as a lieutenant in the 3rd Regiment of York militia during the War of 1812.

[38]Malcolm Wright had a farm on Yonge Street, south of Jonathan Scott's.

[39]James Nash last appears as Poundkeeper of the Town, in 1799.

[40]Frederick Busch (Bush) was one of the Berczy settlers in Markham Township.

[41]Thomas Ward (1770–1861) was born in London, England, and came to Canada with Attorney General John White. He practised law in York, then in Brighton, and in 1808 he moved to Port Hope, where he died. In 1803 he married Mary, daughter of George Playter.

[42]Michael Margh does not appear in any later List of Inhabitants.

[43]Daniel Tiers (Tierce) was a German from Pennsylvania who settled in Berczy's settlement in Markham Township before 1798. In 1802 he advertised as a chairmaker, and in 1808 he opened a Beef-Steak and Beer House in York. He later established the Red Lion Inn in Yorkville, on Yonge Street north of Bloor Street.

[44]Alexander Bell last appears in the List of Inhabitants in 1802.

[45]Thomas Tivey served in the Queen's Rangers, and was granted lands in Etobicoke.

[46]Henry Hutchins was a reduced soldier from the Queen's Rangers.

[47]Probably John Hollaway.

[48]Samuel Nash last appears in the List of Inhabitants in 1802. He may have been the Samuel Nash who was born in Bedford, Conn., in 1778, came to Canada in 1800, married Susanna, daughter of William Gage, and received a lot in Saltfleet Township from her father.

	Males	Females
Amount of Freehold inhabitants in the Town of York	115	97
Amount of Single Men in York	29	
Amount of Inhabitants on the Don	35	24
Amount of Do. on the Humber	29	22
Amount of Do. on Yonge Street	52	34
Total agreeable to the above List	260	177

C 5 RUSSELL TO SIMCOE
[*T.P.L., Peter Russell Papers*]

Upper Canada, Niagara
September 13, 1797

. . . Our Chief Justice,[49] tho' a man of conciliating manners, when he pleases, & of an agreeable Eloquence, and much acquired Information, is unfortunately too impetuous, and apt to be hurried on by every first Impulse; which often leads him into Expressions and Acts that on cooler reflection he repents of, and lessen his consequence with the people.—Tho' I have overlooked much improper Conduct in his Transactions with me, for the sake of keeping upon Terms with him for the good of the Kings Service; I am sorry to observe that his Transgressions in that way are so frequent that I despair of succeeding. Tho' he was told by me on his arrival that your Excellency had removed the Seat of Government to York, and that all the Officers would soon be ordered thither, he obstinately persuaded himself that we should not stir from hence.—and under this Impression he bought Mr. Pilkingtons House and improved it at an Expence of at least £1500 Ster.—this of course nailed him to Niagara, and finding that I was firm in my Intentions of meeting the Parliament at York, he made a formal Requisition as Chief Justice that I would hold the first Session of it at this place, that the Court of Kings Bench and the Sittings for the Home District might remain here.—And on my refusal he insisted on my submitting the Question to a full Council.—The latter I complied with merely to pacify him and their voices (except his own) were unanimous for York. —He then moved that he should be permitted to bring in a Bill to fix the Court of Kings Bench &c. at this place for two years.—This I opposed, because the measure was inexpedient and unnecessary and would throw a damp on the advancement of the Seat of Government, which it could not recover from for years, but as he seemed of opinion that the immediate Removal of the Courts to York might cause Delay in judicial Proceedings injurious to the People, I should not object to a Bill for empowering me to retain the Court of Kings Bench here for as long a period as might be found expedient, not exceeding two years. This was approved by the Council, and acceded to by the Chief Justice. —He notwithstanding carried two Bills thro' both Houses, the one to

[49]John Elmsley.

empower me to hold the Court of Kings Bench at Newark, and the other to fix the Sittings for the Home District there for *two* years.—All this being concealed from me, until I was preparing to give the Royal Assent to the Bills of the Session.—I immediately informed the Chief Justice that I should take the opinion of the Executive Council upon the propriety of passing or rejecting these two Bills, and that I had sent for the Attorney General[50] to advise me on the subject.—He was pleased to be greatly offended with me on this occasion, as he could not see the necessity of my consulting the Attorney Genl., while he was present to advise me. The Attorney Genl. however soon convinced the Chief that the holding the Court of Kings Bench at Newark was unnecessary, and that he himself had the power without a Specific Act for the purpose to open his Commissions of Assize & Nisi prius in any part of the District he pleased.—The Chief could not forgive me for foiling him in his favourite object, and very indecently told me that as he had the power he would retain the Sittings at Newark not only for two years, but for five years.—Ever since he has endeavoured to thwart me on many occasions, and frequently forgets the respect he owes to my present Station. . . .

C 6 Russell to Sheriff Alexander McDonell[51]
[*T.P.L., Peter Russell Papers*]

York 12 May 1798

Fully aware of the indispensible necessity we were under of providing some proper place of Confinement in this Town, to which the civil Magistrate might when called upon commit the disturbers of the public Peace; I had very early recommended it to the Executive Council to take the Police of York into their Consideration and digest some Œconomical plan for preserving Order among its Inhabitants—A Committee of Council to which the business was referred, reported to me in consequence that in consideration of the existing Probability that the Town of York would very soon become the Capital of a District, and being desirous of putting Government to as little Expence as possible it appeared to the Committee to be most Œconomical to erect a District Jail at once. A plan and Estimate for such a building having been thereupon presented by the master builder and approved; the Commissary was directed to Contract for carrying it into execution without loss of time,—but the enormous wages and Expectations of Artificers in this place have hitherto retarded even the commencement of the Business.—

[50]John White.

[51]Alexander McDonell (1762–1842) was the second son of Allan McDonell of Collachie, and brother of Angus McDonell. During the American Revolution he served in Butler's Rangers. He was Sheriff of the Home District, 1792–1805, represented Glengarry in the House of Assembly 1800–12, 1820–3, and was agent for Selkirk's Baldoon settlement. He was Deputy Paymaster General during the War of 1812, and superintendent of the military settlement at Perth after it.

However your Letter of this date and the Conversation I have had with you upon the subject convincing me that it will be very soon impossible to restrain the Enormities of this increasing Town so as to secure the Peace and safety of its Inhabitants unless some other Provision is made which may be executed in less time than a District Jail is likely to require; I judge it to be my Duty during the present recess of the Council to authorise you (after consulting with Capt. Graham) to cause a small log building to be erected of sufficient strength and size to secure three separate Prisoners, and accomodate the Keeper.—You will likewise be pleased to provide Handcuffs and other Irons for binding gross Offenders, and stocks for punishing those who may deserve such Chastisement.—The Expence attending this Service will be discharged on your Requisition by my Warrant on the Receiver General of the Province—

C 7 Statements of Elisha Beman[52] and James Williams [*P.A.O., Miscellaneous, 1798*]

Before us John Small and William Willcocks Esquires two of His Majesty's Justices of the peace in & for the Home District personally came Elisha Beman at present of York Yeoman who being duly sworn made oath and saith that this morning about Sunrising this deponent (having Slept at the House of Abner Miles in the town of York) went down to the water side where his men lay and where several articles of his property had been left in their care that he soon perceived that a great part of such property had been taken away during the preceeding Night and as this deponent verily believes Stolen, among which were a chest containing some Cloathing—*an Iron Tea Kettle—a cooking Kettle an axe a Tea Cannister—a Hat a three Gallon Kegg, with about two quarts of brandy therein & sundry other Articles—that this deponent walked* along by the Water Side towards the Garrison in Search of his property—and after walking for some time this deponent saw four Men come into the Main Road out of the Woods & Walk Towards town—that this deponent Suspecting the said four Men to be the persons who had Stolen his property followed them & when he came up with them—one of them, who now answers to the Name of Wm. Hawkins—entered into a Conversation with a Negro Man whom he met and an other whose name is unknown to deponent went towards the bank of the bay and seemed to look earnestly into the water.—and this deponent maketh oath upon viewing the persons herein after named that they were three of the four men whom he saw enter the main Road out of the woods as aforesaid & whom he followed that is to say—William Hawkins, James Williams and John McLean and deponent having

[52]Elisha Beman (d. 1822) came from New York State and was an early store and tavern keeper in York. About 1806 he moved to Newmarket, where he built a mill. After the death of his first wife, he married the widow of Christopher Robinson in 1805.

Viewed *Joseph Thompson* declared that he was not one of the four men whom he so met & followed unless such Thompson have since changed his apparel.—And this deponent having viewed and well examined an Ax and two bags the one containing pease the other Indian Meal sayth that the Ax is his property and One of the bags.—that he believes the other bag to belong to him likewise but is not positive and that two bags similar to those shewn him and containing Meal & Corn were among the Articles Stolen from him as he verily believes as aforesaid as well as the Said Ax.—

Sworn before us at
York this 27th day of
July 1798.— Elisha Beman
John Small
Will. Willcocks

The Examination of James Williams who voluntarily offers his Evidence in behalf of our Lord the King against—Joseph McCarthy—John McLean,—William Hawkins.—Joseph Thompson—Mathew Dunn. or Michael Dunn—

The said James Williams declares that on the Night of the twenty sixth Instant the said McCarthy—McLean—Hawkins—Thompson and Dunn in consequence of a preconcerted plan to steal a boat and proceed therein towards Kingston met on the Bank of the Bay—nearly opposite to the House of Messrs. Allan & Wood in the Town of York—Hawkins and Dunn went to a shed or Booth erected on the water side & occupied by one Beemans people and property.—and took out thence a chest which they carried some distance Eastward into a Spot where a quantity of Rushes or Flags grew—then they laid down the Chest— & opened the Same—and Dunn Hawkins & McCarthy took out each an arm full of Cloathing from the said Chest & carried the same Westward towards the Garrison of York nearly as far as the Small bridge—first beyond the House of Mr. Willcocks.—being come back Dunn & the Examinant launched a Small Skiff which the parties agreed upon to be more suitable than a larger Boat which had originally been proposed to be taken.—Dunn took & carried into the Skiff out of the large boat two oars and a Sail and this Examinant took and carried into the Same in like Manner two or three Setting poles.—Dunn then proposed to take a Sheep:—and Hawkins proposed taking one out of Beemans Boat then lying moored there on which this Examinant observed that he had no Objection Seeing that they had four Loaves of bread—Examinant & Dunn carried or shoved the boat in the Water about Ten or fifteen Rods towards the Garrison—Hawkins came to examinant and handed to him a Keg which might contain three pints or two quarts of Brandy—

telling him—Williams since you are wet here is a Keg belonging to the Person who owns the Sheep take a Dram—and wee'l take the rest along.—Examinant took a Dram & put the Keg in the boat.—Dunn handed Examinant a pot or kind of Dutch oven & a tea Kettle & Examinant put them into the bow of the Boat—Hawkins—Examinant—McLean—Dunn—and MacCarthy who had gotten drunk by means of the Keg of Brandy (after having carried the Cloaths away) embarked in the Skiff Hawkins set to to Steer—and Examinant & McLean rowed—but the oars being too long Examinant proposed quitting & Dunn & Hawkins joined Examinant in the Same opinion, adding now its day light and about a quarter of a Mile—towards the third bridge—(where the New House is built—the party Landed—McCarthy Williams—Dunn—Hawkins—& McLean carried up or helped to carry up the things to the bank where McCarthy hid them—then Some altercation having arrisen among the party—McLean, Examinant McCarthy and Hawkins went to the brick Kill at the Chief Justices place—and there the two axes and two bags of pease were Sold—*having gotten a quart of rum from Mr. Wood for the order of Six Shillings* & a quarter Dollar Examinant Thompson & Hawkins went into the woods on the lot of John Small Esquire near the Same, and there drank up the greater part of the said Rum untill they were apprehended—Examinant declares that all the parties herein mentioned were equally concerned—& former acquaintances (excepting Hawkins) having been in the Service of the American States.—[53]

James Williams

Taken before us this
27th day of July 1798

John Small.
Will. Willcocks

C 8 CONDITION OF STREETS
[*York,* Upper Canada Gazette, *June 29, 1799*]

The public are much indebted to Mr. John Mc.Dougal, who was appointed one of the path-masters at the last town meeting, for his great assiduity and care in geting the streets cleared of the many and dangerous (especially at night) obstructions therein; and we hope, by the same good conduct in his successors in the like office, to see the streets of this infant town vie with those of a maturer age, in cleanliness and safety.

[53]This case came up for trial on November 12, 1798. Joseph McCarthy was found guilty of grand larceny and was sentenced to be burned on the hand. Hawkins was found guilty of petty larceny and was sentenced to be whipped. The sentences were carried out in the market place at York on November 26, 1798. The others involved were found not guilty, except for Williams who was pardoned because he turned approver.

C 9 REPORT OF COURT OF OYER AND TERMINER AND GENERAL GAOL DELIVERY

[*York,* Upper Canada Gazette, *January 25, 1800*]

On Monday last, 20th inst, the court of Oyer and Terminer and general gaol delivery, for the town and county of York, was opened: before which came John Small, esq. indicted for having mortally wounded the late attorney general in a duel;[54] after a trial of about eight hours—he was acquitted.

On Tuesday last,—Ricks for grand larceny, of which he was acquitted. The indictment appeared to be founded upon the inhuman principles of spite and malice.[55]

Wednesday, Humphrey Sullivan, for having uttered a counterfeit note and knowing it to be such; of which he was convicted.—After the jury had delivered their verdict, his honor the chief justice rose and addressed himself to the unhappy prisoner, in nearly the following words: *Sullivan*, may all who behold you, and who shall hear of your crime, and of your unhappy fate, take warning from your example. But although your crime is great, it does not exceed the boundless mercy of God! to pardon through the all-sufficient atonement of his son. I therefore recommend you to the mercy of God for pardon and salvation, through the merits of his son; and do recommend to you, to employ the few days that shall be allowed, of a life spent in wickedness, in humble and fervent prayer to almighty God, that he would give you a realizing sense of your sins, and misery, true contrition of heart for, and a genuine repentance of them; and that he would enable you, by his grace to be wise in his Son the Lord Jesus Christ unto eternal salvation. He then pronounced sentence of death on him.[56]

C 10 MINUTES OF THE SPECIAL SESSIONS OF THE PEACE, HOME DISTRICT

[*P.A.O., Minutes of the General Quarter Sessions of the Peace, Home District*]

Upper Canada Home District York Sss	At a Special Sessions of the Peace holden in and for said District, in the Town of York in said District on Thursday the 10h. Day of April 1800, at Eleven o'Clock in the forenoon.—

[54]John Small killed John White in a duel on January 3, 1800 (see H 14).

[55]The editor of the *Upper Canada Gazette* apologized for this comment in the February 1, 1800, issue. Reuben Riggs, a carpenter at the Garrison, had been indicted on the evidence of John Dennis, shipbuilder. In the same issue, Dennis testified to Riggs' character, and stated his belief in Riggs' innocence. In the February 8, 1800, issue, the Solicitor General, R. I. D. Gray, and William Weekes, counsel for the Crown, complained of the imputation, and John Dennis' original deposition was printed.

[56]Sullivan was hanged on May 16, 1800 (see H 16).

Justices present
William Jarvis Esq: Chairman,

William Willcocks	Alexander Wood
John Small	William Allan
James Macaulay	James Ruggles

Esquires.

. . . It having been represented that no steps had been taken to guard against Accidents by Fire in the said Town of York and also that it was of public benefit that all nuisances should be removed from thereof,

Ordered—

In pursuance of an Act of the Legislature of said Province, entitled "An Act to guard against Fire," That every Housekeeper in the Town of York aforesaid shall on or before the first day of October next ensuing, provide and Keep Two Buckets for carrying water, when any House shall happen to be on Fire, which Buckets shall be made of Wood, Leather or Canvas, painted on the outside and covered with pitch on the inside, and shall hold, at least, two Gallons of water; and the said Bucketts shall be marked with the Christian and Sirname of the House-keeper to whose House they belong, and shall not be used for any other purpose than the extinguishing of fires.

Ordered, also

That every House Keeper in the said Town, do keep two Ladders, the one to reach from the Ground to the Eaves of the House, the other to be properly secured and fixed with Hooks or Bolts on the roof near the Chimney—

And that Every House Keeper for every neglect of having said Buckets and Ladders or either of them shall forfeit the sum of Five shillings: And in case any House or the Chimney of any House, in or upon which any of the said articles shall be wanting, shall happen to be on fire, the occupier of said House shall forfeit the sum of Forty shillings—

And Whereas the Streets in the said Town of York are frequently obstructed and made dangerous to passengers, by piles of wood and stones placed in them as well as by pits dug in several places; It is notified by order of the Magistrates in Quarter Sessions, assembled; that whosoever shall leave any wood or stone or suffer any nuisance to remain in the said Streets opposite their respective premises after the Twelfth Day of May next, will be prosecuted, as the Law directs—

That the above orders or regulations, be inserted in the Upper Canada Gazette for three weeks.

Adjourned, sine die
Thos: Ridout
Clerk of the Peace Home Dist.

C 11 MINUTES OF THE GENERAL QUARTER SESSIONS OF THE PEACE, HOME DISTRICT

[*P.A.O., Minutes of the General Quarter Sessions of the Peace, Home District*]

Upper Canada
Home District
York Sss.

At a General Quarter Sessions of the Peace holden in and for said District, in the Town of York, on Tuesday the Eighth Day of July in the fortieth Year of the Reign of Our Sovereign Lord George the Third, by the Grace of God of Great Britain, France and Ireland, King, Defender of the faith and so forth, and in the Year of our Lord One Thousand Eight Hundred, before,

William Willcocks Esquire

William Chewett
William Allan
&
Alexander Wood
Esquires

Justices of our said Lord the King, assigned to Keep the peace of our said Lord the King in the said District and also to hear and determine divers felonies, trespasses and other misdemeanors in the said District committed.

Commission opened and read.

The Sheriff returned the precept, with his declaration that he could not cause to come as directed 24 good and lawful men of his District as he was restricted by an Act of the Legislature of the Province from summoning persons to serve on a Jury oftener than once within twelve months—and that most of those whose names appear in the List of Jurors, have served as such twice and some of them three times within Twelve Months—

Robert Wilson[57] who had been nominated at the general quarter Sessions of the Peace of April last to be one of the Constables for the Town of York, having refused to serve, he now appeared and paid his fine of Two pounds into the Hands of the Treasurer of the District—

Andrew Thomson one of the Town Wardens informed the Court, that a woman of the name of Page, (sometime since a Servant to the late John White Esq:) and her two Children, were in great distress, and prayed relief—

The Court was of opinion that the Acts of the Province did not authorize them to make use of the public money, otherwise than as the said Acts precisely allowed, and that the Case now before them did not appear to come within that Statute—

Ordered that the Pound Keeper of the Town of the Town of York be authorise[d] to ask and receive the Sum of Five Shillings, for each and every Hog he shall take up and empound . . .

[57]Robert Wilson appears in the List of Inhabitants, living alone, until 1802.

C 12 Minutes of the Special Sessions of the Peace, Home District

[*P.A.O., Minutes of the General Quarter Sessions of the Peace, Home District*]

Upper Canada }
Home District } At a Special Sessions of the Peace, holden in and for said District, at York, on Monday the 30h Day of March 1801—
Sss. }

Present

William Jarvis Esqre Chairman
John Small }
William Willcocks } Esqrs.
William Allan }

The Undermentioned persons, Inhabitants of the Town of York, applied for recommendations to take out licences for selling wines and spirituous Liquors, and for Keeping Tavern in the Town of York, the year ensuing. vizt

Hannah McBride
James & Eli Playter[58]
John McDougall
William Cooper
Joseph Hunt
Elisha Beman

The above mentioned persons were approved and allowed to apply for Tavern Licences.

John Horton[59] also applied for a recommendation but was not allowed—

The Court are of opinion that Six persons are a sufficient Number, for Keeping Tavern in the Town of York, for the Year Ensuing—

Titus Simons[60] also applied for a Recommendation to take out a Tavern Licence but was not approved—

And in order that the persons who have been recommended for Tavern Licences, might Keep good rule and order in their respective

[58]James (1776?–1809) and Ely (b. 1775) Playter were sons of George Playter. At this time they were keeping the tavern formerly kept by Abner Miles. Both later became farmers, James near Richmond Hill and Ely on Yonge Street. Ely served in the transport service during the War of 1812. From 1825 to 1828 he represented York and Simcoe Counties in the House of Assembly. James married Hannah, daughter of Abner Miles, and Ely married Sophia, daughter of Elisha Beman.

[59]John Horton (d. 1802) was a baker, who also sold groceries. In May, 1802, he committed suicide by drowning in the Don River. Some time previously he had shown evident signs of insanity.

[60]Titus Simons (1743–1824) was a Quartermaster in Peter's Rangers during the Revolution. Afterwards he settled first at Kingston, moving to Niagara, and then York. About 1802 he moved finally to West Flamborough, where he died.

houses; they are appointed Constables, in and for the Town of York, for the Year ensuing—vizt.—

James & Eli Playter
John McDougall
William Cooper
Joseph Hunt
Elisha Beeman

Adjourned
T. Ridout
Clk. of the Peace
H Dt

C 13 Minutes of the General Quarter Sessions of the Peace, Home District

[*P.A.O., Minutes of the General Quarter Sessions of the Peace, Home District*]

Home District Sss. } At a General Quarter Sessions of the Peace, holden in and for said District, by Adjournment, at the Town of York, on Wednesday the 14th day of July 1802, at 8 A.M.

Present
William Jarvis Esqre Chairman

William Willcocks
William Graham
William Allan
James Ruggles } Esqres.

. . . William Hunter of the Town of York, Blacksmith produced an Account for the Board & Lodging of Mary Day, (a pauper and insane woman), from the 25 May last past to the 1 July instant, at the rate of 12/6 P Cy. per week

	£ s d
amounting to which account was approved.	3: 2: 6
He was further allowed the Sum of for his maintenance and attendance of the said Mary Day, in her lying in &c.	6:17. 6
Provce. Cy.	£10: 0. 0

Ordered, That the sd. Sum of Ten pounds, be paid by the District Treasurer—

Also recommended, that a further allowance of Eight Dollars, be appropriated by the District Treasurer, for the purpose of conveying the said Mary Day to the Province of Lower Canada, from whence she came.

Presentment of the Grand Jury—

The Grand Jury present, to the worshipful The Justices in Sessions assembled that it is proper to direct the wardens appointed for the Town of

York to visit the several Keepers of Houses of Public Entertainment therein and represent to them the indecency and impropriety of allowing people to drink intoxicating liquors and be guilty of disorderly behavior during the hours of Divine Service, and generally on the Sabbath days—

The Grand Jury further present, that the Butchers of the Town of York should be obliged to bury the Garbage and useless offal of their Slaughtered Cattle, remove from the Town or otherwise dispose of the same, so that it may cease to be (what it now is) a public nuisance—

The Grand Jury further present that the Joiners, Cabinet Makers & workers in wood by whose Trade, Shavings are made, be obliged to burn or otherwise destroy the same on the Wednesdays & Saturdays of Every week, at or about the Hour of Sunset—

York 13 July 1802 (Signed) Robert Henderson[61]
Foreman.

Approved by the Magistrates in General Quarter Sessions, who direct the Clerk of the Peace to cause the said Presentments to be published Three times in the Upper Canada Gazette.

Adjourned
T. Ridout
Clerk of the Peace
& of Sessions
Home District,

C 14 Gift of Fire Engine

[*York,* Upper Canada Gazette, *December 18, 1802*]

His Excellency the Lieutenant Governor has been pleased to give to the Inhabitants of this Town, the use of a Fire Engine, for which signal mark of his parental concern for the safety and welfare of the King's subjects, all ranks and descriptions of people seem highly grateful.

As a very small token of their sense of this indulgence, a subscription[62] *was most cheerfully set on foot, which immediately filled, for the erection of a proper building in the Town for the preservation of the Engine, and such measures will be immediately adopted, as are best calculated to procure the most easy access to the Engine at all hours of the day and night.*

[61]Robert Henderson (d. 1811) came to York from Kingston in 1801 and became a successful brewer. He also operated a tannery and slaughter house. In 1808 he was an unsuccessful candidate for the House of Assembly. He died after a long illness on Oct. 13, 1811.

[62]A subscription list for this purpose lists Henry Allcock, Peter Russell, William Jarvis, Alexander McDonell, John Beikie, Thomas Scott, John Small, Elisha Beman, R. I. D. Gray, Donald McLean, William Allan, Duncan and John Cameron, J. H. Kahman, W. B. Peters, Mrs. McBride, W. D. Powell, Paul Marian, and Robert Henderson. The amount subscribed was $30.50. (P.A.C., Upper Canada State Papers, v. 99, p. 100.)

C 15 ALEXANDER WOOD TO ALEXANDER AULDJO,[63] MONTREAL
[*T.P.L., Alexander Wood Letter Books*]

York 30th. Decr. 1805.

Your favour of the 2d. came to hand on the 21st. Current & mark the contents.

I have made the determination of ye, Phoenix Compy. known to most of those concerned in this Town, they think with me that it is hard upon us to be laying money almost daily for the purpose of preventing accidental fire & at the same time having our Prem: of Insurance raised; the Situation of this place is by no means similar to the old Town of Detroit,[64] for no two Houses in this Town join each other, nor is the property of any two persons otherwise connected than by a fence which could be cleared away in less than five minutes; no building is erected on less than one fifth of an Acre & few lots short of an Acre square, most of them have a good well within a few yards of the building & by an order of Sessions every house is provided with Laders & fire Buckets.

Mr Chewett says he will furnish a plan of the Town pointing out the situation of the houses & their distance from each other, if the Office will allow him what is moderate for his trouble.

Messrs. A.M. & Co. will please pay my Prem: which falls due I think on the 1st. Proximo, if at the old rate if at the advanced rate I will reduce the sum to One thousd. pounds to wit on a dwelling house described as before . . . £500. On Merchandize in the said House £500

£1,000

C 16 WOOD TO MRS. ELMSLEY[65]
[*T.P.L., Alexander Wood Letter Books*]

York 23d May 1806—

Since I had last this honour We have here been in imminent danger by fire. Most people in the neighbourhood have suffered, some considerably others not so much, you are, Im sorry to say, among the former. On Sunday, or rather between Saturday and Sunday last, the fire (which

[63]Alexander Auldjo was a partner in the Montreal firm of merchants, Auldjo, Maitland and Company, which was the Canadian agent for the Phoenix Assurance Company of London, England. Alexander Wood acted as their unofficial agent in York, until he returned to Scotland in 1810, when William Allan took over the insurance agency.

[64]Detroit was almost destroyed in a disastrous fire on June 11, 1805.

[65]After Chief Justice Elmsley's death in 1805, his widow and children returned to England. Alexander Wood looked after the Elmsley property around York. The farm, Cloverhill, lay between Lot (Queen) Street and Bloor Street, west of the present Bay Street.

had & still continues to rage furiously in the Woods) got to the Fence at Cloverhill & before sufficient assistance could reach the field a large portion of the fence was totally destroyed; I have got hands to repair the damage, the extent of which cannot as ye[t] be ascertained, some difficulty occured in procuring men, as a previous Fire had laid Colonel's Smith & Shanks meadows entirely open, Col: Shaw & Mr. Givens are not exempt, Col. Smith lost about 2,000 Rails or 250 pannels of fence. Colonel Shank all his Hay stacked on the field, it is some consolation that Col: Shaw & Mr Givens from being early apprized of the danger have come off better than any of their neighbours, Mr. McGill at the Mountain suffered but little tho' at one time he was threatned with total destruction, Mr Boulton & Captn McGill are both involved in the common Calamity in a small degree, they owe their preservation to great exertion & the dampness of their grounds; at your Farm the fire had an awful appearance among the Pines & but for Col: Proctors[66] ready assistance by sending seven men of the 41st Regt. who with about twice as many of the towns people (ever ready to lend their aid to save the property of a person whose memory is dear to them) the whole must inevitably have gone & the flames would soon have swallowed up Doctor McAulays property fortunately we got it diverted from that course & a shower of rain two days after has for the present quieted our fears for the present, but the Woods are Im told a continued fire for many miles, it is particularly unfortunate at this season of the year to have the grass exposed to the Cattle, I have as yet been able to keep them from yours & hope the Fences will soon be up again workmen are so much in demand that it is almost impossible to employ them on anything like reasonable terms. Cols Smith & Shank will I fear loss the Crop of this year from not being able to get hands in time to make up their fences. . . .

C 17 Bridge to Peninsula
[*York*, York Gazette, *April 1, 1808*]

The Editors having been called upon by a number of Gentlemen to request a Meeting of such persons as might wish to subscribe towards erecting a Bridge across that part of the River Don which separates the town and the peninsula, give notice that it is desired such Meeting should take place To morrow, at Campbell and Deary's Tavern,[67] at 3 o'clock in the afternoon. They should be wanting to themselves and in their

[66]Lieutenant Colonel Henry Adolphus Procter (1787–1859) commanded the 41st Regiment. During the War of 1812 he was in command of the Amherstburg sector and was court-martialled for his actions during the retreat in the fall of 1813 and at the Battle of Moraviantown.

[67]In December, 1807, Thomas Deary and John Campbell took over Thomas Hamilton's tavern. In September, 1808, the partnership dissolved; the tavern was kept on by Campbell, and Deary became a storekeeper.

duty to the public, were they not to give every encouragement and assistance in their power to so desirable an object. Humanity is interested in the laudable undertaking, and it may promote a more general subscription, to state that for the want of a bridge, several lives (within their knowledge) have been lost. When completed, the Peninsula will answer every purpose of an extensive common to the owners of cattle; to those who may use it for purposes of recreation, it furnishes a most delightful walk or ride; as a race ground or place for field exercises, we know not its equal; the sportsman will find a constant and easy access to the best shooting ground, and the convalescent might find health in an occasional excursion to the opposite beach—and travellers or persons coming to market from below, would at all seasons find the town accessible, which to them at present it frequently is not, but at the imminent hazard of life.

C 18 Bridges over Ravines

[*York,* York Gazette, *August 13, 1808*]

Before any particular work is begun this year either in the streets, or in the public highways leading to this Town; We feel it a relative duty to point to commissioners and overseers of roads and others duly authorised to regulate proceedings of that nature. That we see an evident and expensive impropriety in erecting wooden bridges over the various Ravines and the number of Gullies and small streams falling into the Lake. In a nine years residence in the place, we have seen a number of Bridges of that nature built, with little taste and less profit. Placed in such places as they are, the consequence arising is, they are almost immediately exposed to rotting, against which it is not possible to guard, and a seven years duration is what very few of them can boast of, or exceed. Such of them as are not in a tottering and almost useless state attended with danger & great inconvenience, are permitted, & the decayed works are replaced by others of short service, little lasting and less ornament. In this country where flag stones can be had in great plenty and much facility, their obvious use in the formation of ever during Conductors in Ravines and small Streams, must occur to every person in the least conversant with the subject. A quarter of, or the third part of the ordinary Toise of stone, will generally be sufficient for a water course in any one place, which in or about may require. A mason's labor or extra labor is not necessary in placing them, which may be done perfectly with as much ease as imperfectly, by any person, and when made something longer than our common Bridges are wide, nothing else is required but to cover them with earth, until a perfect level is formed with the road. We are earnest in our recommendation of this to public notice and practice, as our wish is, that works of common utility may be made the least costly, long during, and best method to advance the public and general advantage.

C 19 Mutilation of Livestock
[*York*, York Gazette, *August 31, 1811*]

MR. EDITOR,

A most inhuman practice exists in this town and neighbourhood, at which the human mind ought to revolt with horror and detestation.

If a latent desire of revenge is cherished towards any person who may own cattle, by some miscreant whose mind is rendered callous by the indulgence of vicious inclinations, or if an horse or cow may happen to stray on the premises of those whose breasts are devoid of feeling; the poor animal, whose only desire is the gratifying his appetite, feels the effects of their brutal rage.

Two horses, accustomed to run on the Commons here, one owned by Mr. Murchison[68] and the other by Mr. Cooper, were since Monday last, cut in a most shocking manner with an axe, knife, or some other sharp instrument—If such infernal customs are passed by, we shall by degrees degenerate into such a state of barbarity, that the next course taken will be to mangle one another.

I have been informed, that of late, this practice has become so horribly prevalent, as hardly to excite belief; and it is to be hoped, that every one who possesses the common feelings of humanity, will join in a fervent wish, that the Magistrates of this town will enforce the law (if such there is) which may tend to prevent the recurrence of such atrocities.

AN INHABITANT.

York, August 30, 1811.

C 20 Minutes of the General Quarter Sessions of the Peace, Home District
[*P.A.O., Minutes of the General Quarter Sessions of the Peace, Home District*]

York 12th October 1811

The Court met Pursuant to Adjournment

Present

Thomas Ridout Esquire, Chairman,

and

William Allan Esquire.

Thaddeus Gilbert,[69] and Jacob Smith,[70] the Path Masters in and for the Town of York appeared Pursuant to their Notifications of the 10th Instant.

[68]John Murchison (1778?–1870) was born in Glengarry, the son of a Loyalist from New York. He began tailoring in York in 1808, after experience in Montreal. The same year he married Frances, daughter of Joseph Hunt. During the War of 1812, he served as a sergeant major in the York Militia.

[69]Thaddeus Gilbert first appears on the List of Inhabitants in 1804.

[70]Jacob Smith was a shoemaker. In December, 1808, he entered a partnership with William Curstead.

The said Thaddeus Gilbert produced his Account and there appeared from his Statement to be 145 days Labour Yet due by the Inhabitants within his boundary, which was returned to him, after the Court had Made their remarks thereon, for his guidance until the whole of the Labour should be Completed, then to be returned again to be filed with the Records of the Court—

Ordered that he do first repair the Road between the Town of York and Don Bridge, and also to fix the Plank on the New Bridge, which have shifted from their places, the Labour not to exceed 20 Days on said Road and Bridge.—next to Repair the Bridges in the Town of York which is over Drains Vizt.—One opposite to Mr. Jordans,[71] Alexr Wood Esquire's, and J. Evens'es and any other place in said Town, that the Magistrates may hereafter think necessary—And then what labour remains due to be expended on Yonge Street Road, Commencing at the Corner of *Leaches* Present dwelling House on said street—and to Continue up the said Street to opposite to Doctor McCauley's House—provided the Labour will hold out—

Jacob Smiths return being also laid before the Court their appeared to be 5 Defaulters together with a Sum of Money of £15. 1
Pro: Currency received by him and not Yet expended, the Defaulters were

D'Arcy Boulton the Elder,[72] Esquire,	7 Days
William Willcocks Esquire	12 Do
Marie[73] Do	8 —
T. R. Johnson[74]	6 —
William Flanagan	3 —

Ordered That Jacob Smith do examine the Road which he was directed to repair this Spring and if any Labour is necessary to make it good to do it—next to examine all the Bridges within his Boundary, and where necessary repair them and particularly that near to the North Corner of the Chief Justices House—and when the said Bridges are repaired to expend the then Balance in his Hands on the Road, or Street called Peter Street—if not ordered by the Magistrates to lay out Labour elsewhere—

[71]John Jordan was a baker and hotel keeper. Jordan's York Hotel was for many years the most popular hotel in York.

[72]D'Arcy Boulton (1759–1834) was born in Lincolnshire, England, and came to Upper Canada in 1797. He was called to the Bar in 1803 and in 1805 became Solicitor General. In 1810 he sailed for England, but was captured by a French privateer and imprisoned at Verdun until 1814, when he returned to Canada, and was appointed Attorney General. In 1818 he became a judge of assize and nisi prius.

[73](Susannah) Maria Willcocks (1768?–1834) was the eldest daughter of William Willcocks. She died unmarried and left her share of the Willcocks and Russell property to her sister, Mrs. W. W. Baldwin. From 1806 to 1815 she was Housekeeper to the Executive Council.

[74]Thomas Ridout Johnson was a butcher, who was also jailer from 1804 to 1807.

The Court then Adjourned to Saturday next at Eleven oClock.

S. Heward
Clk of the Peace attending

C 21 MINUTES OF THE SPECIAL SESSIONS OF THE PEACE, HOME DISTRICT

[*P.A.O., Minutes of the General Quarter Sessions of the Peace, Home District*]

Home District }
York to Wit }

At a Special Session of the Peace holden at the Clerk of the Peace's Office in the Town of York, on Saturday the 7th day of December 1811 at ten oClock A.M.

Present
Thomas Ridout Esquire, Chairman,
William Allan, Duncan Cameron
and
Donald McLean[75]
Esquires
Justices of our Lord the King & Cra.

The Chairman Laid before the Court a Letter addressed to him from the Sheriff of the Home District, which was ordered to be Read, and is as follows

Sheriffs Office
York 4th December 1811

Sir

I beg leave to state to you that the Prisoners in the Cells of the Gaol of the Home District suffer much from Cold and Damp, there being no method of communicating heat from the Chimnies, nor any Bedsteads to raise the Straw from the Floors which lie nearly if not altogether on the ground—therefore I have to request that you will represent these matters to Your Brother Magistrates, and suggest, that a small Stove in the Lobby of each range of Cells, a rough Bedstead for each Cell—together with some Rugs, or Blankets will add much to the Comfort of the unhappy Persons confined and it is to be hoped will remove the grievance complained of to

Sir,
Your most obedient
Humble Servant
(Signed) John Beikie[76]
Sheriff

Thomas Ridout Esqr.
Chairman of the Qr Sessions
Home District.

---

[75]Donald McLean (d. 1813) was appointed Clerk of the House of Assembly in 1801. On the morning of the attack on York by the Americans, April 27, 1813, he volunteered with the 8th Regiment, and was killed on the beach resisting the landing.

[76]John Beikie (1767?–1839) was Sheriff of the Home District 1810–15. He was a member of the House of Assembly 1813–16 and succeeded John Small as Clerk of the Executive Council in 1832. He married Penelope, daughter of Colonel John Macdonell (Scotus).

Ordered on reading the above requisition of the Sheriff That the Treasurer do procure two small Mettle Stoves, and pipes and direct them to be put up in the Lobby of each range of Cells, and to furnish such Bedsteads, Blankets, or Rugs as may be found necessary for the Prisoners.

The Court then Adjourned to 28h December Instant.

S. Heward
Clk of the Peace Attendg

C 22 Public Nuisances and Swine
[*York*, York Gazette, *May 1, 1812*]

WHEREAS it has been represented to the Magistrates in General Quarter Sessions, that notwithstanding the many Presentments against Individuals for having Public Nuisances in front of their Premises in the Streets of the Town of York, which still are unremoved—Due Notice is hereby given to all Persons so offending, that if the said Presented Nuisances are not removed immediately, they will be Indicted at the next Quarter Sessions.

The owners of Swine are also cautioned against allowing them to run at large in the said Town or neighbourhood after the date hereof, otherwise prompt measures will be taken to prevent such trespassing.

S. HEWARD, C.P.

York, 28th April, 1812.

C 23 Prison Escape
[*York*, York Gazette, *August 29, 1812*]

To the prompt and spirited Exertions of Mr. D. Tiers, Merchant of this place, is to be ascribed the apprehending of the Selfclep'd Augustus Baron de Diemar[77] and Mr. Stiles, *two interesting Personages,* who *eloped* from Bed and Board alias the Common Gaol on Wednesday last.—We hope that equal alacrity may distinguish each of our townsmen—when public duty requires it; we sincerely regret that whilst joining in this public duty, Doctor Stebbins[78] was thrown from his horse, and a compound fracture of his left arm and other personal hurts were the consequence.

[77]Baron de Diemar advertised that he was commencing a French school, on January 16, 1808. In December, 1808, Maria de Diemar advertised as a mantua maker. A Baron de Diemar had been associated with Berczy in the land company speculation in the Genesee tract.

[78]Dr. Amasa Stebbins (d. 1814) kept a general store and tavern in York.

D. COMMERCIAL DEVELOPMENT

D 1 RICHARD CARTWRIGHT TO J. B. ROUSSEAU, YORK
[*P.A.O., Cartwright Letter Book*]

Kingston 26th. Octr. 1793

I have now shipped on Board the Caldwell the several Articles that you left behind you which were included in your former Invoice; and also a Crate of Earthen Ware & 6 Bbls. jamaica Rum of which the Invoice is inclosed amounting to £87 . . 11 . . 4.— I have addressed these Articles to Mr. Crooks[1] requesting that he would forward them to you as soon as possible; but it may not perhaps be in his Power to send them without a special order from the Governor which you will do well to procure. . . .

D 2 CARTWRIGHT TO BRYAN CRAWFORD[2]
[*P.A.O., Cartwright Letter Book*]

Kingston 21st Decr. 1793

. . . As I know that the Post of Toronto will in future be victualled from this Place, I would recommend to you to pack as much Flour as you can, to have in Readiness as soon as the Communication opens.— I believe few People will go into the Packing Business this Winter; and in that Case by having a Quantity ready for Delivery we shall infallibly secure a Preference.—This is a Hint that you will of Course keep to yourself. . . .

D 3 ROUSSEAU IN ACCOUNT CURRENT WITH THOMAS BARRY
[*P.A.O., Rousseau Papers*]

1794		To Account paid Mr. Cartright S Hafx. 183 9 5	£			£293	11	1¾
Augst.	26th	To Mr. Robisons acct.		8	0			
	29	,, 1 pair half Soals		2	0			
	30	,, paid Capt. Graham	1	1	1			
	,,	,, 1 pint rum		2	0			
	31st	,, ¼ lb. Tobacco		1	0			
Septr.	4th	To 1 Qt. Rum to Segor		4	0			
	,,	,, ¼ lb. Tobacco 1/. pd. Corpl. Hunt 12/		13	0			
						£2	11	1
	,,	,, 1 Yard White Molton		6	0			
	,,	,, Cash 41/. 1 paper Ink powder 2/.	2	3	0			
	,,	paid Mr. Wilcot[3]		16	0			
		,, paid Indian pr. Order		16	0			
		,, 5⅞ Yds. Mode 2/8 Stg. 75 pr. Cent	2	4	0½			
		,, a Draft on Govr. Simcoe £19.10 Halfx. is York	31	4	0			

[1]James Crooks (1778–1860) was a prominent Niagara merchant.

[2]Bryan Crawford managed Cartwright's Napanee mills.

[3]Paul Wilcot came from Pennsylvania and served in the American army during the Revolution. He came to Canada in 1793. His wife was Elizabeth Ashbridge.

			£	s.	d.	£	s.	d.
Novr.	1st	,, 13½ lb. Bread 3/4 ,, 10½ lb. Pork 7/10 } To the man diging Potatoes		11	2			
	6th	Paid for Diging Potatoes		18	0	38	18	2½
Decr.	15th	To paid Nicholas Miller	1	16	2½			
	24th	,, 6 pair Shoe packs 6/	1	16	0			
1795								
Jany.	4th	a Do. Shoes	1	0	0			
Feby.	2nd	,, Cash pr. Mr Bond	17	0	0			
,,		,, Do. from John Smith		17	0			
April	22nd	,, paid Indian		12	0			
	,,	,, 2 Yds. Ribbin		8	0			
	,,	,, Bread & Pork		4	0	23	13	2½
April	23	,, paid Serjt. Major Perry[4]	1	4	0			
	27	,, Do. Serjt. Hannah[5]	1	7	0			
May	1st	,, 2 Yds. Broad Ribbon		8	0			
		,, paid for bringing Potatoes from Browns		8	0			
	21	3 Quarts Porter 2/		6	0			
	,,	,, Cash pr. Mr. Beasley	20	0	0			
	,,	,, Share of a Draft on Russle	32	0	0			
	,,	,, 13 cwt. 0 Qr. 16 lb. flour in Mr. Beasleys acct.	15	15	5			
June	,,	,, 4 Bushels Potatoes fed to your Cow @ 6/.	1	4	0	72	12	5
		To 2 Bushels Turnips @ 2/.		4	0			
	22nd	,, Cash 10/.4 1 Bushel oats Mr. Iredel[6] 5/		15	4			
	,,	,, 1 tin Lanthron		8	0			
	,,	,, 4½ Bushels Indian Corn Philip Horps 4/6		19	1½	2	6	5½
Augst.	27th	an Almanac for Shafer		2	0			
Novr.	15th	Cash received from Mr. Beasley	20	0	0			
		4 cwt. Bran to Horning[7]	1	12	0			
		Cash paid Mr. Ridout in August		4	0			
		an Order on Lottridge[8]	2	8	0			
1796								
April	11th	Cr. Capt. Lippincot[9]	4	0	0			
		Cash in Niagara Bills		8	0			
May	15th	Over paid on Grahams bill		4	0	28	18	0

4 Alexander Perry (d. 1800) had a long service record in the 44th Regiment before he became Quartermaster Sergeant of the Queen's Rangers in 1792. He was living in Montreal in 1800 when he came to York in an unsuccessful attempt to be admitted to the Bar in Upper Canada, and was drowned in the Rouge River on his return journey.

5 Sergeant John Hannah of the Queen's Rangers.

6 Abraham Iredell (1751–1806) was a deputy land surveyor.

7 Abraham Horning settled in Barton Township, on the Dundas highway.

8 Captain Robert Lottridge served as a captain in the Indian department during the American Revolution. He had lands near Niagara and in Barton Township. By July, 1796, he was dead, and his sons, John and William, were disputing possession of his Niagara lands with Thomas Butler, and his Barton lands with Richard Beasley.

9 Richard Lippincott (1745–1826) was born at Shrewsbury, New Jersey. He served as a captain in the American Revolution, and was implicated in the hanging of a prisoner of war. After the Revolution he immigrated to New Brunswick, and about 1793 settled at Richmond Hill. His daughter Esther Borden Lippincott married George Taylor Denison (1783–1853).

June	10th	An order in favour of Mr. Beasley	37	10	0			
July	9th	An order on Doctor Richardson	4	12	9			
		Sturgeon Oil		2	0			
	25	2 Orders on Beasley £50 Each	100	0	0			
		4 Months use of Licence	1	5	4			
		130 lbs. Midlings	1	4	0			
		200 lb. Cornel	1	0	0			
						145	14	1
						£608	4	7¼
To a Balance Due Mr St John NYC						17	12	7¾
York 8th Septr. 1796 Erors Excepted						£625	17	3

Thomas Barry

Contra Cr.

1794		By Amount of Invoice S 196 2 9 Hfx £				£315	15	5
Septr.	2nd	By Mr. Lawrence's Acct.	1	19	8			
Augst.	8th	Cash pr. Mr. Herron	3	1	0			
		Do. pr. Mr. Asbridge		2	6			
		2 cwt. 1 Qr. 0 lb. flour 26/	2	18	0			
	12	Cash recd. from Fredrick Smith[10]		6	0			
Septr.	22nd	Do. Recd. from Parker Mills		4	0			
		1 Barrel sold		5	0			
	8	Do. a Do.		5	0			
Octr.		6 Barrels Do. @ 6/	1	16	0			
		recd. from Mr. Matthews[11]	6	8	0			
		Cash recd. from Mosley[12]	2	1	10			
						19	7	0
		Thomas Barry's acct	£4	2	4			
		Doctor Gambles[13] Do.	5	8	0			
		cwt. 13 Qr 0 lbs 16 flour @ 24/	15	15	5			
		6 Chairs @ 6/	1	16	0			
		An ox Sold	15	0	0			
		Licence	4	16	0			
		Mr. Johnstons Acct.	6	9	11			
						53	7	8
		Cash recd. from Abram Devins		5	3			
March		2 Counterfeit Bills		18	0			
May	1st	1 Mocock Sugar 80 lbs at 1/3	5	0	0			
		62¾ lbs. Butter	4	14	2			
		Mr. Constant	3	0	0			

[10]Frederick Smith had a farm on Yonge Street.

[11]John and Thomas Matthews (Mathews) farmed on Lot 10, first concession, York Township.

[12]Thomas Mosley (1767?–1827) was born in Kent, England. He was a storekeeper and auctioneer in York. He had learned his trade under Alderman Swayne, of London, England. In an advertisement dated July 22, 1815, he stated "although Providence has deprived him of the use of his feet, he has still, through his Divine Mercy, the use of his tongue." He had been crippled by frost-bite.

[13]Doctor John Gamble (1755–1811) was born near Enniskillen, Ireland, and studied medicine at the University of Edinburgh. He emigrated to New York in 1779, and served in the Queen's Rangers in the Revolution. Afterwards, he settled at St. John, N.B., until he once more joined the reorganized Rangers as Assistant Surgeon. When the regiment was disbanded, he moved to Kingston, and practised medicine there until his death.

			£	s	d	
	15	2 Chairs Capt. Graham 6/		12	0	
	17	14 Bushels Potatoes @ 6/	4	4	0	
	21	Charg'd Major Shank 2 Guineas	3	14	8	
		Mr. Cameron	2	13	0	
		22 cwt. 3 Qr. 14 lb. flour 25/	27	19	11	
						53 1 0
		10 Bushels Corn Major Shanks 5/	2	10	0	
		9 Bushels Potatoes Do Do 4	1	16	0	
		2 Bushels Corn Do Do 4/6		9	0	
		Cash on Mr. Seddings Bill 6. 16. 8 Hallx.	10	18	8	
		By 1 Cow £8 1 Half Bushel 8/	8	8	0	
						24 1 8
June	22nd	By Mr. Camerons Note	7	10	0	
July	3rd	Capt. Cox Do.	7	0	0	
Augst.	29th	233½ lbs. Sugar @ 1/4	15	11	11	
		Mr. Camerons Bill on Mr. McCauly	8	8	0	
Novr.		Mr. Wilcots Note	12	13	9	
		paid Abram Horning	7	0	0	
		12 Lights Window Glass @ 2/	1	4	0	
		paid Young for Peak[14]	10	11	7	
						69 18 8
		2 Water Buckets 4/		8	0	
		flour Barrels	1	16	9	
		2–2 Feet Rules 12/	1	4	0	
		56 lbs. Shot /10d.	2	6	8	
		1 pair Hose		6	0	
		Candle Stick		6	0	
		100 Flints		3	0	
		paid Mr. Felman[15]	8	2	3	
						14 12 8
		3 Quire paper		10	6	
		150 lbs. Flour	3	0	0	
		Ditto to Smith		17	0	
		2 Bushels Corn		8	0	
		2 Years Rent	32	0	0	
		59 lb. Sugar Serjt. Cranford[16]	4	8	6	
						£41 3 0
						591 7 1
		By Adjutant McGill				34 10 2
						625 17 3

D 4 Cartwright to Thomas Barry, York

[*Queen's University, Douglas Library, Cartwright Letter Books*]

Kingston 16th. Octr. 1797—

I wrote of 28th & 29th. Septr. by the Industry[17] Capt. McMullen, on Board of whom I shipped at the same Time a very considerable Part

[14]William Peak was an Indian trader near the mouth of Duffin's Creek, in Pickering Township.

[15]John and Conrad Filman (Felman) settled in Barton Township, on the Dundas highway.

[16]Sergeant James Cranford of the Queen's Rangers settled in Etobicoke Township and owned a tavern. He married the widowed mother of Moody and William Farewell of Whitby. For a time he operated the Ferry over the Humber River.

[17]The only *Industry* located was a North West Company sloop built at Detroit in 1786 for use on the Upper Lakes.

of your Goods, & a Number of Packages for Mr. Beasley & Mr. St. John.—She sailed from hence on the Evening of the 29th. Ulto. & not having reached York when Capt. Seleck[18] left it, and the Weather having been very boisterous, we are under very great Anxiety for her Safety.— Should she unfortunately have been lost, you will be a Sufferer to a large Amount: But I hope you will not be discouraged on that Account, as I shall be disposed to afford you any reasonable Indulgence & Aid; and in the unfortunate Event of the loss of the Vessel, will, if you wish it, make you up as far as I am able, an Assortment of Articles similar to those sent you, that you may not be altogether without Goods for the Winter.—

Inclosed is the Invoice of Goods imported for you from Montreal Amontg. to £338 . . 15 . . 9½ to which will be added the Freight & my Commission. Also the Invoice of Articles furnished by myself amounting to £620 . . 18 . . 11½. There are still wanting some Tape & Candles, some Buttons & a few Articles of Hard Ware to complete your Order: But I have not yet recd. these Articles; and they will be sent by the next Opportunity, at which Time I hope to be able to send you some Flour; for I have yet not been able to procure any. I have a few Barrels of Pork and Beef, the former at 26 the latter at 16 Dollars per Bbl.—Should you want any more Crockery Ware I can send you a Cask, the Contents & Price of which you will find in the inclosed Memorandum.— You will also receive inclosed a Copy of the Sales of your Pelteries, Nt. Proceeds £292 . . 9 . . 2 at your Credit. . . .

D 5 A Tailor Arrives

[*York*, Upper Canada Gazette, *May 25, 1799*]

Evean Eveans,
Taylor and Habit-Maker,
(FROM LONDON.)

Having taken a room in a small building belonging to Mr, Willcocks, for the purpose of prosecuting the duties of his trade; begs leave to inform the ladies and gentlemen of York, that he has commenced the above business; and to those, who, may honor him with their commands, he flatters himself from his experience, to afford satisfaction.

York, May 23.

D 6 Potash Wanted

[*York*, Upper Canada Gazette, *December 7, 1799*]

ASHES, ASHES, ASHES.

The subscriber begs leave to inform the public, that he is about to erect a POT-ASH upon lot No. 7, West side of Yong-street; where he

[18]Captain Charles Selleck served during the Revolution with the rank of lieutenant in the army on board armed gunboats. In 1799 he was Captain of the *Duchess of York*. In 1804 he owned a tavern near Presqu' Isle.

will give a generous price for ASHES;—for house-ashes NINE-PENCE per bushel, for field-ashes SIX-PENCE, delivered at his Potash. He conceives it his duty to inform those who may have ashes to dispose of, that it will not be in his power to pay cash, but merchandize at cash price.

DUKE W. KENDRICK.

York, Dec. 7, '99

D 7 A HAIRDRESSER ARRIVES
[*York*, Upper Canada Gazette, *April 5, 1800*]

ROCK,
Hair Dresser, from London,

Begs leave to inform the Ladies and Gentlemen of York and its Vicinity, that he will open Shop on the 25th inst. in Mr. Cooper's House, next the Printing Office. All orders left for him at said place will be punctually attended to. N.B. Shop customers, and others will be dressed on the most reasonable terms.

York, April 5, 1800.

D 8 A WATCHMAKER ARRIVES
[*York*, Upper Canada Gazette, *April 19, 1800*]

Elisha Purdey

WATCHMAKER, begs leave to inform his friends and the public that he has taken a room in the house of Mr. Marther, where he repairs and cleans Watches of all kinds in the best manner and on the most reasonable terms. All orders left for him at said house will be duly attended to. He has a small but elegant assortment of Jewelry for sale.

York, April 19, 1800.

D 9 ANNOUNCEMENT OF AUCTION SALE
[*York*, Upper Canada Gazette, *August 2, 1800*]

FOR SALE
At public Auction,
ON WEDNESDAY THE *6th* of AUGUST,
at Mr. *John M'Dougal's Tavern*, 10
o'clock, A.M.

THE FOLLOWING ARTICLES:

FASHIONABLE Chintz,
one piece of Strip'd Muslin,
Black and White Cotton Stockings,
Ladies' and Gentlemen's Shammy Gloves,
Do. Tanned,
Fashionable Shawls,

Large Silk Handkerchiefs, of various colours,
Ribbons and Edging, of the best quality,
Nun's Thread,
Loaf and Muscovado Sugar,
Starch and fig Blue,
Fool's cap Paper,
Pins and Tape,
Men's Hatts,
Mustard in bottles,
Best quality Green Tea,
5 Silver Watches,
And sundry other articles not mentioned, by

THO'S MOSLEY,
Auctioneer.

York, 30 July.

D 10 A BAKER ADVERTISES
[*York*, Upper Canada Gazette, *August 30, 1800*]

John Horton
BEGS leave to inform his Friends and the Public, that he carries on the
Bakeing business
At his Bake-house, opposite Mrs. Barry's in this town; where he keeps
Bread and Cakes
For sale on the most reasonable terms. Also some excellent
Smoked-beef
Cheap for CASH, together with sundry articles of
Groceries.
York, July 31, 1800.

D 11 THEFT FROM A MERCHANT
[*York*, Upper Canada Gazette, *January 24, 1801*]

On Friday the 16th inst. some villian or villians, allured by the hope of plunder, broke open the stable of Mr. Patrick Mealey, of this town, store-keeper, wherein he lately kept a quantity of liquors and other merchandize; but luckily they were removed a few days before.— In their search they found an old bridle, which not thinking worth carrying off, they left at the outer gate.

Those merchants who are, for the want of room in their stores, obliged to keep part of their goods in out-houses, cannot be too cautious, as this nest of robbers will, most probably, be on the constant watch to see where they can make their prey.

D 12 FRUIT TREES FOR SALE
[*York*, Upper Canada Gazette, *March 7, 1801*]

ABOUT 2000 Fruit trees of various kinds from the best seed; 500 do grafted from the best fruit of Mr. Prince's garden L. island, most of which six and nine years old, some have borne fruit: viz.—Apple, pear, peach, plumb, cherry, apricot, nectarine, quince, goosberry, currant, grape, mulberry, &c. Also a few Lumberdy poplars and areasia or locus trees. — For further particulars apply to the printers of the Oracle.

D 13 William Cooper Opens a Tavern
[*York,* Upper Canada Gazette, *March 7, 1801*]

To the public.

THE subscriber gives notice, that he has taken the house in King-street lately occupied by Mr. M'Murtrie as a tavern, which he is now fitting up, and will be prepared about the first of April next for the accommodation of lodgers, boarders and travellers. Nothing shall be wanting on his part to place it as nearly on the footing of an English Inn, as local circumstances will permit, and to render it pleasant and agreeable to gentlemen who honor him with their countenance and custom,— He flatters himself that from the quality of the liquors he will keep, the conveniencies of the house, and the punctual attendance which he pledges himself to give on all occasions, that his house will have a preference and his undertaking be worthy the patronage of a generous public.

W. COOPER

☞ He will have good provender and stabling for horses.

D 14 Alexander Wood to James Dunlop,[19] Montreal
[*T.P.L., Alexander Wood Letter Books*]

York 17th. June 1801—

. . . I am sorry to observe that the Fame in which my goods were Shipped and to Sail on the 25th March has not as yet, or rather had not on the 6th been heard of but hope ere now she is at your place—and some of the Goods on their Way as I suppose it will not be difficult to procure Freight this year boats being much wanted to carry down Flour.

If my Goods are safe, its probable there may be as much as I can vend here to Advantage the prices being this year beyond measure, extravagant and it will not answer in these times to have a Supply far above the demand in your market goods as it appears to me may be much lower another season but can hardly increase in value, and I am very anxious to see old scores cleared before running too far in a new Debt—

I wait the 30th. Inst. before leaving this in expectation that some of Allan & Woods friends may enable me to carry down a little paper for

[19]James Dunlop (1755?–1815) was born in Scotland, and became one of the wealthiest Montreal merchants.

cash in this place is perfectly out of the question if times do not get better and money more plenty I don't know but the name of Cash may even be forgotten. I'm sorry to see the Exchange so much against English Bills as our customers here have only such to offer us and they would grumble much if we insisted on their paper at the rate of Exchange. . . .

D 15 Counterfeit Money
[*York,* Upper Canada Gazette, *July 18, 1801*]

CAUTION

The public ought to be on their guard how they take dollars of the date of 1796 and 1797, as there is a large number of them in circulation, very handsomely plated, supposed to have been imported this spring into the States from Birmingham and Sheffield, and in all probability may come into circulation here: the milling on the pillar side is rather faint; and they may easily be discovered by sawing on the edge with a knife, and turning it strong up, when the plate will rise.

D 16 Wood to Robert Hamilton,[20] Queenston
[*T.P.L., Alexander Wood Letter Books*]

York 2d. Septr. 1801

. . . With respect to the subject of Flour. I find that at present some might be sold as the Yonge Street Farmers have not been able to bring any to Market, but have been offering to sell at your price, say six dollars per Barrel of two Cwt. if you can send the Washington[21] over or make her touch here and lay down a hundred Barrels at that price I think it might be in my power to sell good part of it before any is brought from the Farmers about the town or head of the Lake, by this it will appear that the sooner you are in the Market the more likely will we be able to dispose of the commodity: you will understand I mean that it should be laid down here at 3 Dr per Cwt. Barrels included, the payment I will take care shall be forthcoming at the day for so much as is disposed of

The Whisky Brewers at the head of the Lake, bring a good deal to this place which they retail by 3 Gallons at a dollar per Gall notwithstanding if you think proper to send a few Barrels I will do my best for your Interest.

If you send the Flour I beg you will let it be of a good quality as

[20]Robert Hamilton (1750–1809), born in Scotland, was a very prominent merchant at Queenston.

[21]The *Washington* was a sloop built near Erie, Pa., in 1797. The following year it was bought by a Canadian, renamed the *Lady Washington,* and brought around Niagara Falls by land for use on Lake Ontario. In November, 1803, it was wrecked in a storm near Oswego.

we are tormented here with returned Flour sometimes, most people get their Bread from the Baker and pay in flour so that it has to undergo his inspection but I dare say this is a caution which might have been left out as you would not send any produce to the Market unmerchantable. . . .

D 17 JOHN STUART[22] TO THE BISHOP[23]

[*Synod of Ontario Archives, Stuart Letters; printed in Preston,* Kingston before the War of 1812, *pp. 351–2*]

Kingston, September 14, 1801

. . . I need not observe to your Lordship, that *York* never was intended by nature for a metropolis; and that nothing but the caprice and obstinacy of Genl Simcoe raised it to that Dignity. The Harbour is not commodious, as the wind that carries a vessel out of it, is a head wind when it enters the Lake.—The *Town* is a Hot Bed, where every Thing is forced, unnaturally, by English money. I know of no Trade now existing, or to be expected at any future Period, to support or enrich it.—The Lands contiguous, to the Distance of some miles, are ingrossed by what we call *the Servants of Government,* so that a Pound of Butter must travel at least four or five miles before it reaches the market. The settlements now forming in its vicinity, are so distant, and thinly peopled, that they have no Produce to spare. The Township of Hope (I think 50 miles to the Eastward) consisting of 40 or 50 Families is by far the most flourishing. And there are few Inhabitants, to the Westward, nearer than the Head of the Lake. There is indeed a Range of Farms on what is called Young Street, a Road that leads to Lake Simcoe, which are expected to produce mighty advantages to the seat of Government. A recent Fact will corroberate what I have said; A Brewer[24] from Kingston removed to York lately and, on application to the Governor, obtained one of the King's vessels to transport wheat and other Grain from Kingston and the Bay of Quintie, before Beer could be made—and almost all the Pork, Beef Butter, Flour, Hams, Mutton, which are used at York are brought by water, from Kingston, Niagara, the Genesee Counttry &c. &c.—In short the Town is supported by the money which the Gentlemen who have Salaries from Government expend in Buildings & other Improvements; and that source begins to fail. And it is the opinion of the most judicious of my acquaintance that there are more people now in York, by one third than the Place can support.

[22]Rev. John Stuart (1740–1811) was born in Pennsylvania and educated at the College of Philadelphia. He was appointed missionary to the Mohawks at Fort Hunter, N.Y. In 1781 he came to Canada and from 1785 was Rector of St. George's Church, Kingston.

[23]The similarity between this letter and G 8, Bishop Mountain to the S.P.G., would suggest that he was the recipient.

[24]Robert Henderson.

D 18 WOOD TO HAMILTON, QUEENSTON
[*T.P.L., Alexander Wood Letter Books*]

York 26th. September 1801

. . . you know a Small parcel [of flour] overstocks the market here and it is so uncertain as to price that its impossible for any one to fix on a medium if the Farmers about the head of Lake Ontario can find outing for the surplus of their Crop elsewhere we may pay pretty high for flour otherwise it will certainly be cheap there will be a good deal to spare amongst the Yonge street people this season and you know it is not in their power to carry it past us. . . .

D 19 WOOD TO IRVINE, MCNAUGHT & CO.,[25] QUEBEC
[*T.P.L., Alexander Wood Letter Books*]

Upper Canada
York 28th. Sepr. 1801.

. . . I am sorry to inform you that three of my packages from Scotland are still amissing I have discovered the rout they are in but owing to bad marking they had got so far up the Country that the expences incurred in carrying them forward and bringing them back will be more than the prime cost of the goods they are Glass Candles & frying pans the former can be easily dispensed with a[s] Messrs. L.M.& Co. sent just double the Quantity ordered Candles are in demand. I might have sold what is now on their rout down from Fort Erie travelling at an expense far beyond any profit that can be expected on such an article the latter Frying pans I might have sold over and over, being entirely out of them some time previous to my leaving this. This is sad complaining about trifles but while we are creeping a small obstacle in the way seems of much consequence. . .

With respect to the State of our Market no difinite account can be given at present, as the Crop for this Year is not as yet in a Merchantable State we however pay 7 dollars per 224w. of fine flour in a Barrel at present tho its my opinion that cannot be quoted as the standard price the crops have been abundant and there's no visible outlet for the surplusage which will be considerable

I cannot state pease and ashes we regulate by your generosity I shall be happy to hear from you when oppy. occurs and beg the prices current with you.

Many of our substantial farmers have a wish to try how hemp will answer in this Province but theres such a scarcity of seed they have it not in their power is there any to be got in your quarter that can be depended on as fresh, and what price.

[25]Irvine, McNaught & Co., under James Irvine, was the Quebec branch of the Glasgow exporting firm, Leslie, McNaught & Co.

D 20 WOOD TO LESLIE, MCNAUGHT & CO., GREENOCK
[*T.P.L., Alexander Wood Letter Books*]

York 1st Octr. 1801.

. . . I now inclose an order for Merchandise which you will please complete and send forward by the first vessel in the spring, the Articles are numerous and small, but we are under the necessity of laying in such triffles to accommodate our Customers and it is the practice in this Country to keep every kind of goods in one store. . . .

If you find convenient to make up the order now sent, I beg your attention to the quality of the goods and to the packing. I would wish to recall to your mind the difficulty a young man finds in establishing a Character; how much more difficult to reestablish himself in the opinion of the Public, when they take it in their heads that damaged goods are imported to impose on them—I do not from this mean to insinuate any inattention of yours in putting up the goods sent this spring, on the contrary I dare say you took what might be thought the necessary steps to procure them of good qualities and on the best terms, and its probable had they been well packed I should have little reason to complain of the quality except the wine, Vinegar and Loaf Sugar these were certainly inferiour in the first instance the later suffered very much on the communication from the insufficiency of the package and particularly from its size. I shall say no more on the subject at present but depend on your generosity to make the necessary allowance and am in hopes if my proposal is accepted the next will be in better plight.

I have been writing to James Wood[26] to procure me a decent young man as a Servant, a lad of about 15 years old would answer very well, he says there is a difficulty in getting one to come out by himself; if it is not imposing a troublesome task on you it would be obliging me very much to indent a young lad to answer the above description: if you can find one willing to engage please have the necessary writings made out and engage on my part for any number of years, and make the remuneration for his services what you conceive to be generous. his work will be mostly indoors and not laboreous. however I would not wish to point out a certain place of his employment as we must have such a Servant as will answer every purpose. . . .

If there is a probability of a Peace in the ensuing Spring, I wish you would assort the goods accordingly, that is, to send such articles as in the event of Peace, will not be much diminished in value, the others may be sent in part only. as to the Spirits if it is very low with you the quantity ordered may be sent. if on the contrary it is high it will be better not to complete this part of the order—when the Crops are good in Jamaica we have their Produce cheaper in this Country than with you. this you can easily ascertain and be governed as you think will

[26]Alexander Wood's brother, living near Aberdeen, Scotland.

answer my purpose best. I mean this as a trial, as we, in the Upper Province are not in the habit of importing Spirits; the import to Lower Canada is, I'm informed, this year, short of the demand, it is of course extravagantly dear say 8/ to 9/ Hx per Gallon for the first sort, and 6/6 to 7/ for reduced Rum. . . .

D 21 WOOD TO HAMILTON, QUEENSTON
[*T.P.L., Alexander Wood Letter Books*]

York 22d Jany. 1802

I duly recd. your esteemed favour of the 16th. Inst. yesterday morng. and have been employed this morng. in trying to get your Flour ashore and believe it may now be accomplished with the assistance lent by Col: Shaw, who was good enough to order one of the Kings Boats to be launched in purpose—in consequence of a keen frost Skinner was last night obliged to fall down to the Garrison, what with paying the men for bringing this Flour to the beach and Sleighing it to town I'm affraid it will not clear your price, and you will see by Mr Clarks[27] taking back a parcel he had in charge, that it is not in demand here just now, indeed there is no money in the Circle if it was—the open weather has enabled the Farmers on the lake side to bring up quantities in Boats which has in some degree gluted the market Notwithstanding yours will have every chance in my power. . . .

I shall not fail from time to time to let you know the state of our Market for Flour. I have possess'd myself of your ham and will treat it as you direct, which when in condition shall be submitted to the judgment of some of your friends—I think it's not unlikely that some might find sale here, particularly if sent pretty early, and let them be well died as I have no place fit to hang them in except the Store which might prove too warm for them when the weather gets hot, but by being well smoked they may resist the heat—Whisky being an Article in no danger of perishing by age, if you are plentifully stocked it would only be risking the Freight to send a parcel of it I find but little sale for it tho' I have some on hand now the very best that has appeared in this place—cost me 7/6 in exchange for other Merchandise, and grain being now reduced so considerably, one would suppose it might fall also.—I have the last 12 Bbls of Flour still on hand.

D 22 A CHAIRMAKER ADVERTISES
[*York,* Upper Canada Gazette, *January 23, 1802*]

THE Subscriber returns his sincere thanks to his Friends and the Public for the great encouragement he has hitherto met with, and begs leave to inform them, that he now intends carrying on his business in

[27]Probably Thomas Clark (1770–1837), merchant, miller, and forwarder of goods at Queenston, Chippawa, and Fort Erie.

all its branches without delay—armed chairs, Sittees, and dining ditto, fan-back and brace-back Chairs. He very shortly expects a quantity of different paints; it will then be in his power to finish his Chairs in the best manner, and by his great attention to perform his promises, hopes to merit protection and support.

DANIEL TEIRS.

York, Jan. 23, 1802.

N.B. He also expects a quantity of common Chairs from below, which he will dispose of on reasonable terms.

D 23 Wood to Leslie, McNaught & Co.
[*T.P.L., Alexander Wood Letter Books*]

Up. C. York 11th. Ap: 1802

. . . I recd. a letter from James Wood dated the 2d. Jany. last which gave me to understand that you decline executing my order for this Spring; I'm sorry this intimation was not given in time to apply else where as you must have known that it would be impossible after the 18th Decr. to arrange matters with a House in London so as to give time to make the shipment by the Spring Fleet, which leaves me in a very awkward state of suspense; and will operate very considerably against me; had you given an answer to the question on the receipt of my letters of the 22d. July and 6th. Augt. I should have been able to alter my plan so as to obviate the difficulty that appears now before me.

Tho' I am a very considerable sufferer by last importation, I lay none of the blame to your charge on the contrary believe you spared no pains to forward my interest and I supposed by pointing out to you where it appeared the attention was wanting that similar mismanagement might be avoided.

I acknowledge my business may at present be more troublesome than profitable, but with the increasing population our wants will increase and of course my orders may be more extensive. When you have in mind that the Capital of U.C. York sprung into existence (if you will allow the term) within 5 years back and that the country round for more than 30 miles within that period an un-inhabited wilderness, tho' now a very promising settlement: you will not wonder at the triffles which make up my order; especially when I tell you that at the time of making it up I had on hand a Moiety of £4,000 NYC. value in Merchandize and upwards of that sum in outstanding debts to collect. with this property a considerable Balance due our correspondent was to liquidate, which is now, thank God, within very decent bounds—had the goods you shipped come safe to hand it would have been in my power to pay off your demand at the end of the Credit without application to my Brother, but being under the necessity of making up the deficiency at Montreal at the Expence of 50 pc it was necessary to make some payments there the little of your shipment that got here in good order has turned out very well, the expence on the whole if only a calculation of what would have been necessary to lay them down here was about 33 which will point out to you the advantage of laying in on your side of the water—

D 24 Minutes of Executive Council
[*P.A.C., Upper Canada State Book C, pp. 257–8*]

Council Chamber at York 7th December 1802.

Present

The Honorable Henry Allcock[28] Chief Justice Chairman
The Honorable Peter Russell
The Honorable John McGill

The Board proceeded to read the following Order of Reference from His Excellency The Lieutenant Governor.

Lieut. Governor's Office York 6th Decr. 1802

It having been Represented to the Lieutenant Governor that as well the Inhabitants of the Town of York and its Neighbourhood, as the Farmers in the several adjoining Townships would be much benefited if a regular Market was established in the Town—The Lieutenant Governor requests the Executive Council to take the subject into their consideration and Report to him their Opinion whether it would be adviseable that any such Market should be established, and whether once a week or oftener and on what particular day or days, together with any other circumstances relative to the subject which they may think material for his information

By Order of the Lieut Governor
(signed) James Green Secy

The Board having taken the subject matter into consideration Report as follows.—
To His Excellency Peter Hunter Esquire Lieutenant Governor of the Province of Upper Canada, and Lieutenant General Commanding His Majesty's Forces in Upper & Lower Canada &c. &c. &c. May it please Your Excellency!

Your Excellency having been pleased by your Order of the 6th day of this Instant December, to require that the Board should consider, and Report to You, whether it would be adviseable that any Market should be established in the Town of York; The Board this day took the said Order of Reference into consideration, and do Report to Your Excellency as their Opinion, that it would be extremely beneficial, as well to the Farmers and Settlers in the Township of York, and the several

[28]Henry Allcock (d. 1808) was called to the English Bar in 1791. In 1798 he was appointed a judge of the Court of King's Bench in Upper Canada, and in 1802 he succeeded Elmsley as Chief Justice. He became Speaker of the Legislative Council in Upper Canada in 1803. He once more succeeded Elmsley as Chief Justice of Lower Canada in 1805.

adjacent Townships, as also to the Inhabitants of the Town of York, that a regular Market should be established in the said Town, and that it would for the present be sufficient if such Market should be holden one day in a week only. That it appears to the Board that Saturday would be the most convenient day to all Parties interested in the subject, and the Board would humbly Recommend, if your Excellency sees fit, that You would be pleased to order that a part of the plot of Ground which was heretofore set apart in the Town for a Market, should be appropriated to the purpose, under such Regulations as to Your Excellency shall seem meet.

(signed) H. Allcock Chairman

Approved (signed) P. Hunter Lt. Govr.

D 25 QUETTON ST. GEORGE[29] & CO. ADVERTISES

[*York,* Upper Canada Gazette, *June 11, 1803*]

Quetton St. George & Co.

LATELY ARRIVED FROM NEW-YORK,

Have brought in with them a valuable and extensive assortment of

DRY GOODS

GROCERIES, HARDWARE,

AND A FEW ARTICLES OF

PERFUMERY, &c &c

Which will be Sold at more reasonable rates than they formerly have done.

—Consisting in the following Articles:—

Cloths, cashmeres, twilled corduroys, flannels and baizes,
Callimancoes, durants, moreens,
Wild bores, white tammies,
Coating, swansdown, Molton's green and blue ratteens, striped cotton,
Cotton check, jeans, fustians, nankeens,
Chintz and callicoes, white and black muslins, printed ditto, book ditto,
Blue muslins, Bufta's hummums,
Shawls, of different qualities,
White camel hair do. with fringe,

[29]Laurent Quetton de St. George (1771–1821) was born at Vérarques, Herault department, France. A Royalist, he joined Mirabeau's legion in the army of the Prince de Condé and served in Alsace and Brisgau. In January, 1795, he joined the legion of the Comte de Béon, in the service of the States General of Holland. From 1795 to 1798 he was an officer in the Catholic and Royal Army of Brittany, taking part in the expedition to Quiberon in 1795. He came to Canada with the Comte de Puisaye in 1798 and received lands in the French royalist colony at Windham. Almost immediately he began trading with the Indians and in 1802 opened a shop in York. He carried on an extensive business and owned stores in York, Queenston, Fort Erie, Lundy's Lane, Dundas, Amherstburg, Kingston, and Niagara, as well as Indian trading posts on Lakes Simcoe and Couchiching. In 1815 he returned to France, and his right to the honorary titles of Lieutenant Colonel and Chevalier of the Order of St. Louis were confirmed by Louis XVIII. His name was originally Laurent de Quetton, but in 1796 he added Saint George.

Bandana handkerchiefs, muslin ditto, cotton ditto,
Madras and pullicat handerchiefs, &c.
Children's ditto, diaper, table cloths,
Napkins, irish linen, white sheeting,
Brown sheeting, creas, brown Holland dowlass, ognaburgs, German rolls,
German bagging, black & colored sattins,
Mens and women's hose,
White and colored long gloves,
Sattin and China ribbons, velvet do.
White and black laces, fans,
White muslin handkerchiefs, cravats,
Mulinetts, black and colored silk,
Thread, of different kinds,
Tape and bobbins,
White cotton night caps, &c. &c.
Half boots, morocco slippers, leather ditto, mens' shoes, children's ditto.

GROCERIES.

Loaf, lump, Muscovado and East-India sugars, Molasses,
Pepper, allspice, ground ginger, race do.
Starch, fig blue, indigo, nutmegs,
Cloves, Cassia, Cayenne pepper,
Sugar candy, brimstone, sulphur,
Salt petre, mustard, chocolate of two qualities, Soap,
Gun powder, cotton wool, hyson tea,
Green tea, souchong and bohea ditto,
Muscatia raisins, bloom ditto, common ditto, prunes, currants,
Cordials, oil, fish sauce, ketchup,
Basket salt, first quality gin, brandy,
Lemon juice, Almonds,
Pipes, Copperas, &c.

HARDWARE & JEWELLERY.

Andirons, shovels and tongs,
Brass tea-kettles, hammers, Hair brooms, chimney ditto,
Clothes brushes, shoe do. white wash do.
Black ball, tea trays, waiters,
Bread baskets, buttons of different sizes and qualities, knives and forks,
Pocket knives, pen-knives, pruning do.
Razors, scissars, snuffers, cork screws,
Fish hooks, plated candlesticks,
Brass candlesticks, snuff boxes,
Ivory combs, dressing ditto,
Crooked ditto, looking glasses,
Razor straps, pocket inkstands,
Ladies and gentlemen's pocket books,
Needle cases, Whitechapel needles,

Iron spoons, necklaces of different kinds,
Ear rings and drops, watch keys,
Gold rings, knee buckles,
Watch ribbons, lamp glasses,
Brass hinges, iron ditto,
Silver thimbles, brass and iron ditto,
Japanned quart and pint mugs,
Pitchers, spectacles, castors,
Children's watches, Spurs,
Chair whips, cowskin ditto,
And different articles of TIN WARE.
Also— a few HATS.

PERFUMERY.

Essences of lavender, bergamot, and peppermint,
Turlington's balsam, Hill's ditto,
Windsor soap, wash balls,
Hair powder and pomatum,
Liquorice ball, tooth brushes & powder,
Shaving boxes, playing cards,
Glauber's salts, Corks,
Letter and writing paper,
Holland quills, ink powder, sealing wax,
A few Spelling Books and Catechisms.

York, 11*th June*, 1803.

D 26 WOOD TO OGILVY, MYLNE & CO.,[30] LONDON
[*T.P.L., Alexander Wood Letter Books*]

York 27th July 1803

I have to acknowledge your letter of the 11th April accompyg. Invoice of Merchd. per the Paget and part of the Goods is at hand in seeming good condition. I have not as yet had time to unpack them but the appearance of the packages gives me reason to believe the contents are as safe as can be expected after the rough treatment they must undergo to get this length—

the amount is rather more than I expected & many articles higher than we have hitherto been charged, but Im confident you have done your best for my Interest & it now only remains for one to try and make a return as speedily as possible, which to effect I assure you is my sincere wish.

The quantity of Sugar is considerably more than necessary, and the very great bulk of the package rendered it impossible to transport the original up the river. Mr. Dunlop being perfectly aware of that had it repacked at the expence of £2.8—after advice it was not practicable

[30]Ogilvy, Mylne & Co. was a London exporting firm, which went bankrupt in 1807.

to give orders to sell any part of it at Montreal as it had left that place before your letters reached me, otherwise I should have had the 2 Cwt. disposed of there, however as things are if Ord & Co. will pay the expense of repacking I shall say nothing further on the subject

Im sorry you have no Agent or correspondent in Lower Canada as I should be able to remit small sums which a Bill cannot be obtained for on England and it would be otherwise advantageous.

I now inclose the 1st of R I D Grays[31] set of Bills & Certificates by Govr. Hunter on Edwd. Firtier Esqr. Agt. for U Canada at Messr. Ransom & Morlands Bankers Pallmall or to Wentworth Brinly Esqr. No 10 New Square Lincolns Inn London for £50 Stg in my favour with which please do the needful and pass the amount to my Credit—Im in no doubt but this will meet due honour—but should there be any demur I will thank you not to Incur the expense of protesting

War is the subject of concern with us here at present, tho' politicians seem to disagree with respect to the truth of the report—I see nothing in which it can be very detrimental to this Colony but in a small measure to affect the value of imported Articles; to overbalance that we may look forward to a better Market for the produce of which we shall have much to spare and in a few years Hemp may be a considerable part of our ways & means—

Notwithstanding the very triffling extent of my business it may be something in my way to know the state of your Market and would be very pleasant to see the price Current if you are subscribers might I request the favour to have your Copy sent to me by the trading vessels during the summer, the expense of postage would over balance the advantage in the winter months

D 27 Wood to Joseph Provan,[32] Montreal
[*T.P.L., Alexander Wood Letter Books*]

York 10th. Augt. 1803—

Yesterday your respectd. favr. of the 8th. Ulto. came to hand with the case mentioned to have left Montreal on the 2d.

The contents of the Case have had a little drenching, but except the Scissors no great damage will be sustained, the Articles on Consignmt. are as unfortunately chosen for me as is possible the waist coating is quite superfluous. I wrote you before that upwards of 100 yds lye on hand, and tho' well laid in will not bring prime cost. Buckle Brushes are seldom called for and of Scissors I am well supplied—with respect to your muslin it remains in an entire state—had you sent any thing in the Fancy line there might have been a chance of disposing of it

[31]Robert Isaac Dey Gray (1772?–1804) came to Canada with his parents in 1776. In 1794 he was appointed Acting Solicitor General and the appointment was confirmed in 1796. From 1796 until his death in the loss of the *Speedy*, he was a member of the House of Assembly.

[32]Joseph Provan (1759?–1814) was a prominent general merchant in Montreal.

D 28 A MARKET IS ESTABLISHED
[*York,* Upper Canada Gazette, *November 5, 1803*]

UPPER-CANADA
PETER HUNTER, *Esquire,*
LIEUTENANT GOVERNOR OF THE PROVINCE OF UPPER CANADA, AND LIEUTENANT GENERAL COMMANDING HIS MAJESTY'S FORCES IN UPPER AND LOWER CANADA, &c. &c.

WHEREAS great prejudice hath arisen to the Inhabitants of the Town and Township of YORK, and of other adjoining Townships, from no place or day having been set apart or appointed for exposing publicly for Sale, Cattle, Sheep, Poultry, and other Provisions, Goods and Merchandize, brought by Merchants, Farmers, and others, for the necessary supply of the said TOWN of YORK;

AND WHEREAS great benefit and advantage might be derived to the said Inhabitants and others, by establishing a Weekly Market within that Town, at a place and on a day certain for the purpose aforesaid—KNOW ALL MEN, That I, PETER HUNTER, Esquire, Lieutenant Governor of the said Province, taking the Premises into consideration, and willing to promote the interest, advantage and accommodation of the Inhabitants of the Town and Township aforesaid, and of others His Majesty's Subjects within the said Province, by and with the advice of the Executive Council thereof, have ordained, erected, established and appointed, and do hereby ordain, erect, establish and appoint, A PUBLIC OPEN MARKET, to be held on SATURDAY, in each and every week during the year, within the said Town of YORK: (The first market to be held therein on SATURDAY, the FIFTH DAY of NOVEMBER next, after the date of these Presents) on a certain piece or plot of Land within the Town, consisting of five Acres and a half, commencing at the South-East angle of the said plot, at the corner of Market-street and New-street, then North Sixteen degrees West five chains seventeen links, more or less, to King's-street; then along King-street South seventy-four degrees West nine chains fifty one links, more or less, to Market-street; then along Market-street North seventy-four degrees East two chains; then North sixty-four degrees East along Market-street seven chains sixty links, more or less, to the place of beginning—for the purpose of exposing for Sale, CATTLE, SHEEP, POULTRY, and other Provisions, GOODS and MERCHANDIZE, as aforesaid.

GIVEN under my Hand, and Seal at Arms, at YORK, this twenty-sixth day of October, in the year of our Lord one thousand eight hundred and three, and in the forty-fourth year of His Majesty's Reign.

P. HUNTER, Lieut. Gov'r.

By His Excellency's Command,
WM. JARVIS, SEC.

D 29 WOOD TO OGILVY, MYLNE & CO., LONDON
[*T.P.L., Alexander Wood Letter Books*]

York 29th March 1804

. . . Sales have been dull with us these past twelve months owing, I believe, to a number of adventurers coming among us from the United States, they being but birds of passage offer the trash they import on very low terms & by that means carry off the little money which gets into circulation, so that the established Mercht. must either vend his goods on long Credit or keep them on hand: As I have quite eno. outstandg. I have chosen the later method, supposg. the goods to be worth themselves.

I am surprised at having no letter from you since the month of July last for tho. the good people in the states generally open british letters, they seldom detain them altogether. . . .

D 30 WOOD TO LESLIE, MCNAUGHT & CO.
[*T.P.L., Alexander Wood Letter Books*]

York 6th Octr. 1804

. . . My intention was to consult with some of my Country Friends on the subject of Pot Ashes but a kind of Epidemick has been raging so generally round this place that people have not been able to come to Town I mean the Ague accompanied with a low but distressing Fever not dangerous tho' painful and lingering. In consequence of your letter of the 18th April I have on the other side ordered some goods for which I mean to pay either in Ashes, if they can be procured or by remitting in Bills to Our Friends in Quebec. . . .

D 31 A HATTER ARRIVES
[*York,* Upper Canada Gazette, *February 2, 1805*]

Samuel Jackson,[33]

INFORMS his friends and the Public in general that he is commencing the Hatting business opposite to Thomas Ridout Esq. in the Town of York, where he will take all kinds of Furs, Lamb's wool, and country produce, or Cash itself will be received for Hats, but no credit need be asked.

York, 1st February, 1805.

[33]Samuel Jackson (b. 1765?) was a Quaker from Pennsylvania. It has been suggested that he was brought to Canada by William Bond who was proposing to establish a hat manufactory on his property at Bond Lake. He later moved to Yonge Street where he continued making hats. During the War of 1812, his open support of the Americans forced him out of the country, but after the war he returned, and made an unsuccessful attempt to regain possession of his Yonge Street property.

D 32 J. Cawthra[34] Opens an Apothecary's Shop
[*York,* Upper Canada Gazette, *June 14, 1806*]

J. CAWTHRA wishes to inform the Inhabitants of York and the adjacent Country, that he has opened an Apothecary's Store in the House of A. Cameron, opposite Stoyles's[35] Tavern, in York, where the Public can be supplied with most articles in that line. He has on hand also, a quantity of Mens', Womens' and Childrens' Shoes, Mens' Hats: also for a few days will be sold the following articles, Table Knives and Forks, Siscars, Silver watches, Maps and Prints, Profiles, some Linen, and a few Bed Ticks, Teas, Tobacco, a few casks of fourth proof Cogniac Brandy, and a small quantity of Lime Juice, about twenty thousand Whitechapel Needles.

York, June 14, 1806.

D 33 Quetton St. George Advertises
[*York,* Upper Canada Gazette, *June 14, 1806*]

MR. ST. GEORGE has just received by Capt. Kendrick, L.P. Madiera Wine, Jamaica Spirits, Rappie Snuff, Nails, best Spanish Segars.

Mr. St. George having missed two pairs of Suwarrow Boots, requests those persons who have purchased some from him to let him know, as he is afraid he has forgot to charge them, or should they have been taken on trial, it is requested they may be returned.

It is also requested that the Gentleman or Lady who has borrowed a Volume of the Revolutionaire, Plutarch, will return it immediately. . . .

York, June 14, 1806.

D 34 Henderson Begins the Butchering Business
[*York,* Upper Canada Gazette, *August 30, 1806*]

NOTICE.

THE subscriber having got the Contract for supplying his Majesty's Troops at the Garrison with fresh Beef, takes the liberty of informing the Public that he has engaged a Person to superintend the Butchering business, and that good fresh Beef may be had three times a week. Fresh Pork and Mutton will be always ready on a day's notice, Poultry, &c. Those Gentlemen who may be pleased to become Customers, may rely on being well served and regularly supplied—If constant Customers,

[34]Joseph Cawthra (1759–1842) was born in Yorkshire and came to York after short stays in Scotland and New York State. He began a shop specializing in drugs, which soon expanded into a general store. As his grandson Henry wrote, "The real prosperity of the family began during the war of 1812, when they were in business." (A. Maude (Cawthra) Brock, comp., *Past and Present, Notes by Henry Cawthra and Others,* p. 12.) Joseph Cawthra's sympathies were with the Reformers up to the outbreak of the Rebellion of 1837.

[35]Dr. Thomas Stoyell (1760?–1832) was a non-practising doctor with American training and radical politics. He owned a tavern and later a brewery. He died without heirs and bequeathed his property to the Methodist Conference.

&c. a note of the weight will be sent along with the article. Families becoming constant Customers, will please to send a Book by their Servant, to have it entered, to prevent any mistakes,—The Business will commence on Monday the first of September next

R. HENDERSON,

York, August 28, 1806.

D 35 Wood to John Grant,[36] Lachine
[*T.P.L., Alexander Wood Letter Books*]

York 2d April 1807

. . . Im Sorry you did not make me acquainted with your inclination to purchase Common Flour—I would have with ease supplied yr. quantity as our roads and traveling has been very uncommonly good during the winter and Sufficiency of Such Flour might have been obtained, but as nothing of the fine is used here—the Farmers never think of bringing it to Market unless they have orders for it—I may probably be able to procure Some from the head of Lake Ontario and shall immediately write on the Subject, but from the Settlements about this place the roads are so very bad that all intercourse with Loads of any Kind is over till the month of June—Should I succeed at the head of the Lake you will be advised—it would answer me well to get Transport for produce. . . .

D 36 Robert Kerr[37] to Wood
[*T.P.L., Alexander Wood Papers*]

Niagara 29th July 1807

I had the Pleasure of receiving your favour yesterday, and haste to inform you, that the articles, for the Lt. Governor, & yourself; came up in the Sloop with me, to Albany; I got them forwarded over to Schenectady with some things of my own, but as they went by water, & I took my route by Land I cou'd not take any more charge of them; but spoke to Mr. Turner agent for Walton,[38] at Utica, to write to his agent at Oswego if there was a Vessel going to York at Oswego, (When they arrived;) to forward them Straight to York. All the articles for the Lt. Governor are directed to you, as well as, a Chest of tea for Mrs. Powell. If they come here I will forward them immediately.

The Champagne, I am afraid the Weather is too warm for it; and the

[36]John Grant engaged in an extensive forwarding business at Lachine. Goods from Europe or the Lower Province were sent from Montreal to Lachine by wagon. Grant sent them up to Kingston in river boats manned by French Canadians.

[37]Robert Kerr (1764?–1824) was surgeon to the Indian Department, stationed at Niagara.

[38]Jonathan Walton was a prominent merchant in Oswego, specializing in supplying the Upper Canadian market.

Bottles may *fly*, it was in good order at Schenectady, it was taken over in a Covered Waggon—and was happy to have it in my Power to serve the Lt. Governor, & yourself. . . .

D 37 QUETTON ST. GEORGE ADVERTISES
[*York*, York Gazette, *November 11, 1807*]

MR. Q. ST. GEORGE begs leave to inform his Friends and Customers that he has arrived from Montreal, and brought with him an ample stock of FALL & WINTER GOODS, also Crockery, Glass Ware, Cutlery and Ironmongery, and a handsome and well chosen assortment of Furriery; having arranged with a respectable Furrier there, all orders for articles in that line, from his friends here, will be forwarded by him, and their execution immediately attended to. He has also received from New-York a variety of Beaver Bonnets, of the newest fashions, and a general assortment of Millinery, among which are elegant and the most fashionable Ostrich Feathers, &c. &c. The length of time he devoted at Montreal to the purchase and selection, has enabled him to lay in his goods, this year, on the most favorable terms, and he can supply Country Store-keepers more advantageously to them than if they made their purchases below—He proposes to receive in payment and barter for Goods, the following articles, so soon as his stores will be fitted for their reception, viz:—Flour, Wheat, Indian Corn, Oats, Pease and Pork. None of these articles will be received unless they are of prime qualities, and he hopes none other will be offered; the Pork must be well cured and packed in sufficient barrels, and warranted for twelve months; the barrel marked with the venders name, and date of delivery.

Cash advanced as usual on account of Sterling Bills, which he will receive in payment from his regular Customers at par, although subject to a large discount in other places. He flatters himself that his Country-Friends and Customers, witnessing his exertions, will, by more regular payments in future, enable him to continue them, to their mutual convenience and advantage. His store at Niagara, under the care of Mr. Fortier, contains nearly a similar assortment with the one at York.

Impelled by motives of gratitude and esteem for Messrs. Boucherville[39] and McDonell[40] (his late Clerks) Mr. St. George has established them at Amherstberg. All support and favors shewn them by his friends and the public, will be considered as personal obligations by him.

York, 10*th Nov.* 1807.

[39]René Thomas Verchères de Boucherville was descended from an old French-Canadian family. After several years' experience in the fur trade, he entered St. George's employ in 1804. In 1806 he was sent to Amherstburg to open a branch of the business there, which became independent of St. George in 1808. His experiences at York and Amherstburg are contained in his *A Merchant's Clerk in Upper Canada: The Journal of Thomas Vercheres de Boucherville, 1804–1811* edited by W. S. Wallace (Toronto, 1935).

[40]John Macdonell was formerly a clerk in St. George's store in York.

D 38 Quetton St. George Advertises
[*York*, York Gazette, *February 20, 1808*]

THE Subscriber has just received the following GARDEN SEEDS, which he will dispose of on moderate terms:—viz.

Red onion, white onion, green marrowfat pease, blood beet, early cabbage, winter cabbage, Savoy cabbage, red cabbage, scarcity, lettuce, cucumber, early cucumber, long cucumber, turnips, sage, carrot, parsnet, radish, French turnips, summer squash, winter squash, watermelon, musk melon, early beans, cranberry beans, early purple beans, asparagus, summer savory, celery, parsley, pepper grass, burnet, saffron, carraway, and pink.

He has also received Hyson skin and Green Teas.

QUETTON ST. GEORGE.

12th February, 1808.

D 39 Loan to Elisha Beman
[*York*, York Gazette, *March 2, 1808*]

We are sorry to learn that Mr. Beman's house (lately burned) was not insured, to those who are acquainted with the great and arduous exertion of Mr. Beman, in furnishing provisions for this Town on its first establishment, and to such as can feel for the losses of an upright and valuable man, an opportunity is now offered to the grateful, as well as the benevolent, to raise, by way of loan, from any person who chuse to subscribe, a fund to enable him to prosecute the business he is engaged in, with such real advantage and convenience to the country.— The terms of the loan might be, one half payable in five years, the other half in five years more.—Lists for this purpose are left with Duncan Cameron, Esq. Mr. Joseph Kendrick and Mr. J. Cameron.[41]

D 40 John Jacob Astor[42] to Quetton St. George, Queenston
[*P.A.O., Baldwin Papers*]

New York April 30, 1808

Your favr. of 2 ulto came to hand I will reserve for you the tea which you have been pleased to order as to the nankeens they are plenty it would be against your Interest to send them now teas will rise but nankeen not the embargo[43] is still to continue for some time I

[41]John Cameron (1776?–1815) was an early York merchant, with a shop near the Garrison at one time. In 1805 he was an unsuccessful candidate for the House of Assembly. From 1807 to 1815 he was King's Printer and editor of the *Upper Canada Gazette*, changing its name to the *York Gazette*.

[42]John Jacob Astor (1763–1848), New York merchant and fur trader, founded the American Fur Company, and the Astor millions.

[43]The Embargo Act was passed by Congress on December 22, 1807, forbidding any ship to sail with cargo from an American port to any foreign port.

wrot you long since that I should be glad if you could pay Some money for me in Montreal & that I would pay it here to your order as I am much in want of it there

D 41 TIMOTHY NIGHTINGALE[44] TO QUETTON ST. GEORGE
[*P.A.O., Baldwin Papers*]

Whitby May 28 1808

As Anderson has disapointed me about taking my farm I am like to disapoint you about the Money due you it is out of my power to pay you unless I sell my farm which if for Sale I have offerd to sell for three or four hundred Dollars less then the Value of it but if you know any body that will buy it plese to send them and I will take the same that Anderson was to give in order that you may get your pay or I will let you have half of it for twelve Shillings an Acre which is worth Double what I offer it to you for or I will deliver my farm to you and you may let it out till you get your pay I cant offer anything more if I cant sell and you wont Comply with these terms to gaol I must go . . .
NB You need not send no officer any more only send a line and I will come up immediatly and go to gaol if you say so

D 42 NIGHTINGALE TO QUETTON ST. GEORGE
[*P.A.O., Baldwin Papers*]

Whitby July 22 1808

I have ben atrying to get the money for you to pay you which you know that twice I have ben disopinted I am agoing to make potash to see if I cant pay you that way if you will Let me alone till I can turn my self to make it part this fall and part in the Spring I shall do my best to pay you I will pay you the Interest of the money from this date you draw no Interest after Judment but if you will wate I am willing to pay you Interest if you put me to gail I cant be in the way to pay you then but to spend what I have and then sarten you wont get your pay from your humble sarvent

D 43 GREEN DESPARD[45] TO QUETTON ST. GEORGE
[*P.A.O., Baldwin Papers*]

Niagara Octr. 11th 1808

it is with pleasure I embrace the opportunity of informing you that I have been Successful in getting every article of your Safe over the River at Queenstown on Saturday night[46]—and will go up this Day with

[44]Timothy Nightingale was assessor for Whitby in 1804. He was living on the Farewell farm in Whitby in 1811.

[45]Green Despard was one of St. George's clerks in York, later managing his Niagara store. He was a nephew of one of the partners in Despard and Thomas, a New York firm with whom St. George did business.

[46]St. George bought most of his goods in New York, unlike Wood and others,

waggons to bring them Down here. I will settle the Duty with Mr. Dickson[47]—they Goods were to have been taken Down to the Garrison on the other side, on Sunday, and I got word, and immediately wrote off to Mr. B.[48] to come up, and he and Mr. Chinica[49] who you are are very much indebted to for their exertions, with a party of Frenchmen and a large Boat, together with a Boat I got up their went off and got into the Store by a window, and Secured the Deputy who was Sleeping in the Store, and brought off all they Goods. theire is a reward of one thousand Dollars offered on the other Side for taking me and the attempted to arrest me on Sunday at Queenstown. So for Gods Sake loose no time in Sending over some body here, and let me go to York, for the will bribe Some body to take me after Dark. . . .

D 44 Wood to Leslie, McNaught & Co.
[*T.P.L., Alexander Wood Letter Books*]

U. Canada York 25th. October 1808.

. . . if a little more attention is paid in marking, packing and shipping Goods and if shipped in a vessel direct for Montreal would save the packages much ill usage they receive in unloading two or three times, however as it is an advantage to have them early as possible, probably the first Ships do not clear out for Montreal but were the same attention paid to the packing & packages marks &c as in London they might be reshipped fifty times without suffering in the least—I also complained of some of the articles and repeat the Complaint the hardware Knives and forks the large Kind Hinges locks &c are the veriest trash that ever workman put out of his hands—for the credit of my country I would wish they had been from any other place. On the Sugar I shall not be able to make up the expenses and duty. the quantity is about three times as much as ordered, and the Quality indifferent badly packed and in every way a disgrace to those who manufactured papered and patched up. On the other hand the Cloths Blankets Callicos &c. were exceedingly well packed came in good order and are excellent goods the looking Glasses are not such as I ordered and came each at the price of a Doz. of the Kind wanted, they will remain a dead Stock on my hands, one of the Cases of hats was so chattered that the Rats had got in and destroyed

---

who bought from Great Britain. With the enforcement of the Embargo Act, his goods were empounded at Lewiston in 1808. A different account of this incident is given in Boucherville's *A Merchant's Clerk in Upper Canada: The Journal of Thomas Vercheres de Boucherville, 1804–1811*, pp. 17–22.

[47]Thomas Dickson was Collector of Customs at Queenston.

[48]Thomas Verchères de Boucherville.

[49]Joseph Cheniquy (b. 1778) studied at the Quebec Seminary 1792–4, considered entering the Anglican priesthood in 1800, and became a lieutenant in the Royal Canadian Volunteers. In 1807 he was appointed Customs Collector at Sault Ste. Marie; in 1813 he was a priest with the Anglican Trappists. He eventually went to Martinique and died a Roman Catholic. He was an uncle of Father Charles Chiniquy.

half the Contents. I before certified the articles short sent to wit 2 pair Japand bed Room Candlesticks, a Japand qt. mug and some triffling thing of Crockery—but on this last articles one Doz. Qt. Queens ware sent more than charged which made up the wastage on that article. . . .

D 45 Henderson Advertises his Property
[*York*, York Gazette, *June 24, 1809*]

MALT HOUSE, BREWERY, &c.

For SALE *by* PRIVATE CONTRACT;

WHICH if not sold by the first of AUGUST next ensuing, will be rented to a good Tenant.—The Premises consist of a complete PLANT for MALTING, BREW HOUSE, WORKING TUBS, COOLERS,Two KILNS for Drying Malt, a GRANARY, PUMPS, a PATENT BREWING MALT MILL, Two Good Wells of Water, Stable, &c.

The Boiler was set up a new last Summer.—The Utensils are adapted to manufacturing Thirty Barrels of Beer Weekly with ease, which has been repeatedly done.—The whole of this Establishment has been perfected within these Nine Years.—There are likewise Two STILLS, with Worms, &c complete.

A TAN HOUSE, completely fitted up, with an Excellent Horse Mill for Grinding Bark, and nearly adjoining the Tan House a small Dwelling House, to lodge and accommodate the workmen, or others.

A SLAUGHTER HOUSE complete—in this House there is a Chimney built, and a sufficiency of room for the reception and operation of Two Stids[50] of any size, with a never failing Well of Water in the building.

There are nearly Three Acres of Cultivated Garden Ground, in high Order, on which the above Buildings, &c. are erected, together with a Good DWELLING HOUSE, convenient, and in perfect repair.—The whole whereof are situate in the Town of York, the Capital of Upper Canada. —The Proprietor thinks it unnecessary to make any Encomiums, as those who are inclined to Purchase or Rent will naturally view the Premises.

N.B. There is Malt on hand to begin Brewing with, and Hops sufficient for a Season; there are also Hydes and Bark to commence Business in the Tannery.

. . . ROBT. HENDERSON

York, 8th June, 1809.

. . .

D 46 Despard to Quetton St. George, Niagara
[*T.P.L., St. George Papers II*]

York June 23d. 1810

. . . I am sorry to find A. R. Lawrence[51] & Co. have disappointed you about forwarding your goods, as nankeens are in great Demand R. sheet-

[50]Probably a misprint for "skids," movable platforms in slaughter houses.

[51]Abram R. Lawrence was a prominent New York merchant.

ing &c. I suppose the goods from the States are arrived with you by this time. . . . Business here has been rather Dull, as the assortment is very much Broken. I Reced. yours by Mr. Land[52] with ninety one Barrels Flour which I answerd by him—the Flour is very much Damaged from the weather. Mr. Jordan told me the he Did not want to buy any at present—I am affraid you will not be able to Dispose of all you have to advantage this Summer—I understand that Mr. Allans Goods were come to Kingston where Monger left them. . . . Your Goods must be at Kingston by this time, and of course will be here in a few Days—I dread the Hurry and fatigue of their arrival—therefore I must give up the Idea of any recreation this Summer, which would be necessary after being near Three years confined to the Shop. I am sorry to see another merchant arrive from the States but as you are in better circumstances you can sell as low as any of them—

I hope you will be able to procure a Servant woman, while you are over, as this Retch here has been in one Continual State intoxication Since Monday morning last—until this never able to Dress a bit of Dinner. Was it not for the old French man, we would have had to Dress it ourselves—I have stop'd some of the Soldiers coming in to the Kitchen with Liquor—and the night before last, her Husband was with her and early in the Morning he attempted to go home but was so Drunk that he fell twice going out of the entry—then she went in to her Room and Drank again, untill she could not Stand or talk a word—Was I to give my opinion, I don't think your House or property safe with such a Drunken Creature in it—She may set Fire to it in the night or may bring a Set of Drunken men about it who may break open any part of the House at night, and carry off your property, and who would be the wiser. . . .

D 47 John Detlor[53] to Quetton St. George, Niagara
[*T.P.L., St. George Papers II*]

York 30 June 1810.

. . . We have been anxiously looking out for vessels from Kingston for some time past, expecting a part of the New Goods by the first, but upon the Arrival of Kendrick was much disappointed when he informed us that not a single package of yours had arrived at Kingston at the time of his departure (the 23d. inst)—the delay of the goods from the States has been unfortunate as it prevents you from giving so essential a Check to the sales of the horde of interlopers that swarm this place as you could have done had they arrived at as early a period as might have been expected—When disappointments come by an Act of Providence we

[52]Robert Land (d. 1822) was a Loyalist from New York State, who became one of the first settlers at the Head of the Lake.

[53]John Detlor was St. George's bookkeeper. He was the son of John Detlor who died from wounds received during the battle of York.

can possibly bear them without complaint but when occasioned by men it requires a considerable degree of fortitude to command our temper. . . .

D 48 DESPARD TO QUETTON ST. GEORGE, NIAGARA
[*T.P.L., St. George Papers II*]

July 14th, 1810

. . . No sign of Kendrick yet, tho 2 Days easterly wind, but I am in hopes of seeing him in the Harbour in the Morning with the Goods, such as you mention, with the whole of your assortment, as Mr. Allan has got a number of Goods, and so many Stores in Town. Cawthera arrived in the Toronto from New York and says he has a number of Goods coming from Oswego, besides what he brought, but from what I could learn from him, he paid very high for them, it is strange what could have delayed that vessell with the Remainder of your Goods, As Scythes & Sicles are in great Demand, I could have sold 200 of them this week, as there are no States Scythes in Town—Sanders[54] & Johnson are also very uneasy about the Riging of their vessell, they have been here almost every day expecting them. I told them that I expected it over in the Toronto, so I suppose one or other of them will be Down on Monday. . . .

I am sorry to observe that Auldjoe & Co. have made the same mistake about the velvet in the Invoices from this place. One piece would have been enough as it comes so high say 14/6/– every thing almost comes very High except the Cutlery, especially Dry Goods, all those Bought in London, besides the exhorbitant prices that they charge for Boxes & Kegs & Casks. We have not one yd. Cotton or Cambrick, which is a great loss but I put the people off with the best Story I can by promising them an elegant assortment a few Days—Mr. Detlor will help me on Monday to make out the advertisement, but as I understand the Toronto is to come back on Tuesday I will defer it until the Invoice of D. & T.[55] . . . I have not sent any Pot Ash Down Since Kendrick left this as there was no Vessell but I have nine Bbl. in the Store. I find Mr. Archibald Thomson dont intend to let you have any this Summer as he brought 3 Bbls. more to Allan this morning. J. Widdifield[56] sent in four yesterday 2 underhand to Allan the other 2 to you, but I wrote him a very smart note about it—to let him see that I found out his tricks, mentioning that was not the kind of treatment you deserved from him. . . .

[54]Matthias Sanders (d. 1813) was a carpenter and shipbuilder. He assisted his father-in-law, John Dennis, in building the *Toronto,* and other vessels. Probably the vessel referred to here was the *Bella Gore,* which he commanded. He was killed in the explosion of the magazine during the capture of York in 1813.

[55]Despard & Thomas, New York merchants.

[56]Probably a relative of Henry Widdifield (1779–1869) who was born in New Jersey, moved to Pennsylvania, and settled in Whitchurch Township in 1801.

D 49 DESPARD TO QUETTON ST. GEORGE
[*T.P.L., St. George Papers II*]

July 23d. 1810

I am sorry to Inform you that las Wednesday I Received letters by Capt. Monger from Montreal, mentioning that the Ship John from Liverpool Bound for Montreal with all your woolens, and a Number, for others, was taken by a French Privateer—this circumstance I suppose will oblige you to go Down to Montreal Sooner than you intended in order replace the loss, as Cloths are very plenty in Montreal, and the sooner as was there the better bargain could be got. . . .

I am sorry that the fine goods have not yet come, as this would help the sale of other Goods, & tend to Stop the Sale of Allans, as well as those Yankees. . . .

the Govr. is expected back the first fair wind, then the People will get their Money, which will halve fall into your Hands, or at least some of it. . . .

Drean[57] who came up in Kendricks has Brought new Goods, and is going establish Totman[58] here, and to commence Business himself in Montreal. he came out by way of New York—he says Cottons could be Bought much lower in New York than in England—and that he purchased 5 Bales in the former place on his way up here—

D 50 DESPARD TO QUETTON ST. GEORGE, MONTREAL
[*T.P.L., St. George Papers II*]

York August 28th 1810—

. . . on Saturday last I Packed up the Furs &c. which consisted of three Packs and put them on Board the Toronto, marked and numbered as per Bill enclosed, and wrote at the same time to Messrs. Hugh & H. Boyd[59] and also to Walton & Co. Desiring the former Gentlemen to keep them until your Arrival there from Montreal, and the latter Directing them to forward them immediately to the former. . . .

this Day a vessell arrived from Oswego with Salt, and the few Goods you expected from D. & T. [Despard & Thomas] & J. Walton & Co. viz. 2 Kegs Raisins, 9 of Nails 1 Barrel Sherry wine 1 Box Chocolate & 2 Baskets of oil. Sooner than let Drean have all the Market to himself, I have Bought 69 Barrels at \$3½ per one half in Cash and the other Half at 60 Days—Davison has arrived in the same vessell with 200 Barrels.

[57]Henry Drean first appeared in the List of Inhabitants in 1808. He was a successful storekeeper, buying most of his goods in England, and his store continued prosperous after the War of 1812. In 1809 he married Jane Brooke.

[58]Joshua B. Totman was Drean's son-in-law.

[59]Merchants in Albany, New York.

... J. Post[60] has given in £14 on his old note—John Doggett [61] his a/c in full—Jas. Henton $ 20—Peter Coon[62] £7—which includes the whole of what I have recd. upon a/c. and not more than $30 a Day, in the Shop. Jordan the Baker wishes you to bring a Keg of Shrub for him, if you can get it good and cheap in Montreal (say 20 Galls.). Mrs. Gore has been at the Shop Twice Since you went I sent them a Sample of the Lime juice, and this Day she told me to send up 4 Galls. She also wants a Box of the Best Bloon Raisins that can be got in New York also a Good white Silk Handkf. for her neck. ...

D 51 DESPARD TO QUETTON ST. GEORGE
[*T.P.L., St. George Papers II*]

York Septr. 25th. 1810—

... Boulton & Robinson[63] have a general assortment but from what I hear they are not quite so cheap as a Person might Expect—& B. is a very stupid Block. I am glad to find that you Bought your Goods in Montreal so low for Goods here are a mere Drug—We sell Green Tea for 6/- a Pound—all other things low in like manner. chocolate and many other things that we want would sell. Port wine has been very much wanting, heretofore. I have not got the Invoices from Montreal yet, but I hope to them & the goods every moment, as the wind has been fair this Four Days, and the new Vessell[64] has been waiting some time for them—

There is a new chap come to the Store which Drean used to keep, who they sells very low—Deary has arrived but his goods are not yet come—Ridout & Mercer[65] expect theirs every Day—they has taken the Yellow House from Miss Russell and intend opening a Store in one end of it—

[60]Jordan Post (b. 1744) was a Loyalist who came to York with his family from Hebron, Conn. He became a baker. His son Jordan Post (1767–1845) was a watchmaker. In 1834 Jordan Post, Junior, moved to Scarborough and built a saw-mill on Highland Creek.

[61]John Doggett served in the Queen's Rangers, was granted land in Etobicoke, and was a servant of William Chewett.

[62]Peter Kuhn (Coon) was an inhabitant in York from 1799.

[63]D'Arcy Boulton, Junior (1785–1846), was born in Lincolnshire, the eldest son of Judge D'Arcy Boulton. He was called to the Bar in 1807, but in the summer of 1810 gave up the law briefly to operate a store in partnership with his brother-in-law, Peter Robinson (1785–1838). Robinson was the eldest son of Christopher Robinson, and is now best known for his superintendence of the Irish settlement around Peterborough. He was Commissioner of Crown Lands from 1827 to 1836.

[64]Probably the *Bella Gore*.

[65]Samuel Smith Ridout (1778–1855) and Andrew Mercer (d. 1871) formed a partnership to operate a distillery, but ran a general store. Ridout was the eldest son of Thomas Ridout, and was Sheriff of the Home District from 1815 and 1827, when he became Registrar. Andrew Mercer was a Scotsman who came to Canada with Chief Justice Scott. At his death there were prolonged legal difficulties over his estate, which eventually passed to the Crown, and was used to establish the Mercer Reformatory.

it is reported that the Parson[66] intends Building a large Store in the of his Garden next to Col. St. George[67] for the Yankee that lives near Jordans—he was speaking [ms. torn] upon Nails—it is reported that he intends helping [ms. torn] Col. St. George is going to live to Niagara and Drean is going to purchase McDonells House. Thomas [68] & the man that lives in Mosleys House are Both gone to Albany for a large supply of winter Goods—so if you Dont buy cheap & Good Goods you will loose custom. . . .

D 52 HENDERSON SELLS HIS BEER
[*York*, York Gazette, *May 25, 1811*]

ADVERTISEMENT

THE Subscriber from the poor state of his health, and the difficulty of collection of Money, lays the following plan before the Public:—

That he intends in the ensuing week, to dispose of his Beer, strong and clear, at Six Dollars per Barrel. Those who wish to have less quantities, may have, by sending their own keggs clean and sweet, filled, from one gallon to any number, from sun-rise to sun-set, at Two Shillings N.Y. Cy. per gallon.

As he has now got a Person whom he can confide in, fit for said purpose, there will be no serving of Beer on the Sabbath Day.

N.B. The Consumer will, by the above plan, save an hundred per cent.—as such, there will be nothing delivered without the cash.

This may be supposed to be a spurt for the moment; but he has Beer on hand and Malt ready made, which will supply York and its vicinity for twelve months; and shall be continued by a Gentleman who is to carry on my Business during my absence.

ROBERT HENDERSON.

P.S. I have a complete Slaughter House to let and a Tannery; if not let in the course of fourteen days, it will be carried on in the same manner as the Beer, with exception also of the Sabbath.

York, May 25, 1811.

D 53 RUNAWAY APPRENTICE
[*York*, York Gazette, *October 30, 1811*]

☞ RUN AWAY.

RAN AWAY from the Subscriber on the 22nd Inst.— An Indented Apprentice to the Wheel Wright's Trade, about 19 years of age, and five

66Rev. George Okill Stuart owned extensive property in York, a cause of dissension with his successor, Rev. John Strachan who thought that Stuart had appropriated land intended for the church.

67This seems somewhat confused. Despard is presumably reporting the local gossip to St. George.

68George Thomas opened a general store in York in 1810. He withdrew during the War of 1812, returning after it only to collect debts.

feet five or six inches high, with light hair and weak eyes; named JOHN BRADY. Had on when he went away, a short blue Coat and Trowsers of the same, white Vest, new fur Hat, and several other new articles which he obtained upon his Master's credit, without his permission on the day previous to his leaving this place. All persons are therefore cautioned not to harbor or trust him on his said Master's account, or employ him.

From his want of good qualities, industry and whatever else can make an Apprentice valuable, the Subscriber will not offer any Reward for the expences of his apprehension.

LADNER BOSTICK[69]

York, 30th Octr. 1811.

D 54 ALEXANDER LEGGE[70] TO JOHN WATSON,[71] LONDON
[*P.A.O., Miscellaneous MSS, Alexander Legge Papers*]

York/U.C./—1 June 1816

I duly received your favor of 13 June 1815 expressing your surprise at my not having remitted you the proceeds of the Cotton Goods per Morton Hardie, and advising your having valued upon me for £152 . . 8 . . 2 Stg in favor of Alexr. & Robt. Tulloch @ 12 /St. which was duly honored and passed to your debit

I now beg leave to hand you an account Sales of these Goods, by which you will observe the net proceeds amount to £270 . . 8 . . 6 British and by an account Current of the transaction which I send herewith, that you have received on their account £287 . . 8 . . 2 Btsh, leaving a balance due to me of £16 . . 19 . . 8 Stg all which I hope you will find correct.

I cannot help observing that this business has been peculiarly unpleasant and troublesome to me; You Sent me a large parcel of Goods to a place which at the best of times affords but a poor Market, Urging me to sell them off immediately upon arrival, either by Public or Private Sale; now, Sir, you must know that when these Goods arrived, such was the dulness of the times and such the scarcity of money, that had I put them up to Auction, and sold them all off they would not have actually nett'd one half the Amount of the Invoice, nay the Auctioneer (the only one we have in the place) positively assures me, that he is of opinion

[69]Lardner Bostwick (1774–1834) was born in Baltimore and came to York about 1810. He was a wheelwright who owned an acre on the southeast corner of Yonge and King Streets. He was elected to the first city council of Toronto in 1834.

[70]Alexander Legge (1768?–1855) was born in Scotland, and first appeared in the List of Inhabitants in 1799. When he took the oath of allegiance in 1802, he spelt his name without the final "e," and gave his occupation as carpenter. He shortly afterwards became a general merchant. He married Grace, eldest child of Joseph Cawthra.

[71]John Watson lived at Mr. William Legge's No. 6 Beech Street, Finsbury Square, London.

that he never would have been able to dispose of one half of the Dresses & Shawls upon any terms whatsoever, and he is confident that had not the War taken place the major part of them would still be on hand. The Trade in Upper Canada is entirely limited to the retail business, you may judge therefore what prospect there was of disposing of your Goods wholesale, in a Country but thinly inhabited and where the circulation of Specie is so limited, so much so, indeed, that before the War, a Merchant scarcely ever could get money for his Goods, but was obliged to Exchange them for produce, which would never have answered your purpose—

The War had the effect of causing immense sums of money to be spent in the Country, and it consequently became a more plentiful commodity, amongst the People, which enabled them to lay it out more liberally: it was at this moment that I seized the favorable opportunity of sending them to Auction, sincerely wishing that they might all go off and at once put an end to so troublesome a business, but I was disappointed, the Auctioneer sold 'till he could sell no more and return'd me the remainder declaring it useless to attempt forcing an article upon the Public, which they look'd upon with so much indifference and for which towards the latter end of the Sale they were only bidding a dollar & even so low as 3/4 of a Dollar a dress previous to my putting them up to Auction I had (in order to give them every chance) distributed them amongst the Merchants in this Town and in the Country, keeping a large proportion myself. They all sold some, but could not get a farthing more than 2½ Dollars a dress at which price I was happy to let them go—for their trouble they demanded 10 per Cent which I was obliged to comply with and even with this Commission they were disatisfied, and many after selling one or two Dresses returned the remainder declaring them almost unsaleable it was at this period (which was before the War) seeing no prospect of disposing of these goods here, that I was about to have them sent down to Montreal to endeavor to get them off by auction there, which I was anxious to do, from your repeatedly urging me to sell and remit, I was advised to take this step by several Merchants of this place, and certainly would have put it into execution had not a House informed me that they had got out Goods of the same description as yours, but finding the impossibility of selling here, repack'd them and sent them down to Montreal where they were sold at Public Sale, for *25 per Cent less than what they cost* in England from whence they had them about the same time as yours arrived these were fully as good as yours, if not better, and were much lower Invoiced, so that you must be mistaken in supposing yours *so very low laid in*—

The Cloth and Shawls I sold my self, the former is an article, that requires much time and patience in selling it, it being only now and then that I could sell a few yards to any person wanting new cloths—it was only till very lately that I sold the last 5 yards @ 15/-. . . .

E. COMMUNICATIONS

E 1 Minutes of Executive Council
[*P.A.C., Upper Canada State Book B, p. 3*]

Council Chamber at Newark 17th January 1797

Present.

His Honor Peter Russell Esqr. Administring the Government
Honl. John Elmsley Chief Justice
Honl. David William Smith

. . . The Administrator having represented to the Board that when the Seat of Government shall be removed to York there will be an absolute necessity of securing some certain and safe means of communicating by water from thence with the other parts of the Province at all times when the occasions of Government may require; but in consequence of the reduction of the Marine establishment on the two Lakes, those communications by means of the King's Vessels can never be depended on as York lies out of the usual Transport line, & they being employed on that service will seldom be able to attend to the requisition of Government for any other from York.

The Board are therefore of opinion that a Vessel[1] of small Tonnage sufficiently large to navigate the Lake with safety, should be provided for the purpose of carrying Dispatches, & Passengers wherever the exigencies of Government may require, & that this Vessel should be entierly under the orders of the Governor or person administring of this Province. . . .

E 2 Russell to Hugh Finlay,[2] Quebec
[*T.P.L., Peter Russell Papers*]

Upper Canada
York 22d November 1797

The Inhabitants of this Town having represented to me that they have hitherto suffered very great Inconvenience from their Letters not being delivered to them by the Winter express before its return from Niagara, which puts it out of their power for want of time to return answers by that opportunity; I am to request you will be pleased in future to order the Letters for York to be put up in a separate Bag and appoint some person in this Town to Act as Postmaster in distributing the Letters it may contain.—Should you not have determined upon the Person you are to invest with this Office, I beg leave to recommend Mr. William

[1]The yacht *Toronto* was finally built and launched in 1799. See E 8.
[2]Hugh Finlay (d. 1801) was Deputy Postmaster for Canada.

Willcocks a Merchant Resident here, as a Gentleman capable and willing to execute the Duties of it.—

E 3 Russell to Major Shank or Officer Commanding
[*T.P.L., Peter Russell Papers*]

York 8 March 1798

The Council having yesterday come to a Resolution to open a Road and make Bridges between the Humber & the River Credit in front next the Lake, and to strike a road from the Credit to the Road which now leads to the Head of the Lake, I am to request you will be pleased to order a Party from the Queens Rangers under your Command, consisting of one Sergeant one Corporal, and 12 privates, to assist the Deputy Surveyor whom the Surveyor General is directed to send on that Service. —But as it may be some days before Mr. Jones can be taken from the Service he is now upon, I beg leave to suggest the propriety of employing a Party in the Interim in making a good Road from the Garrison to this Town, for the purpose of facilitating the Communication, lest fire, an Attack of Indians or other Causes should Call for the Sudden Aid of the Kings Troops, agreeable to a Request I formerly made to you when I proposed your making the Road from the Garrison to the Humber— for the goodness of which I beg to offer my thanks to the party employed upon it.—The parties employed upon all these Services will be paid as before upon the Certificate of the Officer commanding the Regiment by my Warrants on the Receiver General—

E 4 Russell to the Comte de Puisaye
[*T.P.L., Peter Russell Papers*]

York January 1st, 1799

. . . We have raised about 300 Dollars with which the Surveyor Genl. has undertaken to turn Yonge Street[3] into the Town nearer the Garrison by opening a Road thro his own & my land before you come to the three Ravines next the Town, by which those bad Pitches will be avoided— and he has it further in contemplation to give such a course to the Road farther back, that all the Pitches may be escaped—Can this be done the communication with your Settlement will be rendered expeditious and easy. . . .

[3]Work on Yonge Street was begun in the spring of 1794 by the Queen's Rangers, working north from Eglinton Avenue. The usual route from Eglinton south was the Poplar Plains Trail, east of Yonge. In 1796 the Rangers opened Yonge Street south of Eglinton, but it was very bad, and was usually avoided. Russell is writing of an alternative road to be built west of Yonge Street, roughly where St. George and Beverley Streets are now. (See Ontario, Department of Planning and Development, *Don Valley Conservation Report*, 1950.)

E 5 Russell to Portland

[*P.R.O., C.O. 42, v. 324, p. 152; microfilm copy in P.A.O.*]

Upper Canada York
19th, June 1799

. . . After having for more than two years experienced the very great Inconveniences resulting to the public Service from the Want of a free land Communication with the Seat of Government & long lamented that I could not in Consequence comply with the Wishes of the People by assembling the Provincial Parliament in Winter and considering that the Thinness of the Population in these new Settlements precluded all Hopes of the Inhabitants being soon in a Condition of themselves to open sufficient Roads for that purpose; I judged it proper to submit to the Executive Council the propriety of immediately adopting some Measures for removing the difficulties we labored under. I have therefore the Honor of informing your Grace that, as it was the unanimous opinion of the Council as well as myself, that a Contract[4] should be forthwith entered into with some capable and responsible Person for cutting Road from this Town to the Bay of Quinti, a Contract has been accordingly made to that Effect; and the Contractor began his Work on the first Instant. . . .

E 6 Russell to Lieutenant Colonel Smith

[*T.P.L., Peter Russell Papers*]

York 1 July 1799

The Executive Council having recommended it to me to request a party of Fifty men with the adequate compliment of Commissioned and non Commissioned Officers to proceed under the Instructions of the Surveyor General to open and smooth a road for carriages from the Bay by Toronto street thro' Yonge Street as far as the first Lot—But it appearing to me from the Conversation I have had with you on the subject, that the other services on which the Corps under your Command, is at present employed, will not permit you to spare so large a Party—I beg leave to request, that you will be pleased to order a party of half that number with such portion of Officers as you shall judge proper to proceed forthwith on the service mentioned—Mr Smith the Acting Surveyor General, will inform the Officer who shall Command

[4]The contract with Asa Danforth was that the road was to be 33 feet wide, with the centre 16½ feet smooth to the ground. Danforth was to receive $90.00 a mile, and 40 labourers recommended by him were each to get 200 acres. The Townships of Dereham and Norwich were sold to defray the expense. It was to be completed as far as Port Hope by Jan. 1, 1800. Asa Danforth (1746–1836) was born in Dunstable, Mass., and served in the 4th Massachusetts Regiment during the Revolution. He became a major general in the state militia. He moved to Brookline, Mass., and then to Mayfield, N.Y. He was the first settler in the Onondaga Valley, superintended the salt springs at Syracuse, built an early sawmill near Rochester, and contracted for a number of roads.

them, where they are to begin, the different Roads they are to prepare for Carriages; and the manner in which it is expected the work shall be performed—Nothing but the necessity I am under of facilitating as soon as possible a Carriage communication with the French Colony at Windham, in order to lessen the great expence to Government of the carriage thither of Provisions and stores could have induced me to call upon you, before the Muskatoe Season was over; and you had finished, the Huts intended for the Winter accomodation of your regiment, but I flatter myself, that the sparing the number I now solicit will not contribute to impede that very necessary service—

E 7 MEMORIAL[5] OF JOSEPH KENDRICK
[*P.A.C., Upper Canada State Papers, v. 42, p. 3*]

I Humbly beg leave to lay before Your Honor the Awkwardness of my Situation by continuing to keep Charge of the Schooner Peggy. belonging to Messrs. Barry & Cameron, being Purposely for the Accommodations of the Gentlemen & inhabitants of York.—And that as the Passage Money and freight on a trip to Newark and back, Does not Exceed ten or at most twelve Dollars, Out of which the Port charge Exacted is four, a sum far more than ever was exacted before in any British Port—when the Vessel ought only to be considered as a common Passage Boat—being little more than twenty Tons, and at the same time in Carrying a full Freight to Kingston and returning with the same, am not charged near so much, and without Your honors Interference to Prevent such Unusual Charges. I must be Oblidged to Quit said Vessel—the consequence of which, She must be laid up, which of course will Prove highly Detrimental not only to the Owners—but the Gentlemen who are frequently Visiting the Town—

E 8 LAUNCHING OF THE YACHT *Toronto*
[*York,* Upper Canada Gazette, *September 14, 1799*]

The *Toranto Yatch*, Captain BAKER,[6] will, in the course of a few days, be ready to make her first trip. She is one of the handsomest vessels, of her size, that ever swam upon the Ontario; and if we are permited to judge from her appearance, and to do her justice, we must say, she bids fair to be one of its swiftest sailing vessels.—She is admirably well calculated for the reception of passengers, and can, with propriety, boast of the most experienced officers and men. Her master builder was a Mr. *Denison,*[7] an American, on whom she reflects much honor.

[5]This memorial was read by the Executive Council on August 6, 1799, but consideration was deferred until a study of the charges levied at the ports "on this and the Upper Lake" could be made.

[6]William Baker (b. 1755?) was born in Newfoundland, and entered the Provincial Marine in 1787. He was formerly master of the *Caldwell.*

[7]John Dennis.

E 9 Postal Service between York and Niagara
[*York*, Upper Canada Gazette, *December 21, 1799*]

To our PATRONS.

. . . The present size of the Gazette is owing to the great disadvantage which it labors under for the want of a regular mode of conveyance from Niagara to this place. Could we receive our intelligence, regular, from our correspondents in the States, it would be in our power to enlarge the Gazette to a more respectable size, and conduct it with half the trouble that it now requires, for then we should never be difficient of subject matter to fill the paper; but now, it does not come to hand once in a month, in which case if the Gazette was large enough to contain all the intelligence received, we should then be necessitated to suspend the publication of it for a while.

It is astonishing that the postmasters in this province do not exert themselves to establish a post between this town and that of Niagara; it would undoubtedly contribute to their interest and afford a great satisfaction to the public. There is scarcely a person in this, and the town of Niagara that would not contribute his mite in support of so laudable a plan. This being the capital, it is presumed, ought to be a strong inducement to the postmasters for adopting some mode of conveyance, to, and from this town. But we flatter ourselves, when his excellency shall have arrived, that he will remedy the great inconveniency which the inhabitants of this town labor under for the want of a post from this to Niagara.

E 10 George Heriot to Sir Francis Freeling[8]
[*P.A.C., C284, p. 3*]

Quebec 6th March 1800

. . . His Excellency Genl. Hunter has requested me to state a plan now in Contemplation, and which he has proposed to me, for the Establishment of a regular Post by land, from Montreal to York, the Capital of the Province of Upper Canada; with this view, people are now employed in making, from the Bay of Quinte to that place, a road, which will be sufficiently good to allow any of the common Conveyances of the Country to pass along without difficulty—By next Autumn the road will be compleated.—General Hunter who is Lieutenant Governor of Upper Canada, seems to be of Opinion, that the Revenue which will accrue from the conveyance of letters and packets to York by a Courier, will be sufficiently adequate to cover the expence necessary to be incurred.—Should it however fall short, His Excellency assures me, that he will be answerable for any excess of Expence, that may be thereby incurred, as he expects it will be defrayed by the Legislature of Upper Canada.[9] . . .

[8]Sir Francis Freeling (1764–1836) was secretary to the General Post Office, Great Britain.

[9]On July 5, 1800, Freeling refused to consider the request, on the grounds

E 11 Opening Road to Yonge Street[10]
[*York,* Upper Canada Gazette, *December 20, 1800*]

On Thursday last about noon, a number of the principal inhabitants of this town, met together in one of the Government buildings, to consider of the means of opening the road to Yonge-Street, and enabling the farmers there to bring their provisions to market with more ease than is practicable at present.

The Hon. the Chief Justice[11] was called to the chair. He briefly stated the purpose of the meeting, and added, that a subscription had been lately opened, by which something more than two hundred dollars in money and labour had been promised, and that other sums were to be expected from several respectable inhabitants who were well-wishers to the undertaking; but had not yet contributed towards it. These sums would not, he feared, be equal to the purpose, which could hardly be accomplished for less than between five and six hundred dollars; but many of the subscribers were desirous that what was already subscribed should be immediately applied as far as it would go, and that other resources should be looked for. With this view, it had been suggested that a considerable aid might be obtained by shutting up the street[12] which now forms the northern boundary of the town between Torento-street and the Common, and disposing of the land occupied by it. This street, it was conceived, was altogether superfluous, as another street, equally convenient in every respect, run parallel to it at the distance of about ten rods; but it could not be shut up and disposed of by any authority less than that of the Legislature. To consider of an application to Parliament for the purpose, was one of the objects of the meeting.

The subscribers present were unanimously of opinion, that the subscription should be immediately applied, as far as it would go, and that an application should be made to Parliament at its next session, for the purpose abovementioned.

A paper was then produced and read, containing a proposal from Mr. Eliphalet Hale[13] to open and make the road, or so much of it as

---

that the proposed service would not pay for itself; on Oct. 24, 1800, Hunter ordered that it be begun as an experiment, guaranteeing indemnification if necessary. (P.A.C., C284, pp. 4–5.)

[10]Yonge Street ended at Lot (Queen) Street, then north of the town. From Lot Street to the Second Concession (Bloor Street) it was extremely rough, and the usual route south was to the eastward.

[11]John Elmsley.

[12]Lot Street (Queen Street West). The usual route to the west was Hospital (Richmond) Street, rather than Lot Street. When the New Town was laid out in 1797, no provision was made for extending Yonge Street south of Lot Street. It was necessary when going south on Yonge to jog east to Toronto Street.

[13]Eliphalet Hale (d. 1807) moved from Niagara to York in 1799, where he advertised that he was commencing bricklaying, lathing, and plastering. In 1806 he was in the shoemaking business. From 1806 until his death he was High Constable.

might be required, at the rate of twelve dollars per acre, for clearing it where no causway was wanted, four rods wide and cutting the stumps in the two middle rods close to the ground; and 7s. 6d. Provincial Currency per rod, for making a causway 18 feet wide, where a causway might be wanted. He undertook to give security for performing the work by the first of February next.

Mr. Hale's proposal was accepted, and a committee consisting of Mr. Secretary Jarvis, Mr. Allen, and Mr. James Playter, was appointed to superintend the carrying it into execution.

A Petition to the Legislature lies for signature at Mr. M'Dougall's Tavern, and subscriptions will be received by Messrs. Allan and Wood.

E 12 Advantages of Road to Yonge Street
[*York,* Upper Canada Gazette, *March 7, 1801*]

It must be flattering, and in the last degree gratifying to every one interested in the improvements and prosperity of this country, to behold the rapid advances daily made in cultivation, buildings, and the opening of roads to the different and distant parts of the province. Any citizen, or inhabitant of this neighbourhood, who was a witness to the beginning of its settlement, has it now in his power to draw a pleasing contrast: the ground that five years ago was an absolute wild, and haunt for beasts of prey, we now see occupied by works and structures of public and private convenience and utility. Nothing can be a greater ornament, nor of more direct and immediate advantage to the country and the people at large, than safe and convenient roads: they promote and encourage travelling; they enable the farmer to transport his commodities with ease and safety to a market; they make the communications with neighbourhoods expeditious and commodious: in fact, it is unnecessary to enlarge upon the advantages, since they must be obvious to every one at first view.

The citizens and inhabitants of this town and part of the country, have the strongest imaginable inducements to open roads to the interior, and in particular to Lake Simcoe, as well from views of local convenience, as the certain and extensive advantages which will arise, from having the rout of the North West traders transferred to this quarter. It certainly depends upon ourselves to make this a depository to the wealth, and common centre of the province: We have nothing to do but improve upon the situation and advantages with which nature has distinguished it, to make it vie with the most favoured sea port. The views of Government, no doubt, coincide with the intentions of the traders, which leave but little for us to do—and when it is considered, that this place will be a depot to the exports and immense imports (the fruits of the North West trade) every one in the least interested, will contribute something to put us in possession of advantages, which we now enjoy but in prospect.

We have seen that the Hon. Chief Justice Elmsley, and several other gentlemen, (whose independent situations preclude every idea of interestedness or profit on their part) have been the first to propose, and with a praiseworthy liberality to contribute to the public spirited undertaking.

The examples of men, actuated solely by pure patriotism, are well worthy imitation, and will, it is hoped, stimulate such as have the stronger motives of self-interest and personal advantage in view, to promote and encourage to the utmost, a work fraught with so many and such general advantages. There is a second subscription circulating for this desirable purpose, and it is presumed, that whoever considers the object in its right point of view will generously throw in their mite to accomplish it.

A CITIZEN.

York, 5th March, 1801.

E 13 William Willcocks Resigns
[*York*, Upper Canada Gazette, *December 19, 1801*]

To prevent disappointment and trouble, the Public is requested to take notice, that some time ago Mr. WILLCOCKS resigned his place of Post Master for York, his reasonable charges for the rent of an office, stationary, fire, candles, and a servant to attend, being disputed; although by his assiduity and attention, the revenue was productive beyond expectation, as appears by the accounts he rendered, and the money he remitted to the Post Master General at Quebec.

Dec. 16, 1801.

E 14 Further Advantages of Road to Yonge Street
[*York,* Upper Canada Gazette, *March 6, 1802*]

It affords us much pleasure to state to our Readers that the necessary repair of Yonge Street is likely to be soon effected; as the work, we understand, has been undertaken with the assurance of entering upon, and completing it without delay: and to every one, who reflects upon the present sufferings of an industrious community on resorting to a Market, it cannot but prove highly satisfactory to observe a work of such convenience and utility speedily accomplished.—That the measure of its future benefits must be extensive indeed we may reasonably expect; but whilst we look forward with flattering expectations of these benefits, we cannot but appreciate the immediate advantage which is afforded to us in being relieved from the application of the Statute labour circuitous to bye paths and occasional Roads and in being enabled to apply the same to the improvement of the Streets, and the nearer and more direct approaches to the Town.

E 15 Alexander Wood to Ogilvy, Mylne & Co., London
[*T.P.L., Alexander Wood Letter Books*]

York 13th Octr. 1803

. . . I would be extremely obliged to you, if not inconvenient, to receive any letters my relations in Scotland may send and put them in the way of getting straight to New York, as the Packet leaves all letters directed to persons in either of the Canadas, at Halifax from thence they are sent only once a month to Montreal & seldom reach this in less than six months after date, when left at New York, the inland post to Niagara leaves that place once a week & letters are at hand generally in three months, which makes a material difference

E 16 Francis Gore[14] to Sir George Shee[15]
[*P.R.O., C.O. 42, v. 343, p. 100; microfilm copy in P.A.O.*]

York Upper Canada
1st April 1807.

The Dispatches which are sent from the Secretary of States Office by the Rout of Halifax, seldom arrive at the seat of this Government under five months. May I therefore take the liberty to request, that in future, they may be directed to the care of Thomas William Moore Esquire, Agent for British Packets New York; through which channel, private Letters are in general received here from London in about seven or eight weeks.

E 17 Improvement of Yonge Street
[*York,* York Gazette, *December 9, 1807*]

To such of our Yonge Street friends, as feel themselves interested in *its* improvement, and who can foresee the advantages of turning the North-West communication into *this* channel, we recommend industry and alacrity. We beg leave to remind them, that as the next year will produce a general Election, the ensuing session will be the proper time to petition for a Turn-Pike, for the obvious reason, that the present House of Assembly will be proud, by supporting such a beneficial and praiseworthy measure, to leave a great and laudable example to their successors, for imitation.

[14]Francis Gore (1769–1852) entered the army in 1787, retiring in 1802 with the rank of major. In 1804 he was appointed Lieutenant Governor of Bermuda, and in 1806 of Upper Canada, which post he held until 1817. From 1811 to 1815 he was on leave in England.

[15]Sir George Shee (d. 1825) was Undersecretary of State for the Home Department 1800–3, and in 1806 was appointed Undersecretary of State for the War Department.

E 18 Lighthouse on Gibraltar Point
[*York,* York Gazette, *August 5, 1809*]

WE this week have witnessed the Light House on Gibralter Point so far finished, as to be applied to its original purpose. This Beacon so essentially material to our Lake navigation, and to the protection equally of vessels, and their crews and passengers, must be generally acceptable, and much approved of. The Building, from being substantially constructed of handsome Stone, holds out a strong presumption, that its duration will long ensure as well its great utility as its known necessity. The view from the Garrison and Town, being in a great measure bounded by the Timber growing on the Peninsula, to obviate it and to remedy the privation, his Excellency has directed (in addition to the intention of its common use) that signals be hoisted at the Light House, whenever a vessel bears in sight of it, for the desired information of persons here, in any wise interested.

E 19 William McGillivray[16] to Gore, May, 1810
[*P.A.C., Upper Canada Sundries*]

In order to become perfectly acquainted with the proposed Route by York to Lake Huron, so as to be enabled to lay a satisfactory report of the same before the General meeting of the North West Company on Lake Superior—Mr McLeod,[17] one of the Agents of that Concern, and a Partner in our Establishment, takes the Route by York—on his way up, and will have the Honor of delivering you this.—

Mr. McLeod will examine the Ground about the Landing at Penitenguishingue Bay & every other situation which may be useful in the arrangement of the intended Route.—

The North West Company no doubt, must have permanent Establishments & Stores at Penitenguishingue, & also Stores at the Landing on Kempenfelt Bay.—It is presumed there will be no difficulty in providing Storage at York, and either the North West Company, or those with whom they may Contract for the carrying place, must have a proper place to Lodge the Goods at Gwillimbury; I should suppose that two large Boats navigated by a dozen men would be sufficient for transporting the Goods from thence to Kempenfelt Bay.—Such is my present view of the mode of Transport, and as your Excellency has all along patronized the Plan, judging correctly of the beneficial Effects it must produce on the Settlements through which we must pass, we are encouraged to hope for your support in the undertaking—and that we may be allowed to hold such Portions of Land at the different Stations, as may be suitable for our purposes—conforming of course, to the Regulations established by the Provincial Govt.—

[16]William McGillivray (1764?–1825), was a fur trader, and from 1804 the chief director of the North West Company.

[17]Archibald Norman McLeod became a partner in McTavish, McGillivray & Co. in 1808.

E 20 Memorial of North West Company

[*P.R.O., C.O. 42, v. 351, pp. 123-4; microfilm copy in P.A.O.*]

To His Excellency Francis Gore Esquire, Lieutenant Governor of the Province of Upper Canada &ca. &ca. &ca.

The Memorial of William McGillivray, William Hallowell,[18] Roderick McKenzie,[19] Angus Shaw,[20] Archibald Normond McLeod, and James Hallowell Junior,[18] forming the House of McTavish McGillivray & Co. as well for themselves as divers other persons their associates, composing with them, the North-West Company.

Humbly Sheweth,

That your Memorialists in carrying on their Trade to the Indian Country, have been accustomed to forward a great proportion of their Goods intended for their annual outfits by way of Niagara and Detroit to their place of randevous on Lake Superior, for the Transport of which and of the Flour, Corn and High-wines furnished at Detroit and Sandwich, they have an Establishment of Vessels on the Lakes plying to and from Fort Erie and St. Maries—

That your Memorialists since the Cession of the Posts in 1796 by following the above Rout, have on several occasions felt and are continually exposed to the vexatious interference of the American Custom House officers; Your Memorialists having had their Boats and Property seized and detained, to their great annoyance and loss, and always without adequate or even any compensation or redress—

That your Memorialists have been given to understand that it is in the contemplation of your Excellency to open a Road and establishment from Kempenfelt Bay to Petinguishingue Bay on Lake Huron; and your Memorialists humbly conceive and beg leave to suggest to your Excellency, that the establishment of that Road and Settlement would be more safe and eligible for the Transport of Goods and Provisions to the Upper Country than the Route now followed as it will conduct your Memorialists and others His Majesty's Subjects by a Road which will supercede the necessity of their following the Frontier of the Americans and from passing under their Forts and Guns, and free them also from the very vexatious and arbitrary impositions of the American Government: Your Memorialists beg leave further to suggest to your Excellency that the Country adjoining the said Road settled by His Majesty's Subjects is susceptible of raising the Corn and Provisions which is wanted for your Memorialists Trade, to the North West Country—That at the present

[18]William (1771–1838) and James (1778–1816) Hallowell were sons of the fur trader James Hallowell, and like their father partners in McTavish, McGillivray & Co. Shortly after this memorial, William and James, Junior, disagreed with their partners and withdrew from the firm.

[19]Roderick McKenzie (1761?–1844) became a partner of McTavish, Frobisher & Co. in 1800, but retired from active participation in the fur trade in 1801. He remained a dormant partner of McTavish, Frobisher & Co., later McTavish, McGillivray and Co., until its failure in 1825.

[20]Angus Shaw (d. 1832) became a member of McTavish, McGillivray & Co. in 1808.

time your Memorialists are forced to procure their Corn and Provisions in a great measure from the Settlers within the American Government, whereas, of the monies expended by your Memorialists for Corn, Provisions and other necessary articles on the American side, and during their annual transit through part of their Country or on their frontiers, were and could be expended within the Province under your Excellency's Command, and care and on the communication proposed by your Excellency, it might and would certainly be a source of Support and advancement that would make that part of the Country a very flourishing settlement.—That your Memorialist[s] feel a great desire to encourage the said new communication proposed by your Excellency and are ready and willing to give it every support: But inasmuch as your Memorialists have been at a very considerable Expense in establishing a line of communication on the old Route, in erecting Stores and Buildings and in the building and maintaining Vessels on Lake Erie, yet your Memorialists are willing whenever the said new Road can be considered practicable to change the channel of their communication and take all their Trade by the way of York and through the Road proposed by Your Excellency—That in abandoning the present Route, your Memorialists must necessarily make a Sacrifice of their Establishment, Buildings and Vessels on the Old Route, and be put to very considerable Expense in making new Establishments and in erecting new Stores and Building &ca. on the proposed Road and at the landing place at Gwilliamsbury—Taking the premises into consideration your Memorialists trusts that Your Excellency will not deem it improper in them to apply to Your Excellency for a Grant of the waste Lands at each end of the said Road, and at Gwilliamsbury.

And your Memorialists therefore Humbly pray, That your Excellency will be pleased to make to them in such manner as your Excellency's Wisdom may seem proper, a Grant of Two thousand acres of the Waste Lands on the North side of Kempenfelt Bay, where the said proposed Road will leave the said Bay, and Two thousand acres of the Waste Lands on the South Side of Penetinguishingue Bay where the said proposed Road will come out on the last mentioned Bay and also a Grant of Two hundred acres of Land at the Landing place at Gwilliamsbury, for the purpose of making an Establishment there and erecting Store Houses and other Buildings.

And your Memorialists as in duty bound, will ever pray—

(signed) W. McGillivray
Wm. Hallowell
Angus Shaw

Montreal 5th November 1810—

(signed) W. McGillivray —for Roderick McKenzie
Wm. Hallowell —for Archd. N. McLeod
Angus Shaw —for James Hallowell Junr.
and others their associates the North West Company.

E 21 Brock to Liverpool

[*P.R.O., C.O. 42, v. 351, pp. 121-2; microfilm copy in P.A.O.*]

York Upper Canada
23 November 1811—

Previous to the departure of Lieutenant Governor Gore, His Excellency directed a Survey of a tract of Land belonging to the Indians upon Lake Simcoe to be made, with a view of meeting the wishes of the gentlemen engaged in the fur trade, as expressed in their Memorial[21] to His Excellency herewith enclosed, together with his private Secretary's answer[22] thereto.

. . . I shall only presume to detain your Lordship to request, that as the Merchants are particularly anxious in the present uncertain state of our relations, to obtain a route for their goods unconnected with the American territory, I may be honored as soon as convenient with your Lordships Commands on the Subject. . . .

E 22 Captain A. Gray to Prevost

[*P.A.C., C676, p. 79; printed in Wood,* Select British Documents of the Canadian War of 1812, *I, 283–4*]

Montreal 13th January 1812

. . . The next object I turned my attention to was the N. West Company. . . . In the event of War the Route by Detroit and the River Sinclair must be abandoned, and that by York adopted. From York they will proceed by Lake Simcoe to Gloucester Bay, in Lake Huron, and along the North Shore of the Lake to the Straits, or falls, of St. Mary's and from thence into Lake Superior. The only part of this Route that they feel any apprehension of being interrupted, or cut off by the Enemy, is upon Lake Huron. An armament may be fitted out at Detroit to inter[cept] them in their return from the N. West (when their Cargoes are more valuable). It is therefore upon this line of Communication they will probably require our support. It would appear from the information I have received that we might be enabled to afford them the requisite support from York, as the communication from York to Lake Huron is much shorter than that from Detroit to the tract proposed by the N. West. . . .

[21]E 20.

[22]Major Halton wrote that it was proposed to buy from the Indians the land along the traders' route, and to lay out towns at Kempenfelt and Penetanguishene Bays, but that "no hope must be entertained of a Monopoly of the Soil at either Debouche." Lands along the road would be granted to actual settlers only. (P.R.O., C.O. 42, v. 351, pp. 125–6, Halton to William McGillivray, Nov. 29, 1810; microfilm copy in P.A.O.)

F. POLITICAL FERMENT

F 1 Cato in Support of an Eminent Candidate
[*York,* Upper Canada Gazette, *March 15, 1800*]

To the free Electors *of the County of York.*

GENTLEMEN,

At a time that the public anxiety is a little raised, to know who is to represent us in the ensuing parliament.[1] It may not be amiss, to say something general on the subject of representation, of constituents and *Constituted.*—Nothing, it is presumed, can be more true, than that the primary wish of every ELECTOR, is to see himself represented in his country's legislature by an *honest upright man.* Honest and upright indeed, ought that man be, who is entrusted with so HIGH A CHARGE. A charge, gentlemen, of such magnitude and so sacred, that no one should assume it without mature examination of the eventful and interminable consequences. A solemn and unprejudiced review of the duties incumbent on the representative, of the powers vested in his hands, of the many whose rights he voluntarily binds himself to support, should methinks, deter the unwary from aiming at it—and the unequal to it—from wishing it, should establish this prominent, though neglected truth, that something more than plebian honesty, than rugged uprightness is necessary, to qualify an individual for the dignified station. A station, gentlemen, to which is attached, duties, so various and so sacred, so extensive and so complicated, that he who has a just sense of them, will not enter on their discharge but with conscious fear and trembling. The subject, gentlemen, is a field on which volumes might be written, then could not the weight of the awful charge be sufficiently impressed on the minds of mankind.

I shall confine myself, in this place, to opening to your views, a few of the needful qualifications—the efficient qualities and more striking duties of the legislator. At the same time that I pause to admire, and greatfully contemplate that noblest fabric of human wisdom, the *British Constitution.* . . . The representative more particularly, who stands so high in this general order, should look abroad and ask: what are my duties? What my necessary qualifications? What my necessary knowledge? I answer: your duties are, to enact wise and beneficial laws for yourself and your constituents—your country and posterity. You are

[1]In the first two parliaments of Upper Canada, York was represented by the member for Durham, York, and the First Riding of Lincoln, whose constituency extended from just east of Port Hope to the Grand River. By the "Act for the more equal Representation of the Commons" passed in 1800, a new riding of Durham, Simcoe, and the East Riding of York was created, and in the general election of that year, an election was held in York for the first time.

not only to be the guardian of their rights and liberties, but you are to be the guardian of their morals. You are to guard against encroachments from superior orders, and to restrain every symptom of licence and licentiousness in the body which you represent. You are to promote and establish such wholesome regulations as effectually to secure, a free and uninterrupted course to civil and moral order. Regulations, which will benefit and harmonize the present age, and entail to you the blessings of the yet, unborn!

The qualities you should possess to warrant your claim to this preeminence are, honesty, independence of spirit, penetration, an intimate knowledge of the true interests of your country, and an acquaintance with its existing laws. You are not blindly to be led astray by what may be of temporary advantage, yet militate to the incalculable injury of posterity. At no time, will this country, stand more in need of men of abilities, than at the present. You are, as it were, now laying the foundations of its future consequence and its happiness—its dearest interests are involved—its welfare and existence are in a manner submitted to your care and your guidance.

Your knowledge of governments and the constitutions of empires should be general. . . . And here let me assert it, no earthly consideration, whether of interest or friendship, should influence the elector. Let his vote be given to the person whose abilities and inclination to serve his country shall, on examination, appear equal. When he shall find these combined with eminence of station,[2] such an one should be the object of general choice. His station will give weight to his counsels—currency to his opinions and strengthen his desire and endeavors of serving his king and his country. These are the requisites, and these the outlines of character, in the man, who, with justice, aspires to a seat in parliament. Many, however, hurried by a ridiculous vanity, or precipitated by an ill directed emulation, or flattered by a peculiarity of situation or circumstances, (situation and circumstances, which are of themselves a moral assurance of success,) thrust themselves forward, as candidates for the honor. Ignorant of the duties—unequal to their discharge—unpossessed of every quality—acquirement or characteristic, which can either dignify or distinguish the legislator. How, gentlemen, by what means, let me ask you—can we shield ourselves from contempt? How can we avoid becoming a laughing stock to our neighbours? When arrogant stupidity, a total ignorance of the principles of government, of the spirit of legislation, of the interest of the country; nay, of the very principles of their native tongue, are the birth-rights, the confessed characteristics of men, who advance themselves to a seat in parliament. Justly, (yet too often unhappily for our interest, our credit and our consequence,) the majority of votes, constitute the representative; this is a moral evil impossible to obviate. Yet let me conjure this last description

[2]Cato is obviously supporting the candidacy of Henry Allcock.

of men, for the love of God! for the love of their country, for the love of themselves, for the sake of their credit, for their modesty, for the sake of their families, and lastly for the sake of not violating nature, for ever to renounce, the idea, of obtaining seats in parliament—of imposing on the country, or like Falstaff's shadows of filling up the muster roll.

CATO.

York, 15 March.

F 2 A Farmer in Support of an Honest Candidate
[*York,* Upper Canada Gazette, *March 22, 1800*]

To the Electors of the County of York,
FELLOW ELECTORS,

. . .

Without doubt many of you have seen the pompous prolixities of Mr. *Cato,* published in the Gazette of the 15th inst. upon the subject of representation, of constituents and constituted. In this production, fellow electors, you are solicited to give your votes to "the person whose abilities and inclination to serve his king and his country shall, on examination, appear equal;" this, fellow electors, is what I am anxious to instill into your minds, and what I with you strickly to adhere to, and to be your primary and leading motive when you come forward to give your votes. He goes on further to observe "When you shall find these combined with *eminence of station,* such an one should be the object of general choice." this position does not correspond with my sentiments nor my interest; Let me ask, is it then his "eminent station" that entitles him to our votes? no, no fellow electors that is not the man, in justice to ourselves, that we can give in charge our dearest rights and liberties; for there are certain emoluments arising from, and a salary annexed to that "eminence of station" which will ever be a bane to our interest, and which are held, by he who enjoys them, in a much higher estimation, than those rights of the many which he attempts to support. It is our duty to constitute a person who neither directly, or indirectly receives any emoluments from, or in office under government; this is the character that we are in duty to support and who is justly entitled to our suffrage. I verily believe, fellow electors, that there are too many of our candidates who entertain a much greater idea of the honor, than of the sacred duties attached to that person who takes upon himself to preserve inviolate the rights, and privileges of his fellow subjects. If this position is true, which, I believe, few of you will deny, it behoves us to keep a vigilant look-out that we may be enabled to guard against such a description of men. The outlines of character delineated by Cato, are those of a Pitt, a Fox and a Burke; I cannot but admit that such a character would make a respectable figure in our parliament in its present infant state, because there would be no one to oppose his measures, whether calculated for the general interest and welfare or not; such a character, I say, would be as equally dangerous, as he who is "ignorant of the very principles of his native tongue."

Fellow electors, I should not have laid down my axe and take up the quil at this remote period, from the day of election, had not Mr. Cato set the example; and I must confess, that I am fearful, unless we continue united, for if divided we can do nothing, that his superior abilities and sound reasoning will, ere that period arrives (for we suppose that the gazette will be teeming weekly with his productions,) obtain a number of votes for the man, whose *"eminence of station,"* is the only claim which he has to them.

Fellow electors, you without doubt, recollect that Wm. Willcocks, esq, Wm. Jarvis, esq, Mr. Samuel Heron and Wm. Allan, esq. are the persons (as we have been informed) who offer themselves as candidates for this county: Mr. Heron is the person selected out of the number by us, and should he succeed in his election, which there is no doubt of, he will do us that justice which we have a right to expect from the man who represents us in our country's legislature. It is true Mr. Heron has not had the advantage of a refined education, he is nevertheless possessed of a large share of mother wit and good sense; and it can justly be said of him, that he is, "that noblest work of God, an honest, upright and just man."—Now fellow electors, let us be unanimous, and for the love of our country, for the love of ourselves, our interests, our welfare, our rights and liberties, assemble on that day when our dearest interests will be at stake, and with one voice constitute Mr. Samuel Heron.

A. FARMER

York, 19 *March,*

F 3 MINUTES OF THE EXECUTIVE COUNCIL
[*P.A.C., Upper Canada State Book C, pp. 34-5*]

Council Chamber at York 25th March 1800.

Present
The Honl. John Elmsley Chief Justice
The Honl. Peter Russell
The Honl. Æneas Shaw.

Mr. Allan a Merchant in York, complained of an article inserted in the Gazette of the 22d. Inst. and signed "a Farmer"; which states him to be a Candidate for the County of York at the ensuing Election. Mr. Allan stated, that the assertion is entierely without foundation, and is apprehensive that if it reaches the persons with whom he is connected in the Lower Province, and is uncontradicted, it may very materially affect his Interests.

The Board conceives that the Printers are highly culpable in having inserted such an Article in their paper without authority: But on looking at the rest of the article, it thinks it absolutely necessary to direct the Chief Justice immediately to transmit the Paper to His Excellency, with the request of the Board, that the Printers may be immediately dismissed from their office, and that His Excellency will avail himself of his present situation to procure some other person to be King's Printer.[8]

F 4 CATO ATTACKS A FARMER
[*York,* Upper Canada Gazette, *April 26, 1800*]

GENTLEMEN,

I Observe that the exiguous integer of folly, who (pardon the expression) seems affected with a mental CHOLERAMORBUS; who insults common-sense under the signature of "A FARMER," is still tormenting the public with reiterated absurdity.—He must have heard his first monster of this kind (which in his second he gives us to understand was a "parliamentary essay) publicly execrated as the vilest offspring of folly —The idle, the nefarious belchings of an assuming ignoramus; void of reasoning in its substance, of common grammar in its composition, and an outrage on the general sense of mankind. If in his pitiful production he had other aim than of making his folly a public spectacle—that aim has on his part been completely defeated: The worthy person whom he had made the hero of his farce, whose virtues he has gibbeted in a news-paper: him he probably wished to serve; by investing with "a large share of mother-wit," he has hung him out as a scare-crow to the doltish; by his uncommon honesty, as a stumbling block to knaves; by his want of a "refined education," as a standing and conspicuous foil to the learned; and as will be generally acknowledged by the uncommon grossness of his daubing, has as completely succeeded in convincing the world that his hero is not "a Fox, a Pitt and a Burke." Nothing that this THING has either said or wrote on the subject, is worthy animadversion, except his intolerable presumption which can only be exceeded by his stupidity. This at a time that it reminds me of what I advanced in my first address to my fellow electors, to wit: that ignorance not unfrequently produces the effect of evil design, fills me with a painful apprehension that the incautious complacence of the printers, may wring from them, the tears of reprobation, may expose them to suffer from the effects of censure undesignedly incurred.

. . . In his warm, mistaken, and unfortunate attempt to appreciate that candidate whom all esteem for his virtues, he has made him appear more ridiculous than the most malicious invention could have done. His intentions might have been kind, their operation was most uncouth.

[8]On March 27, 1800, the King's Printers, William Waters and Titus Geer Simons, petitioned the Governor, acknowledging their error in printing the article (F 2) and throwing themselves on the Governor's clemency. They were pardoned with a reprimand this time, but were dismissed the following year. (P.R.O., C.O. 42, v. 327, pp. 142–3; microfilm copy in P.A.O.)

Let me assure this tantling of a scribbler, that were he to write till doomsday, my reading ends with his twain. Reason sickens at the idea, memory revolts at the recollection, the emotions they create are too painful to

CATO.

F 5 Samuel Heron Declines Nomination[4]
[*York,* Upper Canada Gazette, *July 12, 1800*]

TO THE PUBLIC.

THE subscriber having seen his name in several of the Gazettes, in this place, as a CANDIDATE for the County of York, and having never determined or declared his intentions on that head till the present instant, and as the ensuing Election will soon arrive takes this opportunity to communicate his intentions to his Friends, and begs leave to dispense with the honor they appear so ready and willing to confer upon him, by offering him as their Representative; and at the same time, assures them, it is with the greatest regret he finds it inconvenient to accept their very kind offer.

York, 11 July.

F 6 William Jarvis' Election Address
[*York,* Upper Canada Gazette, *July 19, 1800*]

BEING fully sensible, as I am persuaded you have been for these SIX months past, of my Intention to become a CANDIDATE for your Suffrages at the ensuing Election; yet conceiving, from the *various* REPORTS which have been circulated with much *indecent confidence,* (and which reports have been founded in *falsehood,*) it may be understood that I have relinquished my former intention to Offer myself a Candidate at the approaching Election; it is true I have not solicited the suffrages of my fellow subjects *from door to door*, such conduct, I am confident, you would think ill became a man who, ardently wishes, shortly to be in the character of your Representative. I have not been urgent in the pursuit of so distinguished a preference, deeming it the most constitutional way for you to exercise your own discretion and judgment in the choice of a person to represent you in the next Provincial Parliament. Such are my sentiments, and should I be so far honored as to be placed in that situation by your votes, rest assured, the object of my ambition would be to prove myself to have been deserving of your choice. . . .

York, 14 July, 1800.

[4]This is one of the mysteries about York's first election; Heron obviously was a candidate (see F 7).

F 7 AN IMPARTIAL BYSTANDER'S ACCOUNT OF THE ELECTION
[*Niagara,* Niagara Herald, *March 14, 1801*]

YORK, July 24th, 1800.

THE returning officer[5] opened the poll at 10 o'clock A.M.—The candidates for the representation, were, the hon. Henry Alcock, Wm. Jarvis, John Small, John Wilcox,[6] esqrs. and messrs. George Playter, and Samuel Heron. Messrs. Wilcox and Playter resigned their pretensions in the presence of the electors, whom mr. Playter addressed in a short harrangue. It was agreed by the candidates to poll by tens, in the following order: first judge Alcock, then messrs. Jarvis, Small and Heron in succession. The poll was adjourned this day at 2 o'clock P.M. and on the 25th opened at 10 A.M. The votes at 11 o'clock stood thus:—for Judge Alcock 30, mr. Heron 30, mr. Small 21, and mr. Jarvis 17.—The voters at this time appeared to be growing scarce, except those for mr. Heron, who were pressing forward by threes and fours. Mr. Weeks,[7] who was Judge Alcock's advocate on the occasion, interrogated all the opposite voters in a manner which the people conceived rude and insulting.—Mr. Angus M'Donell acted the part of advocate also.— His interrogatories were general, but in that mild way which characterises the man:—perhaps his fee was smaller; for the eloquence of mr. Weeks seemed invariably to prevail:—It was of the kind to draw the following answers from some of them: "if their lands were not paid for they would bestow them on the tinker; and that his tongue was rather too long." Capt. Van Hain[8] had been previously dispatched to collect the German settlers of Markham, to whom plenty of favorite cheer had been sent—no less than bread and rum.—Messrs. Weeks and Wilcox jun.[9] paid them a visit on the evening of the 24th. and solicited their votes for mr. Alcock, who, it was held out to them, would make the merchants sell cheaper if he was elected:—they enquired if there were other candidates, and were informed that messrs. Small and Jarvis were the only ones. They were also informed that mr. Alcock would purchase whatever they might in future bring to market. On the morning of the 25th there was a letter dispatched from mr. Alcock to capt. Van Hain, desiring him to lead his friends to the place of election; and not to allow

[5]William Chewett. At later elections, this office was held by William Allan.

[6]There does not appear to be any John Wilcox who could be a candidate. It is probably an error, and William Willcocks was the candidate, because he was the only one of the Willcocks family who received the title Esquire at this time.

[7]William Weekes (d. 1806) was born in Ireland and was said to have studied law in Aaron Burr's office. In 1798 he came to York and was admitted to the Bar. He was a radical Reformer. In 1805 he was elected to the House of Assembly representing Durham, Simcoe, and the East Riding of York. He was killed in a duel by William Dickson of Niagara.

[8]Frederick, Baron de Hoen.

[9]Probably Charles Willcocks. Although Joseph Willcocks was later blamed in connection with this riot, he had only been four months in York.

them to be spoken to till they arrived in town: however, the precaution was ineffectual, and when there the majority declared they would vote for mr. Heron.

Mr. Jarvis appeared discouraged, and told some of his friends that they were at liberty to vote for mr. Alcock. At this time a body of soldiers were approaching the hustings, who it was supposed would have voted for mr. Alcock:—A drunken fellow, who observed them, raised the *hue and cry,* and swore that no soldiers had a right to vote there;—his turbulence was noticed by the magistrates present, who commanded the peace, and ordered the man into custody. It is said that mr. Wilcox, jun. went to the man, shook his fists at him, and menaced him with the jail. The man, when in custody of the constables, promised to be peacable; some of the people ran to him, rescued him from the constables, and one of them, armed with a cudgel, threatened to knock Wm. Allan esq. down if he interposed. "Turn out [ms illegible] this is [ms illegible] was [ms illegible] tered by several; and at this moment of confusion capt. Paxton[10] and Wm. Jarvis esq. gave their votes for mr. Alcock. The poll had been, at the beginning of these appearances, adjourned to the ensuing day. Mr. Weeks, seeing that mr. Alcock had at this juncture a majority, insisted that the poll should be closed, in which he was joined by mr. Alcock and the returning officer, seemingly intimidated and bewildered, complied, after having but a moment before adjourned it. The other candidates, except mr. Heron, were struck silent with this inconsistency, he made a verbal protest against it as being illegal:—mr. Weeks bellowed out, "give him law mr. Alcock!"—Mr. M'Donell argued that it was improper, and mr. Alcock told him he ought not to come forward as an advocate on that business. The riot act was then read by Wm. Wilcox, esq. and the people voluntarily dispersed. Mr. Weeks, who had recovered from his apparent consternation, congratulated his friends on the success of the manoeuvre.—Junior printer[11] and he had [line illegible] the occasion, "this is the way we manage elections; if we cannot do it in one way we can in another."

The people, conceiving their rights had been infringed, were highly dissatisfied; and a petition, signed by ninety-eight freeholders who had not voted, was presented to his excellency the governor.—It was handed in on the 25th at the hour of 5 P.M.—They were desired to call the ensuing day for an answer. Mr. Geo. Playter and capt. B. Wilson accordingly waited on his excellency at the appointed time, when they were informed that it was out of his power to order a new election, but

[10]Captain Thomas Paxton (1754–1804) was born in Newcastle, England, and entered the Marine Department on Lake Ontario on Dec. 25, 1787. He was Captain of the *Speedy* and was lost with his ship.

[11]Titus Geer Simons (1765–1829) was the son of the Loyalist Titus Simons. From 1797 to 1801 the *Upper Canada Gazette* was published by William Waters and T. G. Simons, who explained that his name was second only because of his younger age, and that he did most of the work. About 1802 he moved to West Flamborough, where he died.

referred them to the house of assembly, and recommended to them to take every regular step, and the grievance should be redressed—and assured them that nothing should be wanting on his part to see the inhabitants righted. This news gave new spirits to the people, who were so much affected by the illegal proceedings of some on the day before, that the generality of them declared their intentions of quitting the country.

An impartial Bystander.

F 8 The *Upper Canada Gazette*'s Account of the Election
[*York,* Upper Canada Gazette, *July 26, 1800*]

The poll for the Election of a Member to serve in parliament for the East Riding of the County of York, was closed yesterday, when HENRY ALCOCK, Esq. was declared to be *duly elected.*—The election terminated sooner than was expected, by consequence of a daring Riot instigated by persons inimical to Peace and good Order, and to the *pure exercise* of that valuable privilege of the subject—*the elective franchise.* After the Returning Officer closed the poll, conformably to precedents established in such cases—he called upon the Magistrates to check any further outrage, and by their spirited exertions tranquillity was in the course of the evening restored.

It was a matter of much regret to a large majority of those who were sensible of the advantages to be derived from the election of a character, distinguished for talents and virtue, that they were prevented, (by the acts of the riotous and disorderly) from enrolling themselves among the number of independant electors who supported Mr. Alcock—they have, however, in common with the public, to rejoice that the majority of the poll, has secured to the country his services, and enabled them to look with confidence, to a faithful and an independant representative.

☞ We hear that every legal measure is resorted to, to bring the rioters to exemplary punishment.

F 9 Norval Deplores the Riot
[*York,* Upper Canada Gazette, *August 16, 1800*]

. . . I have my friends, endeavored to convince you by the fairest reasoning, of the impropriety of loading the shoulders of ignorance with a burthen which consummate wisdom finds difficult to bear. I have invariably endeavored to impress your minds with truths, which, if made the means of regulating your votes, will establish in the strongest light, my love to my country, its subjects and laws. It is this love that leads me to lament, that disposition to riot, which was manifested by some, and produced the disagreeable issue to the late election. I here invoke the pity of Infinite Goodness on the people, whose liberties are to be protected and whose rights are to be explained by a wretch, notorious for his insolence, ignorance and brutal intemperance, and whatever else is disgusting and degrading to humanity! If when so large and respectable a body of the people are assembled on so solemn an occasion, their proceedings were to be interrupted and themselves so grossly insulted by the most despicable of mortals—authority would be a mockery, and solemnity a farce, if such an outrage could pass with impunity. To what purpose form we a magistracy? To what end speak of order, or civil subordination?—but to curb the unruly—to correct the turbulent and immoral—and guard public and private peace from insult and breach.

If there are men among us, such enemies to their country and good government, as daringly to thwart the mild operation of authority when exerted for the general good, and general harmony, may they suffer for their presumption—may the intemperance of their conduct, and the wickedness of their designs meet with adequate and merited punishment.

By nature and habit, I am an enthusiastic admirer of liberty—not that mistaken liberty which would protect insult and insolence in a worthless vagrant, whose very appearance is the INSIGNIA of depravity—of wretchedness and contempt. I shall not say, that this object of odium, was tutored for a purpose—I shall however presume to say, that an evil unrestrained is tacitly approved. . . .

When the combustion, (occasioned by this representative of insignificance) had in a measure subsided, how painful was it, to hear many of the people avow their intentions of quitting the country! What superlative absurdity in them to imagine that the gilded opinions and interested efforts of a lawyer[12] (since of all practical lawyers—the fee is the leading star,) was a stab to their liberties! Was the election illegal—the avenue of redress was open—an enlightened and patriotic Governor has pledged himself to aid and patronize the investigation.

I do not wish, and far be it from me, to attempt a justification of what must be left to abler judges to pronounce upon. I console myself in the full assurance that neither illegality or impropriety will be allowed or pass unnoticed, when the subject involves, such incalculable consequences.

NORVAL.

York, 1st Aug. 1800.

F 10 PROCEEDINGS OF THE HOUSE OF ASSEMBLY
[*Niagara,* Niagara Herald, *June 13, 1801*]

June 10

The house spent this day on the petition of Samuel Heron and others.

The petition being read, Angus M'Donnell, esq. counsel for the petitioners, opened the business with a short statement of the grounds

[12] William Weekes?

of complaint, and called nine witnesses only to establish the points. The day being wholly spent in examination on this part, mr. Alcock was requested to produce his witnesses on to-morrow—and adjourned.

(*The testimony was very clear that persons voted who had no right to vote: that the poll adjourned until next day, then took two votes, one of which was without the knowledge of the voter, which gave together a majority of 2 to mr. Alcock, then closed, while from 50 to 100 were waiting to vote,and were thereby deprived of an opportunity, with other unfair measures, by which mr. Alcock was procured to be returned as the member.*)

June 11.

Mr. Alcock not producing any testimony on his part, the house, without debate, nem. con. declared that Henry Alcock esq. is not duly elected, and that the speaker issue out a warrants to the proper officer for a new election in the east riding of York, and the counties of Simcoe & Durham.

(*For singularity of unfairness this election is scarcely to be equalled. —The testimony was lengthy from so many persons, repeating almost the same thing in substance as above. . . .*)

F 11 Cartwright's Account of the Proceedings

[*Cartwright, "Memorandum of transactions in first Session of the third provincial Parliament of Upper Canada," printed in C. E. Cartwright, ed.*, Life and Letters of the Late Hon. Richard Cartwright, *116–18, 121*]

. . . The House of Assembly were next occupied in settling the mode of proceeding on a petition of the inhabitants of York and Northumberland respecting a disputed election, and examining into the merits of the petition. The result was that Mr. Justice Alcock, the sitting member, was declared not duly elected, and the election itself void. It appeared in evidence that very unwarrantable steps had been taken by the friends of Mr. Alcock to procure him to be returned. A large majority of the electors were evidently against him; but while those on his side were giving him votes, a drunken man of the opposite party was ordered to be taken into the custody of a constable for some noisy behaviour which, on such an occasion, might very well have been passed over. This act of authority gave such offence to some of the bystanders that they interposed themselves between him and the officer after he had been arrested, by which means the man made his escape in the crowd. While this was doing, two or three people were hastily called up to vote for Mr. Alcock, which gave him a small majority; and hereupon a Mr. Weeks, an Irish lawyer, the Judge's most active agent, cried out, "A riot! a riot!" and prevailed with the returning officer to close the poll. During the whole of this investigation, Mr. Alcock behaved in a most extraordinary manner, being constantly present in the House and taking notes, but pertinaciously declining to reply to the attorney for the petitioners, or to enter at all upon a vindication of his election. Before the House had come to a determination, he handed to some of the members, while the House was sitting, a paper, drawn up by his friend the Attorney-General, stating doubts of the competency of the House to decide the case, as no law had been enacted in the Province relative to this subject, and the law that regulated such proceedings in England being wholly inapplicable here from the paucity of members, and concluding with the insinuation that the Governor might very probably not agree to the issuing another writ. When all the evidence had been gone through, and the result was to be determined upon, Mr. Alcock was, at the request of the House, desired by the Speaker to withdraw; but he replied that "he was still a member of that House, and would not withdraw unless they threw him out *neck and heels,*" and he actually kept his seat while the resolutions respecting himself were determining. Such conduct requires no comment. It is allowed that some of the members had, individually, little claim to respectability, and that some others held doctrines respecting the extent of their authority that no reasonable man would subscribe to; yet, as a public body, they have, unquestionably, a claim to at least the appearance of respect, and when this is so glaringly withheld by persons high in office, it tends evidently to excite opposition against the Government itself, and to raise an idea that they wish to control, in an authoritative manner, the freedom of their deliberations. It seems hardly proper for a Judge of the Court of King's Bench to become a candidate for a seat in a popular Assembly. The usual mode of canvassing for such a situation but little accords with the gravity and dignity expected in such a character, and it might be feared that in the administration of criminal law he would not be altogether unbaissed should any of his opponents be convicted before him in cases where the penalty is undefined and left to the discretion of the Judge. But there seemed to be a peculiar degree of indecorum in a person of this description taking his seat in the House of Assembly under a return which had been obtained by the most glaring violation of law. . . .

During these proceedings a new writ was issued for the Counties of York and Northumberland, and Mr. Angus McDonell, the late Clerk of the House of Assembly, was elected by a large majority, and took his seat as a member. Mr. Alcock declined becoming a candidate on this occasion, yet the people, whose zeal was occasionally heightened by the effect of ardent spirits during this exercise of their sovereign authority, showed a strong disposition at intervals to insult him and his friends. . . .

F 12 Election Results, 1801

[*York,* Upper Canada Gazette, *July 4, 1801*]

Last Friday at the final close of the Poll, for a Member to represent the county of Durham, East riding of the county of York, and the county of Simcoe, in the present Parliament of this Province, Angus M'Donell, Esq; was declared duly elected; there appearing for him 112 unquestionable votes, and for J. Small, Esq; 32—Majority 80.

F 13 ANGUS MCDONELL'S ELECTION ADDRESS [*York*, Upper Canada Gazette, *May 5, 1804*]

To the Worthy Inhabitants of the East Riding of the County of York, and Counties of Durham and Simcoe.

FRIENDS & FELLOW SUBJECTS,

IN addressing you by Apellations unusual, I believe, on similar occasions, no affectation of singularity has dictated the Innovation; my Terms flow from a more dignified Principle, a purer source of Ideas, from a sentiment of liberal and extensive Affection, which embraces and contemplates not only such of you as by Law are qualified to vote, but also such as a contracted and short sighted Policy has restrained from the immediate enjoyment of that Privilege. Your Interests inseparably the same, and alike dear and interesting to me, have always been equally my care; and your Good Will shall indiscriminately be gratifying, whether accompanied with the Ability of advancing my present Pursuit, or confined to the wishes of my succeeding in it.

The anxious anticipation of Events which has engaged so many Persons into such early struggles to supplant me, forces me also, to anticipate the Dissolution of Parliament, in declaring my disposition to continue, (if supported by my Friends, at the next General Election,) in that Situation which I have now the honor of filling in Parliament; a Situation, which the great Majority of suffrages which places me in it, justifies the honest Pride of supposing, was not obtained without Merit, and inspires the rational confidence of presuming, will not be lost without a Fault.

I stoop with Reluctance, Gentlemen, to animadvert upon some puny Fabrications, circulated to mislead your Judgment, and alienate your Favour. It has been said, that I am Canvassing for a Seat elsewhere; No, Gentlemen, the Satisfaction, the Pride of Representing that Division of this Province, which, comprehending the Capital, is consequently, the Political Head, is to me, too captivating an Object of Patriotic Ambition, to suffer the view of it to be intercepted in my Imagination for a moment, by the prospect of any inferior Representation; be assured, therefore, Gentlemen, that I shall not forsake my Post, until You or Life shall have forsaken me.

Another Calumny of a darker hue, has been fabricated. I have been represented as inimical to the repeal of the Provincial Statute which restrains many worthy Persons migrating into this Province from voting at Elections, under a residence of Seven Years: A more insidious, a more barefaced falsehood, never issued from the lips of Malice; for, during every Session of my sitting in Parliament, I have been the warmest, the loudest Advocate for repealing that Statute, and for rendering Taxation and Representation reciprocal.

I shall notice a third expedient, in attempting which, Detraction (by resort to an Imposture so gross as to carry its own refutation upon the very face of it,) has effectually avowed its own Impotency:—It has been whispered, that I have endeavoured to encrease the general Rate of Assessments within the Home District. Wretched misrepresentation! I should have been my own Enemy indeed, if I had lent myself to such a measure. On the contrary, my Maxim has always been, and shall ever continue to be, that so much of the Public Burthen as possible, should be shifted from the shoulders of the Industrious Farmers and Mechanics, upon those of the more opulent Classes of Community; Persons with large Salaries and lucrative Employments: the shallow artifice of these exploded Fibs, suggests this natural reflection, that Slander could find no real foundation to build upon, when reduced to the necessity of rearing its Fabricks upon Visions.

To conclude, Gentlemen, I have no Interest separate from yours—no Country but that which we inhabit in common.—In all situations, under all circumstances, I have been the Friend of the People, and the Votary of their Rights.—I have never changed with the Times, nor shifted sides with the Occasion, and you may therefore reasonably confide that I shall always be, Gentlemen, Your Most Devoted,

And Most Attached Servant,

A: MACDONNELL.

York, 2*d May*, 1804.

F 14 John Cameron's Election Address
[*York*, Upper Canada Gazette, *January 12, 1805*]

THE much to be lamented, and truly affecting loss[18] sustained by the Public, in the premature fates of so many valuable Citizens, is a calamity of melancholy magnitude and distressing operation; and is to the interests as well as the feelings of this small Community, a wound bordering upon vital; a wound which will long remain unhealed, and a disaster of which the effects will be painfully felt by the Bench, the Bar, Society, the Legislature and the Country.

. . .

Gentlemen, the unfortunate event will consequently produce an Election to the vacant seats in the House of Assembly. For that of York, so ably and so honorably filled by my departed Friend, I offer myself a Candidate. If I succeed to it, my abilities, however slender, I pledge myself religiously to consecrate to the Service of my Country: and may that liberty which is the birthright of Freemen and the gift of our God,

[18]On October 7, 1804, the schooner *Speedy* left York for Presqu'Isle, but was lost in a storm. There were about 20 on board, including R. I. D. Gray, member of the House of Assembly representing Stormont and Russell, and Angus McDonell, member for Durham, Simcoe, and the East Riding of York.

be perpetuated by a well disposed People and a well chosen Legislature. I shall be thankful for Support at the day of Election,

York, *4th January*, 1805.

F 15 William Weekes' Election Address
[*York*, Upper Canada Gazette, *January 26, 1805*]

MR. WEEKES avails himself of this public manner of soliciting the support of the FREE and INDEPENDENT Electors of the East Riding of York and the Counties of Durham and Simcoe, at the next election of a Member to represent the Inhabitants of this Circle in Parliament. It is, he trusts, unnecessary for him to express, that, in aspiring to the honor of being one of the Representatives of the People, he bears in mind the importance of that situation, and the necessity of a faithful discharge of its functions. The particular occurrences in public affairs, whether viewed in the enacting of a law, or in enforcing the letter of it, or in the palpable effects of both, or whether developed in the official arrangements of civil departments, carry with them, in every political hemisphere, this monition, that the vigilance of the legislator over the rights and privileges of his Constituents ought to be incessant; and that a due regard to the interests of the People, and a mild and impartial administration of justice, can best promote the prosperity of a State, and perpetuate its establishments—this observation is not merely founded on the dictate of sentiment, but on the written letter of the law asserted in the wisdom of ancient parliaments, and confirmed amidst the contending factions of later times: for in the great Charter of English liberty it is concisely and emphatically declared that "no freeman shall be arrested, or imprisoned, or disseissed of his tenements, or deprived of his liberties or privileges, or outlawed, or banished, or in any other manner destroyed, except by the judgment of his peers, or in the law of the land" and in that second Charter of personal liberty the HABEAS CORPUS Act, it is propitiously provided that "any person who shall send another, prisoner out of the Realm, or beyond the Seas, Contrary to the law of the land, shall be disabled from bearing any office, shall incur the penalty of a praemunire and be incapable of receiving the King's pardon; and the party suffering shall also have his private action against the person so committing and all his aiders, advisers, abettors and shall recover treble costs besides his damages, which no jury shall assess at less than five hundred pounds."[14]

[14]Weekes is referring to the passage during the previous session of "An Act for the better securing this province against all seditious attempts or designs to disturb the tranquility thereof." Under this Act, any person not having been resident six months in the province, nor having taken the oath of allegiance, who was suspected of seditious words or actions, could be summoned by the Governor or Administrator, or any member of the Executive or Legislative Councils, or any judge, or anyone else designated by the Governor, to prove his innocence. If unable to do so to the satisfaction of this one person, he would be summarily banished. This Act was not repealed until 1829.

In these, as well as in many other acts of legislation, are legibly marked the integrity and Independence with which the Representative in former times conducted himself in the service of the Public; but in none more particularly than in those acts which guard against the imposition of aids, taxes or other charges under the colour of prerogative, in which it is declared that "levying money for or to the use of the Crown by pretence of prerogative without grant of parliament, or for longer time, or in other manner than the same is or shall be so granted, is illegal."[15] and in virtue of which the most invaluable privilege is preserved to the subject, and a barrier erected against the enforcing of contributions either oppressive or unjust. The venerable antiquity of those laws, some of which have withstood the test of several centuries, unaltered and unrepealed, proves their efficacy, and affords this induction that those, who maintain the immunities of the people, do more than render a temporary benefit to their Country, inasmuch as that a security against arbitrary or oppressive measures tends not only to preserve the tranquillity, but also to promote the prosperity of the State, and establishes a monument of worth to the latest posterity. How far it may be laudable at this juncture to emulate the spirit and letter of these acts, in the revision and amendment of provincial laws of no less importance to the people; particularly the act for the qualification of Electors and the Jury Act, and to take a more general view of the management and posture of public affairs, it is not for Mr.WEEKES in the situation of an election Candidate to affirm; but shall he be favored with the efficient support of those who enjoy the freedom of Suffrage, and feel the independence to exercise it, he indulges himself in the hope, that their rights will at least be more generally known, if not more fully asserted.

York, 24*th January*, 1805.

F 16 JUDGE THORPE[16] TO JOSEPH WILLCOCKS[17]
[*P.R.O., C.O.42, v. 343, pp. 194–5; microfilm copy in P.A.O.*]

. . . As to representing the Home District I have written fully to Mr.

[15]General Hunter from 1803 had authorized expenditure for the administration of justice and the civil government, without the sanction of the Legislature. In 1806 when President Grant did the same thing, and authorized the expenditure of £617.13.7, the House of Assembly, in which Weekes was now a prominent member, objected. Gore agreed that the objection was valid and had the money returned to the Treasury. The House then waived claim to it and passed the original expenditure.

[16]Robert Thorpe was called to the Irish Bar in 1781, and was a protégé of Lord Castlereagh. He was appointed Chief Justice of Prince Edward Island in 1802, and a puisne judge of the Court of King's Bench of Upper Canada in 1805. He immediately assumed leadership of the anti-government forces, and in 1807 was suspended by Gore. He was later appointed Chief Justice of Sierra Leone, where he again got into difficulties.

[17]Joseph Willcocks (d. 1814) was a distant relative of William Willcocks and came to York from Ireland in 1800. He was probably sympathetic to the United

Wyatt,[18] and to him and yourself I have left to determine for me, on certain terms, I will not go amongst the people, nor keep open houses for drinking, nor involve myself in expense, but if the people chuse to meet, put me in nomination almost unanimously and appoint Committees to compleat the Election without trouble or expense, I will give my time and labor for the public service and toil incessantly to make them as free and happy as any Nation on the Earth, my Sentiments are fully known, I never will change them, but to be in the House of Representatives, cannot raise me or serve my family, and the trouble, toil, anxiety and fatigue, it must give me, will be immense, therefore surely I ought to avoid it, and if I accept it to serve the public, it must not be by doing any thing, derogatory to the Situation I hold or incompatible with my feelings and principals, I see every annoyance to myself, yet altho' it may drive me from the Province in Six months, I do think I could serve the Country, and could lay the foundation of future good, but my sanguine wish is that the Governor will agree with me, and in that case it is incalculable the advantage that may be obtained.—You know the persons that ought to be consulted, bring them to Mr. Wyatt, and consider what is best to be done, I will slave for the people and if called into action I will fight to the stumps, but your friend is full I hope of high honor, proper pride, and acute feelings, therefore preserve these, tho' I may be about sacrificing every comfort and every Situation. . . .

October 16th, 1806.

F 17 THORPE IS REQUESTED TO STAND
[*York*, Upper Canada Gazette, *November 8, 1806*]

At a Meeting of Freeholders held at Moore's Hotel,[19] on the 20th ult. for the purpose of considering of a proper person to Represent them in Parliament, William Willcocks Esquire, in the Chair, it was resolved

---

Irish movement. Until 1802 he lived with Peter Russell, as a clerk and friend, but a difficulty concerning Elizabeth Russell lost him this patronage, and he transferred his allegiance to Judge Allcock. In 1803 he was appointed Sheriff of the Home District, from which position he was dismissed in 1806 by Gore. In 1807 he founded in Niagara the *Upper Canadian Guardian, or Freeman's Journal,* violently critical of the Government. He represented Lincoln, Haldimand, and the West Riding of York in the House of Assembly from 1808 to 1812. At the beginning of the war he was loyal, but as the war progressed he went over to the Americans, and was killed at the siege of Fort Erie, while serving as a colonel in the American army.

[18]Charles Burton Wyatt was the third son of the famous architect, James Wyatt. He was employed in Calcutta by the East India Company, returning to England in 1801. In 1804 he was appointed Surveyor General of Upper Canada, arriving in York in 1805, after a runaway marriage which alienated his father. He joined the anti-Government group, and, after a series of collisions with the Governor, was dismissed by Gore in 1807. Returning to England, he brought a libel suit against Gore and in 1816 obtained a judgment for £300.

[19]Robert Moore kept the tavern formerly kept by William Cooper.

unanimously, That Mr. Justice Thorpe be requested to Represent the Counties of York, Durham and Simcoe, in the place of our late much lamented William Weekes Esq. deceased;[20]—where it was also resolved, That the Meeting should be adjourned to the 27th, and that notice should appear in the next Gazette.

(Signed)
WILLIAM WILLCOCKS, Chairman.

At the Meeting, pursuant to the said Adjournment, (the Chairman being unavoidably absent) the following Address was unanimously agreed upon:—

To the Honorable Mr. Justice THORPE.

SIR,

OVERWHELMED with grief at the unexpected death of our late able and upright Representative, we Freeholders of the Counties of York, Durham and Simcoe, feel that we have neglected our interests in the season of our sorrow.—Now awake, it is to you we turn; notwithstanding the great portion of consolation which we draw from the dawning of an impartial and energetic administration.

Fully persuaded that the great object of your heart is the advancement of public prosperity, the observance of the laws, and the practice of religion and morality, we hasten with assurances of our warmest support, to invite you from your retreat to represent us in Parliament.

Permit us however, to impress upon you, that as subjects of a gracious and beloved King; as a part of that Great Nation which has for so long a time stood the bulwark of Europe, and is now the solitary and inaccessible asylum of liberty; as the Children of Englishmen, guided, protected, and restrained by English laws; in fine, as members of this community, as fathers and sons we are induced to place this confidence in your virtue, from the firm hope, that equally insensible to the impulse of popular feeling and the influence of power, you will pursue what is right—this has been the body of your decisions, may it be the spirit of your counsels.

Signed by forty-two Persons, residing in the Town and Township of York.

When William Jarvis Esquire, was requested to wait on Mr. Justice Thorpe (who at that instant had arrived from Niagara) to know his pleasure upon the subject of the above Address; Mr. Jarvis returned with a favourable answer, which Mr. Justice Thorpe has since communicated in the following terms:—

GENTLEMEN,

WITH pleasure I accede to your desire, if you make me your Representative I will faithfully discharge my duty; your confidence is not misplaced, may the first moment of dereliction, be the last of my existence.

[20]William Weekes was killed on October 10, 1806.

Your late worthy Representative I lament from my heart; in private he was a warm Friend, at the Bar an able Advocate, and in Parliament a firm Patriot; it is but just to draw consolation from our Governor, when the first act of his administration,[21] granted to those on the U.E. list, and their children what your late most valuable Member so strenuously laboured to obtain; surely from this, we have every reason to expect that the liberal intentions of our beloved Sovereign, (whose chief glory is to reign triumphantly enthroned on the hearts of a free people) will be fulfilled, honoring those who give, and those who receive, enriching the Province and strengthening the Empire.

Let us cherish this hope in the blossom, may it not be blasted in the ripening.

I am, Gentlemen, very truly,
your obliged and obedient
humble servant,
ROBERT THORPE.

York, Nov. 7

P.S. If influence, threat, coercion or oppression should be attempted to be exercised over any individual, for the purpose of controlling the freedom of Election, let me be informed.

R.T.

F 18 Titus Geer Simons' Statement
[*P.R.O., C.O. 42, v. 343, pp. 110–12; microfilm copy in P.A.O.*]

I, Titus Geer Simons of the Township of Flambro' West in the County of York, in the Home District of the Province of Upper Canada, Gentleman, make Oath on the holy Evangelist of Almighty God, before Duncan Cameron Esquire, one of his Majesty's Justices of the Peace in and for the District aforesaid, do declare that on the 27th day of November now last past, having rode in Company with several Gentlemen to the house of Mr. John Mills Jackson,[22] on Yonge Street, and was there invited by the said Mr. Jackson to dine with him and some other Gentlemen, to wit, Captain Richard Ferguson,[23] Mr. Sheriff Willcocks,

[21]On Oct. 31, 1806, Gore proclaimed that persons or descendants of persons who joined the Royal Standard before 1783, were resident in Upper Canada on July 28, 1798, and continued to reside there, but were not on the U.E. List, might upon application have their names added to it.

[22]John Mills Jackson (1764?–1836) was born on the Island of St. Vincent, and educated at Oxford. He came to Upper Canada in 1806 and settled on his farm on Yonge Street, called Springfield, and later on Lake Simcoe at Jackson's Point. In 1809 he published *A View of the Political Situation of the Province of Upper Canada*, which was extremely critical of the Governor and Council.

[23]Richard Ferguson had served in the King's Rangers, and became a captain in the Royal Canadian Volunteers in December, 1798. He was living in York Township, and was appointed a magistrate in 1804.

Baron de Hoen, Lieut. Besserer[24] and Mr. Cheniquy—We sat down to dinner at a late hour. The then approaching Election became the topic of conversation, in which Mr. Jackson and Mr. Willcocks appeared warmly interested—Immediately after removing the Cloth, the King's health was drank, and that of several Noblemen in England of whose friendship and confidence Mr. Jackson boasted. I was asked for a toast, I gave the Lieut. Governor of the Province—"Apropos" said the Sheriff "how is the Governor spoken of in your neighbourhood?" (meaning the head of the Lake) those said I, who have had any business to transact with his Excellency have met with every satisfaction which the nature of their case required, for my part I can only speak from his general character, which I believe to be, an amiable one.—"So do I," said Mr. Sheriff, "and in order to exonerate him from the imputation which report is disseminating through the Country;—That I am most shamefully and most cruelly oppressed, for reasons unknown to myself and my friends—That he is my implacable enemy, and that his persecution will only cease on my being ousted—and I say in order to clear his Excellency from this charge, I will read a letter which I have this day received from the Solicitor General"[25]—he then pulled some papers from his Pocket; when Captain Ferguson rose from his chair and begged of him in the most friendly terms "not to read nor expose any official Papers as he conceived the Company a public or mixed one, and an improper place to exhibit public Papers, which respected his public situation, and much more so to make any comments on them—" The Sheriff then addressed himself to Mr. Jackson, saying, "this is the way that I am always oppressed and cannot say a word in vindication of myself—I have offered several Gentlemen of the first rank, men with fifteen hundred pounds Sterling as my Securities,[26] but they have been rejected, this day I have given in two more, Mr. Samual Thompson[27] and Mr. Addison,[28] if these are rejected the Country is ready to come forward and pay the money for me—" Mr. Jackson cried out, "read what you please—say what you please, you are at my table, I know that the Governor has used you as well as some others in this place, like a damned Rascal, but that his stay in this Country was of a short duration, that his friend was recalled and that he (the Governor) would soon experience the same fate, when things were properly stated at home—" Mr. Cheniquy got enraged, asked

[24]Ranny L. Besserer was a lieutenant in the Royal New Brunswick Regiment, later the New Brunswick Fencibles.

[25]D'Arcy Boulton.

[26]Willcocks as Sheriff was required to give sureties.

[27]Samuel Thompson was a Loyalist living at Niagara. He was a brother of Captain Andrew Thompson of Butler's Rangers, and Timothy Thompson, member of the House of Assembly.

[28]Rev. Robert Addison (1754?–1829) came to Upper Canada in 1791 as a missionary of the Society for the Propagation of the Gospel in Foreign Parts. He settled at Niagara. He and his daughter were suspected of anti-Government opinions.

Mr. Jackson "if he was not ashamed to call the Governor a damned Rascal? recollect" said he, "that you are speaking of the Kings representative—" "Damn the King and him too, what have I to expect from either of them? I have asked for no favors since I have been here, nor do I intend to ask for any.—" "If you make use of such language," said Mr. Cheniquy, "I will leave the room;" "leave it and be damned" said Mr. Jackson, "I care as little for you as I do for the Governor, or his Master—" Mr. Cheniquy left the room—Mr. Sheriff then said "that he did not doubt but that every word that had passed would be carried to the Garrison by the next morning at 10 O'Clock—" Captain Ferguson observed, "and so they ought to be, but I shall not do it, the admonitions which I gave you in the early part of the evening respecting your public papers were from motives of friendship—" "Damn your friendship, I hold it in as much Contempt, as that worthy man, Mr. Thorpe, the friend of the people, does the interest you are making against him" said Mr. Sheriff;—Captain Ferguson replied, "I have made no Interest for, nor against him—" "you have" said Mr. Sheriff "but notwithstanding all the interest which your Scotch faction have and can make, Mr. Thorpe will go into the House—" "I know of no Scotch faction" said Captain Ferguson, "nor am I of any Party, and your abuse, Mr. Sheriff, should not pass with impunity—" "yes" said Mr. Jackson, "that damned Scotch faction, with the Governor at their head are striving to bear down all before them, poor Mr. Wyatt has been most shamefully and most rascally treated by the Governor, both him and Mr. Sheriff have been thrown out of the Governor's house without assigning a Cause to either; but the time is not far distant when Mr. Wyatt shall have a Seat in the Executive Council—Mr. Thorpe Speaker of the House, and before twelve months I shall be returned for this place, to which another Member is to be added,[29] as also one to the London District—then Huzza for the man of the People, he must and will stand; but the Governor, what is his support, when the Country is against him, he must fall, he must come to his marrow bones." Mr. Sheriff then said: "I am determined, with Mr. Jackson's leave, to read this letter, be the future consequences what they may; Mr. Simons as a Stranger will see how I am oppressed without a shadow of cause—I have written to the Solicitor requesting to know what kind of security he required and I would obtain it—and this letter which I am going to read is an answer to it—" I think the Contents were nearly as follows:—"Sir, This is to say that the two Gentlemen whose names you give in for your Securities are deemed insufficient; I therefore hope that you will lose no time in procuring others—I am not authorized to reject or accept of any particular person; the Statutes of the Province are my Authority—" "Here

[29]York did not get a second member until the "Act to provide for Increasing the Representation of the Commons" was passed in 1820. In the 1821 election, the town of York elected one member, John Beverley Robinson, and the Riding of York and Simcoe two members, Peter Robinson and William Warren Baldwin.

you see Gentlemen" said the Sheriff "that the Solicitor General disavows any authority from the Governor for thus oppressing me by rejecting the Gentlemen whose names I have given in—" "Damn the Governor and the Government," said Mr. Jackson, "push about the bottle—" "Well," said Captain Ferguson, "I had it in contemplation to offer you my name, tho' I doubted its acceptance, but your imprudent Conduct this evening forbids it—" "Damn you and your friendship it is not to be depended upon, you dare not breathe without asking some of your damned faction," said Mr. Sheriff. Captain Ferguson immediately collared him and they rose from their chairs—we interfered and parted them, when Mr. Sheriff pulled off his Coat and ran out of the door, the Captain followed and brought him back very peaceable—Mr. Sheriff sat down again, and immediately began with Politics; I begged of him to keep his promise, which was to drop Politics as it only tended to keep the Company in Commotion— "By God," said he, "the Country from repeated infringements upon their rights and liberties, is now ripe for any thing; that Mr. Wyatt had sent home 25 or 26 pages of Manuscript, stating the disaffection of the People of this Province and the Cruelty and ill treatment, which he and his friends had experienced from the Governor—when these facts are properly stated at home, and when we shall have made some other arrangements in the Government, we shall then carry all before us by God.—"

(Signed) Titus G: Simons
February 2d. 1807—

Sworn before me at York, the
2d day of February 1807.
(Signed) D. Cameron, J.P.

F 19 T. B. Gough's[30] Second Election Address
[*York*, Upper Canada Gazette, *December 20, 1806*]

To the Independent Electors of the County of Durham, the East Riding of the County of York, and the County of Simcoe.

GENTLEMEN,

WHEN first I had the honor of Addressing you,[31] it was in a style of

[30]Thomas Barnes Gough (1760–1815) was born in Ireland. Shortly afterwards his family moved to Bristol, where he was educated. His family again returning to Ireland, he was apprenticed to a linen draper there, and entered business. With the outbreak of the Irish Rebellion, he immigrated to the United States, where he was a successful businessman in New York, with several mercantile adventures to South America. He came first to Upper Canada in 1801, bought land, and returned soon after to keep a store in York and Yonge Street. He was an unsuccessful candidate for York in 1806, but was returned in 1808. His obituary in the *York Gazette*, April 22, 1815, begins, "Before he lost sight of the counterpoise between a *Bonvivant* and *Sot*, he was a person of some public interest in this country."

[31]Gough's first conventional election address appeared in the same issue of the *Gazette*.

moderation suited to the fair and honorable Cause I had embarked in, the PUBLIC GOOD—at that time I did not expect to intrude myself further upon you; but on my going through the Country, I found the Agents of another Candidate had spread Calumnies, as false as they are despicable; knowing my Reputation in that part where I reside, and am best known, was unassailable by their impotent attacks, have had recourse to the vile artifice of telling you, that *I was to leave the Country immediately*; which is an infamous Falsehood.—Gentlemen, from the moment I concluded on offering you my Services, I determined, if I should be honored by your choice, on a faithful discharge of the Sacred Trust by a diligent attendance on my Duty. Many of you, Gentlemen, know the stake I have in the Country, which must attach me to it and its welfare.—How desperate and declining must the hopes of a Party be, to be obliged to have recourse to such low subterfuges?

I should not have troubled you with any boast of my Character or Circumstances, being so well known, but lest the imposition might impress those unacquainted with me, if not contradicted.

Yonge Street, 17th Dec. 1806.

F 20 QUETTON ST. GEORGE TO GORE
[*P.R.O., C.O. 42, v. 343, pp. 47–8; microfilm copy in P.A.O.*]

York 22nd December 1806.

I have received so many favors from the British Government that I think myself bound to it in gratitude, and as a loyal subject of the King, my duty obliges me in conscience to make you acquainted with what I know respecting some Individuals of this place.

A few days since I was desired to Call at Mr. Wyatt the Surveyor General, after my arrival there Mr. Wyatt told me that I ought as a man of property join the Opposition to the Government;—that the late Governor had acted improperly—that if Mr. Thorpe got into the House of Assembly, they expected he would have a Majority, and then the Government would go to the Devil.

Mr. Thorpe has stated to me that he condemned the conduct of the Secretary of the Province, in not prosecuting the Chief Justice.

The violent abuses I have heard spoke against the Government and your Excellency personally I will not repeat, as I felt ashamed of myself for having listened to it.

F 21 SAMUEL THOMPSON TO THORPE
[*P.R.O., C.O. 42, v. 350, p. 262; microfilm copy in P.A.O.*]

Niagara 24th Decr. 1806

. . . I am really astonishd. and think it hardly possible that Mr. Gough should take the active part I hear he is taking (Electioneering) however the freeholders must know his choice cant be good when he expended at the last Election 200 hundred dollars in opposing the man they made choice off, and the best they could get

As to the Taverns being kept open I should think by a proper representation that might be made a good handle of I have too good an opinion of the freeholders in the County to think they would sell their Votes for a glass of Grog

I really think it would answer a better purpose for you not to do any thing of that kind, only on the day of Election to have Liquor in some convenient place for the people to drink (and perhaps something to eat)—

Capt. Brant and Mr. Jones & several from the Head of the Lake will be at York—Mr. Jas Secord[32] here & Mr. R. from Chippewa & some others told me they woud. go, and was I able to go out of the door you would either see me or hear of my being laid up by the way. . . .

F 22 William Allan to Gore
[*P.R.O., C.O. 42, v. 347, p. 82; microfilm copy in P.A.O.*]

York, 5th January 1807.

I consider it my duty as Returning Officer at the late Election, to inform your Excellency that Mr. Justice Thorpe, is returned as Member.

Mr. Justice Thorpe, after the closing of the Poll, made a long harangue to the people then present (mostly his voters) as I conceived tending to disseminate principles by no means favorable to the Government of this Country, telling them "they did not know their value to Great Britain; there was no Law in this Country to prevent their meetings; that the Habeas Corpus Act had never been suspended here." He reminded them "of the separation of the United States from Great Britain—He loved the people &ca."—which appeared to me was intended to impress them with an idea, that their Situation in this Country might render them Independent of Great Britain.

As a Magistrate and a loyal subject, I have felt myself called upon to state the above circumstances to your Excellency.

F 23 Thorpe to Sir George Shee[33]
[*P.R.O., C.O. 42, v. 347, p. 34; microfilm copy in P.A.O.*]

. . . The Election of which I informed you in my last was delayed even longer than the Law permitted, the Lt. Governor & Storekeepers with all their force against the people, every species of undue influence,

[32]James Secord (1773–1841) served in the 1st Lincoln Militia during the War of 1812 and was wounded at Queenston Heights. He was the husband of Laura Secord.

[33]This letter is endorsed "Rd. 2d May 1807."

bribery, coercion and oppression, was used by them, the Lt. Governor himself demeaned by trying to seduce both high & low, I never asked a vote, I never left my house, they brought me to the hustings, the Election lasted a week, I was returned by an amazing majority (altho' I requested the people from a distance & the aged might be prevented from coming) the people returned in triumph execrating the Governor, in truth there never was such unconstitutional and such illegal proceedings experienced before. . . .

F 24 GOUGH'S STATEMENT AFTER ELECTION
[*York*, Upper Canada Gazette, *January 10, 1807*]

To the Independent and Respectable ELECTORS of the COUNTY of DURHAM, the East Riding of the COUNTY of YORK, and the COUNTY of SIMCOE, who honored me with their Support at the late ELECTION.

GENTLEMEN,

PERMIT me to return you my most sincere and grateful Thanks, for your exertions in my behalf in the late Contest; exertions as honorable to you as flattering to me; although your efforts have not, on this occasion, obtained their merited success, I pledge myself to pursue my endeavours, where I hope and have a confidence of attaining the object of your wishes.

You went to the Hustings, Gentlemen, under the Banners of Liberty, Loyalty and Union, with hearts animated with pure love of KING and CONSTITUTION, and many of you have proved your attachment thereto by shedding your blood in their support; but your opponents were preceded by the Standard of Discord, Anarchy and Rebellion, which in another part of the Empire had led thousands to a premature Death, and many who escaped the horrid carnage of the field, expiated their Treasons, in the vain attempt to sever the Crown from the Harp, by an ignominious exit at the Gallows, and their heads were affixed as public Spectacles, to warn the deluded; but Charity and the Honor of this Country impels me to hope it was only the incautious Indiscretion of the unthinking.

I have also to return my Thanks to many, who on account of the lateness of my offering myself as a Candidate, had so far previously engaged themselves as not to be able to retreat with consistency, though I had their warmest wishes, I could not avail myself of their Support.

Persevere, my friends, in your attachment to your King, maintain the good Order you have been accustomed to, pursue your industry, and cherish your domestic comforts; follow the dictates of reason but be not deluded by discontented Demagogues and when other parts of the world may be desolated by the ravages of war, or agitated by internal Commotion, you will be tranquil and secure.

York, 8th Jan. 1807.

F 25 Meeting of Thorpe's Supporters
[P.R.O., C.O. 42, v. 347, p. 54]

At a meeting of the independent Freeholders of the East riding of the County of York, and the Counties of Durham & Simcoe, held at Stoyle's Tavern, Janry 13th, 1807.

William Willcocks Esqr in the Chair

The following resolutions were unanimously agreed to.

Resvd. That as part of an Address[84] signed Thomas B. Gough & published in the Gazette of the 10 Janry tends to irritate & inflame the public mind, & as it might be used as an instrument for misrepresenting the loyal independant & constitutional exertions of the Freeholders who voted for Mr. Justice Thorpe, We feel it our duty to declare that the second paragraph of said address, is false, malevolent, & calculated to sow the seeds of discontent, & to diffuse ideas of the most dangerous tendency among the people—

Reslvd. 2 That the aforesaid Electors were not preceded by any flag of Discord, Anarchy, or Rebellion but were preceded by the most appropriate & constitutional flags, neither borrowed or hired for the occasion but constructed by themselves—The first large *flag* was *blue,* with *G.R.* & the *Kings Crown* over it, the Union Cross in the corner, & at the bottom, the Royal motto *Dieu et mon droit;*—The second pink flag with *The Freedom of Election* worked on it—& three smaller ones of dark blue, with the Harp (as taken from a compartment in the British Standard) surrounded with these words *The King, the People, the Law, Thorpe & the Constitution* more loyal or constitutional symbols could not have been displayed upon any occasion.

Resolvd. 3 That we know no discontented Demagogues nor if we did could not be deluded by them, many of us have fought, bled & sacrificed our families & properties for the British Government, we have exerted & ever will exert ourselves to preserve the freedom of Election from all undue influence to the last moment of our lives shall we be ready to support our King, & Constitution.

Resd. That the above Resolutions be published in the York Gazette.

signed W— Willcocks
Chairman

The Printer was not permitted to insert the above Resolutions in the Gazette, nor to print them in any shape—

F 26 Petition against Thorpe's Election
[Journals of House of Assembly; printed in P.A.O. Report, *1911, pp. 127–8]*

Monday, 9th February, 1807.

. . . Read, the Petition of Duncan Cameron, John Beikie, Alexander Wood, George Playter and sundry other Freeholders of the Counties of

[84] F 24.

Durham and Simcoe and the East Riding of the County of York, setting forth the ineligibility of Mr. Justice Thorpe as a Member in this Honorable House, for the aforesaid Counties and Riding, which is as follows.

To The Honorable the Representatives of the Commons of Upper Canada in

Parliament assembled.

The Petition of the undersigned Freeholders of the East Riding of the County of York and Counties of Durham and Simcoe.

Most Respectfully Sheweth:—

That His Majesty's Writ, bearing date the Twenty-first of November now last past, did issue for the election of a Knight to represent the East Riding of the County of York and the Counties of Durham and Simcoe in the Assembly of this Province in the place of William Weekes, Esquire, deceased.

That William Allan, of York, Esquire, was duly appointed Returning Officer for the said Riding and Counties, and did, on the Twenty-ninth day of December, proceed to such election.

That Robert Thorpe, Esquire, one of His Majesty's Judges in the Court of his Bench in this Province, and Thomas Barnes Gough, of York, Esquire, were the only candidates nominated by the respective Freeholders then and there present.

That Your petitioners previous to the closing of the poll, the election not being determined on view, did protest against the return of the said Robert Thorpe for the reason and causes hereafter set forth.

That the said Robert Thorpe has been returned as a Member for the said Riding and Counties, he having a majority of votes, to wit, two hundred and sixty-eight, and the said Thomas Barnes Gough only one hundred and fifty-nine votes, whereas Your Petitioners humbly conceive that the said Thomas Barnes Gough should have been returned Member of the said Riding and Counties for the reasons and causes following to wit.

That the said Robert Thorpe, at the time of such election, was, and still is one of His Majesty's Judges of the Court of his Bench in this Province.

That in England none of the Judges of the Court of King's Bench, Common Pleas, Barrons of the Exchequer who have judicial places, can be chosen Knight, Citizen or Burgess in Parliament.

That having adopted in this Province the law of England as a rule of decision, the said Robert Thorpe was not then and now is not eligible in this Province to sit as a Member in Your Honorable House of Assembly, that in the attainment of such an object as Judge, who decides on the life, liberty and property of His Majesty's subjects, must necessarily be liable to the frailties and passions incident to human nature, and may therefrom imbibe partialities, prejudices or prepossessions repugnant to and at war with the purity of the unsullied ermine, inimical to the independence and dignified administration of the law, and subversive of the free and constitutional liberties of His Majesty's subjects.

That Your Petitioners have further to state with great deference to Your Honorable House that this procedure is unconstitutional, inasmuch as being an attempt to clothe, arm and blend in one person, the conflicting powers, authorities and jurisdiction of the Legislature and Judicial functions contrary to the spirit of good government and the immemorial usage and custom of the Commons of England, whose rules of conduct Your Honorable House has adopted as the criterion of your decisions, where not otherwise specially provided for,

Wherefore your Petitioners, conceiving that the said Robert Thorpe was not lawfully returned, and that Thomas Barnes Gough was duly elected, pray that the said return may be reformed and amended, and the name of Thomas Barnes Gough be inserted on the roll, and the name of Robert Thorpe erased therefrom.

And as in duty bound your Petitioners will ever pray.[35]
York, 4th February, 1807.

F 27 Gore to William Windham[36]

[*P.R.O., C.O. 42, v. 343, pp. 61–2; microfilm copy in P.A.O.*]

York Upper Canada, 13th March, 1807.

. . . On Mr. Thorpes return to Niagara, the same indecent language against Persons, high in authority, and calumnies against the late General Hunter, Mr. President Grant, Chief Justice Allcock and Mr. Justice Powell, though wholly irrelevant to the Cause before the Court, were again heard at the Bar, and passed without reprehension from the Judge.

The indecency of Party Spleen, and private Animosity, being permitted to take place in a Court of Justice, was not allowed to pass without animadversion by one of the Counsel[37] (retain'd in the same cause with Mr. Weekes). This took place on a Monday, and his strictures at the time were little noticed by Mr. Weekes, who the next day made an excursion into the Country, and after passing the Evening and the greater part of the night of Tuesday at a Tavern with the Judge, and some other of his friends, he, on the Wednesday, sent a challenge to his Brother Advocate, and in consequence fell, the victim of his own turbulence and as is generally believed, of the indiscreet suggestions of the Party who met at the Tavern.

The opportunity this gave to Mr. Thorpe of openly standing forth as a Factious Demagogue, was not neglected; he was proposed by the Demo-

[35]The House then read a similar petition from T. B. Gough. On Feb. 10, 1807, it was decided "that the Petition of the Inhabitants of the Home District, complaining of the undue election of Mr. Justice Thorpe, does not contain sufficient grounds, if true, to make the election of the sitting Member for the Counties of Durham and Simcoe and the East Riding of the County of York void." Consideration on Gough's petition was deferred for three months. On February 25, 1807, a second petition from Gough was read protesting this postponement, which, however, was upheld by a majority of two.

[36]William Windham (1750–1810) was Secretary for War 1794–1801.

[37]William Dickson of Niagara.

cratic Party as a proper Person to succeed Mr. Weekes in the House of Assembly; and by the most solemn assurances, that he would pursue the same line of conduct, he secured his Election—The solemn mockery of his invoking, at the opening of the Poll, the shade of his departed friend "as looking down from Heaven with pleasure on their exertions in the cause of liberty"—The seditious emblem of his Party (a Harp without the Crown) Thorpe and the Constitution inscribed on badges, which he distributed to his partisans, and his almost Treasonable allusion to The American Revolution, in his Speech at the close of the Election, are indeed ample proofs, that he was not an unworthy successor to Mr. Weekes.

I had urged to Mr. Thorpe the impropriety of a Judge becoming a Candidate for a Seat in a Popular Assembly, and if such a step, was ever doubtful, the circumstances attending this Election, suffice to shew it, in the strongest point of view—Mr. Thorpe on the Hustings was frequently engaged in Altercations, with a Rival Candidate and his Electors, and was occasionally assailed with the severest and most humiliating sarcasms, on his private character, as well as his Public Conduct—he has lost for ever that respect, which his situation on the Bench ought, and is calculated to inspire, and it is impossible to suppose, that in the exercise of his Judicial Functions, he can be indifferent between his Friends and his Opponents; that he can forget the hostility and abuse of the one, or the favor and support of the other.

Two mechanics of low education and worse characters are among Mr. Thorpes intimate associates, one of them (Eliphatt Hale) was presented by the Grand Jury, for Blasphemy, and as I am informed, escaped conviction only by the removal of witness. . . .

F 28 Denial of Meeting Supporting Thorpe
[*York,* York Gazette, *August 29, 1807*]

Messrs. Printers,

AS a friend of truth, I am induced to request that you will insert in your Gazette for to-morrow the inclosed Declaration of a number of the most independent Electors of the Counties of York, Durham and Simcoe.

E. HALE, *High Constable, Home District.*

York, 28*th August,* 1807.

WE, the undersigned Freeholders, Electors and inhabitants of the Town of York and its vicinity, weighing the violence and indignity offered to Truth, to the Public, and our individual feelings, by the publication at Niagara in a paper calling itself the Upper Canadian Guardian, of a Meeting said to have been held in the town of York on the 24th July last, and of an Address to the Hon. Mr. Justice Thorpe, said to have been formed at the said meeting by the independent Electors of the Counties of York, Durham and Simcoe, do solemnly declare that we do not know any thing of such meeting; that we did not hear of the intention, or taking place of any such meeting—and that, after very diligent enquiry, we do not believe such meeting ever was contemplated, or did take place.

E. Hale,
Benjamin Cozens,
Archibald Thomson,
D. Cameron,
Thomas Hamilton,[38]
Gilbert J. Batchiller,[39]
John Edgell,[40]
Joseph Cawthra,
Paul Marian, [41]
Andrew Davidson,[42]
Lewis Bright,[43]
Bennona Lamson,[44]
John Bassell,[45]
Patrick Ward,[46]
Wm. Hunter,[47]
Joshua Leach,
Parshal Terry,[48]
Thomas Hull,[49]

[38]Thomas Hamilton (1770?–1835?) was born in Nova Scotia. He settled first in Upper Canada at Port Dover, moving to York about 1795. He kept a store and tavern in York, and another store on Yonge Street. He owned a small boat which ran between York and Niagara. For some time he was Coroner and also Deputy Sheriff.

[39]Gilbert John Batchiller appears only once in the List of Inhabitants in 1808, but was a Constable in York in 1807.

[40]John Edgell was born about 1771 in Boston. He first appeared in the List of Inhabitants in 1801.

[41]Paul Marian (d. 1808) was probably the first baker in York; he first appears in the List of Inhabitants in 1799. He was a native Frenchman. His bakery and tavern were continued by his wife Jane, who married in 1806 John Jordan, also a baker and tavern keeper.

[42]Andrew Davidson had a farm on Yonge Street, in Markham Township near Richmond Hill.

[43]Lewis Bright (1747–1842) was born in Gloucestershire, England, enlisted in the 47th Regiment in 1775, and served through the American Revolution. Discharged in 1784, he later enlisted in the Royal Canadian Volunteers. He first appears in the List of Inhabitants of York in 1804. From 1812 until 1840, he was Messenger of the Legislative Council.

[44]Benoni Lamson (Lampson) first appears in the List of Inhabitants in 1807, although he was a constable the previous year.

[45]John Bassell (Bassil) (d. 1813) was appointed Keeper and Crier of the Court of General Sessions in 1803. He suffered a concussion when the magazine blew up in the battle of York, but was placed in charge of the hospital set up by the Loyal and Patriotic Society after the battle. He died in the summer of 1813.

[46]Patrick Ward first appears in the List of Inhabitants in 1800.

[47]William Hunter was a blacksmith. He first appears in the List of Inhabitants in 1799.

[48]Parshall Terry (1756?–1808) was born in Orange County, N.Y., later moving to Wyoming Valley, Pa. He served through the Revolution as a lieutenant in Butler's Rangers, came to Canada as a Loyalist, and after living in Kingston and Niagara settled on the east bank of the Don River where he built a sawmill; he was a member in the first legislature representing the Fourth Riding of Lincoln and Norfolk. He married as his second wife Rhoda, daughter of Timothy Skinner. He was drowned on July 20, 1808, while attempting to cross the Don on a floating bridge.

[49]Probably Thomas Hill is intended. He was a sergeant in the Queen's

Wm. Sterritt,[50]
Robert Lackie,[51]
E. Wright,
Francois Belcour,[52]
Samuel Whelends,
Jacob Wurner,
Hugh M'Phie,[53]
Galor Starkweather,[54]
Hugh Carfrae,[55]
John Hunter, [56]
Henry Hale,[57]
James Crandford,
H. Heward,[58]
George Playter,
Ely Playter,
John Playter,[59]
Hugh M'Lean,
Forbes Mitchell,[60]
Samuel Heron,
F. Westphal,[61]

York, 15*th August*, 1807.

F 29 DENIAL IS CONTRADICTED

[*Niagara,* Upper Canada Guardian, *September 10, 1807; P.R.O., C.O. 42, v. 347, p. 61; microfilm copy in P.A.O.*]

TO THE PUBLIC

Whereas we have well known, that certain persons in office have been busily employed for near three weeks, in prevailing on various descriptions of people to sign a paper purporting their disbelief of a meeting held by independent Freeholders of York, Durham and Simcoe on the 24th

Rangers and served through the Revolution. He kept a tavern on Yonge Street, at Lansing.

[50]William Sterritt first appears in the List of Inhabitants in 1802. About 1808 he moved to Scarborough.

[51]Robert Lackie first appears in the List of Inhabitants in 1807. He was a baker.

[52]François Belcour (d. 1808) was a baker who came to York about 1805.

[53]Hugh McPhie first appears in the List of Inhabitants in York in 1800. In 1802 he was keeping a tavern in York. In 1805 and 1806 he is listed in York Township. He does not appear again.

[54]The Starkweather farm was on Yonge Street in Whitchurch Township north of Aurora.

[55]Hugh Carfrae first appears in the List of Inhabitants in 1804. He was High Constable 1805–6, and jailer from 1807 to 1811. He built the pound and the picketing around the jail.

[56]John Hunter was a blacksmith. He was constable in 1802, 1803, and 1806.

[57]Henry Hale was a builder and contractor. He owned a brickyard at the southeast corner of Duke and George Streets, which was sold in a Sheriff's sale in 1808 at the suit of Elijah Ketchum.

[58]Hugh Heward was the son of Hugh Heward who died in Niagara in 1803. He held a number of small government positions.

[59]John Playter (b. 1774?) was a son of George Playter. His land was across the Don River from his father's.

[60]Forbes Mitchell first appears in the List of Inhabitants in York Township in 1804. He had earlier worked as a clerk for Alexander Wood.

[61]Friedrick Ulrick Emijlius Westphal was born in Hamburg, Germany, in 1771. He was a farmer, and was secretary of Berczy's German settlement in Markham Township.

of July at Stoyle's Tavern, York, to address the Hon. Mr. Thorpe—this paper we paid little attention to then, because we were satisfied the public perfectly understood the object and motive with which it was carried about; however, as we now find the contents of that paper have been published in the York Gazette, under the authority of the High Constable Mr. E. Hale; we feel ourselves called on, as Chairman and Secretary to the meeting, to declare there was not only one, but two meetings,[62] the first held at Yonge street, the second in York; that the principal object of the Freeholders was concealment of their intention from the Judge, until the object was carried into effect; and to call only such to the meeting as could contribute without injury to themselves or families—And we do further declare, that the Freeholders were willing to have their names published with the address, but on the Secretary's waiting on the Judge with a copy, the day before it was presented the Judge himself requested the names might not appear, as he said "too many had already suffered for declaring their attachment to him." However, we now find it is the wish of those, who did sign then, and of others who could not attend at that time, but have since signed, to have all the names published, and we shall send them accordingly by the first safe opportunity, for insertion in the Upper Canada Guardian.

JOSEPH SHEPARD.[63]

Sept. 4, 1807. ALEXANDER MONTGOMERY.[64]

F 30 THORPE ANNOUNCES HIS SUSPENSION

[*Niagara,* Upper Canada Guardian, *November 5, 1807; P.R.O., C.O. 42, v. 347, p. 23, microfilm copy in P.A.O.*]

To the Freeholders of the East Riding of the County of York, and of the Counties of Durham and Simcoe.

GENTLEMEN.

WHEN you called on me to represent you in Parliament, I answered that if you placed me in the House of Assembly I would discharge my duty faithfully; but I am now hurried to England, from the most insidious MISREPRESENTATION of my conduct having induced the Secretary of State to signify his Majesty's pleasure to suspend me from my Judicial Situation in this province. However the noble Lord at the head of the Colonial Department,[65] is actuated by the highest sentiments of honor,

[62]The object of the meetings was to raise a sum of money for Judge Thorpe.

[63]Joseph Shepard (d. 1837) was an Indian trader, who settled on Yonge Street at the corner of Sheppard Avenue. Of radical politics, he and his family were implicated in the Rebellion of 1837, although he died a few months before.

[64]Alexander Montgomery (d. 1841) lived in Stamford, Conn. His father was a Loyalist, and he himself arrived in York in 1799. He was the father of John Montgomery of Montgomery's Tavern.

[65]Robert Stewart, Viscount Castlereagh (1769–1822), was Secretary of State for War and the Colonies, 1805–6, 1807–9.

and the strictest principles of justice; therefore, truth, like the divine rod of Aaron, will quickly overcome the machinations of the Magicians.

Though wretched, even to agony, whilst under the slightest imputation, yet your wellfare, your happiness and the prosperity of the province, shall engage my attention and animate my exertions. The objects dearest to me IN LIFE, I leave behind—that which is dearer THAN LIFE (MY HONOR) I hasten to defend; but if it pleases the Almighty to favor and protect me, my return shall be as rapid as my departure was unexpected.

Niagara, Nov. 2, 1807.

F 31 ROBERT HENDERSON'S ELECTION ADDRESS
[*York*, York Gazette, *April 30, 1808*]

As the period will shortly arrive when the dissolution of the present Parliament will of course take place, agreeable to the Constitution, I take the liberty to offer myself as a Candidate, not in the *common* stile of electioneering.

I think it is incumbent *for* every one who intends to have himself put in nomination to represent so respectable a *body,* but *they* should know *something* of his *creed.*

I am a British born subject, I have lived under the Government, I have *read* that great and wonderful *production,* the Constitution, and admire it. Its *origin* is from *Scripture* in Gothic ages, and after the conquest by William the Norman, it was *improved,* and has been by great and able statemen, preserved and supported by wholesome laws. The *three* estates, or *regal power,* when *united,* are like *three pillars* set apart at the *bottom,* and all joined at the *top,* the one supports the other.

I come now, Gentlemen, to the *arduous* part of my Address. For a Man to say any thing in *favor* of his own character, *assuredly* it must *touch* his *feelings*! I must observe, I have not, like your late honorable Member, been *solicited* to *accept* of the honorable office to represent you.

You will naturally say, why did you not vote and support his Election? My answer is the same I gave on that occasion, "that I did not think it proper *that* a judge should be one of the members to make laws which he himself might one day sit to decide upon."

It was from *principle,* not party spirit; I will say it, that no man or set of men, upon *Earth* should ever *bias* my *mind* contrary to my *conscience.*

Perhaps it may be said I am put in nomination by some party, to answer some purpose; I declare that I never consulted with a single individual on the subject, nor do I know at this moment I shall have *one* to *propose* me at the day of Election; however, if I should *chance* to be the *object* of your *choice,* I will endeavor to act as consistent with the sentiments of my Constituents, as shall *appear* to be for the good of the Province at large, and particularly *matters* that concern the *Home* District.

Gentlemen Electors, I have no *ambitious* views at my time of life; I am untried as a *politician;* but be assured it is nothing but *public good* which has prompted me to offer my service; if I see the majority of the Electors appears to be in favor of any other Candidate, I shall not attempt to stand a contested Election.

These are my sentiments without any *mask*. I might here add that having a desire to leave off the active part of my business, was the *only* motive that induced me thus to make my intentions public.

York, 6th April, 1808.

F 32 Gough Agrees to Stand
[*York,* York Gazette, *April 30, 1808*]

To Lieut. Colonel William Graham, Captain John Wilson, Parshal Terry, Esquire, Mr. John Lyon,[66] and the numerous and respectable Freeholders of the East Riding of the County of York and the County of Simcoe, who signed the foregoing requisition.

GENTLEMEN,

To be thus called upon by so respectable a portion of the Electors of this District, to fill a situation which the most eminent characters in the Province have been ambitious to attain, must be truly grateful to any man not devoid of sensibility, and would be ungenerous in *me*, and a dereliction of my former professions, to hesitate; I therefore cheerfully accept *your* offer of holding me up as a Candidate at the ensuing Election, and of supporting me by every fair and honorable means—by no other means would I wish to obtain the distinguished honor; and shall consider the person, who through too ardent zeal, may exercise any artifice or undue influence of any kind, to promote my election, as no friend of mine, of *yours*, or of the *Freedom of Election*, to maintain which you have so nobly volunteered. I neither have solicited nor shall I solicit a single vote, therefore hope no freeholder will be offended at my not personally calling upon him. You have begun the work, and the completion of it will be more honorable to you, and flattering to me.

I will not attempt to amuse you with the hypocritical professions of which electioneering addresses are mostly composed, or to deceive you with promises impossible to be performed; but with that truth and simplicity which no sophistry can misconstrue. I assure you, if I have the honor of being your Representative, of exerting my best and unceasing endeavours to promote the general interests of the Province, and to protect the civil and religious rights of my constituents of every denomination.

York, 25th April, 1808.

[66]John Lyon (Lyons) had a distillery on Yonge Street, on the east side south of Langstaff.

F 33 GEORGE RIDOUT TO T. G. RIDOUT, QUEBEC
[*P.A.O., Ridout Papers*]

York 25th. June 1812

. . . Among my other news I must not omit letting you know that Father is a Member of Parliament for the East riding of the Cy. of York & Simcoe. he was returned by a Majority of 142 agst. Sheppard the only candidate who opposed him as Hamilton, the morning of the Election, resigned his interest in favour of Mr Sheppard His heart failed him when he saw Father's friends to the amt. of 150. turning Leache's corner, huzzaing &a with their flags flying &ca. and he in the meanwhile surrounded by no more than ten or twelve of his adherents. Only six of the old Members are returned—consequently the remdr. are new, who will compose a very respectable House—John McDonell[67] is one of them—he was returned for Glengarry. Our Election here lasted three days and has cost us bet. 4 and 500 dollars—but we must not mind it as Father now stands a very fair chance for the Speakership[68]—indeed it commonly thought to be the case—Genl. Brock is much pleased with his appointmt. We had a famous electioneering dinner after the Polls closed consisting of most of the Gentlemen in York. . . .

[67]John Macdonell (1785–1812) studied law in York, was called to the Bar in 1808, and opened a law office in York. In 1812 he was appointed Attorney General and was also returned as a member for Glengarry. He was provincial aide-de-camp to General Brock and was killed with him at Queenston Heights.

[68]Allan MacLean (1752–1847), a prominent Kingston lawyer and member for Frontenac from 1804 to 1824, was chosen Speaker of the House of Assembly in the sixth Parliament.

G. RELIGION AND EDUCATION

G 1 WILLIAM COOPER OPENS A SCHOOL
[*York*, Upper Canada Gazette, *November 3, 1798*]

William Cooper

Begs leave to inform his Friends and the Public, that he intends opening a SCHOOL at his house in George-street, on the 19th instant, for the instruction of YOUTH in Reading, Writing, Arethmetic, and English Grammar. Those who chuse to favour him with their Pupils, may rely on the greatest attention being paid to their virtue and morals.

York, Nov. 3

G 2 PRAYERS IN THE GOVERNMENT BUILDING
[*York*, Upper Canada Gazette, *March 9, 1799*]

Notice is hereby given, that Morning Prayers will be read in the North Government Building in this town, on Tuesday the 12th instant, being the day appointed for a general Thanksgiving throughout this province to ALMIGHTY GOD, for the late important Victories[1] over the Enemies of Great Britain. Service to begin at half after eleven o'clock.

G 3 THOMAS RADDISH TO RUSSELL
[*P.A.O.*, *Russell Papers*]

No. 86 Portland Street London
March 9, 1799

From the favourable accounts of York, and its increasing population, the residence of a clergyman must now be highly necessary; I think it therefore my duty to inform you, that I will not trespass longer on your goodness, but am ready to resign in favour of any person, you may be pleased to nominate. I wish it were more lucrative, but the pittance is too inconsiderable, and sorry am I to observe, that the salary is very irregularly paid.—From the negligence of office, my situation has been extremely hard.—Not a shilling has yet reached the hands of the private agent, and had he not been assured of my responsibility, the bills would have been returned.—An indemnification is promised in land, and should a recommendation reach you, I am sure from the friendship and indulgence I have hitherto experienced, that I shall not fail of support.—No intimation of my intent to relinquish will be given

[1]News of the Battle of the Nile, August 1, 1798, first reached York on Jan. 5, 1799. It was followed by exaggerated accounts of Egyptian victories.

at The Duke's[2] office, because the Bishop of Quebec would soon be apprized of the event, and rejoice at an opportunity of presenting. . . .

G 4 Account for Tuition
[*T.P.L., Peter Russell Papers*]

The Honorable Peter Russell Esquire
To W Cooper
To 3 Months Tuition of black Boy £1.4.0
Octr. 28th, 1799
Rec'd the Contents W. Cooper

G 5 Cooper's Certificate as Schoolmaster
[*York Pioneer and Historical Society, William Cooper Papers*]

York Feby 17th. 1800

We do hereby Certify that Mr. Wm. Cooper has Kept a School in this Town upwards of two years,[3] the greater part of which time he has had the Educating of our Children, and in Testimony of our approbation of him as a Preceptor, and of his moral Character, we give him this Certificate

Jas. Macaulay
T. Ridout
W Chewett
John McDougall
Patrick Mealey
Joseph Hunt
Edwd. Wright
Saml. Heron
Thos. Stoyell
George Playter
John Denison

G 6 Bishop Mountain to the Society for the Propagation of the Gospel in Foreign Parts, Dated Woodfield, Canada, September 3, 1800
[*Society for the Propagation of the Gospel (S.P.G.), Journals XXVIII, 131–2; microfilm copy in P.A.C.*]

he expresses his hope, that as Lt. Genl. Hunter has nominated the Revd. George Stuart, a Son of his worthy Official at Kingston, to be Minister at York (vacant by the absence of Mr. Raddish) with the usual Salary from Government of £100 a year, the Society will have no objection to extend the same bounty to him, which they have bestowed upon the other Missionaries in that Province. The necessaries of life are at present very dear in that quarter, & the circumstance of being placed in the first society in the Province will necessarily bring with it some augmentation of annual expence. This very respectable appointment

[2]Duke of Portland, Home Secretary.

[3]Cooper gave up his school early in 1801 when it was taken over briefly by Levi Willard. In 1802 Willard was running a boat between York and the Head of the Lake.

Govr. Hunter has been induced to confer upon Mr. Stuart by the correct conduct, & the excellent character, of that young man.

Agreed in Opinion that the Bishop of Quebec be respectfully informed that the Society are well disposed to assist Mr. Stuart, but previously to any determination of a certain Salary, would wish to be furnished with more particulars respecting the situation & circumstances of York Parish, & of the abilities of the people who reside there.

G 7 REMINISCENCES OF NATHAN BANGS[4]

[*Abel Stevens,* Life and Times of Nathan Bangs, *p. 361*]

. . . What a change has been effected in this place! I believe I was the first Methodist preacher that ever attempted to preach in Little York—as Toronto was then called—and I preached in a miserable half-finished house, on a week-evening, to a few people, for there were not over a dozen houses in the place, and slept on the floor under a blanket. This was in 1801. I was then attempting to form a circuit on Yonge-Street, a settlement west of Toronto, and I was induced to make a trial in this new little village, the settlers of which were as thoughtless and wicked as the Canaanites of old. . . .

G 8 BISHOP MOUNTAIN TO THE S.P.G., DATED QUEBEC, OCTOBER 16, 1801

[*S.P.G., Journals, XXVIII, 209–10; microfilm copy in P.A.C.*]

. . . York is indeed the Seat of Government, where many of the principal people have their residence, but it is very far from being such a place as under this description the Society appear very naturally to have conceived. It is altogether in an infant state; the inhabitants not numerous; & in the opinion of some well informed people[5] not likely from its situation to be enriched by trade. The land around is chiefly the property of the servants of Government who reside in the Town, so that the farmers are thrown to a distance & every article of food must come several miles before it reaches the market. The settlements around thinly peopled, & of those the most flourishing is about 50 miles to the east. Grain is yet so scarce in the neighborhood that a brewer lately established at York has been obliged to transport wheat (for they use it instead of barley) from Kingston & the Bay of Quinte, 150 miles, in one of the King's vessels allowed him for that purpose. The greatest part of the pork, hams, beef, mutton, butter, & flour, consumed at York, is procured at Kingston, Niagara, & the Genesee Country, & some of

[4]Nathan Bangs (1778–1862) was born in Stratford, Conn. He came to Upper Canada, aged 21, and taught school near Niagara. In 1801 he was licensed to preach, and until 1808, when he returned to United States, he worked as a Methodist circuit rider in Ontario and Quebec.

[5]Possibly Rev. John Stuart (see D 17).

these articles so low down as Oswegatchie. It is true many of the inhabitants of York are able to contribute handsomely to the support of their Minister, but unfortunately they are not willing. Much has been said of the income to be raised by pew money, but unhappily the building of a Church is yet future. In the mean time Mr. Stuart, praised & respected by every body, is left to shift as he may. Upon his arrival at York he hired two small rooms at 10 dollars a month; for his dinner he paid 2s/6d daily; besides this, his breakfast, &c., Fire, & the expense of a servant were necessary; & finding that his £100 a year from Government, together with the expected bounty from the Society, would not with the utmost economy equal his expenditure, he has submitted to the labour of teaching a few scholars that he might not be burdensome to his Father. The Bp. trusts that from this representation the Society will be satisfied not only that Mr. Stuart is a proper object for their customary allowance, but that (if he has rightly interpreted the passage of their letter above quoted) the very circumstance of his being fixed at York, would place him among the first of those, to whom they would extend some increase of that allowance; such as they shall think the exigency of the case may call for. . . .

Agreed in Opinion that Mr. George Okill Stuart be appointed Missionary to York Town . . . with a salary of £50 a year: but that it be left to the discretion of the Bishop of Quebec to make such further addition to Mr. Stuart's salary as under all circumstances he may think advisable. . . .

G 9 Rev. G. O. Stuart to the S.P.G., Dated York, November 8, 1802

[*S.P.G., Journals, XXVIII, 337–8; microfilm copy in P.A.C.*]

he returns thanks for his appointment, & gives this account of his Mission. The Town of York consists of 120 houses, & about 70 families; but taking in the Township there may be about 140 families. Among them the different denominations that prevail are the Presbyterian, Episcopalian, & Roman Catholic, the number of the last small. The Methodists are numerous. But notwithstanding the prejudices of those, who nominally dissent from the Church of England, he has the satisfaction of seeing a numerous congregation at Church on Sundays, but Communicants are very few. From July 1st, 1800, when he first came there to the 1st of Novr., 1802, he has baptized 53, married 14, & buried 11. Comms. only 10. The people have not as yet contributed to his support, pleading inability from the high price of labour & the necessaries of life. But they have subscribed to the building of a Church, & they expect an additional sum from Govr. Hunter. There is a reservation of six acres of land in the Town intended for the site of the Church, but no plan is under consideration for a Parsonage House. Under the present circumstances it must be unavoidably delayed until a Church is erected. In the interim he officiates in the Government House. He submits these facts to the consideration of the Society, whose advice & instructions he shall be happy to receive, & whose views & expectations it is his duty to promote by a conscientious discharge of the trust reposed in him.

Agreed in Opinion that Mr. Stuart be informed that the Society lament that there is yet no provision made for a Parsonage House.

G 10 Dr. Baldwin[6] Opens a School

[*York,* Upper Canada Gazette, *December 18, 1802*]

Doctor Baldwin

UNDERSTANDING that some of the Gentlemen of this Town have expressed much anxiety for the establishment of a Classical School, begs leave to inform them and the Public, that he intends on Monday the third day of January next to open a School, in which he will instruct twelve Boys in Writing, Reading, the Classics and Arithmetic.—The terms are, for each Boy eight Guineas per annum, to be paid quarterly; one Guinea entrance, and one cord of Wood to be supplied by each Boy on opening the School.

York, Dec. 17, 1802.

G 11 Resolutions for Erecting a Church

[*York,* Upper Canada Gazette, *January 22, 1803*]

At a Meeting of the Subscribers to a Fund for erecting a CHURCH, *in the Town of York, holden at the Government Buildings, on Saturday, the 8th day of January, instant—*

His Honor the CHIEF JUSTICE,[7] in the Chair:

RESOLVED UNANIMOUSLY, That each subscriber shall pay the amount of his subscription by three installments—the first being one moiety in one month from this day, the second being a moiety of the residue in two months, and the remainder in three months.

RESOLVED UNANIMOUSLY, That Mr. *William Allan* and Mr. *Duncan Cameron,* shall be Treasurers, and shall receive the amount of the said subscriptions; and that they be jointly and severally answerable for all monies paid into their hands upon the receipt of either of them.

RESOLVED UNANIMOUSLY, That his Honor the *Chief Justice,* the Honorable Mr. *Russell,* the Honorable Captain *M'Gill,* the Reverend Mr.

[6]Dr. William Warren Baldwin (1775–1844), born in County Cork, Ireland, studied medicine at the University of Edinburgh, and came to Canada with his family in 1799. They first settled in Clarke Township, but in 1802 Dr. Baldwin came to York. In 1803 he married Phoebe Willcocks, who inherited the Russell property. The same year he was called to the Bar. He was appointed Master in Chancery in 1806, and was Judge of the Surrogate Court, Home District, from 1812 to 1836. From 1821 to 1830 he was a member of the House of Assembly. He and his son Robert originated the concept of colonial responsible government.

[7]Henry Allcock.

Stuart, Doctor *Macaulay,* Mr. *Chewett,* and the two Treasurers, be a committee of the subscribers, with full power and authority to apply the monies arising from subscriptions, to the purpose contemplated —Provided nevertheless, that if any material difference in opinion should arise among them, resort shall be had to a meeting of the subscribers to decide.

RESOLVED UNANIMOUSLY, That the Church be built of stone, brick, or framed timber, as the committee may judge most expedient, due regard being had to the superior advantages of a stone or brick building, if not counterbalanced by the additional expence.

RESOLVED UNANIMOUSLY, That eight hundred pounds of lawful money, be the extent upon which the committee shall calculate their plan;— but, in the first instance, they shall not expend beyond the sum of six hundred pounds, (if the amount of the sums subscribed and paid into the hands of the Treasurers, together with the monies which may be allowed by the British government, amount to so much) leaving so much of the work as can most conveniently be dispensed with, to be completed by the remaining two hundred pounds—provided, however, that the said six hundred pounds be laid out in such manner that Divine Worship can be performed with decency in the Church.

RESOLVED UNANIMOUSLY, That the committee do request the opinion and advice of Mr. *Berczy,* respecting the probable expences which will attend the undertaking, and respecting the materials to be preferred; due regard being had to the amount of the fund, as aforesaid; and that after having obtained his opinion, they do advertise their readiness to receive proposals conformable thereto.[8]

N.B. The propriety of receiving contributions in labour or materials, is suggested to the committee.

A. MACDONELL,
Secretary to the Meeting.

G 12 FURTHER RESOLUTIONS ABOUT A CHURCH
[*York,* Upper Canada Gazette, *July 9, 1803*]

On Wednesday last the 6th instant, a Meeting of the Subscribers to the Fund for erecting a Church in this town, was held at the Government Buildings; on which occasion it was unanimously Resolved,

That the said Church should be built of Stone.

That one Hundred Toises of Stone should accordingly be contracted for without delay.

That a quantity of two inch Pine Plank, not exceeding 6000 feet, should also be laid in; and a reasonable quantity of Oak Studs and Oak Plank for the Window Frames and Sashes.

[8]In the *Upper Canada Gazette* of June 4, 1803, Cameron and Allan advertised for pine, boards, scanting, and lime for building a church.

A future meeting we understand will be held in the course of the Season; at which, when the different Estimates and Proposals have been examined, and the extent which the fund will reach, has been ascertained, something decisive will be settled.

G 13 Stuart to the S.P.G., Dated York, September 17, 1804
[*S.P.G., Journals, XXIX, 58–9; microfilm copy in P.A.C.*]

he assures the Society of his continuing to discharge his duty, & tho' sensible that religious impressions have been made upon several of his Congregation, yet he has cause to lament the general reluctance of the people to receive the Sacrament, tho' he has urged in his discourses the obligation, necessity, & beneficial effects of observing that Institution of Love: which he rather attributes to ignorance than to prejudice & mistaken scruples. He therefore requests the Society to send him some Religious Tracts which may assist exhortations on that subject. The observance of the Sabbath, he says, is not so much neglected as it has been, & he flatters himself that a religious conduct & moral habits are gradually taking [the] place of irreligion & licentiousness.[9] That reformations should be gradual is to be expected among a great proportion of the inhabitants, the labouring class consisting almost wholly of disbanded soldiers, whose manner of life has been ill calculated either to improve, or preserve, their morals. That the Bishop of Quebec visited York last summer, confirmed 18, & preached to a numerous audience. He is happy to inform the Society that a plan has been settled for the building of a Church. The people have subscribed £400 Halifax Curry. A Committee for carrying on the work, consisting of six respectable persons, has been chosen. Two Treasurers appointed. The Chief Justice of the Province Mr. Alcock, presides at the Meetings of the Committee, from whom assurances have been given that Governor Hunter will assist the undertaking. He has already given £50. That his prospect of being useful is more encouraging than hitherto. His Notitia from 1st of Jany to the 1st July comprehends 28 Baptisms, 8 Marriages, & 5 Burials. Comms. 14.

Agreed to recommend that some Tracts on each of the Sacraments be sent to Mr. George Stuart for the use of his Congregation.

G 14 Schoolmaster's Contract
[*T.P.L., Early Toronto Papers*]

Articles of agreement made and entered into at York in the Province of Upper Canada, the Thirtieth day of April in the year of our Lord one thousand Eight Hundred and five. Between William Jarvis—James Mac-

[9]In his report to the S.P.G. on July 10, 1804, Stuart complained of "the vices and irreligion of the one rank, and the ignorance of the other." (S.P.G., Journals, XXIX, 45; microfilm copy in P.A.C.)

aulay—William Chewett—Thomas Ridout—Allan McNabb[10] and others the subscribers hereunto residing in the Town of York of the one part, And Alexander William Carson[11] of the same place—Schoolmaster, of the other part; whereby the said Alexander William Carson, for and in consideration of the Covenants and Conditions herein aftermentioned to be done and performed, by and on the part of the said Subscribers—Doth covenant grant promise and agree to and with the said William Jarvis, James Macaulay, William Chewett—Thomas Ridout Allan McNabb, and others the said subscribers and each and every of them in manner following—That is to say—that he the said Alexander William Carson shall and will, from the first day of May now next ensuing the date hereof—until the first day of May—thence following, well and truly, and to the best of his ability teach and instruct the Children of the said Subscribers, or those of any other person, as may or shall be sent to him by the said Subscribers only—and by them allowed to be taught and instructed by him the said Alexander William Carson, and no other (provided the number of the said Children in the whole, do not exceed Twenty-Five) in the art of spelling—reading—writing and arithmetic——That he will attend his School five days and a half in each and every week during the said term—from the Hours of Eight to Twelve in the morning—and from two to five in the afternoon—from the first day of May to the first of October; and from the first of October to the first of May—from the Hours of Nine to twelve in the forenoon—and from two to four in the afternoon—one half day in each week, only excepted—And the said William Jarvis—James Macaulay—William Chewett—Thomas Ridout—Allan McNabb and others the Subscribers hereunto, do hereby promise and agree, for and in consideration of the Instruction of the Said Children as aforesaid—to pay unto the said Alexander William Carson on the first day of each and every Calendar month, during the time that he shall so teach and instruct their Children or such other as they shall consent for him to receive in his School as aforesaid—to the number of Twenty five and no more the Sum of Three pounds fifteen shillings Halifax Currency Dollars at five shillings—and also will procure and find at their Expence, good and sufficient Board and lodging (Liquors excepted) for the said Alexander William Carson during the time that he shall so teach and instruct the Children as aforesaid——And the said William Jarvis doth hereby over and alone his part of the aforesaid subscription, gratuitously allow and permit the said Alexander William Carson, so long as he shall be subject to this agreement to keep

[10]Allan MacNab (1768–1830) served in the British army and in the Queen's Rangers as a lieutenant during the Revolution. He was Sergeant-at-Arms of the House of Assembly from 1815 to 1830, and was the father of Sir Allan Napier MacNab.

[11]Carson advertised in the *Upper Canada Gazette* of May 3, 1806, that he would commence teaching school on April 28 in the house lately occupied by Nicholas Clingenbrumer where he hoped to receive the same encouragement as before.

his School, in a House belonging to him the said William Jarvis—situate and being on Lot Number three on the North side of Duke Street in the said Town of York—

And in case that any difference should at any time during the period herein beforementioned happen to arise between the said Alexander William Carson and the said Subscribers or any of them, it shall be heard and determined by two persons indifferently chosen, the one by the said Alexander William Carson and the other by the said Subscribers or Subscriber—and should these two persons not happen to agree in opinion—they are hereby required and permitted to appoint an Umpire; and the opinion of and decision of the said two persons—or of the Umpire, shall be final—and to which all parties, hereby agree and promise to abide.

In witness whereof the said Parties have hereunto set their hands and seals on the said Thirtieth day of April in the year of our Lord, one thousand Eight hundred and five.

The word "Calendar" being
interlined before signing

Wm. Jarvis
Jas. Macaulay
Allan McNabb
Alexdr Wm Carson
Witness School-Master

G 15 Stuart to S.P.G., Dated York, July 1, 1805
[*S.P.G., Journals, XXIX, 128–9; microfilm copy in P.A.C.*]

since he last wrote, he has been blessed with good health, & has laboured in the discharge of his duty, & the people more generally attend Public Worship. The building of a Church[12] is in a state of advancement. The materials have been purchased, & are deposited on the ground intended for the site of the Church. The dimensions will be 60 feet in length, 40 feet in breadth, & 22 in height, excluding the foundation which is of stone. The workmen say, that the frame will be erected in the course of three weeks. They wished to have had the Church of stone, but it was found impracticable.

His Notitia commencing the 1st of Septr., 1804, and ending July 1, 1805, comprehends 35 Baptisms; 15 Marriages, & 10 Burials. Communicants 15.

G 16 Stuart to S.P.G., Dated York, July 17, 1806
[*S.P.G., Journals, XXIX, 197; microfilm copy in P.A.C.*]

the Society are informed that several adverse events have concurred to retard the completion of their Church; in particular the death of Governor Hunter, whose influence promoted the work, & a great deficit

[12]The first St. James' Church stood on the site of the present Cathedral and was approached from Church Street.

in the subscription. The expenditures having been found to exceed the Funds considerably, prudence has induced the Committee to stop the work, till ways & means can be devised for annihilating the debt. The religious state of the Mission is the same as represented in former letters. The Communicants have not increased since November last. The Notitia from that date comprehends 30 Baptisms, 13 Marriages, & 9 burials.

G 17 STUART TO S.P.G., DATED YORK, FEBRUARY 8, 1807
[*S.P.G., Journals, XXIX, 289–90; microfilm copy in P.A.C.*]

assuring the Society of his constant exertions in promoting their pious & benevolent designs, which in a degree has been successful; but not to the extent he hoped for. The number of Communicants is 18. The Congregation is enlarged. The Church is nearly complete—the pews were to be finished in a few days; but their fund is not equal to the expense of a pulpit & gallery at the west end. There are 32 pews, 18 of which are called single pews—the rest double. The larger are 6 feet 6 inches by 6 ft. 6 inches, & the smaller 3 feet by 6 feet 6 inches. There are 3 aisles. The middle is 6 feet in breadth, the side 4 feet 4 inches along which the range of the wall pews is extended. The situation of the Church is central, & convenient for the parishioners. He requests of the Society a Bible & Prayer Book for the Church as they are unprovided. From July to Jany. 1807, he had baptized 21 Infants and 2 Adults; married 12; & buried 6.

Agreed to recommend that a Quarto Bible & Prayer Book be sent to Mr. Stuart for the use of his Mission.

G 18 MRS. W. D. POWELL[13] TO GEORGE MURRAY, NEW YORK
[*T.P.L., Powell Papers*]

March 31st, 1807

. . . we thought spring advancing, when a fall of snow on Saturday night enabled me to go to Church yesterday in a Carriole—I never saw such an Easter Sunday—we are got into our new Church, it is a good building, & we have decidedly the best Pew in it[14]—our Friend Wood was the purchaser,—Mrs Gore is to give a Bell, the Governor gives an handsome Pulpit &c. . . .

G 19 ACCOUNTS OF DISTRICT SCHOOL AT YORK
[*T.P.L., G. O. Stuart Account Book*]

An Act was passed into a Law by the Legislature of the Province of Upper Canada to establish Public Schools in each and every District of the Province.

[13]Mrs. Anne (Murray) Powell (1758–1849) was the wife of Judge Powell. She kept up a regular correspondence with her brother George Murray, a New York merchant.

[14]The pews were sold at public auction on March 4, 1807.

His Excellency Governor Gore through Major Halton[15] his Secretary was pleased to appoint me[16] Teacher of the District School in York in the Home District.—The Letter dated the 16th April 1807.

On June 1st 1807 the District School was opened and the Pupils whose names follow were admitted. John Ridout—William A. Hamilton.[17] Thomas G. Hamilton.[17] George H. Detlor.[18] George S. Boulton[19]

June 2d

Entered the District School on this day Robert Staunton,[20] William Staunton[20]

June 9th.

Entered the District School on this day Angus McDonnell—

—24th.

Entered the District School on this day Hannah Jarvis[21] and Eliza Anne Jarvis[22]—

26

Entered the District School on Friday the 26th Mary Ridout—

30

Entered the District School on Tuesday the 30th. Anne McNabb[23] and Hannah M. McNabb[23]

July 1st. Wednesday

Entered the District School Alexander Hamilton[17] & Wilson Hamilton[17]

7th. Tuesday

Entered the District School Allan McNabb[23]

15William Halton (d. 1821) was Gore's secretary. From 1816 to 1821 he was Provincial Agent for Upper Canada in London.

16Rev. George Okill Stuart.

17Thomas Hamilton had ten children. There appears to be some confusion about their Christian names.

18George Hill Detlor later moved to Kingston and was a Reform member of the House of Assembly for Lennox and Addington.

19George Strange Boulton (1797–1869) was the third son of D'Arcy Boulton. He was called to the Bar in 1818 and became a member of the House of Assembly, and later of the Legislative Council.

20William Stanton (1756–1833) was born in Staffordshire and entered the Royal Navy in 1771. From 1811 to 1814 he was Sergeant-at-Arms to the House of Assembly, and after 1828 Deputy Assistant Commissary General at Amherstburg. He left a large family of thirteen, including three sets of twins. One of his sons, Robert (1794–1866), entered government employ during the War of 1812, and became King's Printer and editor of the *Upper Canada Gazette* in 1826, a position he held until the Act of Union. He was later Collector of Customs at Toronto.

21Hannah Owen Jarvis (b. 1797) married Alexander Hamilton of Queenston.

22Eliza Ann Jarvis (1801–65) married W. B. Robinson.

23Children of Lieutenant Allan MacNab. Sir Allan Napier MacNab (1798–1862) was born at Niagara. In 1826 he was called to the Bar. He was knighted for his military exploits in the Rebellion of 1837 and had a long career as a Conservative politician. His first wife was Mary, daughter of Daniel Brooke.

6th

Entered the District School, Maria L. Jarvis[24]

7th

Entered the District School William Jarvis.[25]

Receipts

"Received from Thomas Ridout Esqr. the Sum of eight Dollars for a Quarter's Tuition of John and Mary—$8

"Received from Thomas Hamilton the Sum of twelve Dollars for the Tuition of Gilbert,[17] William and Alexander Hamilton $12

"Received from John Detlor[26] the Sum of four Dollars for a Quarter's Tuition of George H. Detlor in advance—$4

"Received from William Jarvis Esqr. the Sum of sixteen Dollars for a Quarter's Tuition of Maria, Augusta,[27] William and Hannah—$16

"Received from Allan McNabb Esqr. the Sum of twelve Dollars for a Quarter's Tuition of Anne Allan and Hannah—$12

$64[28]

. . .

G 20 G. S. JARVIS[29] TO HENRY SCADDING[30]
[*T.P.L., Scadding Papers*]

Cornwall 5 August 1869

. . . I am the George Jarvis named as one of the pupils of Dr. Stuarts school contemporaneous with the late Sir Allan MacNab. The Honble

[24]Maria Lavinia Jarvis (1788–1826) married George Hamilton, after whom Hamilton is named, in 1811.

[25]William Munson Jarvis (1793–1867) served in the militia during the War of 1812 and was Sheriff of the Gore District for many years.

[26]John Detlor (d. 1813) first appears in the List of Inhabitants in 1804. He died of wounds received during the battle of York.

[27]Augusta Jarvis (1790–1848) married Thomas McCormick of Niagara.

[28]Stuart's total receipts to July 1, 1811 were $624, 1 shilling, and 3¾ pence.

[29]George Stephen Jarvis (1797–1878) was born in Fredericton, the son of Stephen Jarvis. The family came to York in 1809, and George entered the Home District School on September 4. During the War of 1812, he served in the 49th and 8th Regiments, and in 1815 was gazetted a lieutenant in the 104th Regiment. He was called to the Bar in 1823, and became a judge of the County Court of Stormont, Dundas, and Glengarry.

[30]Henry Scadding (1813–1901) was born in Devonshire, where his father John was factor of the estate of the Simcoe family. John Scadding came to Canada with Simcoe, and again about 1818 to York, where his family joined him in 1821. Henry Scadding was educated at Cambridge, and, returning to Canada, taught at Upper Canada College. He was first rector of the Church of the Holy Trinity. He was a keen student of local history, and his *Toronto of Old* is the source of much valuable information.

Wm B Robinson[31] & Mr. Daniel Brooke[32] are the only survivors Sir Allan was the best speaker in the school, and was always ready for either a *frolic* or a *fight*.

Dr Stuart on one occasion paid a visit to some of his wifes relations in the U.S. and prevailed upon the late Sir J. B. Robinson[33] to take charge of the school in his absence and I well recollect the difficulty he had in keeping his brother William my brother William[34] & Sir Allan in any sort of subjection

The Dr was a very amiable man and very averse to use corporal punishment. When he found it necessary to have recourse to it he sent the delinquent out into his garden to cut the rod of course the smallest twig of the current bush was brought in. Sir Allan was sent out on one occasion; and thinking he would escape by perpetrating a *good joke*, brought in a pretty large limb cut from an apple tree The Dr did not however see it in that light, and selecting the small part of it gave Sir Allan the most severe castigation I ever saw him inflict.

The boys were frequently in the habit of appropriating the Drs apples and he assured us that the first one detected in this act would be severely punished. On one occasion he detected Sir Allan eating something and pouncing upon him, just as he was putting the last morsel into his mouth, demanded "What are you eating McNab"?—Bread Sir! said the supposed delinquent, turning the half masticated contents of his mouth into his hand and presenting it for inspection. The Dr it is needless to say sat down rather in discomfiture at the giggle than ran round the school

You have remarked that females were admitted to this School. Poor girls they were subjected to many annoyances and were unwittingly the cause of many battles between jealous boys. In one of these Sir Allan had a small piece of bone of the cheek at the lower part of the eye separated and it remained movable till the day of his death—This was a piece of my handy work. . . .

At this time some criminal was condemned to the pillory. The Schollars got the impression that they would be permitted to pelt him with

[31]William Benjamin Robinson (1797–1873) was the third son of Christopher Robinson. From 1830 to 1857, except for 1841–4, he was the member for Simcoe in the House of Assembly. He had extensive property in Newmarket.

[32]Daniel Brooke (1792?–1872) was the son of Lieutenant Daniel Brooke of the 41st and 49th Regiments, who settled at York. He became a lawyer in Brantford, and married a daughter of John Playter.

[33]Sir John Beverley Robinson (1791–1863) was born at Berthier, Quebec, the second son of Christopher Robinson. He was educated at Kingston and Cornwall under John Strachan, who became his patron. He served as a lieutenant in the York militia during the War of 1812. He became a student at law in 1808, and was called to the Bar in 1815. In 1813 he was appointed Acting Attorney General, in place of D'Arcy Boulton who was a prisoner in France. After Boulton's return, he became Solicitor General. In 1818 he was appointed Attorney General, and in 1830 became Chief Justice. He represented the town of York in the House of Assembly from 1821 to 1830.

[34]William Botsford Jarvis (1799–1864) was the third son of Stephen Jarvis. He was appointed Sheriff of the Home District in 1827. In 1826 he married Mary Boyles Powell, granddaughter of Judge Powell.

rotten eggs; and came provided accordingly. I secured a nest of about a dozen of high odor which I secured in my coat tail pockets and approached the scene of action very cautiously. McNab was there before me and with a bat gave me a rap on the pockets—the event can be better imagined than described—After cutting off the pockets one of them was appropriated to the use of the assailant and of course a battle ensued—Result a black eye to McNab and a bloody nose to your humble servant

A fight in those days was looked upon by the boys as necessary to acquire a Status and in truth parents did not altogether discourage it. We would much rather indulge in a *scrimage* than meet the difficulties of that "d——d little Eutropus" at its first introduction. This propensity was much indulged in at an election[35] that came off between the late Surveyor Genl. Ridout whose motto was "Education for the Million" and a goth from the Country whose flag bore the bore the following "No repeal of the *hab us* corpus act." Sides were taken by the boys and votes polled at the mimic hustings with the usual battles after the fashion of the older children. . . .

G 21 MEETING OF THE CATHOLICS OF YORK

[*Quebec Chancery Archives; printed in Brother Alfred,* Catholic Pioneers in Upper Canada, *pp. 183–4*]

At a meeting of the Catholics of the town of York held in the home of Dr. James Glennon, on the 13th day of July, 1807, resolved:

(a) That Hon. Alexander McDonell, speaker of the House of Assembly, Quetton St. George, and Dr. James Glennon[36] be appointed trustees for the Catholic population of the town of York.

(b) That Paul Marian, Isaac Collumbus[37] and François Belcourt be elected elders of the said congregation.

(c) That the said elders do collect such moneys and pay same into the hands of one or more of the trustees above mentioned.

(d) That a chalice and a set of vestments be purchased from the moneys as also a baptismal register, etc.

(e) That as soon as sufficient funds may be found a chapel shall be erected in the town of York.[38]

(f) That the elders and the congregation convene every Sunday at a convenient place to read the prayers at Mass, etc.

(g) That Catechisms and books of instruction be purchased.

[35]The election of 1812, when the candidates were Thomas Ridout and Joseph Shepard.

[36]Dr. James Glennon (d. 1813) arrived in York in 1807, advertised as lately from Europe, but recommended by a gentleman from Schenectady and another from Albany.

[37]Isaac Columbus (Colombe) (d. 1846) was probably a member of an old Island of Orleans family. He was a blacksmith, locksmith, and gunsmith.

[38]Although a site at the northeast corner of Duke and George Streets had been granted by the Crown on March 25, 1806, the first Roman Catholic Church in York was not built until 1822.

G 22 Rev. G. O. Stuart to S.P.G., Dated York, September 1, 1807

[*S.P.G., Journals, XXIX, 306; microfilm copy in P.A.C.*]

the completion of the Church is so far advanced as to make it convenient for the celebration of Divine Service, & the Congregation are better accommodated than they were in the Government House. The rent of the pews amounts to £35 per annum Halifax Currency, which affords a fund that with judicious management will accelerate the completion of the Edifice. His congregation encreases; but the number of Communicants is the same as he represented in his last letters. Since the month of May, the children of his parishioners have been regularly catechized every Sunday; & as he is much gratified by their proficiency, he is prompted to request of the Society a few Tracts explanatory of the Catechism suitable for children under the age of fourteen years. Lt. Govr. Gore has promised to erect a pulpit at his own expense as soon as a proper artist can be found. His Notitia, commencing the 1st. day of Jany. 1807 & ending the 1st. day of July 1807, is as follows:—Baptisms 22—Marriages 10—Burials 7.—

G 23 Complaint about Strangers' Pews

[*York*, York Gazette, *October 3, 1807*]

Messrs. Printers,

WHEN travelling, it has always been customary with me to take notes of every thing I conceive worth noting.—In the latter part of the month of August last, I passed through the Town of York on my route to the lower Province, and must confess, was highly delighted with its situation and internal as well as external appearance. Its commerce and navigation, considering the infancy of the Settlement appeared to me flourishing in the extreme.—Roads were opening and repairing, and buildings increasing in a considerable degree; one of the latter, however, arrested my particular attention, not merely for its structure, but on account of the regulation and government thereof. I allude to the Church, (for you must know, Messrs. Printers, I have from my infancy, been in the habit of attending a place of Divine Worship, and particularly the Church of England) whose Wardens, and others immediately concerned therewith, appear according to my observation and information, to have omitted, or rather misunderstood a very material part of their duty.

My veneration for that Supreme Being, who is the disposer of all things, as well as my inclination, induced me, during my short stay in York, to visit this hallowed place—Shortly after my entrance, I was not a little surprized at finding there were no Pews, benches or any other such necessary appendages for strangers or transient persons of decent appearance; and was therefore reduced to the uncomfortable necessity, during the service, either of standing as a public spectacle, or of seating myself among the military who compose the garrison. From your knowledge of Church government, Messrs. Printers, however superficial it may be, you cannot be ignorant that in all the principal cities in England, Ireland Scotland and America, the various Churches are carefully and properly provided with comfortable seats for strangers of every description—Why this is not the case in the capitol of Upper Canada remains to me a mystery; sensible I am, however, that a considerable number of religious and well-disposed inhabitants, whose present circumstances will not enable them to rent or purchase pews, are thereby deprived of the benefits derived from the propagation of the Gospel, which may ultimately lead the unwary into vicious and depraved habits not easily to be eradicated, and possibly end in their total destruction.

According to my observation, this deficiency did not appear to arise from a want of room, the building being sufficiently spacious for the purpose, and the result of my enquiries leads me to think, from no insufficiency of funds.

I was credibly informed this structure was chiefly raised and completed by voluntary contributions from the citizens and inhabitants of York and its vicinity, some of whom, in moderate circumstances, liberally subscribed from ten to twelve dollars, and yet a number of these very people are, in a manner, excluded its *walls*—Believe me, Sirs, I speak not from motives of self-interest, as in all probability, a number of years will elapse before I revisit your place, and the polite attention I experienced while among you, will leave an indelible impression on my memory.

Should this hint, Messrs. Printers, be productive of the desired effect, an investigation of the causes, and a remedy of the evil, my intention will be fully answered.

A FRIEND TO RELIGION.

Montreal, 20th Sept. 1807.

G 24 STUART TO S.P.G., DATED YORK, JULY 2, 1808
[*S.P.G., Journals, XXIX, 389; microfilm copy in P.A.C.*]

the Society are informed that they have a very decent Church built, & that the Congregation has encreased. The state of the Mission is as prosperous as could be expected. A pulpit has been erected which cost £25 Currency. The expense is great, but the elegance of the design made it unavoidable. The Catechetical Instruction has been attended to every Sunday afternoon, & the children repeat so correctly as to qualify them for apprehending its principles which are explained in a manner adapted to their capacities.—His half Year's Notitia is—Baptisms 33, Marriages 17, Burials 11—Communicants 18.—

G 25 WILLIAM CASE[39] IN YORK
[*United Church Archives, Journal of William Case*]

Saturday 27 August 1808. This day I am 28 years of age. . . . Came to Mr. Detlors in York in the eve. The next morning I had some concern

[39]William Case (1780–1855) was born in Swansea, Mass., and entered the ministry of the Methodist Episcopal Church. His first appointment was the Bay of

on my mind how we should spend our time that day. No Meeting in many miles, & none appointed in York till 5 OC in the afternoon. For direction in secret prayer Br. Perry[40] & myself retired into the adjoining plains, where we proposed several means which we thot most proper to pursue for the day. At first to go from house to house thro the town & talk to the people, warning them to repent, 2 To request liberty to preach to the Soldiers at the Garrison, 3 To spend the day in prayer & religious conversation with Mr. Detlor's family, & indeavor to bring them to a lively faith in Jesus Christ. One of these we felt determined to proceed on till we went to prayer in that retirement, when we gave ourselves up to God for direction, We had scarcely returned to the house when some brethren came in from 12 miles expecting [a meeting] would be held in York that day. We then saw it would be best to give notice in the city & preach to the people & accordingly obtained a considderable congregation so as to preach at 1 OC which I did from these words, "If we say we have no sin we deceive ourselves &c." & at 5 OC I cryd aloud "Why will ye die." In both these meetings the people were all attention & several appeard much concerned, weeping, &c. . . .

G 26 Stuart to S.P.G., Dated York, 1809
[*S.P.G., Journals, XXX, 24; microfilm copy in P.A.C.*]

they have raised a contribution for the erection of a gallery at the west end of the Church to accommodate the soldiers of the garrison near York, & for many of the poorer inhabitants, as the pews have been purchased by persons of rank. The pew rents from March 4, 1807 to March 4, 1809, has amounted to £73 . . 4 . . 6 Halifax Currency, which has been appropriated to the use of the Church. A very decent & honest man[41] who performs the duties of Clerk & Sexton, receives from that fund a salary of £15 per annum. His Notitia for half a Year comprehends 40 Baptisms including 4 Adults—Marriages 18—Burials 12.

G 27 Opening of a Music School
[*York*, York Gazette, *February 14, 1810*]

NOTICE.

JOSEPH B. ABBOT[42] proposes opening a School in the principles of Church Music, in the house lately occupied by Alfred Barret, and now

---

Quinte district; in 1809 he was at Detroit, and from 1810 to 1827 he was presiding elder of the Methodist Church in Canada and northwestern New York. He was General Superintendent of the Wesleyan Methodists in Canada from 1830 to 1833. He was very active in the field of Indian missions.

[40] Robert Perry was the son of a Loyalist, and brother of Peter Perry. He was licensed as a travelling minister in 1805. In 1811 he located, and about 1816 seceded from the Wesleyan Methodists with the Reformed Methodists.

[41] Joseph Hunt, tavern keeper.

[42] Joseph B. Abbot obtained a licence to keep a tavern in 1812. In November, 1811, he married Christina Papst of York.

occupied by Peter Miller.[43] Music Vocal or Instrumental is universally considered as an elegant accomplishment, not more interesting than useful to the profession. The said Abbot flatters himself he will be able to give satisfaction to all those who may be inclined to encourage him, by teaching it in the most expeditious manner and according to most approved standard of modern times. Any person desirous of promoting the above undertaking are informed that a Subscription list will be left with Mr. Thos. Hamilton, on the 17th inst.

York, 13th Feb. 1810.

G 28 Stuart to S.P.G., Dated York, July 7, 1810
[*S.P.G., Journals, XXX, 117–18; microfilm copy in P.A.C.*]

in the last six months, the Baptisms were 30, the Marriages 14, the Burials 10, and 6 added to the Communicants. A gallery has been erected at the west end of the Church for the accommodation of the soldiers of the garrison near York. It cost £32.17.6 Halifax Currency, which was obtained from a public subscription of the parishioners. He thanks the Society for the gift of a Bible & Common Prayer Book, which is considered as a mark of the Society's attention to the Mission.

G 29 Opening of a Night School
[*York,* York Gazette, *September 19, 1810*]

Nocturnal Study.

FOR the benefit of Young Ladies (or men) Apprentices, and others, who cannot conveniently attend in the Day time to Study; are by this mode notified, that the Subscriber will teach those who choose to attend him where the New-Town Day School is now held, and will meet with every [att]ention which can be paid to pupils. From a desire to settle permanently in Town, his utmost attention will be particularly directed to the instruction of all who are placed under him—his terms are for each day scholar, 8s N.Y. Cy per Month and the same for Evening Scholars—an addition of 2s. per Month for Pupils after entering Reduction (in Arithmetic)—Evening Scholars to furnish severally, 1 lb. Candles per Month; and all Scholars, half a Cord of Fire Wood for the Winter.—The Evening School to commence 24th Inst.—the hours of attendance from 6 to 9 P.M. for 5 days of the week only. Regular monthly payments to be made.

CHARLES M'DONNEL.[44]

York, 18th Sept. 1810.

[43]Peter Miller took over Alfred Barrett's tavern in 1810. In December, 1811, it was taken by Andrew O'Keeffe, a tailor.

[44]On June 9, 1810, McDonell advertised the opening of the New Town Day School. He was a stranger at that time. He closed his school in December, 1811. A Mrs. McDonnell, schoolmistress, bought some groceries at the sale of Gore's possessions on Sept. 12, 1812.

G 30 William Barber[45] Opens a School
[*York*, York Gazette, *October 10, 1810*]

SCHOOL.

THE Subscriber respectfully acquaints the Inhabitants of York, and its vicinity, that he will commence a School at his House in Duke Street, on Monday the 8th inst. in which will be taught the common branches of School Education. Tuition, three Dollars per quarter, each Scholar to furnish half a cord of fire wood; to be paid Monthly.

The subscriber, will also teach an Evening School, four Evenings in a week, at two Dollars the quarter, the scholars finding their own candles. —From his experience in this line of business, and attention to his hours; the subscriber flatters himself, he will be able to render general satisfaction.

WILLIAM BARBER.

York, 4th Octr. 1810.

G 31 Thaddeus Osgood[46] Distributes Tracts
[*York*, York Gazette, *November 14, 1810*]

A Note of thanks, accompanied with some communications and friendly remarks.

THE subscriber in this public manner, returns his sincere thanks to all those Gentlemen and Ladies who have repeatedly aided him in his humble attempt to do good, by Printing and disseminating useful books.

Public notice is hereby given, that a variety of small books and entertaining pieces for children, are left in the care of Mr. ADAMS,[47] at his Book-Store in York.

The terms are good. The poor may have them gratis, and the rich may cast into the CHARITY BOX whatever they please, which shall be faithfully applied to printing more. The poor are however invited to bring what Rags they can spare towards making paper cheaper.

The simple plan of instructing little children in the elements of useful science, which any one may see and have explained, by calling at Mr. Cameron's the Printer, or at the place abovementioned; promises great utility to the public; especially to families of little children in the new settlements.

[45]A week later, Barber married Hester Kendrick. He was Town Clerk in 1816, and drops out of the List of Inhabitants in 1819.

[46]Thaddeus Osgood was born in 1775 in the American colonies. He was educated at Dartmouth College, was licensed to preach in 1804, and ordained a Congregational minister in 1808. He came to Canada in 1809 and travelled about distributing tracts. He went to England twice to raise money for his activities, and taught school for a number of years in Lower Canada.

[47]Green Adams' bookstore was probably the one of which J. B. Robinson wrote, "We have quite a respectable Book-store here from the United States. Good authors, but wretched editions—however I could lay out fifty pounds *very much to my satisfaction* in it." (P.A.O., Macaulay Papers, J. B. Robinson to John Macaulay, July 24, 1810.)

Thousands of little children, it is hoped, will this winter amuse themselves in a manner wholly new and highly entertaining as well as useful —"To make amusement and instruction friends" is the object kept in view, by the plan above hinted at.

To make the path to the field of science and to the temple of honor, easy and delightful to children, is an object not unworthy of the highest orders in society. For even the Saviour condescended to come from Heaven to be the teacher and redeemer of this fallen guilty world. And he commands all his followers to imitate him in doing good, assuring them that their most humble attempts to do good, shall not go unrewarded. With sentiments of respect, I am the public's most devoted servant,

THADDEUS OSGOOD.

G 32 Thomas Ridout to T. G. Ridout
[P.A.O., Ridout Papers]

York. U.C. 31 July 1811.

. . . as Mr. Stewart has resigned the Dist School, I have informed Mr. Cameron & Mr. Small two other of the Trustees of my intention to write Mr. Prince for a gent. Qualified—& I have mend. my Intent to the Govr.—they all approve of it. but it be a subject for my next to Mr. P.—a young gent. who had taken orders. if he could obtain the £50 p. ann. given by the Society for propagating the gospel—with the School. which you know is £100 Cy p ann. & the *good* expectation of a parish here, would I hope induce some one to come hither. . . .

G 33 Strachan to Dr. James Brown,[48] St. Andrews
[P.A.O., Strachan Papers]

Cornwall 3d Novr. 1811

In my last I mentioned, that I had sacrificed my interest to my Friendship, and respect for the Clergyman at Kingston whose son I assisted to become his Successor, altho' I wished the place myself, because it was essential to the success of all my plans respecting Education. By this Gentleman's removal to Kingston York becomes vacant, which in mere point of emolument is £75 per annum better than Kingston, besides being the seat of Government, but altho by removing there, I should be able to pursue my plans of Education on as great Scale as at Kingston; I should be much less independent than here. All provincial Governments are full of little party work, and there is no getting clear of it, when therefore the Governor offered me York I declined, after Mature deliberation. . . .

[48]James Brown was Professor of Natural Philosophy in the University of Glasgow, and later Professor in the University of St. Andrew's. He was a close friend and confidant of John Strachan's.

G 34 Opening of a Writing School
[*York,* York Gazette, *December 11, 1811*]

Penmanship.

MR. C. MASON returns his acknowledgements for the encouragement he has received in this Town.

The term of his first course of lessons will this day expire; and he respectfully gives information that if a sufficient number (convinced of the usefulness of his method of instruction and willing to sacrifice prejudice to reason and utility,) apply, he will commence a second course of exercises on Friday the 13th Inst. at the Room he now occupies at T. Gilbert's, North side of King's Street.

York, 11th Dec. 1811.

G 35 Strachan to J. B. Robinson
[*J. B. Robinson Papers in possession of Christopher Robinson, Ottawa; microfilm copy in P.A.O.*]

Cornwall 8 April 1812

. . . I have been induced to alter my resolution respecting York, and to accept of that living—it was offered me in a manner so handsome by General Brock, and the Chaplaincy of which I was ignorant makes such an addition to the emolument, but above all the appointment coming from a quarter different from that through which it came at first, removed all my scruples I propose being in York by the end of June—but as it will then be too late to make a garden, I have to request you to get that done for me. Mr. Cartwright has rented Mr Stuarts house for me, and you can hire some person to dress the Garden, and sow it with roots &c for the Kitchen and, if there be room, get potatoes planted. . . .

G 36 Strachan Opens his School
[*York,* York Gazette, *October 10, 1812*]

EDUCATION.

THE Subscriber having been nominated Teacher of the School of the Home District, informs the Public that his Seminary is now open for the reception of Pupils. *Rate of Tuition appointed by the Trustees,*

Common Education £6 per annum
Classical " £8 Do.

Anxious to extend the advantages of his School, the Subscriber will even abate somewhat of the above rates to the poorer Inhabitants, provided they keep their Children neat and clean, and supply them with proper Books. N.B. Scholars from other Districts are charged ten pounds per annum.

JOHN STRACHAN.

York, October 10, 1812.

H. LIFE IN YORK

H 1 Extracts from Mrs. Simcoe's Diary
[*P.A.O., Simcoe Papers*]

[1793]

2d of May Coll Simcoe set off accompanied by 7 Officers to go to Toronto, he means to go round by the head of the Lake in a Batteaux.

. . .

13th Coll Simcoe returned from Toronto & speaks in praise of the harbour, & a fine spot near it covered with large Oak which he intends to fix upon as a scite for a Town I am going to send you some beautiful Butterflies

. . .

20th [July] Capt Shaw & 100 men set off in Batteaux for Toronto. . . .

. . .

29th of July We were prepared to sail for Toronto this morng. but the wind changed suddenly, we dined with the Chief Justice[1] & were recalled from a walk at 9 oclock this Eveng as the wind was become fair—we embarked on board the Mississaga the band playing in the Ship—it was dark so I went to bed & slept till 8 oclock the next morning when I found myself in the Harbour of Toronto, we had gone under an easy sail all night for as no person on board had ever been at Toronto Mr. Bouchette was afraid to enter the Harbour till day light when St John Rousseau an Indian trader who lives near came in a Boat to pilot us.

30th Tuesday the Queens Rangers are encamped opposite to the Ship after dinner we went on shore to fix on a spot whereon to place the Canvass Houses, & we chose a rising ground divided by a Creek from the Camp—which is ordered to be cleared immediately, the Soldiers have cut down a great deal of wood to enable them to pitch their Tents, we went in the Boat 2 miles to the bottom of the Bay & walked thro' a grove of fine Oaks where the Town is intended to be built a low spit of sand covered with wood forms the Bay & breaks the Horizon of Lake which greatly improves the view which indeed is very pleasing. the water in the Bay is beautifully clear & transparent

Sunday August 4th 1793 we rode on the Peninsula so I call the spit of sand for it is united to the Main Land by a very narrow neck of ground—we crossed the Bay opposite the Camp, & rode by the Lake side to the end of the Peninsula we met with some good natural meadows, & several Ponds—the trees are mostly of the Poplar kind covered with wild Vines & there are some fir,—on the ground were everlasting Peas creeping in abundance of a purple color, I was told they are good to eat

[1]William Osgoode.

when boiled, & some pretty white flowers like lillies of the Valley—we continued our ride beyond the Peninsula, on the sands of the North shore of Lake Ontario till we were impeded by Large fallen Trees on the Beach, we then walkd some distance till we met with Mr Grants (the Surveyors)[2] Boat, it was not much larger than a Canoe but we ventured into it & after rowing a mile we came within sight of what is named in the Map the high lands of Toronto—the shore is extremely bold & has the appearance of Chalk Cliffs but I believe they are only white sand—they appeared so well, that we talked of building a Summer Residence there & calling it Scarborough—the diversity of scene I met with this Morning made the ride extremely pleasant, the wooded part of the peninsula was like a Shrubbery, the Sands towards the Lake reminded me of the Sands at Weymouth, & the sight of the high Lands presented a totally different Country to any thing near the Bay, tho I was not more than 4 miles from it—I was very near riding into what appeared a quick Sand, which with a little rain & wind we met with for half an hour as we rowed from the Shore to the Mississaga were the only unpleasant incidents that occurred this day—After Dinner we left the Mississaga & slept to night in the Canvass House.

5th of August the Children came on Shore; this afternoon we walked two miles, to the Old French Fort but there are no remains of any building there: it rained very hard and I was as completely wet, as if I had walked thro' a River, for being in a Shower in the woods is quite different from being exposed to it in an open Country—every tree acted as a Shower Bath, as the path was but just wide enough to admit of one person—we passed some Creeks on unhewn Trees thrown across, a matter of some difficulty to those unaccustomed to them; I should think it might be done with less danger of falling with Maacassins on the feet—

6th having been wet thro' these last two days I declined going with the Govr. to see a mill on St Johns Creek 6 miles towards the head of the Lake—the Govr brought me some very good Cakes the Millers Wife is from the United States where the Women excell in making Cakes & bread—

7th I rode on the Peninsula from 1 till four, I saw Loons swimming on the Lake—they make a noise like a Man hollowing in a tone of distress—one of these Birds was sent to me dead at Niagara it was as large as a Swan, black with a few white marks on it—at a distance they appear like small fishing boats—the air on these Sands is peculiarly clear & fine, the Indians esteem this place so healthy that they come & stay here when they are ill—

. . .

10th of August I went again to my favorite Sands, the Bay is a mile across—The Govr thinks from the Manner in which the Sandbanks are

[2]Lewis Grant received a farm in York Township, but apparently did not settle on it.

formed, they are capable of being fortified so as to be impregnable he therefore calls it Gibraltar Point tho' the Land is low—

Sunday 11th Lt Smith of the 5th Regt (who is here as acting Deputy Surveyor Genl:) read Prayers to the Queens Rangers assembled under some Trees near the Parade—this Evening we went to see a Creek which is to be called the River Don, it falls in to the Bay near the Peninsula. After we entered it we rowed some distance among Low lands covered with Rushes, abounding with wild Ducks & Swamp black birds with red wings—about a mile beyond the Bay the banks become high, & wooded, as the River contracts its width—

. . .

13th an Indian named Wablé Casigo supplies us with Salmon which the Rivers & Creeks on this Shore abound with—It is supposed they go to the Sea the velocity with which Fish move makes it not impossible & the very Red appearance & goodness of the Salmon confirm the supposition—they are best in the month of June—I brought a favorite White Cat with grey spots, with me from Niagara, he is a native of Kingston, his sense & attachment are such, that those who believe in Transmigration would think his soul once animated a reasoning being—he was undaunted on board the Ship, sits composedly as Centinel at my door amid the beat of Drums & crash of falling Trees; & visits the Tents, with as little fear, as a Dog would do—there has been a fever at Niagara, this place is very healthy & I think it probable we shall spend the Winter here. . . .

August 24th The Govr has received an official account of the Duke of York having distinguished himself in an action at Famars by which the French were dislodged & driven out of Holland—the Govr ordered a Royal Salute to be fired in commemoration of this event & took the same oppirtunity of naming this Station *York*. there are a few 12 & 18 Pounders which were brought here from Oswegatchie or Carleton Island —the Mississaga & Onondago fired also, & the Regt: there were a party of Gibbeway Indians here who appeared much pleased with the firing, one of them named Canise took Francis in his Arms & was much pleased to find the Child not afraid but delighted with the sound—
It was a damp day & from the heavy atmosphere the smoke from the Ships Guns ran along the water with a singular appearance—

. . .

4th of September I rode to St Johns Creek, there is a ridge of land extending near a mile, beyond St Johns House, 300 feet high & not more than three feet wide, the bank towards the river is of smooth turf—there is a great deal of Hemlock Spruce on this River the banks are dry & pleasant; I gathered a beautiful large species of Polygala—I found a green Caterpillar with tuffts like fir on its back I accidentally touched my face with them & it felt as if stung by a nettle, & the sensation contiued painful for some time—it was extremely calm when we set out, but on our return we were almost seasick the water was so rough—a little breeze on this Lake raises the waves in the most sudden manner—

. . .

W 11th we rowed 6 miles up the Donn to Coons, a farm under a hill covered with Pine I saw very fine Butternut Trees, the nuts are better than Walnut, gathered berries of Cockspur Thorns—I landed to see shingles made which is done by splitting large blocks of Pine into equal divisions—we found the River very shallow in many parts & obstructed by fallen Trees, one of them lay so high above the water that the boat passed under the Rowers stooping their heads it looked picturesque & a bald Eagle sat on a blasted Pine on a very bold Pt just above the fallen Tree the Govr talks of placing a Canvass House on this Point for a summer residence—Vencal the Swede rowed the Boat very intelligent man born at Unterburgh in Sweden

. . .

14th We walked to the spot intended for the scite of the Town—Mr Aitkins (the Surveyors) canoe was there we went into it & himself & his man paddled, we went at the rate of 4 Notts an hour, I liked it very much, being without the noise of Oars is a great gratification I gathered purple berries from a Creeping plant, seeds of Lillies & Spikenard—

. . .

23d I rode on the Peninsula my Horse has spirit enough to wish to get before others—I rode a race with Mr Talbot[3] to keep myself warm —I gathered wild grapes they were pleasant but not sweet. . . .

we dine in a Marquee to day, it is become too cold in the Arbour—the Canvass House we use as a bed Room but the other is going to be Erected for a winter dining Room I have gathered most beautiful White berries with a black Eye from red stalks—I cannot find out its name;

. . .

28th of October the weather has been very cold for some days & the frost very severe nothwithsanding which we feel it quite mild in the Woods; to day we walked 2 miles to a pretty spot by the side of a Creek, where we had a fire made of many large Trees & wild Ducks roasted by it & we dined without feeling the least cold—Coll Pickerings Dish,[4] Chowder, is also easily drest in the woods, being prepared in a Kettle before we left our house

T 29th the Govr having determined to take a lot of 200 acres upon

[3]Thomas Talbot (1771–1853) was born near Dublin. He came to Canada as Simcoe's private and confidential secretary, returning in 1794 to rejoin his regiment. In 1803 he returned permanently to Canada and founded the Talbot settlement in Dunwich Township.

[4]Mrs. Simcoe had met Colonel Timothy Pickering (1745–1829) at Niagara in May and June, 1793, when he was one of the Commissioners sent by the American government to treat with the Indians at Sandusky. He gave her a recipe for chowder, made by stewing salmon, sea biscuit, and pork for 20 minutes.

the River Donn for Francis, & the Law obliges persons having Lots of Land to build a House upon them within a year—we went to day to fix upon the spot for building his House—we went 6 miles by water & landed, climbed up an exceeding steep hill or rather a series of Sugar loafed Hills & approved of the highest spot[5] from whence we looked down on the tops of large Trees & seeing Eagles near I suppose they build there—there are large Pine plains around it which being without underwood & I can ride or walk on, & we hope the height of the situation will secure us from Musquetos—

We dined by a large fire on wild Ducks & Chowder on the side of a hill oposite to that Spot, our long walk made it late before we had dined so that altho we set out immediately afterwards & walked fast it was nearly dark before we reached the Surveyors Tent, from there we went home in a Boat as the stumps & Roots of trees in the Road where so troublesome to walk among in the dark—Mr Littlehales & some Gentlemen lost their way in attempting to return to the Camp an hour after us, they slept in the Woods about a mile distant—

. . .

Novr 1st I walked this Morning—at 8 this dark Eveng. we went in a Boat to see Salmon speared—large torches of white birch bark being carried in the Boat the blaze of light attracts the Fish, which the Men are dextrous in spearing—the manner of destroying the fish is disagreable, but seeing them swimming in shoals around the boat is a very pretty sight.

the flights of wild Pidgeons in the Spring & Autumn is a surprizing sight, they fly against the wind & so low that at Niagara the Men threw sticks at them from the Fort & killed numbers—the air is sometimes darkened by them, I think those we have met with here have been particularly good—Sometimes they fix a bullet to a string tied to a Pole & knock them down—. . .

. . .

9th I went to day for the first time in the N West Canoe—a Beaver blanket & a Carpet where put in it to sit upon—we carried a small table to be used in embarking & disembarking for the Canoe cannot be brought very near the Shore least the Gravel or pebbles injure her—so the table was set in the water & a long Plank laid from it to the Shore enabled me to get in or out the Men carrying the Canoe empty into the water & out of it upon their shoulders—we have less than "boards between us & Eternity" for the Canoe is formed of Birch bark fixt on to thin ribs of very light wood with the Gum or Pitch the Indians make from fir Trees, & of which they always carry some with them least an accident rub off any, or the heat of the Sun melt it—we dined in a Meadow on the Peninsula where I amused myself with setting fire to a

[5]Castle Frank was built on the west side of the Don River, north of St. James Cemetery. After the Simcoes' departure, it was used only occasionally, and was finally burned in 1829.

kind of long dry Grass which burns very quick & the flame & smoke run along the ground very quickly & with a pretty effect—I was delighted with the swift & easy motion of the Canoe, & with its appearance—

14th I went again in the Canoe untill we came in sight of the high Lands but it was so very cold I was very glad to walk part of the way back, we dined on the Peninsula—I passed a spot on the Peninsula where it was supposed an Indian had been buried lately—a small pile of wood was raised a bow & arrow lay on it, & a Dog skin hung near it —some Indians sacrifice Dogs, other Tribes eat them when extremely ill—

. . .

20th we dined in the woods & eat part of a Raccon it was very fat & tasted like Lamb if eaten with mint sauce

. . .

[1794]

18th of Jany the Queens Birthday the weather is mild we breakfasted with the window open—an experiment was made of firing Pebbles from Cannon—a Salute of 21 Guns & a dance in the Eveng in honor of the day—the Ladies much dressed—

Sunday 19th the weather so pleasant we rode to the bottom of the Bay crossed the Don which is frozen & rode on the Peninsula, returned across the Marsh which is covered with ice & went as far as the Settlements which are near 7 Mile from the Camp, there appeared some comfortable Log Houses inhabited by Germans & some by Pensylvanians, some of the Creeks were not frozen enough to bear the Govrs Horse, but mine passed very well, he excells in getting over difficult places, & in leaping over logs which I like very much

25th two Soldiers went to Niagara, these Expresses are to go at regular periods by way of a Post—

26th we went to the Donn to see Mr Talbot skait—Capt Shaws Children sat the Marshy ground below the Bay on fire the long dry grass on it burns with great rapidity this dry weather it was a fine sight & a study for flame & smoke from our House, at night the flames diminished & appeard like the lamps in a dark night in the Crescent at Bath—

27th I walked below the Bay & set the other side of the Marsh on fire for amusement—The Indians have cut holes in the Ice over which they spread a Blanket on poles & they sit under the shed moving a wooden Fish hung to a line in the water by way of attrackting the living fish, which they spear with great dexterety when they approach—the Govr: wished me to see the process—we had to walk half a mile to the place there was no snow on the ice & we were without cloth Shoes, the Govr pushed a large limb of a tree before him which kept him steady & with the assistance of Mr Talbot I reached the Spot where they were catching Maskunonge (a superior kind of Pike) & Pickerell—I was almost frozen while looking on, tho the apprehension of falling kept me warm while I walked—

31st one of the Horses drawing Hay across the Bay fell into an air hole & was drowned—
Scaddings Cottage burnt down—

. . .

1st of March the News received of the death of the Queen of France[6] —Orders given out for Mourning in which every body appeared this Eveng, and the dance was postponed—

March 3d the weather severely cold—

4th Do—tho' I wore 3 fur tippets I was so cold I could hardly hold my Cards this Eveng—this is the first time we have felt the want of a cieling which we have not had made in our drawing Room because the room was rather low—

5th very cold, I divided the Room by hanging across it a large Carpet which made it warmer—
there has so little Snow fallen this winter that it was scarcely practicable to track the Deer, in consequence of which the Indians have been almost starved—a great many of their women & Children come to our windows every day for bread which we cannot refuse them, tho' having but a certain quantity of flour untill the Spring supply arrives, it is inconvenient to give them what they require. . . .

. . .

Jany 1st 1796

the Govr infinitely better can walk 4 or 5 miles without fatigue probably owing to the cold season of the year. An express went to Kingston—Mrs Maccauley came to see me & we had a dance, there are 10 Ladies here & as they dance reels we can make up a Ball.

. . .

23d we walked on the Ice to the House which is building on Francis' 200 acre Lot of land—it is called Castle Frank built on the plan of a Grecian Temple, totally of wood the Logs squared & so grooved together that in case of decay any log may be taken out the large Pine trees make Pillars for the Porticos which are at each end 16 feet high—some Trees were cut & A large fire made near the House by which Venison was toasted on forks made on the Spot & we dined—I returned home in the Cariole—several people were fishing on the River Don thro' holes cut in the Ice, the small Red Trout they catch are excellent—I gathered black haws the roots of the tree boiled are a cure for complants in the Stomack

. . .

2d Feby Mrs Richardson went with me to C. Frank it is not yet floored, the Carpenters are building a Hut for themselves, I gathered fox berries they grow like small red Currants on a delicate plant; the water elder

[6]Marie Antoinette was guillotined on October 16, 1793.

berries are here called tree Cranberries & are less bitter than in England —We had an immense fire to day & dined on Toasted venison—

W 3 We drove on the Ice to Skinners Mill a mile beyond Castle Frank which looked beautiful from the River the ice became bad from the Rapidity of the River near the Mill—at the mouth of the Donn I fished from my Carriole, but the fish are not to be caught as they were last winter several dozen in an hour; it is said the noise occasioned by our driving constantly over this Ice frightens away the fish. which seems probable, for they are still in abundance in the Humber where we do not drive, 15 dozen were caught there a few days ago the Govr finds great benefit by driving out this cold weather & likes my Dormeuse very much—the Children sit in the front of it—

4th we drove 3 miles to the Settlement below the Town & at Mrs Ashbridges saw Callebashes which having holes cut in them served as Bowls to ladl water having a natural handle—I brought away some of the seeds which are to be sown in March in rich ground—might not the use of these Callibashes which are in shape like skulls, have given rise to the story of the Southern Indians drinking out of the skulls of their Enemies?
I saw Mr Richardsons Infant laid in a Box which he held by a Cord, & was skaiting upon the Bay this gave the Child air & exercise

5th Mrs McGill Miss Crookshanks[7] & a large party drove with me in Carrioles to dine on toasted venison by a large fire on the Beach below the Settlements, we sat under the shelter of the root of an immense Pine which had been blown up by the wind & found it very pleasant & returned 6 miles in 32 minutes—had a Card party in the Evening

6 the Ladies did not catch cold, & were delighted with the novelty of dining in the air in winter, so to day we went to C Frank—Mrs MCauley joined the party—the Ice was not quite so good & the Snow melted—it was so mild we could not wear great coats—
Francis has a small sleigh, which the Servants have taught a Goat to draw, he is the handsomest goat I ever saw, & lookes very well in harness—it is a very pretty sight to see Francis drawn in this Car—they used the animal to draw the sleigh by making him draw it full of wood, at first he was very untractable

8th we set out on the Ice with 3 Carrioles but driving too near a large Crack in the Ice near the shore the Horses in the first Cariole broke in, but being quickly whipped, recoverd their footing on the ice & drew the Cariole over the Crack We got out of our Cariage & Mr Givings thought he could drive better & pass safely; but the Horses plunged much Deeper & could not extricate themselves; with difficulty the Harness was unloosed & they were set free without injury, the water not being above

[7]Rachel Crookshank (1775–1840) was a sister of Mrs. John McGill and of George Crookshank. She became the second wife of Dr. James Macaulay.

5 feet deep—we walked to Mr McCauleys Lot & dined in that part of the Woods & in the Eveng I walked home but the Carrioles went very safely across the Bay keeping farther from the Crack, & perhaps the night air made the ice harder John Maccauley[8] who is but four years old, cut thro some large pieces of Wood with an ax which made Francis emulous to become an axman also—he is going to begin tomorrow—

. . .

19th Mr Pilkington went in a Boat to the head of the Lake—We dined in the Woods on Major Shanks farm Lot where an Arbour of branches of Helmock Pine was prepared, a band of Music stationed near; we dined on large Perch & Venison—Jacob the Mohawk was there—he danced Scotch Reels with more ease & grace than any person I ever saw, & had the air of a Prince—the picturesque way in which he wore & held a black blanket, gave it the air of a Spanish Cloak his Leggins were scarlet—on his Head & Arms Silver bands—I never saw so handsome a figure—

. . .

31st [March] walked to C. Frank & returned by Yonge Street from whence we rode—the road is as yet very bad, there are pools of water among roots of trees & fallen logs, in swampy spots, & these pools being half frozen render them still more disagreable when the horses plunge into them.

. . .

18th [April] Francis has not been well—we therefore set off for C. Frank to day to change the air intending to pass some days there—the house being yet in an unfinished state, we divided the large Room by Sail Cloth—pitched the Tent in the inner part where we slept on wooden Beds—

It is quite a Summers day—Musquito's arrived at 3 oclock A large wooden Canoe was launched here to day built by one of the Men who ought to have been busy in Working at Castle Frank

. . .

20th the Porticos here are delightful pleasant & the Room cool from its height & the thickness of the logs of which ye House is built—the Mountain Tea berries in great perfection—Francis is much better & busy in planting Currant bushes & Peach trees—there is an Insect which is not be got rid of, it bores into the Timber, & is heard at night it is like a very large maggot—I have seen them taken from under the bark of Trees to bait fishing hooks

. . .

30th [June] Sent the Children to C Frank in a Boat we rode there thro those pleasant shady Pine Plains, now covered with Sweet scented Fern—there is no under wood under the Pines so it is good riding—

[8]John Simcoe Macaulay (1791–1855) was the eldest son of Dr. James Macaulay. He became an officer in the Royal Engineers and the militia, and was a member of the Legislative Council of Upper Canada from 1839 to 1841.

July 1st a large party from the Garrison to dinner, a boat with Music accompanied them, we heard it in the Eveng untill they had passed the Town it sounded delightfully

3 the Govr went to the Garrison & returned to supper—some heavy thunder showers fell this Eveng, & the Musquitos more troublesome than ever—it is scarcely possible, to write or use my hands which are always occupied in killing them or driving them away. This situation being high does not at all secure us from those knats—

4th I descended the Hill & walked to Skinners Mill thro Meadows which looked like Meadows in England Playter was hay making—going down the Hill some Dragons blood Seed fell out as I passed which I collected—

6th I passed Playters picturesque bridge over the Donn it is a butter Nut Tree fallen across the river the branches still growing in full leaf—Mrs Playter being timerous, a pole was fastened thro the branches to hold by; having attempted to pass it, I was determined to proceed but was frightened before I got half way—

7th the weather excessively hot & we find the under ground Room very comfortable, the windows on one side are cut thro the side of the Hill. . . .

. . .

11th a very wet day & the Musquitos so numerous that smoke would not drive them away, when it grow Dark I take my Candle & set to read on my bed under the Musquito Net, which is the only protection from them

12th we rode to the Town by the New Road opened by the Government Farm & thro the Town it is the shortest way in point of time the road is so much better than Yonge Street. . . .

. . .

18th rode to dine at C Frank so heavy a shower of Rain that we were obliged to quit the lower Room the windows of which are not glazed slept here—

19th Mrs McGill & McCauley breakfasted here, I returned to the Garrison with them in Mr Bouchettes Boat & rode back to dine at C Frank —Mr Pilkington came in the Evening; it was very damp & cold I was glad to stand by the fire—

W 20 took leave of C. Frank called at Playters dined with Mrs McGill slept at the Garrison

21st of July took leave of Mrs McGill & Miss Crookshanks I was so much out of Spirits I was unable to dine with her, she sent me some dinner but I could not eat cried all the day—the Govr dined with Mr

McGill & at 3 oclock we went on board the Onondago, under a Salute from the vessels, little Wind soon became calm—

. . .

H 2 WILLIAM COOPER SELLS HIS HOUSE
[*T.P.L., Early Toronto Papers*]

York Novr 27 1794

That is to Sertify that I William Cooper in Consideration of One yoke of Steers Two years Old and upwards with yoke and Staples and Ring therto belonging, (and One bell, Likwise One barell of Salmon to be Delivered at the Mill and One barell of flower—or Cash to the amount that in Consideration of the above have Sold and Demised to him Miles his hears and asignes forever that Dweling Standing on Lott No/ 6 in the City of York with Lot and all the boards Slabs and Shingles therto belonging farthermore that I am to Look for the above Steers but if not to be found the above Miles is by these writings Obligated to make the Same Good by the first Day of April 1795 in Witness therof
we have Singored our hands
this Twenty Seventh Day of Novr. 1794

H 3 GEORGE PORTER[9] SELLS HIS HOUSE
[*P.A.O., Ridout Papers*]

Know all Men by these Presents that I George Porter of York do bargain and sell unto John Small Esqr. my Logg House & Lot in the Town of York aforesaid Number, for the Sum of Fifty Dollars, for which Sum I promise to shingle the House Complete, and that the sd. John Small shall have immediate Possession of the same to him and His Heirs for ever

George Porter

Augt. 31st. 1795

Recd. of John Small Esq the Sum of fifty Dollars in full for the Lot & Log House above mention'd

George Porter

H 4 WILLIAM CHEWETT TO D. W. SMITH
[*Department of Lands and Forests, Survey Records, Surveyors' Letters, XIV, no. 138*]

York 7th September 1796

I thank you for the Glass which I have received, all whole to one pane.

I cannot get any body to do any thing to the House[10] for want they

[9]George Porter, a former sergeant of militia, had been put in possession of this lot, on the southwest corner of King and Ontario Streets, by Alexander Aitkin, the surveyor. It was later found to be part of the Reserve for the Government Buildings.

[10]William Chewett was superintending the building of Maryville.

say of seasoned Boards of which I intended to have lined the whole of the house, for to fill up the inside with refuse brick, before it was under pinned with stone would be doing nothing, or worse than nothing.

The back part of the Chimney where it projects, in order to form the draft, seems to me to be filled up with blocks of wood, where you remarked the weather boarding must be taken down, and boarded over again with better stuff, and I think it will be requisite, to have it taken down, in order to examine the Chimney.

I intended to have made an addition at the Northern Gable end of twelve, or fourteen feet, by the whole of the breadth of the House about seven feet high, with a pent, in the manner of your Office at Niagara but I am afraid nothing can be done this Season.

The Kendricks promissed, but they seem only to be amusing me, for when I ask them for the Estimate they have not had time to do it—and all the other Workmen are engaged.

H 5 ELMSLEY TO RICHARD CARTWRIGHT
[*Queen's University, Douglas Library, Cartwright Letter Books*]

Niagara 5th Decr. 1797—

. . . [York] is now a very different place from what it appeared to be when we were there last Summer. We hear that the Situation of its inhabitants, particularly Capt. Smith & the Attorney General is wretched beyond Discription: It was bad enough when I was there last Month, but some persons who have lately come from thence give us a picture of it, which is really affecting & the harbour having long since been frozen up, there is very little chance of their getting supplies from us, particularly of flour which I understand they are in great want of, & fresh Meat which from their total want of fodder, they cannot possibly have of their own. . . .

H 6 WILLIAM B. PETERS[11] TO WILLIAM JARVIS
[*T.P.L., William Jarvis Papers*]

York April 25th 1798

I reached this *Metropolis* last Saturday and found all the Inhabitants starving as they say, but not quite so bad as that. . . .

Your House is at a stand for want of materials, the Kitchen is covered, but nothing more, there are no boards to be had; you will have to send over bricks and lime from the other side for the Chimneys, as there

[11]William Birdseye Peters (1774–1817) was the son of Rev. Samuel Peters. His early years were spent with his grandfather in Connecticut; he later joined his father in London, and studied at Oxford. He came to Upper Canada, became an ensign in the Queen's Rangers, and was called to the Bar. His marked American sympathies made him unpopular during the War of 1812, and he returned to the United States, where he ultimately settled in New Orleans or Mobile.

was none of the former made here before July, and the latter at all events cannot be procured here I can get men to cut the Pickets for 12/ the hundred. It will be best to get a number ready cut as they will come in play one way or another—the sooner you come over the better

H 7 McGill to Simcoe
[*T.P.L., Wolford Simcoe Papers*]

Upper Canada, York, June 5th, 1798

. . . Pray what are the arrangements that you would wish to have made in regard to Castle Frank? The Chief Justice has a great partiality for the situation, but he is now erecting a very excellent house in town upon Russell's Creek and Simcoe Place. The improvements in York and its vicinity are rapid and the farms upon Yonge Street and Dutch Settlement both valuable and productive. Our Provincial Parliament meets this day in the two brick Government Buildings, but owing to the insufficiency of members present the house is adjourned until tomorrow. . . .

H 8 Expenses of Celebration of King's Birthday
[*T.P.L., Peter Russell Papers*]

Honorable Presidant Russel Dr

June 4th 1798	To Cards for 70 Bottles wine at 9/	31	10	0
	" 3 Bottles Brandy at 10/	1	10	0
	" 52 Suppers at 4/	10	8	0
	" 52 at Tea at 2/	5	4	0
	" 7 lb lofe Sugar for Singaree at 5/	1	5	0
	" 34 lb Candles at 3/	5	12	0
	" Workmanship Boards & nails by John McDonnell—to light the too houses	5	12	9
	" 7 Dollars Paid musick By Order	2	16	0
	" 1 pint Tumbler broke } broke in the Room one Glass		3	0
	" ½ pint Do		2	0
	" 6 wine glasses		12	0
	" 10 Porter Bottle		10	0
	" 80/ for Servt. Diet	4	0	0
	N.Y. Cy.	£69	4	9
	" Scrubing the room Before the Ball 8/ paid by John McDonnold		8	0
	Balance due	£68	7	9

16 June 98 Approved—
J. Small

68. 7. 9
5

8) 341.18.9 (42.14.10
32

21
16

1.18

York June 26, 1798
Received from the Honble Peter Russell Sixty eight Pounds seven shillings and nine pence New York Currency in full of the above account for a Ball & Supper on His Majesty's Birthday.

Abner Miles

H 9 Russell to Osgoode, Quebec
[*T.P.L., Peter Russell Papers*]

[York, Sept. 13, 1798]

. . . You would be pleased to see this place now as it is really beautiful [and] makes a very different appearance from what it did when we were here together about this time six years ago. I have a very comfortable house near the Bay, from whence I see every thing in the harbor & entering it, & Miss Russell has an extensive poultry yard which keeps her fully amused & contributes somewhat to her Health. I have about 700 Acres two miles from the Town, on which I have put a farmer on shares, in hopes of supplying my Table without searching the Country for Provisions. I have been obliged to turn the Senr Franklin[12] off for villiany & Sam lives now with Mr. White—Mr Gray sent me up two others to supply their Places—one of whom is to be tried in October for theft, and the other is rather too fine a Gentleman for Upper Canada. He lived with General Prescott, his name George Thomas Knight you will oblige me by procuring his Character. Mrs. White has not her health here, and the Attorney General is himself not very robust. His Spirits seem to have left him—I fear he is not happy—Shank is now Commandant of the Queens Rangers, and lives in consequence very liberally —The Chief Justice is building here a very fine House which will cost at least £4000—so that I presume he does not look for a removal— The Expence of living most enormous—Beef 1/—Mutton & Veal 1/6 —fowls a dollar a couple—Flour 7 dollars the Cwt—laborers 12/ & Artificers 16/ per day—& no likelyhood of a fall in any thing. . . .

H 10 Extracts from Alexander McDonell's Diary
[*P.A.O., Miscellaneous Papers, 1795, List of Jurors, Home District*]

2d Jan. '99—Fine clear cold weather—Went to the Council Office at ten—Made entries in the State Book . . . At two O'clock left the Office & walked to the Garrison, met the President,[13] Mr. A. Burns, & my Brother[14] who had been out walking . . . Soon after parting with the President met Mr. & Mrs. White—After them Wilson bringing my horse from the head of the lake—Dined at the Mess with Cols. Shank & Smith, Messrs. D. Burns & Gray—Drank tea at Mr. Givens, wrote to Capt. McGill agreeably to the president's wish—After tea went to Col. Shanks room, played a Rubber at whist—the Two Cols. against Gray & myself

[12]Robert Franklin was Russell's senior employee. He was a free Negro. Through Russell's influence he received a grant of land on Yonge Street and built a hut on it, but the York Report in 1796 recommended it be taken from him because of his "not coming within the description of those proposed to be settled on Yonge Street."

[13]Peter Russell.

[14]Angus McDonell.

—Supped at the Mess room, the same company as at dinner. After supper walked to Town with Mr. Gray—Cold weather & slippery roads. Found A. Burns & Mr. Wood at supper with my brother when I got home. Found a note from the Attorney General inviting me to spend the evening of the next day with him. Sent an apology but declined going on acct. of my brothers[15] death. They retired soon after—Went to bed at half-past 10

3d. A fine, clear, cold morning, & continued so throughout the day—Sent my horse out to Yonge Street to be wintered at Lyons's. He returned in the Evening, saying he could not take him. In going to the C. Office met N. Cameron: paid him 10/ for the feeding of the horse at the head of the Lake—Made entries in the State Book till three O'clock. The official Accts. of Admiral Nielsons Victory over Bruyer & the French Fleet at Alexandria arrived[16]—Dined at Mr. Small's—Company only the family & my Brother—who went in the evening to the Attorney Generals—Remained at Mr. Small's till nine went home. Mr. A. Burns called in—Gave him a tea cup full of honey which he wanted—He went off at ten. I went to bed—did not hear my brother come home—

4th. A fine clear morning & cold throughout the day. After breakfast called on Ruggles, Wright, Clark & Arch Cameron, on the two former to get receipts for money paid for disbursements for the Gaol, on Clark about pay—& on Cameron respecting a Bill drawn on him by Pell in my favor—Went to the Council Office made entries in the State Book—Wrote til two o'clock—Walked to the Garrison, met Mr. Allcock—& shortly after was overtaken by the Solicitor[17] in his Cariole who was also going to the Garrison got in with him—Found the Cols. Shank & Smith & Mr. D. Burns at Dinner—Col. Shank having ordered a feu de joie to be fired in consequence of Admiral Nelsons victory, the Mess agreed to give the following proportion of wood for a bon fire—Col. Shank 2 Chords—Col Smith 1-do. Gray, Burns & myself 2 more. At sunset it was set on fire—Returned from the Garrison with Gray in his Cariole. Found my Brother at home. Went to the Presidents, found A. Burns & McNab there. Informed the President that the people want to illuminate in consequence of Nelson's victory—He orderd his rooms to be illuminated, assisted in doing so. The Miss Willcocks called in & drank tea—Mr. Burns went home with them—Mr. Willcocks windows broke in consequence of his not illuminating—Supped at the President's—left him at ten. Messrs. Burns & McNab came home with me, found my brother alone—They did not stay long. Went to bed about eleven O'clock.

[15]James McDonell was a captain in the 43rd Light Infantry, and died in the West Indies.

[16]The Battle of the Nile, August 1, 1798.

[17]Robert I. D. Gray.

5th. Cold, clear day—The Solicitor called in after breakfast—was informed that Mr. Willcock's windows were broken last night in consequence of his not illuminating—After breakfast rode with the Solicitor to James Playters at the mouth of the Don, to prevail on him to winter my horse—He had not fod[d]er to spare . . . Dined with A. McNabb, my Brother there also—Solicitor step'd in at dusk & asked us to go & spend the Evening with him—A few minutes before we went out Powell junior & Mr. J. Pell arrived in a double sleigh from Niagara—Previous to going to the Solicitor's went home. Nicolas Klingenbruner[18] called with Thomas Smith[19] in custody committed by a warrant from Mr. Willcocks for riotous conduct, &ca, the preceding evening—Told him to procure sureties which he did & he entered with Recognizance accordingly—Went to the Solicitors drank tea—D. Burns called in—The Solicitor, McNab, my Brother & self played a Rubber at whist. The Solicitor & I gained four points, drank a glass of porter & came home—having a severe cold, mull'd some wine, bathed my feet & went to bed—

6th. Pleasant clear weather; after breakfast commenced making up my Accounts against Government—Dr. McCaulay called in & soon after Adjutant McGill—Sent my horse to the Garrison in consequence of an offer of Col. Shanks to allow his groom to take care of him—Paid a visit to the Chief Justice in company with McColey sat there some time —The Chief & Mrs. Elmsley were going to visit Mrs. White—Called at Mr. Small's saw him—Mrs. Small not well, & not to be seen—Went to the Speaker; not at home—then to the President's, neither he nor Miss Russell at Home—Call'd on Gray & Doctor Burns then came home & continued making out my Acct. Burns & Gray dined with me—My Brother dined with Ruggles—An indifferent dinner—drank nearly a bottle of port each besides two bottles of porter—Mr. A. Burns, Mr. McNabb & Mr. Allan called in the Evening—drank three bottles more porter & eat bread & cheese—All retired but A. Burns—Mull'd some wine for old Mary who had been sick all day—Could not make her hear me, sent her one of the blankets off my bed, supposing her cold—Conversation during the evening chiefly about Willcocks windows being broke—Different opinions, mine that he deserved to have them broke—McNabb & Gray uneasy about the business—

7th. Mild weather. After breakfast called on Messrs. Allan & Wood purchased 2 yds. of hair ribbon, tied it on my hair. . .

8th. Got up early. Walked before breakfast & looked at the Gaol—

[18]Nicholas Klingenbrumer (Clinginboomer) is said to have been present at the Battle of the Plains of Abraham. He settled at Niagara, where he worked for William Jones, an army tailor. Prior to 1799 he moved to York, where he practised his trade. He last appears in the List of Inhabitants in 1812.

[19]Thomas Smith (d. 1812) was a son of William Smith, the builder. He was killed during the Battle of Queenston Heights.

Remarked that the lower rooms were strong and secure, but thought those above less so . . . Walked homewards near the Court house lot met Burk with an ax in his hand—Told him he must not cut any wood on that lot or on the Gaol Lot—Call'd at Allan & Woods bought a skain of black sewing silk, & borrowed the Encyclopaedia. Went home, breakfast on the table, made tea, my Brother got up breakfasted—Nott[20] the Taylor, call'd in—Gave him a pair of blue pantaloons . . . & a scarlet waistcoat to make. Went to the Council Office . . . Cald at Herchmer's for a blank book, for red silk & twist. He had neither, Called on Heron, he had neither—Met Messrs. McGill, Givens & McCauley—The latter engaged to go to the Garrison with me—Call'd at home & brought from there the journal of the Queens Rangers[21] which I had borrowed from Col. Shank. Cald at Allan & Woods—Met the Chief Justice & Col. Shaw . . . Walked to the Garrison—the Chief Justice accompanied Col. Shaw, Doctor McCauley & self as far as his own house—He there parted with us. At the Garrison called on Mr. Given; saw him, the Ladies not to be seen—Cald on Col. Shank—gave him his book—Soon after the drum beat for dinner—Shank and Smith, McCauley & self only there—Drank 3 bottles of wine. Walked to Town with McCauley . . . Went to the President's—found him & Miss Russell, Mr. A. Burns & Mr. A. McNabb at their wine; drank two glasses of wine—Thereafter Mr. McNabb soon retired—Conversation general . . . Supper—Retired soon after—. . . Went home. Found Messrs. Weekes & Powell with my Brother—Mr. Weekes in liquor my Brother very drunk Mr. Powell gay—Conversation general about Buonaparte, Nelson & the Duke of York—My brother talked absurdly—Weekes & Powell soon retired, & went to bed at half past eleven—

. . .

H 11 ELIZABETH RUSSELL TO ELIZABETH FAIRLIE, HARWICH
[*T.P.L., Elizabeth Russell Papers*]

York Janry 26—1799

. . . We left Niagara and arrived at this place the 3d of Novr 1797 —and yet are only just beging to be settled. We have a good House which my Brother has built at a very great expence in a most charming situation in the front of the Town with a most Beautiful Bay before us and but a few yards from our door on which in the summer there is charming Fishing and rowing or sailing, particularly up a river called the Don, and in the winter it is all Froze of an amazing thickness, it is Delightful Slaying on the Ice on which about a mile & quarter we go

[20]William Knott (d. 1825) served for six years in the 29th Regiment before enlisting in the Queen's Rangers in 1792. He was a tailor, and jailer from 1811.

[21]*A Journal of the operations of the Queen's Rangers, from the end of the year 1777, to the conclusion of the late American War, by Lieutenant Colonel Simcoe, Commander of that corps* (Exeter, 1787).

across the Bay to the opposite side to the Lake (Ontario) on the sands of which there is charming riding or driving to the Length of eight miles. but with all these advantages we have a great many difficultys to encounter with in this new country, particularly the high prices of every necessary of life the dearness of Labour of all kinds and the want of good servants. What do you think to the paying a woman from three and nine pence to four and sixpence a day only for scrubing your House like a common Chare woman in England, and to a man upwards 5 shillings a day for cuting wood for the Fire Carpenters and Bricklayers 9 shillings per Day. Turkeys & geese a dollar & half a peice and so on with every thing. By this you may Judge what a great expence living must be. . . .

H 12 Swarms of Insects

[*York*, Upper Canada Gazette, *May 18, 1799*]

As the wind blows more frequently from the East at this time of year, and thereby swarms of insects are drove from the adjoining swamp, or marsh, we would recommend to those who have gardens in the town, to set fire to small heaps of horses litter, damp shavings, or any thing that will cause a sharp smoake therein, as the best means of keeping them off, and saving their young vegetables; of which we are in great want.

H 13 Elizabeth Russell to Elizabeth Fairlie

[*T.P.L., Elizabeth Russell Papers*]

May 21 1799

. . . I am now agoing to give you a great deal of trouble. I want to work a gown with the coulord cottons, and there is none to be got in this country so will be obliged to you if when you go next to Town if you will get me some of the following Coulors two kinds of Browns yellow orrange pink scarlet & crimson garter Blue light Blue apple & grass green. I dont know how they are sold but if by the ounce a quarter of an ounce of each sort will be enough, if by the skeen three of each kind will do.—I will also be very thankfull to you if you would get me a muslin gown made as they are worn and as you are pretty much my size I will thank you to have it made as for yourself. I would have it a smart & visiting afternoon but not quite a full dress, also a calico morning dress. The pattern of that and the muslin I leave to your choice only dont let the muslin exceed six shillings a yard for If the French shoud happen to take a liking to it it woud not be great Loss. and be so good as to send me a yard & half of each to repair with and let them be mad quite in the taste in the same way as you woud have them for yourself. and if you could send me a fasionable Bonnet and also, whatever is most worn around the waist. I will also be obliged to you if you will send me six Tomboor neddles & a case. . . .

H 14 Russell to Serjeant Shepherd, Lincoln's Inn
[*T.P.L., Peter Russell Papers*]

I take up my Pen under the deepest Affliction to inform you of the Death of your Brother in Law Mr. White, who was shot in a Duel with Mr. Small Clerk of the Ex. Council of this Province in the Morning of the 3d. Instant, and expired at my House in the Evening of the next day —Tho' under the most excruciating Torture he retained his Senses & understanding in their fullest force to within an Hour of his Death, & wanted for Nothing which the tenderest Affection of my Sister & myself with the best medical Aid to be found here could possibly supply. But the Wound was mortal from the first, the Ball having entered on the right Side between the two lowest Short Ribs & striking the Spine probably partially dividing some of the Bundles of Nerves that pass from the Vetebrae caused an instant Palsy of the lower Extremities & the most painfull Spasms. Knowing his dissolution to be inevitable he submitted to his fate with a most pious & Christian Resignation to the divine Will & forgiveness of all his Enemies. The Circumstances which led to this unfortunate Event are briefly as follows—

Mrs. Small having at one of the Assemblies in the Course of last Winter publicly Slighted Mrs. White in a most pointed Manner—as that Lady can best inform you—Mr. White being exceedingly exasperated was unfortunately impelled by the Violence of his Resentment to Communicate to Mr. Smith the Acting Surveyor Genl who is now in England some Circumstances to the Prejudice of Mrs. Smalls Reputation which that Gentleman very imprudently (tho' in some degree authorised by Mr. White to do so) related to Mrs. Elmsley and the Chief Justice—Insinuations arising out of this Story having lately reached Mrs. Smalls Ears, She urged her Husband it is presumed to do her Justice—and having demanded from the Chief Justice the purport of Mr. Smiths Communication he called upon Mr. White in the afternoon of the 2d. instant to avow or deny it immediately—Mr. White answered that it being very possible that Mr. Smith might have said more or less than he told him he had better obtain from himself the exact Tale he had Communicated to the Chief Justice & he should then very candidly tell him what parts of the Relation were true or false—Mr. Small not satisfied with this insisted on Mr. Whites going out with him immediately, which our friend having unfortunately agreed to, they met the next Morning, Mr. Small accompanied by Mr. Sheriff McDonell & Mr. White by a German Officer of the Name of De Haen—The Event you know.

. . . Mr. Small has surrendered to Justice & is in Custody—Warrants are out for the apprehension of the two Seconds, who I am told propose to surrender before the day of Trial. I shall keep the Boys with me until the Navigation opens when I shall forward them to Mr. Osgoode at Quebec, who I have no doubt will procure them a Commodious & safe passage to England, under the Care of some proper person who may deliver them into your Hands. . . .

York 9th Janry. 1800

H 15 Extracts from Joseph Willcocks' Diary
[P.A.C., Joseph Willcocks Memorandum and Letter Book]

19th. [September, 1800] I went to the Humber on a pleasure party with Mr. & Miss Russell, Mr. and the Miss Willcocks's Mr. Weeks and Doctor Baldwin We left York at 10 oClock and reach'd the Humber in Mr. Jarvis's Boat at half past 12. Walked about for an hour & dined at half past 1 We had for Dinner a piece of Cold Roast Beef, Cold ham cold chickens & hot stewed Wild Ducks. We all arrived safe at home at 5 oClock in the Evening. . . .

. . .

28th. . . . Went to Church the discourse was principly to caution Persons from dreading to Die and how necessary it was to be always prepared for that awfull moment. Returned hom Miss Russell and I went to Mrs. W. Smith's to pay a Visit. We met Mrs. Jarvis on the Way. I was introduced to her. Doctr. Baldwin and I went to the Toronto (she not having Sailed) with a letter of Mr. Russells . . . Dined at Mr. Willcocks it being Sunday Mr. Gamble dined there We had for dinner a piece of roast Beef and a Pudding Returned home to Tea Dennison & his son George[22] spent the Evening with us Mr. Russell and Doctor Baldwin were striving to fix a Microscope but could not do it complete. Mr. Russell read part of Gullivers Travels. The whole of the day there was very fine Weather Bought six salmon for Mr. Russell for a Dollar.

. . .

30th. Went very early in the morning with Doctor Baldwin to the Island where he hid his Goods the night before he set off from thence home in his Canoo I returned by myself in my Canoo the Wind was very Strong against me it was very dangerous to cross the Bay I went after breakfast in Mr. Jarvis's boat to Commadore Bouchette's Vessel for Goods of Mr. Russell's Pompadore[23] and a Man of Mr. Jarvis's rowed the Boat I got for Mr. Russell two Boushels of Timothy seed and a box of Peaches I also brought some Goods for Mr. Jarvis & some for D. W. Smith Esqr. I dined with Mr. Small Rugless was there We had for dinner a Salmon two Perch a piece of Roast Beef a Brace of Pheasant rashers and Peas I spent the Evening at home Willcocks was there Mr. Russell read part of Gullivers Travels, the earlier part of the day was windy but the remainder very fine

[22]George Taylor Denison (1783–1853) was the eldest son of John Denison. He played an important part in the organization of the Canadian militia.

[23]Pompadour (d. 1807) was a free Negro employed by Peter Russell. He was married to Peggy, one of Russell's slaves, and his children were also slaves.

. . .

3rd. [October, 1800] Received a note from Mr. Jarvis Stating that a Gentleman arrived at his House that Put it out of his power to go to the Island to-morrow—Went a shooting to the Island—got nothing—Returned to Dinner and had a Loin of roast Mutten, a Broiled Chicken and Some Pork a Bread Pudding Went to Willcocks's after Dinner & from thence to a Puppet Shew the Performance was very indifferent, the Weather very fine.

. . .

Sunday, 12th. Went to Church The discourse was principly supporting a religious Life and pious Conversations reprobating all immoral discourses. . . . Maria Willcocks came for me to go dine with them it being Sunday I returned home Soon after dinner Drank tea at Home Mr. Russell read part of the 4th volume of Udolpho. . . . The early part of the day was wet the remainder very fine Wore a Gray Coat a Dark waistcoat my gray Nankin trousers & Boots Went to bed at half past 11.

. . .

Thursday, [December] 25. [1800] Went to Church Weekes dined with us we had for dinner soup roast beef boiled Pork Turkey Plumb Pudding & minced pies We had a supper for the first time in my remembrance. I came to bed at 12 It was a very fine day Playter called for some camomile

. . .

Thursday, January 1. [1801] Miss Russell & I went out in the sled We called at Alcocks, McGills McCawleys & Smiths I upset the sled coming home McGill the two Ridouts the Solicitor Gen'l & Ruggles called to pay their respects We had for dinner Boiled beef, a roast Pig & minced meats. Denison called in the evening. It froze the bay across I went to bed at 10.

. . .

Thursday, 19. [February, 1801] Went in the sleigh to the Garrison for Mrs. Peters—She Mrs. Jarvis & family Mr. Givens Mr. Allen & I went to the Block House & dined there there was a Fox Chase The Solicitor Joined us at Dinner I stayed the whole day with the Ladies We returned about 5 oClock & after seeing the Horses done up I returned to Mr. Jarvis's where we stayed until one oClock Began to use the second Ben of Oats

. . .

Saturday, 28. [March, 1801] Rode to the Farm before breakfast There was a Horse Race on the Island between Serjeant Purvis[24] & Mr. McNabb Purvis won Weekes called an[d] borrowed three dollars I staid the most of the day in the office The Doctor called. We tapped a Cask of Madaira—we had for dinner minced veal soup Pigs cheek Eggs & Pudding Mr. Ridout & Mr. Denison called in the evening. I went to bed at

[24]Sergeant George Purvis joined the Queen's Rangers in 1791.

8 oClock. Mr. Willcocks gave a large supper party Mr. Russell hired black Sall at 4 Dollars a Month

. . .

Friday, 3. [April, 1801] Went to Mr. Alcock's farm before breakfast Went to church. a vessell arrived from Kingston the first this year I met Mr. Givens and Mrs. Peters Mrs. Peters & I went to Mr. Jarvis's then to Mr. Alcock's where we met Mrs. Jarvis & Mrs. McGill we came home with Mrs. Jarvis & then went to every store in the town I returned to dinner and had roast veal trout Soup Ducks Pancakes. Mr. Willcocks called in the Evg I went to Mr. Alcock's in the evening. Met Mrs. Smith & Mr. Willcocks there Went home with Mrs. Smith

. . .

Monday, 27. Went before breakfast to the farm staid there until night Returned and saw some Indians fighting I parted them One of them attempted to Strike me I nocked him down they were then quiet Dined when I came home on roast fowl & Pudding. Mr. Willcocks called we play cards.

. . .

Monday, 8. [June, 1801] Wrote in the office for some time I went to Dr. Gamble to buy a Yoke of Oxen but he was too Dear I brought an acct. from the office to the Parliament House I had for Dinner corned beef cold veal fish & Pudding. The whole Town was Illuminated for the victories obtained by the English

. . .

Thursday, 11. It was agreed by the Commons that Mr. Alcock should not be the sitting Memmer. Mr. Weekes and I went that morning to Mr. A. Mr. W. spoke severely to Mr. A—Went to the Governors with Warrants Mr. Russells Farmer arrived We had for dinner a Loin of Veal Fish and Pancakes Mr. Willcocks called in the Evening I went to the Farm and dug a well for ye. Horses

. . .

Thursday, 2. [July, 1801] I went to the Election for a Member for the Home County Mr. Small & Mr. McDonell were candidates Mr. Baldwin[25] came here we voted for Small I Examined McDonnell's Voters Returned to dinner and had Salmon Roast veal & Puddind Mr. Baldwin slept with us

. . .

Sunday, 19. Went to Church with Mrs. Smith Returned home with Mr. & Mrs. McCawley called at McGills returned home to Dinner . . .

[25]Robert Baldwin (d. 1816) was the second son of Alderman John Baldwin of Cork. He farmed the family estates of Knockmore and Moneroo, and was appointed by Lord Shannon the seneschal of his manor, Bever. He was enrolled in one of the volunteer corps of cavalry at the time of Lord Charlemont, and subsequently edited a newspaper, the *Volunteer Journal*, in support of the popular cause. In 1788 he became a bankrupt. He arrived in York with his family in 1799, and settled in Clarke Township. He later moved to York to live with his son, Dr. William Warren Baldwin.

Drank Tea at Mr. McGills on my [way] there I called at Mr. Weekes's & after some conversation he said that I was under the Pay of Government as their Informer & used many other approbious imputations—I gave him the Lye he said I should fight him to Morrow. I agreed to fight but not so soon—

Monday, 20. Captn. De Hean called on me in the morning to know my time and place—I told him 6 Next Morning at the point of the Don —I then went to Mr. Ruggles to get him to be my second he agreed he lay with me that night—the Hour was changed from 6 to 5

Tuesday, 21 At 4 oClock Ruggles and I were going to the Place appointed when the Sheriff met us & Put us under an arest—I gave security before Mr. Jarvis to keep the peace for Six Months

. . .

Thursday, 10. [September, 1801] Wrote the most of the day in the Office. A black fell overboard into the Bay but was not drowned we had for dinner roast beef soup & Pudding A boat-load of Hay & four men was blew off shore into the lake Mr. Peters Hale & I followed it with my Boat many other Boats pursued them but they were all sunk—to Appearance—before we could come up with them[26] it was near 10 oClock before we returned they put up a light at Garrison and fired Canon as signals for us. Mr. & Miss Russell drank Tea at Mr. Willcocks's

. . .

Tuesday, 24. [November, 1801] Went with Doctor Baldwin to the Garrison to see the Union flag hoisted & the Guns firing. Col. Shaw afterwards took us to the Mess where we got wine and Cake. Drs. McCawley and Anderson[27] came home with us, We stoped at Willcocks's, Woods & to see Captn. Brant—had for Dinner roast Mutton & boiled Beef Mr. Willcocks spent the evening with us

. . .

Wednesday, 21. [October, 1802] Went to Court with the Chief. Weekes was rude to him in Court but the Chief reprimanded him—When the Court broke up the Chief Capt. McGill & myself were walking home together Mr. Weekes was walking at some distance before us along with several persons, he returned by himself & met us & said the the Chief, Sir, You insulted me to day in Court dare you do it now—your Conduct is that which the Country shall judge it—the Chief asked him—What is my Conduct—Weekes replied & said Your Conduct is that which the Country shall judge it—We had Company to dinner The Chief spent the latter part of the Evening at Capt. McGills I at Mr. Beikey

. . .

[26]In his entry for Sept. 13, Willcocks records that the four men landed safely at Niagara.

[27]Dr. Cyrus Anderson was Assistant Surgeon in the 2nd Battalion, Royal Canadian Volunteers.

H 16 Joseph Willcocks to Richard Willcocks,[28] Dublin
[*P.A.C. Joseph Willcocks Memorandum and Letter Book*]

Upper Cana York
3d. November 1800

. . . There is no new occurrence here worth relating when there is you shall know it remember me to all my friends, let me know particularly about my dear Fathers health. I wish he knew how much I am respected here, in fact I feel as if I was regenerated, I am here among rational beings, Men tho' they are high in rank & fortune know themselves to be Men & will be friendly & kind to you, but at home a Puppy Ensign A Clerks Clerk or a Sneering Atty such as Master Whisler will because he has unjustly usurped the appearance of Loyalty look down uppon the rest of mankind with contempt, However I shall drop the Subject, tho' you know I have some reason to speak on it, and give you a sketch of my friend Mr Willcockss circumstances & character, which you are not to take notice of in your Letters to me, From the Letter my Father received from him previous to my leaving Ireland we should have supposed that his Property and circumstances were very extensive, particularly his mentioning to be Mayor of Cork. Tis true he was Mayor but at the same time a Bankrupt and I have been since led to understand that from the repeated habit of being so, he was well acquainted with all its concomitant circumstances and left Cork rather at the Debtr side of the Book. On his arrival in this Country he became a Merchant, as they are called, and one of the most respectable of that Tribe, but at Home we would call them little Country Dealers; However by this Species of Huxtry he enroled his name on the real Merchants book for nearly £2000, and from which, his present circumstances would not enable him to expunge a single Guinea, Tis true he has large tracks of Land but they are heavily Leaden with this debt, so much so, that I fear they will all sink under the Burden. . . . Think my Dear Richd, what my fate must have been if solely left to the Guardianship and Dependency of this Family; their utter incapacity to promote my Interest would have I am afraid, reduced me to commit some very desperate act, had not Providence (whose protection and unlimited munificence no man has more right to boast of) stept forward and raised a friend for me who has it both in his power and inclination to assist me I mean Mr Russell. . . .

There are several Irishmen here and to the Honor of our Country the first and only Man that has been hung here[29] was an Irisman, it happened since I came here it was for Forgery, there was no getting a Hangman

[28]Sir Richard Willcocks (d. 1835) was Joseph's elder brother, an attorney in Dublin. In 1827 he was knighted for his services as Inspector of Police in Munster.

[29]Humphrey Sullivan (see C 9).

untill at length an other dear Countryman who was in for Robbery, with the promise of a Pardon & twenty Guineas to carry him out of the Country filled the Office with the most unpardonable Ignorance, the Gentleman who was to die fell three times from the Gallows—it fulfilled the old adage—put an Irishman on the spit and you will get another to turn him—I have met a very great loss by the removal of Coll Smith from York Garrison he was uncommonly attentive to me, he had also a very pretty sister[30] that I would have been uncommonly attentive to if she carried more metal; indeed she is a rarity for there are few Pretty Girls in the Country, but you know beauty will not make the Pot boil, which consideration alone prevented me from assuming an air of Seriousness —Love & runaway matches I never was an advocate for, such proceeding may fill the belly of Women but not of men. . . .

Labourers Wages here are extravagantly high, never less than from 6 to 10 Irish Shillings a day, Carpenters & Masons from 9 to 14 these Wages are general thro' America, sometimes more but never less, so that no Man can make Money except those who have large families that can Labor. In this Province Mutten is 6½d and Beef 4d the pound In Lower Canad Mutten 2½ Beef 1½d a Boushell of Potatoes 2d. bread 1d a lb but Groceries very high and Waring Apparel excessively high I paid 5s a yard for a piece of Irish Linen Yesterday, at home it would be three, Madaira 2s2d per quart & Cheaper, Claret is not drank here, Port good 1s.10d a quart—The heat of Summer is insupportable & the Cold of Winter Intollerable, there are many instances of Persons being frozen to death and a Winter dose not pass by with out several noses, fingers, and feet being lost, for my part I dred the Winter altho I have one of the most Comfortable rooms in this Province there is no such room in Donougmores House, in fact Mr Russell thinks nothing to good for me. We have an elegant pair of Horses, and a Sled that will be fine Sport in Winter if not too Cold, but we have a great many very valuable Skins some of which are for the purpose of Sleding. There was great depredations committed the night before last by a flock of Wolves that came into this Town, one man lost 17 Sheep, several others lost in proportion. The perpetrators escaped with impunity We let lose a Pack of Hounds after them but from their Scattering after the different Scents we had no diversion, but when the Snow comes we will have fine fun tracing them & the Deer of which there are great abundance. I assure you that as for the Wild Ducks and Pidgeons they surpass any mention I could make of them. Fish of all kinds are in this Lake We will get a Salmon of 20lb weight as good as ever was killed at Island Bridge for an Irish Shillg., frequently less, You may think this underrating the matter but I assure you it is a fact. The Indians spear them. . . . the People are divided Politics runs very high. . . .

[30]Anne Smith married Alexander McDonell in 1805.

H 17 MASONIC FUNERAL[31]

[*York*, Upper Canada Gazette, *December 20, 1800*]

EXTRACTS

From the minutes of Harmony Lodge No. 8[32] viz.—

Lodge of emergency, called on Sunday 15th inst. to pay the funeral honors to the body of brother ALEX. PERRY of St. Paul's Lodge No. 12 Montreal. The lodge was opened in due form at half past 2 o'clock P.M. and honored with the attendance of the right W.P.G.M. William Jarvis, esq. secretary of this Province; and a respectable number of visiting bretheren. Before removing the body the following short Oration was pronounced by the worshipful Daniel Cozens, jun'r. master of the said lodge:

ORATION

"Like leaves on trees, the race of man is found,
Now green in youth, now withering on the ground!"

GEN. FELLOWS & BRETHEREN

KNOWING your feelings on this present melancholy occasion, I should conceive it unnecessary for me to urge anything on my part, or to point out to you the necessity of observing a particular decorum in doing the last offices to the remains of this our departed brother, had not his fate whilst living seemed strongly marked for commiseration; and whose untimely end now demands the tribute we are about to pay. The spectacle before us should inculcate the most awful lesson on the minds of us his surviving bretheren, and I doubt not, but that it will leave impressions, whose benignant operation may convince us, that there is nothing terrible in death. To free-masons, more particularly death should not be terrible, to them whose sole object is a moral one, bound by their vows to a moral union, to the practise of charity and cardinal virtues: if their lives but conform to the spirit of free masonry—their deaths however untimely, however accomplished, cannot but be happy. Could our participation alleviate the distresses of a childless mother, or sooth the afflicted mind of an affectionate father, their burden should be light and their cup not overflow. We leave to God and religion the task we cannot accomplish, what is now in our power we piously and affectionately will do. Little farther remains for me to add my bretheren, but that we proceed in the

[31]In his entry for Dec. 14, 1800, Joseph Willcocks wrote, "Councellor Perry was buried it was difficult to get People to carry him to the Grave." Willcocks' gossip is not always accurate.

[32]Harmony Lodge was the third masonic body in York. The first was Rawdon Lodge "between the three Lakes in Upper Canada," chartered by the Grand Lodge of England in June, 1792. Rawdon Lodge gave up its warrant on the English register in 1800, and was absorbed in St. John's Royal Arch Lodge, No. 16. The second lodge in York was the Queen's Rangers' Lodge No. 3. The third lodge, Harmony Lodge, was warranted in 1796. After 1802 it allied itself with the irregular Grand Lodge at Niagara, becoming dormant about 1809. In 1811 its warrant was handed in, and a new warrant issued to the Toronto Lodge, No. 8. (Robertson, *The History of Freemasonry in Canada.*)

most decent order, to discharge the last and only duty which this lifeless mass can expect at our hands. We with his immortal part as much at rest, as this his mortal will shortly be.—With your concurrence we will now convey the body to the grave, that goal of ambition, which priores and people and collective humanity must progressively inhabit.

The procession then moved to the place of enterment in the following order:

Preceded by the Rev'd Geo. Stuart,
CORPS, with six master masons poll-bearers,
Two Tylers,
Two Deacons,
A past master, with the bible, square, and compass,
Sen'r. and Jun'r. Wardens with columns,
Master masons, two by two,
Sec'y and Treasurer,
Past masters two by two,
Masters of Lodges, two by two.

The right worshipful provincial grand master between visiting brothers, Ang. M'Donell esq. and Mr. John Cameron, officiating as D.G.C. and D.G.M.

The most perfect silence and order was observed; after seeing the body deposited in the grave, the procession returned in the same order, and the lodge was closed at 4 o'clock P.M. in due form and perfect harmony.

York, 15th Dec. in the year of the Lord Jesus Christ, the master-builder of our hope, 1800, and of masonry 5800.

H 18 T. G. RIDOUT TO GEORGE RIDOUT, YORK
[P.A.O., Ridout Papers]

Quebec 22nd Decemr. 1815.

I hastily acknowledged your interesting magazine of the 30 Ult. which I assure you gave us great pleasure, as the state affairs, both foreign & domestic is so faithfully narrated.

Sally[33] thought herself at home again, and that she saw the Yankee Lawyer & Deforrest[34] on the ladders busy painting, & discussing on points of Law & Politicks, does human nater & you ever pass a Philosophical hour together? how do I long to make the trio—for instance

[33]Sarah Ridout (1801–17) was at school in Quebec.

[34]William Darius Forrest was an American who had lost both ears. He was High Constable from 1807 to 1809. He owned a large inn, the Mansion House, across King Street from Jordan's York Hotel. Its heyday was after the War of 1812. In 1818 it could accommodate 70 persons with board and lodging, terms 6/3 per day for gentlemen, $5 a week for servants.

Thales seated on the anvil, young Plato on the water trough with his feet to the furnace, and I blowing the bellows gently, by half hitches just to keep the fire going & leaning on the pole, the journeyman at the door shoeing a horse & now & then clapping in a word.—Those were glorious times when old Kahman used to let us blow the bellows for him, & Ira Gilbert made Light Jacks.—in those days our first thoughts in the morning were who should canter the black mare down to the bay to water, but with enough foresight, not to go till some more industrious fellow had cut a hole in the ice first, and in the evening with what satisfaction have we tried the strength of our sleigh, loaded with backlogs & garnished with stove wood; and to make our industry known & felt throughout the house, thundered them in at the back door. then comes Fanny[35] with a long face hush boys: the baby is asleep. Mama says she'll pay you for making such a noise.—Gin & Jack are then fed & fastened up with a stick thro' the staple but first a dispute arises who'll go up in the dark loft to throw down hay one says I wont, I did it this morning, and I always run the shingle nails in my head. I swear I wont do more than you: their's Papa; well boys, is every thing safe, have you shut up the fowls, and fed the horse & cows. yes Sir; but Tom wont go up to throw down hay: I wont be ordered by you Mr George; it is not my turn; so the cattle are to starve between you I see, well I'll throw down to the cows if George will feed the mare—done it is in a twinkling, a stick of wood clapt against the door, the big gate fastened, & the scene closed with a crackling star light night—Oh how cold my feet are. I guess we had better grease our shoes tonight—Nancy[36] 'ant there an apple pye for tea? Yes, in the big tin pan—look what a pile of stove wood we cut today: O My, what a sight, boys.—Yepsesho! my shoes & socks are off, they are as wet as dung—I can turn round three times on my heel. thats more than you can do Mr George. I don't care; but I can stand & jump upon the Table—there says Mary[37] youll break all the plates & dishes I've put to drain—I hear you my Gentlemen making such a noise in the Kitchen shut the door John—there is Mr Horace[38] poking all the lightwood into the fire.—thrash him—you may make houses of it, but burn any if you dare.—Tea is ready; helter skelter, rush & run. George runs over Charles.[39] Tom trod on his fingers. hullebalu!—dont make such a bawling Charley, & you shall have some of my pye. hush! hush: Sir.—Tea is over. the table covered with slops & daddy reading some play book to us, seated round the stove on big & little chairs. At ten oClock feel sleepy warm our feet & go to bed, each drag-

[35]Frances Elizabeth Ridout (1797–1844) married James E. Small, second son of John Small, a lawyer who became a member of the House of Assembly, and was Solicitor General 1842–3.

[36]Anne Ridout (1794–1832) married John R. Spooner of Montreal.

[37]Mary Ridout (1796–1872) married John Radenhurst.

[38]Horatio Ridout (1804–26).

[39]Charles Ridout (1806–31).

ging a Buffaloe skin out of the passage to cover over. thus ended one of the days of former years. . . .

Saturday 23d. . . . This is the fifth Christmas I have passed from home, and brings with it my usual remembrance of the latter end of the last century in those ancient days, our good Parents, always decked out our little carcases with a new suit of clothes—each a like—with 2/ to buy gingerbread from Machefisky.[40] then off we strutted up to the goal to hear Cooper preach. then when we mounted the yellow coats, who could look at us without admiration? and the old lady was so proud of her two sons

You are no doubt by this time heartily tired of my Letter, and well you may, for it contains nothing but nonsense.

Tell the girls to write often, their letters are very amusing, as they relate the little family occurrences, which are highly pleasing for instance in Marys of this morning, she says Frank[41] & Edith[42] are *quarrelling like two devils* behind the Stove.—Mama is busy *making candles* in the Kitchen and the house is all in a *slough.* Oh what charming scenes! would we were there to increase the tumult & confusion—what delightful uproar. Alas I am far away, & cannot enjoy your state of chaos on washing days. . . .

H 19 Fox-Hunting in York

[*York,* Upper Canada Gazette, *February 14, 1801*]

HOICKS! HOICKS! HOICKS!

On Thursday last, William Jarvis, Esq; entertained the inhabitants of this town with a diversion new in itself to many; and in some of its circumstances to all. About noon he caused a fox of full growth to be unbagged, near the center of the fine sheet of ice which now covers the Bay, and when at a suitable distance, turned loose the hounds upon it.—As previous notice had been circulated, the chace was followed by a number of gentlemen on horseback, and a concourse of the beau monde of both sexes in carioles and sleighs.—Poor Reynard was probably the first of his species cavalcaded in this manner to his fate.—A light coat of snow covered the surface of the shining plain, and contributed much to steadiness in driving and confidence in riding.

After the death of the unfortunate poulterer, his remains served as a dragg, to prolong for several hours the sport.—It seemed doubtful whether the horses in harness or in the saddle had the advantage in running, as all indeterminately kept up with the hounds in a promiscuous novelty of group.

[40]John Matchefesky (d. 1808) was one of Berczy's Markham settlers. He was a baker.

[41]Francis Ridout (1808–33?).

[42]Edith Ridout (1811–78) married Thomas Mabon Radenhurst, a lawyer in Perth.

H 20 JOHN BENNETT[43] TO JOHN NEILSON,[44] QUEBEC
[*P.A.C., Neilson Papers*]

York, Upper Canada
Aug. 20th 1801

. . . York contains about 100 houses and upwards, and about 7 years ago was an entire wilderness there are several very handsome buildings two in particular, the Chief Justices[45] house and that of Mr Jarvis Secy of the province the garrison is about a mile from the town; Settlers are coming in every day from difft parts, even from Pensylvania There is a road leading from town called *Yonge* street which is settled for about 30 miles up by the French settlers[46] who came up here some time ago and by Americans. The country round about (which however we cannot see) is thickly settled—provisions of all kinds (excepting flour) are very dear and scarce and every article is in fact about double what it is in Quebec York is just emerging from the woods, but bids fair to be a flourishing town. . . .

H 21 JOHN BENNETT TO JOHN NEILSON
[*P.A.C., Neilson Papers*]

York, U.C. Sept. 18. 1801

. . . I am just recovering from a severe fit of fever and ague which confined me to bed for ten days past—no body can escape it who pretends to live here. Mr McLean Clerk of the Assembly who will deliver you this, has also been extremely ill with it and in some families one person is not able to assist another; there is a marsh about ½ a mile from where I live from which a thick fog arises every morning—people attribute it in great measure to that and to the low and uncultivated state of the Country I have been delirious almost every day, but by taking of bark every hour according to Dr McCaulay's prescription I have missed the ague these two days past—I am still under a course of bark—I hope in God I shall have no more of it it sets me quite crazy—the Chief Justice has lately recovered and the Speaker of the House[47] is now ill with the fever. . . .

[43]John Bennett (1765?–1824) was foreman in John Neilson's printing shop in Quebec. In 1797 he went up to Montreal to found a commercial press with Joseph-Marie Roy, but this venture was unsuccessful. He was appointed King's Printer of Upper Canada in 1801, but in 1807 he left the province because of a financial disagreement with the Government.

[44]John Neilson (1776–1848) came to Quebec in 1790, and from 1797 was publisher of the *Quebec Gazette*.

[45]John Elmsley.

[46]Bennett is overemphasizing the French Royalist settlement, which by 1801 was very small and unimportant.

[47]D. W. Smith.

H 22 RUSSELL TO CAPT. MATHEW ELLIOT,[48] SANDWICH [*P.A.O., Russell Papers*]

York, Septr 19, 1801

My Slave Peggy,[49] whom you were so good to promise to assist in getting rid of,[50] has remained in Prison ever since you left this (in expectation of your sending for her) at an Expence of above Ten pounds Halifax, which I was obliged to pay to the Gaoler—and release her last Week by order of the Chief Justice. She is now at large, being not permitted by my Sister to enter this House, and shows a disposition at Times to be very troublesome, which may perhaps compel me to commit her again to Prison. I shall therefore be glad that you would either taker away immediately, or return to me the Bill of Sale I gave you to enable you to do so. For tho I have received no money from you for her, my property in her is gone from me while you hold the Bill of Sale; and I cannot consequently give a valid Title to any other who may be inclined to take her off my hands. I beg to hear from you soon. . . .

H 23 EXTRACTS FROM ELY PLAYTER'S DIARY [*P.A.O., Ely Playter Diary*]

Feby 26 [1802] . . . The little Snow that had fell brought People to town from the country, and it look quite lively. we had four or five Sleys in the yard[51] that stay'd all night. it was 12 OClock before I got to bed. & just after J. Hunter knock'd at the Door. T. White not being in bed let him in & he plead some time for me to get up & let him have a pt. rum but I answered him very determined. that I would not, and he went of some time after I had got to sleep. A Cameron wakened me knocking at my window wanting a pt. rum. I tried to put him of but he was resolved to have it & I got up & supplyed him, & sent him of

. . .

1st March 1802 . . . The Town-Meeting was held here & commenced about Eleven oclock, ended about one. Father & Mother ware down in the Sley, returned home at the Close of the Meetting

[48]Mathew Elliot (d. 1814), a native of Ireland, came to the United States in 1761, and was engaged in Indian trade and government service at Fort Pitt. During the Revolution he was an active leader of Indians for the Loyalist cause, and after the American occupation of Detroit he settled south of Amherstburg. He became Superintendent of Indian Affairs 1796–7, 1807–14. He was said to have had over 60 slaves.

[49]Wife of Pompadour, mother of Amy, Milly, and Jupiter.

[50]Elliot was to find a buyer, or buy Peggy himself. Russell gave Elliot the bill of sale to cover him "in case any breach of the Peace should happen from her folly & violence in being removed from York." Elliot, however, gave the bill to Joseph Brant, who was on bad terms with Russell. The sale to Brant fell through, and Peggy remained in the Russell family. (P.A.O., Russell Papers, Russell to Elliot, Oct 31, 1801.)

[51]Ely Playter was running Abner Miles' tavern.

About 3 oClock Dinner was served up. Messrs Ward and Heward had previously spoke Dinner for five Gentlemen. The gessts ware the two mentioned, Mr. Boyd, Mr. Heward & Myself. we spent the evening very pleasant with Song's & Toasts till the wine began to opperate. The old gentleman Mr. Heward left us. we ware all in fact quite intoxicated. Mr. Heward being more able to bear Liquor, was capable to see Mr. Boyd Home. The wine taking its usual affect on me I turned very Sick & staggered of to Bed with Mr. Wards asistance, he desired me to go into the Parlour and take a cup of Tea. I knew enough Drunk as I was not to expose myself—and tumbled into bed whare I lay and slep'd round till morning. . . .

. . .

6th. March 1802 . . . I had to call on all the Magistrates of the Town to Day Desireing their attendance at the Coffee House, at 6 oClock in the evening, whare I was oblidge to attend as Town Clark, it was some time in the evening before we ware done the chief busyness was to Point out to the overseers of the roads whare to bestow the Statute Labour for the year. it was 9 oClock when I got home. . . .

. . .

March 17th 1802

. . . This was St. Patricks Day which occasioned a number of Drunken Irishmen in town. . . .

. . .

May 1st [1802] . . . The Schooner Peggy arrived in the afternoon loaded with Passengers and family Baggage. Three covered waggon's from Pensilvania passed through York for Markham. had the house full of lodgers all night.

May 2nd[1802] The Town was so full of Smoke in the Morning that it was impossible to see any Distance and was quite Painful to the eyes. . . . The fire on the Planes back of York was allarming and made it difficult travelling the roads.

. . .

April 13th [1802] . . . The Town has been full of People for two Days but Court being over they had dispersed. . . .

. . .

April 21st[1802] . . . S.H[eward] called and him & me walked into the Park, some ducks ware near Shore. I run back for my gun & shot one of them we took Col. Murrys[52] skiffed to go after it & he hailed us to bring it ashore before we got back & appeard vexed that we should make use of it. . . .

. . .

June 4th [1802] Just after Daybreak we got up took out our Horses & fed them. Miss Miles got up & prepared us some Brakfast we soon

[52]Lieutenant Colonel John Murray (d. 1832) of the 100th Regiment. He commanded the attack on Fort Niagara in 1813.

got of jioned with Mr. B. Arnold[53] and rode on, as fast as we could through the bad roads we ware joined by J. Wilson Junr.[54] three of the Mr. Johnsons, Hollingshead,[55] Hoover,[56] Henrick,[57] & some others, we all stoped at Eversons Tavern[58] and drank some Whiskey, whare more company came up, making 14 Horsemen. Pass'd an number on foot all going into town. at the Mill road I left them and got down to father about 8 OClock. J.P[layter]. soon came up and we walked into Town Dressed ourselves. . . . Hurried to the allarm Post to join the Company. The men attended pretty generally, & we march'd into Town & joined the Battallion in the Park. The Men look'd very well we went throgh no exercise only formed the Line. The Captains gave in their returns to the Colonell & he disimiss'd us offerring a Bever Hatt to the best marksman with the smoothe board guns and another to the best with there Riffles we fired at the Target by Turns in the Companys—Mr. Hale got the first Hatt & Mr. P. Mills the other . . . The Town of Course was full of People, and a great number drunk, whare was restling, Jumping, Boxing, and the like all the evening . . . The House was full of all kinds of People. . . .

. . .

Thursday 1st. July [1802] . . . walk'd down on the bank met Mr. Dean[59] & stop'd some laughfing at a little black boy in a small skift working to get ashore in a very awkard manner & some one waiting for the Boat on shore swearing at him & frittened him out of half his witts. . . .

. . .

Sunday York 1st. August 1802— . . . Mr. Beman inform'd us that there was a man Drowned in the Don at the Bridge. A great number of people gather'd there about 9 OClock, a boat was sent round, and it was some before they came up. after a serch till about 11 OClock the Body was found and proved to be Peter McGregor a Scotchman. the Coronr. summoned 12 of us for the inquest as we thought it useless to attempt his recovery. but Doctr. Macauley sent word to have the body rubed with flannel and kept in the sun till he came. we obey'd his orders and he try'd many experiments but all in vain.—we chose Mr. Beman for the fore-

[53]Bowley Arnold had a farm in Markham Township, on Yonge Street at Richmond Hill.

[54]John Wilson, Junior, farmed on the east side of Yonge Street at York Mills.

[55]Anthony Hollingshead was a Loyalist from New Brunswick with lands on Yonge Street in Markham Township, Isaac and William Hollingshead also had farms on Yonge Street at this period. This family also developed farms in King Township on Highway 27 south of Nobleton.

[56]The Hoover family came from Pennsylvania and settled in Markham Township.

[57]Christian Hendrick first appears in the List of Inhabitants in 1800, living on Yonge Street.

[58]John Everson kept a tavern at the southeast corner of Yonge and Finch Avenue.

[59]Erastus Dean was a clerk employed by Elisha Beman. The family had lands in Haldimand Township.

man of the inquest, & brought our report accidental Death, as to all appearance the Man went into the water to bathe. The Body was sent to town in the boat, and we return'd by Land. . . .

. . .

Saturday 28th. [August 1802] . . . The Town in an uproar about Lawer Weekes as no one had seen him for 12 Day nor knew what had become of him, Saml. Whitesides the authority put in goal yesterday. and Weekes House Keeper today on suspicion.—

. . .

York 2nd. September 1802.— . . . heard the woman who was confined on suspicion with Whitesides for making way with Weekes had confessed that they had murdered him. I felt low spirited and dejected at the thought of such heinous crimes being committed in so new a settlement as York. . . .

. . .

Fryday York 10th. September 1802. . . . while at Tea A Miles & Phillip Cody[60] came in, and when they had suped we all went up to Methodist Meeting at Mr. Hales. I call'd for Mr. Heward but he would not go— The man gave us good Doctrin, took his Text the 46 Psalm & 4 verse, the same I had heard him Discourse upon near a year before at the same house, but I conceited he had improved in his explanation. we got home before 10 OClock and went to bed.—

. . .

Thursday York 16th Septr. 1802 . . . J. Edgell E Hale and others had been in the course of the Day preparing to bury the Bones that had been found supposed to be Mr. Weekes, as J McKay Esqr from Niagara had yesterday brought news of his being alive at Niagara, & had been lost in the wood for many Day's & was quite Insaine.—so those people thought proper, as the Bones were found and known to be Human bones, to bury them, and had a full and handsome Coffin made and intered them about sunsett this evening.

. . .

York 19th. Septr. 1802

Sunday.—The Friends concluded to Hold a Meeting to Day at 11 OClock at my Fathers, so I came into Town about 8 OClock and gave Notice to the people. Dress'd myself, and as I came in heard of Mr Herchmers Boy's running of last night with some of his Money.—Call'd on Mr. Hd. and walked up to my Fathers with some others to Meeting we ware just in Time; after a short setting of Silence one of the Woman friends Anna Mifflin Delivered us a Prayer, and soon after the other Woman friende [space in ms.] Kirkbright, gave us a small Discourse, on the remote situation we lived, the occasion of their Visits and her earnest desire, and prayers for our Wellfare Happyness and growth in serving the most Grasious and Mighty Being to whom all Nations are

[60]The Codys were a Quaker family in King Township. Philip Cody's farm was on Yonge Street north of Aurora.

but as the Dust of the Ballance" as Anna Mifflin Describes Him in Her Prayer, A short Pause ensued, and the last mentioned Friend rise and gave us a lecture on the ill custom of Selling strong Liquor to the innocent & ignorant Indians, and after warning us of the Bad consequences and the Risk of incuring the Divine Displeasure by that pernicious habitt a short Silence ensued, the Friends Certificates ware read and the Meeting closed, The Male friends that ware in Company was a [space] Paxton, a [space] and Thos Hill from Niagara. . . .

Monday York 20th Septr 1802. . . . The House was full of People Raffleing for a Watch & Drinking. . . .

. . .

Wednesday 22nd . . . heard of Mr. Weekes returning to town. . . .

. . .

Monday 4th [October, 1802] . . . as I came home I see Mr. Bond get in some trouble with the centinal for not answering his Challenge. . . .

. . .

Fryday 8th. . . . I call'd at Clark he inform'd me of a Methodist Meeting being at Hales, so I call'd on Dean and a number of us went up—A Mr. Bang was the Preacher and he gave us a good sermon. . . .

. . .

York 12th. Octr. 1802—
Tuesday . . . Capt. Boiton[61] and Miss Willcocks were married this afternoon and the young beaux of the Town remindfull of the happy occasion and the French Custom of Shivierieing the Parties a Number of them in disguise assembled and made a great noise about the old Esquires House, till, the Esquire, his Son and Doctr. Baldwin came in a great Passion with their Guns and threatened to Shoot if the disguised Party did not disperse, some run of, one frenchman was taken, the guard that was in the Town, was sent for, the Constables call'd, and the noisey Party soon ware all gone. about 10 OClock, all was quiet and we went to bed. . . .

Wednesday 13th . . . The weather was wet in the evening a small company of wild rakes gathered to keep up the Shivierie, but the night being rainy & dark they soon gave it up. . . .

Thursday 14th. . . . after Tea all was prepared for continuing the Shivierie and such a noise with drums, Kettles, Cowbells and Horns was never before heard at York. They keep'd it up till Past Midnight, round the town but the old Esqr. nor none of his family made their appearance some of the parties in the appearance of Indians went to McDougalls, calld for Liquor, and danced in the House. Then to A

[61]Augustin Boiton de Fougères was one of the French Royalists who came to Canada with de Puisaye. He married Eugenia Willcocks in 1802; she died in 1804. Shortly after he went to Kingston in charge of St. George's store there, but in 1810 left it suddenly and returned to Europe.

Macdonells Pull'd him out of bed and made him treat, danced all over the House, and staid cutting capers till 2 OClock in the morning.

Fryday 15th. See that the wild crew had thrown over Willcocks Stack of Hay last night heard that the Esquire threatened vengeance on the perpetrators.—

. . .

Sunday 23th. Jany 1803

. . . after Dinr. was over, the Girls wishing to go to meeting which was to be holden in the eveng at Mr. Cooper we started in both Sley's and got down in time the Minister was of the Church of Scotland and gave us a very good discourse—there was three psalms sung the two last was sung by Mr. Ward in which Mr. Hewd. & me assisted him. . . .

. . .

Wednesday 13th. [April 1803] I went to Town . . . walk'd out and joined a number of Men jumping & Playing Ball, perceived a Mr. Joseph Randall[62] to be the most active . . .

Thursday 14th. [April 1803] . . . see the Schooner Peggy Launched into the water. a Large Concourse of people were spectators and it began to rain about Noon. . . . the Court ended & the jurors left town. . . .

. . .

Sunday 4th [September 1803]— All prepaired for Meeting . . . we got to town in time, the Meetting was held at Hale's by Mr. McDole[63] of the Church of Scotland. . . .

. . .

Monday 3rd. October 1803.—

. . . a young man from the States call'd here & told us that the French had taken England, the News he had seen in a New York Paper,—Father & Mother where very much affected with such a report, but I placed little confidence in the Mans assertions. . . .

Sunday 4th. [March 1804] . . . at half past 2 OClock Hugh & me went to the Toronto Coffee House to Meeting Mr. S.H. would not go, but Mr. Mercer & him came after wards. Mr McDole was the Minister & he gave us a long Sermond on those words ("for in the day that thou eatest thereof thou shalt surely Die.—Gen: 2.17). . . .

Monday 5th. March 1804—

As the Annual Town Meeting was to be held to Day, I staid at Mr. Hds. till 10 OClock and then went to the Meeting, the People Assembled & chose the officers according to the Statute, after it was over J Fisk[64]

[62]Joseph Randall had a farm near Newmarket in Whitchurch Township.

[63]Robert McDowall (1769?–1841) was born in the American colonies, and was licensed to preach by the Dutch Reformed Church in 1790. He came to Upper Canada as a missionary in 1798, and in 1800 accepted a call to the Bay of Quinte area. He was later associated with the Church of Scotland.

[64]John Fisk (d. 1804) was lost on the *Speedy*. He was High Constable in 1804.

opened an Auction to sell some goods taken by execution the property of Saml. Chaffer[65] at the Suit of Benjn. Gilbert[66] Fisk ask'd me to be Clerk of the Auction and I remain'd busy till the sale was over which was near night. . . .

. . .

Saturday 28th. April 1804. About 7 OClock we arose Geo & me took our share of the fish which was not many and came out home. We met a number of people going to the Town to see a Woman[67] put in the Pilory &c. I spent the day on the farm, Geo return'd to town on an errand—the day was pleasant and Mr. Fisk, who was chosen High Consbe. made a very rediculous appearance at the impilloring the poor Woman. . . .

. . .

Monday 4th. June [1804] . . . We prepared ourselves for training to Day Mr. Cox[68] came out & I lent him my Coat. he staid Breakfast & Geo. went to town with him, met us at the usual allarm Post where we waited some time for the Men as there had not many assembled—we went to the Town, where more of our Company join'd us, & we join'd the other Companys in close order—the Men with arms where order'd to the right & we fired three Volleys in Honor of the King by order of the Ajudant and where then Dissmiss'd—Geo. & me went & took some whiskey & water with Mr. H. Heward then came to P. Merrians & Drank some beer & eat some Cakes with Jonathan Ashbridge, and then came by the Bridge up home about 2 OClock P.M. . . .

. . .

Thursday 7th. [June 1804] . . . going to turn out our Horses after Supper—John P. call'd to us & when we came to him he inform'd us that his wife's Jaw was dislocated and lock'd and he could not replace it—we all came up to the house and after examining Buchan's Family Phisitian[69] we went with John and soon replaced Mrs. P's Jaw by Buchan's directions, return'd home & went to bed.—

. . .

[65]Samuel Chaffer lived in Etobicoke. He first appears in the List of Inhabitants in 1801.

[66]Benjamin Gilbert, having left the Yellow House in Niagara, moved to York in 1805 and reopened the Toronto Coffee House. On April 30, 1807, the Coffee House "occupied by the late Benjamin Gilbert" was offered for sale. A Benjamin Gilbert was operating the government house for travellers at the Credit River during the War of 1812.

[67]Probably Elizabeth Ellis, who was tried with her husband Stephen for keeping a disorderly house in January, 1804. Ellis was acquitted, but Mrs. Ellis was sentenced to six months' imprisonment and to two sessions of two hours each in the pillory on market days, opposite the Market House. (York, *Upper Canada Gazette*, Feb. 4, 1804.)

[68]Osborn Cox (d. 1815) was born in Youghal, Ireland, and arrived in York about 1800. He kept a tavern in York. In 1809 he was apparently living in Whitchurch Township, but in 1810 he was back at his tavern in York.

[69]William Buchan's *Domestic Medicine, or the Family Physician* was first published in 1769, and went into many editions.

Monday 11th. [June 1804] This was the Day of Election,—I went early in the Morning to work at the fence on my upper flats—came home at 11 OClock, father & Geo had gone to town—and I got down about 12 OClock—The Poll had been opened some time—I gave my vote for Mr. Smith and then went with Jas. P. Geo—John Wilson and some others up to Hind's[70] Hotel to see a little animal call'd the Sagou Brown a Species of the orang outang, it was a curious sight for which we paid 1/.—soon after we heard that they had closed the Poll & A Macdo[ne]ll had a great Majority of votes—some of the People where displeased—I dined at Hind's with a number. . . .

. . .

Sunday, 22nd. July 1804— . . . Jas [Ruggles]& me had a deal of talk about a Library which we wished to Establish &c.

. . .

Tuesday 21st. [August 1804] . . .we Heard a Sheriverie going on in Town occasioned by the Mariage of Miss Fisk. Mr. S.H. and me could not be easey without being with them which we were in a short time, and well disguised, we rallied the House—the old man Shott at us 3 times & then came with his sword—we made some fun and disperced. . . .

Wednesday 22nd. August 1804 . . .after dark the Shiverie began again. Mr. Hugh Geo. & me having our disguise all ready we join'd them, the Magistrates came out to stop the noise and where busy to find out who they were, we had some amusement with them, it came on to rain and before 10 OClock we return'd to Gilberts. . . .

. . .

Saturday 25th. August 1804.— . . . I was inform'd the several People where bound over to Court by the Magistrates for being in the Shivarie the other night. . . .

. . .

Saturday 1st. September 1804. I went to town to attend the auction, but no bidder coming they did not begin, some Gents. from New York had a number of Goods at Gilberts which they proposed selling at Auction but so few people coming they give it up. . . .

. . .

Thursday 25th. Octr. 1804.—

. . .The Town of York was in confusion by the Loss the Schooner Speedy on her way to Newcastle with a Number of Passengers from York; her loss had been supposed some time but now was authenticated. . . .

. . .

Sunday 28th. Octr. 1804 . . . a vessel was to have been launch'd & they started her about 1 OClock but did not get her off that eveng. . . .

. . .

70Thomas Hind appears only once in the List of Inhabitants, in 1805. Thomas Talbot took his children to his settlement as servants.

Tuesday 30th. . . . they got the vessel into the water this eveng. & christened her the Governor Hunter.[71] . . .

. . .

Monday 18th Feby. 1805 . . . about dark all went to town but Mr. S. to Methodist Meeting it was held at Hind's a Mr. Coats[72] spoke and performed very handsomly, the congregation were well pleas'd—and we return'd about 9 OClock.—

. . .

Monday 25th. Feby 1805.—

Geo. & me went to town after Breakfast to the Election. The Streets where crowded with People, some hollowing for Weekes, & some for Cameron, who where the two contending Candidates. The Poll was oppened about 11 OClock and continued till near 4 P.M. when it was adjourn'd till 9 next day. . . .

Tuesday 26th. [Feb 1805] Jas & me went down again after Breakfast —found the People peacable and Quiet. the Poll was oppened and before noon Mr. Cameron gave up, Mr. W. being far before him in number of votes, & was declared duly Elected &c. . . .

. . .

Monday 22nd. [April 1805] . . . Mr. P. Clinger[73] and his new Bride where there the late Mrs. Cameron; there was a Sheriverie commenced but Clinger stop'd it by Treating the Party. . . .

. . .

Tuesday 29th. [October 1805] . . . went with M. & Small to the Billiard Table & Play'd game for the first time.—

. . .

Wednesday 22nd. [January 1806] . . . there had been an Illumination last night in Honor of Nelsons Victory over the combined fleets &c.—

. . .

Monday 16th. [June 1806] . . . I came to town where all where busy viewing the Eclips upon the Sun. . . .

. . .

22nd [August 1809]

Joel B.[74] call'd & took Breakfast on his way to town with a load of Goods from North West—a large Canoe and a Number of Men. . . .

. . .

24 [April 1812] Attended for drill in town with the officers & Sergts.

25. [April 1812] Six Companys of the Militia met today 256 rank &

[71]The *Governor Hunter* was owned by Joseph Kendrick. It was destroyed during the occupation of York in 1813.

[72]Rev. Samuel Coate was a Methodist circuit rider from Burlington, N.J.

[73]Philip Clinger (Klinger) first appears in the List of Inhabitants in 1804. He was a blacksmith, with a shop on Yonge Street south of Market (Wellington) Street.

[74]Joel Beman was a son of Elisha Beman.

file 131 Turned out Volunteers, we exercised till 2 OClock the Kings Arm's ware delivered to the Genl. & we soon after dismissed.—

. . .

4th.[May 1812] was in Town the Flank Company's of Militia ware chosen to Day from the volunteers. . . .

. . .

4th. [June 1812] Went to Town by 9 OClock—8 Companies of Militia met Drilled till past 2 OClock, the officers held a Court Martial on a Man for refusing to obey orders fined him 10/. the Col. forgave him the fine.—Officers Dined at Jordan's about 25 in number all very agreeable. . . .

. . .

6th. [June 1812] . . . The Vessel[75] was to be Launched the P.M. & many attended, I went down 4OClock. She stoped 3 or 4 times on her wayes & they did not get her in the water. the Flank Coys. ware at drill & I staid to see them

June 7th 1812 . . . they ware at work at the Vessel but did not get her off. . . .

. . .

12th [June 1812] . . . We all went to Town after Breakfast to the Election—Mr. Hudson[76] had given up & became active for Mr. Ridout. Hamilton & Shepard tossed up for their standing it fell to the latter & Hamilton became warmly his friend tho' the Electors, who ware Hamiltons friends was so much offended at his Tossing them away as they termed it that many of them voted for Mr. Ridout who run a Majority of 79 at the close of the Poll for the day.

13th. [June 1812] . . . We ware at the Election again today, & Mr. R. had over run Shepard 127 & they adjourned till Monday. . . .

. . .

25th. [June 1812] . . . rumour of War quite loud in York. . . .

H 24 Lord Selkirk's Opinion of York

[*P.A.C., Selkirk Papers, printed in* Lord Selkirk's Diary, 1803–1804, *edited by P. C. T. White, pp. 143–69*]

Sunday 20*th*. [November, 1803] . . . York contains 60 or 70 houses—the first built part is compact the lots being 1/5 acre each—latterly acre lots have been granted & several to one person—also evasions of the condition of building on each have been allowed so that the new or Western part of the Town is very scattered—the roads called streets in-

[75]The *Prince Regent*.

[76]John Hampstead Hudson was an early settler in Markham Township. He was Town Warden of Markham in 1803.

famous & almost impassable—the whole appears very ragged from the Stumps—near the Eastern end of the Town is a blockhouse built by President Russel on an alarm from Brant's Indians—& near it the situation proposed for a Governor's House—where only two rooms are built that serve for the meeting of Assembly, Courts of Justice etc. This situation is found to be unhealthy from the neighbourhood of a marsh of 1000 acres formed by the mouth of the Don (ci-devant Toronto R.)—this marsh is not found to affect the Garrison or more distant part of the Town at about a mile or mile & half distant—A party of Soldiers stationed in the Block house last summer were constantly affected by Fever & Ague, while the Garrison on a dry bank 2 miles off was quite healthy—the old town was also more unhealthy than the new part which is farther from the Marsh—& up in Yonge Street a few miles from the Town no fever at all existed.—The prevalence of Easterly winds last summer blowing off the marsh rendered the Town more than usually unhealthy—the Ague also made its appearance in Lower Canada, which is very uncommon.—The marsh might be embarked & drained—being defended from the Lake by a sand bank thrown up by the Surf—& only exposed a short distance along the River—it is observed to be drier than formerly—some ascribe this to filling up—but it must be owing to the retreat of the Lake—which is 3½ feet lower than when the Town was begun—having left dry a harbour built by Simcoe in 1796—The sand banks in some places have been thrown up about 5 feet above the present level.—The Indians have a tradition that the Lake rises 7 years & falls 7. . . .

The Harbour of York is formed by a continuation of the sand bank which defends the marsh—& at the extremity is a Peninsula formerly called an Island—which Governor Simcoe has named Gibraltar Pt. tho' almost on the level of the water.—there is 14 or 15 feet into the mouth & deep water within on the Gibr side—Shallow towards the Town. There has been talk of making a Key—but doubts whether Ice in Spring would not destroy it. Genl. Hunter make light of the objection & alledges that an artificial harbour might be constructed on any part of the Lake shore, at a few hundred Pounds Expence—founding with logs, & filling up with Stones. . . .

The Seat of Govt. was removed to York in a slap dash manner soon after the Posts were given up—Niagara had been chosen by Genl. Simcoe under the idea of the land to the Genesee & being retained by Britain & when disappointed of this, he would not hold his Parliament under the Guns of an American Fortress—he had an aversion at Kingston, partly because Lord Dorchr approved of it, but principally because all the lands were taken up around it—York had the advantage of being able to afford lots for all his friends round it, & accordingly the lands for scome miles distance are all in the hands of Officers of Govt. etc. etc.—& generally remain unimproved.—The Officers of Govt. were obliged to remove from comfortable houses at Niagara into an absolute wood where people were sometimes losing themselves between one hut & another—some incamped till near Christmas, before they could get Loghouses from the want of hands & the run upon the few workmen that could be got—wages & building materials continued for two or three years at double rates—Genl. S. was careless of personal accomodation himself—Mr. F. also—& he had no mercy on others. The advantage of York besides the harbour lies in the proposed communication to Lake Huron by Matchedash—which is opened as far as Lake Simcoe but not thro'—so that no trade passes that way—but it appears to be a favorite idea to push a Settlement that way, but part of the land is still in the hands of the Indians. Yonge Street is well settled as are a few townships near it, Markham by Berczy's Germans—the deserters from Genesee, Gwillimbury by a Quaker Colony from Pensylvania. . . .

Most of the lands between York & Bay of Quinté are taken up in large lots, & there are so few Settlers that the country is nearly impassable, as it also it thro' the Mississaga lands to the Westward towards the head of the Lake—So that York remains an insulated spot almost detached from both ends of the province,—the roads are so bad that in Summer everybody prefers a passage across the Lake—a strange situation for a Capital! . . .

There is no regular Post to Upper Canada from Quebec except 4 Couriers once a month in Winter—in summer letters are trusted to occasional opportunities—as so many battoes etc. are constantly going it is reckoned that a regular Post would not pay.—The Courier in Winter goes on foot, & is paid 36$ for going from Kingston by York to Niagara & back again, which he does in about 3 weeks—240 measured or 270 computed miles each way, i.e. about 4d Haly. pr. mile each way. —In one Winter York remitted of Postage 40 or 50£: Niagara & Sandwich are reckoned to produce more.—

Firewood at York sells about 1½$ pr Cord—laid down in Town—on Mr. Elmsley's farm ½ a mile out—at 1$ per Cord. . . .

Flour sells at York 4½$ per Barrel, at Montreal 6½$—tho' the charge of transport is not at the utmost 1$—

Fresh pork sells 4$ per 100 lbs simply corned 9$—or at least 9d N.Y.C. per lb.—Barrelled pork has varied from 14 to 20$—in general all articles of new produce seem extremely low—the least degree of work charged very high. All articles in the stores appear to be charged full cent per cent upon the English (wholesale) prices—e.g.—

	$ cts.			$ cts.
Blankets, 3 point	3 00	Axes (felling)	2$ to	2 50
Glass pr. Box (100 ft)	15 50	Spades		1 50
Bar Iron (Cast Iron do)	12½	Tar (Barrel)		10 00
Whip Saws	7 00	Soap cwt.		20 00
Cross Cut 6$ hand	2 00	Cordage per lb.		0 56
Scythes	1 25			

A workman's board at York without liquor may be had from 1½$ per week for 2 or 3 years after the beginning of the Town not under 3½ or 4$—flour was then 16$ per barrel.—
To get an idea of the expense of building, I put a sketch of a house on a common place plan—30 by 40—2 stories (20 feet sidewall) cellar & garret—into two Carpenters hands to give Estimates.—

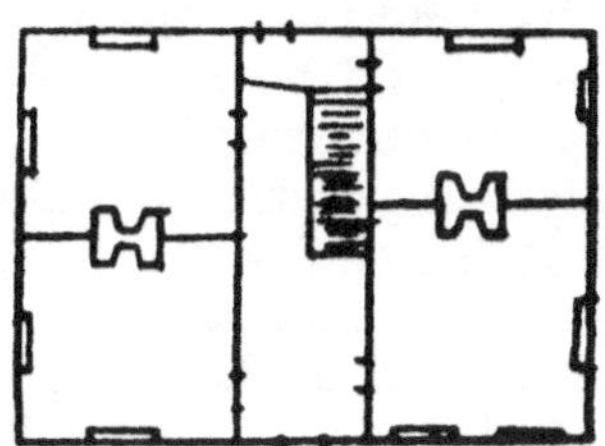

J. Leach estimates—920£ n.y.c. . . .
2 young men—Reuben & Jesse Rici [i.e., Riggs]—offer to burn bricks in a large quantity 50,000 e.g.—at 5$ per 1,000—bricks here do not measure much above 8—4 & 2 inches—the moulds are made 9—etc. but no allowance for shrinking in burning.—Stones are gathered on the Lake beach—& boated:—were 16$ at the beginning of the buildings at York —Lime is brought from Kingston by ships.

Templeton estimates a similar house . . .
N.Y.C. £1065 2 5

Boards are counted superficial feet:—¼ is allowed for wastage in cutting —Glass must be allowed a great breakage often ⅓. A perch of stone wall is 16½ feet long—1 ft. high sometimes paid 1$—: laying 1000 bricks is reckoned a day's work for a mason & 2 labourers— 5$— sometimes more—2 hands (good) will cut 250 feet board pr day with Whipsaw—3 men will fell & score, & 1 hew square 80 or 100 feet of 12 inch log paid 4$ per 100 feet.—1 attendant will do for a mason at Cellar walling.—

The builders here have an idea that a log house cannot be built to last well, as all the Log houses they have seen are apt to settle & get out of shape—owing no doubt to the use of unseasoned wood, & to the want of underpinning or a stone foundation. Some few houses are filled up with brick between the frame, but the generality not—& they have a number of cold windows—the seasons are not severe enough to make them attend to comfort.—

There are some beautiful species of Timber made use of in furniture & ornamental house furnishing—Black Walnut, Curled Maple, & Cherry —these are sometimes sent down St. Lawrence for exportation. . . .

H 25 W. D. Powell to Jeremiah Powell,[77] New York
[*T.P.L., Powell Papers*]

York 16 Decr. 1803

. . . Your Mothers Spectacles which were worn by a Gentleman of 60, & which she has used twelve or fourteen years, do their duty no longer without the aid of a hand Glass which cannot be always used—She wishes for a new pair, but I have two objections to trusting the Commission solely to you, first as your finances may not command the Article & more materially that you are no Judge of the Commodity—Show this to your Uncle Robert & beg him to procure me a pair of the best Glasses for his Sisters Sight, they should be Temple Spectacles with joints of silver gilt light but well made in a good Case to suit a Lady of 48 who has used Spectacles thirty years & now finds insufficient what suited the sight of a Gentleman at 60. . . .

H 26 Mrs. William Jarvis to the Rev. Samuel Peters
[*P.A.C., William Jarvis Papers*]

York 28 Septr 1805
Upper Canada—

. . . Mr. Jarvis is sick, having gone out to suppress a Mob, four men fell upon him and cut his head very bad—and bruised him so much that he is not able to lift his hand to his head or open his left eye—it happened at midnight—he took his Broad sword with him which saved his life—he cut one mans hand off a little below the Fingers, saving the fore Finger & thumb, disarmed another, the others ran away—but have since been taken & thrown into Gaol one who endeavoured to escape is shackled with 50 lb of Iron. . . .

H 27 Mrs. W. D. Powell to George Murray, New York
[*T.P.L., Powell Papers*]

York Novr. 25th.1805—

. . . We have little chance of any inducements to wish a residence in York, except those we find at our own fireside.—I do not consider the new comers[78] as any addition to our society,—indeed I have no intercourse with them,—our neighbours give public dinners twice a week. I had the honor of an invitation to one, but as the Lady knew I never accepted such invitations, & she has not thought proper to return the calls I made her when you were here, & once since, I consider'd her

[77]Jeremiah Powell (1784–1808?) was the fourth son of William Dummer Powell. He was engaged in trading in the West Indies, but in 1806 was arrested by Spanish officials as a pirate. His father was able eventually to get him released in 1807, but he was lost at sea the following year.

[78]Judge Robert Thorpe and his family, and Mr. and Mrs. C. B. Wyatt.

inviting me at all as a piece of insolence, & rejected it accordingly, accustom'd to proper respect from those, who are consider'd by me as far their superiors. I feel no inclination, to submit to their caprice to determine when I am & when I am not to be honor'd by their notice, & tho in public, it is my principle to avoid the appearance of party, by avoiding every thing like incivillity, some concessions must be made before these good people are considered as my private acquaintance—with the *pretty little pair* I am in the same predicament, they are perfectly under the guidance of our neighbours—& as Mrs W has not been here, since her return from Niagara, tho' I call'd the Sunday after you left us, I rejected an invitation to a party this eveng.—I am not sorry on my own account, but on Anne's[79] I should be glad, it had been in my power to pay & receive civilities, but if I forget what is due to myself I have no right to censure any one for not recollecting it—You anticipated my Dear Brother many innovations from these new residents in our savage Country & were not mistaken,—the barbarity of our manners, would by degrees become if not refined at least tolerable, were we taught with moderation,—but an attempt to effect a sudden & entire change will I fear but harden us in error—& the blaze of elegance so new to us will perhaps dazzle our weak sight, a display less splendid, would have enabled us to behold, & in time to imitate & by the end of the season the benefits arising from gentle tuition would have been perceptible to others, & of importance to ourselves, even your old Sister, might have taken advantage of these invaluable lessons, & become a companion for an higher order of Beings than the *Savages* with whom she has so long associated. . . .

H 28 EXTRACTS FROM ELIZABETH RUSSELL'S DIARY[80]

[*T.P.L., Elizabeth Russell Papers*]

Janry 1st, 1806
Wednesday. When I came to breakfast found Dr. Baldwin. He wished the compts of the Season, and wished to look in my throat which is much the same, but I refused as there [is] nothing to be seen—St. George was here before I was up—Miss Sheehan[81] came while at breakfast, and took a dish of chocolate. She was at the Ball last night. (She is at Duncan Camerons.) After chatting some time she went away—After she was gone came Mr. Ridout, then Mr. Saml Ridout, and both went away together. Then came Lucy Stegman[82] with little Robert [Baldwin] —then young Small, then his father who came up to me to wish the

[79]Anne Powell (1787–1822) was the second daughter of William Dummer Powell. She was drowned on a trip to England.

[80]This passage has been punctuated, and spelling has been corrected.

[81]Probably a relative of Colonel John Butler, whose sister married a Sheehan.

[82]Lucy Stegman (Stegmann) (b. 1791) was the third daughter of John Stegmann (1754–1804), land surveyor. She was apparently living with the Baldwins at this time.

compts of the Season. Made a distant curtsey. He did not attempt to take my hand or salute. He gave Robert an apple. His son & he went away together.—Robert did not stay much longer—His mother and father were out airing in the phaeton on the Bank but did not call. St. George came before dinner—Said he was going to dine at Mr. Thorpe's—Then came Willcocks who dined with us, and Mr. Stanton (the paymaster). The last Peter received; I did not see him—Denison came in at dinner time & he & Willcocks stayed the evening.—This was all that called today. Was invited to go to spend the evening at Willcockses, but thinking that Peter would not go I declined it—There was some affront given at the Ball last night, something about a supper being there and some of the Company not asked.

. . .

Saturday 4—

Set off with Dr. Baldwin. It was past two o'clock . . . Went in our phaeton with Burns' horse—When we came to the entrance of the yard we saw Myers boy who lives there & two of Mr. Thorpe's little boys. The Doctor called to them to make a passage for us. There was a small gate through which the children came to us. The entrance for carriages was a gate with draw bars. The boy had vanished. The youngest of the boys was troublesome to us, wanting Baldwin to give him the whip. After a little the boy made his appearance again and drew the bars and let us in. He was bid to tell Mrs. T——— who was at the door. He returned and said she was coming. Met her in the passage and she shewed me in the parlor. After we had sat some time alone with her, then came Miss Featherstone. After she had been with us a while Mr. Thorpe came to us. Was introduced to them all. This is the second or I may say the third time of my being introduced to Miss Featherstone, though this is the first time of my calling on them since they came which was some time in August last.—The first time I saw Miss F———was I think the Sunday after they came to this country. A lady with a white parasol passed near the window with a little boy, and seemed at a loss to find where the Church was. I directed her to it for which she seemed thankful. I afterwards found it was Miss F———. The next time I met with her was one evening when Dr. Baldwin was going with me to Willcockses, she was going to Mr. Wyatt's. She had a little boy then with her, and stopped to speak to Baldwin who introduced me to her.—We sat a little after Mr. Thorpe came in. I made an excuse for Peter, who intended paying his respects, but it being very bad walking he did not go today. They seemed very desirous that we should visit them to join their dinner & evening parties but I made an excuse for Peter & self that we seldom went out anywhere, and that I was not in a state of health to go into company, but it was not taken as an excuse, and the Doctor joined with them in favour of our going out—Mr. Thorpe was muffled up, having a pain in his face. Their family consists of themselves, Miss Featherstone, who is sister to Mrs. Thorpe, & seven children, four of which are girls. Saw none of them except the little boys already mentioned—They came from Prince Edward Island where Mr. Thorpe was Chief Justice. He is here in the place of poor Mr. Cochrane[83]—Our next visit was to Mrs. Wyatt. Mr. Wyatt handed me in, then introduced me to Mr. Boulton who was in the sitting room. Left me a few minutes with him before the Doctor came in. Mrs. Wyatt was preparing to go out but came to us after we had sat a while. She seems a lively good humoured pretty little girl, being only about seventeen.—Mr. Boulton seems a pleasant kind of man, and Mr. Wyatt a very agreeable one.—The former is Solicitor General in place of poor Mr. Gray and the latter in that of Mr. David Smith . . . An eclipse of the moon this evening. I observed it first. Sent to tell the Willcockses of it. Not quite total—

. . .

Wednesday 8
Mr., Mrs. Thorpe, their eldest little girl & Miss Featherstone came to return my visit—Gave them cakes & wine. After chatting a while they went away. They seemed to be a free mannered unreserved people and not formal.—In the evening a little before tea came Mrs. Willcocks entirely by herself. She said she was some time at the Courtyard gate before she could open it. She drank tea and sat great part of the evening. We sent Milly & John home with her. She seldom comes of herself except when she has something to communicate or a favor to ask. Tonight was to express her wish that Charles should succeed to James Clark's[84] place in case of his not being able to do the duty of it from his ill state of health or death. In the former case it would allow him half the salary during his life—Peter told her that he had already applied to the President[85] for a friend (It was Dr. Baldwin but he did not tell her so.) and told him that he had already allotted it to another. My brother did not tell her who, but it is the President's son-in-law; this he told Peter in confidence.—

. . .

Saturday 18
Willcocks was here at dinner time and ate some roasted apple.—He said the evening my brother told him that he of late was thinking of dying. It was mostly in his thoughts, which it was not used to be. He certainly is often out of spirits, seems indifferent about many things such as letting his servants go on as they please without saying much to them, but now and then get out of patience with them & lets them go on again—Peggy & John Beacher are the only ones we have except Milly, and they are certainly very dirty, idle and insolent. John from being always at work does as little as he can help, throws most of the work he used to do on Pompeydore, who is hired by the day, and is also very indolent & dirty.

[83]Thomas Cochrane (1777–1804) was appointed puisne judge of Court of King's Bench in 1803. He was lost on the *Speedy* a year later.

[84]James Clark was Clerk of the Provincial Parliament.

[85]Alexander Grant.

Milly exactly copies their manner. Amy who is at the Farm is rather better than her but is very wild and fond of rambling—& both are very much addicted to pilfering and lying. But it is all owing to the bad example their mother sets them. Peter also has grown quite indifferent about society of late years and goes visiting but very seldom, and invites no one except to take pot luck. Sometimes drinks tea at Willcockses and that not often. His constant application to business and having such bad servants is greatly the cause; and he is rather disgusted at the behavour of some of the people. His wish is to sell his property here & to go home, but there is no likelihood of doing that. If poor Mary[86] was alive I believe I should court society & go into public on her account, but as for myself I have been so long without it that I also grow indifferent about it.

. . .

Fri[day] 24
Tommy Denison[87] came in forenoon for to get some raisins for Betsy,[88] who is still poorly—Robert with us all day. The Doctor came at tea time. I wished him joy of Phoebe's recovery, and he kissed and thanked me. He took one dish of tea & went away. Willcocks came at dinner time and ate roasted apple. After tea was over Mr. St. George came and sat the evening. Willcocks & him were talking about the former's debt to Mr. Gray of Montreal. Willcocks thought that St. George took Mr. Gray's part and began to grow in a passion with St. George, and had he been let go on he would have been in a violent rage & insulted St. George, but I put a check to his going on by speaking a little sharp and telling him that there was quite enough of it. He had got primed with his grog which he often is.—He drinks a great quantity of brandy wine & water mixed together.—However they went away good friends together—St. George was not in fault at all; he goes soon to new York—

Sat[urday] 25
Dr. Baldwin called this morning—Phoebe had a fine night's rest and is continuing mending—Denison called after breakfast. He was come about attending the bail of Jupiter who has been in jail a long time on Denison's account, he having sworn that his & family's lives were in danger from him. Pompydore and John Badger are his Bail, at ten pounds each, but Dr. Baldwin came and told me that Mr. Thorpe whom they went before wished for Mr. Small to also become bail as it might have a greater effect on the boy, but he could not attend today so Jupiter was sent back

[86]Mary Fleming came to Canada with the Russells as a young companion for Elizabeth. She died of tuberculosis in 1797.

[87]Thomas John Denison (1786–1846) was the second son of John Denison. He served in the York militia during the War of 1812.

[88]Elizabeth Sophia Denison (1803–92) was the only daughter of John Denison, and goddaughter of Elizabeth Russell. She had spilt a bowl of boiling water over her face three days previously. She married John Fennings Taylor (1817–82), later Clerk of the Legislative Council and of the Senate.

again to jail, and they are to meet about it again on Monday. Dr. Baldwin declined dining but came & drank tea—Willcocks came at dinner time & ate apple pie and stayed the evening—

. . .

Monday 27th.

. . . Jupiter was released from prison today and contrary to orders was brought into the house, but was sent off home with Pompodore who was very drunk today and impertinent to Peter who was very angry at Jupiter's being brought into the house. He behaved so ill when he was here that I am determined he shall not come at all to the house which Peter is so good as to comply with. He is a thief and everything that is bad, and since he has been in jail he is overrun with lice. He has also behaved so ill at the Farm that Mrs. Denison objects to his going there so he is to remain at Pompys till he is sold.—

. . .

Sunday 9 February, 1806

The President and Capt. Elliot called after they came from Church and sat some time. Sent for Peter (which I don't always do on account of the President as he came so often) but he was too busy to come over—little Robert was here & I took him into the drawing room but he was shy. The President told Capt E— that I intended to leave all my property to the child. This he is almost always at me to do—make a will in its favor. He is a weak man and talks a good deal of nonsense. Poor Burns was buried this afternoon at the Garrison. Peter had an invitation to go, but it was too far for him. Dr. Baldwin here in the forenoon, after which he took his wife and Maria and little Billy[89] up to Mrs. Adjutant McGill's to stay some days to try change of air for Phoebe—

. . .

Thursday 3d [April, 1806]

No one in the morning but Baldwin before I was up, also his little infant Billy, whom Mary brought to my bedside. No one came till Talbot to dinner, then Doctor Baldwin who was invited to meet him. Sent Mary after dinner for Phoebe, Maria, & Robert to come to tea. She returned with him. Talbot took a good deal of notice of him and he was shy but at the same time seemed inclined to be familiar. His mother & Maria came to tea and all stayed the evening. . . .

. . .

Sunday April 20 1806

Lucy came yesterday for Robert, also with a message from Mrs. Baldwin to know whether I would go with her today to see Mrs. Ridout. She had asked me to do this before, & I had disappointed her, & thought she had gone without me, but as I found she had put it off I sent word I would go—The Dr. called before I was out of room. I dressed and went when the people were at Church to Willcockses. The Dr. & Phoebe were

[89]Augustus William Baldwin was born Nov. 13, 1805, and died April 27, 1806.

ready to go. I stopped a few minutes with Mrs Willcocks & then went with them. First paid a visit to Mrs. Wyatt (This is the 3d. visit I have paid her since she came, and she has been four times to call on me.) Mr. Wyatt received us. She after a while came to us. She draws very well. There are some things in the room of her doing, among which are some humorous figures painted on paste board and cut out, one of which is a couple & contending for the breeches. We stayed till Church was coming out and went. Were at the window looking at the Band when a Captain Fuller[90] of the Forty First and a Captain Raye who is not in the Regiment but is the paymaster of it came in. . . .

. . .

Thursday 31st [April, *i.e.* May 1, 1806]

No one to dinner as Mr. Baldwin[91] dined and spent the evening at Mr. Thorpe's. He not coming home I sent John about one o'clock to look if there was still a light at Willcockses. He returned and said there was, by which they were still up & waiting for the doctor who also was at Mr. Thorpe's. We thought at one time we heard him coming, but it was a great sow which had opened the Courtyard & come in. John drove her out. Peter & Mary[92] was gone to Bed some time.

. . .

Saturday May 31 1806

In the forenoon Mrs. Playter came with a Mrs. Lawrence.[93] (She is niece to Mrs. Hill the Quaker of Yonge Street. Her name was Crone. She has been married to Mr. Lawrence between two or three months.) They had called on Mary who was ironing over in her room, and she telling them I was not very well Mrs. Playter wished to see me. Mrs. L— was also desirous of doing so, Mrs. Playter introduced her. I have never seen her but once and that imperfectly some time ago at Mary's room window. Sent over for Mary and we walked some time with them in the garden. The President came there to us. Sat some time in the Arbour, then went in. Gave them cake & wine. After sitting a while in came Miss Cameron with Mrs. Murray of Niagara, the first time she has ever been at York. She has not altered much in her looks except being fatter than when I saw here at Niagara which will be nine years next November.—When they came in Mrs. Playter and her friend went away. After sitting a while went into the garden. (The President went

[90]Richard Thomas Fuller was born in Cork, Ireland, and became a lieutenant in the 68th Regiment in 1787, and a captain in the 41st Regiment in 1796. He was discharged in 1814, and died the same year at Adolphustown. He was the father of Thomas Brock Fuller, first Anglican Bishop of Niagara.

[91]Robert Baldwin, Senior, was staying with the Russells, because of the death of the Baldwin baby.

[92]Mary Thomson was a daughter of David Thomson of Scarborough. In July, 1810, she married John Scarlet of Weston. She was living as a companion to Elizabeth Russell.

[93]Richard Lawrence kept a tavern on Yonge Street. His wife was the daughter of a Loyalist.

away soon after they came in.) (Lucy & Robert came while they were here.)—I went into the house for my bonnet and when I returned into the garden I saw Mrs. Murray had got some white lilac in her hand and Miss Cameron a yellow bachelor's button. These I supposed they had taken of themselves. Mary told me afterwards that Mrs. Murray tore off the flower from the lilac & in her violence had broke another off which I afterwards took. Mrs. M— asked if I had not the snow ball tree. I said I had one, but I took care not to lead them to the part of the garden where it was, lest she should serve it as she did the lilac, and they went in without seeing it. Gave them cake & wine. Mrs. Murray asking if Fiddle who was near her was not the dog I was once going to give her, I told her it was. This introduced my mentioning the little bitch Fanny which Macaulay had some time. I told her that I asked them to leave her with me if did not take it down the country with them. They then told me they did not leave it. I afterwards heard that it was given to them by Mr. Duncan Cameron & when they went away she returned it to him. I therefore now requested Miss Cameron to let me have the refusal of it, if she ever wished to part from it. She immediately said that it was at my service. I expressed my fear of depriving them of it but by what she said they were not very much attached to it, and at parting she promised to send it to me, and I impatiently expected it but it did not come. I hope I shall not have my usual bad luck and something or other happen to disappoint me of it. While we were in the garden watering the plants, message was brought by Charles that tea was ready and the President was there. Peter went in so after a little I left Mary to finish watering and I went to him. While we were at Tea in came the Doctor, Phoebe, and Maria. They had drank Tea so they said they would go into the garden. They returned before we had done. They with the President drank punch & stayed the evening. I bid Lucy when she went home with Robert to tell them at home that I had got what I had long wished for and was going to increase my family and they said they came to know what it was & I told them. This is the first evening I believe that President has come to tea without Allan.—Willcocks came at dinner time and said he had salt pork for dinner, but he was prevailed on to take a second dinner with us. He came from Markham (where he has been about a month) the day before yesterday and dined yesterday with us. Mrs. Moody[94] was also here today.—

. . .

Mon. June 2d

Lost little Fan. Took Mary with me to pay a visit to the Miss Cameron who is lately come, and also to Mrs Murray who is there . . . The new Miss Cameron was in the parlor. I introduced Mary to her. After sitting

[94]Mrs. Mary Moody received a Yonge Street grant in King Township in her own right, for services rendered by her during the Revolution, as well as grants to her children. She was charged with assault at least three times, and contested with her daughter the custody of her granddaughter.

a while the other Miss Cameron came. Mrs Murray was not there. She had gone to Capt. McGill's yesterday and was not returned.— Little Fanny followed me. I took her with me to see how she would act. She followed very well, and when seated she laid herself down by me for a little while, then ran out of the room. Thinking she would not leave the house I did not at first care, but her not appearing again and wanting to go I expressed a wonder where she was. I began to be uneasy about her. The new Miss Cameron went out two or three times about her, but she could not be found, so after waiting a while we took our leave. Mr. Cameron who was in his Store came out of it & escorted us as far as Willcockses where we went in. Invited Mrs Willcocks to drink tea with us this afternoon. She said she would. Also asked Phoebe & Maria. They told us of a sad accident that has happened this morning. A sister[95] of the Widow Ruggles, as she was getting breakfast, her gown or petticoat caught fire and was entirely burnt off her. The waist, her arms and from the waist down is most dreadfuly burnt. Her sister was upstairs and did not hear her shrieks at first, but afterwards gave her assistance, and has her hands a good deal burnt. It is said that Mrs. Moody was passing and was the first that heard her screams, and that the poor creature had run into the street. Doctor Baldwin and Doctor Thom[96] of the 21st Regiment attend her. It is thought she cannot live. Old Mrs. Dudley who has a room to keep school in in the house has lost some of her work, it being burnt by the poor thing's sitting down on it. While we were watering the garden came Mrs. Willcocks, and Phoebe came there to us. When we returned in the house found Charles there. Maria, Lucy, and little Robert came after tea. St. George came just before the things were taken away and took some tea but did not stay long after. The rest spent the evening. The poor girl that was burnt still very bad. Sent her some balm and mint to make drink of, by Peggy who said she wanted rags so sent some old linen, also some Indian meal that they wanted for her.— After we left Willcockses I took Mary to see old Mrs. Ridout's last little boy[97] who is about 2 months old. Did not see Miss Ridout but she is better, but not able to walk yet. Mrs R——— on my praising a little table in the sitting room, she took us into the other parlor to shew us a handsomer. At the same time we saw the fifty pound Carpet which they bought of Allan. It is of a manufacture I never saw before and very handsome but not worth half what it cost.— We went into the garden with her, and asked her for a comfrey root which I am to have. I took her daughter Mary home with me to give her some flower seeds & I sent home with her.—Mr Cameron's boy brought home Fanny. I did not know where she was, but suspect that she was concealed at Francois[98] the Baker's who lives opposite their

[95]Miss W. Dunham, aged about 14, and sister of Mrs. Ruggles, died on June 16, 1806, from the burns she received (York, *Upper Canada Gazette*, June 21, 1806).

[96]Doctor Alexander Thom (d. 1845) came to Canada as Assistant Surgeon of the 41st Regiment. He later settled at Perth, where he died.

[97]Charles Ridout.

[98]François Belcour.

house where Miss Cameron told me she went very often there being children there.

. . .

Saturday 23 Augt 1806

The Earl of Moira arrived this morning with Governor Gore and his lady and attendants. Chief Justice Scott[99] and Mr. Small were here to my brother before he was out of his room to inform him of it. Mr. Stanton, the President's first clerk, also called for the same purpose. Mr. Wyatt called at breakfast time to speak to Peter about an intention he had of taking Mrs. Wyatt on board to pay her respects to the lady & to invite her to dinner, and to beg the loan of our boat to go on board. Peter being some time before he came, he made two or three efforts to go to call another time, but I detained him. Went to Peter to say about the boat and got permission for him to have it. After that Peter not coming he went, but before he was got out of the gate Peter was ready, and I called him back again. He had the key of the boat given him, but on consulting Peter I believe he changed his mind about going on board as the boat still remained at her moorings, but he has not returned the key —Denison came in while Mr. Wyatt was here. After he was gone took some chocolate. Peter had some thoughts of going in our phaeton to the Garrison to pay his respects but on calling on the President he changed his mind & walked up with some others, which I was better pleased at, as I should have been uneasy if he had gone the other way for fear of accident as the roads are in places bad—the President came home with him having drove him from the Garrison in Allan's caleche—They like the Governor very well, who seems about thirty, is tall and handsome and of pleasant manners. I am told that the lady has brought some pets with her, viz. a small French dog a monkey and parakeets. Lucy and Robert here in forenoon, he with a dead scarlet bird in his hand which Milly had picked up by Mr. Wyatt's. I gave him some barley sugar for it and our servant Charles skinned it for me.

. . .

Friday 3d April [1807]

Heard this morning that Mrs. Davidson was brought to bed of a girl and was very unwell and little or no help, some little time ago her mulatto wench having forsaken her & gone to the Governer's to whom they have giving up her time. This girl Mrs. Davidson brought up from an infant, but they are all a bad ungrateful set.—Heward called in before he went home twice. The last time he said that my brother had been taken with an oddness in his speech as if he could not well articulate his words, as if his tongue was swelled. He was not so when he was over since breakfast to take his medicine. Mr. Heward said it was about two hours ago he was taken with it. I sent Mary with an excuse for a bit of paper to

[99]Thomas Scott (1746–1824) was born in Scotland, and educated for the ministry of the Church of Scotland, but studied law, and was called to the English Bar in 1793. He was Attorney General in Upper Canada from 1801 to 1806, and Chief Justice from 1806 to 1816.

see how he was. She said that he looked well & seemed in good spirits, and as I bid her she told him to come over & he said he would directly. He had his pen in his mouth but he spoke so as she understood him. He came over soon after. Found his speech very much altered, but did not seem ill otherwise. Sent for Baldwin but he was in court, but they said that they would send him as soon as he returned. Watch his coming out of court and stayed dinner a little, telling Peter not that I sent for him but that I wished him to take dinner as his own might be over. He not coming it was taken away. Peter seemed to wish to see him, so Mary said she would go and see Robert and tell him (Peter ate pretty good) when the Doctor came. According to custom he put on a solemn countenance, prescribed a blister to be applied to the back of his neck and whey made of mustard. I went out to desire Charles to go & get some milk, and was going to send John to Dr. Davidson,[100] but Charles said he did not think he could come, for Miss Cameron and other ladies were gone to her as she was so bad it was thought she could not live, so I did not send, but telling Baldwin of this he said he would go and call on Dr. Davidson and tell him of Peter and see how she was, so after taking some tea he went.—Willcocks came as did Mr. Heward who both drank tea here—Heward went away after tea. Dr. Baldwin returned & Dr. Davidson with him. Davidson I believe thinks with Baldwin that it is a nervous affection but did not tell my brother so, but wished to ascribe it to some other cause. Told him that his pulse was good and chatted cheerfully to him. Prescribed instead of the blister only hartshorn on a flannel to the back of his neck, white wine whey, and to have his feet well rubbed with flannel when going to bed and wash and gargle with hartshorn and water which he did. The Doctor chatted him into tolerable spirits and seemed pretty well all but his speech. Some times he spoke much better than at others.—There is something at Court happened today against Mr. Thorpe which puts Dr. Baldwin rather out of sorts, being with the Willcockses very much interested about Mr. Thorpe, who is much disliked by most of the people here and at Niagara. Mary & I rubbed Peter's feet, put the hartshorn at the back of his neck, & gave him hot wine whey to drink when he went to bed which was between 11 & 12 with hartshorn in it.—He fell asleep soon after he took it. When just returned from putting him to bed saw somebody come in. It was Dr. Baldwin returned to tell me that it was right he should be watched tonight & desired to be sent for if he was worse. I told him I would and he went away. He is a poor dead hearted creature and always fears the worst. Davidson on the contrary is all cheerfulness and good humour. He said that Mrs. Davidson was a great deal better. Peter after sleeping, asked to gargle his mouth. I got the hartshorn and water and he mixed it himself, but when he put it in his mouth he said it had taken the skin off his tongue, having made it too strong, so got him some water to wash his mouth which made it easier—

[100]Dr. James Davidson was Surgeon of the 2nd Battalion, Royal Canadian Volunteers.

. . .

Sunday May 10th.

Poor Mrs. Willcocks was buried this morning. Dr. Baldwin requested yesterday that John Beacher and Charles our servants should attend, which they did. None of the family but Doctor Baldwin attend the funeral. We wanted Willcocks, Phoebe, and Maria and Baldwin to spend this day with us to be out of the way of seeing or hearing any thing of the funeral but they all declined doing so except Baldwin who said he would yesterday, but he called this morning and also excused himself as he thought it would not be right to leave them.—Davidson called while we were at breakfast and expressed a wish that Betsy Denison should be brought down to him to look at her arm to see if the pock had taken. I told him that it had begun to take but would send for her, so I wrote a note to Mrs. Denison to send Denison down with the child either today or tomorrow, but before I could get it sent Sally Mills (the farm maid) brought the child to me. They had come to Town to see the funeral. I did not keep them long but had her take the child to Doctor Davidson on the way home and told Aex to take the note to Mrs. Denison which would explain my reason for sending her there. The pock has taken and goes on very well. It was this day week that Mrs. Denison brought her down and Doctor Davidson inoculated her with the Cow pock. Doctor Baldwin came after dinner and went after tea with us to see the Willcockses. I dreaded the first meeting. As we were going their little maid Jenny came to meet us. I feared something was the matter. She went up to the Doctor and told him that Robert had hurt himself. He ran on and Mary went on first as did Milly. What it was he had fallen down and cut his face. Only Willcocks was in the parlor when we went in. He saluted me and seemed much calmer than I expected him. Maria then came in with Robert who has a cut just under his eye.

. . .

Th 7 [January, 1808]

In the forenoon Baldwin came and gave Peter the injection after which as soon as I was dressed he drove me in our sleigh to the Garrison to pay my respects to Mrs. Gore. The Servant said she was at home and was ushered into the small parlour. It was not long before she came and was very gracious, gave us some cake and milk punch. The Governor came in and was quite surprised and seemed glad to see me. They were both sorry to hear my brother had been so unwell since he saw him last. The Governor gave some sort of reason by way of apology for not calling when he was last in Town. He did not appear to have taken any offence at anything so hope all is right in that respect. Mrs. Gore also apologised for her not calling on me. I forget what reason she gave. Major Halton did not make his appearance and the Governor did not sit long with us. There were several fancy things and little ornaments in the room, and in two little jars on a table was some feathergrass. It is very like the feather of the bird of paradise. I had seen the sort before. On my admiring it she made me a present of several of them. After sitting a while I made a motion to go, but she asked me to stay longer & I sat down a few minutes & then we drove to Captain Fuller's. . . . In going to the Garrison I got out at Baldwins to speak to Maria & Phoebe while the Doctor put on his boots. When we set off Maria went home on foot. Also stopped there on our return and I stayed to keep house with little Robert while the Doctor drove his wife to Mr. McGill's and some other places. Robert was very good and played with a little boy, Mackintosh's son,[101] who is about nine years old and lives as a servant with them. After staying some time they returned & the Doctor drove me home. Found Peter pretty well and nothing disagreeable happened in my absence. Willcocks dined and spent the evening.

. . .

Sunday 10 [January, 1808]

Peter after breakfast grew very unwell. Baldwin gave him the purging & afterwards the starch injection. Willcocks, Maria and little Robert dined with us. He was very noisy and unruly. His grandfather and Maria spoil him by humouring him. He will be four years old next May. In the forenoon while Peter was busy in the drawing room with Heward (which since my brother has been so unwell) is made an office—Major Halton came as far as the passage to inquire after Peter's health. I asked him to go to him but he declined. The Governor was in a sleigh at the door who declined disturbing my brother and begged I would not come out in the cold, but seeing Mrs. Gore in the sleigh (who also wished me not to come out) I went to her. She still declined getting out. Colonel Claus[102] was in the sleigh with him. After chatting a little they drove off. After that Mr. Stanton called.

. . .

Mar 26 1808 Saturday

My dearest love

Though I sit many hours in your company I have not an opportunity to converse with you on the subject next my heart—We having both agreed on our closer union—the sooner it can be accomplished the better. I am old and you are not growing young. Therefore as little time should be lost as convenience and propriety will admit of.—I do not wish our marriage to take place before the middle of May—but that as you may think best. I leave to your prudence the mentioning it to your good brother. I wish for some conversation with you

Ever your
Willcocks

[Pinned to this page is this note:]

The answer to your very extraordinary letter is that I think you have taken

[101]Probably a son of John McIntosh (1754–1830) who was born in Perthshire, and came to Canada in 1801. After two years in Quebec, the family came to York. He was a blacksmith living at the corner of Yonge and Lot (Queen) Streets and had 11 children.

[102]Colonel William Claus (1763–1826) was appointed Deputy Superintendent of Indian Affairs in 1799.

leave of your senses and beg you will not trouble me any more with such folly—& nonsense

This letter was given to me this forenoon by himself bidding me to read it at my leisure—

I was much astonished at the impudence and folly of the contents, & read it to Mary Thomson. She was equally surprised. It however struck me when he gave it that it alluded to something of the kind, as he has been lately very particular in his manner . . . I avoided speaking to him as much as possible all day, & when he asked me to drink a glass of wine with him at dinner declined doing so.—We had no one else to dine or tea. I sent for Maria to come to tea but she was busy, but said she would come in the evening, which she did and the Doctor with her—Peter was talking at random about going to the Brazils it being so fine a climate. Willcocks asked him if he would take him as his secretary. He said he would not. He then asked me if I would take him as my valet de chamber. I said No.—I thought he seemed mortified. I scarce looked at him, but as I was adozing at one time in the evening Mary said he looked at me in a significant manner.—I wish much to speak to the Doctor on this subject, but did not say anything to him tonight, but mean to shew him the letter tomorrow.—My brother got a very sore throat but the Doctor thinks it of no consequence, but I am uneasy about it. He gargles with sage, honey & port wine—poor Mrs. Willcocks has not been dead a year & the family are still in mourning for her.—

Sunday 27

. . . as I was setting Cato & Fanny after the pigs that were rooting up the grass before the house we saw Mrs. Gore with another person in the phaeton, Major Halton driving them. They drove up to us. She declined getting out. It was her maid that was with her, who is a pretty modest looking girl and whose name is King.—The Governor has got a cold.—After chatting a while they drove away. She fondled little Fanny. Said it put her in mind of her misfortunes—(meaning the loss of her little Spot).[103] . . .

Monday 28—

The Doctor came in the morning as usual to Peter. I asked if Maria had spoke to her father. He had given her the letter, but she declined saying anything to him about it, and would rather that I would do so myself, and wished I would tell my brother of it and beg him to give him a good set down about it, but to do it without being in a passion with him or forbid him the house. . . . It seems the whole of the family wishes to have nothing to do with it, and throw the matter on me and want me to speak severely to him about it. I mean to write and give him a short answer. I wish to get the letter back again from Maria that I may at a

[103]According to H. W. Wilkinson, the death of Mrs. Gore's dog Spot, on March 14, 1808, had a depressing effect on the entire Government. (P.A.O., Macaulay Papers, H. W. Wilkinson to John Macaulay, May 3, 1808.)

proper time shew it to my brother. The Old Fool came as usual to dinner. I talked at him whenever I had an opening to say any thing severe, and was as cool and distant as possible and avoided being alone with him or even look at him. . . . Mrs. Denison with her little Betsy & son Tom came to sit for her profile.[104] Mary went to the man's who does them with them. I ask Tom to sit. After a while they returned. Mrs Denison sat twice, the first without a bonnet, she thought did not look well and had it done in a bonnet. I do not think either of them is much like, but Tom's is very like and makes a good profile. Betsy Detlor came with one of her little sisters and went away with them and then returned alone to see the profiles. Mrs Denison declined staying dinner, so had some cold beef for them as luncheon. They soon after went home. Johnny Denison[105] sat about a week ago at my request and a few days after Denison brought down little Betsy and went with her to have hers & his own done. His is not over like but hers is very much so.—The price [of] each profile framed and glazed is six shillings but without the frame, you can have four profiles for each person, viz. two shades and the blocks that come out of them for two shillings. He gives you three and requests to keep one of the blocks to shew he has taken a great many people's likenesses since he came here. Mary Thomson & her sister Ellen (who was here for a few days) had theirs done (They were both framed.) After that Miss Mary Baldwin[106] and little Robert was taken, all at my request. The latter two were not framed.—I asked Maria to sit for me but she declined it. Mary Thomson sat twice, the first not being like. Had them both framed.

. . .

H 29 Mrs. Powell to George Murray
[*T.P.L., Powell Papers*]

York Janry 19th, 1806

. . . the follies of *little* York will if we meet serve to you who know us, for an hour's ridicule,—the Ball which the President[107] gives tomorrow in honor of the Queen, will I doubt not add to my budget,—there *rank* will be settled & I fear some who claim precedence, will find themselves of less importance than they expect,—for me I am fortunately out of the scrape,—I shall get my Rubber, & whether I eat my supper at the upper or lower end of the table, is a matter of the most perfect indif-

[104]Mr. Bouker advertised his profile likenesses in the *York Gazette,* April 30 and May 7, 1808. He had been staying at Barrett's Tavern, and had made profiles in New England, New Brunswick, Quebec, Montreal, etc. He was on his way to Niagara and Detroit.

[105]John Denison (1796–1826) was the youngest son of John Denison, and the first of the family to be born in Canada.

[106]Mary Warren Baldwin (1791–1871) was the youngest sister of Dr. W. W. Baldwin. In 1816 she married John Breakenridge (1789–1828), a Niagara lawyer.

[107]Alexander Grant (1734–1813) was President from September, 1805, to August, 1806.

ference, perhaps my Neighbour[108] will feel more interest, as wherever I am, she is below me. . . .

H 30 T. G. Ridout to George Ridout, Cornwall
[*P.A.O., Ridout Papers*]

York 19 January 1806

. . . there is to be a ball given here by President Grant on Monday the Twentieth, of this Month, there has been three Balls given this Winter to two of which Papa and Mamma have been, and whilst they are gone, Basil Stays to take care of the house and amuses the children with Stories untill 11 and 12 o Clock, the reason why Papa & Mamma did not go to the last Ball was that Basil got Drunk that Day and did not come and so Mamma would not go because she was afraid of leaving the house alone . . . there has been very little carioling hitherto but I hope there will be as it is snowing pretty well to Day, I am to go to Mr. Stantons on Monday Night to Tea and Supper as Robert[109] is agoing on the 30 of January and I am agoing to take leave of him.

H 31 Mrs. Powell to George Murray
[*T.P.L., Powell Papers*]

York Janry 24th, 1808

. . . the change which has taken place is unpleasant in its consequences, but as it could only be prevented, by a total dereliction of those principles which have actuated my conduct since I was capable of forming an opinion, I am satisfied to meet the event . . .prepared for an assembly & expecting it should be honor'd by the presence of the Govr & his Lady, Mrs Jarvis paid me a visit, just before dinner to say Mrs Small, would certainly be there—I made no comment on her information, but so soon as she was gone ask'd my Daughters if they chose to go—Mary[110] just finishing the trimming of a Gown for the Eveng, laid it aside & with her Sister answer'd in the negative,—no more was said & we staid at home, convinc'd that those who had the same intelligence would do the same,—Mrs McGill had long before determined not to be there, & I was much surpriz'd to find she had been there, & had induced by her example, other ladies to remain, who finding this infamous Woman had obtruded herself were inclined to retire.—the Govr & Mrs G——— were pleas'd during the Eveng to express surprize & regret at our absence & when by accident Mr P met his Excellency the next day, a reserve induced him to suppose offence had been taken.—I treated the Idea as groundless—the following Sunday, Mrs G in seeing me

[108]Mrs. Robert Thorpe.

[109]Robert Stanton, age 11, was going to Cornwall to attend Dr. Strachan's school.

[110]Mary Boyles Powell (1790–1884), daughter of Chief Justice William Dummer Powell, married Samuel Peters Jarvis in 1818.

walking in the Wet urged me to allow her to set me down,—I declined it & the Govr walk'd with me from Church.—a few days after in conversation with Mr P. he express'd great obligation to Mrs McG. for her presence at the assembly, & as much resentment at my absence,—much pass'd & among other things I was charged with having combined with Mr Crookshank[111] to oppose the assembly,—Mr. P. treated with contempt that for which there was not the least foundation. finding before the next public eveng, that Ladies who had positively determined to go no more, were to attend I thought it right to wait on Mrs Gore, & explain the reasons of my Conduct I told her, that when I became a member of this Society, I found a determination that this Woman who had been excluded in consequence of her infamy, should never be admitted, that last Winter Miss Crookshank & another Lady had enter'd the room, with a resolution to retire should she intrude herself—that Mrs. Jarvis had absented herself from understanding she was to be introduced by Mrs G——— & from various circumstances I had reason to imagine the resolutions avow'd some years ago where still in force,—aware of the influence ascribed to my example & unwilling to do what might give offence we had at once determined to remain at home, in consequence of Mrs. Jarvis's visit!—had I withdrawn while Mrs. G——— was one of the Company, she had been justly disgusted, had I remain'd to me had been imputed the deviation from rules I consider'd as fix'd & proper. —if a change had taken place in the sentiments of the general society I as a member of it was ill treated by being allow'd to remain in ignorance, & I trusted she would join in thinking I was the person who had cause of complaint,—she perfectly assented, & after saying the Woman, never was nor ever could be an acquaintance of hers, told me the vexation she & the Govr felt respecting [me?] was in consequence of many things they heard subsequent to the Sunday she had so kindly offer'd to give me a place in her Carriage,—the charge respecting Mr. C——— I ridiculed but beg'd her to name any other,—the only one she knew was my joining Mrs. Jarvis to counteract their endeavours to promote amusement,—this was likewise denied, as previous to that day, I had not exchanged more than a How d'ye for Months,—we parted on her promise of doing away all impressions in my disfavour on the part of the Govr.—convinc'd from circumstances that it was known Mrs. Small was *not* to be at the assembly the evening of the day on which I visited Mrs. G——— I determined to go, & was confirm'd in my opinion by the visible astonishment & reserve in the countenances of my most intimate Friends. The Govr & Mrs G——— treated me civilly & that was all—no Cards were sent for the Birth night, a notification in the paper was the only invitation we threw off for the eveng our lately assumed Sables, &

[111]George Crookshank (1773–1859) was born in New York, the son of the Loyalist George Crookshank, born in the Orkney Islands. After the Revolution the family moved to St. John, N.B. In 1796 George Crookshank the younger came to York and entered the Commissary Department under his brother-in-law, John McGill.

attended at the Kings House—the Govr seem'd surpriz'd at seeing me, & during the eveng treated me with the most mark'd neglect—I may say *us*, for his conduct to Mr P. was as improper—at supper, when the Chief Justice handed me into the room, & I was advancing to the place appointed for me, he call'd & desired me not to approach the fire, & the next instant call'd other Ladies to the seat he had forbad me to take. I waited quietly until the company had pass'd me, (after walking round the table to find an eligible seat) & then placed myself at the foot of the Table.—had not the kind & elegant manners of his Lady, overcome the shock this unjustifiable treatment occasion'd I had left the room immediately after Supper, but her solicitations to permit your Nieces to continue the dance induced me to remain, & no greater punishment could be inflicted upon a Man, to whom my calm & even manners, were a continued reproach.—the truth is, that from whatever motive it arises, *he* has endeavor'd to introduce this Woman, & he does not scruple to express his resentment, that Mrs. P. reject the Society of one who is an acquaintance of his Lady's, while her delicate Mind, & most correct principles, would be shock'd at knowing this reason was given by him. —this affair so foolish in itself is attended with the most unpleasant consequences,—a Man who from his long & zealous performance of his duty, from the services he has render'd to the province, & who has a right to confidence & respect is treated with not only neglect but pursued with malignity, because his Wife disdains to introduce her Daughters into the society of a Woman, who *if she is* married to the Man with whom she lives, was in the face of the Country charged with Adultery,[112] & in consequence excluded from the company of creditable Females. . . . it does appear ridiculous that such a triffle, so beneath the inteference of a Man, should break up a whole society, but this is the case.—the Woman made her appearance for the second time at the assembly last week—so soon as the Ladies knew Mrs. Gore was not to be there, they order'd their Carriole's & went home—thus the only public amusement is destroy'd, & as much offence given as if they had absented themselves in the first instance. . . .

H 32 Queen's Birthday Celebration
[*York,* York Gazette, *January 25, 1809*]

Wednesday last being the anniversary of Her Majestys Birth Day, the Royal Standard was hoisted in the morning at the Garrison.—At twelve o'clock a Royal Salute was fired by the Artillery, and followed by three rounds from the Infantry.

In the evening an elegant Ball and Supper was given at the Government House.—Dancing commenced at ten o'clock,—the Ball Room having been tastefully and elegantly fitted up and decorated for the occasion.—At half past one the Supper Room was thrown open, when

[112]At the trial of her husband, John Small, for murder of John White in a duel on January 3, 1800.

the Company, amounting to about an hundred persons, partook of a very sumptuous Banquet, consisting of every delicacy and a variety of the choicest Wines.

Dancing was resumed after Supper, and kept up with great spirit, till near eight o'clock in the morning—when the Company retired highly gratified with the splendour of the Entertainment and the condescending attention of the Lieutenant Governor and Mrs. Gore.

H 33 Maria L. Jarvis to the Rev. Samuel Peters
[*P.A.C., William Jarvis Papers*]

York, February 12th, 1809
Upper Canada

Well my dear Grand Papa what a surprising circumstance I am about relating. Will you believe that positively there was a Play acted here last Night, and what do you think it was? Nay you dont know how much we admire your New York comic gentry for the happy display of their choice in choosing a Comedy so applicable to this gay metropolis as the School for Scandal well calculated my dear Sir to excite the risible faculties of some tho horrible faces in others—A very applicable one you will say and not the first time it has been transported to York Ill answer for it the Theatre opened at seven which by the by was the Ball room—and I am happy to inform you that many of the York scandal hunters were present—I have nothing to recount very material, such as Coaches run away with, squeesing to death, fainting fits caused by the crowded audience and confined air—headlong tumbles from the Gallery's that to be sure I did not see owing I suppose to my not being very observing at the best of times—particularly at such a critical moment as that in which the most of the inhabitants of York were so admirably Depicted—nay what a stupid animal I am I did not even look to see who sat in the Pits—well next time I enter the Ball room I shall take particular notice, and let nothing escape my notice—Law what an exclamation and what an appearance of grandeur this sentence has—I am going to the Play, do you go? . . .

H 34 Theatrical Performance in York
[*York,* York Gazette, *May 5, 1810*]

EXHIBITION

Messrs. POTTER & THOMPSON,
from LONDON,

TAKE the Liberty of informing the Ladies and Gentlemen of York and its vicinity, that they will perform at Mr. Miller's Assembly-Room, formerly the Toronto Coffee-House, on Monday the 7th instant,

Philosophical, Mathematical and Curious
Experiments,

many of which were never performed in America by any others but themselves; Theatrical performance, consisting of Songs and Recitations and

Ventriloquism.

In the course of the evening will be sung the following Songs, the Straw Bonnet, the much admired song of the Cosmetic Doctor, or the man for the Ladies, Caleb Quotern or the man of all Trades and Giles Crogans Ghost, by Mr. Potter, with an accompaniment on the Violin by Mr. Lyon. Tickets to be had at the place of performance. Front seats half a Dollar, back seats half price. for further particulars see Bills.[113]

York, 4th May, 1810.

H 35 THEATRICAL PERFORMANCE IN YORK
[*York*, York Gazette, *September 12, 1810*]

THEATRICAL PERFORMANCE

Second and last night.

THE Ladies and Gentlemen of York and its Vicinity, are respectfully informed, that the company of *Comedians from Montreal,* will on Thursday Evening, September 13th 1810, perform The Reverend MR. HOME's Celebrated TRAGEDY[114] of

DOUGLAS

OR

The Noble Shepherd!

Lord Randolph, ... *Mr. Turner,*
Glenalvon, ... *Mr. Jones,*
Young Norval, (Douglas) .... *Mr. Kennedy,*
Old Norval, ... *Mr. Douglas,*
Officer, ... *Mr. Cipriani,*
Lady Randolph, ... *Mrs. Turner,*
Anna, ... *Mrs. Cipriani,*

BETWEEN THE PLAY AND FARCE,

Recitation.—Jubilee for Jubilee, or *Fifty* years Shepherd and *Fifty* a King. *Mr. Douglas.*

---

[113]On May 12, 1810, a second performance was announced, with "new Songs and Recitations." Songs to be sung were "The Four and Twenty Fiddlers all in a Row Sheltey the Piper, the Yorkshire Irishman or the Adventures of a Potatoe Merchant, and Giles Scroggins Ghost, with alterations." The advertisement ends, "Persons who honor the Exhibition with their company, need be under no apprehension of accidents by the future giving way of the Gallery, it having been secured under the direction of an obliging Gentleman." (York, *York Gazette,* May 12, 1810.)

[114]Rev. John Home's poetic drama, *Douglas,* was first performed in 1756.

To which will be added, an admired Comic Farce—call'd

The Village Lawyer.

Scout, (*the Lawyer*) .... *Mr. Jones,*
Snarl, (a Rich Merchant,) ...... *Mr. Douglas,*
Charles, (his Son) .... *Mr. Cipriani,*
Justice Mittimus, ... *Mr. Turner,*
Sheepface, (Shepherd to Snarl) ...... *Mr. Kennedy,*
Mrs. Scout, ... *Mrs. Cipriani,*
Kate, ... *Mrs. Turner*

Tickets of Admission—Front Seats, One Dollar—Back Seats, half a Dollar, Children under 12 years of age, half price; to be had at the place of Performance. Curtain to rise at half past 7 o'clock precisely.

H 36 W. W. Baldwin to Quetton St. George, New York
[*T.P.L., St. George Papers II*]

York 22d Septr. 1810

. . . the building goes on slowly my carpenter is unluckily for me the fashionable contractor this year—it is therefore necessary for him to do a little for all his employers and not to complete the business of any —the incessant Rains obstruct the Brick makers—so that fretting has become our lot as well as all others who undertake house building—inclosed I send you a list of some medicines which you will oblige me by bringing from New York—Show my Bill to Mr. Bach,[115] & tell him I hope he will give them to you or other customers not initiated in the mysteries of the divine art—but without jest, I do expect he will be as liberal to me in this respect as he is to apothecaries and surgeons—it is only fair—I have requested him to choose for me a pocket case of Lancets & will thank you to pay for them . . . be so good as to direct the packing of them carefully—I lost some laudanum in the last box—the Phial being broke—and another bottle containing a Powder.

H 37 Entertainment at York
[*York*, York Gazette, *May 23, 1811*]

Some Things Wonderful.

The Public are informed that a gallant Display of various Performances will take place on Monday Evening next, May 25, at Mr. O'Keefe's Assembly Room, which is fitted up on purpose, for the reception of the worthy Inhabitants of York and its Vicinity, when a famous Entertainment will be exhibited of

VARIOUS CURIOSITIES,

which is truly arranged to excite the admiration of every beholder, and to afford a degree of jollity which never has failed in giving general

115Richard Bache (1737–1811) was an extremely successful New York merchant, married to a daughter of Benjamin Franklin.

satisfaction to all competant Judges.—The Performances will begin at early Candle-light.—Front Seats half a Dollar, Gallery a quarter of a Dollar. Particulars in the hand Bills of the Day.

H 38 MRS. POWELL TO GEORGE MURRAY
[*T.P.L., Powell Papers*]

York August 9th, 1811

. . . every thing here wears a face of improvement, the Country smiles, & we are all sociable together;—15 Gentlemen subscribe & with their families meet & dine at a pretty House about two ½ Miles from town, once a fortnight, after dinner the fife & Drum induce the young folks to Dance; & we return home in the Evening in good humor one with another;—each subscriber takes his Cold Dish & Bottle of Wine, & a moderate rent is paid for the House, so we who are seniors purchase the pleasure of seeing our young people happy at a very triffling expence. . . .

H 39 HOUSE AND CONTENTS FOR SALE
[*York,* York Gazette, *August 17, 1811*]

TO BE SOLD BY AUCTION,
Unless disposed of by private Contract;
ALL that spacious and newly Built Mansion called

HOLYROOD HOUSE;[116]

Comprising eleven commodious, large and lofty Rooms on one Floor, and two Chambers, and ample space for four others up one pair of stairs, fit for the reception of a large Family; with two Barns, Stabling, Coach House and extensive Outhouses, together with a small Cottage, and four Acres of Land, three of which are enclosed within a strong Park-Paling eight feet high:—Also, To be sold by Auction on Monday August 19th inst. and continued thence till sold. All the genuine modern and elegant Household Furniture, Plate, China, Linen, Books, Music, Wines, Liquors, &c. &c. the property of

WILLIAM FIRTH,[117] Esqr.

comprising superb Mahogany Four Post Bedsteads on Castors, with Chintz and Dimity Furniture and large bordered, and Prime Goose

[116]Firth's house stood at the corner of Market (Wellington) and York Streets. For two or three years at the end of the War of 1812, it was used for the meetings of the Legislature. In 1817–18 negotiations were carried on with Firth's agent, W. W. Baldwin, to buy it for the Government, but there were difficulties concerning title, and the purchase was never completed. Chief Justice W. H. Draper lived in it for a number of years.

[117]William Firth was a barrister in Norwich, and friend of William Windham, Secretary of State for War and the Colonies, who appointed him Attorney General of Upper Canada in March, 1807. He became involved in a struggle over fees, and finally returned to England without leave in the autumn of 1811, and was dismissed in April, 1812.

Feather Beds and Pillows, Best Whitney Blankets, Board, Table and other Linen, quite new, and Hair Mattrasses of very first quality, Tent and other Bedsteads, Drawing-Room bordered Sofa on Castors, with brown Holland and Chintz Covers, stuff'd back Cheeks and back Cushions and Bolsters complete, Dining, Card and Pembroke Tables, Looking Glasses, Presses, Wardrobes, Chest of Drawers, Hearth Rugs and variety of Carpeting, Dinner Service of Plate, Epergne, &c. Blue and White English China, complete Set, Desert Service, Decanters of best Gloucester shape cut Glasses, Hock Glasses, white and green Finger Glasses, Salver, Tumblers, Jelly Glasses, Water and Pint Decanters, Preserve Pots, capital Eight Day Clock in Black Walnut Case, excellent Mangle, fine toned double Key'd Harpsichord and Piano Forte inlaid with Sattinwood and of beautiful Mechanism, capital English Jack (late Genl Hunter's) with Chain, Weights, Pullies, 3 Spits and Fire Irons, with large Tin Reflector complete, a double sheet Tin Roaster, Mahogany Portable Bidet, capital Boat with Sails, Oars, Tackle and Furniture complete, fine toned Chapel Bell, complete set of Tin, Earthen and White Ware and all culinary Utensils, Pickling, and Washing Tubs, Cart, Wheelbarrows, 3 Sleighs and Cariole, Side Saddle, Harness, Saddles and Bridles, fine Clover Hay, chamber'd, Malt-Mill, Iron horse Traces, Crows, new Cast Iron Pots lined with white Metal, Sauce-Pans, Boilers and camp Ovens, several hundred Volumes of Books, ancient and modern in all Languages, exclusive of an extensive and complete Law Library, Cabinet of curious antique Gems with MSS Catalogue Raisonne, Maps, Atlasses, Prints, Secretary, Vellum Paper for Drawing, Box of Patent Water Colour Paints, Indian Ink, Cahoutchow, Drawing Board, Rule and Pencils, Sealing Wax, Wafers and Quills, Ink-Powder, capital single barrel Gun, with gold touch-hole and Patent Breech, Lock by Twigg & Bass, & case with copper Powder Flask, Shot-Pouch and furniture complete, several pounds of best double refined Canister Powder and several Bags of Patent Shot, Kegs of white and black Paint and Linseed Oil, barrels of Norway Pitch, Spanish White, and Tar, Garden Tools, Rakes, Spades, Shovels, Forks, &c. Also a large quantity of Loaf and Muscovado Sugars, and a variety of other Groceries, Burges's Pickles and Fish Sauces, fine old Port and Madeira Wines, old Jamaica Rum, Cogniac Brandy, Geneva, Whiskey, Cyder, Scotch Ale, 2 Kegs of best white Wine Vinegar, several dozen empty bottles, fine Pocket Telescope, by Dollond, Pocket Thermometer, Pocket Campass, Burning Lens, Horse-Shoe Magnet, Argaud Lamp, beautiful Globe in Case, Mathematical Instruments, Writing and Draft Paper, West India Cooler, capital Fly and other Fishing Rods, Landing, Minnow and Casting Nets, Reels, Hooks, Lines, Fishing-basket, Book-Liggers and Night Lines for Pike, &c. never used, with a great variety of sundry other Articles.

I. YORK AND THE WAR OF 1812

I 1 Extracts from Ely Playter's Diary
[*P.A.O., Ely Playter's Diary*]

27th [June, 1812] . . . On my return from the Mill I met George he had been in town & heard that the Congress had declared War against us.[1] Genl. Brock had gone to Niagara the Troops ware also sent there from York, &c We went to town the P.M. found all York in alarm every one's countenance wore the mark of surprise. the Flank companys ware in the Garrison on duty; Orders for more volunteers to be sent in and all the Militia to hold themselves in readyness to turn out at the shortest notice &c. . . .

. . .

6th Sunday [August, 1812] Sergt Wallis[2] call'd to warn me to attend at Col. Chewetts by 9 OClock, the Officers all met, & our orders was to send in such a number of men to the Garn. according to the strength of our Cos. The Enemy had commenced Hostilities again. there was a prize brot. into York this morng. captured the the Regent, &c.

. . .

York April 24th. 1813.

Genl. Muster as usual by the Pay Master Captn. Robinson rec'd the Money for the Company, and left it with me to pay the Men. On Guard —see Langsdales House burn down at 3 OClock A.M. as I was on the Visiting rounds.

25th Sunday. Made out the Acquittance-roll and pd. all the Men that were in Garrison, the Men near all being employed daily at the Batteries & by the Engineer. we did not attend Church:—

26th. Was busy in Garrison till near sunset—Left Mr Daverne the Acquittance roll of the Dock Yard Men up to the 25th Feby & came out home about dark I was sent for by Major Allen. an Alarm of the Yankey fleet seen off the Highlands—I hasted down George went with me the Troops & Militia were all prepairing Patroles & Guards sent out every direction I was ordered to get 2 Militia Men in readyness and go to Major Givins for some Indians. he was at the Generals. I went there and was detained as the Genl. thought I need not go till near Daylight I laid down a short time on the floor, in the Dining room and about Day I started with my Party

27th. Could see the American fleet when it came light—opposite the Tellegraft.[3] I proceeded with my men about 7 Miles down the lake shore

[1]Congress declared war on June 18, 1812.

[2]Probably Daniel B. Wallis, shoemaker.

[3]The telegraph was probably the lighthouse on Gibraltar Point, from which flag signals were hoisted for the information of the town and Garrison.

met some Horse-Men who had received intelligence 25 Miles from York & no enemy had landed which was what I was sent to discover. I therefore returned & we heard the Guns begin to fire just after we started back we came double-Quick near all the way and was not a little wearied when we came to the Garrison I proceeded up to the Batteries where the Guns were playing Briskly. The Men that had been sent up to oppose their Landing, were retreating from the Woods just as I came up, heard the Granideer Co. of the 8th. Regt. was near all killed their Captn.[4] also and the Yankies had effected their Landing West of the Old-fort. Their Vessels kept a constant fire on our Battries, and about an Hour after 6 or 8 of them hauled in near opposite our Garrison & oppened a brisk fire on us tho, at some distance no doubt they perceived our Gun's were light & kept off, were we could not reach them, I came with some other officers to the Barracks, & we got each of us a Musket, as every one expected a severe attact upon the enemy when they advanced from the Woods, Major Allen ordered me to collect all the men in the Barracks & keep them together by the Guard House but the Balls came so hott that we got under the cover of the Garrison Battery for some time we were then all ordered into the Hollow by the Store Houses & greater part of the forces were drawn up there & we were soon after informed that our Men were retreating from the Batteries west of the Garrison. This was a surprise to many as we expected to have been ordered up to attact near those Batteries. There was an attempt made to form the Militia up the Hollow and some formed but when the Men see the Troops of the line pass they refused to stand & we all passed up and formed outside of the Garrison Picquetts. we still ware in expectation of engaging the enemy & I was much surprised after we had haulted for some time to hear us ordered to face to the right & March. I then perceived we were to leave the Garrison, And I went into it & to our Quarters got my Coat, advised Mrs. Chapman a Woman that Cooked for us to come away & as I returned out at the Gate the Magazine Blew up & for a few Minutes I was in a Horrid-situation, the stone falling thick as Hail & large one's sinking into the very earth. see Captn. Loring[5] a little distance from me fall with his Horse, & Mr. Sanders also with one leg mashed by a stone,—Captn. Loring escaped but his Horse was killed, as I came down by Mr. Crookshanks being in the rear I see some of the enemy come passed the Picquets & form there they fir'd after us a few shott. This was the only sight I had of them, we Halted in front of the Council office and after some consultasion Genl. Sheaffe Marched off—the Officers & Men of the Regulars for Kingston, & Major Allen, Captn. J.B. Robinson went with a flagg to the enemy. They returned and told us they were to go again in 15 Minutes—we came on towards the town, met Captn. Leatcover returning

[4]Captain Neal McNeale.

[5]Robert Roberts Loring (d. 1848) served in the 49th Regiment and the New Brunswick Fencibles. In October, 1812, he was appointed aide-de-camp to Sir Roger Sheaffe. He was taken prisoner at Lundy's Lane.

and desired assistance to set fire to the Marine Store and the New ship,[6] I and some others went with him, and performed the service, came threw the town see a number of Country Ma. just come in, call'd a few minutes at Jordans, a number of persons came and spoke to me saying they heard I was killed—came out home with Captn. Ridout, Mr. Mercer & George, Mr. Ridout S.G.s family Mr. Stantons & Mr. Debtlors family, were all at fathers & staid all night. all with fearful apprehentions, and of course low in spirits not knowing what usage we should receive from the Enemy. I being much fatigued slept sound.

28th. Joel Bemen knock'd us up. he had come down with the waggon hearing I was killed, & Sophia with the Children & some of the things I sent out with him to NewMarket, George & me went with them to Ridouts, he and Mr. Mercer went to town. I did not feel disposed to give myself up and kept away. walk down to the back of the Town met Young Debtlor who told me his father was Dead was wounded in the leg, had it cutt off. & Died soon after. Geo. went in to see him—see T. Ridout Jr. he had gone of with Genl. Sheaffe & was sent back by him. I went in the even'g down with Mr. Stanton's Ridouts & Debtlors family's D. Brooks retn'd went in with us, see Robt. Sn. he was paroled said the Yankies used them well, that the blewing up of the Magazine Killed upwards of 100, and the second General Pike,[7] Genl. Deaborne[8] commanded the expedition. I returned with George & lodged at Fathers

29th. at Home Packing up my things and hideing them D. Brooks Pased on his way to Kingston and many others also as the Enemy kept a Guard at the Don Bridge they came up here to cross. in the P.M. an officer & some men came to Fathers. George and me went away as we did not intend to be taken—they came to my House, Broke the Door and took many things away. We watched them till dark and suposing they staid all night at fathers we went back to Mr. Ridouts were we staid all night.

30th. Help'd Mr. R. & Mr. Mercer secure some of their things & Mr. Mercer & myself went to town. Major Allen advised me to go & get Paroled. I went to the Garrison with Mr. Mercer and signed my Parole and got a pass. we then went back to Higgins & see Andw. Borland & Doctr. Hartney.[9] Borland had 6 Wounds & Hartney 3, but both likely to

[6]The *Sir Isaac Brock* was a 30-gun frigate being built at York to be ready for the opening of navigation in 1813. It was not ready, and was destroyed unfinished on the stocks by the British.

[7]General Zebulon Pike (1779–1813), born at Trenton, N.J., was well known as a western explorer, and was sent by the army to the source of the Arkansas and Red Rivers. He was killed in the explosion of the magazine at York.

[8]General Henry Dearborn (1751–1829), born at Hampton, N.H., was originally a doctor. He had a distinguished military career in the Revolution, and was Secretary of War, 1801–9. In January, 1812, he was appointed senior Major General in the army, in command of the northeast sector, from the Niagara to the Atlantic. On July 6, 1813, he was relieved of his command.

[9]Patrick Hartney was Barrack Master at York from about 1806 to 1829, and was wounded at the battle of York. Why Playter called him Doctor is obscure.

recover, we returned. I spoke to Genl. Dearborn of his Men Plundering my House. he said it was contrary to his orders he had station'd an officer in Town to prevent it. That he would enquire into it & have them Punished. The appearance of the Town & Garrison were dissmal. the latter shattered and rent by the Balls & the explosion of the Magazine not a building but shew some marks of it & some all torn to pieces. the Town thronged with the Yankies many busy getting off the publick-stores the Council Office with every Window Broke & pillaged of every thing that it contained the Government Building, the Block House and the Buildings adjacent all burned to Ashes; I got some of my thing's Mrs. Chapman had saved for me in Garrison, we call'd at Jordan's took a cold-cut and came out to Fathers met a Party of Men the officer ask'd us if we were paroled and I Questioned him on the supposition it was the Party that was out Yesterday but found they went back this Morning. The officer that was with them Lieut. Riddle of the 6th. Regt. & those we met were the Rifle Co.—I went back with Mr. M. as I rode Mrs. R's. Mare and took Mrs. R. the side Saddle. Geo. was still there & we came back together at dark.

1st. May Mr. J. Denis was at Fathers since 29th. had started for Kingston but returned, dare not go home for fear of being taken. I intended to have gone to the Garrison to inquire more after my Things, but felt unwell & lowspirrited, went over to John's the P.M. Denis was there heard the Yankies were all going off. Dennis went to town.

2nd. May Sunday. I went to town the Yankies were all on board their vessels. Call'd at Dennis, see Sanders. Geo. was there I went up to see how the Garrison look'd, great numbers were up to look at the ruins. The Yankies had buried all the Dead & I perceived they had done it very ill. see Mrs. Cook, George, & John P. by the store House. I hasted out Home got Dinr. & rode out to NewMarket. It was late when I got out found Sophia in a little School House and the Children ill with the Coughf. . . .

. . .

31st. [July, 1813] The Yankie Fleet came into York Geo was in town, came out in the eveng told me of two Boats he had conducted up the Don one with 3 Dragoons & Stores he had got up but the other lay by the Park, he went to town at Dark the Yankies had landed—opened Major Allen's & St. Georges Store Houses & were taken away the flour &c. the Boat loaded with Arms & Ammunition was still at the Park. & after Midnight Geo & me went down to it had much Difficulty to get her off as she was large—but we got her up above Longreach by sunrise the Dragoons we found at their Boat & we Brot. her further up & came home to Breakfast. 1st. August 1813.—Geo. Hanh. & me went to town they rode—I went into the Park—see the Am. fleet—one of which was coming up the bay & set of from her 5 boats up the Don. I then hastened home Geo. & Hanh. was out before me The Dragoons had gone down to the boat, we had word that the Yankies were coming up after the Stores &c. Captn. J.B. Robinson was out to help us, S. Sinclair[10] & J. Kendrick also—we got the Amunition all out of the boat & secreted the Arms & some Boxes of shot we sunk scuttled the boat & let her go—the Draggoons got their Loading all out & hiden also, we heard in the eveng that the Yankies came some Distance above the bridge but finding it difficult to get the Guards along on Shore they returned back—

. . .

5th [August, 1813] . . . A party of Men came up after the Ammunition Sinclair & me went with them & we collected it all they were to hasten with it to the Army. This was on the 3rd. p.m.

. . .

12th. [August, 1813] . . . I went in the P.M. with a party to get up the Arms that were sunk.—

. . .

28th. [September, 1813] . . . I ploughed till noon—heard heavy Canonading—I went in. the fleets were engaged & in sight, but at such a distance little could be discovered, a heavy East wind drove them towards the Head of the Lake, I attended eveng Parade

. . .

30th. Septr. 1813. At Parade as usual a great number of the men had gone home. the Yanky fleet was seen of standing in this way, & thot. to be coming in the Publick stores were all moved away, all bustle & alarm, I had 3 Boats with flour in my charge, & Brot them up the Don—But the fleet was seen to put about & bear off—all apprehention ceased. —I halted with the boats by the bridge & kept a gd. over them all night.—

1st. Octr. I went to Mr. Crookshank, & he desired the boats to return, I got some more men & we took the Boats back & unloaded them.—. . .

. . .

26th. [October, 1813] . . . every House in town full of Soldiers—

. . .

16th. [November, 1813] An American Vessell came in with a flagg this Morning had some Books &c for the Chief Justice—supposed to be an excuse only to see what was going on, she didn't stay long; the little Vessel came here from Kingston & been to Burlington came in just before the Am. Flagg.—

I 2 Militia at the Garrison

[*York*, York Gazette, *July 4, 1812*]

The Editor is pleased to hear from all ranks of People so many flattering enconiums pronounced on the Volunteer Militia who garrison this Post—well may our mother country be styled the triumphant bulwark of

[10]Samuel Sinclair (Sinckler) (1767–1852) came from New England and served in the Royal Fencible American Regiment during the Revolution. After a time in New Brunswick, he settled above the Terrys on the Don.

Liberty, when her subject Sons thrive to rival each other in proud examples of patriotism and Loyalty. If any thing the Editor could say, could add to the declaration of a Veteran Commander, whose opinion he had the honor of hearing yesterday, to wit, "that the present Garrison were a set of active and well behaved young men—whose conduct did honor to their King, their country, and themselves," he would say, that he believes them men who would ably distinguish themselves in preserving the sacred rights of Religion, Property, and Liberty, which we now under the blessings of Providence enjoy.

I 3 Regimental Orders by Lieut. Colonel Chewett Commanding 3rd Regiment York Militia
[*P.A.C., Upper Canada Sundries*]

York, 5h. September 1812.

In Consequence of the Flank Companies of said Regiment now in the Garrison of York under the Command of Major Allan, having been ordered by Major General Scheaffe on the 4th. Instant, to proceed with all possible speed to Fort George.—The following Officers Number of Non Commissioned Officers and Privates detached by their respective Quotas from the Battalion Companies of said Regiment, are hereby directed to Compose the following Companies and to do Duty in the Garrison until further Orders.

1st. Captain Denison	2nd. Captain Ridout	3rd. Captain Hamilton
Lt. Endicott	Lt. Kendrick	Lieut. Playter
Ensn. McArthur[11]	Ensn. Brooks	Ensn. Jarvis
3 Serjeants	3 Serjeants	3 Serjeants
42 Rank & file	42 Rank & file	42 Rank & file

I 4 Strachan to Dr. Owen,[12] Chaplain General
[*P.A.O., Strachan Letter Books; printed in* John Strachan Letter Book, *ed. Spragge, pp. 19–20*]

Upper Canada 1 Novr 1812

On my arrival at this place in the beginning of July last Mr Stuart then removing to Kingston communicated to me your letter of the 24th March enclosing a circular from the Commander in Chief. As I was just entering upon my duties, and knew nothing of the place it appeared unnecessary or perhaps improper for me to trouble you till I was able from actual observation and experience to answer your several inquiries.

Answer to Question 1st

At present we have forty regulars in Garrison, and two hundred Militia.

[11]Donald McArthur was a clerk in Alexander Wood's store. During Wood's absence in Scotland in 1810–12 he managed the concern, and after Wood's return he opened a shop of his own in York and later on Yonge Street.

[12]Ven. Archdeacon John Owen, M.A., was Chaplain General to the Forces.

In a few weeks we shall have the crews of the ships of war employed on Lake Ontario consisting of nearly three hundred more. This place is now become the general Depot of the Province, and therefore the number of troops on the return of peace will be greater than formerly but just now all our disposable force is upon the lines resisting invasion.

Answer to Question 2nd

The Troops always attend the Parish Church. They are accommodated with a large convenient gallery. Should their numbers increase I shall be ready to read prayers & preach for them separately.

Question 3rd is answered in the affirmative

Answer to Question 4th

My first object in the composition of my sermons is to be clearly understood by all ranks, and as the Soldiers are not inferior to many of my Parishioners I can have no doubt but that they fully comprehend what is said if they lend me their attention.

Answer to Question 5

I visit the Hospital twice every week and oftener when it seems necessary. After conversing with every patient a little I walk up into the middle of the Ward, and beginning with two or three of the most appropriate prayers from the Common Prayer Book I give a short exhortation. I have been for some time proceeding with the Catechism as a sort of text book commenting upon every question as I go along. I speak as much to the heart as I can, and I trust chiefly to my recollection at the moment that it may have the greater weight. It is to be hoped that duties so important are performed with a sincerity that conscience may approve.

Answer to Question 6th

I have had as yet very little opportunity of conversing with the Soldiers except the sick. The unhappy war in which we are engaged has called all the regulars to the lines, and the Militia after remaining a week or two in garrison here are marched off and replaced by raw Militia from the Country so that the garrison is continually changing—It is however a subject which I shall never fail impressing on the minds of the serious

I have given several copies of Dr Porteous' Evidences to the Ward and some other tracts I have also given a new Testament, a prayer book, and some sermons. We sometimes find a person convalescent who is willing to read to the rest. Should you require any particular information in addition to what your questions have produced I shall be happy in giving it, and from my situation at the seat of government I have the means of becoming acquainted with every remarkable occurrence that happens in the Province. . . .

I 5 Alexander Wood to John Stevens,[13] London
[*T.P.L., Alexander Wood Letter Books*]

York 9th. Novr. '12

I have at last just recd. accts. of ye. Ralph Nicholson, she was a few Miles below Montreal on ye. 5th Ulto. Mr Leslie[14] writes me on that day ye. probabty. of his beg. able to get ye. goods sent on in ye. course of ye. week, whether he effected it or not I am unable to say havg. no advice from that quarter since owg. to the prest. unhappy state of ye. country. You will readily believe we feel much anxiety when I mention that ye. River St. Lawrence forms our boundary for nearly 200 miles below Kingston, where our property is exposed in open boats & often in the rout within gun shot of the enemy's posts & are frequently annoyed by parties of Americans who endeavour to intercept our supplies and carry on a predatory war greatly against us tho' they seldom succeed in their plundering designs.

What is to be our fate we know not, We have hitherto been able to keep them off and frustrate all their attempts to gain a lodgement on our side

I 6 Strachan to Lt. J. B. Robinson, Browns Point, Near Niagara
[*J.B. Robinson Papers in possession of Mr. Christopher Robinson, Ottawa; microfilm copy in P.A.O.*]

York 22nd Novr 1812

In consequence of a hint in the letters of Mr. G Ridout & Mr Robt Stanton to their respective Fathers, the Gentlemen of York met in the Church to day for the purpose of subscribing towards the comforts of the Militia belonging to this District on actual service, especially the Flank Companies—Our Subscription tho not yet paid amounts to nearly £150, and we wish your & Capt Hewards advice how to dispose of it, for the most advantage to the men. Your Brother Capt Robinson thinks, that the Captains of the York Militia should make a requisition from the Quarter Master General for Flannel sufficient to make two shirts for every one that wants them (and thread &c to make them up) together with a pair of Stockings for each, and we will supply the Captains with the amount, and thus save the men from the pressure of paying for their necessaries. If this appear the best mode the sooner it is done the better because, if there be any difficulty in making them up we can get it done here instantly and the flannel in that case should be sent over. Capt. Robinson says he does not think, that there are above 100 men from this District, but tho' there be more we can go the length of one pound York in finding necessaries. You will advise with Capt. Heward to whom

[13]London merchant.

[14]James Leslie (1786–1873) was a Montreal merchant, and from 1809 head of Irvine, Leslie, & Co., a branch of Wood's Glasgow correspondents, Leslie, McNaught & Co.

I was going to write, but I have nothing to say but what this letter contains which you will shew him. The Militia will be much pleased when they know with what alacrity the Subscription proceeded. We are told that the men are expected to pay for their Flannel Shirts Stockings & Great Coats. Tell us how much it would cost per man to furnish all these, for altho' we dare not as yet go farther than shirts and stockings yet as I intend to push the Subscription as much as possible, we may be able to add some great coats also—There are I believe a couple of companies here, who will expect to share in our attentions. You will be aware, that this letter requires an immediate answer. We have heard of your firing and are anxious to learn the result—

P.S. Should requisitions for the articles we mean to pay for have been already made by the Captains we can still supply the amount which will make it the same to the men[15]

I 7 T. G. RIDOUT TO ELIZABETH WARD,[16] LONDON
[*P.A.O., Ridout Papers*]

Toronto Upper Canada.
January 5th, 1813—

. . . Our Canadian winter has set in to be very severe. all the great rivers & Lakes are frozen over. & the snow is four feet deep in our tractless Forests, which makes the sleighing excellent for about 1,200 miles thro' the country . . . here I am upon the north shore of Lake Ontario, whose great surface is frozen as far as the eye can reach, & appears like an immense desart of snow, on the land side we are surrounded by an impenetrable forest of Pines &ca 180 or 90 feet in heighth, & five Indian nations who have come down to the war are encamped on the skirts of the woods back of the Town. they keep us alive with their war dances & make the dark cedar woods echo with many savage yells, of which my brothers & I expect to know more than enough to please us next Spring & Summer. . . .

. . . the excellent musket your Father presented me with I take the greatest care of. it has not seen any actual service further than an affair between the Royal George & American fleet, in which I happened to be present by going on board to see my brother John who is a midshipman & behaved himself very well on that day. I continued cruizing on the Lake 10 days, when we returned to Port. and I was obliged to finish my journey by a march of 238 miles along the banks of this Lake with a knapsack & musquet on my shoulders & a young Messessaugā Indian for a companion. since the snow fell I received about a fortnight ago

[15]On Dec. 7, 1812, Strachan sent to Captain D. Cameron, 184 shirts, leather for 70 or 80 pair shoes, 4 pair stockings, 4 pair socks, and 2 pair mittens, with detailed instructions for their disposal among the flank companies. (P.A.O., Strachan Letter Books, Strachan to Cameron, Dec. 7, 1812; printed in *The John Strachan Letter Book*, ed. Spragge, p. 28.)

[16]Daughter of Thomas Ridout's sister.

the rest of my things by John who came up & now goes to a school for the winter, during which all navigation is at an end the waters being frozen up

My brother George & myself have the honor to be Lieutenants in the Toronto Volunteers & we have just returned from Niagara (where I joined them *about a* month ago) to this place where we spend our winter at home quarters. *wide awake* is the word for the spring.

. . . We have two large Frigates[17] upon the Stocks in this Town, at which 400 Workmen are employed. they will be rigged & finished notwithstanding the cold weather in 12 weeks & are to be mann'd by 500 Officers & seamen from Halifax who are now on their way thro' the woods & snow to this country. . . .

Tell your Father that yesterday George & I cut a hole in the ice & caught with hooks 16 dozen of fine trout & speared a large maskinungee . . . this minute there are 7 Indians chasing 2 red deer out upon the Lake. they'll overtake them in a very short time as the snow is deep & is now falling like a cloud. . . .

I 8 BRUYÈRES TO PREVOST
[P.A.C., C729, pp. 69–71]

Fort George 28th. January 1813

On my arrival at York Saturday Inst. the 23rd. Inst. I found the establishment for the Naval Yard, and building of the Ship in so disorganized a state owing to the total difference of opinion of Captn. Gray, and Mr. Plunknett[18] relative to the spot necessary for this purpose, that I considered it most beneficial for the Service to proceed here without loss of time, and to bring Mr. Plunknett with me in order to obtain the final decision, and opinion of Major Genl. Sheaffe, and that of Lt. Col. Myers as Head of the Quarter Master Genl's department on this point that no further delay or obstruction should take place in carrying on this very important Service. It is necessary to explain to Your Excellency the facts of this unfortunate difference.—Captn. Gray on his arrival at York selected a spot about half a Mile up the Harbor which he considered best calculated for the purpose of Building; and in the selection of this spot the Master Builder, and the Officer commanding the Prince Regent concurred in opinion, notwithstanding the Water was very Shoal to some distance from the Shore. but in order to counteract this defect, and to obtain sufficient height for the inclination necessary to Launch the Ship it was proposed to erect a Wharf 25 feet high; 100 feet wide to extend nearly 800 feet from the shore, and thereon to lay the Keel of the Ship.—When Mr. Plunknett came to take charge he objected to

[17]The *Sir Isaac Brock* was the only frigate on the stocks at this time. Possibly Ridout refers to the *Duke of Gloucester*, a schooner built at Kingston in 1807, which was undergoing repairs at York when the Americans landed in April.

[18]Thomas James Plunknett came from Quebec to become Storekeeper and Superintendent of the Marine Department at York. His ability was questioned by Bruyères, Gray, and Myers.

this situation, as he considered it totally impossible that a Vessel could be built there and immediately employed himself in sounding the Harbor, in order to obtain a more eligible place. this he found about a quarter of a Mile farther up the Bay, where there is sufficient depth of water at 300 feet from the shore, and by excavating the Bank for a short distance could obtain a solid foundation on the Ground at a sufficient height from the level of the Water to lay the Keel of the Vessel without the risk or necessity of building on a Wharf.

This work he actually began; and would have been prepared to lay the Keel in two or three days when a positive order arrived from Captn. Gray that the work must be continued on the original spot.—On my arrival at York I found matters in this situation with the Timber nearly divided between the two places, and a general stagnation to every exertion in the progress of this Work.—Mr. Plunknett immediately waited on me to say that he considered himself totally divested of all further responsibility, and that rather than risk his reputation in building a Ship on so uncertain a fabric (where the whole might in an instant fall to the ground) he would return to Quebec, notwithstanding his utmost desire and zealous wishes to do every thing in his power to forward the service he had in charge.—Having myself examined both situations, and heard the local objections to which each are liable I determined to have the subject referred as soon as possible to Head Quarters at Fort George, and it is decided to proceed on the spot[19] fixed by Mr. Plunknett. I earnestly hope no further delay will now occur tho' I must candidly observe to Your Excellency that I have a much more unfavorable opinion of the possibility of obtaining our ascendancy on this Lake than I had when at Kingston. . . .

. . . York may undoubtedly in time of Peace be made an excellent Harbor, and dock yard much preferable to Kingston, but under present circumstances it is totally incompetent for the purpose, and the latter must be made use of untill York can be well established. . . .

I 9 Alexander Wood to John Stevens
[*T.P.L., Alexander Wood Letter Books*]

York 3d. Feby. 1813

I had this pleasure on the 9th Novr. last when I had just heard of the Ralph Nicholson.

I now inclose the 2d of W. H. Robinsons set of Exchange on the Lords of the Treasury at 30% in favr. of Edwd Couch[20] for £100 Sterling, the precarious and even dangerous state of our inland conveyance renders it uncertain whether our letters reach even the lower Province.

In my last I accounted to you for the distant date of the Bills, Specie being so scarse the Commy Genl. was obliged to put paper of this

[19]The *Sir Isaac Brock* was built slightly west of Bay Street.

[20]Edward Couche was Deputy Commissary General.

description into the hands of his Deputies in this Province to enable them to pay the disbursements of that Department & to collect what money could be got by a Sacrifice as you see by the great discount on this Bill.

I'm sorry to inform you that my goods after being I may say almost at hand, the Vessel being in sight of this port and only a few miles to Leeward was obliged to bear away and return to Kingston,[21] when within about thirty miles of that Harbour she was observed by some of the American Ships of War & pursued they keeping up a constant fire upon her, one 24 Shot went through her hold, but by her Superior sailing she made her port tho' full of water & immediately went down on getting to the wharf the goods were got up as quickly as possible thoroughly drenched as you may suppose, many things are entirely lost others so damaged as to render them unsaleable, to complete the misfortune the navigation was altogether shut to us as nothing would venture again on the Lake, the Americans having a Superior force, more able Officers & better Seamen obtained the entire command of the Waters and the advanced Season added to the difficulty. Our land roads are impassable at that time of the year and the distance, 200 Miles makes the expense so great to carry by Land that hardly any kind of Merchandize will bear it. We have however been obliged to to take the advantage of a severe Winter, which facilitates the intercourse, to get such articles from Kingston as were absolutely necessary. I went down and got together such of the Articles in my collection as were worth bringing up, the cost in some instances far exceeds the original price but we must make the best we can of it. I trust this will be a sufficient apology for my backwardness in remitting together with the deranged state of the Country which operates so powerfully against the recovery of debts that it is only adding to the embarrassment to prosecute for property of all kinds is at present a dead Stock.

I 10 Bruyères to Prevost

[*P.A.C., C387, p. 15; printed in Wood,* Select British Documents of the Canadian War of 1812, *II, 75*]

Kingston 13th February 1813

. . . In my Letter of the 28th Ulto. from Fort George I expressed the unfavorable opinion I had respecting York as a Naval establishment under the present pressure of the public Service, as it is much too remote

[21]Wood's goods were shipped from Kingston on the schooner *Simcoe,* Captain James Richardson. The *Simcoe* came down the lake with the *Earl of Moira* and the sloop *Elizabeth,* and all three arrived safely at Niagara. The *Earl of Moira* and the *Elizabeth* left Niagara the next day, the *Simcoe* not until the following day, when it crossed to York, but the wind not being fair, it was forced to continue to Kingston, and was attacked. Wood unsuccessfully tried to claim damages from the ship's owner, Hon. John Richardson, on the grounds that the captain had lingered overlong at Niagara. He was also unsuccessful in claiming compensation from the government as a war loss.

and distant a Port to obtain the necessary resources to carry on any great undertaking. I am more fully confirmed in this opinion since my last visit there.—Nature has done very little to the position as a Military Post,—or to the Harbor for the purposes of a Dock Yard; every thing must be created which will require considerable time, and Expence. . . .

I 11 Sir R. H. Sheaffe to Bathurst

[P.R.O., C.O. 42, v. 354, p. 95; microfilm copy in P.A.O.]

York 5th. April 1813

Many motives, both of a Civil and a Military nature, have combined to detain me here longer than I expected; but I hope to be able to return to Fort George in the course of a few days;—I wish particularly to see this place put into a more respectable state of defence before my departure, as I think it probable that the Enemy will make some attempt on it in the spring; at present his flotilla is locked up in ice in Sackett's harbour; it would be an object of no small importance to him, to destroy the Ship building here, it being larger than any which was floated on these Lakes. . . .

I 12 Minutes of the General Quarter Sessions of the Peace, Home District

[P.A.O., Minutes of the General Quarter Sessions of the Peace, Home District]

General Quarter Sessions of the Peace York 26th April 1813.

The Court met pursuant to Adjournment.
Present
Thomas Ridout, Esquire, Chairman,
Donald McLean, Esquire.

Benjamin Mosley[22] employed to repair the Bridge at the River Rouge, by an Order of this Court of 21st Instant produced his Account to the Court, together with Mr. G. W. Post's[23] charge for securing the said Bridge—the whole amounting to £10.6.0 Provincial Currency—which was Approved and Audited by the Chairman—

The Court also Ordered, that in Consequence of Mr. B. Mosley's exertions in the speedy repair of the Bridge over the River Rouge, that he be employed to examine the state of the Bridges over the River Humber and Sixteen Mile Creek, and to report to this Court, on or before Saturday next the state of both Bridges and the probable expense of the repairs required for the same.

[22]Benjamin Mosley first came to Upper Canada with his father, Sergeant George Moseley of the 45th Regiment, about 1793. He is listed as an inhabitant of the Don and marsh from the first List of Inhabitants in 1797.

[23]George Washington Post (1779–1828) was the youngest son of Jordan Post, baker. He kept a tavern in Scarborough. He later moved to Pickering Township and kept a tavern about three miles west of Whitby.

Ordered that the Slaughter House built near to the Bay at York, lately occupied by the late Daniel Laughlin,[24] be either not used as a Slaughter House, or be removed to such place as the Magistrates may direct on or before the 15th. day of May next—And they do also direct that all Houses used as Slaughter Houses in the Town of York be kept perfectly clean, or that they shall on the first complaint be removed—and that the Clerk do write copies of this Order for Pub: information.

The Court then Adjourned to Saturday next.

S. Heward
Clk attending

NB. In Consequence of the Enemy having possession of the Town of York the Court could not meet on the 27th of April

I 13 Isaac Wilson to Jonathan Wilson[25]

[*P.A.O., Copy of Isaac Wilson Letter Book*]

Young Street Decem 5th 1813.

. . . The day after I wrote the last letter that I sent to England (it was directed to my Uncle) I went to the Garrison at York and continued there until it was taken on the 26th of April. I took much better with that way of life than I thought I would have done. We had plenty of provisions and good beds but sometimes the duty came hard being one night in bed and another on guard then sometimes we had 4 or 5 nights in bed according to the number of men in the Garrison. It was very cold in the nights standing sentry but I acted as sergeant the latter part of my time and had only to relieve the sentries every two hours and the rest of the time I could sit by a good fire. I thought I could stay there over summer very well but most of the men were very discontented and had come to a determination to go home as soon as they got their pay. But they were set at liberty in a way they little expected on the 26th of April. In the evening the American fleet were seen off York and next morning they were standing in for the land The first time I saw them they were passing close to the point of land that forms the Bay of York which you may see in Thos. Stanton's maps. There were 15 sail and they had a very pretty appearance it being a clear still morning. The garrison is nearly opposite that point and they landed their men about 1½ miles above it where the land is uncleared and they came close to the waters edge. The company that I was in was stationed in some barracks near the head of this Bay being about 3 miles from where they were landing their men. We were paraded early in the morning and kept there waiting for orders. At last word came for us to march up to the garrison. When we had gone about a mile we saw the flash of the first gun they fired on board the

[24]Daniel Laughlin (d. 1811) came from northern Ireland. He was a butcher. In 1798 he was allowed to build a slaughter house on the Market Square.

[25]Jonathan Wilson, Isaac's brother, lived in Cumberland, England.

vessels. They were firing grape shot on the men who opposed their landing and immediately heard the reports of small arms. It was well for us that we were not there for the men were falling fast. We went on as fast as we could and soon began to meet the wounded men some one way and some another such a bloody sight made me wish for the first time that I was safe at "Birkbank" again. We kept marching on till we met the Militia, who had been at the place of landing, on their retreat the Americans having made good their landing. One company of the 8th Regiment was nearly all killed. The Batteries and the vessels kept firing on each other for some time without much damage being done on either side. One bad accident happened in one of the batteries, a box of powder blew up and killed and wounded about 30 men. All was now confusion every man going where he would I had one very narrow escape from some of the American rifle men. I was going through a corner of the woods that I might have a better view of the ships firing on the batteries when I saw 8 or 10 men 30 or 40 yards from me. One of them saw me and immediately cocked his rifle and levelled at me and fired. I do not know how many of them fired I heard several shots as I ran through among the bushes. But they all missed me and I came off safe. Their whole army very soon after appeared in the open ground advancing towards the garrison. When they were about ¼ mile from it the magazine to which a match had been placed some time before blew up with a terrible explosion. The air seemed full of stones, some large ones came near me but I got under a large tree that was fallen down. The Americans suffered much. They told me they had 1000 men killed and wounded by it. Had they been nearer they would have been mostly destroyed for the ground was nearly covered with stones. They used the people with great civility. They did not allow their men to plunder any property that could be prevented In the night they put a sentry over every store but they could not keep the inhabitants from it who made shameful work in some peoples houses. But the Americans were greatly praised for their good conduct. There was a large quantity of farming utensils which were sent for the use of settlers in this country. The authorities would not allow these to be given out except to favorites. The Americans distributed these generally to all settlers so their visit to York was very useful in this respect. Many Americans like the country very much and said they would come and settle in it if the war was over. It struck my mind very forcibly the evening after the battle was over to see men who two hours before were doing their utmost to kill one another now conversing together with the greatest familiarity. In the evening all seemed as settled and quiet in York as if nothing had happened. The Americans remained at York until they had the Government property on board and then left. The British are now very busy erecting fortifications to prevent the Americans coming again. The Militia who were taken prisoners were sent home on their parole not to bear arms till exchanges but the regulars about 40 in number were taken to the States. . . .

I 14 STRACHAN TO DR. JAMES BROWN, ST. ANDREWS
[*P.A.O., Strachan Papers*]

York. 26 April, 1813

We were looking for an attack when your affecting letter arrived for owing to the mismanagement of our little Navy we lost the command of the Lake last summer, and shall not regain it till we procure good Officers from England, those we have do not belong to the Royal Navy and not having seen service and without any experience. . . .

I am interrupted an express has come in to tell us the enemys flotilla is within a few miles steering for this place all is hurry, and confusion, and I do not know, when I shall be able to finish this. I am not afraid, but our Commandant is weak—It is now the 14th day of June and what with losses alarms &c I did not feel inclined to continue my letter, I could only give you bad news and I waited for something pleasing. This we have in some measure obtained, and I have copied off the first part of my letter, as I found the paper blotted and I shall give a short account of events since it was begun in the way of [a] journal

April tuesday 27th Got up at four. The enemy in sight mount my horse & ride up to the garrison—The ships fourteen in number approach the shore, about two miles above the garrison—proceed towards them, discover them anchoring—return to the garrison—Look through a glass find the vessels decks thickly covered with troops—from which I infer, that they are come prepared to land in great force. The troops already in their boats—wonder that no troops are ordered to march up to prevent their landing. At length two companies of the eight, and as many of the Newfoundland Regts are ordered to march along the defile. The Militia & one company of the Glengarry Regt. follow our force of all sorts about 650 or 700—Return to town leave my horse, & walk back to the Garrison. The Militia of the town only a head—proceed to the upper battery badly placed—the ships of the enemy too distant. About seven meet the wounded coming towards the Hospital, help some of them along—Attend at the Hospital—perceive our troops retreating—the General in front—disagreeable presages. Inquire of several officers, what stand & when was it to be made. They had no orders—no plan of attack—Capt. M. declared there was no plan—no future point of resistance mentioned. Went again to the upper Battery nothing doing, return to the Hospital & while there heard a violent shock, think a ship of the enemy had blown[26] No! the portable magazine of the Upper Battery had blown[26] which killed a great number of men & wounded many most fright[fully][26] The wounded being now all come in, & the ships getting into the harbour, and[26] firing briskly, I go to town to look after the Ladies &c Soon after I reach town a tremendous explosion takes place. I consider all over as it must be the grand magazine. On going home find that Mrs Strachan had been terrified by the explosion, & run with the children to one of the Neighbours Send her to a Friends a little out of town—Go up towards the Garrison, which we had by this time abandoned, find the General &

[26]Manuscript torn.

his troops in a ravine, the Militia scattering. The General determines to retreat to Kingston with the regulars, & leaves the command with Col Chewett & Major Allan two militia officers, & desires them to make the best conditions they could With the enemy for the town—Offer my services to assist them. Go to Mr Crookshank's house meet Major King & Col Mitchell[27] on the part of the enemy. Our Attorney General Mr Robinson also went with us, & assisted us to discuss the points of capitulation. Difficulty arose from a ship, and Naval store having been set on fire during our negociation, this considered very dishonourable. At length a capitulation is agreed upon, subject to the ratification of their Commanding Officer—broken—Major Allan tho' under the protection of a flag of truce is made prisoner, & deprived of his sword—I accompany him to town in the middle of the Enemie's Column. The Militia on our side ground their arms. The enemy return to the Garrison except the rifle corps, which is left under the pretence of protecting the town. Wednesday April 28 Meet Major King at the Honble Mr. Selbys,[28] complain of the indignity offered Major Allan—complain that the capitulation had not been ratified, and a copy so ratified returned in a few minutes according to his promise, and declared that the whole appeared a deception. Major King was sorry, would do every thing that laid in his power, desired us to go to the Garrison & everything should be amicably adjusted. Went to the Garrison. The Commanding Officer Col Pierce[29] can do nothing—The Militia had been detained in the block house without victuals & the wounded without medicine or nourishment. complain to Col Pierce, who ordered rations for the prisoners. Meet a deputation from Genl Dearborn to rediscuss the articles of capitulation find that they cannot parole the Militia Officers & men. Demand an officer to take me on board the principal ship, where Dearborn was. Meet him coming on shore present him with the articles of capitulation—he read them without deigning an answer—request to know when he will parole the Officers & men & demand leave to take away our sick & wounded—He treats me with great harshness, tells me that we had given a false return of officers, told me to keep off—not to follow him as he had business of much more importance to attend to—Complain of this treatment to Commodore Chauncey[30] the Commander of the flotilla—

[27]George Edward Mitchell (1781–1832) was born in Cecil County, Maryland, and was a doctor. In May, 1812, he was appointed Major of the 3rd Maryland Artillery, and rose steadily in rank. In the closing months of the war he was in command of the centre of the Army of the Niagara. He was a United States Congressman for many years after the war.

[28]Prideaux Selby (d. 1813) came to Canada as a subaltern in the 5th Regiment, and was employed in the Indian Department, and as judge in the District Court in the Western District. From 1808 he was Receiver General. He died in May, 1813, during the American occupation of York.

[29]Colonel Cromwell Pearce (1772–1852) was born and died in Willistown, Pa. He resigned from the army in 1815 and for a number a years was an associate justice of the County Court in Chester County, Pa. After General Pike's death, he was the ranking American officer on shore at York.

[30]Commodore Isaac Chauncey (1772–1840) born in Fairfield County, Conn.,

Declare, that, if the capitulation was not immediately signed, that we would not receive it, that the delay was a deception calculated to give the riflemen time to plunder, and after the town had been robbed they would then perhaps sign the capitulation, and tell us they respected private property; but we were determined, that this should not be the case, & that they should not have it in their power to say, that they respected private property after it had been robbed. After saying this I broke away —Soon after Genl Dearborn came to the room where his deputation were sitting & having been told what I had said settled the whole amicably. The officers & men were released on their parole & we began to remove the sick & wounded 29th Spent the whole of this day in removing the sick & wounded & getting comforts for them. 30th The Govt. buildings on fire, contrary to the articles of capitulation. The Church robbed. Call a meeting of the Judges & Magistrates. draw up a short note stating our grievances, wait upon General Dearborn with it. He is greatly embarrassed promises every thing—visit the Hospital—get a poor Soldier buried. May 1st Go to visit Mrs Givins, whose house had been pillaged—in great danger of being shot by the Rascal, who was pillaging. Accompany Mrs Givins to Genl Dearborn state the insults and injuries she had received. He confesses that he is not able to protect any family connected with the Indians. Embark towards evening May 2d All on board except some stragglers, who are taken up by one of their officers sent on shore on purpose. After their departure we had some difficulty with our own disaffected, of which we have too many All my time was taken up with the Hospital. . . .

I 15 Terms of Capitulation of York
[*T.P.L., York, Papers relating to the Capitulation*]

Terms of Capitulation entered into on the 27th April one thousand eight hundred and thirteen for the surrender of the Town of York in Upper Canada to the Army and Navy of the United States under the command of Major General Dearborn and Commodore Chauncey.

That the Troops Regular and Militia at this Post and the Naval officers and Seamen shall be surrendered Prisoners of War. The Troops Regular and Militia to ground their arms immediately on Parade, and the Naval officers and Seamen be immediately surrendered.

That all Public Stores Naval & Military shall be immediately given up, to the Commanding Officers of the Army and Navy of the United States. That all Private Property shall be guaranteed to the Citizens of the Town of York.

That the Papers belonging to the Civil Officers shall be retained by them. That such Surgeons as may be procured to attend the Wounded of the British Regular and Canadian Militia shall not be considered Prisoners of War.

entered the American navy in 1779. Early in September, 1812, he was made commander of the naval forces on Lakes Ontario and Erie, a position he held throughout the war.

That one Lieutenant Colonel One Major, thirteen Captains, nine Lieutenants, Eleven Ensigns, & one Quarter Master, one Deputy Adjutant General—of the Militia, namely

1 Lt. Coll. Chewett
1 Major W Allan
1 Captain John Willson
2 " John Button[31]
3 " Peter Robinson
" Reuben Richardson[32]
4 " John Arnold
5 " James Fenwick[33]
6 " James Mustard
7 " Duncan Cameron
8 " David Thomson
9 " John Robinson
10 " Samuel Ridout
11 " Thomas Hamilton
12 " John Burn[34]
13 " William Jarvie[35]

Quarter Master 1. Charles Baynes[36]

Lieutenants, John H. Schultz[37]
2 George Mustard[38]
3 Barnet Vanderburgh[39]
4 Robert Stanton
5 George Ridout
6 William Jarvis
7 Edward McMahon[40]
8 John Willson
9 Ely Playter

Ensigns 1 Andrew Thomson
2 Ared Smalley[41]
3 Donald McArthur
4 William Smith
5 Andrew Mercer
6 James Chewett[42]
7 George Kuck[43]
8 Edward Thompson
9 Charles Denison
10 George Denison
11 D'Arcy Boulton

[31] John Button (1772–1861), a cooper by trade, came into Upper Canada in 1798, and settled in Markham Township. He commanded a troop of cavalry attached to the 1st Regiment of York Militia during the War of 1812, and for some years after.

[32] Reuben Richardson was captain of the flank company of the 1st Regiment of York Militia. He was present at Detroit, and was mentioned in despatches for his conduct at Queenston Heights. He had a farm in East Gwillimbury north of Sharon.

[33] James Fenwick came from Scotland and settled in Markham Township.

[34] John Burn was an early settler in Hope Township.

[35] William Jarvie was lieutenant in Captain Cameron's flank company of the 3rd Regiment, York Militia, resigning in 1816. From May, 1811, to June, 1812, he had been in partnership with William Allan. He died in Scotland.

[36] Charles Baynes settled in York about 1809.

[37] John Henry Schultz was one of Berczy's settlers in Markham Township.

[38] George Mustard (d. 1854) was born in Scotland and pressed into the Royal Navy. After he left the service, he settled in the United States, and then moved to Markham Township.

[39] Barnet Vanderburgh was lieutenant in Captain Thomas Selby's flank company of the 1st Regiment, York Militia.

[40] Edward McMahon had been one of Brock's civil secretaries, and was employed in the government office for a number of years as Chief Clerk.

[41] Ared Smalley was Lieutenant Colonel of the 6th North York Regiment in 1838–9.

[42] James Grant Chewett (1793–1862) was born in Cornwall, the eldest son of William Chewett. He worked in the Surveyor General's Department for 30 years, becoming Deputy Surveyor General. After his retirement at the Union, he was active in the Bank of Upper Canada.

[43] George Kuck had been a sergeant. He was possibly a son of the innkeeper in York, Gerhard Kuck, who died in 1812.

Nineteen Serjeants four Corporals & two hundred and four rank and file.
Of the Field Train Department 1. Wm. Dunbar
& the Provincial Navy

1 Capt. Francis Gauvreau[44]
1 Lt. ——— Green
Midshipmen 1. John Ridout
2 Louis Beaupre
Clerk 1 James Langsdon

One Boatswain, fifteen naval Artificers—
Of His Majestys Regular Troops 1 Lt. ——— De Koven[45]
one Serjeant Major
and of the Royal Artillery One Bombardier and three Gunners shall be surrendered as Prisoners of War and accounted for in the Exchange of Prisoners between the United States and Great Britain—

G E Mitchell of Md.
Lt. Col. 3d Artillery
USA

Sam S. Conner, Maj
ADC to Majr Gen. Deaborn.

Will. King
Major 15 U.S. Infy.

Jesse D Elliott[46]
Lt U.S. Navy
W Chewett Lt Coll
Comdg 3rd Regt York Militia

W Allan Major
3d Regt York Militia

F Gauvreau
Lt. N. Dpt.

York April 28th. 1813
the foregoing agreement or terms of Capitulation, is approved by us
H Dearborn Majr. Genl.
Isaac Chauncey Commodore

I 16 MEETING OF THE MAGISTRATES

[*P.A.C., C679, p. 17; printed in Wood,* Select British Documents of the Canadian War of 1812, *II, 94–5*]

At a meeting[47] of the Magistrates resident in the Town of York,

[44]Francis Gauvreau was appointed a second lieutenant in the Provincial Marine in 1805. He was in command of the *Duke of Gloucester* which was captured by the Americans at York.

[45]John Louis de Koven, lieutenant in the Royal Newfoundland Fencibles, was wounded in action during the Battle of York.

[46]Jesse Duncan Elliott (1782–1845), born in Hagerstown, Md., entered the navy in 1804. For part of the war he was second in command under Commodore Perry on Lake Erie, and his conduct at the Battle of Lake Erie has been questioned.

[47]This meeting was held on May 3, 1813.

attended by the Judges, the Sheriff, and the Reverend Doctor Strachan.

The actual situation of the Town & District was taken into consideration.

The Enemy's Fleet and Army lying in the harbour, all our Military defences at the Post destroyed, the Inhabitants disarmed and on parole, it is obvious that measures of as much energy as our circumstances admit should be instantly adopted to preserve order and prevent anarchy; to support & encourage the loyal; to suppress the disloyal and to confirm the wavering.

It is therefore, unanimously declared, that by the irruption of the Enemy and temporary possession of this Post, no change has taken place in the relation of the Subject to His Majesty's Government & Laws, except as to such who were parties to the Capitulation as prisoners of war, and are under parole of honor not to bear Arms until exchanged—

That it is equally now, as before the invasion, high treason to aid, assist, counsel or comfort the Enemy—That all Felons and evil doers are equally amenable to the laws as before—That the power of the Magistrates and Ministers of the law are unimpaired, and continued to be so even during the actual possession of the Enemy, as the Commander of their Forces declared, by a Military General Order to his troops.—That private property having remained unchanged not only in construction of the law, but by the express terms of the Capitulation: the Enemy himself disclaims the right, assumed by some Individuals to transfer it from the owner.—That it is the duty of every good subject to declare to the Magistrate all instances of such unjust possession as may come to their knowledge, and of the Magistrate to enforce the restitution.

That persons desirous to signify their abhorrence of anarchy, which must prevail if principles adverse to the above declaration gain ground, are called upon to associate in support of the laws and to afford their aid to the civil Magistrates and their Ministers.

That the high Sheriff do publish & enforce this declaration.

I 17 MRS. JOHN BEIKIE TO JOHN MACDONNELL[48]

[*Thomas*, History of the Counties of Argenteuil, Que. and Prescott, Ont., *p. 480*]

[York, May 5, 1813]

I am told you are low spirited since you were surprised by the Yankees at St. Regis; but I think it was a providential surprise for you to save your life, for, had not that been the case, I am convinced you would not have suffered yourself to be taken alive. We all have reason to be thankful to Providence, for never did I pass so awful a day as the 27th of April, with my two poor fellows in the heat of the battle. I never prayed more fervently, or said that beautiful psalm ("He that dwells in the help of the Highest shall abide in the protection of the God of Heaven, etc.")

[48]A North Wester, who retired in Hawkesbury. He was Mrs. Beikie's brother.

more devoutly, since my father's death, than I did that day. It is a beautiful psalm, and He who strengthens the weak gave me more strength and fortitude than all the other females of York put together; for I kept my Castle, when all the rest fled; and it was well for us I did so,—our little property was saved by that means. Every house they found deserted was completely sacked. We have lost a few things, which were carried off before our faces; but, as we expected to lose all, we think ourselves well off. Will you believe it? I had the temerity to frighten, and even to threaten, some of the enemy, though they had the place and me in their power. Poor William Swan was one of their majors, and behaved by no means like an enemy; he came without leave, and staid a night with us. I believe that through him we were treated with civility by their officers. Should he fall into our hands, I hope it will not be forgotten of him. They so overloaded their vessels with the spirits of this place, that I am told they have thrown quantities of pork and flour into the lake. I really attribute this visit to the vengeance of heaven on this place, for quantities of stores, farming utensils, etc., sent from England in the time of General Simeon [i.e., Simcoe], were allowed to remain in the King's stores, and nothing of them did they ever get. Now, our enemies have them, to do with them as they please. I think we deserve all we have got. Keep up your spirits, my dear John, for God seems to be on our side.

I 18 Names of American Officers
[*P.A.C., Claus Papers, v. 13, p. 74*]

Names of Several American Officers who came with the Army under the Command of General Dearborn and landed on the ground of the old Fort Toronto—were an awful Battle was fought on Tuesday 27th April 1813—

1 Colonel Ripley
2 Major William Swan
3 Major Forsyth
4 Captain Grafton
5 Captain Young
6 Captain Sadler
7 Captain Pearson
8 Captain Burtsell
9 Lieutenant Sumpter
10 Lieutenant Hall
11 Lieutenant Hansen
12 Mr Pelham
13 Mr. Orr
14 Mr. Chauncy
15 Mr Norton
16 Mr. Fry
17 Mr. Matthews

Memorandums

Captain Young and Lieutenant Sumpter were Officers of the Guard on the 28th. April 1813—They came in the most kind and gentleman[l]y manner and offered me their Services to protect my House and Premises took a Shakedown in the Dining Room & most Providentially prevented me from insult and plunder and perhaps from being murdered by some scoundrels who broke into the House in the Night.

John Beikie

Mr. Matthews was a very attentive fine young man—

I 19 Statement of Major Givins' Losses
[*P.A.C., War of 1812, Losses Claim No. 234*]

Statement of the Losses Sustained by Major Givins, from the Enemy, at the Capture of York the 27th. April 1813—

One Carpet	9	6	8
One ditto	7	10	0
Six Window Curtains of furniture Callicoe 9 yds. in each besides the drapery	14	4	0
Three Curtains of White Cotton 15 yards	1	7	6
One Silver Tea Pot & Stand cost 11 Guineas in London	12	16	8
One Silver Toast rack	2	10	0
Six pairs of Sheets 10 yards in each pair	11	5	0
One Globe Lamp	3	0	0
One Dressing Glass	2	10	0
Crockery & Glass	15	0	0
Two dozen Knives & forks (Ivory handles)	4	0	0
Two large Table Cloths	7	0	0
Two Small do.	2	12	6
Three Breakfast do.	1	10	0
Groceries	20	0	0
One English Saddle & Bridle	10	0	0
The whole of the Wearing Apparel of Mrs. Givens & 7 Children	100	0	0
One double Sett of Harness	12	10	0
Currency	£237	2	4

York 3 Octr 1815

The Subscriber saw several of the above mentioned articles in possession of the enemy and afterwards visited Mrs. Givens and from every appearance and his knowledge of the depredations of the Enemy to which Major Givens as belonging to the Indian department was particularly exposed he is of opinion that the amount of his loss was in all greater than the sum specified above

John Strachan D.D.

A Supplimentary Statement of Losses sustained by Major Givins from the Enemy on the Capture of York the 27th April 1813

Paid for repairs to the House	£50	5	0
Great Atlas & Books	25	0	0
One Large Looking Glass	6	5	0
One Small Do.	3	0	0
Sundry articles of furniture Chairs Tables Bedding &c	2	0	0
A Childs Cott with Dimity Curtains	3	15	0
Kitchen Utensils	6	0	0
Wines and other Liquors	30	0	0
	£151	5	0

I Certify that during the possession of York by the Enemy, I met Mrs. Givens, wife of James Givens Esquire indian Agent, in great Distress having been driven from her House by a Party of Plunderers who had threatened her Life. That one of them was apprehended in my Presence

who had returned loaded with Plunder & from whom a Silver Cup & Mirror was taken by the Guard; That I accompanied Mrs. Givens to the U.S. Head Quarters to claim Protection for herself, family & property, in virtue of the Capitulation of York; that the Commander in Chief General Dearborn personally declared to the Lady in my Presence that it was not in his Power to protect her in her own House & recommended strongly that she would not return to it, but take refuge with some Citizen in Town; That I have good reason to suppose from what I did see that the House was entirely plundered.
at York this 3rd. October 1815—

Wm Dummer Powell J

I 20 William Allan's War Loss Claim
[*P.A.C., War of 1812, Losses Claim No. 1454*]

Home District } William Allan of York Esq
York Court }

came Personally before me Grant Powell[49] one of His Majesty Justices of the Peace for the said District—and made Oath that on 28 & 29th of April 1813. the day following the Capture of this Place by the Enemy under the Command of General Dearborn, while he was necessarily detained at the Garrison, some of the American soldiers broke into his Store House at the Water side—& took several Packages, of Goods to wit Six Cases of Shot, 2 Casks of best Quality Coppeas, One large Case English Soap & Box best Crown Glass, a Barrel of Gun Powder & two Casks of Jamaca Spirits, besides several other Articles he could not Particularise—And that before he could leave the Garrison where he was detained till Sun down, in trying to get some of our own wounded Soldiers & Militia Men, who were lying in a miserable State & Prisoners taken care of and dress'd—He saw them carting several of those boxes & Cases—up to where they had collected all their Plunder, and made application to the Person. which he then understood was the Senior Officer on *Shore*; and endeavoured to remonstrate about taking those things away which was Contrary to the terms of the Capitulation only made the day before. He answered me that there was amunition in my Store & which was always considered lawfull Capture, whether private property or not & that I could get none of those things again—and on the 30th. July & 1 Augt. when they visited this place with their Fleet—I was obliged to withdraw, to avoid being carryed away as a Prisoner They Broke open my Store House & took away burnt or distroyed every thing that was in it:—none of the things then there could be ascertained

[49]Grant Powell (1779–1838) was the third son of William Dummer Powell. He practised medicine on an East Indian merchantman, at Ballston Springs, N.Y., and Montreal, coming to York in 1812. He virtually retired from practice in 1817 and held a number of government positions until his death.

but a large *Cask* of Flour Casks of Nails—altho there was very many other things which had occasionally been moved back & forward to make Room for the Baggage of the troops then going to the Frontier (& which they were obliged to leave behind them—according to a General Order then given—There was some Barrels of Pot Ash—all destroyed and a large Quantity of Hemp burnt but I have no Person about my Place that had a Knowledge the Particulars of any thing more—

W Allan

Sworn before me at York
the 23 day of Augt. 1823—
Grant Powell J.P.

I 21 Colonel Cromwell Pearce's Account of the Battle
[*Historical Society of Pennsylvania, Memoirs of Colonel Pearce*]

. . . There were assembled, at Sackett's Harbor, about 4000 Regulars and Marines. About this time, active preparations were being made for *the Expedition.*

The 6th, 15th, and 16th Regiments of Infantry were organized in one Brigade, commanded by General *Pike:* the 6th on the right, the 16th on the left, and the 15th in the centre. One Company of Light Artillery, One company of the 14th Infantry, a Detachment of the 21st Infantry, *Forsyth's* Rifle Corps, and the New York and Baltimore Volunteers; total 1700 Men.

A few days before the departure of the Fleet, General *Dearborn* arrived. On the 23rd, the ice having disappeared, so that the Fleet was able to leave the Harbor, the troops embarked in a squadron of 13 vessels, commanded by Commodore *Chauncey*. At 10 Oclock, A.M. made sail, and cleared the bay. After a few hours sail, the wind suddenly changed, and commenced blowing a violent gale. There being an appearance of a stormy night, the squadron returned to the Harbor. April 24th, the storm continued, and the Fleet remained at anchor, no communication allowed with the shore. April 25th, the wind being fair, at 8 Oclock, A.M. weighed anchor, and stood out. April 26th, light breezes from the North-East. At 5 Oclock, P.M. we were 25 miles South of York Light-House. All Commanding Officers of Corps summoned on board the Ship Madison. Being within 3 miles of York harbor, the Fleet lay off and on. April 27th, at half past 5 Oclock, by signals stood for shore. At 6 Oclock, A.M. anchored one half mile therefrom, and within one mile and a half of the Fort. At 7 Oclock, A.M. by signals began to disembark,—each vessel having been previously supplied with small boats for that purpose. At 8 Oclock, A.M. the boats—being filled with *Forsyth's* Rifle Corps, & some of the 15th and 16th Regiments of Infantry—rowed toward the shore. It was intended to land in an open field, where a few acres of ground had been cleared (the site of the old

French Fort *Toronto*); but the violence of the wind compelled the boats to approach the shore below it. From this open field, the road passes through the woods to the first battery; and from that the ground is cleared to the Town of Little York,—distant about one mile: The Enemy had constructed batteries to command this road. The Enemy's troops were seen emerging from the woods, marching and forming in the open field. They consisted of 400 Regulars, 300 Militia, and about 200 Indians,—the Regulars occupying the centre, and the Militia and Indians the flanks. Our landing was covered by the fire of our Schooners,—which served to frighten the Militia and Indians, and prevent the Regulars from forming on the plain. Our boats were now steadily rowing to the shore; and being full of men, received a deadly fire from the Enemy, who advanced to the water's edge, and fired into the boats. This served only to quicken our approach; and as soon as the boats touched ground, our troops sprang into the water—waded to the shore—rushed up the beach—and returned the Enemy's fire. Now, nothing was to be heard but an incessant rattle of small arms. The British Regulars advanced with charged bayonet; but the concentrated fire of our troops soon compelled them to fall back. When the Infantry landed, they were formed in platoons. General *Pike* directed them to charge the Enemy,—who immediately retreated, and were rapidly pursued by our troops.The woods now enveloped both parties. Nothing could be heard, but the shouts of the rival combatants, the war-whoop of the Savages, and the echo of the Bugles, mingling with the scattering reports of the Musketry. Thus, for some minutes, were our troops opposed victoriously to more than twice their number, while the boats were returning for, and conveying reinforcements; who, as soon as they landed, dashed into the woods to assist their comrades,—and, in a few minutes, the firing entirely ceased. The Schooners, after having landed the troops, anchored in the bay, and commenced a heavy fire on the battery. About 10 Oclock, A.M. when the troops were forming in the open plain, the Enemy's battery, nearest the Lake, exploded with a tremendous noise. A 11 Oclock, the Artillery having landed, the troops commenced their march toward the Town,—having a swamp and thick wood on their right and left; and had advanced about half a mile, when they received several discharges from an 18-pounder at the battery recently exploded. This battery was hastily thrown up, a few days previous, and was in an unfinished state. It mounted two long 18-pounders: One commanded the road in which the column was advancing; the other, the harbor. By the explosion of this battery, in the morning, the gun that commanded the road was dismounted, and 25 to 30 of the Enemy were killed. The other gun of this battery was raised on a plat-form, and could not be brought to bear on the column in the road. The only injury it did, was cutting off some of the Muskets of the advancing column. The troops advanced; and the few who remained in this battery were made prisoners. The Column had proceeded about one fourth of a mile, and had arrived at a second battery, which was deserted, and within 400 yards of the magazine, in full view of the Town. Not seeing the Enemy, General *Pike* ordered the column to halt, and the Artillery, which was drawn by Soldiers, to be brought in front to fire into the principal Fort, to discover where the Enemy were. At this time, while some Riflemen who had advanced from the rear with a British Serjeant, were speaking to General *Pike,* who was standing near the head of the Brigade, the Magazine exploded. Colonel *Pearce* was sitting on a stump, facing General *Pike,* who was about 15 paces distant. Seeing the General wounded, Colonel *Pearce* went to him, & assisted in removing him. General *Pike* observed that he was mortally wounded, and that Colonel *Pearce* must take command of the troops. Thirty eight men were killed, and 222 wounded, many of them mortally: Among the latter, the lamented General *Pike,*—who was wounded on the side, while questioning the British Serjeant.

The command now devolved on Colonel *Pearce,* as the senior officer. The troops, giving three cheers, advanced; and the Enemy, losing all hopes, set fire to their naval store-house, also to a ship on the stocks, and then made a final retreat. The dense volumes of smoke, which blew violently in our faces, rendered it impossible to proceed for some minutes. The commanding officer deemed it proper to send two of his officers to obtain the necessary information, and to demand the immediate surrender of the Town. They were met by persons authorized by the Citizens of York, and the terms of capitulation agreed on. They were, in substance, that the citizens and their private property should be protected, and that all public property should be delivered to the Commanding Officer; and all the troops—regular and Militia—to be surrendered Prisoners of war. These terms of capitulation were signed by the Parties, delivered to Colonel *Pearce,* and the commanding officer took possession of Little York.

The Brigade had halted, and the Officers were directed to secure the public property. Colonel *Pearce* was engaged in superintending the removal of the public stores, when General *Dearborn* rode up, and asked Colonel *Pearce* what had been done. The Colonel delivered to him the terms of capitulation; and the General immediately rode off without speaking, or issuing an Order that day. The Brigade returned to the Fort, and the Guards were detailed for the night. At this time, the sun had nearly set, and a heavy rain commenced. The Soldiers had been on active service, from 5 Oclock in the morning until sunset,—during which time they had eaten nothing. Many of them had leaped from the boats into 3 feet water, and waded to the shore. From the time when General *Pike* was wounded, the whole responsibility of the Army on shore devolved on Colonel *Pearce,* who had every guard stationed, and sentinel posted; which was not finished until late at night.

About 11 Oclock, next day, the drums were beating to arms,—when the commanding Officer came and demanded who ordered the drums to beat. An Aid of General *Dearborn* advanced, appearing much agitated, and said *he* had,— that the British were coming. The commanding officer replied—Let them come; we are ready for them: and ordered the drums to cease beating. The Aid ran in great haste to General *Dearborn*, & brought an Order to parade the troops. This was the first Order given by General *Dearborn*, after the arrival of the army in Canada.

The troops were accordingly formed, & marched in the direction whence the Enemy were said to be advancing,—General *Dearborn* walking in the rear, with his hands behind his back, and his staff in his hands. After proceeding a short distance, the troops halted; and Colonel *Pearce* observed to General *Dearborn* that he did not think the Enemy were advancing. The General assented, and agreed to return; when the troops were marched to their quarters.

The public property, found in York, was considerable; consisting of Cannon, Clothing, Provisions, &c. and a part of General *Sheaff*'s baggage, including a handsome assortment of Wines,—which, no doubt, were highly relished at Head Quarters.

I 22 Extracts from Dr. William Beaumont's[50] Diary

[*Myer*, Life and Letters of Dr. William Beaumont, *pp. 43–6*]

27th. [i.e., April 26, 1813] Wind pretty strong in the morning, increasing to a strong blow, so that the swells run high, tossing our vessels smartly about. Several seasick—was myself. At half-past four o'clock passed by the mouth of Niagara River. This circumstance baffled our imagination where we were going. We were first impressed with the idea of Kingston, then to Niagara, but now our destination must be Little York. At sunset came in view of York Town & the Fort, where we lay off all night within 3 or 4 leagues.

27th. Sailed into harbor and came to anchor a little below the British Garrison. We now filled the boats and affected a landing, though not without some difficulty and the loss of some men. The British marched their troops from the Garrison down the [hill] to cut us off in landing, and then they had every advantage. They could not effect their [plan]. A hot engagement ensued, in which the enemy lost nearly a third of their men and were soon compelled to quit the field, leaving their dead and wounded strewed in every direction. We lost but very few in the engagement. The enemy returned into garrison, but from the loss sustained in the 1st engagement, the undaunted courage of our men, and the brisk firing from our fleet into the Garrison with 12 and 32-pounders, they were soon obliged to evacuate it and retreat with all possible speed.

[50]William Beaumont (1785–1853), born in Lebanon, Conn., was licensed as a doctor in Vermont in June, 1812. During the occupation of York he was Surgeon's Mate with the 6th U.S. Infantry. He later made important discoveries about gastric juices by studying the digestive system of a young French Canadian, Alexis St. Martin, who had an open gunshot wound.

Driven to this alternative, they devised the inhuman project of blowing up their Magazine (containing 300 Bbls. powder), the explosion of which, shocking to mention, had almost totally destroyed our Army. Above 300 were wounded, and about 60 killed dead on the spot by stones of all dimensions falling like a shower of hail in the midst of our ranks. The enemy had about 20 killed and wounded by the explosion, tho the main body had retreated far out of the Garrison. After this sad disaster our Army marched into the Garrison, hawled down the British coat of arms (which they were too haughty to do), and raised the American Standard on its place. Our Army was about 1,500 strong— Their about the same. Encampt in Garrison this night, mounting a guard 500 strong to secure our safety through the night. A most distressing scene ensues in the Hospital—nothing but the Groans of the wounded and agonies of the Dying are to be heard. The Surgeons wading in blood, cutting off arms, legs, and trepanning heads to rescue their fellow creatures from untimely deaths. To hear the poor creatures crying, "Oh, Dear! Oh, Dear! Oh, my God, my God! Do, Doctor, Doctor! Do cut off my leg, my arm, my head, to relieve me from misery! I can't live, I can't live!" would have rent the heart of steel, and shocked the insensibility of the most hardened assassin and the cruelest savage. It awoke my liveliest sympathy, and I cut and slashed for 48 hours without food or sleep. My God! Who can think of the shocking scene when his fellow-creatures lie mashed and mangled in every part, with a leg, an arm, a head, or a body ground in pieces, without having his very heart pained with the acutest sensibility and his blood chill in his veins. Then, who can behold it without agonizing sympathy!

28th, 10 Ock. A.M. Just got time to suspend capital operation, whilst I can take a little refreshments to sustain life, for the first time since four o'clock yesterday. Return again to the bloody scene of distress, to continue dressing, Amputating and Trepanning. Dressed rising of 50 patients, from simple contusions to the worst of compound fractures, more than half of the last description. Performed two cases of amputation and one of trepanning. 12 Ock. P.M., retired to rest my much fatigued body and mind.

29th. Dressed most of wounds over, Trepanned two. This day ordered to get the sick and wounded on board the fleet, to be transported to Sacketts Harbor. Sent them to the ships, and the most of them were sent back again, very much to the injury of the patients. One of those amputated yesterday does well; the other died in about 12 hours, the fracture being in the thigh and very much contused.

30th. Dressed the wounded, most of them doing well; the two cases of trepanning doing well. The Militia and people giving themselves up to be paroled, nearly 1,700 since the 27th.

May 1st. About my professional employment, dressing the wounded, the most of them doing well. Amputated an arm. On orders for getting all the sick and wounded on board prevents any more operations today. Several more will have to be performed. The wounded on board. All the troops ordered to embark. All on board at six o'clock. Brought off public property taken from his Majesty's stores, estimated to the amount of 2,000,000 and a half dollars. Burnt the ruins of the Government house, the Block-house, one or two public stores and an old sloop.[51]

2nd. Wind unfavorable to sailing out—consequently we remain in the fleet where we were today. The sick and wounded lying distributed among the fleet. I can not note their several conditions—those on board this (The Julia) doing well.

3rd. Still lying at anchor, waiting for a fair wind, or something else. The wounded do well.

4th. At anchor in York harbor, waiting for the storm to subside.

5th. Still at Anchor, wind high, men sickening and miserably crowded in the hold of the ship.

6th. Not weighed anchor yet, wind high, weather stormy and boisterous.

7th. Storm subsiding at night, cold and chilly. Men complaining much of Diarrhoea and Dysenteries. The wounded doing far better than could be expected in such a miserable condition.

8th. Weighed anchor and got under way for Niagara. Arrived here at 5 Ock. Landed the troops. This morning one man died in the hold, mainly, I believe, from suffocation, as he had not been much ill, except a slight wound on the back by a stone from the explosion. Had not time to examine him.

9th. Tents struck at Four Mile Creek, four miles the Garrison. Genl. Boice takes comd. of the Brigade.

10th. The Fleet sailed for Sacketts Harbor this morning before sunrise, carrying part of the sick and wounded, and are expected to bring on more troops from the harbor.

May 11th. This morning arrived from Oswego in Sail-boats part of the 2d Regt. Artillery, between three and four hundred. In the afternoon I attended the sale of Genl. Sheaffe's baggage at public auction taken at York. Saw his most superb Scarlet coat sold for $55, which I presume cost not less than $300. It was the most elegant thing I ever saw—it was most elegantly embroidered in Gold and of the finest quality.

[51]Probably Joseph Kendrick's *Governor Hunter,* which was destroyed during the occupation. General Dearborn gave Kendrick £300 compensation from the public money he received at York.

His other things sold very high, being good and much wanted by our officers—I purchased nothing.

I 23 DEPOSITION OF WILLIAM KNOTT CONCERNING HOWARD
[P.A.C., Upper Canada Sundries]

Home District } The information of Wm. Knott taken before me Thos. Ridout Esqr. one of his Majestys Justices of the peace in and for the said District who says that on the thirtieth of April last Wm. Howard came into the house of the deponent and seizing him by the collar insisted on taking his boots from him and saying at the same time that he had got a party & would have his head shivered from his shoulders if the boots were not given up immediately, that the deponent requested the said Hoard to be quiet for fear of disturbing or hurting some wounded men lying on the floor, but he grew the more outragious untill some American Soldiers came in who drove him out and took him up as a deserter and sent him on board their fleet, after which the deponent never saw the said Hoard untill the American fleet returned on the last day of July

his
William × Knott
mark

Sworn before me
at York this twenty
first day of Augt
1813.
Sigd. Thos Ridout J.P.

I 24 DEPOSITION OF DUNCAN CAMERON CONCERNING THRALL
[P.A.C., Upper Canada Sundries]

Home District The Information of Duncan Cameron of the Town of York Esquire taken on oath before me Thos Ridout Esquire one of his Majestys Justices of the Peace in and for the Said District who saith that some time in the beginning of may last, he went to the House of Jesse Ketchum,[52] of the Town of York Tanner where he understood some Public Property had been deposited and found one Benjamin Thrall of Markam Yeoman in the yard putting some Public Property consisting of Iron Works into a Waggon to carry them off. The Deponent ordered him immediately to Desist, and directed some men who were with him to collect the things and put them into the Tan house. The said Benjamin Thrall answered that those things had been given him by the Americans, and if he the Deponent Interfered, he would go on board

[52]Jesse Ketchum (1782–1867), born in Spencertown, N.Y., came to York in 1799, to join his brother Seneca (1772?–1850) who had arrived in 1796 and taken up lands on Yonge Street. Jesse Ketchum became a tanner, with extensive property southwest of Yonge and Newgate (Adelaide) Streets. He was a Reformer, and noted for philanthropy. He moved to Buffalo in 1845.

the Madison (the Enemys Fleet then lying in the Harbour) and soon have the business settled or words to that Effect

D Cameron

Sworn before me this
sixteenth day of August
1813—
Thos Ridout JP.

I 25 Total Killed, Wounded, Prisoners & Missing at York April 27, 1813[53]

[*P.R.O., C.O. 42, v. 354, p. 125; microfilm copy in P.A.O.*]

Distribution	Captains	Lieutenants	Ensigns	Serjt. Major	Serjeants	Drummers	RK & File	Bombr.	Gunners	Drivers
Killed	1			1	4	1	52		3	
Wounded			1		2	1	30			
Wounded and Prisoners		1			4	1	36			1
Prisoners							6	1	3	
Missing							6		1	
Total	1	1	1	1	10	3	130	1	7	1

I 26 Mrs. Powell to W. D. Powell, Kingston

[*T.P.L., Powell Papers*]

York May 10th 1813

. . . we are as when you left us leading a life of uncertainty without feeling it possible to form or pursue any plan even for a day;—the Fleet so hostile to our comforts departed on Saturday morning, and by removing our apprehensions for ourselves, excited them for the fate of our Friends at Niagara; the opinions as to their destination have been various; and I suspect by their manoevering they designed to conceal their intentions—however we have heard nothing like Cannon therefore it is thought they are probably gone to Sackets Harbour to disembark their sick, and their Plunder;—I will hope that the time is not far distant, when their hateful Flag will yield to the British Lion;—such an event will be some alleviation to the killing reflection, that a lawless mob can boast of having obliged our gallant Troops to retreat before them . . . our excellent Pastor visits us daily; and if any difficulty occurred I should without scruple apply to him; he seems much gratified by the well doing of the wounded men; those under our particular care, are I hear to be

[53]This table includes losses in the Royal Artillery, 8th and 49th Regiments, the Royal Newfoundland Regiment, and the Glengarry Light Infantry. It does not include losses in the militia. Five citizens of York died: John Detlor, Daniel Murray, Matthias Sanders, Donald McLean, and John Bassell.

removed today to the Hospital; the Serjeant was well enough to walk to the Garrison yesterday;—Kerr says milk diet is good for them, so I shall daily prepare a Kettle of Milk Broth and send to them. . . .

I 27 Mrs. Powell to W. D. Powell
[*T.P.L., Powell Papers*]

York May 12th, 1813

. . . the disgrace is I fear indelible, but it will be an alleviation to know that the discomfort we have experienced is a solitary instance of misfortune, or, as it is generally pronounced, of mismanagement; indeed the latter is a more gentle term than is applied to the disastrous event;—you will I suppose hear by the AAG of the steps taken to express the opinion of the inhabitants of this place; for the sake of all parties I hope undue warmth has been avoided, and that all representations are free from the vindictive spirit which always actuates illiberal minds,—yet I cannot but wish the business had been delayed until an investigation had been proposed from the proper quarter;—our Neighbour has I hear given great offence by declining to add his signature, to the list of detailed errors[54] in the conduct of Sr R; he was surely right to avoid the risque of committing himself . . . Dr Strachan and the Gentlemen of the Town proceeded to the melancholy spots where the remains of our brave defenders were deposited a few inches below the earth;— the good Dr gave them christian burial, and all assisted to secure their graves from further disturbance . . . it seems to be well ascertained that Genl Pike died with the Royal Standard as a Pillow for his Head; I can scarcely believe, that various as were the errors of that disastrous day, any thing so nationally important could have been left to the mercy of a rabble;—if it was, much blame must rest upon those who ought to have preserved it at any risk. . . .

I 28 Sheaffe to Bathurst
[*P.R.O., C.O. 42, v. 354, p. 107; microfilm copy in P.A.O.*]

Kingston, U Canada
13 May 1813

I regret to have to state to Your Lordship, that the Money in the Provincial Treasury fell into the Enemy's hands when he obtained possession of York:—it having been concealed, but the Enemy having

[54]A copy of this document in Strachan's handwriting, signed by William Chewett, William Allan, Duncan Cameron, Samuel Smith, John Strachan, Alexander Wood, and W. W. Baldwin, is in the Toronto Public Library. It is of course extremely critical of Sir Roger Sheaffe. The neighbour who refused to sign was possibly John Beikie. It was sent on May 10, 1813, with a covering letter from Strachan, to the Hon. John Richardson, with the suggestion that it be published after being shown to Prevost. The letter itself is published in Cruikshank, *Documentary History of the Campaign upon the Niagara Frontier*, III, pt. 3, pp. 192–203; the covering letter is printed in *The John Strachan Letter Book*, ed. Spragge, p. 37.

threatened to destroy the Town unless it were produced, it was given up:[55]—I do not know the exact Amount, but from the best information I have been able to obtain, it was about two thousand pounds:—Mr. Selby was at the time in a State of insensibility from the illness which soon afterwards proved fatal to him.

I 29 MRS. POWELL TO W. D. POWELL
[*T.P.L., Powell Papers*]

York June 6th 1813

. . . I sicken at the prospect of a total loss of this fine Colony; the dread of such an event is the more galling as it might have been prevented, and the single circumstance of destroying the depot at S Harbor[56] would in all human probability have given us all the advantage the Enemy now possesses . . . every day draws us much nearer the point which cannot fail to decide our fate; and as I cannot yet admit the fear of personal danger, I am prepared as much as possible for what may happen;—under the Govt of the US. I might perhaps have resolution to continue till I had made such arrangements as would serve to secure some of our property; but if our lives are spared the ensuing winter will I trust find us, either under our own Government in this Province or safe in some humble retreat in my native land;—at best our actual situation is almost hopeless, and our future prospects vague and uncertain . . . one ray of the spirit of Wellington would have saved us from those dangers which surround and threaten to overwhelm us;—now a miracle can alone extricate us . . . I think I shall have the Wine drawn off and packed in sawdust tomorrow; at least I shall have a chance of saving some of it if we do fly. . . .

I 30 MINUTES OF THE SPECIAL SESSIONS OF THE PEACE, HOME DISTRICT
[*P.A.O., Minutes of the General Quarter Sessions of the Peace, Home District*]

Special Sessions of the Peace York 10th June1813

Present
Thomas Ridout, Esquire, Chairman
Alexander Wood & Duncan Cameron Esquires

One of the Court A. Wood Esq:, informed the Court, that he had two days ago Billeted two Convalescent Soldiers at the House of Mr. John Jordan Innkeeper in the Town of York—they being only his proportion with other Tavern Keepers in this Town—and that Mr. Jordan

[55]On April 29, Major King requested the public money, agreeable to the terms of capitulation. Strachan gave £2144.11.4 in army bills to Captain Armstrong of the U.S. Infantry.

[56]Sackett's Harbour.

had refused to receive them, and had treated his Authority as a Magistrate with Contempt—The Chairman issued a Warrant for to bring said Jordan before the Court, who on appearing acknowledged that he had refused to receive said Soldiers as Billeted on him—stating his reasons that his House was too full—The Court considered his Excuse as insufficient and Ordered that he do pay a Fine of *Two Pounds* Sterling, (to be paid to the Sheriff), which he then to the Court promised to do immediately.

The Court then adjourned Sine Die.

S. Heward
Clk there attending

I 31 Mrs. Powell to W. D. Powell, Kingston
[*T.P.L., Powell Papers*]

York June 12th 1813

. . . a Boat is just coming round the point; its Colors cannot yet be ascertained; I sicken at the Idea of its being 13 Stripes . . . the Boat is gone past, apparently to the Head of the Lake . . .

2 oclock, Dr. Strachan and Mr Allan called before dinner to tell me of the reinforcements at hand; God grant success to the efforts now made to save this fine Country from the grasp of a crafty and bitter foe;—a small Vessel (our Boy says the Belle Gore) has just passed up to the Town;—her appearance was an attraction to great and small;—the Bank was covered with people and foremost just at the corner of our Street was D Cameron with a party of Indians just come from Lake Simcoe; several of our own Soldiers being on guard dispelled all apprehension of hostility and I conjecture it comes from Niagara with some of our wounded defenders;—Col Plenderleath[57] and the Gentlemen are doing well; he paid us a visit on Friday, and says he is as well as he was in his life, only reduced to use Crutches. . . .

I 32 W. D. Powell to Prevost
[*P.A.C., C679, pp. 148–50*]

Private York 28th. June 1813—

Your Excellency's Commands of the 21st. Instant[58] receive the earliest Attention: There can be no doubt that if required Provision of Beef and

[57]Lieutenant Colonel Charles Plenderleath, of the 49th Regiment.

[58]Prevost had written, "In your leisure moments would you have the goodness to ascertain the resources which the neighbourhood of York affords for the maintenance of an Army—the accomodation remaining in the town for Troops & the probable effect which the appearance there of a military force would produce.—It would also be very satisfactory to me to obtain your sentiments on the degree of confidence to be reposed in the functionaries of Government residing at York, I mean, in their energy, also, upon the state of the public mind on important points." (P.A.C., Powell Papers, Prevost to Powell, June 21, 1813.)

flour for the support of an Army, short of 2000 Men can be furnished from the Country depending for a market on this place—The scarcity of Salt is such that little dependance can be had on a regular supply of salt pork and the issue of fresh pork would probably be injurious to the health of the Soldier—There will be abundance of forage; large Crops of Rye have been raised for the purpose of distillation, which the first act of Genl. De Rottenburgs Administration has prohibited; this Grain affords a wholesome food both for Men and Horse, and will enable a larger proportion of wheat flour and Oats to be offered to the Commissary.—

The Accommodation for Troops is very little diminished, the two block Houses being the only Soldiers Quarters destroyed—There is Timber on the Ground, prepared for building ways and wharf for the Ship, sufficient to throw up a coarse but warm Cover for a great many Men at little expense—The Town could not billet 1000 Men without great Inconvenience.—

The nature of our population is sufficiently known to your Excellency: the March of Troops through the Country has occasioned an obvious Change in the Manners and language of the People, and there can be no doubt that the permanent Station of a body of Troops here would have an excellent Effect in confirming the loyal and over aweing the disaffected, especially if a Party of Dragoon would occasionally make Excursion through the Settlements—

It is an invidious Task to give opinions on individual character, but your Excellency's wish is a Command—

The greater or less energy of public functionaries will ever take its tone from the Head.—In the absence of Genl de Rottenburgh[59] we should not expect any thing decisive in the civil administration, if the Measures depended upon any Individual, but the President has authorized the Council to deliberate on any proposition supposed to be important, without waiting for a special reference, so that little delay need interpose between the necessity for any vigorous proceeding and its Sanction; I think I may assure your Excellency that, under this arrangement, there will be no display of weakness.—The Sheriff[60] is a man of personal Intrepidity, but extremely cautious of responsibility—our police is weak as must be the Case where a numerous body of Individuals have an equal voice—

Major Allan of the Militia, although on parole, fulfills, with promptitude and decision, the duties of governmental Agent in this place—

The Commissary[61] is laborious and well acquainted with the resources

[59]Francis, Baron de Rottenburg (1757–1832), was born at Danzig. After service in French and Polish armies he entered the British army in 1794. He came to Canada in 1810, and was appointed Commander of the Forces in Lower Canada the following year. From June 19 to Dec. 12, 1813, he was Administrator of Upper Canada.

[60]John Beikie.

[61]George Crookshank.

of the Country, but the habits of his department restrain in some Degree the energy of personal Character by its rigid regulations to insure Œconomy & Accuracy

The Secretary[62] of the province is a distressed Man who has no duties to perform which call for Energy. The same may be said of the Surveyor General.[63]

The public mind as far as I am able to judge is elevated or depressed by the alternate Apprehension of preserving or losing the Superiority on the Lake—There seems to be but one Opinion as to keeping this post, that it depends upon the fleet, and there is some regret expressed that it became necessary for the Commodore to destroy the Town of Sodus, from the apprehension that this place may be the subject of retaliation—

In the Event of any serious disaster to his Majesty's Arms little reliance is to be had on the power of the well disposed to repress and keep down the Turbulence of the disaffected who are very numerous—

I have replied to the several Paragraphs of your Excellencys letter with that frankness of a single mind, which takes every thing at the Letter—should I have mistaken your Excellencys wish, and wandered from its Object I assure myself that it will be excused in proceeding from an implicit obedience to your supposed desire

I 33 EDWARD MCMAHON TO J. B. ROBINSON
[*P.A.O., J. B. Robinson Papers*]

St. David's 9th July 1813.

His Honor, the President having received information that the undermentioned persons, Inhabitants of York, and it's vicinity—had traitorously afforded to the enemy upon his late visit to that place information highly injurious to His Majesty's service—I have it therefore in command from His Honor to signify to you his desire, should there be found upon inquiry sufficient grounds, that those persons be immediately arrested, and secured, and that the necessary steps may be taken for the immediate appointment of a special Commission before which those, as well as any other persons of the same description who have not been reported to His Honor are to be tried—

——— Stebbins, Tavern-keeper John Young, Store-keeper Jesse Ketchum, Tanner ——— Gilbert, Blacksmith[64]	York
William B Peters	Yonge Street

[62]William Jarvis.
[63]Thomas Ridout.
[64]Ira Gilbert.

I 34 THE SECOND CAPTURE OF YORK[65]
[*Kingston,* Kingston Gazette, *August 10, 1813*]

KINGSTON, August 5

(The following account of the Enemy's late visit to York, is published by Authority.)

At eleven o'clock on Saturday morning, the 31st ult. the Enemy's Fleet, consisting of 12 sail, were seen standing for the harbor—about half past three the *Pike,* the *Madison* and *Oneida* came to anchor in the offing— the Schooners continuing to pass up the harbor with their sweeps—about 4 o'clock three of them came too abreast of the town, and the remainder near the Garrison, and immediately afterwards several boats full of troops landed at the Garrison, and proceeded from thence to the town, of which they took possession.—They then opened the Gaol, liberating the prisoners, & taking three Soldiers confined for felony. They then went to the Hospitals and paroled the few men that could not be removed. They next entered the Stores of Major Allan and Mr. St. George, and seized the contents, consisting chiefly of Flour, the same being private property. Between 11 and 12 o'clock on Saturday night, the three Schooners which had anchored abreast of the town towed out, and it was supposed that the fleet would have sailed immediately—but information having been given by some traitors, whose names it is hoped will be discovered, that valuable Stores had been sent up the River Don, the Schooners went up the harbor on Sunday morning, the troops were again landed, and 3 armed boats proceeded up the Don in search of the Stores. In consequence however, of the very meritorious exertions of a few young men, amongst whom were two of the name of Platter,[66] every thing was conveyed away, and the boats sunk before the Enemy reached the place. Two or three boats containing trifling articles, which had been hid in the marsh, were discovered and taken, but in their main object the Enemy was compleately disappointed. —As soon as the armed boats had returned, the troops went on board, and by sunset both Sailors and Soldiers had evacuated the town, the Barracks, Wood Yard, and Store Houses on Gibraltar Point, having been first set on fire by them, and at day light on the following morning the Enemy's fleet sailed.

The troops which were landed were acting as Marines, and appeared to be all they had on board the fleet, and did not exceed 240 men. They were under the command of Commodore Chauncey and Lt. Col. Scott,[67] an unexchanged prisoner of war on his parole, both of whom

[65]This account is based on a letter from Strachan and Grant Powell to Colonel Edward Baynes (P.A.C., C679, p. 324, Strachan and Powell to Baynes, Aug. 2, 1813; printed in Wood, *Select British Documents of the Canadian War of 1812,* II, 190–3.)

[66]I.e.Playter (see I 1).

[67]Windfield Scott (1786–1866) entered the army in 1808. He was captured at the Battle of Queenston Heights and placed on parole. In December, 1812, an

landed with the troops. The town upon the arrival of the enemy was totally defenceless, the Militia were still on parole, and the principal Gentlemen had retired from an apprehension of being treated with the same severity used towards several of the inhabitants near Fort George, who had been made prisoners and sent to the United States. Lt. Col. Battersby[68] with the troops under his command, had upon the first appearance of the enemy's fleet off York on the 29th, proceeded from thence with his guns to Burlington Heights, where he had joined Major Maule,[69] and concentrated his force on the following Evening. The enemy had during the course of the day landed from the fleet 300 men near Brandt's house, with an intention of storming the Heights, which they hoped to carry, but finding Major Maule well prepared to receive them, and being informed of Lieut. Col. Battersby's march, they re-imbarked and stood away for York.

The plunder obtained by the enemy upon this predatory expedition has been indeed trifling, and the loss has altogether fallen upon individuals, the Public Stores of every description having been removed; and the only prisoners made by them being confined felons and invalids in Hospital.—We are sorry to be obliged to observe that there is too much reason to believe that the Enemy was furnished with exact information respecting the movements of our troops, and of the state of York and of the position at Burlington Heights, from traitors amongst ourselves, from men too who are holding Public situations in the Country, and whose names we trust, when correctly known, will lead to their conviction and punishment, and hold them up to the just detestation of every loyal subject of his Majesty.

I 35 Powell to Prevost

[*P.A.C., C679, p. 309; printed in Wood,* Select British Documents of the Canadian War of 1812, *II, 189–90*]

Near York, 1st August 1813.

Yesterday about noon the American Squadron consisting of two Ships a Brig & 12 Sail of other vessels entered the Harbour of York and landed Troops computed at 2000 Men—as they seized upon the flour in Messrs. Allan & St. Georges Store & shared it out to the Inhabitants it is to be presumed that they do not mean to remain long enough to consume it

---

exchange was arranged for the officers taken at Queenston, but it was not accepted by Prevost. Thus, they were regarded as on parole by the British and as restored to belligerent status by the Americans. At a later period Scott became Commander in Chief of the Army, and unsuccessful Presidential candidate.

[68]Lieutenant Colonel Francis Battersby of the Glengarry Light Infantry Fencibles. He enters local legend as having shot his horses when he returned to England after the war, interring them beside the burying-ground at York.

[69]John Maule entered the army in 1794. He was in command at Burlington Heights in the summer of 1813.

themselves—The Male Inhabitants very generally dispersed although most on parole allarmed at the Transfer of paroled Militia & some Combattants from Newark to the Interior of the U.S. Major Allan was considered so obnoxious that He quitted the Town early.—It is said this morning that a reward is offered to apprehend him—The Commissary proceeded to Genl. D. Rottenberg. The Cattle which had been provided for Beef were driven off towards the Head of the Lake—The ammunition was removed to the safest place that could be devised; the Baggage of the 19 Dragoons was also secured as well as the Circumstances admitted—Col. ONiel with three officers entered the Town as the Shipping was coming to & proposed risquing to gallop through—

A Message has been sent to the Carrier of your Dispatches not to take them through York & another to Major Herriot[70] to use his discretion in advancing with the Voltigeurs. . . .

I 36 William Allan to Colonel Edward Baynes[71]

[*P.A.C., C688c, p. 84; printed in Wood,* Select British Documents of the Canadian War of 1812, *II, 193–6*]

Darlington Township 44
Miles below York 3d August 1813.

Having received accounts from York, very difft. to what I expected; I am induced to return for a day or so—from Mr. Justice Powell; His Excellency the Commander in Chief would receive the information of the Enemy Fleet and troops to the Number of 340 (only) having reached there on Saturday about 12 oClock—upon their near approach everybody withdrew from Town; myself among the Number; they soon after getting into the Harbour land their force; and the first thing that was done; by Colonel Scott—the Gentn. I conducted down along with all the Other Officers and Men made Prisoners at Queenstown last Octr. was to offer a Reward of 500 dollars to any person who would deliver me up to them—difft. partys went into my House and broke open every door, Chest Trunk & Drawer looking & searching for me; at the moment they were coming into the Harbour I recd. an Express from the Head Quarters which I forwarded on I also recd. a letter from—Burlington Heights which mentioned that they were then attempting to land Men at the Beach from thirteen Vessells, but made very slow Progress having very few Boats, they also atempted to take an Arm'd Schooner through the outlet into the little Lake; our Force was at that time about 320 exclusive of a few Militia & Indians—& more Indians expected—However they embarked all their Men again on the same day without atempt-

[70]Frederick G. Heriot (d. 1843) commanded the Canadian Voltigeurs, the regiment raised by Major de Salaberry in Lower Canada in 1812.

[71]Edward Baynes (d. 1829) entered the army in 1790, and in 1807 was appointed Adjutant General to the forces in British North America.

ing any thing (that was on Friday)—The last thing I did before I left Town was to get a Boat load of Ball Catradges of about 5000 Secured and a Boat load of baggage &c. belonging to a Detachment of 19 Dragoons—all of which are safe by the Exertions of some of a Mr. Playter families to whose house I first retreated.—Mr. Justice Powell by a Note I have just recd. from him says he was informed those two boats were found and begs me to explain it—Before they found them the things were all removed. The baggage of the Light Brigade also got up safe notwithstanding his information to the Contrary—

It is not a New thing for me to tell you that not a Single transaction has been done by any individual but what was made known to them.—They broke open my Store because they were informed it contained Flour belonging to Govt. they took everything that was in it broke open several Trunks and gave away all their Contents to any person who would take them they burnt a large Quantity of Hemp and other things took all my Flour away. This was owing to their being informed that I was in the Constant habit of using & sending information to our Army and Aiding the forwarding of troops &c altho I am returning for a day or two—I cannot remain wh any Safety—the Number of Enemys & Spys are beyond all conception they are allowed to remain and have been all this season altho' well known—without a Military Establishment & Power & that severely exerted—there is no posability of living in Safety at all—They have destroyed all the Barracks Provisions Store Wood Yard—& Blockhouses on Gibralter Point—After they had embarked all their troops they land wh their Boats loaded wh Men to execute some further information they got.—There was several of the Inhabitants constantly wh them who are notoriously known to be as great Enemys as are in the Country to wt a Mr. John Young Mercht. Mr. Stebbins a Tavernkeeper Mr. Gilbert Blacksmith *Mr. Peters a Lawyer who receives half Pay & a Pension besides*, a notorious man—and a great many in the country well known—In short Commodore Chancy own'd to the Revd. Dr. Strachan that he neaver heard of any place that contained half the Number of persons Publickly known & avowadly to be Enemys to the Government & Country to be allowed to remain at rest in there[?] and for own part—I can posatively assert if immediate Steps (more ready than by Civil process) is not taken to apprehend & send away those people from the Country the Consequences will be cerious—

I take the Liberty of Enclosing Dr. Strachan two notes Incd.

This is a very confused letter & perhaps troubling you improperly; but, had I proceeded on my journey at this time I could have given a great deal of more information. I most fervently pray as does several fond and faithfull Subjects—that some Establishment may be kept at York and that something may be done about taking up those Caracters otherwise neither our life or Property is safe when so many surround us as long as we are liable to visited by the Enemys Vessels or Boats.

I 37 Deposition of William Knott Concerning Lyon, Hastings, and Wheeler

[*P.A.C., Upper Canada Sundries*]

Home District } The Information of William Knott of the Town of York
ss. } in the Home district Goaler of the said district taken on Oath before Thomas Ridout Esquire one of his Majestys Justices of the Peace in and for the Home District aforesaid, who saith that on Sunday the first day of August last; while the Enemys forces were in York he saw John Lyon of the Township of Vaughan distiller drawing with his waggon Public Stores down to the Water Side for the Enemy, he saw no appearance of Compulsion, and for all that appeared Lyon did it voluntarily.—That on the Same day one Nathanuel Hastings[72] of the township of York Yeoman, who was liberated from the Goal of this District by the Enemy came back to the Goal, and took by force several Green Rugs belonging to the Public for the use of the Goal and carried them off with him—That also on the Same day, Timothy Wheeler of the Township of Markham Yeoman came with Lyon to the Goal and insisted upon taken a Pair of Dog Irons and other Articles belonging to Government which the Said Wheeler had taken when the Enemy where at York in the Spring, and had been forced to return. The Deponent desired him to leave them, but Wheeler answered that he would take them and stand the Consequences "That" John Lyon on the said first day of August, came to take off a pair of Wheels which he claimed, and finding the Goal Gate locked, Broke open the Padlock that he might take them out

his
William × Knott
mark

Sworn before me at York
the Seventeenth day of
August 1813—
Thos Ridout JP.

I 38 Bruyerès to Freer

[*P.A.C., C387, p. 100; printed in Wood,* Select British Documents of the Canadian War of 1812, *II, 204–5*]

York 26th August 1813.—

I beg leave to report my arrival at this Post early this morning. I have made every enquiry to know if any Instructions had been left for my future proceedings, but as I cannot learn that any Orders have been given respecting me, and your Letter to the Adjutant General having stated that it was His Excellency's desire I should hasten to York, I

[72]Nathaniel Hastings farmed on the east side of Yonge Street, south of the Newmarket road.

shall remain here to receive any further commands; in the meantime I shall occupy myself in examining the position, and establishing a Block House for the Troops with Store room sufficient to serve as a Dèpot for a supply of Provisions, and stores.—Under existing circumstances I beg leave to submit the expediency of establishing these Buildings rather retired from the Lake as owing to the difficulty of procuring Cannon, it will be very hazardous to venture any public Buildings or Stores within reach of the Enemy's Armed Vessels. There is an excellent position which I am now going to examine retired about two Miles that will be very desireable for this purpose, which will reduce the Enemy in the event of attack to have recourse to an extensive Land operation.—Any Dèpot that may be formed here can be defended at a much less expence, and with more certainty of success than what can possibly be accomplished near the Lake, particularly as the want of every article of Materials, and the difficulty of procuring Workmen will make it most immoderately Expensive, and tedious, and nearly impossible to erect any efficient Work capable of resisting a combined attack against a Naval, and Land Force. I would therefore in the present instance confine myself to Buildings least expensive and retired from the risk of immediate destruction.

On leaving Kingston I made every arrangement for the Detachment of Royal Sappers, and Miners to proceed here as expeditiously as possible with a full proportion of Tools necessary for them, and I hope they may soon be sent. The difficulty of obtaining transport will I fear cause much delay. Colonel Baynes assured me that no time should be lost to forward them, and I trust they will not be retarded. . . .

I 39 FOUNDING OF THE YORK ASSOCIATION

[*Kingston*, Kingston Gazette, *November 13, 1813*]

YORK ASSOCIATION.

AT a Meeting held at the Clerk of the Peace Office in the town of York, on the 22d September, 1813, by the Subscribers, the following resolutions have been unanimously agreed upon.

1st. That an association be formed, to be called the York Association, for the purpose of issuing Bills for the convenience of making change.

2. That William Allan, Esquire, be President, Stephen Jarvis,[73] Darcy Boulton, Esqrs. and Mr. Henry Drean, be Directors and Alexander Wood, Esq. Cashier.

3. That any person shall be entitled to receive Bills from the Cashier,

[73]Stephen Jarvis (1756–1840) was born in Danbury, Conn. and served in the South Carolina Dragoons during the Revolution. After it, he settled at Fredericton, moving to York in 1809, where he opened a store. He later became Registrar of the Home District, and Gentleman Usher of the Black Rod to the Legislative Assembly.

by depositing in his hands their amount either in Army Bills or Specie.

4. The Money so deposited shall remain in the hands of the Cashier for the express purpose of answering the demands that may be made on the Association.

5. That the interest or profit arising from the money so deposited, after deducting the necessary expences of the Issue, shall be appropriated for the Poor of the Parish, and be paid over to the Rev. Dr. Strachan for that purpose.

6. That a meeting of the members of the Association be held at Mr. Roch's[74] Hotel on the first Monday of each Month for the purpose of examining into the state of the funds, and making such regulations as may be found expedient, and that the presence of at least the President, or two of the Directors, and three of the members, shall be requisite to form any resolution relative to the society.

7. That the President may have the power of calling a meeting of the members of the association whenever he may think it expedient for the good of the Association.

8. That from the Issuing of the Bills of the Association, no individual's Bill whatever that exceeds the sum of half a dollar, shall be taken by any member of the Association.

9. That the sum of three hundred pounds currency, be issued in Bills under a Dollar.

10. That the said Bills be signed by the President and Cashier.

11. That each subscriber to the above resolutions, shall consider himself bound to the performance of them.

W. ALLAN, President.
STEPHEN JARVIS, Director.
D. BOULTON, Jun.
ALEX. WOOD, Cashier.
D. TIERS.
JOHN YOUNG.
QUETTON ST. GEORGE,
JORDAN POST, Jun.
JOSEPH HUNT,
JOSEPH HUNT, for T. DEARY,
THOMAS HAMILTON,
S. BRIGHT.[75]

I 40 ISAAC CHAUNCEY TO JUDGE SCOTT OR JUDGE POWELL
[*New York Historical Society, Isaac Chauncey Letter Book*]

U.S. Ship General Pike
Off Niagara, 14th Novem. 1813

When the Squadron under my Command visited York in April last, much to my mortification I discovered that Some of the Men had pillaged a number of Books belonging to the Toronto Library,[76]—as soon

[74]James Odell Roch came to York after keeping a tavern in Niagara. He advertised as an importer in October, 1801, but shortly afterwards began to keep a tavern in York.

[75]The only Brights in the Lists of Inhabitants for 1813 and 1814 are Lewis Bright and Thomas Bright, a butcher.

[76]The Toronto Library was a private subscription library founded on Dec. 9, 1810. Its directors were Thomas Scott, Alexander Wood, D'Arcy Boulton Sr., and

as the circumstance was made known to me I interdicted all intercourse with the Shore untill a general Search was made and all the Books in the Fleet collected and boxed up with the intention of having them returned immediately, but circumstances in Some degree beyond my controul have prevented my carrying those wishes into execution before this late period. I have now the pleasure of Sending you (by the Lady of the Lake, flag of Truce) Two Boxes containing all the Books that were taken from York by any person belonging to the fleet. I have no doubt however, but that many others were taken by the Soldiers and will be finally lost to the Library but I am confident that it was owing to the extreme indisposition of General Dearborn that they were not collected and returned.

I beg you Sir to assure the Trustees of the Toronto Library that it has been a source of great mortification to myself and Officers that so useful an institution should not have been deemed Sacred by every person under our command—you however Sir must be aware, that it is not always in the power of Officers with the best disposition to controul those placed under them Situated as they were at York.

I 41 Kitson's[77] "Report on the Defence and the Accommodation of the Troops at York 22nd November 1813" [*P.A.C., C388, p. 136–8*]

A battery of two long 24 Ps. and 24 Prs. carronade is constructed on the edge of the bank near six hundred yards westward of the present Garrison; this battery is nearly enclosed by a Cedar Palisade of 10 feet high, they are so placed as to form loop holes for the infantry to fire through when raised by a banquette; at the N.W. angle of this battery is built a musket proof guard house capable of containing forty men and being loop holed it gives a flank fire upon the ditch and Palisading. This battery is more at present intended against Vessels entering the Harbour: but it is necessary to observe the wood should be cleared for 500 yards, as now an enemy may advance to within 50 yards perfectly under cover; therefore I beg leave to propose that a party of militia should be employed constantly during the winter in clearing this wood. As felling axes are not to be had each Militia should if possible provide himself with an Axe.

Upon the garrison ground and near the scite of the late Gouvernment house is constructed a mortar battery of two 8 inch Mortars; this work is not enclosed as the rear is defended by the Blockhouse.

William Dummer Powell, its treasurer William Allan, and its librarian William Chewett and later John Macdonell. Its books were kept in Elmsley House, and were looted during the occupation. Apparently it never recovered; in 1822 Allan complained that the books Chauncey returned were still in his possession. These were finally sold at auction in December, 1822.

[77]Lieutenant John S. Kitson, Royal Engineers.

On the edge of the water in the ravine is a gun battery consisting of one long 12 Pr. & (one long 9 Pr. without Cascable or Trunnions but mounted on a block carriage) the utility of this battery is very great being low and particularly as the Channel stands on & recedes from it—therefore the guns will rake any Vessel attempting to enter the Bay—

The Blockhouses on account of the badness of weather and the want of materials have been delayed however they are raised to the second floor and should the weather prove favorable I have every reason to believe that one of 60 feet by 40 feet and one of 40 feet square will be roofed and shingled by the 30th Instant

The Council Buildings are now preparing for Barracks and one of them will be finished on the 27th Instant & to contain about one hundred & thirty Men.

I 42 STRACHAN TO DR. OWEN

[*P.A.O., Strachan Letter Books; printed in,* John Strachan Letter Book, *ed. Spragge, p. 55*]

York 1 Jany 1814

I was much gratified to find that my answer to your questions proved satisfactory. Since my last we have been twice in the power of the enemy, had the barracks & hospitals burnt & many depredations committed. I remained after the Military & Surgeons had retreated & demanded the sick & wounded from the American General whom I conveyed from the garrison to the town to a house, which I procured for their reception, a distance of nearly two miles. We had many difficulties to encounter. York was first taken on the 27th April and the Enemy did not leave the harbour till the 9th May. For some time our situation was deplorable, but at length we got medical aid. Nowithstanding their own calamities the Inhabitants were exceedingly kind to the sick & wounded, supporting them entirely, till a regular military hospital was again established. The town was a second time taken possession of by the enemy on the last day of July, but they did not commit much injury. On this occasion the principal inhabitants retreated but I remained to protect the Hospital, the women and children. Since the last visit of the enemy we have been placed in a rather better posture of defence, and this has been the general Hospital. So great was the number of sick for some time upwards of 400 that I was obliged to give up the Church for their reception, a step which could only be justified by the most imperious necessity. There was in truth no other place as all the public buildings had been destroyed by the enemy.

I visit the hospitals regularly twice a week, & oftener when necessary. While the enemy were present, I was there nearly the whole time. I meet with great ignorance & indifference, but I am sometimes gratified with proofs of better things & have experienced on several occasions the truth of your observations. My regular days of visiting are Wednesday

& Sundays. On Wednesday I content myself with kindly inquiring into the state of their health dropping something concerning their spiritual welfare, as I find it useful, and their minds properly disposed. Besides doing this on Sunday I read some prayers & give an exhortation the whole taking up from 15 to twenty minutes. For some time I had five such Exhortations to make every Sabbath, then four & at present three. It seemed to me that those Exhortations have more effect when delivered on Sunday than on any other day, altho' the exertion added to my regular duty becomes severe, especially during the warm weather, as the hospitals were at a distance from each other, & I had service twice in Church. It is now less fatiguing as I have public service only once, and the weather is cool. At present my habit in the hospital is this—after pronouncing as many prayers selected from the Common Prayer Book as I judge proper, I read either the Gospel or Epistle of the day or of the preceding Sunday, & comment upon it or make a short discourse from one of the most striking passages. I trust for words to the time of delivery —I change the subject in each ward, because convalescents frequently follow & and it would lessen the effect did they suppose that I was obliged to repeat the same to all. I have kept my health well through the blessing of God—and notwithstanding the labour I have had much satisfaction this summer, having been the instrument of much comfort to the temporal & I hope in God to the spiritual wants of many. I am badly off for books for the Hospital, those I had were pillaged or burnt. I have purchased a few at my own expence, but they are not now to be had, and I have been forced to refuse several applications for prayer-books with much sorrow. . . .

I 43 General Account of Subscription Assemblies 1814
[*P.A.O., J. B. Robinson Papers*]

Received	£	s	d
31 full Subscriptions 10$ each	77	10	0
Broken Subscriptions	12	5	0
From Mr. Kitson Officers Subscriptions	15	0	0
	£104	15	0
Due 6 full Subscriptions 10$ each	15	0	0
	£119	15	0
Paid	104	15	0
Recd Mr. Harrison's Subscn.	2	10	0
Mr Strachans	5		
	112	5	0

Paid	£	s	d
Paid Brown for going several times round with Subs: paper	1	2	6
Paid Music for the season	22	15	0
Paid Charles (a black man) for waiting	2	5	0
Paid Hunter & others for him for superintending	3	5	0
Paid Lackie the Baker for Cakes furnished during the season	19	7	6
Paid female Attendants for the season	1	10	0
Paid for milk		2	6

Paid Rogers for 5½ lbs loaf Sugar at 6/ NYC		17	6
Paid O'Keeffe for the use of his room	28	5	0
Paid Mr. McIntoshs[78] Account for Wine &c	55	15	7½
Paid A. Wood Esqr. for Sugar	4	2	6
	£139	8	1½
	112	5	
	27	3	1½

The Managers of the York Assemblies
To Angus Mackintosh

				Dr. £	s	d
1814						
Janụy	11	To 4 Gallons L:P: Teneriffe wine	36/	7	4	–
		12 packs playing cards	4/	2	6	–
		6 Nutmegs	1/		6	–
		½ lb best Hyson tea & 4 bottles	1/6	1	2	–
	18	To 1 Loaf refined sugar 7.3	5/	1	19	0¾
		¼ lb Hyson tea			8	–
		2¼ Gallons L:P: Teneriffe Madeira	36/	4	1	–
		4¾ " London Market do.	40/	9	10	–
Feby	1	7 " " " do.	40/	14	"	"
		2 Nutmegs & ¼ Lb Hyson tea	8/		10	–
		½ doz playing cards		1	4	–
	17	8 Gallons London Market Madeira	40/	16	"	"
		6 Nutmegs & ½ lb Hyson tea		1	2	–
		NY Curry		£59	14	0¾
		Sent 1 dble doz cups & saucers if not returned	56/			
Mar	3	To 6 Gallons Lon: P Madeira wine	40/	12	"	"
		3 Nutmegs, ¼ lb. Hyson tea		"	11	"
		6 packs playing cards		1	4	"
				£73	9	0¾

Recd—in part 61 . 9 . 6
Subscription 4

65 . 9 . 6

				£	s.	d
Mar	17	½ lb Hyson tea			16	0
		4 Nutmegs	1/		4	0
		6 Gallons Wine	40/	12	0	0
		1 doz cups & saucers		2	16	0
				89	5	0
		By cash & subscription		65	9	6
				£23	15	6
				20	6	9
				£ 3	8	9

Recd payment of the above balance of
three pounds, eight shillings & nine pence
Angus Mackintosh

[78]Angus Mackintosh (1762–1833) was born in Inverness, the son of the head of the clan, and immigrated to Detroit in early manhood. On the American occupation of Detroit he moved across the river, and became a prominent merchant. During the War of 1812 he was apparently living in York. In 1831 he returned to Scotland where he died.

I 44 Bruyères to Prevost
[*P.A.C., C732, pp. 10–11*]

York 23rd. January 1814

. . . The total want of Artificers, and Labourers of every description has retarded the progress of all the public Works here, and unless some efficient means are taken to procure Men nothing effectively can be done towards the defence of the place. Lieut. Kitson has exerted himself to the utmost but personal exertion is of no use without assistance. Only 13 Carpenters are now employed whereas four times the number are required. The want of Snow has also retarded the supply of Materials being brought but the Roads are now more practicable, and I have directed Requisitions to be immediately made for all that is necessary. . . .

I 45 Minutes of the General Quarter Sessions of the Peace, Home District
[*P.A.O., Minutes of the General Quarter Sessions of the Peace, Home District*]

York 19th March 1814

The Court met pursuant to Adjournment
Present
Thomas Ridout Esqr, Chairman

William Allan } Esquires
Duncan Cameron }

The following Persons had been summoned to attend Court this day and shew cause why they have not sent forward their Teams with Sleighs as regularly impressed and directed so to do, for Government Service, vizt—

1. Christian Troyer[79] 2. John Oister 3. Michael Kiffer[80] 4. John Shank[81] 5. John Snider[82] 6. Joseph Michler	The Constable, Samuel Arnold, who impressed the Sleighs with Teams belonging to the above named persons, did not attend, they consequently were dismissed by the Court.

[79]Christian Troyer was a Mennonite preacher who came from Somerset County, Pa., and settled in Vaughan Township in 1804.

[80]Michael Keefer (1766?–1852) came with his family from Berlin, Pa., arriving in York in December, 1806. He settled in Vaughan Township.

[81]Probably John Shunk (d. 1829) from Pennsylvania, who settled in Vaughan Township about 1805.

[82]John Snider came from near the Susquehanna River in Pennsylvania, and settled in Vaughan Township in 1800.

A Letter from Lieut: Thomas Taylor[83] Fort Major at York was read as follows:—

York 9th March 1814

Sir—

"A Military guard being required to do duty at the Gaol for the security of Prisoners there confined, Colonel Stewart[84] has directed me to apprize you of the inefficient state of that place.—The outside Gate as well as most of the inner doors being without fastenings renders the securing the prisoners more difficult and indeed more doubtful than if they were provided with Locks Keys—This circumstance has been reported to the Gaoler for some time but no measures having been taken to repair them, the Commanding Officer considered it as incumbent upon him to direct the same to be mentioned to you.

I have the Honor to be
Sir,
Your most obedient
humble servant,
(signed) Thos. Taylor, Lieut:,
Fort Major.

T. Ridout Esquire,

Ordered as the Gaol was taken possession of by the Military, and is still in their possession, which excludes the Magistrates from any authority, or access to it at present—and unless a proportion of the Gaol is given up to be at their disposal with free access to it, they do not conceive that they have any right to expend any monies in making the necessary repairs

The Court then Adjourned to Saturday next the 26th Instant

S. Heward, Clk. Peace Home Dist: there attending.

I 46 John Beikie to Miles Macdonell
[*P.A.C., Selkirk Papers, p. 9238*]

York 19th. March 1814

. . . on the 26th. of April alarm Guns were fired that the Enemy's Fleet was seen from the Scarborough Heights. At the peep of day on the 27th. I descried from the Bedroom Window the whole Yankie Fleet 13 in number off the Light House, I called Donald and we armed ourselves with Muskets[85] provided the Evening before, went to the Garrison where we found the Grenadiers of the 8th. Regt. 110 Strong, a few of the Newfoundland Regt. and some Militia already on the Parade. The fleet

[83]Thomas Taylor (1778–1838) was a lieutenant in the 41st Regiment. In 1817 he was called to the English Bar, and in 1819 to the Bar of Upper Canada. The same year he was appointed Judge of the Gore District Court, and in 1823 the first official reporter of the Court of King's Bench.

[84]Colonel Archibald Stewart of the 1st Regiment was on the Staff in Canada.

[85]Beikie had no military command, but volunteered with the Grenadier Company of the 8th Regiment.

came gradually to anchor off the old French Fort & prepared to Land, we opposed but could not prevent, 70 of ye Grenadiers were killed & wounded besides others, the Indians took fright ran away and never stopt 'till they got to Matchedash neither Donald nor me were hurt—finding it idle to remain near the old Fort any longer we retreated to the Batteries, which we were shortly afterwards obliged to abandon, the Enemy coming up in such Force, having Landed 4000 men, our whole strength did not amount to more than 450 half of whom were not engaged. Poor Donald McLean was killed, fighting as a volunteer, at length General Sheaffe ordered the Powder Magazine to be blown up, His Majesty's Colours to be struck, and the Bugle to sound a general retreat—the enemy advanced and were wofully cut up by the Explosion, 250 killed upon the spot the numbers wounded not known but it is clear in the whole more of them were killed and wounded than we were altogether. The Town capitulated & His Majesty's Troops retreated to Kingston. . . . The moment they [the Yankies] got in they began to plunder and burn the public Buildings which they continued for four days when they went on Board where they rode at Anchor from the 1st. to the 8th. of May inclusive. The public Buildings burnt on this occasion were—The Govemt. House, The Block House at the Garrison, The Naval Barracks lately built on the Beach, opposite Crookshank's, The Count De Puisaye's House used as a Naval Store, the Brick Buildings at the East end of the Town and Mr. Russell's Block House. They plundered all my poultry & some few things from the House which we considered as triffling being glad to get off so.—On the 11th. of May Mr. Selby was Buried.

The next thing that occured was the reappearance of the Yankie Fleet on the 31st. July 1813 coming under full Sail for the Harbour, all the Officers of the Civil Government fled, they remained two days, took all the public stores they could find, burnt the Barracks & the Store House on Gibralter Point and put the Soldiers who were sick in Hospital on Parole.—Penelope staid at Home both times by which means our Property was saved, those who abandoned their Houses found nothing but the bare walls at their return— . . .

Elmsley House is converted into an Hospital, & the Stable into Barracks, the Fences all Burnt owing to the scarcity of Wood the Teams being all employed in the transport of Provisions Stores & Troops first one way and then another as the movements of the Enemy required—all dry Goods are just double the price they were—Wood when it can be got 24/- a Cord, Beef 2/- a pound, Mutton 2/- Eggs 6/- Veal 2/6. Cheese 4/- Butter 6/- N.Y. Currcy and 24 Dollars a Ton for Hay.— It was so late last year before we could determine whether to make a Garden or not that very little was done, and what was done did not succeed owing to the season being so Rainy—You may then easily imagine a scarcity of Vegetables the cheapest Potatoes are a Dollar—

Liqurs are very dear Whisky 3½ Dollars a Gallon and little to be got Rum 5 Dollars, Wine 6, Loaf Sugar ½ a Dollar, Green Tea 4 Dollars, Tobacco a Dollar and a half.—Add to all this, every now and then both Public and Private Houses (of necessity) are crammed full of Troops, who not only destroy everything in their way, but carry of whatever they take a liking to.—

Vast preparations are making here to defend the place about a quarter of a mile west of the site of the Government House is a Battery of 2 long 24 pounders & 1 Eighteen pound Carronade—Two Block Houses are just finished on the square where stood the Government House, the Garden is gone to the Devil, The Guns yet to be put into Batteries are 2 long 12s—3 long 18s and 10—18 pound Carronades, besides some others hourly expected. The number of Troops now here are 1300 (exclusive of sedentary Militia)—say the 41st. Regiment 1st & 2nd Battalions in one now called the 1st. Battn. 600—The Incorporated Militia 500—The remains of the Newfoundland Regiment 150 and Artificers & Royal Artilly 50 Men—A Block House is to be put up on Gibralter Point and one is Building at the Corner of Colonel Shank's Farm to command the Ravine and the High road—the whole of the woods are cut down between the Garrison & Colonel Shaw's & Captn. Givin's Farms. . . .

I 47 PRICES OF PROVISIONS

[*P.A.O., Minutes of the General Quarter Sessions of the Peace, Home District*]

By the Magistrates of the Home District at a Special Session holden at the Town of York, in and for the said District, on Monday the 25th day of April, 1814.

WHEREAS His Honor Gordon Drummond,[86] Esquire, President administering the Government of the Province of Upper Canada, and Lieutenant General Commanding His Majesty's Forces within the same, hath judged it expedient by His Proclamation bearing date at Kingston on the 12th day of the present Month of April to declare MARTIAL LAW, to be in force within the said Province, as far as relates to the procuring of Provisions and Forage for said Forces

AND WHEREAS it has been thought proper that prior to the putting in force of the said Law, the Magistrates in their respective Districts should affix a fair and equitable price upon each Article of Produce, Provision, and Forage, at which the same should be sold and delivered.—

[86]Sir Gordon Drummond (1771–1854), born in Quebec, entered the army in 1789. He was Administrator of Upper Canada 1813–15, and of both Canadas, 1815–16. In 1813 he became second in command to Prevost, commanding on the Niagara frontier until the autumn of 1814, when he returned to Quebec to succeed Prevost as Commander in Chief.

THE MAGISTRATES of the HOME DISTRICT, in Special Sessions assembled, having taken the said Proclamation into their serious Consideration, have therefore in conformity thereto agreed upon the following prices, as fair and reasonable in their opinion, for the present to be taken and received for the Articles herein after specified,

That is to say—

Provincial Currency, Dollars at five Shillings.

	Delivered at York or at the Commissariat Stores	Delivered at the Mills or residence of the Farmer.
For Good & Merchantable Flour per Barrel	Three Pounds ten Shillings.	Three Pounds
Do. Do. Wheat per Bushel,	ten Shillings	ten Shillings
Do. Do. Pease per do.	Seven Shillings & Sixpence.	Six Shillings & three pence
Do. Do. Barley per do.	Do. Do.	Do. Do.
Do. Do. Rye per do.	Do. Do.	Do. Do.
Do. Do. Oats per do.	Five Shillings	Three Shillgs. & Ninepence.
Do. Hay per Ton,	Five Pounds	Three Pounds fifteen Shillings
Do. Straw per Do.	Three Pounds	
Do. Beef on Foot per Cwt	Two Pounds five Shillgs.	
Do. Do. slaughtered per lb	Seven pence half penny	
Do. Pork Salted per Barrel	Seven Pounds ten Shillgs.	
Do. Carcass per lb	Seven pence half penny	
Do. Mutton per lb	Nine Pence	
Do. Veal per lb	Eight Pence	
Do. Butter per lb	One Shillg & threepence.	
Do. Bread per Loaf of four Pounds	One Shilling & Six pence.	

By Order of the Court
S. Heward
Clk. Peace Home Dist.

I 48 REGIMENTAL ORDERS, 3RD REGIMENT, YORK MILITIA
[*T.P.L., Copy of Orderly Book, 3rd Regt., York Militia*]

York Regtl Orders York 17th July 1814.

It having been represented to the Lieut. Colonel that many of the Militia while in upon Guard and placed as Sentrys behave in an unsoldier like manner by sitting down, leaving their Muskets in their Sentry Boxes and walking about in a careless manner as if they were on their own private business. This is therefore a caution that it behooves the Men while upon Guard, and Sentry, to be careful not to be found upon their Posts in a careless manner as the Guards will be regularly inspected and any Men so found will be confined and tried by a Court Martial for disobedience of Orders, and unsoldier like conduct.

It is the duty of the Non Commissioned Officers to see the Centinals well posted, and alert while on duty.

I 49 W. W. BALDWIN TO QUETTON ST. GEORGE, MONTREAL
[*T.P.L., W. W. Baldwin Papers*]

York 20 July 1814—

Lest you should relapse into your suspicions of my forgetting my friends I write a few lines by the express—to say we are all, thank God well and as yet unmolested by the Yankees—but I only say as yet, for at this moment there is nothing to prevent them destroying this place—one would suppose Sir G. Prevost still thinks this place unworthy of protection. We have now but about 200 regulars here and the mob of the country Militia—The East wind now blowing puts us in great fear—I put up all my papers last night and kept my horse in to send them off—poor Miss Russell is so dejected that it appears like mental derangement—Mrs. Baldwin came in to town[87] the other day and prevailed on her to go to Markham. Miss Willcocks remains for a day or two to put her house &c in order & pack up such things as Miss Russell may esteem most—She seems somewhat better since she went to the Country, but yet a strong tendency to derangement—it is impossible not to feel for her—

The Melville[88] & Moira are now here separated from the rest of our fleet—a necessary sacrifice to the Enemy if he choose to come for them—It is well for us who may suffer that we do not know the objects and reasons of those at the head of affairs—supposing they know more than ourselves we are inclined to think them right—was it not from a fear that my ignorance might make me err, I would say that there is some dreadful misconduct some where—Providence has protected us hitherto—and in Providence alone I rest. . . .

I 50 THOMAS RIDOUT TO T. G. RIDOUT, CORNWALL
[*P.A.O., Ridout Papers*]

York 9th August 1814—

On Saturday last the 6th Inst. I hastily enclosed to your care, a letter I had written to my Brother, informing you at the same time that the American Fleet were off this place they made their appearance on the preceeding day about ten sail, standing towards Niagara, with a fine easterly breeze, and at no great distance from that shore—I had gone down towards the Bay, and was standing near Coxe's door conversing with Capt. McDonell, who has lost his left arm at the Battle at Lundys—when I felt a violent concussion of the air, and presently after heard an explosion towards Niagara, much greater, than the explosion of our magazine—on looking over the Lake where the enemy's vessels were—I saw a prodigious cloud of smoke, rising to a great height—I then concluded, and do now that one of the enemys vessels has blown up—but of

[87]The Baldwin family were at Millbrook, William Willcocks' establishment in Markham Township.

[88]The *Lord Melville* was a brig built at Kingston, and launched in July, 1813.

this, we have not received any information—when I enclosed my letter—the American Fleet were lying off this Place, about 8 miles off it and the Lady of the Lake, was attempting to come into this Harbour, as a Flag of Truce—but not permitting such insidious policy, a shot from one of our Batteries was fired at this Vessel, she then hoisted her proper Colours and fired at the Garrison, & afterwards another shot we fired three or four more, but all fell short of her—she put out to join her fleet—and a visit was expected from them—at this time, we had only a few convalescent & lame soldiers, & 2 or 300 of the sedentary or Home Militia in the course of the afternoon 300 men or 1st. detachment of the 82—came in having marched at the rate of 4 miles an Hour—and on Sunday the residue of that regiment came in also this morng a part of that corps have proceeded towards Niagara by Land, & the 1st division of the 6th. are expected in the course of this day—four of the enemys Vessels are now in sight about 8 miles off on Friday Saturday & Sunday people were busy in moving their effects into the country—on Saturday I removed the remainder of my office papers & some Family necessaries—with much difficulty I walked as far as Sams, having been laid up some days with a Lumbago—I came in this morng—& tho' not in pain when I sit or lye—yet I can walk but very slowly . . .

I 51 JOHN DOUGLAS'[89] ACCOUNT OF THE WOUNDED AT YORK

[*Douglas*, Medical Topography of Upper Canada, *pp. 15–17, 82–5, 104–5*]

York, the seat of government, and capital of the province, is built on a level plain, along the northern bank of an extensive bay, which communicates on its west side with the lake. This bay is long and narrow, and fed by many streams from the contiguous soil, which in summer supply its waste of evaporation. It is navigable to vessels of considerable burden; and its shores in many parts are overgrown with rushes. Those winds which at times agitate the surface of the lake, seldom or never disturb its stagnant waters. The site which the town occupies appears to have been once a deep meadow, interspersed with pools of water. Some spots of ground which border upon the town are as yet in a state of nature. Even those fields which have been cultivated, are not sufficiently intersected with drains to carry off the collections of water, which, in the rainy season of the year, often inundate the soil. The inhabitants of the town do not exceed six hundred, a number extremely small when contrasted with the whole population of the province. The town on its west side is defended by a fort, which is erected on a dry and level spot of ground. Here was established the general hospital, in rear of the army, to which the sick and wounded were conducted as necessity or contingency required. In sickly seasons the inhabitants of York are liable to be attacked by intermittent fever. . . .

[89]John Douglas (1788–1861) was Assistant Surgeon in the 8th Regiment. His account of his experiences in Canada was published in 1819.

The active services of the troops were continued for a period of nearly three years. The campaign of 1814, which preceded the ratification of peace in the following spring, was rendered important by the successful achievements of the army. Being stationed at York in charge of the general hospital during the greater part of that year's campaign, a favourable opportunity was afforded me of witnessing the state of the sick and wounded who were sent thither from the army. That part of the province, I may observe, which stretches from Fort George to Fort Erie was the principal field of active operation. After the several actions which were fought in that tract of the country, the wounded were immediately conducted to the rear as far as Fort George, from whence they were shipped on board small vessels, conveyed across the western extremity of Lake Ontario, to be landed at York, and admitted into hospital. On the evening of the second or third day after an action, they generally reached their place of destination. After the battle of Chippawa, which took place on the 5th of July, a considerable number of wounded were disembarked at York, and admitted into hospital. Sufficient accommodation being afforded them, the routine of medical duty had not as yet met with any obstruction. The battle of Lundey's Lane, which was fought on the 17th of the same month, being more sanguinary than that of Chippawa, filled the general hospital at York, and its adjacent buildings, with its numerous wounded. After the latter period, the duty of the medical department, not only at York, but along the Niagara frontier, became serious and laborious. The skirmishes and casual engagements which occurred during the remainder of the campaign, kept the hospitals more or less filled with wounded till the beginning of winter, when the enemy, evacuating Fort Erie, passed over the river Niagara to the peaceful possession of his own territory. Our troops, though opposed to a force much greater in number, generally maintained their ground; and in almost every rencounter had the scale of victory on their side. The task, however, is not mine, either to applaud the well-conducted enterprises of an army, or to censure those precipitated measures, which, in their fatal consequences, often obscure the brightest prospects of success.

The general hospital at York, though a commodious building, was deficient in size for the accommodation of the sick and wounded. Its apartments being originally intended for family use, were too small for the wards of an hospital, and did not admit of a free ventilation. Neither were the adjoining houses of the hospital, which were fitted up for temporary accommodation, any way suitable for the reception of the wounded. When, in the course of the summer, the wounded became so numerous as not to be contained within the general hospital and its outhouses, the church, a large and well-ventilated building, was dismantled of its seats, and, for the time being, converted into a hospital. . . .

The wounded who were admitted into the church hospital, had all the advantages of a free ventilation. This building became extremely serviceable to the recovery of those men whose injuries were of a serious kind. From the pure air which the sick and wounded enjoyed in it, their progress to a state of convalescence was often rapid. Men whose wounds put on an unpromising aspect in the general hospital, were at times transferred to this establishment. Intermittent fever, however, with all its fatality, prevailed in the latter, as well as in the former building. . . .

I 52 ALEXANDER WOOD TO ROBERT ARMOUR,[90] MONTREAL
[*T.P.L., Alexander Wood Letter Books*]

York 12th [December, 1814]

. . . I'm happy to have it in my power to inform you that the goods were safely landed at the Head of Lake Ontario on the 29th or 30th Novr. the Boats got here on the 27th & Conductor Dugan with some difficulty was prevailed upon to proceed which he did on the 28th. Alexander[91] had left this by land on the 26th & passing at the Beach left directions there respecting the Six Boats

Dugan and his men passed here on his return on the 2d Inst. they were furnished with provisions to carry them to Kingston which I advised Mr. Grant of LaChine to whose acct. I placed the money by his orders—

Some days ago a Canadian came here to say that his Boats three in number were wrecked about 40 Miles below that the loading was upon the Beach His Bill Lading was directed to Messrs. Alexander & forwarded by a Mr Smith of Kingston. . . .

I 53 ALEXANDER WOOD TO MAITLAND, GARDEN, & CO.,[92] MONTREAL
[*T.P.L., Alexander Wood Letter Books*]

York 15 Decr. 1814

. . . As I have no Spirits on hand the rise in the Market is no very pleasing news to me.

I fear it will not be possible to procure either Flour or Pork in this neighbourhood for Mr Ermatinger the Commy buys not only all that comes for sale but sends his people into the Country to examine what the inhabitants can spare and lays his hand upon it either manufactured or in Grain. as to Pork Salt is so scarse that I do not think many Barrels will be put up in this quarter. Govrt. buy it fresh and having salt in store they salt it for themselves however say to Mr. Ermatinger with my respects that I shall make every effort tho' I'm certain it will be in vain. . . .

[90]Robert Armour (b. 1780) came to Canada from Kilmarnock, Scotland, in 1798, and became a prominent merchant in Montreal.

[91]Possibly Hugh Alexander, merchant at Stamford.

[92]Maitland, Garden, Auldjo & Co. was the successor of Auldjo, Maitland & Co.

I 54 ALEXANDER WOOD TO JOHN STEVENS, LONDON
[*T.P.L., Alexander Wood Letter Books*]

Upper Canada York 23d. Decr. 1814

I have this day received your respected favours of the 18th & 25th August conveying Invoice of Goods per: the Wm. Nelson and Enterprize, the former arrived at Quebec, I understand about the 7th Nov. and the goods had been shipped in River Craft for Montreal where they must remain untill our winter roads are in a state to suffer them to be sent on with sledges, a very expensive hazardous and slow mode of transport, however being the only conveyance at this season of the year we must addopt it without complaining ye Enterprize had not got to Quebec on the 9th Inst. and would not of course reach that port this season where she is or what has been her fate I know not . . . had ye goods got in so as to have reached me by water carriage much time expense & trouble would have been saved besides a more advantageous Market large supplies have this year been sent to some of my neighbours by Messr. Phyn Inglis & Co.[93] they have been at hand some time and came to an empty Market & accordingly met rapid sale. Waiting long for my Invoice to see the prices intending to have sent an order for the ensuing spring I have been very much disappointed in not receiving them & fear they will come too late for me to have the goods sent by first Fleet which is a very great advantage in such a navigation as ours. . . .

I 55 REGULATIONS CONCERNING SELLING PRACTICES
[*York,* York Gazette, *December 24, 1814*]

Forestalling, Regrating, and Extortion,

Home District } WHEREAS at a Special Sessions of the Peace, holden at the Town of York on Saturday the 17th day of the present month of December 1814. It was represented to the Magistrates that sundry persons residing in the said Town, make it a practice of intercepting and buying up the Provisions and other necessaries coming to the said Town for sale—and that the said persons sell the same at very advanced prices to the Inhabitants, who are compelled to purchase from them.

Notice is hereby given, that any person or persons who shall, after the date thereof, intercept any provision on its way to the said Town, or purchase the same on its way in or after it shall be brought into the Town, with a view to sell the same again, will be prosecuted to the utmost rigor of the Law, for each and every time he, she, or they shall so offend.

[93]Phyn, Ellices and Inglis was founded in 1787, in succession to the fur trading company, Phyn, Ellice and Company.

I 56 ALEXANDER WOOD TO WILLIAM MITCHELL, KINGSTON
[*T.P.L., Alexander Wood Letter Books*]

York 3d Jany. 1815

Your favour of the 20th. has been at hand some days and that of the 27th this moment recd. I'm really very sorry to hear that you are so incommoded & had hoped my Friends below, to whom I wrote long ago on the subject, would have saved you at least on my part, but I suppose they find it impossible to engage the Canadians to come above Kingston.

It grieves me seriously to be obliged to say that my own efforts have met with as little success, the roads in this neighbourhood are entirely bare & untill yesterday that we had rain our weather had been for a week as mild as April after the rain last night it froze a little and a powdering of snow fell I trust it will now be more seasonable & that I shall be able to engage some Teams to go down your length, should you however obtain transport be so kind as disencumber yourself of such of my goods as are most in the way. Sleighs from Kingston & Cornwall are daily coming in here with Rum &c. this after noon I see McArthurs goods has got up I hope the press will soon be over, the first of the roads seem always eagerly seized. Adventurers with hope of advantaging by being here while the Market is empty probably occasion the difficulty and extravagance. were you not so uncomfortably encumbered I feel no desire to be in such a violent hurry but I know well how you are situated & had done my endeavour to save you as much as lay in my power

On Friday last I gave Bates of the Township of Clark a note to you he and another engaged to go down immediately for two loads & I think in a little I may induce some more. . . .

I 57 ALEXANDER WOOD TO GEORGE AND WILLIAM GORDON, LACHINE
[*T.P.L., Alexander Wood Letter Books*]

York 7th April 1815

On the other side is a Copy of what I wrote you on the 3d Inst. to go by Express, the Post got in yesterday & I have merely to say that the sale of your Spirits will be advertised in the Gazette tomorrow, the sale to be some day next Week as the Auctioneer may think best, it was necessary to give this Notice that the Country Innkeepers may know as I expect they will be the purchasers, I wish you had fixed a price which no Sale was to take place under, the Americans are already bringing loads of Liquor, Salt Shoes &c. &c. &c. three of their Craft have been at this post, which tho' not suffered to enter, Smuggling goes on rapidly

I 58 LOCAL REMARKS
[*York,* York Gazette, *April 15, 1815*]

The Ontario uncommonly high—The ice disappeared from the bay of York a fortnight earlier than in the two preceding seasons—The roads in the neighbourhood never in a worse state, or more nearly impassable—Immense flights of the wild pidgeon, from west to east on the 27th ult.—No conviction of the supposed murderers of the late J. P. Rademuller[94]—One person sentenced to death for cow-stealing—another to pillory and imprisonment for misdemeanors.—An annual Register Ship to Botany Bay wanted—The wild duck revisit our waters since peace was made.

[94]John Paul Radelmüller (1763?–1815) had been a servant in the royal family, first in the household of the Duke of Gloucester, then of the Duke of Kent. He first settled in Vaughan Township, where he wished to establish a government-supported school for the German settlers. In 1809 he was appointed the first keeper of the lighthouse at Gibraltar Point, and was murdered, probably by some drunken soldiers, on Jan. 2, 1815.

BIBLIOGRAPHY AND INDEX

BIBLIOGRAPHY

MANUSCRIPTS

CANADA

Public Archives of Canada

Claus Papers.
H. H. Farmar Papers.
William Jarvis Papers.
Neilson Papers.
Powell Papers.
Selkirk Papers, vols. 31, 74–5.
Shepherd-White Papers.
John Walworth Papers.
War of 1812 Losses Claims.
Joseph Willcocks Memorandum and Letter Book.
R.G. 1, E 1, Upper Canada State Books A–F.
R.G. 1, E 3, Upper Canada State Papers.
R.G. 1, L 1, Upper Canada Land Book C.
R.G. 5, A 1, Upper Canada Sundries.
R.G. 8, C Series, Military Papers.
Society for the Propagation of the Gospel, Journals, vols. 27–30, microfilm of originals in Society for the Propagation of the Gospel Archives, London.

ONTARIO

Archives of the United Church, Victoria College, Toronto

Journal of William Case.

Department of Public Records and Archives (P.A.O.)

Baldwin Papers.
H. J. Boulton Papers.
Cartwright Papers, Cartwright Letter Book, Business Affairs, 1793–6.
Colonial Office Papers, C.O. 42, microfilm of originals in Public Record Office, London.
Crown Land Papers, York Township.
Minutes of the General Quarter Sessions of the Peace, Home District.
Alexander Hamilton Letter Book.
Solomon Jones Papers.
Macaulay Papers.

Miscellaneous MSS
Alexander Legge Papers.
List of Jurors, Home District.
1796, State of Case against Charles McCuen.
1798, Statements of Beman, Humberstone, and Williams concerning theft.
1799, Papers concerning thefts by Pitney.
Ely Playter Diaries.
Ridout Papers.
J. B. Robinson Papers.
Percy Robinson Papers.
Rousseau Papers.
Russell Papers.
Simcoe Papers.
Elias Smith Letter Book.
F. P. Smith Papers.
Strachan Papers.
Isaac Wilson Letter Book (copy).
J. B. Robinson Papers, microfilm of originals in possession of Christopher Robinson, Esq., Ottawa.

Department of Lands and Forests
Survey Records, Surveyors' Letters, vol XIV.

Queen's University, Douglas Library
Cartwright Letter Books.

Royal Canadian Military Institute, Toronto
Account Books of the Garrison at York, 1812–15.

Synod of Ontario Archives, Kingston
Stuart Letters.

Toronto Public Library
Allan Papers.
Robert Baldwin Papers II.
W. W. Baldwin Papers I & II.
Inventory of sale of Brock's possessions.
John Elmsley Letter Book.
Accounts of sale of Gore's possessions.
S. P. Jarvis Papers.
William Jarvis Papers.
John McGill Papers.
Abner Miles Account Books.
Oaths of Allegiance before Baldwin.

Oaths of Allegiance before Willcocks.
Powell Papers.
T. A. Reed Papers.
J. Ross Robertson Scrapbooks and Picture Collection.
Elizabeth Russell Papers.
Peter Russell Papers.
St. George Papers I & II.
Scadding Papers.
Wolford Simcoe Papers.
D. W. Smith Papers.
Strachan Papers.
G. O. Stuart Account Book of School.
Early Toronto Papers.
Alexander Wood Papers.
Alexander Wood Letter Books.
Minutes of Town Meetings and Lists of Inhabitants of York, 1797–1822.
Papers relating to the Capitulation of York.
Correspondence, etc. of York Militia.
Orderly Book of the 3rd. Regiment, York Militia (typescript copy).

York Pioneer and Historical Society, Toronto
William Cooper Papers.

UNITED STATES

Detroit Public Library, Burton Historical Collection
Henry Dearborn Letter Book.

Historical Society of Pennsylvania, Philadelphia
Memoirs of Colonel Pearce.

New York Historical Society, New York
Isaac Chauncey Letter Book.

University of Michigan, William L. Clements Library
Clinton Papers.

NEWSPAPERS

Canada Constellation, Niagara.
Kingston Gazette.
Niagara Herald.
Upper Canada Gazette, Niagara and York. Renamed *York Gazette* from 1807 to 1815.
Upper Canada Guardian, Niagara.

PUBLISHED DOCUMENTS AND COLLECTIONS

ASKIN, JOHN, *The John Askin Papers,* ed. M. M. QUAIFE (2 vols., Detroit, 1928–31).

BOUCHERVILLE, R. T. VERCHÈRES DE, *A Merchant's Clerk in Upper Canada: The Journal of Thomas Verchères de Boucherville, 1804–1811,* ed. W. S. WALLACE (Toronto, 1935).

BREAKENRIDGE, M. W. "Recollections . . . written by her daughter Maria Murney, from her mother's own words, in 1859," Women's Canadian Historical Society of Toronto, *Transactions,* no 11 (1920), pp. 12–23.

CARTWRIGHT, C. E., ed., *Life and Letters of the Late Hon. Richard Cartwright . . .* (Toronto, 1876).

CRUIKSHANK, E. A. ed., *The Documentary History of the Campaign upon the Niagara Frontier,* vol. III, pt. 3 (Welland, 1902).

"Grants of Crown Lands in Upper Canada," 1792-8, Upper Canada Land Books A–D, Eighteenth–Twentieth *Report of Department of Public Records and Archives of Ontario,* 1929–31 (Toronto, 1930–2).

HODGINS, J. G., *Documentary History of Education in Upper Canada, 1796–1876,* vol. I (Toronto, 1894).

"Journals of the Legislative Assembly of Upper Canada," 1792–1814, Sixth, Eighth and Ninth *Report of the Bureau of Archives . . . Ontario,* 1909, 1911–12 (Toronto, 1911–13).

"Journals of the Legislative Council," 1792–1814, *Seventh Report of the Bureau of Archives . . . Ontario, 1910* (Toronto, 1911), pp. 1–457.

"Letters from W. Jarvis, Secretary for Upper Canada and Mrs. Jarvis to the Rev. Samuel Peters . . . ," Women's Canadian Historical Society of Toronto, *Transactions,* no. 23 (1922–23), pp. 11–61.

"Minutes of the Court of General Quarter Sessions of the Peace for the Home District, 1800–1811," *Twenty-first Report of the Department of Public Records and Archives of Ontario, 1932* (Toronto, 1933).

"Political State of Upper Canada in 1806–7," Note D, *Report on Canadian Archives, 1892* (Ottawa, 1893), pp. 32–135.

POWELL, A. M., "Letters of Mrs. Wm. Dummer Powell, 1807–1821," Niagara Historical Society *Papers,* no. 14 (1906), pp. 1–39.

PRESTON, R. A. ed., *Kingston before the War of 1812* (Toronto, 1959).

RUSSELL, PETER, *Correspondence,* ed. E. A. CRUIKSHANK (3 vols., Toronto, 1932–6).

SELKIRK, THOMAS, EARL OF, *Lord Selkirk's Diary, 1803–1804 . . . ,* ed. P. C. T. WHITE (Toronto, 1958).

SIMCOE, E. P., *The Diary of Mrs. John Graves Simcoe . . . ,* ed. J. ROSS ROBERTSON (Toronto, 1934).

SIMCOE, J. G., *Correspondence,* ed. E. A. CRUIKSHANK (5 vols., Toronto, 1923–30).

STRACHAN, JOHN, *The John Strachan Letter Book*, ed. G. W. SPRAGGE (Toronto, 1946).

WOOD, W. C. H., ed., *Select British Documents of the Canadian War of 1812* (3 vols., Toronto, 1920–8).

TRAVEL NARRATIVES AND CONTEMPORARY WORKS

BEARDSLEY, C. E., *The victims of tyranny* (Buffalo, 1847).

BOULTON, D'ARCY, *Sketch of His Majesty's Province of Upper Canada* (London, 1805).

DOUGLAS, JOHN, *Medical Topography of Upper Canada* (London, 1819).

EDGAR, MATILDA, *Ten years of Upper Canada, 1805–15* (Toronto, 1890).

FINAN, P., *Journal of a voyage to Quebec in the year 1825, with recollections of Canada during the late American war in the years 1812–13* (Newry, 1828).

GOURLAY, R. F., *A Statistical Account of Upper Canada . . .* (2 vols., London, 1822).

HERIOT, GEORGE, *Travels through the Canadas . . .* (London, 1807).

LANDMANN, G. T., *Adventures and recollections* (London, 1852).

LA ROCHEFOUCAULD-LIANCOURT, F. A. F., DUC DE, *Voyage dans les Etats-Unis d'Amérique fait en 1795, 1796 et 1797* (8 vols., Paris, 1799).

A Letter from a Gentleman to his Friend in England, descriptive of the different Settlements in the Province of Upper Canada (Philadelphia, 1795).

LOYAL AND PATRIOTIC SOCIETY OF UPPER CANADA, *Explanation of the Proceedings . . .* (Toronto, 1841).

———*The Report . . .* (Montreal, 1817).

SMITH, D. W., *A Short Topographical Description of His Majesty's Province of Upper Canada in North America* (London, 1799).

SMITH, MICHAEL, *A Geographical View of the Province of Upper Canada . . .* (Hartford, 1813).

SELECTED SECONDARY WORKS

ALFRED, BROTHER, *Catholic Pioneers in Upper Canada* (Toronto, 1947).

ASHBRIDGE, W. T., *The Ashbridge Book . . .* (Toronto, 1912).

BEERS, J. H. & CO., *Commemorative Biographical Record of the County of York* (Toronto, 1907).

BETHUNE, A. N. *Memoirs of the Right Reverend John Strachan* (Toronto, 1870).

BOYLE, DAVID, *The Township of Scarboro, 1796–1896* (Toronto, 1896).

BROCK, A. M. (CAWTHRA), comp., *Past and Present, Notes by Henry Cawthra and Others,* ed A. H. YOUNG (Toronto, 1924).

CARROLL, JOHN, *Case and his Contemporaries, or the Canadian Itinerants Memorial* . . . (5 vols., Toronto, 1867–77).

CHADWICK, E. M., *Ontarian Families: Genealogies of United-Empire-Loyalist and Other Pioneer Families of Upper Canada* (2 vols., Toronto, 1894–98).

CRUIKSHANK, E. A., "The Garrisons of Toronto and York, 1750–1815," Royal Canadian Military Institute, *Selected Papers from the Transactions,* no. 31, pp. 17–65.

——— "A Study of Disaffection in Upper Canada in 1812–5," *Proceedings and Transactions of the Royal Society of Canada,* 3rd Series, VI (1912), Section II, pp. 11–64.

CUMBERLAND, F. B., *The Battle of York* . . . (Toronto, 1913).

CUTHBERSTON, G. A., *Freshwater: A History and Narrative of the Great Lakes* (Toronto, 1931).

GREGG, WILLIAM, *History of the Presbyterian Church in the Dominion of Canada* . . . (Toronto, 1885).

GUILLET, E. C., *Pioneer Life in the County of York* (Toronto, 1946).

——— *Toronto from Trading Post to Great City* (Toronto, 1934).

HATHAWAY, E. J., "Early schools in Toronto," Ontario Historical Society, *Papers and Records,* XXIII (1926), pp. 312–27.

——— *Jesse Ketchum and his Times* (Toronto, 1929).

——— *The Story of the Old Fort at Toronto* (Toronto, 1934).

History of Toronto and the County of York, Ontario (2 vols., Toronto, 1885).

HUMPHRIES, C. W., "The Capture of York," *Ontario History,* LI (1959), pp. 1–21.

HUNTER, A. T., *History of the 12th Regiment, York Rangers, with Some Account of the Different Raisings of Militia in the County of York, Ontario* (Toronto, 1912).

IRVING, L. H., *Officers of the British Forces in Canada during the War 1812–15* (Welland, 1908).

IVISON, E. H. S., and ROSSER, F. T., *The Baptists in Upper and Lower Canada before 1820* (Toronto, 1956).

JACKSON, H. M., *The Queen's Rangers in Upper Canada* . . . (Montreal, 1955).

JARVIS, JULIA, *Three Centuries of Robinsons: The Story of a Family* (Toronto, 1953).

JONES, J. E., *Pioneer Crimes and Punishments in Toronto and the Home District* . . . (Toronto, 1924).

KERR, W. B.,"The Occupation of York (Toronto), 1813" *Canadian Historical Review,* V (1924), pp. 9–21.

LIZARS, K. M., *The Valley of the Humber, 1615–1913* (Toronto, 1913).

MEREDITH, A. G., *Mary's Rosedale and Gossip of "Little York"* (Toronto, 1928).

MIDDLETON, J. E., *The Municipality of Toronto* . . . (3 vols., 1923).
——— "York, Canada, in the War of 1812," *Americana* (Jan., 1924), pp. 1–33.
MIDDLETON, J. E., and LANDON, FRED, *The Province of Ontario: A History, 1615–1927* (4 vols., Toronto, 1927).
MILES & CO., PUB., *Illustrated Historical Atlas of the County of York* (Toronto, 1878).
MILLMAN, T. R., *Jacob Mountain, First Lord Bishop of Quebec* . . . (Toronto, 1947).
MURPHY, ROWLEY, "Gibraltar Point Light" *Inland Seas,* III (July, 1947), pp. 150–4.
MYER, J. S., *Life and Letters of Dr. William Beaumont* . . . (St. Louis, 1912).
ONTARIO, DEPARTMENT OF PLANNING AND DEVELOPMENT, *Don Valley Conservation Report* (Toronto, 1950).
——— *The Humber Valley Report* (Toronto, 1948).
——— *Upper Holland Conservation Report 1953* (Toronto, 1953).
QUAIFE, M. M., *The Yankees Capture York* (Detroit, 1955).
RIDDELL, W. R., "Joseph Willcocks, Sheriff, Member of Parliament and Traitor," Ontario Historical Society, *Papers and Records,* XXIV (1927), pp. 475–99.
——— *The Life and Times of William Dummer Powell* (Lansing, 1924).
——— *The Life of John Graves Simcoe* . . . (Toronto, 1926).
——— "Mr. Justice Thorpe, the Leader of the First Opposition in Upper Canada" *Canadian Law Times* (Nov., 1920), pp. 907–24.
——— *Old Province Tales, Upper Canada* (Toronto, 1920).
——— "Toronto in Cartography," Ontario Historical Society, *Papers and Records,* XXVIII (1932), pp. 143–5.
——— "Toronto in the Parliaments of Upper Canada, 1792–1841," Women's Canadian Historical Society of Toronto, *Transactions,* no. 22 (1921–2), pp. 11–20.
——— *Upper Canada Sketches* (Toronto, 1922).
ROBERTSON, J. ROSS, *The History of Freemasonry in Canada* . . . (2 vols., Toronto, 1900).
——— *Landmarks of Toronto* (6 vols., Toronto, 1894–1914).
ROBINSON, SIR C. W., *Life of Sir John Beverley Robinson* (Edinburgh, 1904).
ROBINSON, PERCY, *Toronto during the French Régime* (Toronto, 1933).
——— "The Toronto Carrying-place and the Toronto Purchase," Ontario Historical Society, *Papers and Records,* XXXIX (1947), pp. 41–9.
——— "Yonge Street and the North West Company," *Canadian Historical Review,* XXIV (1943), pp. 253–65.
SCADDING, HENRY, *Memoirs of the Four Decades of York, Upper Canada* (Toronto, 1884).

——— *Toronto of Old* (Toronto, 1873).

STEVENS, ABEL, *Life and Times of Nathan Bangs* (New York, 1863).

THOMAS, CYRUS, *History of the Counties of Argenteuil, Que., and Prescott, Ont.* . . . (Montreal, 1896).

YOUNG, A. H., "The Rev'd George Okill Stuart, M.A., L.L.D.," Ontario Historical Society, *Papers and Records,* XXIV (1927), pp. 512–34.

INDEX

www.ingramcontent.com/pod-product-compliance
Lightning Source LLC
LaVergne TN
LVHW090758070826
844660LV00022B/1021

* 9 7 8 1 4 8 7 5 9 8 5 5 6 *